13TH EDITION
PART ONE

College Accounting

10A1 – 10A3

13TH EDITION
PART ONE

College Accounting

JAMES A. HEINTZ, DBA, CPA
Professor of Accounting
Indiana University
Bloomington, Indiana

ARTHUR E. CARLSON, PhD
Professor of Accounting
School of Business Administration
Washington University, St. Louis

ROBERT W. PARRY JR., PhD
Associate Professor of Accounting
Indiana University
Bloomington, Indiana

AV80MA1
PUBLISHED BY
SOUTH-WESTERN PUBLISHING CO.
CINCINNATI, OH   WEST CHICAGO, IL   DALLAS, TX   LIVERMORE, CA

AV80MA1   ISBN: 0-538-80401-7

1 2 3 4 5 6 7 8 9 Ki 7 6 5 4 3 2 1 0 9

Printed in the United States of America

Developmental Editor: Dave Robinson
Associate Editors: Jean Privett
                  Mark Sears
Editorial Associates: Nancy Watson
                      Laurie Merz
                      Mary Mullins
Senior Staff Designer: Barb Libby
Internal Design: Designworks
Production Artist: Darren Wright
Marketing Manager: G. M. "Skip" Wenstrup
Cover quilt artwork: © Carol Keller 1988

Library of Congress Cataloging-in-Publication Data

Heintz, James A.
   College accounting.   Part 1 / James A. Heintz, Arthur E. Carlson,
Robert W. Parry, Jr. — 13th ed.
       p.   cm.
   Carlson's name appears first on the earlier edition.
   ISBN 0-538-80401-7   ISBN 0-538-80408-4 (soft)
   1. Accounting.   I. Carlson, Arthur E.   II. Parry, Robert W.,
        III. Title.
HF5635.C227   1990b
657'.044—dc20   89-21953
                                                                  CIP

PREFACE

This textbook is designed for career oriented students of accounting, business administration, computer science, and office technology. An understanding of accounting is essential for anyone who desires a successful career in business, in many of the professions, and in many branches of government. This book provides a thorough and efficient introduction to fundamental accounting concepts and principles. The emphasis throughout the text is on student understanding. Toward this end, the use of professional jargon and references to official accounting pronouncements are minimized, while the content is kept totally consistent with current accounting standards.

Important Features of the Thirteenth Edition

The basic foundation that made this text continually successful for many years has been retained in the thirteenth edition. However, in response to user feedback and independent reviews by accounting educators, there have been numerous improvements to the last edition. The text material has been reorganized both as a whole and within specific chapters, and new materials have been added.

▨ **Chapter Objectives.** As in the twelfth edition, each chapter begins with the chapter objectives. These objectives have been refined and are keyed to text material throughout each chapter by the use of marginal captions. This aids the learning process by keeping the student focused on the relevant objectives at each point in the chapter.

▨ **Illustrations.** Accounting documents and records, diagrams, and flow-charts are used throughout the text to help students visualize important concepts. There is increased use of illustrations in the thirteenth edition, particularly when any new accounting principles or procedures are introduced.

NEW

▨ **Demonstration Problem and Solution.** A complete demonstration problem and solution are provided at the end of the last module in each chapter. The problem is a comprehensive application of key concepts and principles introduced in the chapter. It is designed to give the students guidance and confidence in their ability to solve the exercises and problems based on the chapter material.

Key Terms—Expanding Your Business Vocabulary. Each key term in a chapter appears in boldfaced color type to help students recognize its importance. An Expanding Your Business Vocabulary section is then provided at the end of each chapter, listing all key terms in the chapter and the pages on which definitions can be found. In this way, the student can see the terms used in context rather than defined in isolation.

Building Your Accounting Knowledge. Building Your Accounting Knowledge review questions are provided at the end of each chapter module. The questions provide students with an opportunity to immediately test their recall of important chapter concepts.

NEW

Exercises and Problems. Two complete sets of exercises and problems (Series A and B) have been prepared to facilitate instructor usage and student learning. At the end of each chapter module, an assignment box directs students to the related section of the study guide and to the appropriate exercises and problems provided at the end of the chapter.

NEW

Mastery Problem. A comprehensive mastery problem follows the exercises and problems at the end of each chapter. This problem is usually similar to the demonstration problem in content and purpose, except that no solution is provided. This problem can be used either to test or to further strengthen the students' overall grasp of the chapter materials.

Important Changes and Additions in the Thirteenth Edition

In addition to the features noted above, numerous changes have been made in the organization and content of the thirteenth edition. These changes were made to facilitate student learning of the fundamental accounting process, to give increased emphasis to material that is important to first-year accounting students, to address new financial reporting requirements, and to improve the efficiency of the presentation. Some of the more important changes are as follows.

Reorganization. While the entire thirteenth edition has been reorganized, the restructuring of the first ten chapters is of particular importance in two respects. First, the chapters provide a clear progression from cash to modified cash to accrual basis accounting. This approach facilitates learning of the accounting process by focusing first on the simplest setting—accounting for cash movements. Basic accounting concepts are more readily grasped because the student can identify with the cash basis setting. The modified cash basis is then presented with limited "exceptions" to the cash basis. Once again, the student can readily understand such a system. The presentation gradually builds to a complete accrual accounting system. This provides a realistic yet pedagogically sound progression from a simple to a relatively complex accounting environment.

The second important aspect of the reorganization is that the complete accounting cycle is presented before addressing the details of accounting for such items as cash and payroll. Accounting for cash is now covered in Chapter 5, after the modified cash basis system has been explained and the illustration of the accounting cycle has been completed. Payroll has been moved to Chapter 8, after the accrual accounting system has been presented. This sequencing enables the teacher and student to focus on the fundamental accounting process first and then to build on the fundamentals with related details.

NEW

Receivables. A new chapter (11) has been added on accounting for accounts receivable. The coverage is more thorough than in the twelfth edition. Material that was addressed piecemeal in the twelfth edition is now contained in a single, more complete chapter.

NEW

Departmental Accounting. A new module on departmental accounting has been added as part of Chapter 18, effectively replacing the consolidated operations topic covered in the twelfth edition. The consolidations materials are appropriate for a more advanced course, while departmental accounting is likely to be more useful to an introductory accounting student. The usefulness of departmental reports for management decision making is emphasized. Key issues covered include the difference between direct and indirect expenses, assignment and allocation of expenses, and measurement and interpretation of departmental operating income and direct operating margin.

Accounting for Investments and Intangible Assets. Chapter 25 has been expanded and reorganized to include coverage of short- and long-term investments in stocks and bonds. Major topics include application of the lower of cost or market method of accounting for short-term debt and equity securities and passive, long-term investments, and the use of the equity method of accounting for active, long-term investments. As noted above, accounting for a controlling interest in the securities of another firm through the preparation of consolidated financial statements has been eliminated.

NEW

Statement of Cash Flows. A new chapter (26) on the statement of cash flows has been added. This chapter illustrates the direct method of preparing the statement of cash flows for a merchandising company. In addition, a new section has been added to Chapter 29 illustrating the indirect method of preparing the statement of cash flows for a manufacturing company. These chapters expand the coverage provided in the twelfth edition and are consistent with new reporting requirements.

▓▓▓ Cost Accounting and Manufacturing Companies. The three-chapters (27-29) covering cost accounting for a manufacturing business have been reorganized and rewritten. Job order cost accounting and process cost accounting are covered more thoroughly than in the twelfth edition, and the distinction between the two accounting systems is clarified. Presentation of both the job order and process cost systems emphasizes the underlying documentation, the flow of charts through the system (using flowcharts, journal entries, and T accounts), and the accounting reports generated. The functioning of a job order cost accounting system in a small manufacturing company is illustrated.

▓▓▓ Financial Statement Analysis. The financial statement analysis chapter (30) has been repositioned as the final, capstone chapter in the text. This chapter has also been rewritten to provide more thorough coverage of the interpretation, rather than just the computation, of key financial statement data. In addition, a brief introduction to the analysis and interpretation of financial statement variables is provided in both Chapter 10 and Chapter 20.

▓▓▓ Practice Sets. The dependency of the practice sets on the text has been greatly reduced. Chapters 3-4, 9-10, 19-20, and 28-29 offer background material that can be used to introduce a practice set. However, the coverage of practice set related material in the chapters is only sufficient to demonstrate the use of accounting in a particular type of business. Additional details needed for using the practice sets are provided with the sets themselves. This greatly increases the user's flexibility in using the text and any of the following practice sets: Andrea Marree, Computer Consultant; Northern Micro, a wholesale/retail microcomputer supplier; Mitchell & Jenkins a retail/wholesale sporting goods store and WeMake Toys Inc., a toy manufacturer using a job order cost system.

NEW

▓▓▓ Study Guide. A completely new study guide has been prepared for the thirteenth edition. For each chapter module,, the study guide begins with a brief discussion of the important learning objectives. This helps students recall the key points from the chapter. The written assignments consist of a series of questions, exercises, and problems tailored to facilitate achieving the related learning objectives. The exercises are designed to focus on specific learning objectives and the problems pull together related concepts within the chapter module. Upon completion of the study guide material, the Mastery Problem at the end of each chapter may be used to draw together concepts from the entire chapter. By completing the study guide assignments, students should master the important materials from the chapter.

NEW

▓▓▓ Software. Two new educational software programs are available. The Electronic Problem Solver is a general ledger program designed to solve selected end-of-chapter problems. It is also designed to allow an instructor to add additional problems. The second software program is a spreadsheet application template diskette of selected end-of-chapter problems using Lotus™ 1-2-3™.[1]

NEW

▨ **Working Papers.** A bound set of forms for end-of-chapter exercises, problems, and mastery problems is available for the student.

▨ **Check Figures.** There are two sets of check figures—an abbreviated form for end-of-chapter materials and a more comprehensive set for study guide activities.

Resources Available to the Instructor

▨ **Instructor's Resource Guide.** This manual contains a variety of teaching resources. Each chapter contains a condensed overview of the subject matter followed by a brief chapter outline and then specific teaching suggestions relating to the content of the chapter. Also included is a lesson plan with lecture notes for each chapter. Teaching transparency masters are provided to support major chapter concepts.

▨ **Solutions Manual—Text.** This manual contains solutions to all end-of-chapter materials including the questions, exercises, problems, and mastery problem. The solutions have been developed to parallel the student working papers.

▨ **Solutions Manual—Study Guide.** This manual contains solutions to the questions, exercises, and problems in the study guide. The format parallels the student edition of the study guide with solutions inserted.

▨ **Transparencies.** Solution transparencies are available for all exercises, problems, and mastery problems in the text.

▨ **Test Bank.** This book contains true or false questions, multiple choice questions, and problems with solutions. A microcomputer version (MicroSWAT III) of this printed material is also available.

▨ **Achievement Tests.** Two sets (A and B) of preprinted tests are available for each chapter. In addition, two preprinted placement tests are available.

NEW

▨ **HyperGraphics.** HyperGraphics is an instructional delivery system employing software. The delivery system is achieved through the use of a

---

[1]Lotus™ 1-2-3™ are registered trademarks of the Lotus Development Corporation. Any references to Lotus or 1-2-3 refers to this footnote.

personal computer, a liquid crystal display, and an overhead projector. Student response pads are optional items. The resulting computer-based teaching and learning environment can enhance both classroom instruction and self study. A student study guide called Accounting Notes is used in conjunction with this system.

Acknowledgments

We thank the following reviewers of our manuscript for their valuable contributions:

Mary Dianne Bridges
South Plains College

Robert Campbell
Montcalm Community College

Ted A. Duzenski
Augusta Technical College

Michael A. Evans
MTI Business School

Richard A. Fornicola
South Hills Business School

Jo Ann Frazell
Southeast Community College

Stephen S. Hamilton
Lane Community College

Mildred A. Lanser
Santa Barbara Business College

Shirley W. Leung
Los Medanos College

Joan Ryan
Lane Community College

Albert J. Walczak
Linn-Benton Community College

We also thank all faculty whose suggestions contributed in a substantive way to the development of this textbook and Jane Parry for her verification and proofreading of the end-of-chapter and study guide materials.

James A. Heintz, DBA, CPA
Indiana University

Arthur E. Carlson, PhD
Washington University, St. Louis

Robert W. Parry, Jr., PhD
Indiana University

Contents

CHAPTER 1

The Nature and Structure of Accounting

Careful study of this chapter should enable you to:

- Describe accounting as it applies to profit-seeking enterprises.
- Define the elements of the accounting equation.
- Show the effects of selected business transactions on the accounting equation.
- Explain the function of and prepare a simple balance sheet.
- Explain the function of and prepare a simple income statement.
- Enter selected business transactions in T accounts using debits and credits.
- Explain the function of and prepare a trial balance.

The purpose of accounting is to provide financial information about the current operations and condition of an enterprise to individuals, agencies, and organizations who have the need and the right to be so informed. These user groups normally include:

1. The *owners* of the business—both present and prospective.
2. The *managers* of the business—who may or may not own the business.
3. The *creditors* or *suppliers* of the business—both present and prospective. Creditors or suppliers are those who supply goods and services on account. This category also includes banks and individuals who lend money to the business.
4. *Government agencies*—local, state, and national. For purposes of regulation and taxation, various government agencies must be given certain financial information.

In connection with many businesses, some or all of the following users also need accounting information: customers or clients, labor unions, competitors, trade associations, stock exchanges, commodity exchanges, financial analysts, and financial writers.

Most types of users want data regarding (1) the results of operations—net income or loss—for the most recent period and (2) the financial condition of the business as of the most current date available. There are differences among users, however, in exactly what they want to know about the results of operations and the financial condition of the business.

The demand for the greatest quantity and variety of information usually comes from the managers of the business. These managers utilize managerial accounting because it focuses on detailed, up-to-date information about different parts of the business. Managerial accountants provide information to management in many forms to aid in decision making and evaluation. A managerial accountant can achieve professional status as a **Certified Management Accountant** (CMA) by passing a uniform examination offered by the Institute of Management Accounting of the National Association of Accountants.

One way management ensures that it obtains the information it needs is through internal auditors. The main functions of an internal auditor are to review the operating and accounting control procedures adopted by management and to see that accurate and timely information is provided. An internal auditor can achieve professional recognition as a **Certified Internal Auditor** (CIA) by passing the uniform examination offered by the Institute of Internal Auditors.

The information needs of owners and groups external to the business, such as creditors and suppliers, are satisfied by financial accounting procedures. These users generally need reports regarding operations and financial condition prepared according to specific accounting policies and practices. These financial reports often are audited (verified) by independent public accountants.

The **auditing** function involves the application of standard review and testing procedures to the records of an enterprise to be certain that proper accounting policies and practices have been followed. The purpose of the audit is to provide an independent opinion that the financial information about a business is fairly presented. A public accountant can earn the professional designation of **Certified Public Accountant** (CPA) by meeting various prescribed requirements, including the passing of a uniform examination prepared by the American Institute of Certified Public Accountants.

The previous paragraphs have discussed accounting in connection with profit-seeking organizations. There are thousands of governmental and not-for-profit organizations such as states, municipalities, educational institutions, churches, and hospitals that also need to accumulate and report information. These organizations employ a large number of accountants. While the "rules of the game" are somewhat different for governmental and not-for-profit organizations, many accounting procedures are similar to those found in profit-seeking enterprises.

Government agencies are another group of users with specific information needs. Probably the most familiar of these agencies is the Internal Revenue Service (IRS). The IRS has its own set of regulations for determining income or loss and the amount of tax a business must pay. Because of the detailed nature of the tax rules and information required by the IRS and various state taxation authorities, many accountants specialize in the tax area.

The accountant is responsible for accumulating and reporting the financial information needed by users. Since such activities touch upon nearly every aspect of business operation and since financial information is communicated in accounting terms, accounting is said to be the "language of business." Anyone intending to engage in any type of business activity should learn this language.

The Accounting Process

Describe accounting as it applies to profit-seeking enterprises.

Accounting is the art of analyzing and recording financial transactions and certain business-related economic events, classifying and summarizing that information, and reporting and interpreting the results. These six major phases of the accounting process that provide the basis for this definition are explained below.

Analyzing is the first phase of the accounting process. The accountant must look at a transaction or event that has occurred and determine its fundamental significance to the business so that the relevant information can be properly processed.

Recording traditionally meant writing something by hand. Much of the record keeping in accounting still is done manually; however, technological advances have introduced a variety of machines which typically combine the major attributes of typewriters, calculators, cathode-ray tubes, and electro-mechanical printing. The initial processing can take the form of (1) terminal keyboard input directly into a computer, (2) diskettes prepared by keyboard input on personal or microcomputers for possible later transfer to larger, main-frame computers, or (3) special characters that can be magnetically or electronically "read" from source documents and thus used to feed information directly into a computer. Because of the multiple ways information can be processed, the term "data entry" can be substituted for the term "recording" in the accounting process.

Classifying relates to the process of sorting or grouping like things together rather than merely keeping a simple, diary-like narrative record of numerous and varied transactions and events.

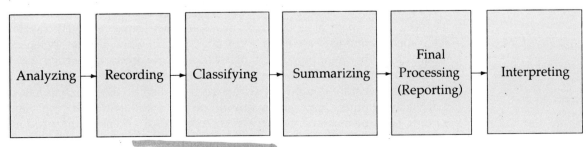

The Accounting Process

Summarizing is the process of bringing together various items of information to determine or explain a result.

Final processing, or **reporting**, refers to the process of communicating the results. In accounting, it is common to use tables of numbers rather than narrative-type reports. Sometimes, a combination of the two is used.

Interpreting refers to the steps taken to direct attention to the significance of various matters and relationships. Percentage analyses and ratios often are used to help explain the meaning of certain related bits of information. Footnotes to financial reports and special captions also may be valuable in the interpreting phase of accounting.

Accounting and Bookkeeping

A person involved with or responsible for such functions as accounting information systems design, accounting policy making, data analysis, report preparation, and report interpretation may be referred to as an accountant. A person who records or enters information in accounting records may be referred to as a bookkeeper. Bookkeeping is the processing phase of the accounting information processing system. That term goes back to the time when formal accounting records were in the form of books—pages bound together. While this still is sometimes the case, modern practice favors the use of loose-leaf or computer-generated records and cards. When the language catches up with practice, the designation **information processor** may replace "bookkeeper."

Accounting Elements

Define the elements of the accounting equation: assets liabilities, and owner's equity.

Before the accounting process can begin, the entity to be accounted for must be defined. A **business entity** is a specified individual, association, or organization with control over economic resources and which engages in economic activities. This flexible definition allows the personal and business finances of an owner, and even the finances of different businesses of the same owner to be accounted for separately.

Three basic accounting elements exist for every business entity: assets, liabilities, and owner's equity.

Assets. Any item a business owns that will provide future benefits is called an **asset**. Items such as money, merchandise, furniture, fixtures, machinery, buildings, and land are common examples of business assets.

It is possible to conduct a business or a professional practice with very few assets. A medical doctor, for example, may have relatively few assets, such as money, accounts receivable, instruments, laboratory equipment, and office equipment. In many cases, however, numerous assets are necessary. A merchant must have a large selection of merchandise to sell as well as store equipment with which to display the merchandise. A manufacturer must have an inventory of parts and materials, tools and various sorts of machinery with which to make or assemble the product.

Liabilities.   A probable future outflow of assets by a business as a result of a past transaction or event is called a liability. Liabilities are debts or obligations of the business that can be paid with money, goods, or services, but usually are paid with cash. They represent one type of interest in a business—an "outside" interest.

The most common liabilities are accounts payable and notes payable. An account payable is an unwritten promise to pay a supplier for assets purchased or for a service rendered. Formal written promises to pay suppliers or lenders specified sums of money at definite future times are known as notes payable. A business may also have one or more types of taxes payable classified as a liability.

Owner's Equity.   The amount by which the business assets exceed the business liabilities is termed the owner's equity in the business. The word "equity" used in this sense represents another type of interest in a business—an "inside" interest. Owner's equity represents the owner's interest in the assets of the business which remains after deducting the liabilities. The terms proprietorship, net worth, and capital are sometimes used as synonyms for owner's equity. If there are no business liabilities, the owner's equity in the business is equal to the total amount of the assets of the business.

Traditionally a business that is owned by one person is called a proprietorship. The person owning the business is known as the proprietor. A proprietor may have business assets and liabilities as well as nonbusiness assets and liabilities. For example, the proprietor probably owns a home, clothing, and a car, and perhaps owes the dentist for dental service. These are personal, nonbusiness assets and liabilities and they will not be included on the formal accounting records of the enterprise.

If the owner invests money or other assets in the business, the item invested is reclassified from a nonbusiness asset to a business asset. If the owner withdraws money or other assets from the business for personal use, the item withdrawn is reclassified from a business asset to a nonbusiness asset. These distinctions are important and allow the owner to make decisions based on the financial condition and results of the business apart from nonbusiness affairs.

The Accounting Equation

The relationship between the three basic accounting elements—assets, liabilities, and owner's equity—can be expressed in the form of a simple equation known as the accounting equation.

$$\text{Assets} = \text{Liabilities} + \text{Owner's Equity}$$

This equation reflects the fact that outsiders and insiders have an interest in all of the assets of a business. When the amounts of any two of these elements are known, the third can always be calculated.

$$\text{Liabilities} = \text{Assets} - \text{Owner's Equity}$$
$$\text{Owner's Equity} = \text{Assets} - \text{Liabilities}$$

For example, assume that Andrea Hopper has business assets on December 31 that total $60,400. The business liabilities on that date consist of $5,400 owed for equipment purchased on account. The owner's equity element of the business may be calculated by subtracting the total liabilities from the total assets, $60,400 − $5,400 = $55,000. These facts about the business can also be expressed in equation form as follows:

$$\text{Assets} = \text{Liabilities} + \text{Owner's Equity}$$
$$\$60,400 = \quad \$5,400 \quad + \qquad \$55,000$$

A closer examination of the elements of the accounting equation shows how the equation maintains equality. One way to increase the assets of the business is for the owner to invest more money or other property in the business. For example, if Hopper invests an additional $6,000 in cash in the business, the status of the business as shown by the accounting equation would be as follows:

Assets	=	Liabilities	+	Owner's Equity
$60,400	=	$5,400	+	$55,000
+6,000				+6,000
$66,400	=	$5,400	+	$61,000

The additional investment by Hopper increased the assets by $6,000 and increased Hopper's ownership interest (owner's equity) by $6,000.

A second way to increase the assets of the business is to borrow money. If Hopper borrows $5,000 for the business from the bank by signing a note, the accounting equation would change again, as follows:

Assets	=	Liabilities	+	Owner's Equity
$66,400	=	$ 5,400	+	$61,000
+5,000		+5,000		
$71,400	=	$10,400	+	$61,000

The money borrowed from the bank increased the assets by $5,000 and increased the outside interest (liabilities) by $5,000.

If the transactions and events of the business are not properly accounted for, the elements of the accounting equation will not balance. It is essential that the business records correctly show the effects of the activities of the business on the elements of the accounting equation.

Transactions

Any activity of an enterprise which involves the exchange of values is referred to as a **transaction**. These values typically are expressed in terms of money, but may also be expressed as the market values of goods and services. Buying and selling assets and borrowing money are common transactions. The following typical business transactions are analyzed to show that each represents an exchange of values.

Typical Transactions	*Analysis of Transactions*
a. An individual invested $6,000 cash in a business.	In exchange for money, the individual's interest in the business was increased.
b. Office equipment was purchased on account, $2,700.	A liability known as an account payable was incurred in exchange for office equipment.
c. Cash of $4,000 was borrowed from a bank.	A liability known as a note payable was incurred in exchange for money.
d. Office equipment was purchased for cash, $900.	Money was exchanged for office equipment.
e. Payment of $2,000 was made on account to a supplier.	Money was given in settlement of a debt that resulted from a purchase on account.

Effect of Transactions on the Accounting Equation

Show the effects of selected business transactions on the accounting equation.

Each transaction affects one or more of the three basic accounting elements. For example, in transaction (b) the office equipment was purchased on account, thereby resulting in an increase in assets (office equipment) with a corresponding increase in liabilities (accounts payable). In transaction (d) the purchase of office equipment for cash represents both an increase and a decrease in assets. The assets increased because office equipment was acquired; the assets decreased because cash was disbursed. Neither of these transactions has any effect upon the owner's equity element of the equation.

The effect of a transaction on the basic elements of the accounting equation may be indicated by increasing or decreasing a specific asset, liability, or owner's equity account. To illustrate, assume that transactions like the five described above took place during June, 19--, the first month of operations for John Wendt, an attorney. The effect of these transactions on the accounting equation can be analyzed as follows:

Transaction (a)

An Increase in an Asset Offset by an Increase in Owner's Equity

Wendt opened a bank account with a deposit of $6,000 for his business. This transaction caused the new business to receive the asset, cash; and since Wendt contributed the assets, the owner's equity element, John Wendt, Capital, was increased by the same amount. As a result, the equation for the business would appear as follows:

Assets	=	Liabilities	+	Owner's Equity
Cash	=			John Wendt, Capital
(a) $6,000				$6,000

Total Assets: $6,000 = Total Liabilities + Owner's Equity: $6,000

Transaction (b)

An Increase in an Asset Offset by an Increase in a Liability

Wendt purchased office equipment (desks and chairs) for $2,700 on account. This transaction caused the asset, office equipment, to increase by $2,700 and resulted in an equal increase in the liability, accounts payable. Updating the previous equation by this transaction results in the following:

	Assets		= Liabilities	+ Owner's Equity
		Office	Accounts	John Wendt,
	Cash +	Equipment =	Payable +	Capital
Bal. $6,000				$6,000
(b) _____		$2,700	$2,700	_____
Bal. $6,000		$2,700	$2,700	$6,000

Total Assets: $8,700 = Total Liabilities + Owner's Equity: $8,700

Transaction (c)

An Increase in an Asset Offset by an Increase in a Liability

Wendt borrowed $4,000 at a bank by signing a 90-day note. This transaction caused the asset, cash, to increase by $4,000 and resulted in the creation of the liability called notes payable, for the same amount. The effect of this transaction on the equation is as follows:

	Assets		=	Liabilities		+ Owner's Equity
		Office		Notes	Accounts	John Wendt,
	Cash +	Equipment =		Payable +	Payable +	Capital
Bal. $ 6,000		$2,700			$2,700	$6,000
(c) 4,000		_____		$4,000	_____	_____
Bal. $10,000		$2,700		$4,000	$2,700	$6,000

Total Assets: $12,700 = Total Liabilities + Owner's Equity: $12,700

Transaction (d)

An Increase in One Asset Offset by a Decrease in Another Asset

Wendt purchased office equipment (filing cabinets) for $900 cash. This transaction caused a $900 increase in the asset, office equipment, that exactly offset the $900 decrease in the asset, cash. The effect on the equation is as follows:

	Assets		=	Liabilities		+ Owner's Equity
		Office		Notes	Accounts	John Wendt,
	Cash +	Equipment =		Payable +	Payable +	Capital
Bal. $10,000		$2,700		$4,000	$2,700	$6,000
(d) −900		900		_____	_____	_____
Bal. $ 9,100		$3,600		$4,000	$2,700	$6,000

Total Assets: $12,700 = Total Liabilities + Owner's Equity: $12,700

Transaction (e)

A Decrease in an Asset Offset by a Decrease in a Liability
Wendt paid $2,000 on account to the company from which $2,700 of office equipment was purchased. (See transaction (b).) This payment caused the asset, cash, and the liability, accounts payable, both to decrease by $2,000. The effect on the equation is as follows:

	Assets		=	Liabilities		+ Owner's Equity
		Office		Notes	Accounts	John Wendt,
	Cash +	Equipment =		Payable +	Payable +	Capital
Bal.	$ 9,100	$3,600		$4,000	$ 2,700	$6,000
(e)	−2,000				−2,000	
Bal.	$ 7,100	$3,600		$4,000	$ 700	$6,000

Total Assets: $10,700 = Total Liabilities + Owner's Equity: $10,700

The Balance Sheet

Explain the function of and prepare a simple balance sheet.

A set of business records that make up an accounting data base is maintained to fill a variety of needs. Primarily, business records provide source data for use in preparing various reports, including those referred to as financial statements. One of these financial statements is the **balance sheet**, which is sometimes called a **statement of financial position** or **statement of financial condition**. The balance sheet shows the assets, liabilities, and owner's equity of a business at a specified date. If the five transactions described above were the only ones that took place during June, the balance sheet for Wendt's business as of June 30, 19--, would appear as follows:

John Wendt, Attorney
Balance Sheet
June 30, 19--

Assets		Liabilities	
Cash	$ 7,100	Notes payable	$ 4,000
Office equipment	3,600	Accounts payable	700
		Total liabilities	$ 4,700
		Owner's Equity	
		John Wendt, capital	6,000
		Total liabilities and	
Total assets	$10,700	owner's equity	$10,700

Expanding the Accounting Equation

Define two additional elements of the accounting equation: revenues and expenses.

In the preceding sections, the three key accounting elements of every business entity were defined and explained: assets, liabilities, and owner's equity. In order to complete the explanation of the accounting process, two additional elements must be added to the discussion: revenues and expenses.

The term **revenue** generally means an inflow of assets (or decrease in liabilities) as a result of selling a product or providing a service. Revenue directly affects owner's equity. It is one of the two ways that owner's equity can be increased, as follows:

1. As illustrated on page 7, the owner may invest additional money or other assets in the enterprise. Such investments result in an increase in both the assets of the enterprise and in the owner's equity, but they do not further enrich the owner. The owner now has more assets invested in the enterprise and fewer assets outside of the enterprise.
2. Revenue that is derived from sales of goods or services, or from other sources also increases owner's equity.

When revenue occurs, either the assets are increased or the liabilities are decreased. In either case, owner's equity is increased. If a transaction causes an increase in owner's equity and is not an investment of assets by the owner, the transaction involves revenue.

The term **expense** generally means an outflow of assets (or increase in liabilities) as a result of efforts made to produce revenues. As with revenue, expense directly affects the owner's equity. It is one of the two ways that owner's equity can be decreased, as follows:

1. The owner may withdraw money or other assets from the business enterprise.
2. Expenses that are incurred in operating the enterprise also decrease owner's equity.

When an expense is incurred, either the assets are reduced or the liabilities are increased. In either event, owner's equity is reduced. If a transaction causing a reduction in owner's equity is not a withdrawal of assets by the owner, an expense is incurred. Common examples of expense are rent of office or store, salaries of employees, telephone service, supplies consumed, and many types of taxes.

If during a specified period of time, the total increases in owner's equity resulting from revenue exceed the total decreases resulting from expenses, the excess represents the **net income** or net profit for the period.

$$\text{Revenue} > \text{Expenses} = \text{Net Income}$$

On the other hand, if the expenses of the period exceed the revenue, such excess represents a **net loss** for the period.

$$\text{Expenses} > \text{Revenue} = \text{Net Loss}$$

The time interval used in the measurement of net income or net loss can be determined by the owner. It may be a month, a quarter (three months), a year, or some other period of time. Any accounting period of twelve months' duration is usually referred to as a **fiscal year.** The fiscal year frequently coincides with the calendar year.

The accounting equation is expanded to include revenue and expenses in the following manner:

$$\text{Assets} = \text{Liabilities} + [\text{Owner's Equity} + \text{Revenue} - \text{Expenses}]$$

In this expanded form the equation clearly shows that revenue and expenses directly affect owner's equity, because they are part of owner's equity.

Effect of Revenue and Expense Transactions on the Accounting Equation

Show the effects of selected business transactions on the accounting equation: revenue and expenses.

To show the effects of revenue and expense transactions, the example of John Wendt, Attorney, will be continued. Assume that the following revenue and expense transactions took place in Wendt's business during June, 19--.

Transaction (f)

An Increase in an Asset Offset by an Increase in Owner's Equity Resulting from Revenue
Wendt received $2,000 cash from a client for professional services rendered. This transaction caused the asset, cash, as well as owner's equity to increase by $2,000, since the cash was received for services performed by the business. This increase in owner's equity is shown by increasing the revenue element called client fees by $2,000. The effect on the equation is as follows:

Assets		=	Liabilities		+	[Owner's Equity	+	Revenue]
Cash	Office + Equipment	=	Notes Payable	+ Accounts Payable +		John Wendt, Capital	+	Client Fees
Bal. $7,100	$3,600		$4,000	$ 700		$6,000		
(f) $2,000								$2,000
Bal. $9,100	$3,600		$4,000	$ 700		$6,000		$2,000

Total Assets: $12,700 = Total Liabilities + [Owner's Equity + Revenue]: $12,700

Transaction (g)

A Decrease in an Asset Offset by a Decrease in Owner's Equity Resulting from Expense
Wendt paid $800 for office rent for June. This transaction caused the asset, cash, to be reduced by $800 with an equal reduction in owner's equity. This decrease in owner's equity is shown by increasing an expense called rent expense by $800. The effect on the equation follows:

	Assets	=	Liabilities		+	[Owner's Equity	+ Revenue	− Expenses]
		Office	Notes	Accounts		John Wendt,	Client	Rent
	Cash +	Equipment =	Payable +	Payable +		Capital	+ Fees	− Expense
Bal.	$9,100	$3,600	$4,000	$ 700		$6,000	$2,000	
(g)	−800							$800
Bal.	$8,300	$3,600	$4,000	$ 700		$6,000	$2,000	$800

Total Assets: $11,900 = Total Liabilities + [Owner's Equity + Revenue − Expenses]: $11,900

Transaction (h)

A Decrease in an Asset Offset by a Decrease in Owner's Equity Resulting from Expense
Wendt paid a bill for telephone service, $69. This transaction, like the previous one, caused a decrease in the asset, cash, with an equal decrease in the owner's equity. This decrease in owner's equity is shown by increasing an expense called telephone expense by $69. The effect on the equation is as follows:

	Assets	=	Liabilities		+	[Owner's Equity	+ Revenue	− Expenses]	
		Office	Notes	Accounts		John Wendt,	Client	Rent	Telephone
	Cash +	Equipment =	Payable +	Payable +		Capital	+ Fees	− Expense −	Expense
Bal.	$8,300	$3,600	$4,000	$ 700		$6,000	$2,000	$800	
(h)	− 69								$69
Bal.	$8,231	$3,600	$4,000	$ 700		$6,000	$2,000	$800	$69

Total Assets: $11,831 = Total Liabilities + [Owner's Equity + Revenue − Expenses]: $11,831

The Income Statement

Explain the function of and prepare a simple income statement.

The second financial statement regularly prepared by every business entity is the **income statement,** which is sometimes called the **profit and loss statement** or **operating statement**. The income statement shows the net income or net loss for a specified period of time and how it was calculated. Based on the three revenue and expense transactions described above, the income statement for Wendt's business for the month of June would appear as follows:

John Wendt, Attorney
Income Statement
For Month Ended June 30, 19--

Revenue:		
Client fees		$2,000
Expenses:		
Rent expense	$800	
Telephone expense	69	869
Net income		$1,131

The Updated Balance Sheet

Explain the function of and prepare a simple balance sheet.

The revenue and expense transactions described above also affected the asset and owner's equity accounts. A new balance sheet can now be prepared, as follows:

John Wendt, Attorney
Balance Sheet
June 30, 19--

Assets		Liabilities	
Cash	$ 8,231	Notes payable	$ 4,000
Office equipment	3,600	Accounts payable	700
		Total liabilities	$ 4,700
		Owner's Equity	
		John Wendt, capital	7,131
		Total liabilities and	
Total assets	$11,831	owner's equity..........	$11,831

The comparison of this balance sheet with the one on page 9 reveals that assets are increased by $1,131 ($11,831 – $10,700) and owner's equity is increased by $1,131 ($7,131 – $6,000). Notice the net income on the income statement of $1,131 is the exact amount by which the owner's equity increased. This illustrates the direct effect of revenue and expenses on owner's equity.

Summary of the Accounting Process

The complete accounting process described in the preceding sections is illustrated in the following diagram:

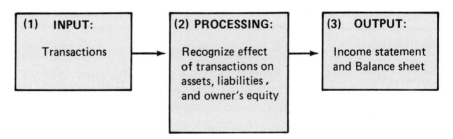

1. Transactions in which assets or services are bought or sold by an enterprise provide the necessary input for the accounting information system.
2. Recognizing the effect of these transactions on the assets, liabilities, owner's equity, revenue, and expenses of an enterprise is the processing function of the accounting information system.

3. The accounting data base that is updated in the processing function provides the source data for the **output** of the accounting information system—the income statement and the balance sheet.

Building Your Accounting Knowledge

1. Identify four user groups normally interested in financial information about a business enterprise.
2. Which group of users usually demands the greatest quantity and variety of information?
3. What are the main functions of an internal auditor?
4. What is the purpose of an audit by an independent public accountant?
5. Why is accounting called the "language of business"?
6. Identify the six major phases of the accounting process and explain each phase.
7. Why is it necessary to distinguish between business assets and liabilities and nonbusiness assets and liabilities of a single proprietor?
8. What is the function of a balance sheet?
9. In what way other than by investing additional assets can the owner's equity in a business be increased?
10. In what way, other than by withdrawing assets, can the owner's equity in a business be decreased?

Assignment Box

To reinforce your understanding of the preceding text materials, you may complete the following:

Study Guide: Part A
Textbook: Exercises 1A1 through 1A6 or 1B1 through 1B6
Problems 1A1 through 1A2 or 1B1 through 1B2

The Double-Entry Framework

Enter selected business transactions in T accounts using debits and credits.

The terms asset, liability, owner's equity, revenue, and expense were explained in the preceding pages. Examples were given to show how individual business transactions cause a change in one or more of these basic accounting elements. Each of the transactions had a dual effect. An increase or decrease in any asset, liability, owner's equity, revenue, or expense was always accompanied by an offsetting change within the basic accounting elements. This is always true. The fact that each transaction has a dual effect upon the accounting elements provides the basis for what is called **double-entry accounting**. This term describes a processing system that involves entering the two effects of every transaction. Double-entry accounting does not mean that a transaction is entered twice; instead, it means that both of the aspects of each transaction are entered.

Double-entry accounting has been practiced for at least 500 years. The method has endured largely because it has several virtues: it is orderly, fairly simple, and very flexible. There is no transaction that cannot be entered in a double-entry manner. Double-entry accounting promotes accuracy. Its use makes it impossible for certain types of errors to remain undetected for very long. For example, if one aspect of a transaction is properly entered but the other aspect is overlooked, it will soon be found that the records as a whole are "out of balance." The accountant then knows that something is wrong, reviews the records to discover the trouble, and then makes the needed correction.

The Account

It has been explained previously that the assets of a business may consist of a number of items, such as cash, accounts receivable, merchandise, equipment, buildings, and land. The liabilities may consist of one or more items, such as accounts payable and notes payable. Similarly, owner's equity may consist of the owner's investments and various revenue and expense items. A separate record should be kept of each type of asset, liability, owner's equity, revenue, and expense.

A form or record used to keep track of the increases and decreases in each item is known as an **account**. There are many types of account forms in general use. Some may be on ruled sheets of paper bound in book form or kept in loose-leaf binders. Others may be in the form of cards kept in files or information stored in computers. The following is an illustration of a standard account form.

ACCOUNT							ACCOUNT NO.	
DATE	ITEM	POST. REF.	DEBIT	DATE	ITEM	POST. REF.	CREDIT	

The three major parts of the standard account form are (1) the title and the account number, (2) the debit or left side, and (3) the credit or right side. This account form is designed to make it simple to enter essential information regarding each transaction that affects the account. Each account should be given an appropriate title that will indicate whether it is an asset, a liability, or an owner's equity account. Before any entries are made in an account, the title and number of the account should be entered on the horizontal line at the top of the form. The standard account form is divided into two equal parts or sections which are ruled identically for entering increases and decreases. The left side is called the debit side, and the right side is called the credit side. The Date columns are used for entering the dates of transactions. The Item columns may be used for entering a brief description of a transaction. The Posting Reference columns will be discussed later. The amount column on the left is headed "Debit" while that on the right is headed "Credit." The Debit and Credit columns are used for entering the amounts of transactions.

To determine the balance of an account at any time, total the amounts in the Debit and Credit columns, and calculate the difference between the two totals. To save time, a **T account** is commonly used for instructional purposes. It consists of a two-line drawing resembling the capital letter T and is sometimes referred to as a skeleton form of account.

Title

| Debit side | Credit side |

Debits and Credits

To **debit** an account means to enter an amount on the left or debit side of the account. To **credit** an account means to enter an amount on the right or credit side of the account. The abbreviation for debit is Dr. and for credit Cr. (based on the Latin terms "debere" and "credere"). Sometimes the word **charge** is used as a substitute for debit. In entering transactions, the debits always must equal the credits. Increases in assets are entered on the left (debit) side of an account and decreases are entered on the right (credit) side. These rules are the opposite in liabilities and owner's equity accounts because liabilities and owner's equity are on the opposite side of the accounting equation. Specifically, increases in liabilities and owner's equity are entered on the right (credit) side of an account and decreases are entered on the left (debit) side. By following these rules the basic equality of assets to liabilities plus owner's equity will be maintained (Assets = Liabilities + Owner's Equity). Likewise, equality will be maintained between the total amounts debited to all accounts and the total amounts credited to all accounts (Total Debits = Total Credits). These basic relationships are shown on the next page.

Because revenue and expenses are part of owner's equity, transactions involving revenue and expenses always cause a change in the owner's equity element. Such transactions could be entered by debiting an account called Owner's Equity for expenses and crediting it for revenue. If this practice were followed, however, the credit side of the owner's equity account would contain a mixture of increases due to revenue and to the investment of assets in the business by the owner, while the debit side would contain a mixture of decreases due to expenses and to the withdrawal of assets from the business by the owner. In order to determine net income or net loss for each accounting period, a careful analysis

Assets   =   Liabilities
+
Owner's Equity

All Asset Accounts		All Liability Accounts	
Debit to enter increases (+)	Credit to enter decreases (−)	Debit to enter decreases (−)	Credit to enter increases (+)

All Owner's Equity Accounts	
Debit to enter decreases (−)	Credit to enter increases (+)

Total Debits   =   Total Credits

of the owner's equity account would be required. Therefore, it is better practice to enter revenue and expenses in separate accounts.

The credit side of each revenue account serves temporarily as part of the credit side of the owner's equity account. Increases in owner's equity are entered as credits. Thus increases in owner's equity resulting from revenue are credited to revenue accounts. Likewise, the debit side of each expense account serves temporarily as part of the debit side of the owner's equity account. Decreases in owner's equity are entered as debits. Thus decreases in owner's equity resulting from expense are debited to expense accounts. The key relationship between the revenue and expense accounts and the owner's equity account is illustrated as follows:

All Owner's Equity Accounts	
Debit to enter decreases (−)	Credit to enter increases (+)

All Expense Accounts		All Revenue Accounts	
Debit to enter increases (+)	Credit to enter decreases (−)	Debit to enter decreases (−)	Credit to enter increases (+)

The revenue and expense accounts are called **temporary owner's equity accounts** because they are closed into the owner's equity account at the end of each accounting period. The closing process transfers the revenue and expense account balances to the owner's equity account. This process sets the temporary account balances back to zero.

The Use of Asset, Liability, and Owner's Equity Accounts

The application of the double-entry process in handling transactions that affect asset, liability, and owner's equity accounts will be explained using the transactions discussed on pages 18-19. These transactions will be analyzed and their effect on the accounting elements will be indicated by showing the proper entries in T accounts.

Transaction (a)

An Increase in an Asset Offset by an Increase in Owner's Equity
John Wendt, an attorney, started a business by investing $6,000 in cash.

Assets	=	Liabilities	+	Owner's Equity
Cash				**John Wendt, Capital**
(a) 6,000				(a) 6,000

Analysis: As a result of this transaction the business acquired an asset, cash. The interest given by the business in exchange for the asset is owner's equity, entitled John Wendt, Capital. Thus the amount of the asset, cash, is equal to the owner's equity in the business. Separate accounts are kept for the asset, cash, and for the owner's equity. To enter the transaction as an increase in an asset and an increase in owner's equity, the cash account was debited and Wendt's capital account was credited for $6,000.

Transaction (b)

An Increase in an Asset Offset by an Increase in a Liability
Purchased office equipment (desks and chairs) for $2,700 on account.

Assets	=	Liabilities	+	Owner's Equity
Office Equipment		**Accounts Payable**		
(b) 2,700		(b) 2,700		

Analysis: As a result of this transaction the business acquired a new asset, office equipment. The debt incurred as a result of purchasing the equipment on account is a liability, accounts payable. Separate accounts are kept for office equipment and for accounts payable. To show the increase in the assets of the business, the asset account, Office Equipment, was debited for $2,700. To show the increase in the liabilities of the business, the liability account, Accounts Payable, was credited for $2,700. This liability represents an increase in the outside interest in the business.

Transaction (c)

An Increase in an Asset Offset by an Increase in a Liability
Borrowed $4,000 at a bank by signing a 90-day note.

Assets	=	Liabilities	+	Owner's Equity
Cash		**Notes Payable**		

```
(a)  6,000                      (c)   4,000
(c)  4,000
```

Analysis: As a result of this transaction the business increased the asset, cash. The debt incurred in order to obtain this additional cash is a liability, notes payable. Cash is debited for $4,000 because that asset has increased. A new account, Notes Payable, is credited for $4,000 to recognize the increase in the liability. The outside interest in the business, thus, increased by an additional $4,000 (Accounts Payable of $2,700 plus Notes Payable of $4,000).

Transaction (d)

An Increase in One Asset Offset by a Decrease in Another Asset
Purchased office equipment (filing cabinets) with cash, $900.

Assets		= Liabilities + Owner's Equity
Cash	**Office Equip.**	

```
(a)  6,000 (d)    900 (b)  2,700
(c)  4,000         (d)    900
```

Analysis: As a result of this transaction the business increased the asset, office equipment. To obtain this asset, the business gave up $900 of the asset, cash. Notice that there is no change in total assets. The increase in one asset, office equipment, was offset by a decrease in another asset, cash. To enter the transaction properly, Office Equipment was debited and Cash was credited for $900.

Transaction (e)

A Decrease in an Asset Offset by a Decrease in a Liability
Paid $2,000 on account to the company from which the office equipment was purchased. (See transaction (b).)

Asset	=	Liabilities	+	Owner's Equity
Cash		**Accounts Payable**		

```
(a)  6,000 (d)    900    (e)  2,000 (b)  2,700
(c)  4,000 (e)  2,000
```

Analysis: This transaction resulted in a decrease in the liability, accounts payable, with a corresponding decrease in the asset, cash. Thus, it was entered by debiting Accounts Payable and by crediting Cash for $2,000. As a result of this transaction, the outside interest in the business has decreased by $2,000.

Use of Revenue and Expense Accounts

The application of the double-entry process in handling transactions that affect revenue and expense accounts will be shown using the transactions discussed on pages 20-21. These transactions will be analyzed and their effect on the accounting elements will be indicated by showing the proper entries in T accounts. These transactions are a continuation of the transactions completed by John Wendt, an attorney.

Transaction (f)

An Increase in an Asset Offset by an Increase in Owner's Equity Resulting from Revenue

Received $2,000 in cash from a client for professional services rendered.

Assets			=	Liabilities	+	Owner's Equity	
Cash						Client Fees	
(a)	6,000	(d)	900				(f)	2,000
(c)	4,000	(e)	2,000				
(f)	2,000						

Analysis: This transaction resulted in an increase in the asset, cash, with a corresponding increase in owner's equity because of revenue from professional fees. To enter the transaction properly, Cash was debited and the revenue account, Client Fees, was credited for $2,000. In this case the revenue account was given the title, Client Fees, since accounts should always be given a descriptive title that will aid in classifying them in relation to the accounting elements.

Transaction (g)

A Decrease in an Asset Offset by a Decrease In Owner's Equity Resulting from Expense

Paid $800 for office rent for one month.

Assets			=	Liabilities	+	Owner's Equity	
Cash						Rent Expense	
(a)	6,000	(d)	900			(g)	800	
(c)	4,000	(e)	2,000				
(f)	2,000	(g)	800				

Analysis: This transaction resulted in a decrease in the asset, cash, with a corresponding decrease in owner's equity because of expense. To enter the transaction properly, Rent Expense was debited and Cash was credited for $800.

Transaction (h)

A Decrease in an Asset Offset by a Decrease In Owner's Equity Resulting from Expense

Paid a bill for telephone service of $69.

Assets			= Liabilities +	Owner's Equity
Cash				**Telephone Expense**

(a)	6,000	(d)	900	(h)	69	
(c)	4,000	(e)	2,000			
(f)	2,000	(g)	800			
		(h)	69			

Analysis: This transaction is identical with the previous one except that telephone expense rather than rent expense was the reason for the decrease in owner's equity. To enter the transaction properly, Telephone Expense was debited and Cash was credited for $69.

The Trial Balance

Explain the function of and prepare a trial balance.

It is a fundamental principle of the double-entry framework that the sum of the assets is always equal to the sum of the liabilities plus owner's equity. In order to maintain this equality in entering transactions, the sum of the debit entries must always be equal to the sum of the credit entries. To determine whether this equality has been maintained, it is customary to take a trial balance periodically. A **trial balance** is a list of all accounts showing the title and balance of each account.

The **balance** of any account is the difference between the total debits and the total credits. To determine the balance of each account, first the debit and credit amount columns should be totaled. This procedure is called **footing** the amount columns as shown in the following illustration:

Cash			
(a)	6,000	(d)	900
(c)	4,000	(e)	2,000
(f)	2,000	(g)	800
	12,000	(h)	69
	8,231		*3,769*

Once the columns are totaled, the balance of the account is determined by finding the difference between the footings. This balance should be entered on the side of the account that has the larger total. The footings and balances of accounts should be entered in small figures just below the last entry, preferably in pencil. If there are entries on only one side of an account, the balance is shown by simply footing that side of the account. If there is only one item entered in a column, no footing is necessary.

Since asset and expense accounts are debited for increases, these accounts normally have **debit balances** Since liability, owner's equity, and revenue accounts are credited for increases, these accounts normally have **credit balances**

The accounts of John Wendt are reproduced below. To show their relationship to the fundamental accounting equation, the accounts are arranged in three columns under the headings of Assets, Liabilities, and Owner's Equity. The footings and the balances are printed in italics. Note that (1) the footings are directly under the debit and credit amount columns of the cash account and under the debit column of the office equipment account, (2) the balance is shown on the left side of the cash account and on the right side of the accounts payable account, and (3) the footing serves as the balance of the office equipment account. It is not necessary to enter the balances of the other accounts because there is only a single entry in those accounts.

Assets = Liabilities + Owner's Equity

Cash

(a)	6,000	(d)	900
(c)	4,000	(e)	2,000
(f)	2,000	(g)	800
	12,000	(h)	69
	8,231		*3,769*

Notes Payable

(c)	4,000

John Wendt, Capital

(a)	6,000

Office Equipment

(b)	2,700
(d)	900
	3,600

Accounts Payable

(e)	2,000	(b)	2,700
			700

Client Fees

(f)	2,000

Rent Expense

(g)	800

Telephone Expense

(h)	69

The following is a trial balance of John Wendt's accounts. The trial balance was taken on June 30, 19--; therefore, this date is shown on the third line of the heading. The trial balance shows that the debit and credit totals are equal in amount. This is proof that in entering transactions (a) to (h) inclusive the total of the debits was equal to the total of the credits.

A trial balance is not a formal statement or report. Normally, it is never seen by anyone except the accountant. It is used as an aid in preparing the income statement and the balance sheet. If John Wendt's trial balance is studied in conjunction with his income statement and balance sheet shown on pages 12 and 13, it will be seen that these state-

Account	Dr. Balance	Cr. Balance
John Wendt, Attorney		
Trial Balance		
June 30, 19--		
Cash	8 2 3 1 00	
Office Equipment	3 6 0 0 00	
Notes Payable		4 0 0 0 00
Accounts Payable		7 0 0 00
John Wendt, Capital		6 0 0 0 00
Client Fees		2 0 0 0 00
Rent Expense	8 0 0 00	
Telephone Expense	6 9 00	
	12 7 0 0 00	12 7 0 0 00

John Wendt's Trial Balance

ments could have been prepared quite easily from the information on the trial balance. This use of the trial balance will be demonstrated in the next chapter.

Building Your Accounting Knowledge

1. Identify three ways in which account forms may be stored.
2. What are the three major parts of the standard account form?
3. What is the left side of the standard account form called? the right side?
4. Explain the origin of the abbreviations "Dr." for debit and "Cr." for credit.
5. What word is sometimes used as a substitute for debit?
6. What is the relationship between the revenue and expense accounts and the owner's equity account?
7. What is the function of the trial balance?

Assignment Box

To reinforce your understanding of the preceding text materials, you are able to complete the following:
Study Guide: Part B
Textbook: Exercises 1A7 through 1A8 or 1B7 through 1B8
Problems 1A3 through 1A4 or 1B3 through 1B4

Expanding Your Business Vocabulary

What is the meaning of each of the following terms?

account (p.15)
accountant (p.4)
accounting (p.3)
accounting equation (p.5)
account payable (p.5)
asset (p.4)
auditing (p.2)
balance (p.21)
balance sheet (p.9)
bookkeeper (p.4)
business entity (p.4)
capital (p.5)
charge (p.16)
credit (p.16)
credit balances (p.21)
debit (p.16)
debit balances (p.21)
double-entry accounting (p.14)
expense (p.10)
fiscal year (p.11)
footing (p.21)
income statement (p.12)

information processor (p.4)
input (p.13)
liability (p.5)
net income (p.10)
net loss (p.10)
net worth (p.5)
notes payable (p.5)
operating statement (p.12)
output (p.14)
owner's equity (p.5)
processing (p.13)
profit and loss statement (p.12)
proprietorship (p.5)
revenue (p.10)
statement of financial condition (p.9)
statement of financial position (p.9)
temporary owner's equity accounts
  (p.17)
transaction (p.6)
trial balance (p.21)
T account (p.16)

Demonstration Problem

Patti Gearing owns and operates Gearing Image Coordinators, a hair and beauty styling salon for men and women. The assets and liabilities of the business as of September 1 of the current year are as follows: Cash, $30,000; Styling Equipment, $17,000; Accounts Payable, $900. Patti operates the business in a rented building and pays the electric and telephone bills of the business. She also has a temporary assistant. The transactions for the month of September are as follows:

(a) Paid rent for September, $800.00.
(b) Purchased beauty aids from Model Beauty Materials Co., $1,100.00, on account (Beauty Aids Expense).
(c) Received $1,200.00 revenue from styling services.
(d) Paid electricity bill, $65.25.
(e) Purchased two new hair dryers (styling equipment), at $675.00 each from Venus Products Co., on account.
(f) Paid temporary assistant (wages) for first half of month, $600.00.
(g) Received $1,500.00 revenue from styling services.
(h) Paid telephone bill, $37.80.
(i) Paid $500.00 to Model Beauty Materials Co. on account.
(j) Received $1,350.00 revenue from styling services.
(k) Paid temporary assistant (wages) for last half of month, $600.00.
(l) Received $1,300.00 revenue from styling services.

Required:

1. Find the amount of owner's equity (Patti Gearing's Capital) as of September 1 of the current year.

2. Enter the September 1 balances in T accounts.
3. Enter the transactions for September in the same T accounts as the September balances.
4. Foot the T accounts and determine their balances as necessary.
5. Prepare a trial balance of the accounts as of September 30 of the current year.
6. Prepare an income statement for Gearing Image Coordinators for the month ended September 30 of the current year.
7. Prepare a balance sheet for Gearing Image Coordinators as of September 30 of the current year.

Solution

1. Assets   − Liabilities   = Owner's Equity
                               (Patti Gearing, Capital)
    $47,000 − $900   = $46,100

2, 3, & 4.

Cash

Bal.	30,000.00	(a)	800.00
(c)	1,200.00	(d)	65.25
(g)	1,500.00	(f)	600.00
(j)	1,350.00	(h)	37.80
(l)	1,300.00	(i)	500.00
	35,350.00	(k)	600.00
	32,746.95		*2,603.05*

Styling Equipment

Bal.	17,000.00
(e)	1,350.00
	18,350.00

Accounts Payable

(i)	500.00	Bal.	900.00
		(b)	1,100.00
		(e)	1,350.00
			3,350.00
			2,850.00

Patti Gearing, Capital

	Bal.	46,100.00

Styling Revenue

	(c)	1,200.00
	(g)	1,500.00
	(j)	1,350.00
	(l)	1,300.00
		5,350.00

Beauty Aids Expense

(b)	1,100.00

Wages Expense

(f)	600.00
(k)	600.00
	1,200.00

Rent Expense

(a)	800.00

Electricity Expense

(d)	65.25

Telephone Expense

(h)	37.80

5.

Gearing Image Coordinators
Trial Balance
September 30, 19--

Cash	$32,746.95	
Styling Equipment	18,350.00	
Accounts Payable		$ 2,850.00
Patti Gearing, Capital		46,100.00
Styling Revenue		5,350.00
Beauty Aids Expense	1,100.00	
Wages Expense	1,200.00	
Rent Expense	800.00	
Electricity Expense	65.25	
Telephone Expense	37.80	
	$54,300.00	$54,300.00

6.

Gearing Image Coordinators
Income Statement
For Month Ended September, 19--

Revenue:		
Styling revenue		$5,350.00
Operating expenses:		
Beauty aids expense	$1,100.00	
Salary expense	1,200.00	
Rent expense	800.00	
Electricity expense	65.25	
Telephone expense	37.80	
Total operating expenses		3,203.05
Net income		$2,146.95

7.

Gearing Image Coordinators
Balance Sheet
September 30, 19--

Assets		Liabilities	
Cash	$32,746.95	Accounts payable ...	$ 2,850.00
Styling equipment	18,350.00		
		Owner's Equity	
		Patti Gearing, capital,	
		September 30, 19--	48,246.95
		Total liabilities and	
Total assets	$51,096.95	owner's equity....	$51,096.95

*Note: Now that you have reviewed the Demonstration Problem and Solution you may complete the **Mastery Problem** at the end of the chapter activities.

Applying Accounting Concepts

Series A

Exercise 1A1—Effect of Transactions on Accounting Equation; Balance Sheet Accounts. Joyce Berg has started a business. During the first month (February, 19--), the following transactions occurred. Show the effect of each transaction on the basic elements of the accounting equation: Assets = Liabilities + Owner's Equity. Show the new amounts in the accounts after each transaction.

(a) Invested $20,000 cash in the business.
(b) Purchased office equipment on account, $3,500.
(c) Borrowed $5,000 from a bank.
(d) Purchased office equipment for cash, $1,200.
(e) Paid $1,500 on account to a supplier.

Exercise 1A2—Effect of Transactions on Accounting Equation; Income Statement Accounts. Assume that Joyce Berg completed the following additional transactions during February. Show the effect of each transaction on the basic elements of the expanded accounting equation: Assets = Liabilities + [Owner's Equity + Revenue − Expenses]. Once again, show the new amounts in the accounts after each transaction.

(f) Received $2,500 from a client for professional services.
(g) Paid $900 office rent for February.
(h) Paid $73 for February telephone services.

Exercise 1A3—Effect of Transactions on Accounting Equation; Income and Balance Sheet Accounts. Albert Hirson has started a business. During the first month (April 19--), the following transactions occurred. Show the effect of each transaction on the basic elements of the accounting equation: Assets = Liabilities + [Owner's Equity + Revenue − Expenses]. Show the new amounts in the accounts after each transaction.

(a) Invested $18,000 cash in the business.
(b) Purchased office equipment for $4,600 on account.
(c) Purchased office equipment for cash, $1,200.
(d) Received $3,300 cash from a client for services rendered.
(e) Paid $4,600 on account to the company that supplied the office equipment in (b) above.
(f) Paid $750 office rent for the month.

Exercise 1A4—Analysis of Changes in Owner's Equity. Refer to Exercise 1A3 and answer the following questions:

1. Hirson's initial cash investment in the business was $_____.
2. Hirson's net income for the first month of operations was $_____.
3. Hirson's total owner's equity at the end of the first month of operations was $_____.

Exercise 1A5—Income Statement Preparation. Refer to Exercise 1A3 and prepare an income statement for Albert Hirson for the month of April 19--.

Exercise 1A6—Balance Sheet Preparation. Refer to Exercise 1A3 and prepare a balance sheet for Albert Hirson as of April 30, 19--.

Exercise 1A7—T Account Transaction Analysis. For each of the May transactions of Allison Young given below, show the effect on the accounting elements by preparing the necessary entries in the appropriate asset, liability, owner's equity, revenue, and expense T accounts.

(a) Invested $16,000 cash in the business.
(b) Purchased office equipment for $3,600 on account.
(c) Purchased office equipment for cash, $1,400.
(d) Received $2,300 cash from a client for services rendered.
(e) Paid $3,600 on account to the company that supplied the office equipment in (b) above.
(f) Paid $550 office rent for the month.

Exercise 1A8—Trial Balance Preparation. Refer to Exercise 1A7. Prepare a trial balance for Allison Young's business at the end of the first month of operations (May 19--).

Series B

Exercise 1B1—Effect of Transactions on Accounting Equation; Balance Sheet Accounts. Don Coursey has started a business. During the first month (March, 19--), the following transactions occurred. Show the effect of each transaction on the basic elements of the accounting equation: Assets = Liabilities + Owner's Equity. Show the new amounts in the accounts after each transaction.

(a) Invested $30,000 cash in the business.
(b) Purchased office equipment on account, $4,500.
(c) Borrowed $8,000 from a bank.
(d) Purchased office equipment for cash, $1,600.
(e) Paid $2,000 on account to a supplier.

Exercise 1B2—Effect of Transactions on Accounting Equation; Income Statement Accounts. Assume that Don Coursey completed the following additional transactions during March. Show the effect of each transaction on the basic elements of the expanded accounting equation: Assets = Liabilities + [Owner's Equity + Revenue − Expenses]. Once again, show the new amounts in the accounts after each transaction.

(f) Received $3,000 from a client for professional services.
(g) Paid $1,000 office rent for March.
(h) Paid $68 for March telephone services.

Exercise 1B3—Effect of Transactions on Accounting Equation; Income Statement and Balance Sheet Accounts. Lee Bernstein has started a business. During the first month (October, 19--), the following transactions occurred. Show the effect of each transaction on the basic elements of the accounting equation: Assets = Liabilities + [Owner's Equity + Revenue − Expenses]. Show the new amounts in the accounts after each transaction.

(a) Invested $15,000 cash in the business.
(b) Purchased office equipment for $3,800 on account.

(c) Purchased office equipment for cash, $1,000.
(d) Received $2,700 from a client for services rendered.
(e) Paid $3,800 on account to the company that supplied the office equipment in (b) above.
(f) Paid $650 office rent for the month.

Exercise 1B4—Analysis of Changes in Owner's Equity. Refer to Exercise 1B3 and answer the following questions:

1. Bernstein's initial cash investment in the business was $_____.
2. Bernstein's net income for the first month of operations was $_____.
3. Bernstein's total owner's equity at the end of the first month of operations was $_____.

Exercise 1B5—Income Statement Preparation. Refer to Exercise 1B3 and prepare an income statement for Lee Bernstein for the month of October 19--.

Exercise 1B6—Balance Sheet Preparation. Refer to Exercise 1B3 and prepare a balance sheet for Lee Bernstein as of October 31, 19--.

Exercise 1B7—T Account Transaction Analysis. For each of the November transactions of Mary Calais given below, show the effect on the accounting elements by preparing the necessary entries in the appropriate asset, liability, owner's equity, revenue, and expense T accounts.

(a) Invested $22,000 cash in the business.
(b) Purchased office equipment for $5,700 on account.
(c) Purchased office equipment for cash, $1,500.
(d) Received $4,000 cash from a client for services rendered.
(e) Paid $5,700 on account to the company that supplied the office equipment in (b) above.
(f) Paid $950 office rent for the month.

Exercise 1B8—Trial Balance Preparation. Refer to Exercise 1B7. Prepare a trial balance for Mary Calais' business at the end of the first month of operations (November 19--).

Series A

Problem 1A1   Analysis of Changes in Accounting Equation

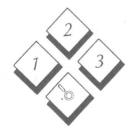

Dr. John Schleper is a chiropractor. As of December 31, Schleper owned the following property that related to the professional practice:

Cash, $4,750   X-ray Equipment, $11,680
Office Equipment, $6,200   Laboratory Equipment, $7,920

As of the same date Schleper owed business suppliers as follows:

Chouteau Gas Company, $2,420
Aloe Medical Supply Company, $3,740

Required:

1. On the basis of the preceding information, compute the amount of the accounting elements, and record them in equation form by filling in blank spaces such as in the equation below.

   Assets $_____ = Liabilities $_____ + Owner's Equity $_____

2. Assuming that during January there is an increase of $7,290 in Dr. Schleper's business assets and an increase of $4,210 in the business liabilities, give the resulting accounting equation.

   Assets $_____ = Liabilities $_____ + Owner's Equity $_____

3. Assuming that during February there is a decrease of $2,920 in Dr. Schleper's business assets and an increase of $2,200 in the business liabilities, give the resulting accounting equation.

   Assets $_____ = Liabilities $_____ + Owner's Equity $_____

Problem 1A2   Detailed Analysis of Changes in Accounting Equation

Kim Petrich is a CPA. As of July 1 Petrich owned the following business assets:

> Cash, $6,260
> Office Equipment, $8,500
> An automobile, used for business purposes only, $16,000

On the same date, Petrich owed Equipo Co. a final installment on the office equipment amounting to $1,500.

The following transactions were completed by Petrich during the month of July. Indicate the effect of each transaction on the accounting equation by inserting the amounts under the proper headings on lettered lines such as those below. Each amount should be preceded by a plus sign if it represents an increase or by a minus sign if it represents a decrease.

(a) Bought additional office equipment on account, $1,800.
(b) Paid the final installment due on equipment, $1,500.
(c) Paid cash for office safe, $450.
(d) Paid $800 for office rent for July.
(e) Received $3,000 revenue from clients.

	Assets			=	Liabilities	+	(Owner's Equity	+	Revenue	−	Expenses)
	Cash	+	Office Equip.	+	Auto- mobile	=	Accounts Payable	+	Kim Petrich, Capital	+	Client Fees	−	Rent Expense
Bal.	$6,260		$8,500		$16,000		$1,500		$29,260			
(a)												
Bal.												
(b)	etc.											

Problem 1A3   T Account Transaction Analysis; Trial Balance

Steven Wong has decided to go into the lawn maintenance business and to operate as Wong's Lawn Maintenance Service. The following transactions were completed during the first month of operations (March):

    (a) Invested $50,000.00 cash in the business.
    (b) Purchased lawn maintenance equipment for $20,000.00 cash.
    (c) Paid $750.00 rent for garage and office quarters.
    (d) Purchased chemicals for $1,000.00 from Catalyst Chemical Co. on account (Chemical Expense).
    (e) Received $650.00 revenue from lawn maintenance service.
    (f) Paid electricity bill, $45.95.
    (g) Paid temporary assistant's wages for first half of month, $400.00 (Wages Expense).
    (h) Received $575.00 revenue from lawn maintenance service.
    (i) Paid telephone bill, $33.95.
    (j) Paid license fee for truck, $110.00.
    (k) Paid $450.00 to Catalyst Chemical Co. on account.
    (l) Paid $101.75 for gas and oil purchased.
    (m) Received $1,200.00 revenue from lawn maintenance service.
    (n) Received $840.00 revenue from lawn maintenance service.
    (o) Paid temporary assistant's salary for second half of month, $400.00.

Required:

1. Enter the transactions in T accounts.
2. Foot the accounts where necessary and enter the total of each column immediately under the last entry in small figures. If an account has entries on both sides, determine the balance and enter it in small figures on the side with the larger total.
3. Prepare a trial balance of the accounts as of March 31, 19--. After listing the account balances, rule a single line across the amount columns immediately below the last item. Enter the totals on the next horizontal line and rule a double line across the amount columns immediately under the totals.

Problem 1A4   Analysis of Net Income and Change in Owner's Equity

Refer to the trial balance of Wong's Lawn Maintenance Service (Problem 1A3) and select the information needed to fill in the blank spaces in the following statements:

1. (a) Total revenue for the month ....   _____
    (b) Total expenses for the month ....   _____
    (c) Net income for the month ....   _____
2. (a) Wong's original investment in the business ......   _____
        + the net income for the month ....   _____
        = owner's equity at the end of the month ......   _____
    (b) End-of-month accounting equation:
        Assets $_____ = Liabilities $_____ + Owner's Equity $_____

Series B

Problem 1B1   Analysis of Changes in Accounting Equation

Dr. Patricia Parsons is a dentist. As of January 31, Parsons owned the following property that related to the professional practice:

Cash, $3,560   X-ray Equipment, $8,760
Office Equipment, $4,600   Laboratory Equipment, $5,940

As of the same date Parsons owed business suppliers as follows:

Cupples Gas Company, $1,815
Swan Dental Lab, $2,790

Required:

1. On the basis of the preceding information, compute the amount of the accounting elements, and record them in equation form by filling in the blank spaces in the equation below.

Assets $_____ = Liabilities $_____ + Owner's Equity $_____

2. Assuming that during February there is an increase of $5,465 in Dr. Parsons' business assets and an increase of $3,910 in the business liabilities, give the resulting accounting equation.

Assets $_____ = Liabilities $_____ + Owner's Equity $_____

3. Assuming that during March there is a decrease of $2,190 in Dr. Parsons' business assets and an increase of $1,650 in the business liabilities, give the resulting accounting equation.

Assets $_____ = Liabilities $_____ + Owner's Equity $_____

Problem 1B2   Detailed Analysis of Changes in Accounting Equation

Harry Flenner is an attorney. As of August 1, Flenner owned the following business assets:

Cash, $4,690
Office Equipment, $6,375
An automobile, used for business purposes only, $12,000

On the same date, Flenner owed Peeper-Clark Co. a final installment on the office equipment amounting to $1,025 and had no other business debts.

The following transactions were completed by Flenner during the month of August. Indicate the effect of each transaction on the accounting equation by inserting the amounts under the proper headings on lettered lines such as those below. Each amount should be preceded by a plus sign if it represents an increase or by a minus sign if it represents a decrease.

(a) Bought additional office equipment on account, $1,350.
(b) Paid the final installment due on equipment, $1,025.
(c) Paid cash for office safe, $375.
(d) Paid $600 for office rent for August.
(e) Received $2,500 revenue from clients.

		Assets			=	Liabilities	+	(Owner's Equity	+	Revenue	−	Expenses)
	Cash	+	Office Equip.	+	Auto-mobile	=	Accounts Payable	+	Harry Flenner, Capital	+	Client Fees	−	Rent Expense
Bal.	$4,690		$6,375		$12,000		$1,025		$22,040				
(a)	etc.												

Problem 1B3   T Account Transaction Analysis; Trial Balance

Jennifer Zulanch has decided to go into the insect extermination business and to operate as Jenny's Exterminating Service. The following transactions were completed during the first month of operations (May):

(a) Zulanch invested $60,000.00 cash in the business.
(b) Purchased extermination equipment for $24,000.00 cash.
(c) Paid $900.00 rent for garage and office quarters.
(d) Purchased chemicals for $1,200.00 from Chemsearch Co. on account (Chemical Expense).
(e) Received $760.00 revenue from extermination service.
(f) Paid electricity bill, $54.25.
(g) Paid temporary assistant's wages for first half of month, $500.00 (Wages Expense).
(h) Received $690.00 revenue from extermination service.
(i) Paid telephone bill, $40.65.
(j) Paid license fee for truck, $125.00.
(k) Paid $550.00 to Chemsearch Co. on account.
(l) Paid $121.20 for gas and oil purchased.
(m) Received $1,500.00 revenue from extermination service.
(n) Received $990.00 revenue from extermination service.
(o) Paid temporary assistant's salary for second half of month, $500.00.

Required:

1. Enter the transactions in T accounts.
2. Foot the accounts where necessary and enter the total of each column immediately under the last entry in small figures. If an account has entries on both sides, determine the balance and enter it in small figures on the side with the larger total.
3. Prepare a trial balance of the accounts as of May 31, 19--.
   After listing the account balances, rule a single line across the amount columns immediately below the last item. Enter the totals on the next horizontal line and rule a double line across the amount columns immediately under the totals.

Problem 1B4   Analysis of Net Income and Change in Owner's Equity

Refer to the trial balance of Jenny's Exterminating Service and select the information needed to fill in the blank spaces in the following statements:

1. **(a)** Total revenue for the month .... _____
   (b) Total expenses for the month .... _____
   (c) Net income for the month .... _____
2. **(a)** Jennifer Zulanch's original investment in the business .... _____
      + the net income for the month .... _____
      = owner's equity at the end of the month ...... _____
   (b) End-of-month accounting equation:
      Assets $_____ = Liabilities $_____ + Owner's Equity $_____

Mastery Problem

Cecil Pints owns and operates We-Buy, You-Pay Shopping Services. For a fee that is based on the amount of research and shopping time required, Cecil or one of his associates will shop for most anything from groceries to home furnishings. Business is particularly heavy around Christmas and in early summer when many wedding anniversaries are celebrated. The business is operated out of a rented store. The associates are paid a commission based on the revenues they generate and a mileage reimbursement for the use of their personal automobiles for shopping trips. The assets and liabilities as of December 1 of the current year are as follows:

Cash... $25,000
Office Equipment 9,000
Accounts Payable 5,000

The transactions for the month of December are as follows:

(a) Paid rent for December, $500.
(b) Received $5,200 for shopping fees.
(c) Paid telephone bill, $90.
(d) Borrowed $5,000 from the bank by signing a note payable.
(e) Purchased a computer, $4,800.
(f) Paid commissions to associates for revenues generated during the first half of the month, $3,500.
(g) Paid electric bill, $600.
(h) Paid $2,000 on account.
(i) Received $11,200 for shopping fees.
(j) Paid associates for last half of month $7,000.
(k) Paid mileage reimbursements for the month, $1,500.
(l) Paid $1,000 on note payable to bank.

Required:
1. Calculate the amount of owner's equity (Cecil Pints, Capital) as of December 1 of the current year.
2. Enter the December 1 balances in T accounts.
3. Enter the transactions for December in the T accounts.
4. Foot the T accounts and determine their balances, as necessary.
5. Prepare a trial balance of the accounts as of December 31 of the current year.
6. Prepare an income statement for We-Buy, You-Pay Shopping Services for the month ended December 31 of the current year.
7. Calculate the amount of owner's equity (Cecil Pints, Capital) as of December 31 of the current year.
8. Prepare a balance sheet for We-Buy, You-Pay Shopping Services as of December 31 of the current year.

CHAPTER 2

Accounting Procedure

Chapter Objectives

Careful study of this chapter should enable you to:

- Describe the flow of financial data through an accounting information system.
- Describe and explain the purpose of a book of original entry.
- Describe the chart of accounts as a means of classifying

financial information, using an account numbering system.
- Perform the journalizing and posting process.
- Prepare the trial balance.
- Prepare the income statement, statement of owner's equity, and balance sheet from the trial balance.

The double-entry framework of accounting was explained and illustrated in the preceding chapter. To avoid complicating that framework, the mechanics of collecting and classifying information about business transactions were ignored. In actual practice, the first record of a transaction, sometimes called a source document, usually is in the form of a business paper, such as a check stub, receipt, cash register tape, sales ticket, or purchase invoice. These source documents provide information used in determining the effects transactions have on accounts.

This chapter traces the flow of financial data from source documents through the accounting information system. The functions of a book of original entry and a set of accounts are described, and their uses in the journalizing and posting process are explained and illustrated. The use of the chart of accounts in classifying financial information also is described and illustrated. Finally, the procedures for preparing the trial balance, the income statement, statement of owner's equity, and balance sheet from the trial balance information, are explained and illustrated.

Journalizing and Posting Transactions

A chronological listing of the transactions of a business is called a journal. The act of entering the transactions in a journal is called journalizing. It is necessary to analyze each transaction before it can be journalized properly. The purpose of a journal is to provide a record of all transactions completed by the business showing the date of each transaction, titles of the accounts to be debited and credited, and the amounts of the debits and credits. This information is then used to transfer the debits and credits to the proper accounts.

A collection of the accounts of a business is called a **ledger**. The flow of data from the source documents through the journal to the ledger in an accounting information system can be illustrated in the following manner:

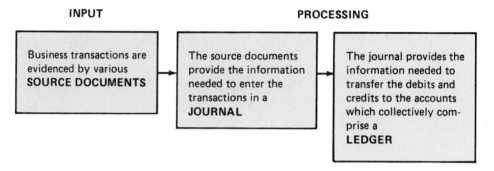

Source Documents

The term *source document* covers a wide variety of forms and papers. Almost any document that provides information about a business transaction can be called a **source document**.

Source Documents

Examples:	*Provide information about:*
1. Check stubs or carbon copies of checks	Cash payments
2. Receipt stubs, carbon copies of receipts, cash register tapes, or memos of cash register totals	Cash receipts
3. Copies of sales tickets or sales invoices issued to customers or clients	Sales of goods or services
4. Purchase invoices received from suppliers	Purchases of goods or services

The Journal

A journal is commonly referred to as a **book of original entry** because the first formal accounting record of a transaction is made in a journal from source document information. The format of the pages in a journal varies with the type and size of an enterprise and the nature of its operations. Although a wide variety of journals are used in business, the simplest form of journal is a two-column journal. The following is an example of such a journal.

	DATE	DESCRIPTION	POST. REF.	DEBIT	CREDIT	
1						1
2	(1)	(2)	(3)	(4)	(5)	2
3						3
4						4

JOURNAL   PAGE

Journal pages usually are numbered in sequence, and the appropriate number is entered after the word "Page" in the upper right-hand corner of each page of the journal. A **two-column journal** has only two amount columns, one for debit amounts and one for credit amounts. In the illustration, the columns have been numbered for the following discussion.

Column 1 is the Date column. The year is entered in small figures at the top of the column immediately below the column heading. The year only needs to be repeated at the top of each new page unless an entry for a new year is made later on the page. The **Date column** is a double column, the perpendicular single rule being used to separate the month from the day. Thus in entering the date, the month should be entered in full or abbreviated to the left of the single line and the day of the month should be entered to the right of this line. The name of the month need only be shown for the first entry on a page unless an entry for a new month is made farther down on the page.

Column 2 is generally referred to as the Description or explanation column. The **Description column** is used to enter the titles of the accounts affected by each transaction, together with a description of the transaction. Two or more accounts are affected by each transaction, and each of these accounts must be recorded. The accounts to be debited are entered first at the extreme left of the column while the accounts to be credited are usually indented one-half inch (about 1.3 centimeters). A separate line should be used for each account title. The description should then be entered immediately following the last credit entry and indented an additional one-half inch.

Column 3 is the **Posting Reference column** sometimes referred to as a folio column. No entries are made in this column at the time of journalizing; such entries are made only at the time the debit and credit elements are transferred to the proper accounts in the ledger. This procedure will be explained in detail later in this chapter.

Column 4, the **Debit amount column**, is used to enter the amount that is to be debited to an account. The amount should be entered on the same line as the title of that account.

Column 5, the **Credit amount column**, is used to enter the amount that is to be credited to an account. The amount should be entered on the same line as the title of that account.

Journalizing

Journalizing involves entering the significant information concerning each transaction in the chronological order in which it and the other transactions occurred. For every transaction, the entry should include the date, the title of each account affected, the amounts, and a brief description. Before a transaction can be entered properly, it must be analyzed in order to determine:

1. Which accounts are affected by the transaction.
2. What amount affects each account.
3. Whether the balance of each account is increased or decreased.

To illustrate the journalizing process, assume that a business purchased an electronic calculator on August 25 for $125 in cash. This transaction caused an increase in Office Equipment and a decrease in Cash. The following information would be entered in a two-column journal.

Aug. 25	Office Equipment	125.00	
	Cash		125.00
	Purchased an electronic calculator.		

The Chart of Accounts

Describe the chart of accounts as a means of classifying financial information, using an account numbering system.

In analyzing a transaction prior to journalizing it, the accountant must know which accounts are being used by the business. When an accounting information system is established for a new business, the first step is to decide which accounts are required. The accounts used will depend upon the information needed or desired. Ordinarily, it is desirable to keep a separate account for each type of asset and each type of liability, since information will be needed regarding what is owned and what is owed. A permanent owner's equity or capital account should be kept so that information regarding the owner's interest in the business is available. It is also advisable to keep separate accounts for each type of revenue and each kind of expense. The revenue and expense accounts are temporary accounts that are used to enter increases and decreases in owner's equity. Revenue accounts reflect increases as a result of selling a product or providing a service, while expense accounts reflect decreases as a result of efforts made to produce revenues. The specific revenue and expense accounts that should be kept for entering increases and decreases in owner's equity depend upon the nature and sources of the revenue and expenses.

A professional person or an individual engaged in operating a small enterprise may need to keep relatively few accounts. On the other hand, a large business may need to keep a great many accounts because of the complexity of the operation. Regardless of the number, accounts can be separated into the three major classes, assets, liabilities, and owner's equity, and should be grouped according to these classes in the ledger.

Asset accounts are placed first, liability accounts second, and owner's equity accounts, including revenue and expense accounts, last. A list of all the accounts used by a business enterprise is called a **chart of accounts.** It is common practice to number each account and to keep the accounts in numerical order. The numbering usually follows a consistent pattern and becomes a code. For example, asset accounts may be assigned numbers that always start with "1," liability accounts with "2," owner's equity accounts with "3," revenue accounts with "4," and expense accounts with "5."

To illustrate, assume that John Wendt, the attorney whose business was considered in Chapter 1, wanted to establish a chart of accounts on June 1, 19--, the start of his business. Wendt would not need many accounts initially because the business is new. Additional accounts can easily be added as the need arises. The following is a chart of accounts for John Wendt, Attorney:

John Wendt, Attorney—Chart of Accounts

Assets*
  111 Cash
  191 Office Equipment
Liabilities
  216 Notes Payable
  218 Accounts Payable
Owner's Equity
  311 John Wendt, Capital
  312 John Wendt, Drawing

Revenue
  411 Client Fees
Expenses
  541 Rent Expense
  544 Travel and Entertainment Expense
  545 Telephone Expense
  572 Miscellaneous Expense

*Words in heavy type represent headings and not account titles.

Most of the accounts listed above were explained and illustrated in Chapter 1. The owner's equity account, John Wendt, Drawing, is new and needs to be explained. When the owner of a business enterprise withdraws assets for personal use, a decrease in owner's equity occurs. Although the amounts withdrawn could be entered as debits to the owner's capital account, it is better practice to enter withdrawals in a separate owner's equity account called Drawing. This practice makes it easier to summarize the owner's withdrawals during a period. The use of the drawing account is illustrated on page 43.

Journalizing Procedure Illustrated

Perform the journalizing and posting process.

To illustrate journalizing procedures, transactions for the first month of operations of John Wendt, Attorney will be journalized. In addition to the eight (a through h) transactions considered in Chapter 1, a few more transactions will be included here. Since you are already familiar with the transactions from Chapter 1, the journalizing process should be easier to understand. A narrative of the transactions, containing all of the information needed in journalizing them, is provided. Some of the transactions are analyzed to explain their effect upon the accounts. This analysis will immediately follow the journal entry.

JOHN WENDT, ATTORNEY—*Narrative of Transactions*

Friday, June 1, 19--

John Wendt, an attorney, started a business by investing $6,000 in cash.

June 1 Cash	6,000.00	
John Wendt, Capital		6,000.00
Original investment in law office.		

Analysis: As a result of this transaction, the business acquired cash in the amount of $6,000 in exchange for an ownership interest of the same amount. There was an increase in the asset, cash, and an increase in owner's equity. The entry for the transaction is a debit to Cash and a credit to John Wendt, Capital, for $6,000.

Note that the following steps are involved:

1. Since this was the first entry on the journal page, the year is entered at the top of the Date column.
2. The month and day are entered on the first line in the Date column.
3. The title of the account to be debited, Cash, is entered on the first line at the extreme left of the Description column. The amount of the debit, $6,000, is entered on the same line in the Debit column.
4. The title of the account to be credited, John Wendt, Capital, is entered on the second line indented one-half inch from the left side of the Description column. The amount of the credit, $6,000, is entered on the same line in the Credit column.
5. The explanation of the entry is entered on the next line indented an additional one-half inch. The second line of the explanation is also indented the same distance as the first.

Saturday, June 2

Purchased office equipment (desks and chairs) for $2,700 on account from Bynum Office Supply.

June 2 Office Equipment.........................	2,700.00	
Accounts Payable		2,700.00
Purchase equipment from Bynum Office		
Supply.		

Analysis: As a result of this transaction, the business acquired office equipment in exchange for a promise to pay for it at a later date. There was an increase in the asset, office equipment, and an increase in the liability, accounts payable. The transaction is entered by debiting Office Equipment and crediting Accounts Payable for $2,700. The name of the supplier to whom Wendt owes the money is noted in the explanation of the entry.

Wednesday, June 6

Borrowed $4,000 at First State Bank by signing a 90-day note.

```
June   6  Cash ....................................  4,000.00
              Notes Payable...........................               4,000.00
              First State Bank, 90-day note.
```

Analysis: This transaction caused an increase in the asset, cash, and a corresponding increase in a liability called notes payable. The proper entry for the transaction is a debit to Cash and a credit to Notes Payable.

Thursday, June 7

Purchased office equipment (filing cabinets) for cash, $900.

```
June   7  Office Equipment..........................   900.00
              Cash ...................................                 900.00
              Paid for office equipment.
```

Analysis: In this transaction, the business simply exchanged one asset, cash, for another asset, office equipment. There was an increase in office equipment and a decrease in cash. The transaction is entered by debiting Office Equipment and crediting Cash.

Friday, June 8

Paid Bynum Office Supply $2,000 on account for a portion of the office equipment purchased on June 2.

```
June   8  Accounts Payable..........................  2,000.00
              Cash ...................................               2,000.00
              Made partial payment to Bynum Office Supply.
```

Analysis: This transaction caused a decrease in the liability, accounts payable, with a corresponding decrease in the asset, cash. The transaction is entered by debiting Accounts Payable and crediting Cash for $2,000.

Monday, June 11

Received $2,000 from James Losch for legal services rendered.

```
June  11  Cash ...................................  2,000.00
              Client Fees ............................               2,000.00
              Received from James Losch.
```

Analysis: This transaction resulted in an increase in the asset, cash, with a corresponding increase in revenue from client fees. The increase in revenue represents an increase in owner's equity. The transaction is entered by debiting Cash and crediting Client Fees for $2,000.

Tuesday, June 12

Paid office rent for June, $800.

June 12 Rent Expense 800.00
         Cash 800.00
            Paid June rent.

Analysis: This transaction resulted in an increase in an expense, with a corresponding decrease in the asset, cash. The increase in the expense represents a decrease in owner's equity. The transaction is entered by debiting Rent Expense and crediting Cash for $800.

Thursday, June 14

Paid the General Telephone Co. $69 for the cost of installing a telephone in the office and for the first month's service charges.

June 14 Telephone Expense 69.00
         Cash 69.00
            Paid telephone bill.

Analysis: This transaction caused an increase in an expense and a corresponding decrease in the asset, cash. The transaction is entered by debiting Telephone Expense and crediting Cash for $69.

In the eight preceding journal entries the Posting Reference column has been left blank. (It is not used until the amounts are posted to the accounts in the ledger.) The journal illustrated on pages 43 and 44 shows the account numbers in the Posting Reference column as they would appear after the posting has been completed.

Note that in the journal illustration there are no blank lines between the entries. Although some accountants leave a blank line after the explanation of each entry, this practice is not recommended, because it provides an opportunity for dishonest persons to alter one or more entries.

The journal entries for the following transactions (as well as for those to this point) are illustrated on pages 43 and 44.

Tuesday, June 19

Paid $36 for current issues of business and law journals for use in the office.

Analysis: This transaction resulted in an increase in an expense and a corresponding decrease in the asset, cash. The transaction is entered by debiting Miscellaneous Expense and crediting Cash for $36.

Friday, June 22

Received $500 from Nita Erskine for legal services rendered.

Friday, June 22

Paid Diamond Travel Service $235 for an airplane ticket for a lawyer's convention trip.

Analysis: This transaction resulted in an increase in an expense and a corresponding decrease in the asset, cash. The transaction is entered by debiting Travel and Entertainment Expense and crediting Cash for $235.

Monday, June 25

Received $650 from James DeBruin for legal services rendered.

Wednesday, June 27

Paid $90 membership dues in the State Bar Association.

Friday, June 29

Wendt withdrew $400 for personal use.

Analysis: This transaction resulted in a decrease in cash and a corresponding decrease in owner's equity. The transaction is entered by debiting the separate owner's equity account, John Wendt, Drawing, and crediting Cash for $400.

JOURNAL

PAGE *1*

	DATE		DESCRIPTION	POST. REF.	DEBIT	CREDIT	
1	*June*	*1*	Cash	*111*	6 0 0 0 00		1
2			*John Wendt, Capital*	*311*		6 0 0 0 00	2
3			*Original investment in law office.*				3
4		*2*	*Office Equipment*	*191*	2 7 0 0 00		4
5			*Accounts Payable*	*218*		2 7 0 0 00	5
6			*Purchased equipment from Bynum Office*				6
7			*Supply.*				7
8		*6*	*Cash*	*111*	4 0 0 0 00		8
9			*Notes Payable*	*216*		4 0 0 0 00	9
10			*First State Bank, 90-day note.*				10
11		*7*	*Office Equipment*	*191*	9 0 0 00		11
12			*Cash*	*111*		9 0 0 00	12
13			*Paid for office equipment.*				13
14		*8*	*Accounts Payable*	*218*	2 0 0 0 00		14
15			*Cash*	*111*		2 0 0 0 00	15
16			*Made partial payment to Bynum Office*				16
17			*Supply.*				17
18		*11*	*Cash*	*111*	2 0 0 0 00		18
19			*Client Fees*	*411*		2 0 0 0 00	19
20			*Received from James Losch.*				20
21		*12*	*Rent Expense*	*541*	8 0 0 00		21
22			*Cash*	*111*		8 0 0 00	22
23			*Paid June Rent.*				23
24		*14*	*Telephone Expense*	*545*	6 9 00		24
25			*Cash*	*111*		6 9 00	25
26			*Paid telephone bill.*				26
27		*19*	*Miscellaneous Expense*	*572*	3 6 00		27
28			*Cash*	*111*	18 5 0 5 00	3 6 00 18 5 0 5 00	28
29			*Purchase of journals.*				29

JOURNAL

PAGE **2**

	DATE		DESCRIPTION	POST. REF.	DEBIT	CREDIT	
1	June	22	Cash	111	5 0 0 00		1
2			Client Fees	411		5 0 0 00	2
3			Received from Nita Erskine.				3
4		22	Travel & Entertainment Expense	544	2 3 5 00		4
5			Cash	111		2 3 5 00	5
6			Paid airplane fare for convention.				6
7		25	Cash	111	6 5 0 00		7
8			Client Fees	411		6 5 0 00	8
9			Received from James DeBruin.				9
10		27	Miscellaneous Expense	572	9 0 00		10
11			Cash	111		9 0 00	11
12			Paid Bar Association dues.				12
13		29	John Wendt, Drawing	312	4 0 0 00		13
14			Cash	111		4 0 0 00	14
15			Withdrawn for personal use.		1 8 7 5 00	1 8 7 5 00	15

Proving the Journal

Because a double entry is made for each transaction, the equality of the debits and credits on each page of the journal can be proved by totaling the amount columns. The total of each column is entered as a footing immediately under the last entry. When a page of the journal is filled, the footings are entered just under the last single horizontal ruled line at the bottom of the page as shown in the illustration on page 43.

Posting to the Ledger

The purpose of a journal is to provide a chronological record of financial transactions expressed as debits and credits to accounts. Accounts are kept to supply management with desired information in summary form. When the accounts are grouped together, they are known collectively as the **general ledger**, or often simply as "the ledger." The accounts should be classified properly in the ledger; that is, the asset accounts should be grouped together, the liability accounts together, and the owner's equity accounts together. Proper grouping of the accounts in the ledger facilitates the preparation of the various reports desired by the owner.

Although there are many ways to keep account forms Wendt has chosen to keep all of the accounts for the business in a loose-leaf ledger. The numbers shown in Wendt's chart of accounts on page 39 were used as a guide in arranging the accounts in the ledger. The ledger is reproduced on pages 46-48. Note that the accounts are in numerical order.

The process of transferring the debits and credits from the journal to the ledger accounts is known as **posting**. All amounts entered in the journal should be posted to the accounts kept in the ledger in order to summarize the results. Such posting can be done daily or at frequent intervals. The ledger is not a reliable source of information until all of the transactions entered in the journal have been posted. Since the accounts provide the information needed in preparing financial statements, an accurate posting procedure must be maintained.

Posting from the journal to the ledger involves the following four steps:

1. Enter the date of each transaction in the accounts.
2. Enter the amount of each transaction in the accounts.
3. Enter the page of the journal from which each transaction is posted in the accounts.
4. Enter the account number in the Posting Reference column of the journal for each transaction that is posted.

Step 4 shows that each journal transaction has been posted to the ledger accounts. Steps 3 and 4 together make it possible to identify the journal page from which each account was posted, and the account to which each entry was posted. The information in the posting reference columns of the journal and ledger provides a link between the journal and ledger known as a **cross-reference.**

The first entry of Wendt's business to be posted from the journal occurred on June 1, 19--, and required a debit to cash of $6,000. The posting to the cash account is accomplished, as shown in the following illustration, by four steps:

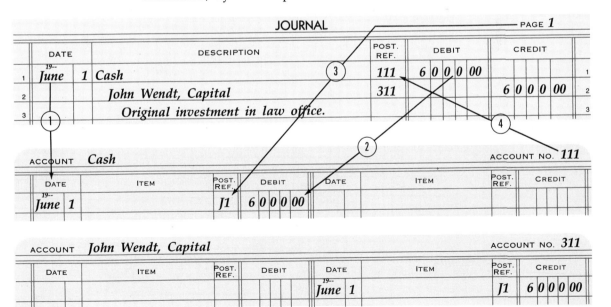

Posting from the Journal to the General Ledger

1. Enter the year, "19--," the month, "June," and the day, "1," in the Date column of the cash account.
2. Enter the amount, $6,000, in the Debit column.
3. Enter "J1" in the Posting Reference column since the posting came from Page 1 of the journal.
4. Enter the cash account number 111 in the Posting Reference column of the journal on the same line as the debit to Cash for $6,000.

The same pattern is followed in posting the credit part of the journal entry, $6,000, to John Wendt, Capital, Account No. 311.

As shown in the journal of John Wendt, Attorney (reproduced on pages 43 and 44) and the ledger (reproduced below and on pages 47-48), a similar procedure is followed in posting every amount from the journal. Note also that in the ledger, the year "19--" is entered only at the top of each Date column, and that the month "June" is entered only with the first posting to an account.

ACCOUNT *Cash* ACCOUNT NO. **111**

DATE		ITEM	POST. REF.	DEBIT	DATE		ITEM	POST. REF.	CREDIT
19-- June	1		J1	6 0 0 0 00	19-- June	7		J1	9 0 0 00
	6		J1	4 0 0 0 00		8		J1	2 0 0 0 00
	11		J1	2 0 0 0 00		12		J1	8 0 0 00
	22		J2	5 0 0 00		14		J1	6 9 00
	25		J2	6 5 0 00		19		J1	3 6 00
		8,620.00	13	1 5 0 00		22		J2	2 3 5 00
						27		J2	9 0 00
						29		J2	4 0 0 00
									4 5 3 0 00

ACCOUNT *Office Equipment* ACCOUNT NO. **191**

DATE		ITEM	POST. REF.	DEBIT	DATE	ITEM	POST. REF.	CREDIT
19-- June	2		J1	2 7 0 0 00				
	7		J1	9 0 0 00				
				3 6 0 0 00				

ACCOUNT *Notes Payable* ACCOUNT NO. **216**

DATE	ITEM	POST. REF.	DEBIT	DATE		ITEM	POST. REF.	CREDIT
				19-- June	6		J1	4 0 0 0 00

ACCOUNT **Accounts Payable**   ACCOUNT NO. **218**

DATE	ITEM	POST. REF.	DEBIT	DATE	ITEM	POST. REF.	CREDIT
19-- June 8		J1	2 0 0 0 00	19-- June 2	700.00	J1	2 7 0 0 00

ACCOUNT **John Wendt, Capital**   ACCOUNT NO. **311**

DATE	ITEM	POST. REF.	DEBIT	DATE	ITEM	POST. REF.	CREDIT
				19-- June 1		J1	6 0 0 0 00

ACCOUNT **John Wendt, Drawing**   ACCOUNT NO. **312**

DATE	ITEM	POST. REF.	DEBIT	DATE	ITEM	POST. REF.	CREDIT
19-- June 29		J2	4 0 0 00				

ACCOUNT **Client Fees**   ACCOUNT NO. **411**

DATE	ITEM	POST. REF.	DEBIT	DATE	ITEM	POST. REF.	CREDIT
				19-- June 11		J1	2 0 0 0 00
				22		J2	5 0 0 00
				25		J2	6 5 0 00
							3 1 5 0 00

ACCOUNT **Rent Expense**   ACCOUNT NO. **541**

DATE	ITEM	POST. REF.	DEBIT	DATE	ITEM	POST. REF.	CREDIT
19-- June 12		J1	8 0 0 00				

ACCOUNT **Travel & Entertainment Expense**   ACCOUNT NO. **544**

DATE	ITEM	POST. REF.	DEBIT	DATE	ITEM	POST. REF.	CREDIT
19-- June 22		J2	2 3 5 00				

ACCOUNT **Telephone Expense**   ACCOUNT NO. **545**

DATE	ITEM	POST. REF.	DEBIT	DATE	ITEM	POST. REF.	CREDIT
19-- June 14		J1	6 9 00				

ACCOUNT	*Miscellaneous Expense*										ACCOUNT NO. *572*	
DATE	ITEM	POST. REF.	DEBIT		DATE	ITEM	POST. REF.	CREDIT				
19-- June 19		J1	3 6 00									
27		J2	9 0 00									
			1 2 6 00									

As shown in the preceding illustrations, when the posting is completed, the information in both the journal and the ledger as to the date, the amount, and the effect of each transaction is the same. A cross-reference between the journal and the ledger is provided by the Posting Reference column. Each entry in the journal can be traced to the ledger accounts by referring to the account number indicated in the Posting Reference column of the journal. Also, each entry in any ledger account can be traced to the journal by referring to the page number indicated in the Posting Reference column of the ledger account.

Building Your Accounting Knowledge

1. Name a source document that provides information about each of the following types of business transactions:
   (a) Cash payment
   (b) Cash receipt
   (c) Sale of goods or services
   (d) Purchase of goods or services
2. Where is the first formal accounting record of business transactions usually made?
3. What information usually is entered in each of the following columns of the journal?
   (a) Date column
   (b) Description column
   (c) Debit amount column
   (d) Credit amount column
4. What is the first step in establishing an accounting information system for a new business?
5. Name the five types of financial statement items for which it is ordinarily desirable to keep separate accounts.
6. Which two types of accounts are temporarily used to enter increases and decreases in owner's equity from most day-to-day business transactions?
7. In what order are the accounts customarily placed in the ledger?
8. Describe how to prove the journal.
9. What must be done in order for the ledger to be a reliable source of information?
10. In posting from the journal to the ledger, what information is entered in the accounts?
11. What information is entered in the Posting Reference column of the journal as each amount is posted to the proper account in the ledger?

■ **Assignment Box**

To reinforce your understanding of the preceding text materials, you may complete the following:
     Study Guide: Part A
     Textbook: Exercises 2A1 through 2A4 or 2B1 through 2B4
                Problems 2A1 through 2A3 or 2B1 through 2B3

The Trial Balance and the Financial Statements

Prepare the trial balance.

    As indicated in Chapter 1, the purpose of a trial balance is to prove that the totals of the debit and credit balances in the ledger accounts are equal. A trial balance can be taken daily, weekly, monthly, or whenever desired. Before taking a trial balance, all transactions should be journalized and posted so that the effect of all transactions to date will be reflected in the ledger accounts.

Footing Accounts

    Prior to taking a trial balance, it is necessary to (1) **foot**—add the amounts entered on the debit and credit side of each account, and (2) determine the balance of each account. As illustrated in the cash account shown below, the footings are entered immediately below the last item in both the debit and credit amount columns of the account. The footings should be entered in small figures close to the preceding line so that they will not interfere with an entry on the next ruled line. At the same time,

ACCOUNT **Cash**   ACCOUNT NO. **111**

DATE		ITEM	POST. REF.	DEBIT	DATE		ITEM	POST. REF.	CREDIT
19-- June	1		J1	6 0 0 0 00	19-- June	7		J1	9 0 0 00
	6		J1	4 0 0 0 00		8		J1	2 0 0 0 00
	11		J1	2 0 0 0 00		12		J1	8 0 0 00
	22		J2	5 0 0 00		14		J1	6 9 00
	25		J2	6 5 0 00		19		J1	3 6 00
		8,620.00		13 1 5 0 00		22		J2	2 3 5 00
						27		J2	9 0 00
						29		J2	4 0 0 00
									4 5 3 0 00

    the **balance** (the difference between the footings) is computed and entered in small figures in the Item column of the account just below the line on which the last regular entry appears. If the total of the debits exceeds the total of the credits (referred to as a debit balance), the balance should be entered in the Item column on the debit or left side of the account. If the total of the credits exceeds the total of the debits (referred to as a credit balance), the balance should be entered in the Item column on the credit or right side of the account. If an account has entries on only the debit or credit side, the footing is used as the balance and no amount is entered in the Item column.

In the ledger shown on pages 46-48, the accounts have been footed and the balances entered. No footing is necessary when only one item has been posted to an account, regardless of whether it is a debit or a credit amount.

Care should be taken when entering transactions or when computing the balances of the accounts because most accounting errors result from carelessness. For example, an account balance might be entered on the wrong side of a ledger account by mistake or figures might be entered so carelessly that they might be misread later. Errors also can be made in adding the amount columns or in determining the difference between the footings. In either case, the error may be carried to the trial balance and considerable time may be required to locate the mistake.

Preparing the Trial Balance

The following procedures should be followed in preparing a trial balance:

1. Head the trial balance by showing (a) the name of the individual, firm, or organization, (b) the title of the report, "Trial Balance," and (c) the date. The date shown is the day of the last transaction that is included in the accounts, which is usually the last day of a month. A trial balance dated December 31 might actually be prepared on January 3, but the account balances should reflect only transactions through December 31.
2. List the account titles in numerical order, showing each account number.
3. Enter the account balances, placing debit balances in the left amount column and credit balances in the right amount column.
4. Place a single line across the amount columns below the last balance, add the columns and enter the totals. Then place a double line below the totals in the manner shown in the illustration on page 51.

A trial balance is usually prepared on ruled paper though it can be prepared on plain paper. The illustration on page 51 shows the trial balance of the ledger of John Wendt, Attorney as of June 30, 19--.

Even though the trial balance indicates that the ledger is in balance, there still can be errors in the ledger. For example, if a journal entry has been made in which the wrong accounts were debited or credited, or if an item has been posted to the wrong account, the ledger will still be in balance. It is important, therefore, that extreme care be used in preparing the journal entries and in posting them to the ledger accounts.

The Financial Statements

Describe the flow of financial data through an accounting information system.

The transactions completed by John Wendt, Attorney during the month of June were entered in a two-column journal (see pages 43 and 44). The debits and credits were subsequently posted to the proper accounts in a ledger (see pages 46-48). At the end of the month, a trial balance was taken as a means of proving that the equality of debits and credits had been maintained throughout the journalizing and posting process (see below).

John Wendt, Attorney

Trial Balance

June 30, 19--

Account	Acct. No.	Dr. Balance	Cr. Balance
Cash	111	8 6 2 0 00	
Office Equipment	191	3 6 0 0 00	
Notes Payable	216		4 0 0 0 00
Accounts Payable	218		7 0 0 00
John Wendt, Capital	311		6 0 0 0 00
John Wendt, Drawing	312	4 0 0 00	
Client Fees	411		3 1 5 0 00
Rent Expense	541	8 0 0 00	
Travel & Entertainment Expense	544	2 3 5 00	
Telephone Expense	545	6 9 00	
Miscellaneous Expense	572	1 2 6 00	
		13 8 5 0 00	13 8 5 0 00

Trial Balance

The trial balance taken as of June 30 lists all of the accounts, shows the amounts of their debit and credit balances, and proves the equality of these debit and credit balances. However, the trial balance does not clearly present all of the information that Wendt might need regarding the results of operations during the month or the status of the business at the end of the month. To meet these needs, it is the usual practice for a small service enterprise to prepare three financial statements—the income statement, the statement of owner's equity, and the balance sheet. The preparation of financial statements is the last step in the flow of financial data through an accounting information system. This flow can be illustrated as shown on the next page.

Financial statements are usually prepared first on ruled paper. From the ruled paper, they can be typed or word processed on a microcomputer so that multiple copies can be easily obtained.

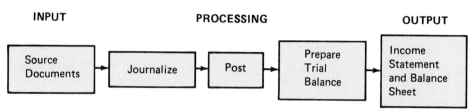

The Income Statement

An **income statement** is an itemized statement that provides information regarding the results of operations during a specified period of time. It is a statement of the changes in owner's equity resulting from the revenue and expenses of a specific period (month, quarter, or year). Such changes are originally entered in temporary owner's equity accounts known as revenue and expense accounts. Changes in owner's equity resulting from investments or withdrawals of assets by the owner are not included in the income statement because they do not involve either revenue or expenses.

The heading of an income statement consists of the following:

1. The name of the business
2. The title of the statement
3. The period of time covered by the statement

The body of an income statement consists of (1) an itemized list of the sources and amounts of revenue earned during the period, and (2) an itemized list of the various expenses incurred during the period. The income statement reflects the **matching concept**, which means that expenses incurred to earn particular revenues should be matched with those revenues. It is said that this matching process is the "heart" of income measurement.

The following income statement shows the results of operations of John Wendt, Attorney for the month ended June 30, 19--. The trial balance was used to determine the revenue and expenses.

John Wendt, Attorney										
Income Statement										
For Month Ended June 30, 19--										
Revenue:										
Client fees						$3	1	5	0	00
Expenses:										
Rent expense	$ 8	0	0	00						
Travel & entertainment expense	2	3	5	00						
Telephone expense		6	9	00						
Miscellaneous expense	1	2	6	00						
Total expenses						1	2	3	0	00
Net income						$1	9	2	0	00

Income Statement

The income statement shown is on two-column paper; however, the columns do not have any debit or credit significance. Dollar signs are placed beside the first amount in each column and the first amount below a ruling in each column. The only source of revenue was client fees that amounted to $3,150. The total expenses for the month amounted to $1,230. The revenue exceeded the expenses by $1,920. This represents the amount of the **net income** for the month. If the total expenses had exceeded the total revenue, the excess would have represented a **net loss** for the month. The information provided by the income statement of John Wendt, Attorney can be summarized in equation form as follows:

$$\text{Revenue} - \text{Expenses} = \text{Net Income}$$
$$\$3,150 \quad - \quad \$1,230 \quad = \quad \$1,920$$

It is apparent that the income statement is more informative than the trial balance in presenting the results of operations for June. Although the trial balance contains the necessary data for preparing the income statement, the income statement presents the data in a more meaningful way.

The Statement of Owner's Equity

A **statement of owner's equity** is a statement summarizing all of the changes in owner's equity during a specified period of time. In Chapter 1 it was explained that owner's equity can be increased in two ways: (1) investments of assets by the owner, and (2) revenues. It was also explained that owner's equity can be decreased in two ways: (1) withdrawals of assets by the owner, and (2) expenses. A statement of owner's equity summarizes the effects these four factors have on owner's equity of a business.

The heading of a statement of owner's equity consists of the following:

1. Name of the business
2. Title of the statement
3. The period of time covered by the statement

The body of the statement of owner's equity consists of (1) the balance in the capital account at the beginning of the period, (2) additional investments (if any) by the owner, (3) the net income or loss for the period, (4) withdrawals (if any) by the owner, and (5) the balance in the capital account at the end of the period.

The sources of information needed in preparing a statement of owner's equity for John Wendt are the trial balance and the income statement. The trial balance on page 51 shows that Wendt's equity on June 1 amounted to $6,000. This amount appears as a credit balance in the capital account. The income statement on page 52 shows that the net income of the business for June amounted to $1,920. The trial balance also shows that the amount withdrawn by Wendt for personal use during the month amounted to $400. This amount appears as a debit balance in the drawing account. On the basis of this information, the statement of owner's equity for John Wendt, Attorney, for the month ended June 30, 19--, is as follows:

John Wendt, Attorney										
Statement of Owner's Equity										
For Month Ended June 30, 19--										
John Wendt, capital, June 1, 19--							$6	0	0	0 00
Net income for the month	$1	9	2	0 00						
Less withdrawals		4	0	0 00						
Increase in owner's equity							1	5	2	0 00
John Wendt, capital, June 30, 19--							$7	5	2	0 00

Statement of Owner's Equity

The Balance Sheet

A **balance sheet** is an itemized statement of the assets, liabilities, and owner's equity of a business enterprise as of a specified date. Its purpose is to provide information regarding the status of these basic accounting elements as of the close of business on the date indicated in the heading.

The heading of a balance sheet contains the following:

1. The name of the business
2. The title of the statement
3. The date of the statement as of the close of business on that day

The body of a balance sheet consists of an itemized list of the assets, liabilities, and owner's equity. A balance sheet for John Wendt, Attorney, showing the status of the business at the end of the day on June 30, 19--, is reproduced on page 55. The balance sheet illustrated is arranged with the assets listed on the left side and the liabilities and owner's equity listed on the right side. Dollar signs are placed beside the first amount in each column and the first amount below a ruling in each column. This presentation is called an account form of the balance sheet. The information provided by the balance sheet can be summarized in equation form as follows:

$$\text{Assets} = \text{Liabilities} + \text{Owner's Equity}$$
$$\$12,220 = \$4,700 + \$7,520$$

The trial balance is used to determine the assets and liabilities for the balance sheet. The amount of the owner's equity is the ending balance shown in the statement of owner's equity. The amount of the owner's equity can also be determined by subtracting the total liabilities from the total assets. Thus, Wendt's equity as of June 30, 19--, is as follows:

Total assets $12,220
Less total liabilities 4,700
Owner's equity .... $ 7,520

Owner's equity calculated in this manner must be equal to the ending balance shown in the statement of owner's equity.

Assets							Liabilities						
							John Wendt, Attorney						
							Balance Sheet						
							June 30, 19--						
Cash	$	8	6	2	0	00	*Notes payable*	$	4	0	0	0	00
Office equipment		3	6	0	0	00	*Accounts payable*			7	0	0	00
							Total liabilities	$	4	7	0	0	00
							Owner's Equity						
							John Wendt, capital		7	5	2	0	00
							Total liabilities and owner's						
Total assets	$12	2	2	0	00		*equity*	$12	2	2	0	00	

Balance Sheet—Account Form

Building Your Accounting Knowledge

1. Where should the footings of an account be entered?
2. Where should the balance of an account be entered?
3. Explain why there still can be errors in the ledger even though the trial balance indicates that the ledger is in balance. Give examples of two such types of errors.
4. What information is provided by an income statement?
5. Why are changes in owner's equity resulting from investments or withdrawals of assets by the owner not included in the income statement?
6. What are the three parts of the heading of an income statement?
7. What is the source of information for preparing the income statement?
8. What information is provided by the statement of owner's equity?
9. What are the three parts of the heading of the statement of owner's equity?
10. What are the sources of information for preparing the statement of owner's equity?
11. What is the purpose of a balance sheet?
12. What are the three parts of the heading of a balance sheet?
13. What are the sources of information for preparing the balance sheet?
14. Owner's equity can be calculated by subtracting total liabilities shown on the balance sheet from total assets shown on the balance sheet. In what other way can the owner's equity balance be determined?

Assignment Box

To reinforce your understanding of the preceding text materials, you may complete the following:

> Study Guide: Part B
> Textbook: Exercises 2A5 through 2A8 or 2B5 through 2B8
>   Problems 2A4 through 2A6 or 2B4 through 2B6

Expanding Your Business Vocabulary

What is the meaning of each of the following terms:

balance (p. 49)	journal (p. 35)
balance sheet (p. 54)	journalizing (p. 35)
book of original entry (p. 36)	ledger (p. 36)
chart of accounts (p. 39)	matching concept (p. 52)
Credit amount column (p. 37)	net income (p. 53)
cross reference (p. 45)	net loss (p. 53)
Date column (p. 37)	posting (p. 45)
Debit amount column (p. 37)	Posting Reference column (p. 37)
Description column (p. 37)	source document (p. 36)
foot (p. 49)	statement of owner's equity (p. 53)
general ledger (p. 44)	two-column journal (p. 37)
income statement (p. 52)	

Demonstration Problem

Mark Clayton has been practicing law since August 1 of last year. During the month of July of the current year, he completed the following transactions in connection with his law practice:

July 3 Paid office rent for July, $900.00.

     5 Purchased office equipment from Grogan Co., $2,600.00, on account.

     6 Purchased stationery from Bradburn Office Supplies, $750.00, on account. (Stationery Expense)

     7 Received $3,500.00 in client fees.

   10 Paid electricity bill, $73.35.

   12 Paid $1,000.00 to Grogan Co. on account.

   13 Paid telephone bill, $42.60.

   14 Received $4,000.00 in client fees.

   14 Paid $500.00 to Bradburn Office Supplies on account.

   14 Gave the Epilepsy Foundation $50.00. (Charitable Contributions Expense)

   14 Paid temporary secretary for first half of month, $550.00.

   17 Paid to have office windows washed, $25.00. (Miscellaneous Expense)

18 Paid expenses of trip to testify before state legislature, $112.75. (Traveling Expense)

21 Received $3,800.00 in client fees.

21 Gave the American Red Cross $25.00. (Charitable Contributions Expense)

28 Received $4,500.00 in client fees.

31 Paid temporary secretary for last half of month, $550.00.

Clayton had the following account balances as of July 1:

Cash, No. 111	$ 8,826.55	Stationery Expense,	
Office Equipment, No. 191	5,567.99	No. 543	$493.42
Accounts Payable, No. 218	1,004.95	Travel & Entertainment	
Mark Clayton, Capital,		Expense, No. 544	460.20
No. 311	4,645.38	Telephone Expense,	
Mark Clayton, Drawing,		No. 545	278.55
No. 312	6,000.00	Electric Expense No. 549	418.73
Legal Fees, No. 411	28,732.46	Charitable Contributions	
Rent Expense, No. 541	5,400.00	Expense, No. 557	175.00
Salary Expense, No. 542	6,600.00	Miscellaneous Expense,	
		No. 572	162.35

Required:

1. Open a T account ledger for Mark Clayton as of July 1 of the current year. Enter the July 1 balance of each of the accounts in the T accounts on the appropriate side, with a check mark to the left of each balance. Then, prove the equality of the debit and credit balances before proceeding further. (Hint: The totals should be $34,382.79.)

2. Record each transaction.

3. Post the journal to the ledger, and foot and balance the T accounts.

4. Prepare a trial balance as of July 31.

5. Prepare an income statement for the seven-month period ended July 31.

6. Prepare a statement of owner's equity for the seven-month period ended July 31.

7. Prepare a balance sheet as of July 31.

Solution

1 and 3.

Mark Clayton's Ledger

Cash——Acct. No. 111						
19--						
July	1	Bal.	√	8,826.55	July 3 J12	900.00
	7		J12	3,500.00	10 J12	73.35
	14		J12	4,000.00	12 J12	1,000.00
	21		J13	3,800.00	13 J12	42.60
	28		J13	4,500.00	14 J12	500.00
					14 J12	50.00
				24,626.55	14 J13	550.00
			20,797.85		17 J13	25.00
					18 J13	112.75
					21 J13	25.00
					31 J13	550.00
						3,828.70

Office Equipment——Acct. No. 191				
19--				
July	1	Bal.	√	5,567.99
	5		J12	2,600.00
				8,167.99

Accounts Payable——Acct. No. 218

19--				19--				
July	12	J12	1,000.00	July	1	Bal.	√	1,004.95
	14	J12	500.00		5	J12		2,600.00
					6	J12		750.00
			1,500.00					4,354.95
								2,854.95

Mark Clayton, Capital——Acct. No. 311

				19--				
				July	1	Bal.	√	4,645.38

Mark Clayton, Drawing——Acct. No. 312

19--				
July	1	Bal.	√	6,000.00

Legal Fees——Acct. No. 411

				19--				
				July	1	Bal.	√	28,732.46
					7	J12		3,500.00
					14	J12		4,000.00
					21	J13		3,800.00
					28	J13		4,500.00
								44,532.46

Rent Expense——Acct. No. 541

19--				
July	1	Bal.	√	5,400.00
	3	J12		900.00
				6,300.00

Salary Expense——Acct. No. 542

19--				
July	1	Bal.	√	6,600.00
	14	J13		550.00
	31	J13		550.00
				7,700.00

Stationery Expense——Acct. No. 543

19--				
July	1	Bal.	√	493.42
	6	J12		750.00
				1,243.42

Travel & Entertainment Exp.——Acct. No. 544

19--				
July	1	Bal.	√	460.20
	18	J13		112.75
				572.95

Telephone Expense——Acct. No. 545

19--				
July	1	Bal.	√	278.55
	13	J12		42.60
				321.15

Electric Expense——Acct. No. 549

19--				
July	1	Bal.	√	418.73
	10			73.35
				492.08

Charitable Contributions Exp.——Acct. No. 557

19--				
July	1	Bal.	√	175.00
	14	J12		50.00
	21	J13		25.00
				250.00

Miscellaneous Expense——Acct. No. 572

19--				
July	1	Bal.	√	162.35
	17	J13		25.00
				187.35

2. _____ **JOURNAL**   PAGE 12

19--				
July	3 Rent Expense.....................	541	900.00	
	Cash	111		900.00
	Paid rent.			
	5 Office Equipment	191	2,600.00	
	Accounts Payable	218		2,600.00
	Grogan Co.			
	6 Stationery Expense	543	750.00	
	Accounts Payable	218		750.00
	Paid Bradburn Office Supplies.			
	7 Cash.............................	111	3,500.00	
	Legal Fees	411		3,500.00
	Fees from clients.			
	10 Electric Expense	549	73.35	
	Cash	111		73.35
	Paid electricity bill.			
	12 Accounts Payable	218	1,000.00	
	Cash	111		1,000.00
	Grogan Co.			
	13 Telephone Expense..................	545	42.60	
	Cash	111		42.60
	Paid telephone bill.			
	14 Cash.............................	111	4,000.00	
	Legal Fees	411		4,000.00
	Fees from clients.			
	14 Accounts Payable	218	500.00	
	Cash	111		500.00
	Bradburn Office Supplies.			
	14 Charitable Contributions Expense	557	50.00	
	Cash	111		50.00
	Epilepsy Foundation.			
	14 Salary Expense	542	550.00	
	Cash	111		550.00
	Paid secretary's salary for first half of			
	month.		_13,965.95_	_13,965.95_

2. _____ **JOURNAL**   PAGE 13

19--				
July	17 Miscellaneous Expense	572	25.00	
	Cash	111		25.00
	Paid window washers.			
	18 Travel & Entertainment Expense........	544	112.75	
	Cash	111		112.75
	Expert witness.			
	21 Cash.............................	111	3,800.00	
	Legal Fees	411		3,800.00
	Fees from clients.			
	21 Charitable Contributions Expense	557	25.00	
	Cash	111		25.00
	American Red Cross.			

28 Cash	111	4,500.00	
Legal Fees	411		4,500.00
Fees from clients.			
31 Salary Expense	542	550.00	
Cash	111		550.00
Paid secretary's salary for end of month.			
		9,012.75	*9,012.75*

4.

Mark Clayton
Trial Balance
July 31, 19--

Account	Acct. No.	Dr. Balance	Cr. Balance
Cash	111	$20,797.85	
Office Equipment	191	8,167.99	
Accounts Payable	218		$ 2,854.95
Mark Clayton, Capital	311		4,645.38
Mark Clayton, Drawing	312	6,000.00	
Legal Fees	411		44,532.46
Rent Expense	541	6,300.00	
Salary Expense	542	7,700.00	
Stationery Expense	543	1,243.42	
Travel & Entertainment Expense	544	572.95	
Telephone Expense	545	321.15	
Electric Expense	549	492.08	
Charitable Contributions Expense	557	250.00	
Miscellaneous Expense	572	187.35	
		$52,032.79	$52,032.79

5.

Mark Clayton
Income Statement
For Seven Months Ended July 31, 19--

Revenues:		
Legal fees.................................		$44,532.46
Expenses:		
Rent expense	$6,300.00	
Salary expense...........................	7,700.00	
Stationery expense	1,243.42	
Travel and Entertainment expense	572.95	
Telephone expense	321.15	
Electric expense...........................	492.08	
Charitable contributions expense	250.00	
Miscellaneous expense.....................	187.35	
Total expenses...........................		17,066.95
Net income		$27,465.51

6.

Mark Clayton
Statement of Owner's Equity
For Seven Months Ended July 31, 19--

Mark Clayton, Capital, January 1, 19--		$ 4,645.38
Net income January-July 19--	$27,465.51	
Less withdrawals	6,000.00	
Net increase in owner's equity		21,465.51
Mark Clayton, Capital, July 31, 19--		$26,110.89

7.

Mark Clayton
Balance Sheet
July 31, 19--

Assets		Liabilities	
Cash	$20,797.85	Accounts payable	$ 2,854.95
Office equipment	8,167.99		
		Owner's Equity	
		Mark Clayton, capital..	26,110.89
		Total liab. & owner's	
Total assets	$28,965.84	equity	$28,965.84

Applying Accounting Concepts

Series A

Exercise 2A1—Journal Entries for Transactions. Jim Kimes operates a placement service. Journalize the following transactions which occurred during the first month of operations (April, 19--). Identify the entries by inserting the transaction number in the Date column.

1. Invested $30,000 cash in the business.
2. Paid office rent, $1,200.
3. Purchased office furniture from Mound City Office Supply on account, $6,400.
4. Received $1,600 from Mary Kearns' employer for placement services rendered.
5. Paid Mound City Office Supply $3,000 on account.

Exercise 2A2—Posting to T Accounts; Trial Balance. (a) Using T accounts, post the journal entries from Exercise 2A1 to appropriate accounts. (b) Foot the accounts and enter the balances. (c) Prepare a trial balance.

Exercise 2A3—Journal Entries for Transactions. Arlene Boxerman operates a consulting business. Journalize the following transactions which occurred during the first month of operations (January, 19--). Identify the entries by inserting the transaction number in the Date column.

1. Invested $34,000 in the business.
2. Paid office rent, $1,400.

3. Paid Silver Mountain Telephone Company $104 for telephone installation and first month's service charges.
4. Paid $30 for several copies of trade journals (Miscellaneous Expense).
5. Received $5,600 from Deborah Hackett for consulting services rendered.
6. Purchased office materials from EDC Co. on account, $1,300. (Office Materials Expense.)
7. Paid temporary office secretary $1,700 covering her salary for the first month.

Exercise 2A4—Posting to T Accounts; Trial Balance. (a) Using T accounts, post the journal entries from Exercise 2A3 to appropriate accounts. (b) Foot the accounts and enter the balances. (c) Prepare a trial balance.

Exercise 2A5—Income Statement; Statement of Owner's Equity; Balance Sheet. Using the trial balance given below: (a) Prepare an income statement for the Jim Kimes Placement Service for the month ended April 30, 19--; (b) Prepare a statement of owner's equity for the Jim Kimes Placement Service for the month ended April 30, 19--; and (c) Prepare a balance sheet in account form for the Jim Kimes Placement Service as of April 30, 19--.

Jim Kimes Placement Service
Trial Balance
April 30, 19--

Account	Acct. No.	Dr. Balance	Cr. Balance
Cash	111	$27,400	
Office Furniture	192	6,400	
Accounts Payable	218		$ 3,400
Jim Kimes, Capital	311		30,000
Placement Fees	411		1,600
Rent Expense	541	1,200	
		$35,000	$35,000

Exercise 2A6—Income Statement; Statement of Owners Equity; Balance Sheet. Using the trial balance given below: (a) Prepare an income statement for the Arlene Boxerman Consulting Service for the month ended January 31, 19--; (b) Prepare a statement of owner's equity for the Arlene Boxerman Consulting Service for the month ended January 31, 19--; and (c) Prepare a balance sheet in account form for the Arlene Boxerman Consulting Service as of January 31, 19--.

Arlene Boxerman Consulting Service
Trial Balance
January 31, 19--

Account	Acct. No.	Dr. Balance	Cr. Balance
Cash	111	$36,366	
Accounts Payable	218		$ 1,300
Arlene Boxerman, Capital	311		34,000
Consulting Fees	411		5,600
Rent Expense	541	1,400	
Salary Expense	542	1,700	
Office Materials Expense	543	1,300	
Telephone Expense	545	104	
Miscellaneous Expense	572	30	
		$40,900	$40,900

Exercise 2A7—Income Statement. Tami Combs operates a beauty salon. The following is the trial balance for the business as of July 31, 19--, the first month of operations.

Tami Combs Beauty Salon
Trial Balance
July 31, 19--

Account	Acct. No.	Dr. Balance	Cr. Balance
Cash	111	$ 3,366	
Store Equipment	181	8,300	
Accounts Payable	218		$ 638
Tami Combs, Capital	311		12,000
Tami Combs, Drawing	312	1,250	
Customer Fees	411		2,902
Rent Expense	541	800	
Beauty Aids Expense	543	1,740	
Telephone Expense	545	84	
		$15,540	$15,540

Prepare an income statement for the Tami Combs Beauty Salon for the month of July.

Exercise 2A8—Statement of Owner's Equity; Balance Sheet. Refer to Exercise 2A7 and prepare (a) a statement of owner's equity for the month of July and (b) a balance sheet in account form for the Tami Combs Beauty Salon as of July 31.

Series B

Exercise 2B1—Journal Entries for Transactions. Christine Jackson operates a travel agency. Journalize the following transactions which occurred during the first month of operations (October, 19--). Identify the entries by inserting the transaction number in the Date column.

1. Invested $25,000 cash in the business.
2. Paid office rent, $1,000.
3. Purchased office furniture from Quad City Office Supply on account, $5,300.
4. Received $1,200 from Teresa Fry for travel services rendered.
5. Paid Quad City Office Supply $2,500 on account.

Exercise 2B2—Posting to T Accounts; Trial Balance. (a) Using T accounts, post the journal entries from Exercise 2B1 to appropriate accounts. (b) Foot the accounts and enter the balances. (c) Prepare a trial balance.

Exercise 2B3—Journal Entries for Transactions. Duncan Seay operates a barber shop. Journalize the following transactions which occurred during the first month of operations (January, 19--). Identify the entries by inserting the transaction number in the Date column.

1. Invested $20,000 cash in the business.
2. Paid shop rent, $1,000.
3. Paid West Coast Telephone Company $86 for telephone installation and first month's service charges.
4. Paid $25 for several copies of trade journals. (Miscellaneous Expense)

5. Received $6,200 from various customers for barber services rendered.
6. Purchased hair accessories from SGA Co. on account, $1,100. (Hair Accessories Expense)
7. Paid temporary assistant $1,275 covering his salary for the first month.

Exercise 2B4—Posting to T Accounts; Trial Balance. (a) Using T accounts, post the journal entries from Exercise 2B3 to appropriate accounts. (b) Foot the accounts and enter the balances. (c) Prepare a trial balance for Seay's Barber Shop.

Exercise 2B5—Income Statement; Statement of Owner's Equity; Balance Sheet. Using the trial balance given below: (a) Prepare an income statement for the Christine Jackson Travel Agency for the month ended October 31, 19--; (b) Prepare a statement of owner's equity for the Christine Jackson Travel Agency for the month ended October 31, 19--; and (c) Prepare a balance sheet in account form for the Christine Jackson Travel Agency as of October 31, 19--.

Christine Jackson Travel Agency
Trial Balance
October 31, 19--

Account	Acct. No.	Dr. Balance	Cr. Balance
Cash	111	$22,700.00	
Office Furniture	192	5,300.00	
Accounts Payable	218		$ 2,800.00
Christine Jackson, Capital	311		25,000.00
Travel Fees	411		1,200.00
Rent Expense	541	1,000.00	
		$29,000.00	$29,000.00

Exercise 2B6—Income Statement; Statement of Owner's Equity; Balance Sheet. Using the trial balance given below: (a) Prepare an income statement for Seay's Barber Shop for the month ended January 31, 19--; (b) Prepare a statement of owner's equity for Seay's Barber Shop for the month ended January 31, 19--; and (c) Prepare a balance sheet in account form for Seay's Barber Shop as of January 31, 19--.

Seay's Barber Shop
Trial Balance
January 31, 19--

Account	Acct. No.	Dr. Balance	Cr. Balance
Cash	111	$23,814.00	
Accounts Payable	218		$ 1,100.00
Duncan Seay, Capital	311		20,000.00
Service Fees	411		6,200.00
Rent Expense	541	1,000.00	
Salary Expense	542	1,275.00	
Hair Accessories Expense	543	1,100.00	
Telephone Expense	545	86.00	
Miscellaneous Expense	572	25.00	
		$27,300.00	$27,300.00

Exercise 2B7—Income Statement. Tanda Norvell operates a dance studio. The following is the trial balance for Norvell's business as of March 31, 19--, the first month of operations.

Norvell Dance Studio
Trial Balance
March 31, 19--

Account	Acct. No.	Dr. Balance	Cr. Balance
Cash	111	$ 5,366	
Equipment	191	10,300	
Accounts Payable	218		$ 638
Tanda Norvell, Capital	311		14,000
Tanda Norvell, Drawing	312	1,250	
Student Fees	411		4,902
Rent Expense	541	800	
Instructors' Salaries Expense	543	1,740	
Telephone Expense	545	84	
		$19,540	$19,540

Prepare an income statement for the Norvell Dance Studio for the month of March.

Exercise 2B8—Statement of Owner's Equity; Balance Sheet. Refer to Exercise 2B7 and prepare (a) a statement of owner's equity for the month of March and (b) a balance sheet in account form for the Norvell Dance Studio as of March 31.

Series A

Problem 2A1   Journal Entries for Transactions

Presented below are the chart of accounts for K.A. Buckler, a certified public accountant and a narrative of the transactions completed during the month of February.

Chart of Accounts

Assets
111 Cash
191 Office Equipment

Liabilities
218 Accounts Payable

Owner's Equity
311 K.A. Buckler, Capital
312 K.A. Buckler, Drawing

Revenue
411 Professional Fees

Expenses
541 Rent Expense
542 Salary Expense
543 Stationery Expense
544 Travel & Entertainment Expense
545 Telephone Expense
557 Charitable Contributions Expense
572 Miscellaneous Expense

Feb. 1 Paid telephone bill, $84.60.
     1 Paid February office rent, $780.00.
     2 Gave the Heart Assn. $200.00. (Charitable Contributions Expense)
     5 Paid traveling expense, $222.50.

8 Paid Carol House Furniture Co. (a supplier) $492.00, the full amount owed them.

9 Received $800.00 from Carl Nowacki for professional service.

12 Paid $30.00 for window cleaning. (Miscellaneous Expense)

12 Received $1,300.00 from Nancy Mayfield for professional service.

17 Received $630.50 from C. Penn for professional service.

19 Buckler withdrew $400.00 for personal use.

22 Received $220.00 from Shirley Emerson for professional service.

23 Received $600.00 from John Berra for professional service.

26 Purchased new office desk on account from Lammert's Furniture, $900.00.

26 Purchased stationery on account from Bargain Office Supply Co. (a supplier), $348.60. (Stationery Expense)

26 Paid temporary secretary's monthly salary, $1,450.00.

Required:

1. Prepare a journal entry for each transaction. The account titles should be selected from the chart of accounts. (Do not forget to indent each credit entry about one-half inch.)

2. Prove each journal page by footing the debit and credit amount columns in small figures.

Problem 2A2   Journal Entries for Transactions

Following is a narrative of the transactions completed during the month of March by K.A. Buckler, a certified public accountant.

Mar. 1 Paid Bargain Office Supply Co. $348.60 in full payment of account.

1 Paid March office rent, $780.00.

5 Paid $331.50 for new office chair.

9 Received $450.50 from Mary Wurtz for professional service.

12 Paid traveling expense, $270.00.

15 Received $800.00 from Michael Newquist for professional service.

16 Purchased typewriter for office use from Walker's Typewriter Co. (a supplier) on account, $950.00.

17 Received $2,100.00 from G. Gabriella for professional service.

19 Paid $135.30 for new filing cabinet.

23 Buckler invested $8,000.00 additional cash in the business.

26 Paid Walker's Typewriter Co. $600.00 on account.

29 Gave to United Way, $100.00. (Charitable Contributions Expense)

29 Buckler withdrew $1,200.00 for personal use.

30 Paid $120.00 for custodial service. (Miscellaneous Expense)

31 Paid temporary secretary's monthly salary, $1,450.00.

Required:

1. Prepare a journal entry for each transaction. The account titles should be selected from the chart of accounts listed on page 66 for Problem No. 2A1.

2. Prove each journal page.

Problem 2A3   Posting to Ledger Accounts and Finding Balances

If the working papers for this textbook are not used, omit Problem 2A3.

P.C. Schoen operates a real estate office under the name of the Schoen Realty Agency, which handles the sale of commercial and residential property. Schoen employs a temporary secretary at a salary of $1,400.00 a month to handle all correspondence, files, and accounts. The accounting records consist of a two-column journal and a ledger. Revenue is recorded when received in cash and expenses are recorded when paid in cash. The agency begins the accounting year on April 1 and ends it on the following March 31. Following is a trial balance of the agency as of April 30.

Schoen Realty Agency
Trial Balance
April 30, 19--

Account	Acct. No.	Dr. Balance	Cr. Balance
Cash..	111	$ 4,514.80	
Automobile..................................	185	16,500.00	
Office Equipment	191	1,440.00	
Accounts Payable	218		$ 7,520.00
P.C. Schoen, Capital	311		13,993.50
P.C. Schoen, Drawing	312	2,000.00	
Revenue from Commissions	411		5,671.20
Rent Expense	541	650.00	
Salary Expense..............................	542	1,400.00	
Telephone Expense	545	136.70	
Automobile Expense	546	251.00	
Miscellaneous Expense.......................	572	292.20	
		$27,184.70	$27,184.70

The agency's journal for the month of May is reproduced in the working papers. Note that the amount columns have been footed and proved.

Required:

1. Open ledger accounts with the May 1 balances as indicated in the trial balance.
2. Post the journal entries for May, foot the accounts, and enter the balances.

Problem 2A4   Journal Entries; Posting to T Accounts; Trial Balance

Neil Jacobs operates a humorous messenger service under the name "Neil's Nutty Messages," which specializes in birthdays, anniversaries and other special occasions. The charge for performing thirty minutes is $100; for fifteen minutes, $50. Jacobs has two temporary employees: an experienced performer who receives a salary of $1,100 a month; and a novice, who also keeps the agency accounts, at a salary of $900 a month. Revenue is not recorded until received in cash, and expenses are not recorded until paid in cash. A trial balance taken as of April 30, appeared as follows:

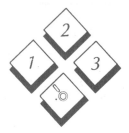

Neil's Nutty Messages
Trial Balance
April 30, 19--

Account	Acct. No.	Dr. Balance	Cr. Balance
Cash	111	$ 9,641.75	
Costumes & Equipment	191	12,439.25	
Accounts Payable	218		$ 1,543.50
Neil Jacobs, Capital	311		5,638.00
Neil Jacobs, Drawing	312	4,950.00	
Performance Revenue	411		47,550.00
Rent Expense	541	3,300.00	
Salary Expense	542	22,000.00	
Telephone Expense	545	602.40	
Electric Expense	549	424.62	
Advertising Expense	551	916.00	
Charitable Contributions Expense	557	300.00	
Miscellaneous Expense	572	157.48	
		$54,731.50	$54,731.50

The transactions completed during May were as follows:

May 1 Paid $300 for office rent for one month.
2 Paid telephone bill, $63.75.
2 Paid electric bill, $42.68.
4 Paid for window cleaning, $45.00. (Miscellaneous Expense)
7 Paid for advertising, $75.00.
9 Received $1,250.00 for 10 thirty-minute performances and 5 fifteen-minute performances during the past week.
14 Received $200.00 from the local Dental Association for a special one-hour show.
16 Donated $30.00 to the YMCA. (Charitable Contributions Expense)
21 Paid Larry's House of Laughs $400.00 to apply on account.
23 Received $1,650.00 for 12 thirty-minute performances and 9 fifteen-minute performances during the past two weeks.
28 Received $350.00 from Carrie's Child Care Service for a special two-hour show.
29 Jacobs withdrew $450.00 for personal use.
31 Paid temporary employees' salaries, $2,000.00.

Required:

1. Journalize the May transactions and prove the journal.
2. Open the necessary accounts as of May 1 and enter the balances as shown in the April 30 trial balance. Post the journal entries to the ledger. Foot the accounts where necessary and enter the balances.
3. Prove the account balances by taking a trial balance as of May 31.

Problem 2A5   Income Statement; Statement of Owner's Equity; Balance Sheet

---

Following is a trial balance of the accounts of Yee Insurance Agency as of December 31:

Yee Insurance Agency
Trial Balance
December 31, 19--

Account	Acct. No.	Dr. Balance	Cr. Balance
Cash	111	$14,710.92	
Office Equipment	191	9,279.98	
Accounts Payable	218		$ 1,674.92
Pat Yee, Capital	311		7,772.30
Pat Yee, Drawing	312	10,200.00	
Agency Fees	411		51,554.78
Rent Expense	541	6,360.00	
Salary Expense	542	14,000.00	
Stationery Expense	543	2,423.10	
Telephone Expense	545	1,222.58	
Advertising Expense	551	2,234.30	
Miscellaneous Expense	572	571.12	
		$61,002.00	$61,002.00

Required:
1. Prepare an income statement for Yee Insurance Agency for the year ended December 31, 19--.
2. Prepare a statement of owner's equity for Yee Insurance Agency for the year ended December 31, 19--.
3. Prepare a balance sheet in account form for Yee Insurance Agency as of December 31.

Problem 2A6   Trial Balance and Financial Statements

On December 1, Pamela Marsden started in business as a financial consultant, using the name Marsden's Financial Consultants. Marsden's accounting records consisted of a two-column journal and a ledger. A reproduction of the accounts as they appeared in the ledger on December 31 are provided in the working papers.

Required:
1. Foot the accounts where necessary and enter the balances in small figures.
2. Prepare a trial balance.
3. Prepare an income statement for the month of December.
4. Prepare a statement of owner's equity for the month of December.
5. Prepare a balance sheet in account form as of December 31.

Series B

Problem 2B1   Journal Entries for Transactions

Presented on the following page are the chart of accounts for A.J. Blocha, an architect and a narrative of the transactions completed during the month of September.

Chart of Accounts

Assets	Revenue
111 Cash	411 Professional Fees
191 Office Equipment	
	Expenses
Liabilities	541 Rent Expense
218 Accounts Payable	542 Salary Expense
	543 Stationery Expense
	544 Travel & Entertainment Expense
Owner's Equity	545 Telephone Expense
311 A.J. Blocha, Capital	557 Charitable Contributions Expense
312 A.J. Blocha, Drawing	572 Miscellaneous Expense

Sept. **1** Paid telephone bill, $63.45.

     1 Paid September office rent, $570.00.

     4 Gave the Lung Association $150.00. (Charitable Contributions Expense)

     5 Paid traveling expense, $166.75.

     8 Paid Crossroads Furniture Co. (a supplier) $369.00, the full amount owed them.

   11 Received $600.00 from Joseph Guenther for professional service.

   12 Paid $22.50 for window cleaning. (Miscellaneous Expense)

   12 Received $975.00 from Patricia Wiltse for professional service.

   18 Received $472.85 from V. Thompson for professional service.

   19 Blocha withdrew $300.00 for personal use.

   22 Received $165.00 from Carol Shearer for professional service.

   25 Received $450.00 from Don Fuentes for professional service.

   26 Purchased new office desk on account from Carafiol Furniture, $675.00.

   29 Purchased stationery on account from Botz Supply Co. (a supplier), $61.45. (Stationery Expense)

   30 Paid temporary secretary's monthly salary, $1,025.00.

Required:

1. Prepare a journal entry for each transaction. The account titles should be selected from the chart of accounts. (Do not forget to indent each credit entry about one-half inch.)

2. Prove each page by footing the debit and credit amount columns in small figures.

Problem 2B2   Journal Entries for Transactions

Following is a narrative of the transactions completed during the month of October by A.J. Blocha, an architect.

Oct. **1** Paid Botz Supply Co. $61.45 in full payment of account.

     1 Paid September office rent, $570.00.

     5 Paid $248.65 for new office chair.

     9 Received $337.75 .from Ana Galutera for professional services.

   12 Paid traveling expense, $210.00.

   13 Received $600.00 from Michael McGrath for professional service.

16 Purchased typewriter for office use from Block Typewriter Co. (a supplier) on account, $725.00.

19 Received $1,575.00 from Jeannette Garber for professional service.

20 Paid $101.25 for new filing cabinet.

23 Blocha invested $6,000.00 additional cash in the business.

26 Paid Block Typewriter Co. $450.00 on account.

27 Gave the Salvation Army $75.00. (Charitable Contributions Expense)

27 Blocha withdrew $900.00 for personal use.

30 Paid $90.00 for custodial service. (Miscellaneous Expense)

30 Paid temporary secretary's monthly salary, $1,075.00.

Required:

1. Prepare a journal entry for each transaction. The account titles should be selected from the chart of accounts listed on page 70 for Problem 2B1.
2. Prove each journal page.

Problem 2B3   Posting to Ledger Accounts and Finding Balances

If the working papers for this textbook are not used, omit Problem 2B3.

E.O. Maes operates an insurance office under the name of Maes Insurance Agency, which handles the sale of automobile, fire, and life insurance. Maes employs a temporary secretary at a salary of $1,050 a month to handle all correspondence, files, and accounts. The accounting records consist of a two-column journal and a ledger. Revenue is recorded when received in cash and expenses are recorded when paid in cash. The agency begins the accounting year on May 1 and ends it on the following April 30. Following is a trial balance of the agency as of May 31:

Maes Insurance Agency
Trial Balance
May 31, 19--

Account	Acct. No.	Dr. Balance	Cr. Balance
Cash	111	$ 3,386.10	
Automobile	185	12,375.00	
Office Equipment	191	1,080.00	
Accounts Payable	218		$ 5,640.00
E.O. Maes, Capital	311		10,507.65
E.O. Maes, Drawing	312	1,500.00	
Revenue from Commissions	411		4,253.40
Rent Expense	541	500.00	
Salary Expense	542	1,050.00	
Telephone Expense	545	102.55	
Automobile Expense	546	188.25	
Miscellaneous Expense	572	219.15	
		$20,401.05	$20,401.05

The agency's journal for the month of June is reproduced in the working papers. Note that the amount columns have been footed and proved.

Required:

1. Open the ledger accounts with the June 1 balances as indicated in the trial balance.
2. Post the journal entries for June, foot the accounts, and enter the balances.

Problem 2B4   Journal Entries; Posting to T Accounts; Trial Balance

Ernest Last operates a service under the name of Ernie's Delivery Service, which specializes in delivering urgent packages. Last has two temporary employees: an experienced employee who receives a salary of $1,000 a month; and a new employee, who also keeps the service accounts, at a salary of $750 a month. Revenue is not recorded until received in cash, and expenses are not recorded until paid in cash. A trial balance taken as of November 30 appeared as follows:

Ernie's Delivery Service
Trial Balance
November 30, 19--

Account	Acct. No.	Dr. Balance	Cr. Balance
Cash.....................................	111	$12,855.00	
Delivery Equipment	185	26,732.00	
Accounts Payable	218		$ 1,164.70
Ernest Last, Capital	311		10,536.30
Ernest Last, Drawing........................	312	6,600.00	
Delivery Revenue	411		63,450.00
Rent Expense	541	5,500.00	
Salary Expense..............................	542	19,250.00	
Telephone Expense	545	802.40	
Truck Expense	546	2,216.00	
Electric Expense.............................	549	576.72	
Charitable Contributions Expense	557	400.00	
Miscellaneous Expense.......................	572	218.88	
		$75,151.00	$75,151.00

The transactions completed during December were as follows:

Dec. 1 Paid $500.00 for office rent for one month.
    4 Paid telephone bill, $84.75.
    4 Paid electric bill, $56.64.
    5 Paid for window cleaning, $60.00 (Miscellaneous Expense)
    6 Paid for truck repairs, $205.80.
    8 Received $2,000.00 for delivery services during the past week.
  15 Received $2,250.00 for delivery services during the past week.
  15 Gave $40.00 to Boy's Town as a donation. (Charitable Contributions Expense)
  20 Paid Delivery Supply Co. $600.00 to apply on account.
  22 Received $2,700.00 for delivery services during the past week.
  29 Received $2,500.00 for delivery services during the past week.
  29 Last withdrew $600.00 for personal use.
  30 Paid salaries of temporary employees, $1,750.00.

Required:

1. Journalize the December transactions and prove the journal by footing the debit and credit amount columns.
2. Open the necessary accounts as of December 1 and enter the balances as shown in the November 30 trial balance. Post the journal entries to the ledger. Foot the accounts where necessary and enter the balances.
3. Prove the account balances by taking a trial balance as of December 31.

Problem 2B5   Income Statement; Statement of Owner's Equity; Balance Sheet

Following is a trial balance of the accounts of Bondo Realty Agency as of December 31:

Bondo Realty Agency
Trial Balance
December 31, 19--

Account	Acct. No.	Dr. Balance	Cr. Balance
Cash.......................................	111	$11,032.74	
Office Equpment	191	6,959.98	
Accounts Payable	218		$1,256.19
J.H. Bondo, Capital	311		5,825.77
J.H. Bondo, Drawing	312	7,650.00	
Agency Fees.................................	411		38,669.08
Rent Expense	541	4,770.00	
Salary Expense	542	11,500.00	
Stationery Expense	543	817.32	
Telephone Expense	545	916.94	
Advertising Expense	551	1,675.72	
Miscellaneous Expense.......................	572	428.34	
		$45,751.04	$45,751.04

Required:

1. Prepare an income statement for Bondo Realty Agency for the year ended December 31, 19--.
2. Prepare a statement of owner's equity for Bondo Realty Agency for the year ended December 31, 19--.
3. Prepare a balance sheet in account form for Bondo Realty Agency as of December 31.

Problem 2B6   Trial Balance and Financial Statements

If the working papers for this textbook are not used, omit Problem 2B6.

On December 1, Timothy Pierce started in business as a management consultant, using the name Pierce's Business Consulting. Pierce's records consisted of a two-column journal and a ledger. A reproduction of the accounts as they appeared in the ledger on December 31 is provided in the working papers.

Required:

1. Foot the accounts where necessary and enter the balances in small figures.
2. Prepare a trial balance.
3. Prepare an income statement for the month of December.
4. Prepare a statement of owner's equity for the month of December.
5. Prepare a balance sheet in account form as of December 31.

Mastery Problem

Jane Tarry lives in a town with a major university and several large businesses. These employers experience high faculty and executive turnover which creates a bustling housing market. Jane started her own business on April 1 called Dream Home Exploration. Through contacts at the university and several businesses, Jane learns of families that will be moving to town. For a flat fee, she offers the following services.

(a) After developing a profile of a client's dream home, Jane follows the housing market to identify potential homes. Information on prospective homes is sent to the client for a three-month period preceding the first house-hunting trip.

(b) During the house-hunting trip, Jane will arrange transportation and hotel accommodations, take the clients on a tour of the town, and arrange for the clients to see homes of interest.

(c) Jane also provides a current survey of local mortgage rates and borrowing requirements.

A trial balance as of April 30, 19-- is provided below, followed by transactions for the month of May.

Dream Home Exploration
Trial Balance
April 30, 19--

Account	Acct. No.	Dr. Balance	Cr. Balance
Cash	111	$5,000	
Computer Equipment	191	6,000	
Office Furniture	192	2,000	
Computer Software	193	1,500	
Notes Payable	216		$5,000
Accounts Payable	218		3,000
Jane Tarry, Capital	311		6,600
Jane Tarry, Drawing	312	500	
Client Fees	411		2,500
Rent Expense	541	600	
Salary Expense	542	300	
Telephone Expense	545	100	
Limo/Transportation Expense	546	300	
Utilities Expense	549	200	
Legal Expense	561	400	
Courtesy Gift Expense	563	50	
Postage Expense	564	150	
		$17,100	$17,100

May	2	Paid Ellis Floral for flowers sent to clients that recently moved into their new homes, $120.
	5	Paid postage on materials sent to clients, $45.
	8	Paid rent for the month, $600.
	10	Received payment from clients for services rendered, $1,500.
	14	Paid for limo services used to transport clients to and from the airport, $500.
	18	Purchased a new printer for the computer from Privett Co. on account, $1,200.
	20	Paid salary for temporary secretary, $200.
	22	Paid telephone bill, $120.
	26	Paid utility bill, $180.
	28	Received payment from clients for services rendered, $3,000.
	30	Paid legal expenses, $150 cash.
	30	Made payment on note payable, $1,000.
	30	Made payment to Privett Co. on account, $800.
	30	Jane withdrew $400 cash for personal use.

Required:

1. Enter the transactions in a two-column journal. Foot each page of the journal.
2. Open general ledger accounts and enter the May 1 balances.
3. Post the May transactions to the general ledger accounts.
4. Foot and balance the accounts.
5. Prepare a trial balance as of May 31, 19--.
6. Prepare an income statement for the two months ended May 31, 19--.
7. Prepare a statement of owner's equity for the two months ended May 31, 19--.
8. Prepare a balance sheet as of May 31, 19--.

CHAPTER 3

Accounting for a Personal Service Enterprise

Careful study of this chapter should enable you to:

- Describe the cash basis of accounting and explain the limits of its application.

- Apply the accounting concepts and procedures described and illustrated thus far in an accounting system for a personal service enterprise.

- Explain and prepare a multi-column book of original entry (the combination journal) and a four-column ledger account.

- Explain and prepare an end-of-period work sheet.

- Explain and prepare adjustments to the accounts at the end of the accounting period.

In the first two chapters, the purpose and nature of business accounting, transaction analysis, and the double entry framework were introduced. Explanations and illustrations were given of (1) journalizing (entering transactions in a two-column journal—a book of original entry), (2) posting (transferring entries to the accounts that comprise the general ledger), (3) taking a trial balance, and (4) using the latter to prepare an income statement and a balance sheet. In this chapter, the accounting procedures for a personal service enterprise are explained using a multi-column combination journal and a four-column ledger account. In addition, the use of an eight-column work sheet is explained and illustrated.

A **personal service enterprise** is one in which the principal source of revenue is compensation for services rendered to a business firm or to a person. This is in contrast to a **merchandising enterprise** which buys merchandise for resale and a **manufacturing enterprise** which makes and sells one or more products. There are two major types of personal service enterprises:

1. Business enterprises
2. Professional enterprises

Personal service **business enterprises** include real estate, insurance, advertising, transportation, storage, entertainment, brokerage, and various other firms. Personal service **professional enterprises** include attorneys, physicians, dentists, public accountants, management consultants, engineers, architects, artists, and educators. The principal source of revenue for individuals engaged in these two types of enterprises is usually the compensation received for rendering personal services.

Accounting Procedures for a Personal Service Enterprise

Describe the cash basis of accounting and explain the limits of its application.

Accounting for revenue on the cash basis (**cash basis revenue**) means that revenue is not entered in the accounts until the cash is received for the services performed. Some services may be performed in one period but the revenue from them will not be accounted for until received in the following period. The business or professional person using the cash basis of accounting takes the view that there is no revenue until cash is actually received. One cannot "spend" the promise of a customer or client to pay some money.

Accounting for expenses on the cash basis (**cash basis expense**) generally means that expenses are not entered in the accounts until they are paid for in cash. Consequently, a certain expense may be incurred in one period but not entered until the following period, when it is actually paid. In the case of most expenses of a recurring nature, using this accounting method is not a significant problem. For example, assume that twelve monthly telephone bills of about the same amount are paid during each year. It is of little importance that the bill that is paid and entered as an expense in January is really for service that was received in December.

A **complete cash basis** of accounting means that all revenues and all expenses are recognized only when cash is received or spent. Except for very small businesses, this method of accounting generally does not provide a sufficiently useful measure of income. A method commonly used by personal service enterprises to provide a more useful measure of income is the modified cash basis of accounting. Under the **modified cash basis**, most revenues and expenses are recognized on the cash basis, but exceptions are made for certain types of economic transactions and events. Two examples of such exceptions are the purchase and use of plant and equipment, and supplies.

In accounting for plant and equipment, it is unreasonable to consider the entire cost of a building or piece of equipment to be an expense of the period in which it was purchased. These assets are expected to serve for a number of years; therefore, their cost less any expected scrap or salvage value should be allocated over their estimated useful lives. The method used to allocate this expense is called depreciation. **Depreciation expense** represents the part of the original cost of the asset that is assigned as an expense to each period expected to benefit from its use. Although such expense cannot be calculated with precise accuracy, this allocation results in a far more equitable periodic net income (profit) or loss measurement than one that simply considers the entire cost of such assets to be an expense of the period in which they were purchased.

In accounting for supplies, it is also sometimes unreasonable to consider the entire cost of the supplies purchased to be an expense of the period. If a large dollar amount of supplies is still on hand at the end of the period, an effort should be made to determine the cost of those items which are on hand. When this is done, only the cost of the supplies used is treated as an expense of the period.

Illustration of Accounting Procedure

Apply the accounting concepts and procedures described and illustrated thus far in an accounting system for a personal service enterprise.

In this chapter the concepts and procedures involved in keeping the accounts of a personal service enterprise on the modified cash basis are applied to a system of accounts for Andrea Marree, a computer consultant. The system of accounts used by Marree can readily be adapted to the needs of any personal service enterprise regardless of whether it is of a professional or a business nature.

Chart of Accounts

The chart of accounts for Andrea Marree is shown below. Note that all account numbers beginning with 1 relate to assets; 2, liabilities; 3, owner's equity; 4, revenue; and 5, expenses. Account numbers that have four digits with a decimal point between the third and fourth digit represent **contra accounts** meaning "opposite" or "offsetting" accounts. A contra account is used with a related account to bring about a decrease in the net amount of the two account balances. This system of account numbering permits the addition of new accounts as they may be needed without disturbing the numerical order of the existing accounts.

Andrea Marree, Computer Consultant
Chart of Accounts

Assets*
111 Cash
151 Supplies
191 Office Equipment
191.1 Accum. Depr.—Office Equipment
Liabilities
218 Accounts Payable
Owner's Equity
311 Andrea Marree, Capital
312 Andrea Marree, Drawing
331 Expense and Revenue Summary

Revenue
411 Professional Fees
Expenses
541 Rent Expense
542 Salary Expense
543 Supplies Expense
544 Travel and Entertainment Expense
545 Telephone Expense
546 Automobile Expense
547 Depreciation Expense
551 Advertising Expense
557 Charitable Contributions Expense
572 Miscellaneous Expense

*Words in bold type represent headings and not account titles.

Many of the accounts in Marree's chart of accounts have been discussed and their use illustrated in the preceding chapters. New accounts that are particularly important are: Supplies (No. 151), Accumulated Depreciation—Office Equipment (No. 191.1), Expense and Revenue Summary (No. 331), Supplies Expense (No. 543), and Depreciation Expense (No. 547). Each of these new accounts will be explained and illustrated as the need for the account arises.

Except for Supplies Expense and Depreciation Expense, every debit to an expense account arises in connection with a cash payment. For example, the car that Marree uses for business purposes is leased. The monthly car rental and the costs of gasoline, oil, lubrication, washing, and automobile insurance are debited to Automobile Expense and credited to Cash.

Accounting Records

Marree uses the following accounting records in operating the business:

1. General records
   (a) Combination journal
   (b) General ledger
2. Auxiliary record
   Copies of statements rendered to clients (billings for fees) with collections noted on them

Explain and prepare a multi-column book of original entry (the combination journal) and a four-column form of balance-column ledger.

■■■ **Combination Journal.** The two-column journal illustrated in Chapter 2 can be used to enter every transaction of a business enterprise. However, in most businesses, there are many similar transactions that involve the same account or accounts. Outstanding examples are receipts and payments of cash. Suppose that in a typical month there are 30 transactions that result in an increase in cash and 40 transactions that cause a decrease in cash. In a two-column journal, this would require entering the account "Cash" 70 times, using a journal line each time. A considerable amount of time and space is saved if a journal contains a special column for cash debits and one for cash credits. At the end of the month, the special columns for cash debits and credits are totaled. The total of the Cash Debit column is posted as one amount to the debit side of the cash account and the total of the Cash Credit column is posted as one amount to the credit side of the cash account. Thus, instead of receiving 70 postings, Cash receives only two, one debit and one credit. This method requires much less time and the danger of posting error is reduced.

There is no reason to limit special journal columns to only the cash account. If there are other accounts frequently used, then the special columns should be used to collect the amounts that have the same effect on the account. When accounts are infrequently used, the only columns necessary are a General Debit column and a General Credit column. A journal with such special and general columns is called a **combination journal**.

Marree uses a combination journal as the record of original entry. The following is a reproduction of a portion of this journal. It has seven amount columns, two at the left and five at the right of the Description column. The headings of the amount columns (reading from left to right on the journal page) are as follows:

Cash
    Debit
    Credit
General
    Debit
    Credit
Professional Fees Credit
Salary Expense Debit
Automobile Expense Debit

Each of the five special columns is needed to help make the data entry process more efficient, since there are many transactions requiring entries in each of the accounts. A narrative of transactions completed by Marree during the month of December, 19--, is given on pages 82-88. These transactions are entered in the combination journal on pages 86-87. Note that before any transactions are entered in this journal, a memo notation of the cash balance at the start of the month, "Balance $6,993.65," is entered in the Description column just after the words "Amounts Forwarded."

In addition to providing the "Amounts Forwarded" information, the Description column is used for two purposes. (1) When a transaction affects the General Debit or Credit column, the name of the account debited or credited is entered in the Description column. (2) When a transaction affects the special columns, information about the transaction can be entered in the Description column. For example, if cash is paid to another business for goods or services, the name of that business can be entered in the Description column. If cash is received from a client, the client's name can be entered in the Description column.

Immediately to the right of the Cash Debit and Credit columns is a "Ck. No." column. Marree has a business checking account and makes all payments by check. When payments are entered in the combination journal, the appropriate check number is entered in the Ck. No. column.

COMBINATION JOURNAL

PAGE		CASH					
	DEBIT	CREDIT	CK. No.	DAY	DESCRIPTION	POST. REF.
1					AMOUNTS FORWARDED	
2						
3						
4						

■■■ **General Ledger.** Marree's general ledger is comprised of **four-column account forms** like the one illustrated below. This account form has four amount columns: a debit column, a credit column, and two balance columns—one for debit balances and one for credit balances.

ACCOUNT						ACCOUNT NO.	
						BALANCE	
DATE	ITEM	POST. REF.	DEBIT	CREDIT		DEBIT	CREDIT

Four-Column Account Form

The four-column account form has the advantage of providing a specific place for the account balance to be entered after each amount is posted. Posting to the ledger may be done after each transaction, at the end of the week, or at month end. Marree posts the General column accounts of the combination journal at the end of the week and the column totals at the end of the month.

Marree's general ledger is reproduced on pages 88-91. In each instance, the balance of the account as of December 1 has been entered. This is done by (1) entering the date (Dec. 1, 19--) on the first line in the Date column of each account, (2) entering the word "Balance" in the Item column, (3) entering a check mark ($\sqrt{}$) in the Post. Ref. column (to show that each balance amount was not posted from the combination journal), and (4) entering the amount of the balance in the appropriate (Debit or Credit) Balance column of each account. The balance should **not** be entered in either the Debit or Credit amount column.

Expense and Revenue Summary (No. 331), Supplies Expense (No. 543), and Depreciation Expense (No. 547) are not included in the ledger because they had zero balances on December 1 and did not receive any debits or credits as a result of the cash receipt and payment transactions in December. These accounts are not used until the end-of-year process of adjusting and closing the accounts occurs. This procedure will be explained and illustrated later in this chapter and in Chapter 4.

FOR MONTH OF				**19**	**PAGE**			
GENERAL				PROFESSIONAL FEES CREDIT	SALARY EXPENSE DEBIT	AUTOMOBILE EXPENSE DEBIT		
DEBIT		CREDIT						
								1
								2
								3
								4

Auxiliary Record. Marree keeps a file for each client which includes a copy of the contract or agreement with the client. This agreement stipulates the fee for the engagement and the time of payment (or payments, if the fee is to be paid in installments—which is the usual case). A copy of each statement or billing for fees earned is also placed in each client's file. When money is received from a client, the date and amount are noted on the copy of the billing in addition to the formal entry made in the combination journal. The auxiliary record included in Marree's accounting information system is not reproduced in this chapter.

Transactions and Entries During the Fiscal Period

ANDREA MARREE, COMPUTER CONSULTANT—Narrative of Transactions

The following transactions have been entered in the combination journal illustrated on pages 86-89, and posted to the general ledger accounts illustrated on pages 88-91.

Monday, December 3

Issued Check No. 432 for $910 to Bryan Reid for December office rent.
The account title Rent Expense was entered in the Description column and $910 was debited in the General Column and credited in the Cash column.

Tuesday, December 4

Received a check for $1,400 from Phyllis Davis, a client, for services billed Nov. 23 and deposited it in the bank.
The client's name was entered in the Description column. Also, since the individual posting of professional fees revenue is not required, a check mark was placed in the Posting Reference column of the combination journal at the time the transaction was entered. The check mark shows that there is nothing entered in the General Debit and Credit columns on that line.

Wednesday, December 5

Issued Check No. 433 for $58.40 to the News-Talk in payment for a business advertisement in the newspaper.

Friday, December 7

Issued Check No. 434 for $260 to Tempaid Co. in payment for the part-time secretarial services obtained through them for the week.

End-of-the-Week Work

(1) Proved the footings of the combination journal.

To be sure that the debits entered in the journal are equal to the credits, the journal must be **proved.** Each amount column is footed and the sum of the footings of the debit columns and the sum of the footings of the credit columns compared. This is known as a **proof of footings.** The footings are entered in small figures immediately below the last regular entry. If these sums are not the same, the journal entries must be examined to discover and correct the errors. The footings should be proved frequently. When the transactions are numerous, it is advisable to prove the footings daily. The footings must be proved when a page of the journal is filled to be sure that no error is carried forward to a new page.

Proof of the footings is essential at the end of the month before the journal is ruled or any column totals are posted. The following is a proof of the footings of Marree's combination journal at the end of the first week of December.

	Debits	=	Credits
	$1,400.00		$1,228.40
	968.40		1,400.00
	260.00		
Totals	$2,628.40	=	$2,628.40

(2) Proved the cash balance (Beginning balance, $6,993.65 + cash debits $1400.00 − cash credits $1,228.40 = $7,165.25, end-of-week balance), and entered the new balance in the Description column following the transaction of December 7.

(3) Posted each entry individually from the General Debit column of the combination journal to the proper general ledger account. The December 3 entry was posted to the rent expense account in the general ledger, Account No. 541 (see page 90). The date, "3," was entered in the Date column of this account; the code, "CJ28," was entered in the "Post. Ref." column; the amount, $910.00, was entered in the Debit column, and the updated balance, $10,920.00, was entered in the Debit Balance column. The code, "CJ28," in the Post. Ref. column indicates that this entry was posted from page 28 of the combination journal. Finally, the number, "541," was entered in the Post. Ref. column of the combination journal on the line with Rent Expense, to show that the ledger account was posted.

The December 5 entry was posted to the advertising expense account, Account No. 551, in a similar manner.

Monday, December 10

Received a check for $2,000 from Goods Stores, Inc., a client, for services billed Dec. 3 and deposited it in the bank.

Issued Check No. 435 for $38.47 to Craig's Service Center in payment for gasoline purchased during the past week. These purchases related to operating a leased automobile used for business purposes.

Tuesday, December 11

Issued Check No. 436 for $239.21 to UARCO Business Forms Co. in payment for supplies.

Marree charges all purchases of supplies to the supplies account (No. 151). At the end of the year Marree takes an inventory of the supplies on hand and determines the unused portion. These unused supplies are an asset, while the used supplies must be recognized as supplies expense. Procedures for entering this information in the accounting records are explained and illustrated on pages 92-94.

Wednesday, December 12

Received a check for $3.60 from the News-Talk to whom Marree had sent a check (No. 433) on December 5 in the amount of $58.40 in payment for a business advertisement. The check for $3.60 was accompanied

PAGE

COMBINATION JOURNAL

CASH				CK. No.	DAY	DESCRIPTION	POST. REF.	
DEBIT		CREDIT						
1						AMOUNTS FORWARDED *Balance 6,993.65*		
2		9 1 0 00	432	3		*Rent Expense*	541	
3	1 4 0 0 00			4		*Phyllis Davis*	✓	
4		5 8 40	433	5		*Advertising Expense*	551	
5		2 6 0 00	434	7		*Tempaid Co.*	✓	
6	1 4 0 0 00	1 2 2 8 40					7,165.25	
7								

by a letter from the News-Talk explaining that a clerical error was made in preparing the invoice for the advertisement. The correct amount was $54.80—not $58.40. Marree's check for $58.40 had been deposited by the News-Talk before the mistake was discovered. The check for $3.60 was a refund of the excess billing and the check was deposited by Marree in the bank.

This advertising refund check was entered in the combination journal as a debit to Cash and a credit to Advertising Expense, Account No. 551, in the amount of $3.60. Check No. 433 had already been entered on December 5 as a debit to Advertising Expense for $58.40. After entering $3.60 as a credit to Advertising Expense, the net amount entered in this account was a debit of $54.80 ($58.40 debit − $3.60 credit), which is the correct amount of advertising expense incurred. Note that the error resulted from the fact that the clerk in the News-Talk office had made a **transposition error**—a mistake well known to accountants. The intention was to type $54.80 but $58.40 was typed instead. The "4" and the "8" were placed in the wrong order—they were transposed.

Issued Check No. 437 for $2,100 to Marree for personal use.

This check represented a withdrawal of assets from the business by Marree. The amount was entered as a debit to Andrea Marree, Drawing, Account No. 312, and a credit to Cash.

Thursday, December 13

Issued Check No. 438 for $320.00 to the O'Daniel Auto Leasing Co. in payment of one month's rent for the leased automobile used by Marree for business purposes.

This payment was entered as a debit to Automobile Expense, Account No. 546, and a credit to Cash.

Friday, December 14

Issued Check No. 439 for $255.00 to Tempaid Co. in payment for the part-time secretarial services obtained through them for the week.

Issued Check No. 440 for $100.00 to American Heart Association.

End-of-the-Week Work

(1) Proved the footings of the combination journal. Total debits ($3,403.60 + $3,407.61 + $515.00 + $358.47 = $7,684.68) equal total credits ($4,281.08 + $3.60 + $3,400.00 = $7,684.68).

(2) Proved the cash balance ($6,993.65 + $3,403.60 − $4,281.08 =

FOR MONTH OF *December*   19--   PAGE *28*

GENERAL		PROFESSIONAL FEES CREDIT	SALARY EXPENSE DEBIT	AUTOMOBILE EXPENSE DEBIT	
DEBIT	CREDIT				
					1
9 1 0 00					2
		1 4 0 0 00			3
5 8 40					4
			2 6 0 00		5
9 6 8 40		1 4 0 0 00	2 6 0 00		6
					7

$6,116.17), and entered the new balance in the Description column following the second transaction of December 14.

(3) Posted each entry individually from the General Debit and General Credit columns of the combination journal to the proper general ledger accounts.

Monday, December 17

Issued Check No. 441 for $58.35 to Craig's Service Center in payment for gasoline, oil and lubrication purchased during the past week. All of these purchases related to the expense of operating the leased automobile used for business purposes.

Issued Check No. 442 for $24.75 to Falk Typewriter Service in payment of charges for cleaning and repairing the office typewriter.

The amount of this check was charged to Miscellaneous Expense, Account No. 572.

Tuesday, December 18

Issued Check No. 443 for $79.60 to Triumph Telephone Co. in payment of the statement just received showing charges for local and long-distance business calls during the past month.

Wednesday, December 19

Received a check for $1,600 from L. R. Frames, a client, for services billed Dec. 10 and deposited it in the bank.

Issued Check No. 444 for $178.22 to Corporate Enterprise Systems in payment for supplies purchased.

Friday, December 21

Issued Check No. 445 for $275.00 to Tempaid Co. in payment for the part-time secretarial services obtained through them for the week.

Issued Check No. 446 for $370.60 to Axel Office Supply for supplies purchased on account last month.

Issued Check No. 447 for $400.00 to Marree for personal use.

End-of-the-Week Work

(1) Proved the footings of the combination journal.

(2) Proved the cash balance ($6,329.65).

(3) Posted each entry individually from the General Debit column of the combination journal.

PAGE 28

COMBINATION JOURNAL

CASH DEBIT	CASH CREDIT	CK. NO.	DAY	DESCRIPTION	POST. REF.
				AMOUNTS FORWARDED **Balance 6,993.65**	
	9 1 0 00	432	3	Rent Expense	541
1 4 0 0 00			4	Phyllis Davis	✓
	5 8 40	433	5	Advertising Expense	551
	2 6 0 00	434	7	Tempaid Co.	✓
1 4 0 0 00 / 2 0 0 0 00	1 2 2 8 40		10	Goods Stores, Inc. 7,165.25	✓
	3 8 47	435	10	Craig's Service Center	✓
	2 3 9 21	436	11	Supplies	151
3 60			12	Advertising Expense	551
	2 1 0 0 00	437	12	Andrea Marree, Drawing	312
	3 2 0 00	438	13	O'Daniel Auto Leasing Co.	✓
	2 5 5 00	439	14	Tempaid Co.	✓
	1 0 0 00	440	14	Charitable Contributions Expense	557
3 4 0 3 60	4 2 8 1 08 / 5 8 35	441	17	Craig's Service Center 6,116.17	✓
	2 4 75	442	17	Miscellaneous Expense	572
	7 9 60	443	18	Telephone Expense	545
1 6 0 0 00			19	L. R. Frames	✓
	1 7 8 22	444	19	Supplies	151
	2 7 5 00	445	21	Tempaid Co.	✓
	3 7 0 60	446	21	Accounts Payable	218
	4 0 0 00	447	21	Andrea Marree, Drawing	312
5 0 0 3 60	5 6 6 7 60 / 2 4 8 75	448	26	Travel & Entertainment Expense 6,329.65	544
	4 1 53	449	26	Craig's Service Center	✓
	3 6 00	450	27	Miscellaneous Expense	572
			27	Supplies	151
				Accounts Payable 6,003.37	218
5 0 0 3 60	5 9 9 3 88		27	Carried Forward	

Wednesday, December 26

Issued Check No. 448 for $248.75 to Memorial Country Club in payment of food and beverage charges for one month.

Marree uses the facilities of the club to entertain prospective clients. The amount of this check was charged to Travel and Entertainment Expense, Account No. 544.

Issued Check No. 449 for $41.53 to Craig's Service Center for gasoline purchased during the past week.

Thursday, December 27

Issued Check No. 450 for $36.00 to Computer News to renew the subscription to a computer newsletter.

FOR MONTH OF December   19--   PAGE 28

	GENERAL DEBIT	GENERAL CREDIT	PROFESSIONAL FEES CREDIT	SALARY EXPENSE DEBIT	AUTOMOBILE EXPENSE DEBIT
1					
2	9 1 0 00				
3			1 4 0 0 00		
4	5 8 40				
5				2 6 0 00	
6		9 6 8 40	1 4 0 0 00 / 2 0 0 0 00	2 6 0 00	
7					3 8 47
8	2 3 9 21				
9		3 60			
10	2 1 0 0 00				
11					3 2 0 00
12				2 5 5 00	
13	1 0 0 00				
14	3 4 0 7 61	3 60	3 4 0 0 00	5 1 5 00	3 5 8 47 / 5 8 35
15	2 4 75				
16	7 9 60				
17			1 6 0 0 00		
18	1 7 8 22				
19				2 7 5 00	
20	3 7 0 60				
21	4 0 0 00				
22	4 4 6 0 78 / 2 4 8 75	3 60	5 0 0 0 00	7 9 0 00	4 1 6 82
23					4 1 53
24	3 6 00				
25	2 6 7 41				
26		2 6 7 41			
27	5 0 1 2 94	2 7 1 01	5 0 0 0 00	7 9 0 00	4 5 8 35
28					

The amount of the check was charged to Miscellaneous Expense, Account No. 572.

Purchased supplies from Axel Office Supply for $267.41 on account. The amount of this purchase was entered as a debit to Supplies and a credit to Accounts Payable. Note that two lines were needed to enter this transaction because both the General Debit and General Credit columns had to be used.

Because a page of the combination journal was filled after this transaction was entered, the footings of the columns were proved and entered as totals on the last line of the page, and the words "Carried Forward" were placed in the Description column. The totals were entered in the

PAGE 29

COMBINATION JOURNAL

CASH DEBIT	CASH CREDIT	CK. NO.	DAY	DESCRIPTION	POST. REF.
5 0 0 3 60	5 9 9 3 88			AMOUNTS FORWARDED *Balance 6,003.37*	
9 0 0 00			28	*F & M Seafood Markets*	✓
	1 8 0 00	451	28	*Tempaid Co.*	✓
5 9 0 3 60	6 1 7 3 88			6,723.37	
(1 1 1)	(1 1 1)				

appropriate columns on the top line of the next page. The cash balance was entered in the Description column of the new page just after the words "Amounts Forwarded."

Friday, December 28

Received a check for $900 from F & M Seafood Markets, a client, for services billed Dec. 17 and deposited it in the bank.

Issued Check No. 451 for $180.00 to Tempaid Co. in payment for the part-time secretarial services obtained through them for the week.

Routine-End-of-the-Month Work

(1) Proved the footings and entered the totals in the combination journal.

(2) Proved the cash balance ($6,723.37).

(3) Completed the individual posting from the General Debit and General Credit columns of the combination journal.

(4) Completed the summary posting of the five special-column totals of the combination journal and ruled the journal as illustrated on pages 86-89. Note that the number of the account to which the total is posted was written in parentheses just below the total, and that check marks in parentheses were placed below the General Debit and General Credit column totals to indicate that these amounts were not posted. Also note that the ledger account balance was entered after each entry was posted.

(5) Prepared a trial balance of the ledger accounts.

Usually a trial balance at the end of a month is prepared using two-column paper. However, because Marree has chosen the calendar year for the fiscal year (a common, but by no means universal practice), the trial balance at the end of December is placed in the first two amount columns of a form known as a work sheet. The need for and preparation of a work sheet are explained and illustrated on pages 92-95.

ACCOUNT *Cash* ACCOUNT NO. 111

DATE		ITEM	POST. REF.	DEBIT	CREDIT	BALANCE DEBIT	BALANCE CREDIT
19-- Dec.	1	*Balance*	✓			6 9 9 3 65	
	31		CJ29	5 9 0 3 60		12 8 9 7 25	
	31		CJ29		6 1 7 3 88	6 7 2 3 37	

FOR MONTH OF *December*   **19--** **PAGE** *29*

GENERAL DEBIT	GENERAL CREDIT	PROFESSIONAL FEES CREDIT	SALARY EXPENSE DEBIT	AUTOMOBILE EXPENSE DEBIT	
5 0 1 2 94	2 7 1 01	5 0 0 0 00	7 9 0 00	4 5 8 35	1
		9 0 0 00			2
			1 8 0 00		3
5 0 1 2 94	2 7 1 01	5 9 0 0 00	9 7 0 00	4 5 8 35	4
(√)	(√)	(4 1 1)	(5 4 2)	(5 4 6)	5

ACCOUNT **Supplies**   ACCOUNT NO. *151*

DATE		ITEM	POST. REF.	DEBIT	CREDIT	BALANCE DEBIT	BALANCE CREDIT
19-- Dec.	1	Balance	√			7 0 3 3 86	
	11		CJ28	2 3 9 21		7 2 7 3 07	
	19		CJ28	1 7 8 22		7 4 5 1 29	
	27		CJ28	2 6 7 41		7 7 1 8 70	

ACCOUNT **Office Equipment**   ACCOUNT NO. *191*

DATE		ITEM	POST. REF.	DEBIT	CREDIT	BALANCE DEBIT	BALANCE CREDIT
19-- Dec.	1	Balance	√			45 2 1 0 80	

ACCOUNT **Accumulated Depr.—Office Equipment**   ACCOUNT NO. *191.1*

DATE		ITEM	POST. REF.	DEBIT	CREDIT	BALANCE DEBIT	BALANCE CREDIT
19-- Dec.	1	Balance	√				9 6 5 4 70

ACCOUNT **Accounts Payable**   ACCOUNT NO. *218*

DATE		ITEM	POST. REF.	DEBIT	CREDIT	BALANCE DEBIT	BALANCE CREDIT
19-- Dec.	1	Balance	√				3 7 0 60
	21		CJ28	3 7 0 60		- 0 -	- 0 -
	27		CJ28		2 6 7 41		2 6 7 41

ACCOUNT **Andrea Marree, Capital**   ACCOUNT NO. *311*

DATE		ITEM	POST. REF.	DEBIT	CREDIT	BALANCE DEBIT	BALANCE CREDIT
19-- Dec.	1	Balance	√				24 1 5 2 00

Andrea Marree, Computer Consultant—General Ledger

ACCOUNT **Andrea Marree, Drawing**   ACCOUNT NO. *312*

DATE		ITEM	POST. REF.	DEBIT	CREDIT	BALANCE DEBIT	BALANCE CREDIT
Dec.	1	Balance	✓			27 21 0 75	
	12		CJ28	2 1 0 0 00		29 31 0 75	
	21		CJ28	4 0 0 00		29 71 0 75	

ACCOUNT **Professional Fees**   ACCOUNT NO. *411*

DATE		ITEM	POST. REF.	DEBIT	CREDIT	BALANCE DEBIT	BALANCE CREDIT
Dec.	1	Balance	✓				83 24 0 00
	31		CJ29		5 90 0 00		89 14 0 00

ACCOUNT **Rent Expense**   ACCOUNT NO. *541*

DATE		ITEM	POST. REF.	DEBIT	CREDIT	BALANCE DEBIT	BALANCE CREDIT
Dec.	1	Balance	✓			10 01 0 00	
	3		CJ28	9 1 0 00		10 92 0 00	

ACCOUNT **Salary Expense**   ACCOUNT NO. *542*

DATE		ITEM	POST. REF.	DEBIT	CREDIT	BALANCE DEBIT	BALANCE CREDIT
Dec.	1	Balance	✓			9 13 0 00	
	31		CJ29	9 7 0 00		10 10 0 00	

ACCOUNT **Travel & Entertainment Expense**   ACCOUNT NO. *544*

DATE		ITEM	POST. REF.	DEBIT	CREDIT	BALANCE DEBIT	BALANCE CREDIT
Dec.	1	Balance	✓			3 32 5 95	
	26		CJ28	2 4 8 75		3 57 4 70	

ACCOUNT **Telephone Expense**   ACCOUNT NO. *545*

DATE		ITEM	POST. REF.	DEBIT	CREDIT	BALANCE DEBIT	BALANCE CREDIT
Dec.	1	Balance	✓			1 41 8 04	
	18		CJ28	7 9 60		1 49 7 64	

ACCOUNT **Automobile Expense**   ACCOUNT NO. *546*

DATE		ITEM	POST. REF.	DEBIT	CREDIT	BALANCE DEBIT	BALANCE CREDIT
Dec.	1	Balance	✓			4 86 0 73	
	31		CJ29	4 5 8 35		5 31 9 08	

Andrea Marree, Computer Consultant—General Ledger *(Continued)*

ACCOUNT **Advertising Expense** ACCOUNT NO. **551**

DATE		ITEM	POST. REF.	DEBIT	CREDIT	BALANCE DEBIT	BALANCE CREDIT
19-- Dec.	1	Balance	✓			9 2 8 40	
	5		CJ28	5 8 40		9 8 6 80	
	12		CJ28		3 60	9 8 3 20	

ACCOUNT **Charitable Contributions Expense** ACCOUNT NO. **557**

DATE		ITEM	POST. REF.	DEBIT	CREDIT	BALANCE DEBIT	BALANCE CREDIT
19-- Dec.	1	Balance	✓			7 3 5 00	
	14		CJ28	1 0 0 00		8 3 5 00	

ACCOUNT **Miscellaneous Expense** ACCOUNT NO. **572**

DATE		ITEM	POST. REF.	DEBIT	CREDIT	BALANCE DEBIT	BALANCE CREDIT
19-- Dec.	1	Balance	✓			5 6 0 12	
	17		CJ28	2 4 75		5 8 4 87	
	27		CJ28	3 6 00		6 2 0 87	

Andrea Marree, Computer Consultant—General Ledger *(Concluded)*

Building Your Accounting Knowledge

1. How does a personal service enterprise differ from a merchandising enterprise? From a manufacturing enterprise?
2. Describe the process of accounting for revenue on a cash basis.
3. Describe the process of accounting for expenses on a cash basis.
4. How does the modified cash basis of accounting differ from the cash basis of accounting?
5. How does the use of the combination journal save time and space in entering cash transactions?
6. What is the principal advantage of the four-column account form over the two-column account form?
7. What is the purpose of the proof of footings of the combination journal?
8. When an entry is posted from the combination journal to a ledger account, what information is entered in the "Post. Ref." column of the combination journal? In the "Post. Ref." column of the ledger account?

Assignment Box

To reinforce your understanding of the preceding text materials, you may complete the following:
   Study Guide: Part A
   Textbook: Exercises 3A1 through 3A4 or 3B1 through 3B4
         Problems 3A1 through 3A2 or 3B1 through 3B2

Work at Close of the Fiscal Period

As soon as possible after the end of the fiscal period, the owner (or owners) of an enterprise wants to be provided with (1) an income statement, (2) a statement of owner's equity covering the period just ended, and (3) a balance sheet as of the last day of the period. To provide these statements, the accountant must consider certain matters that have not been entered in the daily routine of events. For example, in the case of Marree's enterprise, usage of supplies and depreciation of office equipment must be recognized. Furthermore, the revenue accounts, the expense accounts, and the account showing the owner's withdrawals have performed their function for the period just ended and need to be made ready for the new period. In the language of accountants, "the books must be adjusted and closed." Actually, only the temporary owner's equity accounts—those for revenue, expense and the owner's drawings—are closed.

The End-Of-Period Work Sheet

Explain and prepare an end-of-period work sheet.

To facilitate (1) the making of needed adjustments in the accounts, (2) the preparing of financial statements, and (3) the closing of the temporary owner's equity accounts, it is common practice to prepare an **end-of-period work sheet**. Because of the nature of Marree's enterprise, an eight-column work sheet like the one shown on page 96 is adequate. Note that the heading states that it is for the year ended December 31, 19--. The income statement columns relate to the full year, and the balance sheet columns show the financial position as of the last day of the fiscal period.

Explain and prepare adjustments to the accounts at the end of the accounting period.

The first pair of columns of the work sheet illustrated on page 96 shows the trial balance taken after the routine posting for the month of December has been completed. Note that the accounts Supplies Expense (No. 543) and Depreciation Expense (No. 547) are included in the list of accounts and account numbers even though these accounts have zero balances at this point. The second pair of columns, headed "Adjustments," is used to make entries for changes in the accounting elements that have occurred during the year but have not yet been recognized.

An abbreviated version of Marree's eight-column work sheet is illustrated on page 94. This partial work sheet is presented here to help focus attention on the adjustment process.

Adjustment (a) shows the cost of supplies used during the year. The balance of $7,718.70 in Supplies (No. 151) in the trial balance is the cost of supplies on hand at the beginning of the year plus the cost of supplies purchased during the year. A physical count of the supplies on December 31 determined that the cost of supplies on hand was $736.00. Therefore, the cost of supplies used during the year must have been $6,982.70 ($7,718.70 − $736.00). This expense is entered on the work sheet by placing $6,982.70 in the Adjustments Debit column on the line for Supplies Expense, and placing the same amount in the Adjustments Credit column on the line for Supplies, as shown on page 94. Note that the related debit and credit of each adjustment is identified by letter. This makes the work sheet easy to review and is helpful later when the adjusting entries are entered in the journal and posted to the ledger accounts.

Adjustment (b) shows the estimated depreciation of the office equipment for the year. In the trial balance columns, Office Equipment (No. 191) has a balance of $45,210.80, and the balance of Accumulated Depreciation—Office Equipment (No. 191.1) is $9,654.70. No new equipment was purchased during the year and there were no sales or retirements of such property during the year. Accordingly, the balances of these two accounts have not changed during the year. The two accounts are closely related: the debit balance of the office equipment account indicates the original cost of the assets, and the credit balance of the accumulated depreciation account indicates the amount of this cost that has been charged off as depreciation in past years—that is, up to January 1 of the current year. The difference between the cost of the asset and the accumulated depreciation, $35,556.10 ($45,210.80 − $9,654.70), is described as the **undepreciated cost** of the office equipment. This amount is also called the **book value** of the equipment.

To compute the amount of depreciation expense for the year, Marree estimates that the various items of office equipment have average useful lives of ten years and that any scrap or salvage value at the end of that time is likely to be so small that it can be ignored. Accordingly, estimated depreciation expense for the year is calculated to be $4,521.08 as follows:

$$\frac{\text{Original cost}}{\text{Average useful lives}} \quad \frac{\$45,210.80}{10 \text{ years}} = \$4,521.08 \text{ depreciation for one year}$$

This expense is entered as adjustment (b) in the work sheet by placing $4,521.08 in the Adjustments Debit column on the line for Depreciation Expense and placing the same amount in the Adjustments Credit column on the line for Accumulated Depreciation—Office Equipment, as shown on page 94. Since there are no more adjustments, the Debit and Credit columns are totaled to prove the equality of the debit and credit entries.

The next step is to combine each amount in the Trial Balance columns with the amount, if any, in the Adjustments columns and to extend the total into the Income Statement or Balance Sheet columns. This process is illustrated in the full work sheet on page 96. Revenue and expense account balances are extended to the Income Statement columns. Asset, liability, and owner's equity account balances are extended to the Balance Sheet columns. Note that the new amount for Supplies, $736.00

Andrea Marree, Computer Consultant
Work Sheet
For the Year Ended December 31, 19--

	ACCOUNT TITLE	ACCT. NO.	TRIAL BALANCE DEBIT	TRIAL BALANCE CREDIT	ADJUSTMENTS DEBIT	ADJUSTMENTS CREDIT	INCOME STATEMENT DEBIT	INCOME STATEMENT CREDIT	BALANCE SHEET DEBIT	BALANCE SHEET CREDIT
1	Cash	111	672337						672337	
2	Supplies	151	771870			(a)698270			73600	
3	Office Equipment	191	4521080						4521080	
4	Accum.Depr.-Office Equip.	191.1		965470		(b)452108				1417578
11	Supplies Expense	543			(a)698270		698270			
12	Travel & Entertainment									
13	Exp.	544	357470				357470			
14	Telephone Expense	545	149764				149764			
15	Automobile Expense	546	531908				531908			
16	Depreciation Expense	547			(b)452108		452108			
19			12321411	12321411	1150378	1150378	4535427	8914000	8238092	3859519
20	Net Income						4378573			4378573
21							8914000	8914000	8238092	8238092
22										
23										
24										

($7,718.70 − $6,982.70), appears in the Balance Sheet Debit column, and that the new amount for Accumulated Depreciation—Office Equipment, $14,175.78 ($9,654.70 + $4,521.08), appears in the Balance Sheet Credit column. In addition, the Supplies Expense of $6,982.70 and the Depreciation Expense of $4,521.08 appear, along with all other expenses, in the Income Statement Debit column.

The Income Statement columns and Balance Sheet columns are then totaled. The total of the Income Statement Credit column exceeds the total of the Income Statement Debit column by $43,785.73. Since revenues are entered in the credit column and expenses in the debit column, this difference represents the net income for the year. The label "Net Income" is entered in the Account Title column and the amount is placed in the Income Statement Debit column to bring the pair of Income Statement columns into balance. The total of the Balance Sheet Debit column exceeds the total of the Balance Sheet Credit column by this same amount, $43,785.73. This is because the owner's equity in the Balance Sheet Credit column has not yet been increased by the net income of $43,785.73. This amount is placed in the Balance Sheet Credit column to bring the Balance Sheet columns into balance. The final totals of the last four columns are entered at the bottom of the work sheet.

The reason the net income for the year, $43,785.73, is equal to the difference between the Balance Sheet Debit and Credit columns is explained as follows. The amounts for the assets and liabilities in the last pair of columns are up-to-date amounts. However, Marree's owner's equity account is not up-to-date. In this example, the Andrea Marree, Capital account of $24,152.00 reflects only the balance of the account at the beginning of the year. Marree's owner's equity is affected during the year by withdrawals and net income. The drawing account balance of $29,710.75 has been extended to the debit column of the Balance Sheet. However, it is also necessary to enter the net income of $43,785.73 in the credit column of the Balance Sheet to show the increase in the owner's equity due to the successful operation of the business during the year. There has been a profit from operations during the year (increasing owner's equity) as well as withdrawals for personal expenses (decreasing owner's equity) that have caused the owner's equity element to increase to $38,226.98. These relationships can be expressed in the form of the following equation:

Owner's Equity at + Net Income for − Withdrawals = Owner's Equity at
  Start of Period   the Period   End of Period
     $24,152.00   + $43,785.73   − $29,710.75   = $38,226.98

The correct amounts for assets, liabilities, owner's equity at start of period, and withdrawals are already in the Balance Sheet columns. Therefore, the net income for the year has to be included so that those columns will reflect the basic equation: Assets = Liabilities + Owner's Equity.

Andrea Marree, Computer Consultant
Work Sheet
For the Year Ended December 31, 19--

	ACCT. NO.	TRIAL BALANCE		ADJUSTMENTS		INCOME STATEMENT		BALANCE SHEET	
ACCOUNT TITLE		DEBIT	CREDIT	DEBIT	CREDIT	DEBIT	CREDIT	DEBIT	CREDIT
1 Cash	111	6 7 2 3 37						6 7 2 3 37	
2 Supplies	151	7 7 1 8 70			(a) 6 9 8 2 70			7 3 6 00	
3 Office Equipment	191	45 2 1 0 80						45 2 1 0 80	
4 Accum.Depr.-Office Equip.	191.1		9 6 5 4 70		(b) 4 5 2 1 08				14 1 7 5 78
5 Accounts Payable	218		2 6 7 41						2 6 7 41
6 Andrea Marree, Capital	311		24 1 5 2 00						24 1 5 2 00
7 Andrea Marree, Drawing	312	29 7 1 0 75						29 7 1 0 75	
8 Professional Fees	411		89 1 4 0 00				89 1 4 0 00		
9 Rent Expense	541	10 9 2 0 00				10 9 2 0 00			
10 Salary Expense	542	10 1 0 0 00				10 1 0 0 00			
11 Supplies Expense	543			(a) 6 9 8 2 70		6 9 8 2 70			
12 Travel & Entertainment Exp.	544	3 5 7 4 70				3 5 7 4 70			
13 Telephone Expense	545	1 4 9 7 64				1 4 9 7 64			
14 Automobile Expense	546	5 3 1 9 08				5 3 1 9 08			
15 Depreciation Expense	547			(b) 4 5 2 1 08		4 5 2 1 08			
16 Advertising Expense	551	9 8 3 20				9 8 3 20			
17 Charitable Cont. Expense	557	8 3 5 00				8 3 5 00			
18 Miscellaneous Expense	572	6 2 0 87				6 2 0 87			
19		123 2 1 4 11	123 2 1 4 11	11 5 0 3 78	11 5 0 3 78	45 3 5 4 27	89 1 4 0 00	82 3 8 0 92	38 5 9 5 19
20 Net Income						43 7 8 5 73			43 7 8 5 73
21						89 1 4 0 00	89 1 4 0 00	82 3 8 0 92	82 3 8 0 92

Building Your Accounting Knowledge

1. Identify the headings of the four pairs of columns of an eight-column work sheet.
2. Explain how the amount of supplies expense for the year is determined by Marree.
3. What does the credit balance in the accumulated depreciation account represent?
4. In completing the work sheet, what is the reason for adding the net income for the year to the balance sheet credit column?

Assignment Box

To reinforce your understanding of the preceding text materials, you may complete the following:
        Study Guide: Part B
        Textbook: Exercises 3A5 through 3A8 or 3B5 through 3B8
               Problems 3A3 through 3A5 or 3B3 through 3B5

Expanding Your Business Vocabulary

What is the meaning of each of the following terms?

book value (p. 93)
business enterprises (p. 77)
cash basis expense (p. 77)
cash basis revenue (p. 77)
combination journal (p. 79)
complete cash basis (p. 77)
contra accounts (p. 78)
depreciation expense (p. 77)
end-of-period work sheet (p. 92)
four-column account forms (p. 81)

manufacturing enterprise (p. 76)
merchandising enterprise (p. 76)
modified cash basis (p. 77)
personal service enterprise (p. 76)
professional enterprises (p. 77)
proof of footings (p. 82)
proved (p. 82)
transposition error (p. 84)
undepreciated cost (p. 93)

Demonstration Problem

Maria Vietor is a financial planning consultant. She completed the following transactions during the month of December of the current year:

Dec. 3 Issued Check No. 721 for $1,000.00 to Katie DeNourie for December office rent.
    4 Received a check for $2,500.00 from Aaron Bisno, a client, for services and deposited it in the bank.
    6 Issued Check No. 722 for $75.60 to Union Electric for December heating and light.

7   Received a check for $2,000.00 from Will Carter, a client, for services and deposited it in the bank.

12   Issued Check No. 723 for $73.74 to Smith's Super Service for gasoline and oil purchases.

14   Issued Check No. 724 for $600.00 to Comphelp in payment for temporary secretarial services obtained through them during the past two weeks.

17   Purchased supplies from Cleat Office Supply Co. for $286.47 on account.

20   Issued Check No. 725 for $96.40 to Cress Telephone Co. in payment of charges for local and long distance business calls during the past month.

21   Issued Check No. 726 for $1,100.00 to Vietor for personal use.

24   Issued Check No. 727 for $100.00 to the National Multiple Sclerosis Society.

27   Received a check for $1,500.00 from Ellen Thaler, a client, for services and deposited it in the bank.

28   Issued Check No. 728 for $600.00 to Comphelp in payment for temporary secretarial services obtained through them during the past two weeks.

Required:

1.   Record the preceding transactions in a seven-column combination journal like the one illustrated in the chapter. The balance in the Cash account on Dec. 1 is $20,490.48.

2.   Prove the end-of-month footings and enter the totals in the combination journal. Then, rule the journal.

3.   Post the entries and the totals from the combination journal to the necessary ledger accounts, and show posting references as needed both in the journal and in the ledger. (The Dec. 1 balances are already entered in the ledger accounts. Do not post the totals of the General Debit and Credit columns.) Foot and balance the ledger accounts.

4.   Prepare a trial balance in the first two columns of a work sheet for the year ended Dec. 31, 19-- for Maria Vietor. Allow a line for each of the following account titles in their proper sequence:
Supplies Expense   Acct. No. 543
Depreciation Expense   Acct. No. 547

5.   Prepare the necessary adjusting entries in the work sheet to record the following:
(a)   the cost of supplies used, when the December 31 count of supplies on hand was $13,630.
(b)   the estimated depreciation of office equipment for the year, $6,781.62, based on a ten-year average useful life. Total the Adjustments columns.

6.   Complete the work sheet by extending the Trial balance and Adjustments columns to the Income Statement and Balance Sheet columns

of the work sheet. Then, total the last four columns, determine the net income (or loss), and total and rule all columns of the work sheet.

7. Calculate Maria Vietor's owner's equity at year end as follows:

$$\begin{array}{c} \text{Owner's Equity} \\ \text{at Start of Period} \\ \text{(from capital account)} \end{array} + \begin{array}{c} \text{Net Income} \\ \text{for the Period} \end{array} - \text{Withdrawals} = \begin{array}{c} \text{Owner's Equity} \\ \text{at End of Period} \end{array}$$

Solution

1 & 2 can be found on the next page

3.   **GENERAL LEDGER**

Account Cash   *Account No.* 111

Date	Item	Post. Ref.	Debit	Credit	Balance Debit	Credit
Dec. 1 Balance		√			20,490.48	
31		CJ18	6,000.00		26,490.48	
31		CJ18		3,645.74	22,844.74	

Account Supplies   *Account No.* 151

Date	Item	Post. Ref.	Debit	Credit	Balance Debit	Credit
Dec. 1 Balance		√			20,550.79	
17		CJ18	286.47		20,837.26	

Account Office Equipment   *Account No.* 191

Date	Item	Post. Ref.	Debit	Credit	Balance Debit	Credit
Dec. 1 Balance		√			67,816.20	

Account Accumulated Depreciation Office Equipment   *Account No.* 191.1

Date	Item	Post. Ref.	Debit	Credit	Balance Debit	Credit
Dec. 1 Balance		√				14,482.05

Account Accounts Payable   *Account No.* 218

Date	Item	Post. Ref.	Debit	Credit	Balance Debit	Credit
Dec. 1 Balance		√				555.90
17		CJ18		286.47		842.37

Account Maria Vietor, Capital   *Account No.* 311

Date	Item	Post. Ref.	Debit	Credit	Balance Debit	Credit
Dec. 1 Balance		√				48,052.50

1, 2 & 3.

COMBINATION JOURNAL

	CASH DEBIT	CASH CREDIT	CK. NO.	DAY	DESCRIPTION	POST. REF.
1					AMOUNTS FORWARDED 20,490.48	
2		1 0 0 0 00	721	3	Rent Expense	541
3	2 5 0 0 00			4	Aaron Bisno	✓
4		7 5 60	722	6	Heating & Lighting Expense	549
5	2 0 0 0 00			7	Will Carter	✓
6		7 3 74	723	12	Smith's Super Service	✓
7		6 0 0 00	724	14	Comphelp	✓
8				17	Supplies	151
9					Accounts Payable	218
10		9 6 40	725	20	Telephone Expense	545
11		1 1 0 0 00	726	21	Maria Vietor, Drawing	312
12		1 0 0 00	727	24	Charitable Contributions Expense	557
13	1 5 0 0 00			27	Ellen Thaler	✓
14		6 0 0 00	728	28	Comphelp	✓
15	6 0 0 0 00	3 6 4 5 74				
16	(1 1 1)	(1 1 1)				

Proof of Footings

	Debit Footings	Credit Footings
Cash	$6,000.00	$3,645.74
General.	2,658.47	286.47
Professional Fees		6,000.00
Salary Expense	1,200.00	
Automobile Expense	73.74	
	$9,932.21	$9,932.21

Account Maria Vietor, Drawing   *Account No.* 312

Date		Item	Post. Ref.	Debit	Credit	Balance Debit	Balance Credit
Dec. 1	Balance		✓			40,816.12	
21			CJ18	1,100.00		41,916.12	

Account Professional Fees   *Account No.* 411

Date		Item	Post. Ref.	Debit	Credit	Balance Debit	Balance Credit
Dec. 1	Balance		✓				124,860.00
31			CJ18		6,000.00		130,860.00

1, 2 & 3.   **FOR MONTH OF** *December*   **19--**   **PAGE** *18*

	GENERAL		PROFESSIONAL FEES CR.	SALARY EXPENSE DR.	AUTOMOBILE EXPENSE DR.	
	DEBIT	CREDIT				
						1
	1 0 0 0 00					2
			2 5 0 0 00			3
	7 5 60					4
			2 0 0 0 00			5
					7 3 74	6
				6 0 0 00		7
	2 8 6 47					8
		2 8 6 47				9
	9 6 40					10
	1 1 0 0 00					11
	1 0 0 00					12
			1 5 0 0 00			13
				6 0 0 00		14
	2 6 5 8 47	2 8 6 47	6 0 0 0 00	1 2 0 0 00	7 3 74	15
	(√)	(√)	(4 1 1)	(5 4 2)	(5 4 6)	16

Account Rent Expense   *Account No.* 541

Date	Item	Post. Ref.	Debit	Credit	Balance Debit	Credit
Dec. 1 Balance		√			11,000.00	
3		CJ18	1,000.00		12,000.00	

Account Salary Expense   *Account No.* 542

Date	Item	Post. Ref.	Debit	Credit	Balance Debit	Credit
Dec. 1 Balance		√			12,000.00	
31		CJ18	1,200.00		13,200.00	

Account Travel & Entertainment Expense   *Account No.* 544

Date	Item	Post. Ref.	Debit	Credit	Balance Debit	Credit
Dec. 1 Balance		√			4,988.92	

Account Telephone Expense   *Account No.* 545

Date	Item	Post. Ref.	Debit	Credit	Balance Debit	Credit
Dec. 1 Balance		√			2,127.06	
20		CJ18	96.40		2,223.46	

Accounts are continued on page 103.

4, 5 & 6.

Maria Vietor, Financial Planning Consultant

Work Sheet

For Year Ended December 31, 19--

	ACCOUNT TITLE	ACCT. NO.	TRIAL BALANCE DEBIT	TRIAL BALANCE CREDIT	ADJUSTMENTS DEBIT	ADJUSTMENTS CREDIT	INCOME STATEMENT DEBIT	INCOME STATEMENT CREDIT	BALANCE SHEET DEBIT	BALANCE SHEET CREDIT	
1	Cash	111	22 844 74						22 844 74		1
2	Supplies	151	20 837 26			(1) 7 207 26			13 630 00		2
3	Office Equipment	191	67 816 20						67 816 20		3
4	Accum. Depr.—Office Equipment	191.1		14 482 05		(2) 6 781 62				21 263 67	4
5	Accounts Payable	218		842 37						842 37	5
6	Maria Vietor, Capital	311		48 052 50						48 052 50	6
7	Maria Vietor, Drawing	312	41 916 12						41 916 12		7
8	Professional Fees	411		130 860 00				130 860 00			8
9	Rent Expense	541	12 000 00				12 000 00				9
10	Salary Expense	542	13 200 00				13 200 00				10
11	Supplies Expense	543			(1) 7 207 26		7 207 26				11
12	Travel & Entertainment Expense	544	4 988 92				4 988 92				12
13	Telephone Expense	545	2 223 46				2 223 46				13
14	Automobile Expense	546	4 899 34				4 899 34				14
15	Depreciation Expense	547			(2) 6 781 62		6 781 62				15
16	Heating & Lighting Expense	549	1 468 20				1 468 20				16
17	Charitable Contribution Expense	557	1 202 50				1 202 50				17
18	Miscellaneous Expense	572	840 18				840 18				18
19			194 236 92	194 236 92	13 988 88	13 988 88	54 811 48	130 860 00	146 207 06	70 158 54	19
20	Net Income						76 048 52			76 048 52	20
21							130 860 00	130 860 00	146 207 06	146 207 06	21
22											22

Account Automobile Expense　　　　　　　　　　　　　　*Account No.* 546

Date	Item	Post. Ref.	Debit	Credit	Balance Debit	Credit
Dec. 1 Balance		✓			4,825.60	
31		CJ18	73.74		4,899.34	

Account Heating & Lighting Expense　　　　　　　　　　*Account No.* 549

Date	Item	Post. Ref.	Debit	Credit	Balance Debit	Credit
Dec. 1 Balance		✓			1,392.60	
6		CJ18	75.60		1,468.20	

Account Charitable Contributions Expense　　　　　　　*Account No.* 557

Date	Item	Post. Ref.	Debit	Credit	Balance Debit	Credit
Dec. 1 Balance		✓			1,102.50	
24		CJ18	100.00		1,202.50	

Account Miscellaneous Expense　　　　　　　　　　　　*Account No.* 572

Date	Item	Post. Ref.	Debit	Credit	Balance Debit	Credit
Dec. 1 Balance		✓			840.18	

7.

Owner's equity at Start of Period	+	Net Income for the Period	−	Withdrawals	=	Owner's Equity at End of Period
$48,052.50	+	$76,048.52	−	$41,916.12	=	$82,184.90

*Note: Now that you have reviewed the Demonstration Problem and Solution you may complete the **Mastery Problem** at the end of the chapter activities.

Applying Accounting Concepts

Series A

Exercise 3A1—Combination Journal Entries. The Gary Arlen Company completed the following transactions during the first week of January, 19--:

Jan. 2 Received a check for $1,200.00 from Maria Skye, a client, for services rendered.

5 Issued Check No. 120 for $483.65 to JD Supply Co. in payment of supplies purchased.

13 Issued Check No. 121 for $128.50 to Giovanni's Restaurant in payment of a bill for dinner to entertain customers.

16 Issued Check No. 122 for $1,000.00 to Arlen for personal use.

17 Received a check for $1,150.00 from Tom Rich, a client, for services rendered.

20 Issued Check No. 123 for $150.00 to the Epilepsy Foundation.

26 Issued Check No. 124 for $275.00 to Sectemps in payment for the part-time secretarial service obtained through them for the week.

30 Issued Check No. 125 for $26.32 to Hi-Points Service Center in payment of gasoline purchased during the past week.

Prepare a combination journal using the same format and column headings as illustrated in the chapter. The balance in the cash account on January 1 is $4,280.77. Enter the preceding transactions in the combination journal.

Exercise 3A2—Combination Journal Entries. Steven Burch, a management consultant, completed the following transactions during the month of January of the current year:

Jan. 2 Issued Check No. 541 for $800.00 to Sarah Smithers for January office rent.

3 Received a check for $1,600.00 from Mark Reidy, a client, for services rendered.

6 Issued Check No. 542 for $73.20 to Garden Restaurant in payment of bill for dinner to entertain client.

9 Received a check for $2,500.00 from Good Buys, Inc., a client, for services rendered.

13 Issued Check No. 543 for $33.62 to Nowak's Service Palace for gasoline and oil purchases.

13 Issued Check No. 544 for $560.00 to Helptemps in payment of part-time secretarial services obtained through them during the past two weeks.

16 Purchased supplies from S. G. Adams Co. for $342.67 on account.

18 Issued Check No. 545 for $83.20 to Blue Line Telephone Co. in payment of charges for local and long distance business calls during the past month.

20 Issued Check No. 546 for $1,000.00 to Burch for personal use.

24 Issued Check No. 547 for $100.00 to American Lung Association.

27 Received a check for $2,000.00 from Judy Meador, a client, for services rendered.

30 Issued Check No. 548 for $560.00 to Helptemps in payment of part-time secretarial services obtained through them during the past two weeks.

Prepare a combination journal using the same format and column headings as illustrated in the chapter. Number the journal page 28. The balance in the cash account on January 1 is $7,342.45. Enter the preceding transactions in the combination journal.

Exercise 3A3—Proof of Combination Journal Footings; Totaling and Ruling Journal. Refer to Exercise 3A2. Foot the column totals of Steven Burch's combination journal. Show the proof of footings below the journal. Then, total and rule the journal.

Exercise 3A4—Posting from Combination Journal to Four-Column Ledger Accounts. Refer to Exercise 3A3. Post the entries and the totals from Steven Burch's combination journal to the general ledger. Open four-column ledger accounts as necessary. Be sure to show posting references both in the combination journal and in the ledger accounts. Do not post the totals of the General Debit and Credit columns.

Exercise 3A5—Trial Balance Columns of Work Sheet. The following are the general ledger account balances for Allison Gunn's Consulting Service at December 31, 19--:

		Debit Balances	Credit Balances
Cash	111	$ 9,281.08	
Supplies	151	6,547.68	
Office Equipment	191	42,800.10	
Accum. Depr.—Office Equipment	191.1		$ 8,569.30
Accounts Payable	218		750.00
Allison Gunn, Capital	311		35,250.00
Allison Gunn, Drawing	312	31,897.49	
Professional Fees	411		78,914.79
Rent Expense	541	12,600.00	
Salary Expense	542	14,300.00	
Supplies Expense	543		
Travel & Entertainment Expense	544	607.50	
Telephone Expense	545	1,140.30	
Automobile Expense	546	3,312.25	
Depreciation Expense	547		
Charitable Contributions Expense	557	850.00	
Miscellaneous Expense	572	147.69	

Prepare the trial balance columns of an eight-column work sheet for the year ended December 31, 19-- by entering the preceding general ledger account balances and totaling the debit and credit amount columns.

Exercise 3A6—Adjustments Columns of Work Sheet. Refer to Exercise 3A5. In the Adjustments columns of Allison Gunn's work sheet, make the necessary adjustments to record: (a) the cost of supplies used, when the December 31 count of supplies on hand was $562.00; and (b) the estimated depreciation of office equipment for the year, $4,280.01, based on an average useful life of ten years. Total the Adjustments columns.

Exercise 3A7—Completion of Work Sheet. Refer to Exercise 3A6. Complete Allison Gunn's work sheet by extending the Trial Balance and Adjustments columns to the Income Statement and Balance Sheet columns of the work sheet. Then, total the last four columns, determine the net income (or loss), enter the final totals, and total and rule all columns of the work sheet.

Exercise 3A8—Calculation of Year-End Owner's Equity. Refer to Exercise 3A7. Calculate Allison Gunn's owner's equity at year end, using the following model:

Owner's Equity		Net Income				Owner's Equity
at Start of Period	+	for the Period	−	Withdrawals	=	at End of Period

Series B

Exercise 3B1—Combination Journal Entries. The Anita Tobin Company completed the following transactions during the first week of January, 19--:

Jan. 3   Received a check for $1,800.00 from Lee Landers, a client, for services rendered.
  6   Issued Check No. 330 for $725.50 to GQ Supply Co. in payment of supplies purchased.
  9   Issued Check No. 331 for $64.90 to Spiro's Restaurant in payment of bill for dinner to entertain customers.
 12   Issued Check No. 332 for $2,000.00 to Tobin for personal use.
 15   Received a check for $1,700.00 from David Pittman, a client, for services rendered.
 18   Issued Check No. 333 for $200.00 to Shelter House as a charitable contribution.
 23   Issued Check No. 334 for $260.00 to Computemps in payment for the part-time word processing services obtained through them for the week.
 30   Issued Check No. 335 for $34.77 to Clayton Shaw Service in payment of gasoline purchased during the past week.

Prepare a combination journal using the same format and account titles as illustrated in the chapter. The balance in the cash account on January 1 is $6,421.32. Enter the transactions in the combination journal.

Exercise 3B2—Combination Journal Entries. Esther Léal, an information systems consultant, completed the following transactions during the month of January of the current year:

Jan. 2   Issued Check No. 621 for $900.00 to Frank Cornwell for January office rent.
  4   Received a check for $1,800.00 from Barbara Burke, a client, for services rendered.
  7   Issued Check No. 622 for $68.40 to Anthony's Restaurant in payment of bill for dinner to entertain client.
 10   Received a check for $2,700.00 from Tent City, Inc., a client, for services rendered.
 11   Issued Check No. 623 for $41.74 to Roger's Service Station for gasoline and oil purchases.
 16   Issued Check No. 624 for $550.00 to Fasthelp in payment of part-time secretarial services obtained through them during the past two weeks.
 21   Purchased supplies from Otte Supplies for $427.63 on account.
 23   Issued Check No. 625 for $62.70 to Temple Telephone Co. in payment of charges for local and long distance business calls during the past month.
 25   Issued Check No. 626 for $900.00 to Léal for personal use.
 28   Issued Check No. 627 for $75.00 to American Cancer Society.
 29   Received a check for $2,500.00 from Kay Christensen, a client, for services rendered.
 31   Issued Check No. 628 for $550.00 to Fasthelp in payment of part-time secretarial services obtained through them during the past two weeks.

Prepare a combination journal using the same format and account titles as illustrated in the chapter. Number the journal page 32. The balance in the Cash account on January 1 is $6,937.75. Enter the preceding transactions in the combination journal.

Exercise 3B3—Proof of Combination Journal Footings; Totaling and Ruling Journal. Refer to Exercise 3B2. Foot the column totals of Esther Léal's combination journal. Show the proof of footings below the journal. Then total and rule the journal.

Exercise 3B4—Posting from Combination Journal to Four-Column Ledger Accounts. Refer to Exercise 3B3. Post the entries and the totals from Esther Léal's combination journal to the general ledger. Open four-column ledger accounts as necessary. Be sure to show posting references both in the combination journal and in the ledger accounts. Do not post the totals of the General Debit and Credit columns.

Exercise 3B5—Trial Balance Columns of Work Sheet. The following are the general ledger account balances for John Lotshaw's Financial Planning Service at December 31, 19--:

		Debit Balances	Credit Balances
Cash	111	$ 4,640.54	
Supplies	151	3,273.84	
Office Equipment	191	21,400.05	
Accum. Depr.—Office Equipment	191.1		$ 4,284.65
Accounts Payable	218		375.00
John Lotshaw, Capital	311		17,625.00
John Lotshaw, Drawing	312	15,948.75	
Professional Fees	411		39,457.43
Rent Expense	541	6,300.00	
Salary Expense	542	7,150.00	
Supplies Expense	543		
Travel & Entertainment Expense	544	303.75	
Telephone Expense	545	570.15	
Automobile Expense	546	1,656.15	
Depreciation Expense	547		
Charitable Contributions Expense	557	425.00	
Miscellaneous Expense	572	73.85	

Prepare the trial balance columns of an eight-column work sheet for the year ended December 31, 19-- by entering the preceding general ledger account balances and totaling the debit and credit amount columns.

Exercise 3B6—Adjustments Columns of Work Sheet. Refer to Exercise 3B5. In the Adjustments columns of John Lotshaw's work sheet, make the necessary adjustments to record: (a) the cost of supplies used, when the December 31 count of supplies on hand was $281.00; and (b) the estimated depreciation of office equipment for the year, $2,140.01, based on an average useful life of ten years. Total the adjustments columns.

Exercise 3B7—Completion of Work Sheet. Refer to Exercise 3B6. Complete John Lotshaw's work sheet by extending the Trial Balance and Adjustments columns to the Income Statement and Balance Sheet columns of the work sheet. Then, total the last four columns, determine the net income (or loss), enter the final totals, and total and rule all the columns of the work sheet.

Exercise 3B8—Calculation of Year-End Owner's Equity.   Refer to Exercise 3B7. Calculate John Lotshaw's owner's equity at year end, using the following model:

Owner's Equity at Start of Period	+	Net Income for the Period	−	Withdrawals	=	Owner's Equity at End of Period

---

Series A

Problem 3A1   Combination Journal Entries; Proof of Footings; Totaling and Ruling Journal

---

Kenneth Schwartz is an attorney. During the month of February, you are employed to keep Schwartz's books on a temporary basis. The following transactions were completed by Schwartz during the month of February, 19--:

Feb. 2   Issued Check No. 201 for $1,000.00 to Todd Tobiasz for February office rent.
   2   Received a check for $1,360.00 from Peggy Chin, a client.
   2   Issued Check No. 202 for $149.40 to Illinois Power for February heating and lighting.
   3   Issued Check No. 203 for $408.22 to Cloverleaf Office Supplies in payment of office supplies.
   3   Received a check for $5,000.00 from Diana Ortiz, a client.
   3   Issued Check No. 204 for $400.00 to Richard Klott, temporary paralegal, in payment of his weekly salary.
   3   Issued Check No. 205 for $200.00 to Lauri Levine, temporary secretary in payment of her weekly salary.
   5   Issued Check No. 206 for $100.00 to the Arthritis Foundation.
   6   Issued Check No. 207 for $138.80 to Car Care Service Station in payment for gas, oil, and lubrication charges for the past month on the car that Schwartz leases for business purposes.
   7   Received a check for $2,200.00 from Mary Grana, a client.
   9   Issued Check No. 208 for $400.00 to Richard Klott and Check No. 209 for $200.00 to Lauri Levine in payment of weekly salaries.
   9   Issued Check No. 210 for $1,000.00 to Schwartz for personal use.
   12   Issued Check No. 211 for $320.00 to Mallory Buick for one month's rent of the car leased to Schwartz for business purposes.
   13   Received a check for $16,000.00 from Wallis Bayer, a client.
   14   Issued Check No. 212 for $38.40 to Eppler's Typewriter Shop for typewriter repairs. (Charge to Miscellaneous Expense.)
   14   Issued Check No. 213 for $264.80 to Ozark Telephone Co. for monthly statement.
   16   Issued Check No. 214 for $400.00 to Richard Klott and Check No. 215 for $200.00 to Lauri Levine in payment of weekly salaries.

21 Issued Check No. 216 for $196.18 to Bond Supply Co. in payment of supplies purchased.

23 Issued Check No. 217 for $400.00 to Richard Klott and Check No. 218 for $200.00 to Lauri Levine in payment of weekly salaries.

28 Issued Check No. 219 for $296.00 to Bel Aire Country Club in payment of food and beverage charges for February. (Charge to Travel and Entertainment Expense.)

28 Purchased supplies from Gem Office Supply Co., $137.42 on account.

Required:

1. Prepare a combination journal using the same format and column headings as illustrated in the chapter. Number the journal page 24. The balance in the cash account on February 1 is $12,496.42.
2. Enter the preceding transactions in the combination journal.
3. Foot, prove, total, and rule the combination journal.

Problem 3A2   Posting Combination Journal to Four-Column Ledger Accounts

Kenneth Schwartz keeps a four-column general ledger like the one illustrated in the chapter. This ledger contains the following accounts and balances as of February 1:

Account	Account No.	Feb. 1 Balance
Cash	111	$12,496.42 dr.
Supplies	151	1,500.00 dr.
Office Equipment	191	12,000.00 dr.
Accum. Depr.—Office Equipment	191.1	4,050.00 cr.
Accounts Payable	218	902.40 cr.
Kenneth Schwartz, Capital	311	21,044.02 cr.
Kenneth Schwartz, Drawing	312	0.00
Professional Fees	411	0.00
Rent Expense	541	0.00
Salary Expense	542	0.00
Supplies Expense	543	0.00
Travel & Entertainment Expense	544	0.00
Telephone Expense	545	0.00
Automobile Expense	546	0.00
Depreciation Expense	547	0.00
Utilities Expense	549	0.00
Charitable Contributions Expense	557	0.00
Miscellaneous Expense	572	0.00

Required:

1. Open the accounts in Kenneth Schwartz's general ledger and enter the February 1 balances.
2. Refer to Problem 3A1. Post the combination journal to the ledger accounts. Update each account balance after each entry is posted. Be sure to include all necessary posting references both in the combination journal and in the ledger.

Problem 3A3

Eight-Column Work Sheet; Calculation of Year-End Owner's Equity

The following are the balances of Kenneth Schwartz's general ledger accounts as of the close of business on February 28 of the current year:

	Acct. No.	Debit Balance	Credit Balance
Cash......................................	111	$30,744.62	
Supplies...................................	151	2,241.82	
Office Equipment	191	12,000.00	
Accum. Depr.—Office Equipment	191.1		$ 4,050.00
Accounts Payable	218		1,039.82
Kenneth Schwartz, Capital	311		21,044.02
Kenneth Schwartz, Drawing	312	1,000.00	
Professional Fees	411		24,560.00
Rent Expense	541	1,000.00	
Salary Expense	542	2,400.00	
Supplies Expense	543	-0-	
Travel & Entertainment Expense	544	296.00	
Telephone Expense	545	264.80	
Automobile Expense	546	458.80	
Depreciation Expense	547	-0-	
Utilities Expense	549	149.40	
Charitable Contributions Expense	557	100.00	
Miscellaneous Expense......................	572	38.40	

Required:

1. Prepare a trial balance of Schwartz's ledger as of February 28 in the first two columns of an eight-column work sheet for the period ended February 28, 19--.
2. Prepare the necessary adjustments in the Adjustments columns of the work sheet, based on the following information:
    (a) An inventory of supplies on hand February 28 amounts to $1,250.00.
    (b) Depreciation of office equipment, 1% per month, amounts to $120.00.
    Then, total the Adjustments columns of the work sheet.
3. Complete the work sheet for the month ended February 28, 19-- by extending all amounts in the Trial Balance and Adjustments columns to the Income Statement and Balance Sheet columns. Then, total all remaining columns and determine the net income (or net loss).
4. Calculate the owner's equity as of February 28, based on the following equation:

Owner's Equity at Start of Period	+	Net Income for the Period	−	Withdrawals	=	Owner's Equity at End of Period

Problem 3A4

Eight-Column Work Sheet

The following are the Trial Balance columns of the work sheet of Carr Trovillion, Certified Public Accountant, for the month ended September 30, 19--.

Account	No.	Debit	Credit
Cash	111	$ 61,489.24	
Supplies	151	4,483.64	
Office Equipment	191	24,000.00	
Accum. Depr.—Office Equipment	191.1		$ 8,100.00
Accounts Payable	218		2,079.44
Carr Trovillion, Capital	311		42,088.24
Carr Trovillion, Drawing	312	2,000.00	
Professional Fees	411		49,120.00
Rent Expense	541	2,000.00	
Salary Expense	542	4,800.00	
Supplies Expense	543		
Travel & Entertainment Expense	544	592.20	
Telephone Expense	545	529.40	
Automobile Expense	546	917.60	
Depreciation Expense	547		
Heating & Lighting Expense	549	298.40	
Charitable Contributions Expense	557	200.00	
Miscellaneous Expense	572	77.20	
		$101,387.68	$101,387.68

Required:

Complete an eight-column work sheet, assuming the following adjustment data:
- (a) Supplies expense $1,983.64
- (b) Depreciation of office equipment   240.00

Problem 3A5   Eight-Column Work Sheet

The following are the Trial Balance columns of the work sheet of Sandra Evans, Computer Consultant, for the month ended April 30, 19--.

Account	No.	Debit	Credit
Cash	111	$15,372.31	
Supplies	151	1,120.91	
Office Equipment	191	6,000.00	
Accum. Depr.—Office Equipment	191.1		$ 2,025.00
Accounts Payable	218		519.91
Sandra Evans, Capital	311		10,522.01
Sandra Evans, Drawing	312	500.00	
Professional Fees	411		12,280.00
Rent Expense	541	500.00	
Salary Expense	542	1,200.00	
Supplies Expense	543		
Travel & Entertainment Expense	544	148.00	
Telephone Expense	545	132.60	
Automobile Expense	546	229.20	
Depreciation Expense	547		
Heating & Lighting Expense	549	74.60	
Charitable Contributions Expense	557	50.00	
Miscellaneous Expense	572	19.30	
		$25,346.92	$25,346.92

Required:

Complete an eight-column work sheet, assuming the following adjustment data:

(a) Supplies expense $495.91
(b) Depreciation of office equipment   60.00

Series B

Problem 3B1   Combination Journal Entries; Proof of Footings; Totaling and
                   Ruling Journal

James Rhea is an orthodontist. During the month of January, you are employed
to keep Rhea's books on a temporary basis. The following transactions were
completed by Rhea during the month of January, 19--:

Jan. 2   Issued Check No. 311 for $900.00 to Richard Barre for January office
rent.

2   Received a check for $1,020.00 from Thomas Findley, a patient.

3   Issued Check No. 312 for $152.30 to Ozark Electric Co. for January
heating and lighting.

4   Issued Check No. 313 for $306.16 to Ideal Dental Supplies in payment
of dental supplies.

4   Received a check for $3,000.00 from Sandra Madow, a patient.

5   Issued Check No. 314 for $350.00 to Janice Patrick, temporary assistant,
in payment of her weekly salary.

5   Issued Check No. 315 for $175.00 to Judith Brooks, temporary recep-
tionist, in payment of her weekly salary.

8   Issued Check No. 316 for $75.00 to the Cystic Fibrosis Foundation.

10 Issued Check No. 317 for $173.80 to U-Gas, Inc. in payment for gas,
oil, and lubrication charges for the past month on the car that Rhea
leases.

11 Received a check for $1,600.00 from Edward Lyss, a patient.

12 Issued Check No. 318 for $350.00 to Janice Patrick and Check No. 319
for $175.00 to Judith Brooks in payment of weekly salaries.

15 Issued Check No. 320 for $1,500.00 to Rhea for personal use.

16 Issued Check No. 321 for $325.00 to Darr Pontiac for one month's rent
of the car leased to Rhea for business purposes.

17 Received a check for $6,000.00 from Sam Medina (son and daughters
are patients).

18 Issued Check No. 322 for $26.40 to Melcher's Repair Shop for type-
writer repairs. (Charge to Miscellaneous Expense.)

19 Issued Check No. 323 for $248.60 to Easy Exchange Telephone Co. for
monthly statement.

19 Issued Check No. 324 for $350.00 to Janice Patrick and Check No. 325
for $175.00 to Judith Brooks in payment of weekly salaries.

23 Issued Check No. 326 for $88.93 to Office Supply Co. in payment of
office supplies purchased.

26 Issued Check No. 327 for $350.00 to Janice Patrick and Check No. 328
for $175.00 to Judith Brooks in payment of weekly salaries.

31 Issued Check No. 329 for $179.00 to Algonquin Country Club in payment of food and beverage charges for January. (Charge to Travel and Entertainment Expense.)

31 Purchased dental supplies from Ideal Dental Supplies on account, $168.59.

Required:

1. Prepare a combination journal using the same format and column headings as illustrated in the chapter. Number the journal page 32. The balance in the cash account on January 1 is $9,372.31.

2. Enter the preceding transactions in the combination journal.

3. Foot, prove, total, and rule the combination journal.

Problem 3B2   Posting Combination Journal to Four-Column Ledger Accounts

James Rhea keeps a four-column general ledger like the one illustrated in the chapter. This ledger contains the following accounts and balances as of January 1:

Account	Account No.	Jan. 1 Balance
Cash	111	$ 9,372.31 dr.
Supplies	151	1,125.00 dr.
Office Equipment	191	9,000.00 dr.
Accum. Depr.—Office Equipment	191.1	3,037.50 cr.
Accounts Payable	218	676.80 cr.
James Rhea, Capital	311	15,783.01 cr.
James Rhea, Drawing	312	0.00
Professional Fees	411	0.00
Rent Expense	541	0.00
Salary Expense	542	0.00
Supplies Expense	543	0.00
Travel & Entertainment Expense	544	0.00
Telephone Expense	545	0.00
Automobile Expense	546	0.00
Depreciation Expense	547	0.00
Utilities Expense	549	0.00
Charitable Contributions Expense	557	0.00
Miscellaneous Expense	572	0.00

Required:

1. Open the accounts in James Rhea's general ledger and enter the January 1 balances.

2. Refer to Problem 3B1. Post the combination journal to the ledger accounts. Update each account balance after each entry is posted. Be sure to include all necessary posting references both in the combination journal and in the ledger.

Problem 3B3   Eight-Column Work Sheet; Year-End Owner's Equity

The following are the balances of James Rhea's general ledger accounts as of the close of business on January 31 of the current year:

Account	Acct. No.	Debit Balance	Credit Balance
Cash	111	$14,917.12	
Supplies	151	1,688.68	
Office Equipment	191	9,000.00	
Accum. Depr.—Office Equipment	191.1		$ 3,037.50
Accounts Payable	218		845.39
James Rhea, Capital	311		15,783.01
James Rhea, Drawing	312	1,500.00	
Professional Fees	411		11,620.00
Rent Expense	541	900.00	
Salary Expense	542	2,100.00	
Supplies Expense	543	-0-	
Travel & Entertainment Expense	544	179.00	
Telephone Expense	545	248.60	
Automobile Expense	546	498.80	
Depreciation Expense	547	-0-	
Utilities Expense	549	152.30	
Charitable Contributions Expense	557	75.00	
Miscellaneous Expense	572	26.40	

Required:

1. Prepare a trial balance of Rhea's ledger as of January 31 in the first two columns of an eight-column work sheet for the period ended January 31, 19--.
2. Prepare the necessary adjustments in the Adjustments columns of the work sheet, based on the following information:
   (a) an inventory of supplies on hand January 31 amounts to $937.50.
   (b) depreciation of office equipment, 1% per month, amounts to $90.00.
   Then, total the Adjustments columns of the work sheets.
3. Complete the work sheet for the period ended January 31, 19-- by extending all amounts in the Trial Balance and Adjustments columns to the Income Statement and Balance Sheet columns. Then, total all remaining columns and determine the net income (or net loss).
4. Calculate the owner's equity as of January 31, based on the following equation:

   Owner's Equity   Net Income   Owner's Equity
   at Start of Period   +   for the Period   −   Withdrawals   =   at End of Period

Problem 3B4   Eight-Column Work Sheet

The following are the Trial Balance columns of the work sheet of Robert Karn, M.D., for the month ended April 30, 19--.

Account	No.	Debit	Credit
Cash	111	$29,834.24	
Supplies	151	3,377.36	
Office Equipment	191	18,000.00	
Accum. Depr.—Office Equipment	191.1		$ 6,075.00
Accounts Payable	218		1,690.78
Robert Karn, Capital	311		31,566.02
Robert Karn, Drawing	312	3,000.00	
Professional Fees	411		23,240.00
Rent Expense	541	1,800.00	
Salary Expense	542	4,200.00	
Supplies Expense	543		
Travel & Entertainment Expense	544	358.00	
Telephone Expense	545	497.20	
Automobile Expense	546	997.60	
Depreciation Expense	547		
Heating & Lighting Expense	549	304.60	
Charitable Contributions Expense	557	150.00	
Miscellaneous Expense	572	52.80	
		$62,571.80	$62,571.80

Required:

Complete an eight-column work sheet, assuming the following adjustment data:

    (a) Supplies expense $1,502.36

    (b) Depreciation of office equipment   180.00

Problem 3B5   **Eight-Column Work Sheet**

The following are the Trial Balance columns of the work sheet of Flo Martin, a Financial Planning Consultant, for the month ended November 30, 19--.

Account	No.	Debit	Credit
Cash	111	$ 7,458.56	
Supplies	151	844.34	
Office Equipment	191	4,500.00	
Accum. Depr.—Office Equipment	191.1		$ 1,518.75
Accounts Payable	218		422.69
Flo Martin, Capital	311		7,891.51
Flo Martin, Drawing	312	750.00	
Professional Fees	411		5,810.00
Rent Expense	541	450.00	
Salary Expense	542	1,050.00	
Supplies Expense	543		
Travel & Entertainment Expense	544	89.50	
Telephone Expense	545	124.30	
Automobile Expense	546	249.40	
Depreciation Expense	547		
Heating & Lighting Expense	549	76.15	
Charitable Contributions Expense	557	37.50	
Miscellaneous Expense	572	13.20	
		$15,642.95	$15,642.95

Required:

Complete an eight-column work sheet, assuming the following adjustment data:

(a)	Supplies expense	$375.59
(b)	Depreciation of office equipment	45.00

Mastery Problem

William Byrd owns and operates a summer basketball camp for children ages 10 through 18. It is open the months of June and July. Campers typically register for one week arriving on Sunday afternoon and returning home the following Saturday afternoon. College players are hired to serve as cabin counselors and to assist the local college and high school coaches who run the practice sessions. The registration fee includes room and board as well as basketball instruction. In the off-season, the facilities are used for weekend retreats and coaching clinics. The following transactions took place during the month of June:

June   1   Received registration fees, $15,000.

2   A new basketball court was completed at a cost of $12,000. The estimated life of the facility is 5 years at which time the court will have to be resurfaced and the basketball standards, backboards and hoops will have to be replaced. Arrangements were made to pay the bill in July.

3   Purchased food supplies on account from Acme Super Market, $5,000.

5   Purchased office supplies on account from Gordon Office Supplies, $300.

7   Received registration fees, $16,200.

10   Purchased food supplies on account from Acme Super Market, $6,200.

10   Issued Check Nos. 334 to 338 for $100 each to pay camp counselors: D. Fields, G. Headley, P. Kerr, A. Pierani, C. Shapiro.

14   Received registration fees, $13,500.

17   Purchased food supplies on account from Acme Super Market, $4,000.

17   Issued Check Nos. 339 to 343 for $100 each to pay camp counselors: D. Fields, G. Headley, P. Kerr, A. Pierani, C. Shapiro.

18   Issued Check No. 344 to pay postage expense, $85.

21   Received registration fees, $15,200.

24   Purchased food supplies on account from Acme Super Market, $5,500.

24   Issued Check Nos. 345 to 349 for $100 each to pay camp counselors: D. Fields, G. Headley, P. Kerr, A. Pierani, C. Shapiro.

28   Received registration fees, $14,000.

30   Purchased food supplies on account from Acme Super Market, $6,000.

30   Issued Check Nos. 350 to 354 for $100 each to pay camp counselors: D. Fields, G. Headley, P. Kerr, A. Pierani, C. Shapiro.

30   Issued Check No. 355 for $28,700 to Acme Super Markets in payment on account.

30   Issued Check No. 356 for $500 to Midwest Electric for the utility bill.

30   Issued Check No. 357 for $120 to Tri City Telephone Co. for the telephone bill.

30   Issued Check No. 358 to William Byrd for personal use, $2,000.

Additional information at the end of June:

(a) A physical inventory of food supplies indicated that $8,000 in supplies were still available.

(b) Office supplies not yet used came to $100.

(c) Depreciation expense on the basketball facilities for one month is $200.

Required:

1. Enter the above transactions in the combination journal.
2. Foot, prove, total, and rule the combination journal.
3. Prove the cash balance and enter it in the Description column following the last transaction.
4. Post the General Debit and Credit columns of the combination journal to the appropriate accounts in the general ledger.
5. Post the special column totals of the combination journal to the appropriate accounts in the general ledger.
6. Complete a work sheet for the month of June.

The Personal Service Enterprise: Completing the Accounting Cycle

Chapter Objectives

Careful study of this chapter should enable you to:

- Prepare financial statements with the aid of a work sheet.

- Journalize and post adjusting entries.

- Journalize and post closing entries.

- Prepare a post-closing trial balance.

- List and describe the steps in the accounting cycle.

An examination of the accounting procedures for a personal service enterprise was begun in Chapter 3. Chapter 4 completes this examination by further illustrating these accounting procedures. The eight-column work sheet, introduced in Chapter 3, is used to facilitate the preparation of the income statement, the statement of owner's equity, and the balance sheet. Procedures for formally journalizing and posting the adjustments made on the work sheet are shown. The process of closing the temporary owner's equity accounts is demonstrated. Also, the purpose and preparation of a post-closing trial balance are explained and illustrated. Finally, the steps in the accounting cycle are summarized.

The Financial Statements

Prepare financial statements with the aid of the work sheet.

The work sheet prepared in Chapter 3 supplies all of the information needed to prepare an income statement, a statement of owner's equity, and a balance sheet for Andrea Marree, Computer Consultant. These statements for Marree's enterprise are shown on pages 119-121.

The Income Statement

The Account Title and Income Statement columns of the work sheet provide the information needed to prepare an income statement for Marree. The format of Marree's income statement is similar to that illustrated in Chapter 2. Revenue is shown first, followed by an itemized and totaled list of expenses. Net income is calculated and presented as the last item in the statement.

The expenses are listed in Marree's income statement in the same order that they appeared on the work sheet and in the chart of accounts and general ledger. This approach is used because it is convenient to simply list the expenses on the income statement in the same order they appear on the work sheet. An alternative approach that is often used is to list the expenses in descending order by dollar amount.

Andrea Marree, Computer Consultant
Income Statement
For the Year Ended December 31, 19--

Revenue:		
Professional fees		$89,140.00
Professional expenses:		
Rent expense	$10,920.00	
Salary expense	10,100.00	
Supplies expense	6,982.70	
Travel and entertainment expense	3,574.70	
Telephone expense	1,497.64	
Automobile expense	5,319.08	
Depreciation expense	4,521.08	
Advertising expense	983.20	
Charitable contributions expense	835.00	
Miscellaneous expense	620.87	
Total professional expenses		45,354.27
Net income		$43,785.73

Andrea Marree, Computer Consultant—Income Statement

The Statement of Owner's Equity

The Account Title and Balance Sheet columns of the work sheet, and possibly the income statement shown above provide the information needed to prepare a statement of owner's equity for Marree. Marree's capital account balance on January 1, 19-- and the drawing account balance at year end appear in the Balance Sheet columns of the work sheet. The net income for the year can be found either on the work sheet as the balancing item at the bottom of the Balance Sheet columns, or on the income statement. With these three items of information, the statement of owner's equity shown on page 120 can be prepared. The format of this statement is the same as that illustrated in Chapter 2.

If Marree had made any additional investments during the year, an additional source of information would have been needed to prepare the statement of owner's equity—the ledger account for Andrea Marree, Capital. This account is needed because the work sheet shows only the updated capital account balance. *after* the additional investment had been made, rather than the balance on January 1, 19--. The January 1, 19-- balance in Marree's capital account is found in the general ledger account. Additional investments would be shown on the statement of owner's equity as "Add: Additional Investments" on the line immediately after net income for the period.

The owner of a small personal service enterprise makes periodic withdrawals for personal needs during the year in anticipation of a certain net income for the year. Marree's net income of $43,785.73 not only was enough to allow her to withdraw $29,710.75 during the year, but it also enabled her to increase her investment in the business by $14,074.98. This increase of $14,074.98 in Marree's owner's equity is a good sign for the business.

Andrea Marree, Computer Consultant
Statement of Owner's Equity
For the Year Ended December 31, 19--

Andrea Marree, capital, January 1, 19--		$24,152.00
Net income for year	$43,785.73	
Less withdrawals	29,710.75	
Increase in owner's equity		14,074.98
Andrea Marree, capital, December 31, 19--		$38,226.98

Andrea Marree, Computer Consultant—Statement of Owner's Equity

The Balance Sheet

The work sheet and possibly the statement of owner's equity shown above are used to prepare the balance sheet for Marree. The asset and liability amounts can be found in the Balance Sheet columns of the work sheet. The ending balance in Andrea Marree, Capital, must be computed by taking the beginning balance, subtracting the balance in Andrea Marree, Drawing, and adding net income. Each of these three amounts can also be found in the Balance Sheet columns of the work sheet. Alternatively, the Andrea Marree, Capital, ending balance can be found on the statement of owner's equity. Each of these approaches to computing the ending owner's equity should yield the same amount.

There are two important features of the balance sheet on page 121 that should be noted. First, it is a **report form of balance sheet,** which means that the liabilities and owner's equity sections are shown below the assets section. It differs from an account form of balance sheet in which the assets are at the left, and the liabilities and the owner's equity sections are at the right. (See the balance sheet of John Wendt, Attorney on page 55.)

Andrea Marree, Computer Consultant
Balance Sheet
December 31, 19--

Assets

Current assets:

Cash	$ 6,723.37	
Supplies	736.00	
Total current assets		$ 7,459.37

Property, plant, and equipment:

Office equipment	$45,210.80	
Less accumulated depreciation	14,175.78	31,035.02
Total assets		$38,494.39

Liabilities

Current liabilities:

Acounts payable		$ 267.41

Owner's Equity

Andrea Marree, capital		38,226.98
Total liabilities and owner's equity		$38,494.39

Andrea Marree, Computer Consultant—Balance Sheet

Second, it is a classified balance sheet, which means that the items of a balance sheet are classified by similarities. Assets are classified as current assets and property, plant, and equipment assets. Current assets include cash and assets that will be converted into cash or consumed within either one year or the normal operating cycle of the business, whichever is longer. An operating cycle, for example, is the period of time required to purchase supplies and services and convert them back into cash. The property, plant, and equipment assets are assets which are expected to serve the business for many years. Liabilities are classified as current liabilities and long-term liabilities (Marree has no long-term debts). Current liabilities are liabilities that are due within either one year or the normal operating cycle of the business, whichever is longer, and which are to be paid out of current assets. Accounts payable are classified as current liabilities. All liabilities that are not current liabilities are considered long-term liabilities. Long-term liabilities are obligations that need not be paid for a long time, usually more than one year. A mortgage on an office building is an example of a long-term liability. If

Marree had any debts of this type, they would be listed on the balance sheet in a section immediately following the current liabilities.

Rounded Amounts in Statements and Schedules

Financial statements for any business enterprise can be presented by rounding to the nearest dollar. This is done because amounts less than a dollar are unimportant in these financial statements, and it makes the statements more efficient to read. The rule for rounding is: If the cents in the amount are 50 cents or more, raise the first digit left of the decimal point by one; if 49 cents or less, drop the cents. Thus, $37.73 would become $38; $37.38 would become $37. For larger businesses, financial statement amounts often are rounded to the nearest $100 or $1,000.

Building Your Accounting Knowledge

1. Identify the source of the information needed to prepare the income statement for Marree.
2. Describe two approaches to listing the expenses in the income statement.
3. Identify the sources of the information needed to prepare the statement of owner's equity for Marree.
4. If Marree had made additional investments during the year, what information in addition to the work sheet would be needed to prepare the statement of owner's equity?
5. Identify the sources of the information needed to prepare the balance sheet for Marree.
6. Describe two different ways to determine the ending balance in Andrea Marree, Capital, in preparing the balance sheet.

Assignment Box

To reinforce your understanding of the preceding text materials, you may complete the following:
    Study Guide: Part A
    Textbook: Exercises 4A1 through 4A3 or 4B1 through 4B3
        Problems 4A1 through 4A4 or 4B1 through 4B4

Adjusting And
Closing The
Accounts;
Completion of
The Cycle

To complete the accounting cycle for a personal service enterprise, three additional accounting procedures must be performed for Andrea Marree, Computer Consultant. First, the adjusting entries on the work sheet must be formally entered in the accounting records. Second, the temporary owner's equity accounts must be closed. Third, a post-closing trial balance must be prepared.

Adjusting Entries

Journalize and post adjusting entries.

The amounts in the financial statements must agree with the ledger account balances. To speed up the preparation of the statements, a work sheet is used to informally adjust accounts and accumulate income statement, statement of owner's equity, and balance sheet information. Subsequently, these adjustments need to be formally entered in the journal and posted to the accounts. Such entries are called adjusting entries.

Two adjusting entries were made on the work sheet in Chapter 3—for (a) supplies expense and (b) depreciation expense. As shown in the partial combination journal below, to enter these adjustments, the heading "Adjusting Entries" is centered in the Description column of this journal. For each adjustment, the title of the account debited is entered in the Description column on the next available line, along with the debit amount in the General Debit column. The title of the account credited is indented in the Description column on the following line, and the credit amount is entered in the General Credit column. The account numbers in the Post. Ref. column are entered later when these entries are posted to the general ledger.

COMBINATION JOURNAL FOR MONTH OF *December 19--*

DAY	DESCRIPTION	POST. REF.	GENERAL DEBIT	GENERAL CREDIT
	Adjusting Entries			
31	*Supplies Expense*	543	6 9 8 2 70	
	Supplies	151		6 9 8 2 70
31	*Depreciation Expense*	547	4 5 2 1 08	
	Accumulated Depr.—Office Equipment	191.1		4 5 2 1 08

The following illustration shows how the four accounts affected by the entries—Supplies Expense (No. 543), Supplies (No. 151), Depreciation Expense (No. 547), and Accumulated Depreciation-Office Equipment (No. 191.1)—appear after the entries are posted. After these postings are completed, the balances of the supplies expense and depreciation expense accounts agree with the amounts shown in the income statement, and the balances of the supplies and accumulated depreciation accounts are the same as the amounts shown in the balance sheet.

ACCOUNT *Supplies*   ACCOUNT NO. *151*

DATE		ITEM	POST. REF.	DEBIT	CREDIT	BALANCE DEBIT	BALANCE CREDIT
19-- Dec.	1	*Balance*	✓			7 0 3 3 86	
	11		CJ28	2 3 9 21		7 2 7 3 07	
	19		CJ28	1 7 8 22		7 4 5 1 29	
	27		CJ28	2 6 7 41		7 7 1 8 70	
	31		CJ30		6 9 8 2 70	7 3 6 00	

ACCOUNT **Accumulated Depr.—Office Equipment**   ACCOUNT NO. **191.1**

DATE	ITEM	POST. REF.	DEBIT	CREDIT	BALANCE DEBIT	BALANCE CREDIT
19-- Dec. 1	Balance	✓				9 6 5 4 70
31		CJ30		4 5 2 1 08		14 1 7 5 78

ACCOUNT **Supplies Expense**   ACCOUNT NO. **543**

DATE	ITEM	POST. REF.	DEBIT	CREDIT	BALANCE DEBIT	BALANCE CREDIT
19-- Dec. 31		CJ30	6 9 8 2 70		6 9 8 2 70	

ACCOUNT **Depreciation Expense**   ACCOUNT NO. **547**

DATE	ITEM	POST. REF.	DEBIT	CREDIT	BALANCE DEBIT	BALANCE CREDIT
19-- Dec. 31		CJ30	4 5 2 1 08		4 5 2 1 08	

Closing Entries

Journalize and post closing entries.

The revenue and expense accounts and the account for Andrea Marree, Drawing (No. 312) have accumulated information for the year 19--. The balance of each of these temporary accounts needs to be reduced to zero, or closed, in order to make the accounts ready for entries in the following year. This is accomplished by closing entries that will have to be formally entered in the journal and posted to the ledger accounts. The expense and revenue summary account will assist in closing the expense and revenue accounts.

As in the case of the adjusting entries, the closing entries are made as of December 31. Note that the work sheet provides all of the data needed to prepare the adjusting and closing entries. The purpose and use of Expense and Revenue Summary, Account No. 331, is to summarize the amounts of expense and revenue.

The procedures for closing the temporary accounts are:

1. For revenue accounts with credit balances: debit the account for its balance and credit the expense and revenue summary account.
2. For expense accounts with debit balances: debit the expense and revenue summary account and credit the expense account for its balance.
3. Close the expense and revenue summary account to the Andrea Marree capital account.
4. Close the Andrea Marree drawing account to the capital account.

These procedures are shown in the following diagram:

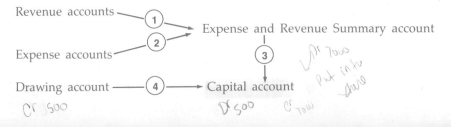

The journal entries reflecting the above procedures are as follows:

1. The $89,140 credit balance of Professional Fees, Account No. 411 is closed to Expense and Revenue Summary, Account No. 331, by debiting Professional Fees and crediting Expense and Revenue Summary.

2. The debit balances of all ten expense accounts (Nos. 541 through 547, 551, 557, and 572) which, in total, amounted to $45,354.27, are closed to Expense and Revenue Summary (No. 331) by debiting Expense and Revenue Summary and crediting each expense account.

3. The result of entries (1) and (2) is a credit balance of $43,785.73—the net income for the year—in Expense and Revenue Summary (No. 331). This is closed to Andrea Marree, Capital (No. 311) by debiting Expense and Revenue Summary and crediting Andrea Marree, Capital.

4. The $29,710.75 debit balance of Andrea Marree, Drawing (No. 312) is closed to Andrea Marree, Capital (No. 311) by debiting Andrea Marree, Capital and crediting Andrea Marree, Drawing.

These journal entries are shown in T account form on page 126.

The closing entries are shown in the partial combination journal below. The heading "Closing Entries" is centered in the Description column immediately below the adjusting entries, and the closing entries are placed on the following lines.

The combination journal is followed by an illustration of the effects of the closing procedures on Andrea Marree's capital and drawing accounts,

COMBINATION JOURNAL FOR MONTH OF December 19--

DAY	DESCRIPTION	POST. REF.	GENERAL DEBIT	GENERAL CREDIT
	Closing Entries			
31	*Professional Fees*	411	89 140 00	
	Expense and Revenue Summary	331		89 140 00
31	*Expense and Revenue Summary*	331	45 354 27	
	Rent Expense	541		10 920 00
	Salary Expense	542		10 100 00
	Supplies Expense	543		6 982 70
	Travel and Entertainment Expense	544		3 574 70
	Telephone Expense	545		1 497 64
	Automobile Expense	546		5 319 08
	Depreciation Expense	547		4 521 08
	Advertising Expense	551		983 20
	Charitable Contributions Expense	557		835 00
	Miscellaneous Expense	572		620 87
31	*Expense and Revenue Summary*	331	43 785 73	
	Andrea Marree, Capital	311		43 785 73
31	*Andrea Marree, Capital*	311	29 710 75	
	Andrea Marree, Drawing	312		29 710 75

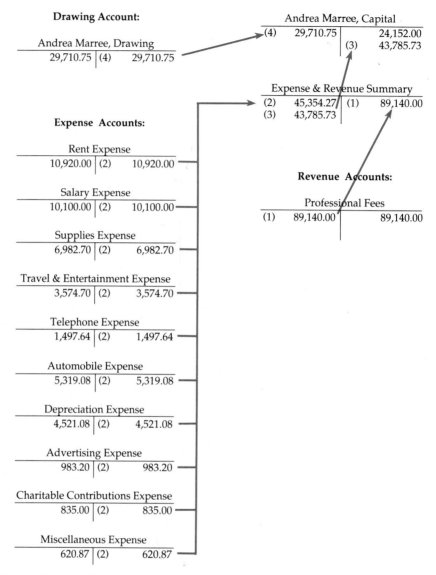

Closing Entries—T Account Form

the expense and revenue summary account, and all of the revenue and expense accounts on page 127. (As part of the closing process, zeros are entered in the Debit Balance and Credit Balance columns of each account that is closed.) Note that the net effect of the four closing entries is an increase in the credit balance of the account for Andrea Marree, Capital (No. 311) of $14,074.98. This amount is the excess of the net income for the year over withdrawals for the year, ($43,785.73 − $29,710.75). This $14,074.98 increase in the Andrea Marree, Capital balance is the same amount that was calculated on the statement of owner's equity on page 120.

ACCOUNT **Andrea Marree, Capital**   ACCOUNT NO. *311*

DATE		ITEM	POST. REF.	DEBIT	CREDIT	BALANCE DEBIT	BALANCE CREDIT
19-- Dec.	1	Balance	✓				24 15 2 00
	31		CJ30		43 7 85 73		67 9 37 73
	31		CJ30	29 7 10 75			38 2 26 98

ACCOUNT **Andrea Marree, Drawing**   ACCOUNT NO. *312*

DATE		ITEM	POST. REF.	DEBIT	CREDIT	BALANCE DEBIT	BALANCE CREDIT
19-- Dec.	1	Balance	✓			27 2 10 75	
	12		CJ28	2 1 00 00		29 3 10 75	
	21		CJ28	4 00 00		29 7 10 75	
	31		CJ30		29 7 10 75	-0-	-0-

ACCOUNT **Expense and Revenue Summary**   ACCOUNT NO. *331*

DATE		ITEM	POST. REF.	DEBIT	CREDIT	BALANCE DEBIT	BALANCE CREDIT
19-- Dec.	31		CJ30		89 1 40 00		89 1 40 00
	31		CJ30	45 3 54 27			43 7 85 73
	31		CJ30	43 7 85 73		-0-	-0-

ACCOUNT **Professional Fees**   ACCOUNT NO. *411*

DATE		ITEM	POST. REF.	DEBIT	CREDIT	BALANCE DEBIT	BALANCE CREDIT
19-- Dec.	1	Balance	✓				83 2 40 00
	31		CJ29		5 9 00 00		89 1 40 00
	31		CJ30	89 1 40 00		-0-	-0-

ACCOUNT **Rent Expense**   ACCOUNT NO. *541*

DATE		ITEM	POST. REF.	DEBIT	CREDIT	BALANCE DEBIT	BALANCE CREDIT
19-- Dec.	1	Balance	✓			10 0 10 00	
	3		CJ28	9 1 00		10 9 20 00	
	31		CJ30		10 9 20 00	-0-	-0-

ACCOUNT **Salary Expense**   ACCOUNT NO. *542*

DATE		ITEM	POST. REF.	DEBIT	CREDIT	BALANCE DEBIT	BALANCE CREDIT
19-- Dec.	1	Balance	✓			9 1 30 00	
	31		CJ29	9 70 00		10 1 00 00	
	31		CJ30		10 1 00 00	-0-	-0-

ACCOUNT **Supplies Expense** ACCOUNT NO. **543**

DATE	ITEM	POST. REF.	DEBIT	CREDIT	BALANCE DEBIT	BALANCE CREDIT
Dec. 31		CJ30	6 9 8 2 70		6 9 8 2 70	
31		CJ30		6 9 8 2 70	-0-	-0-

ACCOUNT **Travel & Entertainment Expense** ACCOUNT NO. **544**

DATE	ITEM	POST. REF.	DEBIT	CREDIT	BALANCE DEBIT	BALANCE CREDIT
Dec. 1	Balance	✓			3 3 2 5 95	
26		CJ28	2 4 8 75		3 5 7 4 70	
31		CJ30		3 5 7 4 70	-0-	-0-

ACCOUNT **Telephone Expense** ACCOUNT NO. **545**

DATE	ITEM	POST. REF.	DEBIT	CREDIT	BALANCE DEBIT	BALANCE CREDIT
Dec. 1	Balance	✓			1 4 1 8 04	
18		CJ28	7 9 60		1 4 9 7 64	
31		CJ30		1 4 9 7 64	-0-	-0-

ACCOUNT **Automobile Expense** ACCOUNT NO. **546**

DATE	ITEM	POST. REF.	DEBIT	CREDIT	BALANCE DEBIT	BALANCE CREDIT
Dec. 1	Balance	✓			4 8 6 0 73	
31		CJ29	4 5 8 35		5 3 1 9 08	
31		CJ30		5 3 1 9 08	-0-	-0-

ACCOUNT **Depreciation Expense** ACCOUNT NO. **547**

DATE	ITEM	POST. REF.	DEBIT	CREDIT	BALANCE DEBIT	BALANCE CREDIT
Dec. 31		CJ30	4 5 2 1 08		4 5 2 1 08	
31		CJ30		4 5 2 1 08	-0-	-0-

ACCOUNT **Advertising Expense** ACCOUNT NO. **551**

DATE	ITEM	POST. REF.	DEBIT	CREDIT	BALANCE DEBIT	BALANCE CREDIT
Dec. 1	Balance	✓			9 2 8 40	
5		CJ28	5 8 40		9 8 6 80	
12		CJ28		3 60	9 8 3 20	
31		CJ30		9 8 3 20	-0-	-0-

ACCOUNT *Charitable Contributions Expense*   ACCOUNT NO. *557*

DATE		ITEM	POST. REF.	DEBIT	CREDIT	BALANCE DEBIT	BALANCE CREDIT
19-- Dec.	1	Balance	√			7 3 5 00	
	14		CJ28	1 0 0 00		8 3 5 00	
	31		CJ30		8 3 5 00	-0-	-0-

ACCOUNT *Miscellaneous Expense*   ACCOUNT NO. *572*

DATE		ITEM	POST. REF.	DEBIT	CREDIT	BALANCE DEBIT	BALANCE CREDIT
19-- Dec.	1	Balance	√			5 6 0 12	
	17		CJ28	2 4 75		5 8 4 87	
	27		CJ28	3 6 00		6 2 0 87	
	31		CJ30		6 2 0 87	-0-	-0-

Post-Closing Trial Balance

Prepare a post-closing trial balance.

After posting the closing entries, it is advisable to take a **post-closing trial balance** to prove the equality of the debit and credit balances in the general ledger accounts. The following is the post-closing trial balance of Marree's ledger:

Andrea Marree, Computer Consultant
Post-Closing Trial Balance
December 31, 19--

Account	Acct. No.	Dr. Balance	Cr. Balance
Cash	111	$ 6,723.37	
Supplies	151	736.00	
Office Equipment	191	45,210.80	
Accumulated Depr.—Office Equip.	191.1		$14,175.78
Accounts Payable	218		267.41
Andrea Marree, Capital	311		38,226.98
		$52,670.17	$52,670.17

Andrea Marree, Computer Consultant—Post-Closing Trial Balance

The Accounting Cycle

List and describe the steps in the accounting cycle.

The steps involved in handling all of the transactions and events completed during an accounting period, beginning with placing data in a book of original entry and ending with a post-closing trial balance, are referred to collectively as the **accounting cycle**. Together, Chapters 3 and

4 have illustrated a complete accounting cycle. A brief summary of the various steps follows:

1. Journalize the transactions
2. Post to the ledger accounts
3. Prepare a trial balance
4. Determine and prepare the needed adjustments on the work sheet
5. Complete an end-of-period work sheet
6. Prepare an income statement, statement of owner's equity, and balance sheet
7. Journalize the adjusting and closing entries
8. Post the adjusting and closing entries
9. Prepare a post-closing trial balance

These nine steps are illustrated, by number, in the diagram shown below.

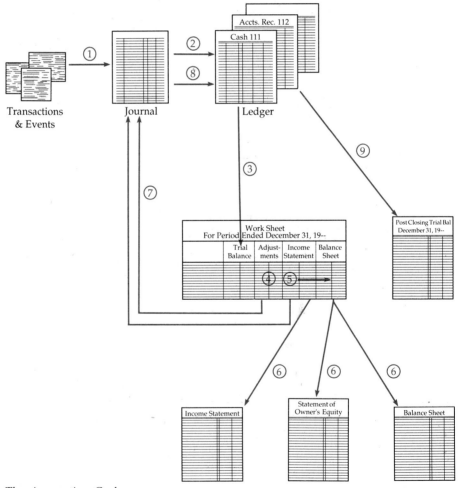

The Accounting Cycle

In visualizing the accounting cycle, it is important to realize that steps (3) through (9) in the preceding list are performed as of the last day of the accounting period. This does not mean that they are actually done on the last day. The accountant may not be able to do any of these things until the first few days (sometimes weeks) of the next period. Nevertheless, the work sheet, statements, and entries are prepared as of the closing date. While the journalizing of transactions in the new period proceeds in regular fashion, entries relating to the new period are normally not posted to the general ledger until the steps relating to the period just ended have been completed.

Building Your Accounting Knowledge

1. List the four procedures for closing the temporary accounts.
2. Describe the net effect of the four closing entries on the balance in Andrea Marree, Capital. Where else is this same amount calculated?
3. What is the purpose of the post-closing trial balance?
4. List the nine steps in Andrea Marree's accounting cycle.

Assignment Box

To reinforce your understanding of the preceding text materials, you may complete the following:
>   Study Guide: Part B
>   Textbook: Exercises 4A4 through 4A8 or 4B4 through 4B8
>   Problems 4A5 through 4A7 or 4B5 through 4B7

Expanding Your Business Vocabulary

What is the meaning of each of the following terms?

account form of balance sheet (p. 121)
accounting cycle (p. 129)
adjusting entries (p. 123)
classified balance sheet (p. 121)
closing entries (p. 124)
current assets (p. 121)

current liabilities (p. 121)
long-term liabilities (p. 121)
post-closing trial balance (p. 129)
property, plant, and equipment assets (p. 121)
report form of balance sheet (p. 120)

Demonstration Problem

Carolyn Mears is a small business consultant. The following is her work sheet for the year ended December 31, 19--:

Carolyn Mears, Business Consultant
Work Sheet
For Year Ended December 31, 19—

	ACCT. NO.	TRIAL BALANCE DEBIT	TRIAL BALANCE CREDIT	ADJUSTMENTS DEBIT	ADJUSTMENTS CREDIT	INCOME STATEMENT DEBIT	INCOME STATEMENT CREDIT	BALANCE SHEET DEBIT	BALANCE SHEET CREDIT	
Cash	111	6 960 81						6 960 81		1
Supplies	151	4 910 76			a 4 489 26			4 21 50		2
Office Equipment	191	32 100 08						32 100 08		3
Accum. Depr. Office Equipment	191.1		6 426 98		b 3 210 01				9 636 99	4
Accounts Payable	218		5 62 50						5 62 50	5
Carolyn Mears, Capital	311		26 237 50						26 237 50	6
Carolyn Mears, Drawing	312	23 923 15						23 923 15		7
Professional Fees	411		59 186 15				59 186 15			8
Rent Expense	541	9 450 00				9 450 00				9
Salary Expense	542	10 725 00				10 725 00				10
Supplies Expense	543			a 4 489 26		4 489 26				11
Telephone Expense	545	855 22				855 22				12
Automobile Expense	546	2 284 22				2 284 22				13
Depreciation Expense	547			b 3 210 01		3 210 01				14
Utilities Expense	549	455 63				455 63				15
Charitable Contributions Expense	557	637 50				637 50				16
Miscellaneous Expense	572	110 76				110 76				17
		92 413 13	92 413 13	7 699 27	7 699 27	32 217 60	59 186 15	63 405 54	36 436 99	18
Net Income						26 968 55			26 968 55	19
						59 186 15	59 186 15	63 405 54	63 405 54	20
										21
										22

Required:

1. Prepare an income statement for Carolyn Mears for the year ended December 31, 19--.
2. Prepare a statement of owner's equity for Carolyn Mears for the year ended December 31, 19--.
3. Prepare a balance sheet for Carolyn Mears as of December 31, 19--.
4. Make the necessary adjusting entries at year end, using the General Debit and Credit columns of a combination journal.
5. Make the necessary closing entries at year end to produce zero balances in all of the temporary owner's equity accounts (including the drawing account).
6. Post the adjusting entries to the affected accounts in a four-column ledger. Show the posting references both in the combination journal and in the ledger. (December 31 balances do not appear in the affected expense accounts.)
7. Post the closing entries to the affected accounts in a four-column ledger. Show the posting references both in the combination journal and in the ledger, and "zero out" the balance columns of the affected ledger accounts. (December 31 balances already appear in all accounts except Expense and Revenue Summary.)
8. Prepare a post-closing trial balance for Carolyn Mears as of December 31, 19--. Use the Balance Sheet columns of the work sheet, except for account numbers 311 and 312. Replace these two balances with the updated balance of account number 311 from that ledger account.

Solution

1.

Carolyn Mears, Small Business Consultant
Income Statement
For the Year Ended December 31, 19--

Revenue:		
Professional fees		$59,186.15
Professional expenses:		
Rent expense	$ 9,450.00	
Salary expense	10,725.00	
Supplies expense	4,489.26	
Telephone expense	855.22	
Automobile expense	2,284.22	
Depreciation expense	3,210.01	
Utilities expense	455.63	
Charitable contributions expense	637.50	
Miscellaneous expense	110.76	
Total professional expenses		32,217.60
Net income		$26,968.55

2.   **Statement of Owner's Equity is on page 135.**

3.   **Carolyn Mears, Small Business Consultant**
Balance Sheet
December 31, 19--

Assets

Current assets:

Cash	$ 6,960.81	
Supplies	421.50	
Total current assets.......................		$ 7,382.31
Property, plant, and equipment:		
Office equipment	$32,100.08	
Less accumulated depreciation	9,636.99	22,463.09
Total assets		$29,845.40

Liabilities

Current liabilities:

Accounts payable		$ 562.50

Owner's Equity

Carolyn Mears, capital........................		29,282.90
Total liabilities and owner's equity		$29,845.40

---

4 & 5.   Partial Combination Journal For Month Of December 19--   Page 6

Day	Description	Post Ref.	Debit	Credit
	Adjusting Entries			
31	Supplies Expense	543	4,489.26	
	Supplies	151		4,489.26
31	Depreciation Expense	547	3,210.01	
	Accum. Depr.—Office Equip.	191.1		3,210.01
	Closing Entries			
31	Professional Fees	411	59,186.15	
	Expense and Revenue Summary	331		59,186.15
31	Expense and Revenue Summary	331	32,217.60	
	Rent Expense	541		9,450.00
	Salary Expense	542		10,725.00
	Supplies Expense	543		4,489.26
	Telephone Expense	545		855.22
	Automobile Expense	546		2,284.22
	Depreciation Expense	547		3,210.01
	Utilities Expense	549		455.63
	Charitable Contributions Expense	557		637.50
	Miscellaneous Expense	572		110.76
31	Expense and Revenue Summary	331	26,968.55	
	Carolyn Mears, Capital	311		26,968.55
31	Carolyn Mears, Capital	311	23,923.15	
	Carolyn Mears, Drawing	312		23,923.15
			149,994.72	*149,994.72*

2.

Carolyn Mears, Small Business Consultant
Statement of Owner's Equity
For the Year Ended December 31, 19--

Carolyn Mears, capital, January 1, 19--		$26,237.50
Net income for the year	$26,968.55	
Less withdrawals	23,923.15	
Increase in owner's equity		3,045.40
Carolyn Mears, capital, December 31, 19--		$29,282.90

6 & 7.   **General Ledger**

Account Supplies   Account No. 151

Date	Item	Post. Ref.	Debit	Credit	Balance Debit	Balance Credit
19--						
Dec. 31 Balance		√			4,910.76	
31		CJ6		4,489.26	421.50	

Account Accumulated Depreciation—Office Equipment   Account No. 191.1

Date	Item	Post. Ref.	Debit	Credit	Balance Debit	Balance Credit
19--						
Dec. 31 Balance		√				6,426.98
31		CJ6		3,210.01		9,636.99

Account Carolyn Mears, Capital   Account No. 311

Date	Item	Post. Ref.	Debit	Credit	Balance Debit	Balance Credit
19--						
Dec. 31 Balance		√				26,237.50
31		CJ6		26,968.55		53,206.05
31		CJ6	23,923.15			29,282.90

Account Carolyn Mears, Drawing   Account No. 312

Date	Item	Post. Ref.	Debit	Credit	Balance Debit	Balance Credit
19--						
Dec. 31 Balance		√			23,923.15	
31		CJ6		23,923.15	-0-	-0-

Account Expense and Revenue Summary   Account No. 331

Date	Item	Post. Ref.	Debit	Credit	Balance Debit	Balance Credit
19--						
Dec. 31		CJ6		59,186.15		59,186.15
31		CJ6	32,217.60			26,968.55
31		CJ6	26,968.55		-0-	-0-

Account Professional Fees   *Account No.* 411

Date	Item	Post. Ref.	Debit	Credit	Balance Debit	Balance Credit
19--						
Dec. 31 Balance		√				59,186.15
31		CJ6	59,186.15		-0-	-0-

Account Rent Expense   *Account No.* 541

Date	Item	Post. Ref.	Debit	Credit	Balance Debit	Balance Credit
19--						
Dec. 31 Balance		√			9,450.00	
31		CJ6		9,450.00	-0-	-0-

Account Salary Expense   *Account No.* 542

Date	Item	Post. Ref.	Debit	Credit	Balance Debit	Balance Credit
19--						
Dec. 31 Balance		√			10,725.00	
31		CJ6		10,725.00	-0-	-0-

Account Supplies Expense   *Account No.* 543

Date	Item	Post. Ref.	Debit	Credit	Balance Debit	Balance Credit
19--						
Dec. 31		CJ6	4,489.26		4,489.26	
31		CJ6		4,489.26	-0-	-0-

Account Telephone Expense   *Account No.* 545

Date	Item	Post. Ref.	Debit	Credit	Balance Debit	Balance Credit
19--						
Dec. 31 Balance		√			855.22	
31		CJ6		855.22	-0-	-0-

Account Automobile Expense   *Account No.* 546

Date	Item	Post. Ref.	Debit	Credit	Balance Debit	Balance Credit
19--						
Dec. 31 Balance		√			2,284.22	
31		CJ6		2,284.22	-0-	-0-

Account Depreciation Expense   *Account No.* 547

Date	Item	Post. Ref.	Debit	Credit	Balance Debit	Balance Credit
19--						
Dec. 31		CJ6	3,210.01		3,210.01	
31		CJ6		3,210.01	-0-	-0-

Account Utilities Expense   Account No. 549

Date	Item	Post. Ref.	Debit	Credit	Balance Debit	Credit
19--						
Dec. 31 Balance		✓			455.63	
31		CJ6		455.63	-0-	-0-

Account Charitable Contributions Expense   Account No. 557

Date	Item	Post. Ref.	Debit	Credit	Balance Debit	Credit
19--						
Dec. 31 Balance		✓			637.50	
31		CJ6		637.50	-0-	-0-

Account Miscellaneous Expense   Account No. 572

Date	Item	Post. Ref.	Debit	Credit	Balance Debit	Credit
19--						
Dec. 31 Balance		✓			110.76	
31		CJ6		110.76	-0-	-0-

8.
Carolyn Mears, Business Consultant
Post-Closing Trial Balance
December 31, 19--

Account	Acct. No.	Dr. Balance	Cr. Balance
Cash	111	$ 6,960.81	
Supplies	151	421.50	
Office Equipment	191	32,100.08	
Accumulated Depreciation—Office			
Equipment	191.1		$ 9,636.99
Accounts Payable	218		562.50
Carolyn Mears, Capital	311		29,282.90
		$39,482.39	$39,482.39

*Note: Now that you have reviewed the Demonstration Problem and Solution you may complete the **Mastery Problem** at the end of the chapter activities.

Applying Accounting Concepts

Series A

Exercise 4A1—Income Statement Preparation. The following are the Income Statement and Balance Sheet columns of the work sheet for Allison Gunn's Consulting Service for the year ended December 31, 19--:

Account Title	Acct. No.	Income Statement Debit	Income Statement Credit	Balance Sheet Debit	Balance Sheet Credit
Cash...............	111			$ 9,281.08	
Supplies............	151√ +			562.00	
Office Equipment	191			42,800.10	
Accum. Depr.—Office Equip.	191.1√				$12,849.31√
Accounts Payable	218				750.00
Allison Gunn, Capital..	311				35,250.00
Allison Gunn, Drawing	312			31,897.49	
Professional Fees	411		$78,914.79		
Rent Expense	541	$12,600.00			
Salary Expense........	542	14,300.00			
Supplies Expense	543√	5,985.68			
Telephone Expense	545	1,140.30			
Automobile Expense ...	546	3,312.25			
Depreciation Expense..	547√	4,280.01			
Utilities Expense	549	607.50			
Charitable Contrib. Expense	557	850.00			
Miscellaneous Expense	572	147.69			
		$43,223.43	$78,914.79	$84,540.67	$48,849.31
Net Income		35,691.36			35,691.36
		$78,914.79	$78,914.79	$84,540.67	$84,540.67

Prepare an income statement for Allison Gunn's Consulting Service for the year ended December 31, 19--.

Exercise 4A2—Statement of Owner's Equity Preparation. Refer to Exercise 4A1. Prepare a statement of owner's equity for Allison Gunn's Consulting Service for the year ended December 31, 19--.

Exercise 4A3—Report Form Balance Sheet Preparation. Refer to Exercises 4A1 and 4A2. Prepare a balance sheet in report form for Allison Gunn's Consulting Service as of December 31, 19--.

Exercise 4A4—Adjusting Entries in Combination Journal. The Adjustments columns of the work sheet for Allison Gunn's Consulting Service for the year ended December 31, 19-- are on the following page.

Using the General Debit and Credit columns of a combination journal, make the adjusting entries to record (a) the supplies expense for the year, $5,985.68; and (b) the depreciation expense for the year, $4,280.01. Number the journal page 5.

Exercise 4A5—Posting Adjusting Entries to Ledger. Refer to Exercise 4A4. Post the adjusting entries from the combination journal to the affected four-column ledger accounts. These accounts should show the following December 31 balances prior to adjustment:

Supplies, Acct. No. 151	$6,547.68 dr.
Accum. Depr.—Office Equip., Acct. No. 191.1	8,569.30 cr.

Account Title	Acct. No.	Adjustments Debit	Adjustments Credit
Cash....................................	111		
Supplies................................	151		(a)$ 5,985.68
Office Equipment	191		
Accum. Depr.—Office Equip..............	191.1		(b) 4,280.01
Accounts Payable	218		
Allison Gunn, Capital	311		
Allison Gunn, Drawing	312		
Professional Fees	411		
Rent Expense	541		
Salary Expense	542		
Supplies Expense.......................	543	(a)$ 5,985.68	
Telephone Expense	545		
Automobile Expense	546		
Depreciation Expense...................	547	(b) 4,280.01	
Utilities Expense	549		
Charitable Contributions Expense	557		
Miscellaneous Expense..................	572		
		$10,265.69	$10,265.69

Exercise 4A5 (Concluded)

Supplies Expense, Acct. No. 543	-0-	
Depreciation Expense, Acct. No. 547	-0-	

Be sure to update account balances in the ledger as necessary and show posting references both in the combination journal and in the ledger accounts.

Exercise 4A6—Closing Entries in Combination Journal. Refer to Exercise 4A1 for the Income Statement and Balance Sheet columns of the work sheet for Allison Gunn's Consulting Service.

Using the General Debit and Credit columns of a combination journal, make the entries necessary to close Allison Gunn's temporary owner's equity (revenue, expense, and drawing) accounts as of December 31, 19--. Number the journal page 6. In making these closing entries, you will need to use a new account, Expense and Revenue Summary, Acct. No. 331. This account does not appear on the work sheet.

Exercise 4A7—Posting Closing Entries to Ledger. Refer to Exercise 4A6. Post the closing entries from the combination journal to the affected four-column ledger accounts. These accounts should show the following December 31 balances prior to closing:

Allison Gunn, Capital, Acct. No. 311	$35,250.00	cr.
Allison Gunn, Drawing, Acct. No. 312	31,897.49	dr.
Expense & Revenue Summary, Acct. No. 331	-0-	
Professional Fees, Acct. No. 411	78,914.79	cr.
Rent Expense, Acct. No. 541	12,600.00	dr.
Salary Expense, Acct. No. 542	14,300.00	dr.
Supplies Expense, Acct. No. 543	5,985.68	dr.
Telephone Expense, Acct. No. 545	1,140.30	dr.
Automobile Expense, Acct. No. 546	3,312.25	dr.

Depreciation Expense, Acct. No. 547   4,280.01 dr.
Utilities Expense, Acct. No. 549   607.50 dr.
Charitable Contributions Expense, Acct. No. 557   850.00 dr.
Miscellaneous Expense, Acct. No. 572   147.69 dr.

Be sure to enter zeros in the balance columns of each of the temporary owner's equity accounts (including the drawing account) as each closing entry is posted.

Exercise 4A8—Post-Closing Trial Balance Preparation. Refer to Exercises 4A1 and 4A7. Using the Balance Sheet columns of Allison Gunn's work sheet, prepare a post-closing trial balance as of December 31, 19--. For this purpose, use the amounts shown in the Balance Sheet columns of the work sheet for each asset account and each liability account, but use the updated balance of the capital account from Exercise 4A7 in place of the amounts shown in the work sheet for the capital and drawing accounts.

Series B

Exercise 4B1—Income Statement Preparation. The following are the Income Statement and Balance Sheet columns of the work sheet for John Lotshaw's Financial Planning Service for the year ended December 31, 19--:

Account Title	Acct. No.	Income Statement Debit	Credit	Balance Sheet Debit	Credit
Cash	111			$ 4,640.54	
Supplies	151			281.00	
Office Equipment	191			21,400.05	
Accum. Depr.—Office Equip.	191.1				$6,424.66
Accounts Payable	218				375.00
John Lotshaw, Capital	311				17,625.00
John Lotshaw, Drawing	312			15,948.75	
Professional Fees	411		$39,457.43		
Rent Expense	541	$6,300.00			
Salary Expense	542	7,150.00			
Supplies Expense	543	2,992.84			
Telephone Expense	545	570.15			
Automobile Expense	546	1,656.15			
Depreciation Expense	547	2,140.01			
Utilities Expense	549	303.75			
Charitable Contrib. Expense	557	425.00			
Miscellaneous Expense	572	73.85			
		$21,611.75	$39,457.43	$42,270.34	$24,424.66
Net Income		17,845.68			17,845.68
		$39,457.43	$39,457.43	$42,270.34	$42,270.34

Prepare an income statement for John Lotshaw's Financial Planning Service for the year ended December 31, 19--.

Exercise 4B2—Statement of Owner's Equity Preparation. Refer to Exercise 4B1. Prepare a statement of owner's equity for John Lotshaw's Financial Planning Service for the year ended December 31, 19--.

Exercise 4B3—Report Form Balance Sheet Preparation. Refer to Exercises 4B1 and 4B2. Prepare a balance sheet in report form for John Lotshaw's Financial Planning Service as of December 31, 19--.

Exercise 4B4—Adjusting Entries in Combination Journal. The following are the Adjustments columns of the work sheet for John Lotshaw's Financial Planning Service for the year ended December 31, 19--:

Account Title	Acct. No.	Adjustments Debit	Adjustments Credit
Cash	111		
Supplies	151		(a)$2,992.84
Office Equipment	191		
Accum. Depr.—Office Equip.	191.1		(b) 2,140.01
Accounts Payable	218		
John Lotshaw, Capital	311		
John Lotshaw, Drawing	312		
Professional Fees	411		
Rent Expense	541		
Salary Expense	542		
Supplies Expense	543	(a)$2,992.84	
Telephone Expense	545		
Automobile Expense	546		
Depreciation Expense	547	(b) 2,140.01	
Utilities Expense	549		
Charitable Contrib. Expense	557		
Miscellaneous Expense	572		
		$5,132.85	$5,132.85

Using the General Debit and Credit columns of a combination journal, make the adjusting entries to record (a) the supplies expense for the year, $2,992.84, and (b) the depreciation expense for the year, $2,140.01. Number the journal page 7.

Exercise 4B5—Posting Adjusting Entries to Ledger. Refer to Exercise 4B4. Post the adjusting entries from the combination journal to the affected four-column ledger accounts. These accounts should show the following December 31 balances prior to adjustment:

Supplies, Acct. No. 151	$3,273.84 dr.
Accum. Depr.—Office Equip., Acct. No. 191.1	4,284.65 cr.
Supplies Expense, Acct. No. 543	-0-
Depreciation Expense, Acct. No. 547	-0-

Be sure to update account balances in the ledger as necessary and show posting references both in the combination journal and in the ledger accounts.

Exercise 4B6—Closing Entries in Combination Journal. Refer to Exercise 4B1 for the Income Statement and Balance Sheet columns of the work sheet for John Lotshaw's Financial Planning Service.

Using the General Debit and Credit columns of a combination journal, make the entries necessary to close John Lotshaw's temporary owner's equity (revenue, expense, and drawing) accounts as of December 31, 19--. Number the journal page 8. In making these closing entries, you will need to use a new account, Expense and Revenue Summary, Acct. No. 331. This account does not appear on the work sheet.

Exercise 4B7—Posting Closing Entries to Ledger. Refer to Exercise 4B6. Post the closing entries from the combination journal to the affected four-column ledger accounts. These accounts should show the following December 31 balances prior to closing:

John Lotshaw, Capital, Acct. No. 311	$17,625.00 cr.
John Lotshaw, Drawing, Acct. No. 312	15,948.75 dr.
Expense & Revenue Summary, Acct. No. 331	-0-
Professional Fees, Acct. No. 411	39,457.43 cr.
Rent Expense, Acct. No. 541	6,300.00 dr.
Salary Expense, Acct. No. 542	7,150.00 dr.
Supplies Expense, Acct. No. 543	2,992.84 dr.
Telephone Expense, Acct. No. 545	570.15 dr.
Automobile Expense, Acct. No. 546	1,656.15 dr.
Depreciation Expense, Acct. No. 547	2,140.01 dr.
Utilities Expense, Acct. No. 549	303.75 dr.
Charitable Contributions Expense, Acct. No. 557	425.00 dr.
Miscellaneous Expense, Acct. No. 572	73.85 dr.

Be sure to enter zeros in the balance columns of each of the temporary owner's equity accounts (including the drawing account) as each closing entry is posted.

Exercise 4B8—Post-Closing Trial Balance Preparation. Refer to Exercises 4B1 and 4B7. Using the Balance Sheet columns of John Lotshaw's work sheet, prepare a post-closing trial balance as of December 31, 19--. For this purpose, use the amounts shown in the Balance Sheet columns of the work sheet for each asset account and each liability account, but use the updated balance of the capital account from Exercise 4B7 in place of the amounts shown in the work sheet for the capital and drawing accounts.

Series A

Problem 4A1   Financial Statement Preparation

Given on page 143 are the Income Statement and Balance Sheet columns of the work sheet for Carr Trovillion, CPA, for the month ended September 30, 19--.

Required:

1. Prepare an income statement for Carr Trovillion, CPA, for the month ended September 30, 19--. (Round all amounts to the nearest dollar.)
2. Prepare a statement of owner's equity for Carr Trovillion, CPA, for the month ended September 30, 19--. (Round all amounts to the nearest dollar.)
3. Prepare a balance sheet in report form for Carr Trovillion, CPA, as of September 30, 19--. (Round all amounts to the nearest dollar.)

Account Title	Acct. No.	Income Statement Debit	Income Statement Credit	Balance Sheet Debit	Balance Sheet Credit
Cash................	111			$61,489.24	
Supplies.............	151			2,500.00	
Office Equipment	191			24,000.00	
Accum. Depr.—Office Equipment..........	191.1				$ 8,340.00
Accounts Payable	218				2,079.44
Carr Trovillion, Capital	311				42,088.24
Carr Trovillion, Drawing	312			2,000.00	
Professional Fees	411		$49,120.00		
Rent Expense	541	$2,000.00			
Salary Expense	542	4,800.00			
Supplies Expense	543	1,983.64			
Travel & Entertainment Expense	544	592.20			
Telephone Expense	545	529.40			
Automobile Expense ...	546	917.60			
Depreciation Expense ..	547	240.00			
Heating & Lighting Expense	549	298.40			
Charitable Contrib. Expense	557	200.00			
Miscellaneous Expense	572	77.20			
		$11,638.44	$49,120.00	$89,989.24	$52,507.68
Net Income		37,481.56			37,481.56
		$49,120.00	$49,120.00	$89,989.24	$89,989.24

Problem 4A2   Financial Statement Preparation

Given on page 144 are the Income Statement and Balance Sheet columns of the Work Sheet for Sandra Evans, Computer Consultant, for the month ended April 30, 19--.

Required:

1. Prepare an income statement for Sandra Evans, Computer Consultant, for the month ended April 30, 19--. (Round all amounts to the nearest dollar.)
2. Prepare a statement of owner's equity for Sandra Evans, Computer Consultant, for the month ended April 30, 19--. (Round all amounts to the nearest dollar.)
3. Prepare a balance sheet in report form for Sandra Evans, Computer Consultant, as of April 30, 19--. (Round all amounts to the nearest dollar.)

Account Title	Acct. No.	Income Statement Debit	Income Statement Credit	Balance Sheet Debit	Balance Sheet Credit
Cash	111			$15,372.31	
Supplies	151			625.00	
Office Equipment	191			6,000.00	
Accum. Depr.—Office Equipment	191.1				$ 2,085.00
Accounts Payable	218				519.91
Sandra Evans, Capital . .	311				10,522.01
Sandra Evans, Drawing	312			500.00	
Professional Fees	411		$12,280.00		
Rent Expense	541	$500.00			
Salary Expense	542	1,200.00			
Supplies Expense	543	495.91			
Travel & Entertainment Expense	544	148.00			
Telephone Expense	545	132.60			
Automobile Expense . . .	546	229.20			
Depreciation Expense . .	547	60.00			
Heating & Lighting Expense	549	74.60			
Charitable Contributions Expense	557	50.00			
Miscellaneous Expense	572	19.30			
		$ 2,909.61	$12,280.00	$22,497.31	$13,126.92
Net Income		9,370.39			9,370.39
		$12,280.00	$12,280.00	$22,497.31	$22,497.31

Problem 4A3   Financial Statement Preparation

Given on the next page are the Income Statement and Balance Sheet columns of the work sheet for Judy Meadors, Investment Consultant, for the quarter ended March 31, 19--.

Required:

1. Prepare an income statement for Judy Meadors, Investment Consultant, for the quarter ended March 31, 19--. (Round all amounts to the nearest dollar.)
2. Prepare a statement of owner's equity for Judy Meadors, Investment Consultant, for the quarter ended March 31, 19--. (Round all amounts to the nearest dollar.)
3. Prepare a balance sheet in report form for Judy Meadors, Investment Consultant, as of March 31, 19--. (Round all amounts to the nearest dollar.)

Account Title	Acct. No.	Income Statement Debit	Income Statement Credit	Balance Sheet Debit	Balance Sheet Credit
Cash	111			$ 92,233.86	
Supplies	151			3,750.00	
Office Equipment . . .	191			36,000.00	
Accum. Depr.—					
Office Equipment . .	191.1				$ 12,510.00
Accounts Payable . . .	218				3,119.56
Judy Meadors,					
Capital	311				63,131.96
Judy Meadors,					
Drawing	312			3,000.00	
Professional Fees	411		$73,680.00		
Rent Expense	541	$ 3,000.00			
Salary Expense	542	7,200.00			
Supplies Expense	543	2,975.56			
Travel &					
Entertainment					
Expense	544	888.00			
Telephone Expense . .	545	794.30			
Automobile Expense	546	1,376.40			
Depreciation Expense	547	360.00			
Utilities Expense	549	447.60			
Charitable					
Contributions					
Expense	557	300.00			
Miscellaneous					
Expense	572	115.80			
		$17,457.66	$73,680.00	$134,983.86	$ 78,761.52
Net Income		56,222.34			56,222.34
		$73,680.00	$73,680.00	$134,983.86	$134,983.86

Problem 4A4   Financial Statement Preparation

Given on page 146 are the Income Statement and Balance Sheet columns of the work sheet for Kenneth Schwartz, Attorney at Law, for the period ended February 28, 19--.

Required:

1. Prepare an income statement for Kenneth Schwartz, Attorney at Law, for the period ended February 28, 19--. (Round all amounts to the nearest dollar.)
2. Prepare a statement of owner's equity for Kenneth Schwartz, Attorney at Law, for the period ended February 28, 19--. (Round all amounts to the nearest dollar.)
3. Prepare a balance sheet in report form for Kenneth Schwartz, Attorney at Law, as of February 28, 19--. (Round all amounts to the nearest dollar.)

Account Title	Acct. No.	Income Statement Debit	Income Statement Credit	Balance Sheet Debit	Balance Sheet Credit
Cash................	111			$30,744.62	
Supplies.............	151			1,250.00	
Office Equipment	191			12,000.00	
Accum. Depr.—Office Equipment..........	191.1				$ 4,170.00
Accounts Payable	218				1,039.82
Kenneth Schwartz, Capital............	311				21,044.02
Kenneth Schwartz, Drawing	312			1,000.00	
Professional Fees	411		$24,560.00		
Rent Expense	541	$ 1,000.00			
Salary Expense........	542	2,400.00			
Supplies Expense......	543	991.82			
Travel & Entertainment Expense	544	296.00			
Telephone Expense	545	264.80			
Automobile Expense ...	546	458.80			
Depreciation Expense ..	547	120.00			
Utilities Expense	549	149.40			
Charitable Contributions Expense	557	100.00			
Miscellaneous Expense	572	38.40			
		$ 5,819.22	$24,560.00	$44,994.62	$26,253.84
Net Income		18,740.78			18,740.78
		$24,560.00	$24,560.00	$44,994.62	$44,994.62

Problem 4A5   Adjusting and Closing Entries in Combination Journal

Given on the next page are the Adjustments, Income Statement, and Balance Sheet columns of the work sheet for Kenneth Schwartz, Attorney at Law, for the period ended February 28, 19--.

Required:

1. Prepare a partial combination journal with only the General Debit and Credit amount columns. Number the journal page 8.
2. Make the necessary adjusting entries.
3. Make the necessary closing entries.

Account Title	Acct. No.	Adjustments Debit	Adjustments Credit	Income Statement Debit	Income Statement Credit	Balance Sheet Debit	Balance Sheet Credit
Cash	111					$30,744.62	
Supplies	151		(a)$ 991.82			1,250.00	
Office Equipment	191					12,000.00	
Accum. Depr.—Office Equipment	191.1		(b) 120.00				$ 4,170.00
Accounts Payable	218						1,039.82
Kenneth Schwartz, Capital	311						21,044.02
Kenneth Schwartz, Drawing	312					1,000.00	
Professional Fees	411				$24,560.00		
Rent Expense	541			$ 1,000.00			
Salary Expense	542			2,400.00			
Supplies Expense	543	(a)$ 991.82		991.82			
Travel & Entertainment Expense...............	544			296.00			
Telephone Expense	545			264.80			
Automobile Expense	546			458.80			
Depreciation Expense	547	(b) 120.00		120.00			
Utilities Expense	549			149.40			
Charitable Contributions Expense...............	557			100.00			
Miscellaneous Expense	572			38.40			
		$1,111.82	$1,111.82	$ 5,819.22	$24,560.00	$44,994.62	$26,253.84
Net Income				18,740.78			18,740.78
				$24,560.00	$24,560.00	$44,994.62	$44,994.62

Problem 4A6   Posting Adjusting and Closing Entries to Ledger

Refer to Problem 4A5. The following are the general ledger accounts with their balances as of February 28 prior to adjustment:

Accounts	Acct. No.	Balance
Supplies...................................	151	$ 2,241.82 dr.
Accum. Depr.—Office Equipment	191.1	4,050.00 cr.
Kenneth Schwartz, Capital	311	21,044.02 cr.
Kenneth Schwartz, Drawing	312	1,000.00 dr.
Expense and Revenue Summary	331	-0-
Professional Fees...............................	411	24,560.00 cr.
Rent Expense	541	1,000.00 dr.
Salary Expense.................................	542	2,400.00 dr.
Supplies Expense...............................	543	-0-
Travel & Entertainment Expense	544	296.00 dr.
Telephone Expense	545	264.80 dr.
Automobile Expense	546	458.80 dr.

Depreciation Expense	547	-0-
Utilities Expense	549	149.40 dr.
Charitable Contributions Expense	557	100.00 dr.
Miscellaneous Expense	572	38.40 dr.

Required:

1. Post the adjusting entries from the combination journal to the affected four-column ledger accounts.
2. Post the closing entries from the combination journal to the affected four-column ledger accounts.
3. Be sure to:
   (a) Update account balances in the ledger as necessary.
   (b) Show posting references both in the combination journal and in the ledger accounts.
   (c) Enter zeros in the balance columns of each temporary owner's equity account (including the drawing account) as each closing entry is posted.

Problem 4A7   Post-Closing Trial Balance Preparation

Refer to Problems 4A4 and 4A6.

Required:

Using the Balance Sheet columns of Kenneth Schwartz's work sheet given in Problem 4A4, prepare a post-closing trial balance as of February 28, 19--. For this purpose, use the updated balance of the capital account from the statement you prepared in Problem 4A4, and omit the balances of the capital and drawing accounts as shown on the work sheet.

Series B

Problem 4B1   Financial Statement Preparation

Given on the next page are the Income Statement and Balance Sheet columns of the work sheet for Robert Karn, M.D., for the month ended June 30, 19--.

Required:

1. Prepare an income statement for Robert Karn, M.D., for the month ended June 30, 19--. (Round all amounts to the nearest dollar.)
2. Prepare a statement of owner's equity for Robert Karn, M.D., for the month ended June 30, 19--. (Round all amounts to the nearest dollar.)
3. Prepare a balance sheet in report form for Robert Karn, M.D., as of June 30, 19--. (Round all amounts to the nearest dollar.)

Account Title	Acct. No.	Income Statement Debit	Income Statement Credit	Balance Sheet Debit	Balance Sheet Credit
Cash	111			$29,834.24	
Supplies	151			1,875.00	
Office Equipment	191			18,000.00	
Accum. Depr.—Office Equipment	191.1				$ 6,255.00
Accounts Payable	218				1,690.78
Robert Karn, Capital . . .	311				31,566.02
Robert Karn, Drawing	312			3,000.00	
Professional Fees	411		$23,240.00		
Rent Expense	541	$ 1,800.00			
Salary Expense	542	4,200.00			
Supplies Expense	543	1,502.36			
Travel & Entertainment Expense	544	358.00			
Telephone Expense	545	497.20			
Automobile Expense . . .	546	997.60			
Depreciation Expense . .	547	180.00			
Heating and Lighting Expense	549	304.60			
Charitable Contributions Expense	557	150.00			
Miscellaneous Expense	572	52.80			
		$10,042.56	$23,240.00	$52,709.24	$39,511.80
Net Income		13,197.44			13,197.44
		$23,240.00	$23,240.00	$52,709.24	$52,709.24

Problem 4B2   Financial Statement Preparation

Given below are the Income Statement and Balance Sheet columns of the work sheet for Flo Martin, Financial Planning Consultant, for the month ended November 30, 19--.

Required:

1. Prepare an income statement for Flo Martin, Financial Planning consultant, for the period ended November 30, 19--. (Round all amounts to the nearest dollar.)
2. Prepare a statement of owner's equity for Flo Martin, Financial Planning Consultant, for the month ended November 30, 19--. (Round all amounts to the nearest dollar.)
3. Prepare a balance sheet in report form for Flo Martin, Financial Planning Consultant, as of November 30, 19--. (Round all amounts to the nearest dollar.)

38785.00
cr.

Account Title	Acct. No.	Income Statement Debit	Income Statement Credit	Balance Sheet Debit	Balance Sheet Credit
Cash...................	111			$ 7,458.56	
Supplies...............	151			468.75	
Office Equipment	191			4,500.00	
Accum. Depr.—Office Equipment............	191.1				$ 1,563.75
Accounts Payable	218				422.69
Flo Martin, Capital	311				7,891.51
Flo Martin, Drawing.....	312			750.00	
Professional Fees........	411		$5,810.00		
Rent Expense	541	$ 450.00			
Salary Expense..........	542	1,050.00			
Supplies Expense........	543	375.59			
Travel & Entertainment Expense	544	89.50			
Telephone Expense	545	124.30			
Automobile Expense	546	249.40			
Depreciation Expense	547	45.00			
Heating & Lighting Expense	549	76.15			
Charitable Contributions Expense	557	37.50			
Miscellaneous Expense...	572	13.20			
		$2,510.64	$5,810.00	$13,177.31	$ 9,877.95
Net Income		3,299.36			3,299.36
		$5,810.00	$5,810.00	$13,177.31	$13,177.31

Problem 4B3   Financial Statement Preparation

Given on the following page are the Income Statement and Balance Sheet columns of the work sheet for Patricia Schoen, Realtor, for the quarter ended June 30, 19--.

Required:

1. Prepare an income statement for Patricia Schoen, Realtor, for the quarter ended June 30, 19--. (Round all amounts to the nearest dollar.)
2. Prepare a statement of owner's equity for Patricia Schoen, Realtor, for the quarter ended June 30, 19--. (Round all amounts to the nearest dollar.)
3. Prepare a balance sheet in report form for Patricia Schoen, Realtor, as of June 30, 19--. (Round all amounts to the nearest dollar.)

Account Title	Acct. No.	Income Statement Debit	Income Statement Credit	Balance Sheet Debit	Balance Sheet Credit
Cash................	111			$44,751.36	
Supplies.............	151			2,812.50	
Office Equipment	191			27,000.00	
Accum. Depr.—Office Equipment..........	191.1				$ 9,382.50
Accounts Payable	218				2,536.17
Patricia Schoen, Capital	311				47,349.03
Patricia Schoen, Drawing	312			4,500.00	
Professional Fees	411		$34,860.00		
Rent Expense	541	$ 2,700.00			
Salary Expense........	542	6,300.00			
Supplies Expense......	543	2,253.54			
Travel & Entertainment Expense	544	537.00			
Telephone Expense	545	745.80			
Automobile Expense ...	546	1,496.40			
Depreciation Expense..	547	270.00			
Utilities Expense	549	456.90			
Charitable Contributions Expense	557	225.00			
Miscellaneous Expense	572	79.20			
		$15,063.84	$34,860.00	$79,063.86	$59,267.70
Net Income		19,796.16			19,796.16
		$34,860.00	$34,860.00	$79,063.86	$79,063.86

Problem 4B4   Financial Statement Preparation

Given on page 152 are the Income Statement and Balance Sheet columns of the work sheet for James Rhea, Orthodontist, for the period ended January 31, 19--.

Required:

1. Prepare an income statement for James Rhea, Orthodontist, for the period ended January 31, 19--. (Round all amounts to the nearest dollar.)
2. Prepare a statement of owner's equity for James Rhea, Orthodontist, for the period ended January 31, 19--. (Round all amounts to the nearest dollar.)
3. Prepare a balance sheet in report form for James Rhea, Orthodontist, as of January 31, 19--. (Round all amounts to the nearest dollar.)

Account Title	Acct. No.	Income Statement Debit	Income Statement Credit	Balance Sheet Debit	Balance Sheet Credit
Cash.................	111			$14,917.12	
Supplies.............	151			937.50	
Office Equipment	191			9,000.00	
Accum. Depr.—Office					
Equipment..........	191.1				$ 3,127.50
Accounts Payable	218				845.39
James Rhea, Capital ...	311				15,783.01
James Rhea, Drawing ..	312			1,500.00	
Professional Fees	411		$11,620.00		
Rent Expense	541	$ 900.00			
Salary Expense	542	2,100.00			
Supplies Expense	543	751.18			
Travel & Entertainment					
Expense	544	179.00			
Telephone Expense	545	248.60			
Automobile Expense ...	546	498.80			
Depreciation Expense ..	547	90.00			
Utilities Expense	549	152.30			
Charitable Contributions					
Expense	557	75.00			
Miscellaneous Expense	572	26.40			
		$ 5,021.28	$11,620.00	$26,354.62	$19,755.90
Net Income		6,598.72			6,598.72
		$11,620.00	$11,620.00	$26,354.62	$26,354.62

Problem 4B5   Adjusting and Closing Entries in Combination Journal

Given on the next page are the Adjustments, Income Statement, and Balance Sheet columns of the work sheet for James Rhea, Orthodonist, for the period ending January 31, 19--. (The business started January 1.)

Required:

1. Prepare a partial combination journal with only the General Debit and Credit amount columns. Number the journal page 9.
2. Make the necessary adjusting entries.
3. Make the necessary closing entries.

Account Title	Acct. No.	Adjustments Debit	Adjustments Credit	Income Statement Debit	Income Statement Credit	Balance Sheet Debit	Balance Sheet Credit
Cash	111					$14,917.12	
Supplies	151		(a)$751.18			937.50	
Office Equipment	191					9,000.00	
Accum. Depr.—Office Equipment	191.1		(b)90.00				$ 3,127.50
Accounts Payable	218						845.39
James Rhea, Capital	311						15,783.01
James Rhea, Drawing	312					1,500.00	
Professional Fees	411				$11,620.00		
Rent Expense	541			$ 900.00			
Salary Expense	542			2,100.00			
Supplies Expense	543	(a)$751.18		751.18			
Travel & Entertainment Expense	544			179.00			
Telephone Expense	545			248.60			
Automobile Expense	546			498.80			
Depreciation Expense	547	(b)90.00		90.00			
Utilities Expense	549			152.30			
Charitable Contribution Expense	557			75.00			
Miscellaneous Expense	572			26.40			
		$841.18	$841.18	$ 5,021.28	$11,620.00	$26,354.62	$19,755.09
				6,598.72			6,598.72
				$11,620.00	$11,620.00	$26,354.62	$26,354.62

Problem 4B6   Posting Adjusting and Closing Entries to Ledger

---

Refer to Problem 4B5. The following are the general ledger accounts with their balances as of January 31 prior to adjustment:

Accounts	Acct. No.	Balance
Supplies	151	$ 1,688.68 dr.
Accum. Depr.—Office Equip.	191.1	3,037.50 cr.
James Rhea, Capital	311	15,783.01 cr.
James Rhea, Drawing	312	1,500.00 dr.
Expense and Revenue Summary	331	-0-
Professional Fees	411	11,620.00 cr.
Rent Expense	541	900.00 dr.
Salary Expense	542	2,100.00 dr.
Supplies Expense	543	-0-
Travel & Entertainment Expense	544	179.00 dr.
Telephone Expense	545	248.60 dr.
Automobile Expense	546	498.80 dr.

Depreciation Expense.............................	547	-0-
Utilities Expense	549	152.30 dr.
Charitable Contributions Expense	557	75.00 dr.
Miscellaneous Expense...........................	572	26.40 dr.

Required:
1. Post the adjusting entries from the combination journal to the affected four-column ledger accounts.
2. Post the closing entries from the combination journal to the affected four-column ledger accounts.
3. Be sure to:
   (a) Update account balances in the ledger as necessary.
   (b) Show posting references both in the combination journal and in the ledger accounts.
   (c) Enter zeros in the balance column of each temporary owner's equity account (including the drawing account) as each closing entry is posted.

Problem 4B7   Post-Closing Trial Balance Preparation

Refer to Problems 4B4 and 4B6.

Required:
Using the Balance Sheet columns of James Rhea's work sheet given in Problem 4B4, prepare a post-closing trial balance as of January 31, 19--. For this purpose, use the updated balance of the capital account from the statement you prepared in Problem 4B4, and omit the balances of the capital and drawing accounts as shown on the work sheet.

Mastery Problem

A completed work sheet for Kiddie Kollege Nursery School is provided on the next page.

Required:
1. Prepare an income statement for the year ended December 31, 19--.
2. Prepare a statement of owner's equity for the year ended December 31, 19--. (Check the capital account for additional investments.)
3. Prepare a balance sheet as of December 31, 19--.
4. Record adjusting entries in the General Debit and Credit columns of a combination journal. Number the journal page 6.
5. Record the closing entries in the combination journal.
6. Post the adjusting and closing entries to the general ledger accounts.
7. Prepare a post-closing trial balance.

Kiddie Kollege Nursery School
Work Sheet
For the Year Ended December 31, 19--

Account Title	Acct. No.	Trial Balance Debit	Trial Balance Credit	Adjustments Debit	Adjustments Credit	Income Statement Debit	Income Statement Credit	Balance Sheet Debit	Balance Sheet Credit
Cash	111	$ 2,355.66						$ 2,355.66	
Supplies	151	13,255.99			$(b) 11,200.25			2,055.74	
Play Equipment	191	24,987.66						24,987.66	
Accum. Depr.—Play Equip.	191.1		$ 9,995.06		(a) 4,997.53				$14,992.59
Accounts Payable	218		2,000.00						2,000.00
Mary Jane Hook, Capital	311		15,985.87						15,985.87
Mary Jane Hook, Drawing	312	12,000.00						12,000.00	
Registration Fees	411		85,344.00				$85,344.00		
Rent Expense	541	12,000.00				$12,000.00			
Salary Expense	542	40,000.00				40,000.00			
Supplies Expense	543			$(b) 11,200.25		11,200.25			
Field Trips Expense	544	5,668.87				5,668.87			
Telephone Expense	545	1,345.87				1,345.87			
Depreciation Expense	547			(a) 4,997.53		4,997.53			
Advertising Expense	551	445.88				445.88			
Education Workshops Expense	558	1,265.00				1,265.00			
		$113,324.93	$113,324.93	$16,197.78	$16,197.78	$76,923.40	$85,344.00	$41,399.06	$32,978.46
Net Income						8,420.60			8,420.60
						$85,344.00	$85,344.00	$41,399.06	$41,399.06

CHAPTER 5

Accounting for Cash

Careful study of this chapter should enable you to:

- Explain the meanings of the term "cash" as it is used in accounting.
- Describe internal control over cash receipts, cash payments, and cash balances.
- Explain the operation of a petty cash fund and prepare a petty cash payments record.
- Describe banking procedures for use of commercial bank checking accounts.
- Reconcile a bank statement.
- Describe procedures for use of a bank savings account.

This chapter is devoted to a discussion of the handling of and accounting for cash receipts and cash payments. Included in the discussion are the nature of the cash account, proving cash, and the operation of and accounting for a petty cash fund. Also included in the discussion are the operation of both bank checking and savings accounts, the functions performed by commonly used bank forms, and the process of reconciling the bank statement.

Cash Receipts and Cash Payments; Petty Cash

Explain the meanings of the term "cash" as it is used in accounting.

The term "cash" has several meanings. In a very narrow sense, cash means currency and coins. In a broader sense, cash also includes cash items, such as checks, drafts, credit card receipts (discussed in Chapter 7), and money orders payable to the business. Usually, any reference to the cash receipts of a business relates to the receipt of cash and cash items. The cash account balance, as well as the amount reported for cash on the balance sheet, normally includes cash and cash items on hand plus the amount on deposit in one or more bank accounts. Cash on hand includes cash and cash items currently held by the business. A distinction between "cash on hand" and "cash in bank" is seldom made on the balance sheet.

A good policy for a business enterprise to adopt is a system of **internal control** (a set of procedures intended to ensure proper processing of business transactions) which requires that all cash and cash items received be deposited daily in a bank. When this system is used, the enterprise's total cash receipts equal its total deposits in the bank. It is also a good policy for a business enterprise to have all its checks and other cash deposits accepted by the bank for deposit only. This will ensure that the cash receipts records of the business agree item by item with the bank's record of deposits.

The Cash Account

Describe internal control over cash receipts, cash payments, and cash balances.

The cash account is debited when cash is increased and credited when cash is decreased. This account normally has a debit balance.

Cash Receipts. Cash and cash items received by a business are known as cash receipts. It is essential that an accurate and timely record be kept of cash receipts to avoid the possibility of errors. When the volume of receipts is large both in number and in amount, specific procedures designed to reduce the danger of mistakes and **embezzlement** (the unauthorized taking of business cash by an employee) should be followed.

When numerous receipts of currency and coins are accepted from customers who have purchased goods or services, it is convenient for a business to use a **cash register**. Such a machine classifies items and amounts sold. A cash register may also have the capability of accumulating subtotals by departments and calculating sales taxes. Many cash registers today are actually small computer terminals that have the ability to accumulate large amounts of information about cash transactions.

A business often receives payments by mail (nearly always as checks). These payments are usually accompanied by the top or bottom portion of a customer's monthly statement which is supplied by the business. The returned form contains the remitter's name, address, and account number (preprinted by the business) and the amount of the enclosed payment (handwritten by the customer). An example of the top portion of a customer's monthly statement is shown in the illustration on page 158.

Sometimes a written receipt must be prepared by the business when a remittance is received from a customer. A copy of this receipt or the returned portion of the monthly statement provides the source document for the cash received. In any case, the initial document or record of each amount received should be prepared by someone other than the accountant or the person who makes bank deposits to provide good **internal control**. The initial records are given to the accountant to use in preparing proper journal entries for cash receipts. The money received, including checks and money orders, is given to the person authorized to handle bank deposits and cash on hand. Under such a plan, the accountant does not actually handle any cash; instead cash receipts are entered

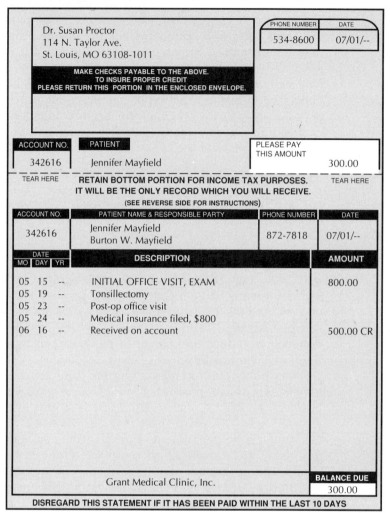

Monthly Statement

by the accountant from documents prepared by other persons. The procedure of having transactions involving cash handled by two or more persons reduces the danger of embezzlement and is one of the important features of a system of internal accounting control.

Cash Payments. Cash and cash items paid by a business are known as **cash payments**. Payments can be made in cash or by bank check. For good internal control, all cash payments should be made by check, except for payments from petty cash, as explained later in this chapter. This ensures that the cash payments' records of the business agree with the bank's record of withdrawals. When a payment is made in cash, a receipt should be obtained as evidence of the payment. When a payment is made by check, it is not necessary to obtain a receipt since the canceled check that is returned by the bank serves as a receipt.

▂▂ **Keeping a Ledger Account for Each Bank.** If a business has more than one bank account, it may keep a ledger account for each bank. The title of such an account often includes the name of the bank. Sometimes, more than one account is kept with a bank, in which case each account should be correctly labeled. Such terms as "commercial," "executive," and "payroll" are used to identify the accounts.

The bank account is debited for the amount of each deposit and credited for the amount of each check written. The account should also be debited or credited for any other transactions that may have been handled directly by the bank, including collections and service charges.

When both a cash on hand account and a bank account are kept in the ledger, the following procedures should be used in entering transactions affecting these accounts:

1. Cash receipts are entered as debits to Cash on Hand.
2. Cash payments and bank deposits are entered as credits to Cash on Hand.
3. Bank deposits and bank collections are entered as debits to Cash in Bank.
4. Checks written and bank charges are entered as credits to Cash in Bank.

These procedures are illustrated in T account form as follows:

Cash on Hand		Cash in Bank	
Debit	Credit	Debit	Credit
(1) For all receipts of cash and cash items.	(2) For all payments in cash. For all bank deposits.	(3) For all bank deposits. For collection of amounts for the depositor.	(4) For all checks written. For all bank services and other charges.

Under this method of accounting for cash and banking transactions, the cash on hand account will have a zero balance when all cash on hand has been deposited in the bank.

The cash on hand account is not needed when a cash in bank account is kept in the ledger and all cash receipts are deposited daily in the bank. All payments except small amounts paid from a petty cash fund are made by check. If all cash received during the month has been deposited before the accounts are closed at the end of the month, the total amount of the bank deposits will equal the total cash receipts for the month. If all payments during the month are made by check, the total amount of checks issued will be the total cash payments for the month.

▂▂ **Proving Cash.** The process of determining whether the amount of cash, both on hand and in the bank, is the same as the amount entered in the accounting records is called **proving Cash**. Cash should be proved at least once a week, and more often if the volume of cash transactions is large. The first step is to determine from the ledger the amount of the cash account balance. The most recent cash account balance is determined by adding the total of the receipts since the beginning of the period to the opening balance and subtracting the total of the payments. This cash account balance should be equal to the amount of cash on deposit in the bank as reflected in the checkbook stubs plus the total of the cash and cash items on hand. An up-to-date record of cash on deposit in the bank is maintained by using check stubs to show deposits as well as checks drawn. (See check stubs illustrated on page 174.) The amount of cash on hand must be determined by actual count.

To illustrate proving Cash, assume the following information for Zed Plumbing.

General ledger cash account balance, June 1, 19--	$6,420
Cash receipts per combination journal, June 1-6	5,190
Cash payments per combination journal, June 1-6	5,865
Cash and cash items on hand, June 6, 19--	477
Cash in bank, June 6, 19--, per check stubs	5,268

Cash would be proved for Zed Plumbing as of June 6, 19--, as follows:

Cash account balance per ledger:	
Balance, June 1, 19--	$ 6,420
Add cash receipts per combination journal, June 1-6	5,190
	$11,610
Less cash payments per combination journal, June 1-6	5,865
Balance, June 6, 19--	$ 5,745
Cash on deposit and on hand:	
Balance, June 1, 19--, per check stubs	$ 5,268
Add cash and cash items on hand, June 6, 19--	477
Balance, June 6, 19--	$ 5,745

Cash Short and Over. If the effort to prove Cash is not successful, either (1) the records of receipts, payments, and cash on deposit contain one or more data entry errors, (2) the physical count of cash not deposited is incorrect, or (3) a shortage or an overage exists. If verifications of the records and the physical count of cash do not uncover any error, it is evident that some mistake must have been made in handling cash.

Finding that Cash is slightly short or over is not unusual. If there are numerous cash transactions, it is difficult to avoid occasional errors in making change. There is always the danger of shortages due to dishonesty, but most discrepancies are the result of mistakes. Many businesses have a special ledger account entitled **Cash Short and Over** which is used to keep track of day-to-day shortages and overages of cash. If, in the effort to prove Cash, a shortage is found, the amount is treated as a cash decrease involving a debit to Cash Short and Over and a credit to Cash. Any overage discovered is regarded as a cash increase involving a credit to Cash Short and Over and a debit to Cash.

To illustrate, if the amount of cash was $2 short at the end of the day, the entry would be as follows:

Cash Short and Over...........................	2.00	
Cash...		2.00

Conversely, if the amount of cash was $3 over, the entry would be as follows:

Cash...	3.00	
Cash Short and Over...........................		3.00

By the end of the fiscal year, it is likely that the cash short and over account will have both debits and credits. If the total of the debits exceeds the total of the credits, the balance represents an expense or loss; if the reverse is true, the balance represents revenue.

The Petty Cash Fund

Explain the operation of a petty cash fund and prepare a petty cash payments record.

When all cash receipts are deposited in a bank, an office fund known as a **petty cash fund** may be established for paying small items. ("Petty" means small or little.) Such a fund eliminates the necessity of writing checks for relatively small amounts.

Operating a Petty Cash Fund. To establish a petty cash fund, a check is written for the amount that is to be set aside in the fund. The amount may be $50, $100, $200, or any amount considered necessary. The check is made payable to the person in charge of the fund. That person's name, followed by a comma and the words, "Petty Cash Fund Cashier" appears on the check as the payee. The cashier cashes the check and places money in a cash drawer, a cash register, or a safe used for the petty cash fund. Since the cashier is the only person authorized to make payments from the fund, the cashier should be able to account for the full amount of the fund at any time.

Payments from the fund should be recorded on some sort of receipt. A special form of receipt, showing the name of the payee, the purpose of the payment, and the account to be charged for each petty cash payment, is known as a **petty cash voucher**. A type of petty cash voucher is shown on page 162. Such a voucher should be prepared for each expenditure. These vouchers should be numbered consecutively and signed by the petty cashier and the person receiving the cash.

The check written to establish the petty cash fund is entered in the journal by debiting Petty Cash Fund and crediting Cash. To replenish the

attached all receipts

```
┌─────────────────────────────────────────────────────────┐
│                 Petty Cash Voucher                        │
│                                                           │
│                          No. 4                            │
│                          Date December 11, 9--            │
│                                            ┌──────┬─────┐ │
│    Paid to Deborah Douglas                 │  $   │  ¢  │ │
│    For American Cancer Society             │ 25   │ 00  │ │
│                                            └──────┴─────┘ │
│    Charge to Charitable Contributions Expense             │
│                                                           │
│    Remittance received          Approved by               │
│    Deborah Douglas              John E. Buna               │
└─────────────────────────────────────────────────────────┘
```

Petty Cash Voucher

fund, the petty cashier usually prepares a statement of the payments and a check is then written for the exact amount of the total payments. This check is entered in the journal by debiting the proper accounts indicated in the statement and crediting Cash.

To illustrate, assume that on June 1, Fiona's Fashions established a petty cash fund for $100, and that on June 30 the fund was replenished for $85.25 after classifying and totaling the petty cash vouchers. The journal entries for these transactions are:

June	1 Petty Cash Fund	100.00	
	Cash		100.00
	To establish petty cash fund.		
	30 Automobile Expense	22.00	
	Supplies Expense	32.00	
	Postage Expense.........................	26.00	
	Miscellaneous Expense	5.25	
	Cash		85.25
	Replenishment of petty cash fund.		

The petty cash fund is thus a revolving fund. The petty cash account balance does not change in amount unless the fund is increased or decreased. The actual amount of cash in the fund plus the total of the petty cash vouchers should be equal to the amount originally deposited in the petty cash fund. This method for handling petty cash is referred to as the **imprest method**

Petty Cash Payments Record. When a petty cash fund is maintained, it is good practice to keep a formal record of all payments from the fund. The petty cash payments record is a special multi-column record that supplements the regular accounting records. No posting is done from this special record. In a petty cash payments record, the headings of the Distribution columns may vary, depending upon the types of expenditures. These headings represent accounts that are charged for the expenditures. Often, account numbers instead of account titles are used in the headings to indicate the accounts to be charged. One type of petty cash payments record is illustrated on pages 164 and 165.

The petty cash payments record reproduced on pages 164 and 165 is a part of the records of James Michaels, a business consultant. Michaels established a petty cash fund since he is out of the office much of the time. His administrative assistant, Tina Blank, is authorized to make petty cash payments not to exceed $35 each. A narrative of the petty cash transactions completed by Blank during the month of December follows:

JAMES MICHAELS—Narrative of Petty Cash Transactions

Dec. 1   Michaels issued a check for $200 payable to Tina Blank, Petty Cash Fund Cashier. Blank cashed the check and placed the money in a secure cash drawer.

This transaction is entered in the journal by debiting Petty Cash Fund and crediting Cash, as shown below. A notation of the amount received is also made in the Description column of the petty cash payments record reproduced on pages 164 and 165.

Dec. 1 Petty Cash Fund	200.00	
Cash		200.00
To establish petty cash fund.		

During the month of December, the following payments were made from the petty cash fund:

Dec. 5   Paid $22.80 to Jerry's Auto for having the company automobile serviced. Petty Cash Voucher No. 1.

8   Reimbursed Michaels $15.75 for the amount spent in entertaining a client at lunch. Petty Cash Voucher No. 2.

9   Gave Michaels $30 for personal use. Petty Cash Voucher No. 3.

The $30 given to Michaels is entered in the Amount column provided at the extreme right of the petty cash payments record since no special distribution column has been provided for entering amounts withdrawn by the owner for personal use.

11   The American Cancer Society was given a $25 donation. Petty Cash Voucher No. 4. (See voucher illustrated on page 162.)

15   Paid $18.25 for typewriter repairs. Petty Cash Voucher No. 5.

17   Reimbursed Michaels $14.50 for traveling expenses. Petty Cash Voucher No. 6.

19   Paid $8.00 to Big Red Car Care for having the company automobile washed. Petty Cash Voucher No. 7.

22   Paid $9.50 for mailing a package. Petty Cash Voucher No. 8.

23   Donated $15 to the local orphanage. Petty Cash Voucher No. 9.

PAGE *1*   **PETTY CASH PAYMENTS**

	DAY	DESCRIPTION	VOU. NO.	TOTAL AMOUNT		Tel. Exp.		Auto Exp.	
1		AMOUNTS FORWARDED							
2	1	Received in fund　　　Bal.　200.00							
3	5	Automobile repairs	1	22	80			22	80
4	8	Client luncheon	2	15	75				
5	9	James Michaels, personal use	3	30	00				
6	11	American Cancer Society	4	25	00				
7	15	Typewriter repairs	5	18	25				
8	17	Traveling expense	6	14	50				
9	19	Washing automobile	7	8	00			8	00
10	22	Postage expense	8	9	50				
11	23	The local orphanage	9	15	00				
12	29	Postage stamps	10	30	00				
13	30	Long distance call	11	4	80	4	80		
14				193	60	4	80	30	80
				193	60	4	80	30	80
15	31	Balance		6.40					
16	31	Replenished fund		193.60					
17		Total		200.00					

James Michaels' Petty Cash Payments Record (Left Page)

29　Paid $30 for postage stamps. Petty Cash Voucher No. 10.
30　Reimbursed Michaels $4.80 for a long distance business telephone call made from a public telephone. Petty Cash Voucher No. 11.

▪▪▪ **Proving the Petty Cash Payments Record.**　The petty cash fund should be replenished whenever the fund runs low, and at the end of each accounting period so that the accounts are brought up to date. To prove the petty cash payments record, it is first necessary to foot all of the amount columns. The sum of the footings of the Distribution columns should equal the footing of the Total Amount column. After proving the footings, the totals are entered and the record is ruled as shown in the illustration. The illustration shows that a total of $193.60 was paid out during December. Since this is an appropriate time to replenish the petty cash fund, the following statement of the payments for December is prepared:

Statement of Petty Cash Payments for December

Telephone expense	$ 4.80
Automobile expense	30.80
Postage expense	39.50
Charitable contributions expense	40.00
Travel and entertainment expense	30.25
Miscellaneous expense	18.25
James Michaels, Drawing	30.00
Total payments	$193.60

FOR MONTH OF December 19--   PAGE 1

	Post. Exp.		Char. Cont. Exp.		Travel & Ent. Exp.		Misc. Exp.			Account	Amount		
													1
													2
													3
					15	75							4
										James Michaels, Drawing	30	00	5
			25	00									6
							18	25					7
					14	50							8
													9
	9	50											10
			15	00									11
	30	00											12
													13
	39	50	40	00	30	25	18	25			30	00	14
	39	50	40	00	30	25	18	25			30	00	
													15
													16
													17

James Michaels' Petty Cash Payments Record (Right Page)

The statement of petty cash payments provides the information needed to replenish the petty cash fund. On December 31, Michaels issued a check for $193.60 payable to Tina Blank, Petty Cash Fund Cashier to replenish the petty cash fund. This transaction was treated as a compound entry in the journal by debiting the proper accounts and crediting Cash for the total amount of the expenses. A **compound entry** is one that affects more than two accounts, with the sum of the debits equal to the sum of the credits. Such an entry is usually required for petty cash fund replenishment. The entry is then posted from the journal to the affected ledger accounts.

Dec. 31	Telephone Expense	4.80
	Automobile Expense	30.80
	Postage Expense.............................	39.50
	Charitable Contributions Expense	40.00
	Travel & Entertainment Expense	30.25
	Miscellaneous Expense	18.25
	James Michaels, Drawing	30.00
	Cash	193.60
	Replenishment of petty cash fund.	

After the petty cash payments record is footed and ruled, the balance in the fund and the amount received to replenish the fund can be entered in the Description column below the ruling as shown in the illustration. It is customary to carry the total forward to the top of a new page on the "Amounts Forwarded" line before entering any of the transactions for the following month.

Building Your Accounting Knowledge

1. What is the usual source documentation of cash receipts when they are numerous and presented in person? What form of source documentation usually accompanies money that comes in by mail?
2. Why should transactions involving cash be handled by two or more persons?
3. Why is it not unusual to find that the cash balance at the time of proof is slightly short or over?
4. What does a debit balance in the cash short and over account represent? What does a credit balance in this account represent?
5. What is the purpose of a petty cash fund?
6. What should be obtained from the receiving party each time a petty cash payment is made?
7. From what source is the information obtained for issuing a check to replenish the petty cash fund?
8. At what two times should the petty cash fund be replenished?

Assignment Box

To reinforce your understanding of the preceding text materials, you may complete the following:

> Study Guide: Part A
> Textbook: Exercises 5A1 through 5A4 or 5B1 through 5B4
> Problems 5A1 through 5A2 or 5B1 through 5B2

Banking Procedures

A **bank** is a financial institution that receives deposits, lends money, makes collections, and provides a variety of other services. A bank may provide vaults for the safekeeping of valuables, handle trust funds, and buy and sell securities and insurance for its customers. Most banks offer facilities for both checking accounts and savings accounts.

Checking Account

Describe banking procedures for using commercial bank checking accounts.

The majority of all money payments in the United States are made by checks. A piece of commercial paper drawn on funds in a bank account and payable on demand is called a **check**. A check involves three parties: (1) the depositor who orders the bank to pay a certain amount of money—known as the **drawer**; (2) the bank in which the drawer has money on deposit—known as the **drawee**; and (3) the person directed to receive the money—known as the **payee**. The drawer and payee may be the same person, though the payee named on the check in such a case usually is "Cash."

A check is **negotiable** (meaning that the right to receive the money can be transferred to someone else) if it complies with the following requirements: (1) it is in writing; (2) it is signed by the drawer; (3) it contains an unconditional order to pay a specified amount of money; (4) it is payable on demand; and (5) it is payable to the order of another party or to the bearer. The payee transfers the right to receive the money by **endorsing** the check. This procedure requires stamping or writing his or her name and sometimes other pertinent information on the back of the check. If the payee simply signs on the back of the check, customarily near the left end, the signature is called a **blank endorsement**. This makes the check payable to any bearer. If there are added words such as "For deposit," "Pay to any bank," or "Pay to Daryl Beck only," it is called a **restrictive endorsement**. A widely used business practice when endorsing checks for deposit is to use a rubber stamp on the back of the check. A check that has been stamped with a restrictive endorsement is shown in the following illustration:

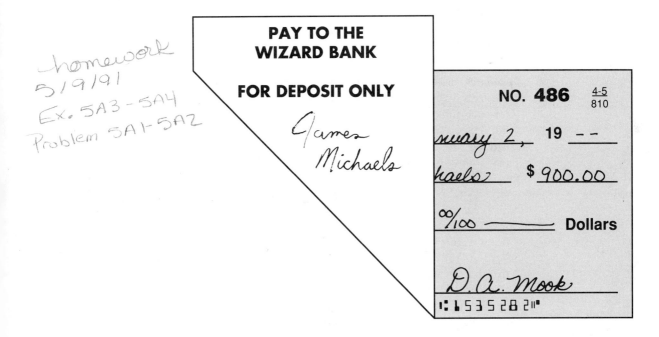

Important activities in connection with using a checking account are: (1) opening the account, (2) making deposits, (3) making withdrawals, (4) entering banking transactions, and (5) reconciling the bank statement.

Opening a Checking Account. To open a checking account with a bank, it is necessary to obtain the approval of an official of the bank and to make an initial deposit. Money, checks, bank drafts, money orders, and other cash items usually are accepted for deposit, subject to their verification as to amount and validity.

Banks usually require new depositors to sign their names on a card or form called a **signature card**. This card is used in verifying the depositor's signature on checks that may be issued, on cash items that may be endorsed for deposit, and on other business papers that may be presented to the bank. The depositor's social security number is also shown on the card for identification purposes. All persons authorized to use the account must sign signature cards. A signature card is one of the safeguards that a bank uses to protect its own interests as well as the interests of its depositors.

Making Deposits. To make a deposit with a bank, it is necessary to use certain forms provided by that bank and to observe the rules of that bank with regard to acceptable and unacceptable deposit items. In preparing the deposit, paper money should be arranged in the order of the denominations, the smaller denominations being placed on top. The bills should be all stacked face up and top up. Coins (pennies, nickels, dimes, quarters, half dollars and dollars) that are to be deposited in considerable quantities should be wrapped in coin wrappers, which the bank provides, unless the bank has a coin-sorting machine. Also, all checks being deposited must be endorsed.

Deposit Ticket. A printed form with a detailed listing of items being deposited is called a **deposit ticket**. Banks provide these forms for depositors. A filled-in deposit ticket is reproduced on page 169. Note that the depositor's account number is preprinted at the bottom in numbers that can be "read" by electronic equipment. These numbers are called **MICR** (magnetic ink character recognition) **numbers**. This series of digits, which is also preprinted at the bottom of all of the depositor's checks, is actually a code used in sorting and routing deposit slips and checks. In the first set of digits, 063112094, the "6" indicates that the bank is in the Sixth Federal Reserve District. The third digit "1" is the reserve bank or branch serving the district. The fourth digit "1" indicates whether the item is for immediate credit or deferred credit. The number "20" is a number assigned to the Wizard Bank. The last number position ("4" in this case) is a check digit position and may be used to verify the accuracy of the eight preceding digits in computer processing. This numbering method, known as **ABA numbers**, was established by the American Bankers Association, for use in sorting and routing deposit tickets. The second set of digits, 16-3247-5, is the number assigned by the Wizard Bank to James Michaels' account.

In preparing a deposit ticket, the date and signature (if required) should be written in the spaces provided. The amounts of cash repre-

JAMES MICHAELS
4112 WEBER ST.,
ORLANDO, FL 32818-1123

DEPOSIT TICKET

$\frac{63\text{-}1209}{631}$

WIZARD BANK
3711 Buena Vista Dr.
Orlando, FL 32811-1314

DATE _____ October 13 _____ 19 --

CHECKS AND OTHER ITEMS ARE RECEIVED FOR DEPOSIT SUBJECT TO
THE TERMS AND CONDITIONS OF THIS FINANCIAL INSTITUTION'S
ACCOUNT AGREEMENT.

James Michaels
SIGN HERE ONLY IF CASH RECEIVED FROM DEPOSIT

CURRENCY	934	00
COIN	42	63
C H E C K S 4-21	320	80
80-459	680	00
4-5	590	00
TOTAL FROM OTHER SIDE		
SUB-TOTAL	2,567	43
LESS CASH RECEIVED		
TOTAL DEPOSIT	2,567	43

⑆063112094⑆ 0001632475

Deposit Ticket

sented by currency, coins, and checks should be entered in the amount column of the deposit ticket on the lines provided for these items. Each check to be deposited should be listed on a separate line of the deposit ticket as shown in the illustration. The instructions of the bank should be observed in describing the checks for identification purposes. Banks usually prefer that depositors identify checks being deposited by showing the ABA number of the bank on which the check is drawn. This number is frequently located in the upper right hand corner of the check. The ABA number for the first check listed on the deposit ticket is 4-21/810. The number "4" is the number assigned to the city in which the bank is located and the number "21" is assigned to the specific bank. The denominator "810" is the check routing number, but only the numerator is used in identifying the deposit.

After the amounts on the deposit slip are totaled, the deposit ticket, together with the cash and the other items deposited, should be delivered to the receiving teller of the bank. The teller processes the deposit ticket and gives the depositor either a duplicate deposit ticket as a receipt or, more commonly today, a machine-printed receipt.

A depositor may obtain cash at the time of making a deposit by indicating on the deposit ticket what amount is to be returned to him or her. Alternatively, a check may be drawn payable to the depositor, or usually, just payable to "Cash."

Most banks use teller-operated machines in preparing receipts for deposits. The use of such machines saves the time required to make manual entries and eliminates the need for making duplicate copies of deposit tickets. Such machines are not only timesaving, but they also assure accuracy in the handling of deposits.

The deposits handled by each teller during the day are accumulated in the teller-operated machine. At the end of the day the total amount of the deposits received by the teller is automatically recorded by the machine. This amount may be proved by counting the cash and cash items accepted by a teller for deposit during the day.

Deposits by Mail. Bank deposits can be made by mail since it is not always convenient to make deposits over the counter. Such deposits should consist exclusively of checks. When deposits are made by mail, the bank may provide the depositor with a supply of deposit tickets, and a self-addressed, pre-stamped envelope. A machine-printed receipt for the deposit is subsequently returned by the bank.

Night Deposits. Many banks provide night-deposit service. A common practice is for the bank to have a night safe with an opening on the exterior of the bank building. Upon signing a night depository contract, the bank supplies the depositor with a key to the outside door of the safe, a numbered bag in which valuables can be placed, and two keys to the bag itself. Once the deposit is placed in the night deposit safe, it cannot be retrieved because it moves to a vault in the bank that is only accessible to bank employees. Since only the depositor is provided with keys to the bag, the depositor or an authorized representative must go to the bank to unlock the bag. The depositor may or may not at this time deposit the funds that had been placed previously in the night deposit safe.

Night-deposit service is especially valuable to those individuals and businesses that accumulate cash and other cash items which they cannot take to the bank during regular banking hours. If the individual or business has no safe facilities, the night deposit banking service provides the needed protection.

Dishonored Checks. A check that a bank refuses to pay is called a **dishonored check**. A depositor guarantees all items deposited and is liable to the bank for any dishonored item. When a check or other cash item that is deposited is not honored, the depositor's bank may charge the amount of the dishonored item to the depositor's account or may present it to the depositor for reimbursement. It is not uncommon for checks that have been deposited to be returned to the depositor for various reasons accompanied with a statement sometimes called a **debit advice**. As indicated on the debit advice (page 171), the most common reason for checks being returned unpaid is that they are **NSF checks** ("not sufficient funds" remain in the drawer's account to cover them).

Issuance of a check without sufficient funds in the account when it is presented for payment is called an **overdraft**. Under the laws of most states, issuance of such a check is illegal. When a dishonored check is deducted from the depositor's account by the bank, the amount should be deducted from the balance shown on the depositor's checkbook stub.

Most overdraft checks are not the result of any dishonest intent on the part of the drawer. Sometimes the drawer believes that there is enough money in the account when the check is written, due to an error in keeping the checkbook. Other times the drawer expects to get a deposit to the bank in time to "cover" the check before it reaches the bank for payment. It is commonly considered to be something of a disgrace to the drawer of a check if the bank will not honor (pay) it. It is possible to

Debit	⚡ **WIZARD BANK** *3711 Buena Vista Dr.* *Orlando, FL 32811-1314*

Statement Copy	**Date** June 16, 19--

Dishonored check - not sufficient funds	$84.75

Debit			
	Account No.	**Total**	$84.75
James Michaels	16-3247-5	Dept.	Checking
		By	_MM_

⑆063112094⑆ 0001632475⑈

Debit Advice

arrange to have all checks, within prescribed limits as to amount, be honored even if the depositor's balance is too low. This amounts to a prearrangement with the bank to make a loan to the depositor, and in some cases, interest may be automatically computed and charged against the depositor's account.

Postdated Check.   A check dated after the date that the check was actually written and issued is known as a **postdated check**. For example, a check written and issued on March 1 is dated March 15. The recipient of the postdated check should not deposit it before the date specified on the check (March 15) because it is not legally acceptable as cash until that date. One reason for issuing a postdated check may be that the maker does not have sufficient funds in the bank at the time of issuance, which in this case is March 1, but expects to have a sufficient amount on deposit by the time the check is presented for payment (March 15). When a postdated check is presented to the bank on which it is drawn and payment is not made, it is handled by the bank in the same manner as any other dishonored check and the payee should treat it as a dishonored check. Generally, it is not considered good practice for a business to issue postdated checks.

Making Withdrawals.   The amount on deposit in a bank checking account may be withdrawn either by the depositor or by any other person who is properly authorized to make withdrawals from the depositor's account. Such withdrawals can be made by the use of bank issued plastic cards inserted in automated teller machines or by the use of checks signed by the depositor or by others having the authority to sign checks drawn on the account.

Automated Teller Machines.   Many banks now make **automated teller machines** available at all times to depositors. Although such machines may be used to make deposits, they are used far more frequently to make withdrawals.

Each depositor electing to use automated teller machines is provided with a bank issued plastic card and a secret code number. The depositor inserts the card into the machine and keys in the "password" code number. The depositor is then asked to indicate the type of transaction, either (1) a withdrawal or (2) a deposit, from either a (1) checking account or (2) savings account. Then the depositor keys in the amount. The machine next asks for a keyed-in verification ("yes" or "no") of the amount and—after a slight pause—instructs the depositor to open a drawer or door on the front of the machine.

If the transaction is a withdrawal, the cash requested can be found and removed. If a deposit, the deposit ticket and deposit items are placed in the drawer or compartment. The machine then asks the depositor whether another transaction will take place, and if the keyed-in answer is "no," the drawer or compartment locks automatically. The depositor then removes the plastic card from the machine and the machine deactivates until the next depositor arrives.

Checkbook.   Checks used by businesses are usually bound in the form of a book with two or three blank checks to a page and perforated so that they may be removed singly. Checks may be provided by the bank (often for a charge) or purchased directly from firms that specialize in the manufacture of check forms.

In some checkbooks, to the left of each check is a small form called a **check stub** that contains space to record all relevant information about the check. Other times the depositor is provided with a checkbook that, instead of containing stubs, is accompanied by a small register book in which the relevant information is noted. The information contained on the stub or on the register includes the check number, date, payee, amount, the purpose of the check and often the account to be charged. In addition, the stub shows the bank balance before the check was issued, current deposits if any, and the resulting balance after issuing the check.

The depositor's name and address normally are preprinted on each check. The MICR numbers are shown along the bottom edge and the check number is preprinted in the upper right corner. Some checks come bound in the form of a pad with a blank page after each check for use in making a carbon copy of the check. The copy is not a check; it is merely a copy of what was typed or written on the original check and provides the information needed for making an entry in the formal records.

Preparing a Check.   The first step in preparing a check is to complete the check stub or check register. This insures that the drawer will retain a record of each check issued. Second, the name of the payee is entered on the check. Third, the amount of the check is entered on the check in both figures and words. If the amount shown on the check in figures does not agree with the amount shown in words, the bank usually contacts the drawer for the correct amount or returns the check unpaid.

Care must be used in entering the amount on the check in order to avoid any possibility that the payee or a subsequent holder may change the amount. If the instructions below are followed in the preparation of a check, it will be difficult to change the amount.

(a)   The amount shown in figures should be entered so that there is no space between the dollar sign and the first digit of the amount.

(b)   The amount stated in words should be entered beginning at the extreme left on the line provided for this information. The cents should be entered in the form of a common fraction; if the check is for an even number of dollars, use two dashes or the word "no" as the numerator of the fraction. If a vacant space remains, a line should be drawn from the amount stated in words to the word "Dollars" on the same line with it, as shown in the illustration on page 174.

A machine frequently used to print the amount of a check in figures and in words is known as a **checkwriter**. The use of a checkwriter is desirable because it practically eliminates the possibility of changing the amount of a check.

The fourth step in preparing a check is to note the purpose for which the check is drawn in the lower left-hand corner of the check itself. Indicating the purpose on the check provides information for the benefit of the payee and provides a specific receipt for the drawer. In the fifth step, the signature of the drawer is written on the lower right hand corner of the check in the same manner as on the signature card.

Each check issued by a depositor will be returned by the bank on which it is drawn after the check has been paid. Canceled checks are returned to the depositor with a bank statement, which is usually sent by mail each month. Canceled checks will have been endorsed by the payee and any subsequent holders. They constitute receipts that the depositor should retain for future reference. They may be attached to the stubs from which they were removed originally or they may be filed.

Electronic Processing of Checks.   It is now nearly universal practice to use checks that, like deposit tickets, contain MICR (magnetic ink character recognition) numbers that permit processing by MICR equipment. In processing checks with electronic equipment, the first bank that handles the check imprints the amount in magnetic ink characters to further aid in the processing of the check. The amount is printed directly below the signature line in the lower right-hand corner of the check.

Checks imprinted with the bank's number, the depositor's number, and the amount—all in MICR characters—can be posted electronically to the customer's account. The two checks reproduced on page 174 illustrate magnetic ink characters along the lower margins.

NO. **207**			JAMES MICHAELS 4112 WEBER ST. ORLANDO, FL 32818-1123			NO. 207	63-1209 631
DATE *April 3* 19 --			PAY				
TO *Linclay Corp.*			TO THE			*April 3* 19 --	
FOR *April Rent*			ORDER OF *Linclay Corporation*			$ *300.00*	
ACCT. *Rent Expense*			*Three-hundred 00/100*			DOLLARS	
	DOLLARS	CENTS	FOR CLASSROOM USE ONLY				
BAL. BRO'T FOR'D	3,625	41	**WIZARD BANK**				
AMT. DEPOSITED			3711 Buena Vista Dr.				
TOTAL			Orlando, FL 32811-1314	BY	*James Michaels*		
AMT. THIS CHECK	300	00	⑆063112094⑆ 000⑆632475⑆				
BAL. CAR'D FOR'D	3,325	41					
NO. **208**			JAMES MICHAELS 4112 WEBER ST. ORLANDO, FL 32818-1123			NO. 208	63-1209 631
DATE *April 4* 19 --			PAY				
TO *Continental Mfg. Co.*			TO THE			*April 4* 19 --	
FOR *Inv. March 31*			ORDER OF *Continental Mfg. Co.*			$ *1,478.18*	
ACCT. *Accounts Payable*			FOR CLASSROOM USE ONLY				
	DOLLARS	CENTS	*One-thousand four hundred seventy-eight 18/100*			DOLLARS	
BAL. BRO'T FOR'D	3,325	41	**WIZARD BANK**				
AMT. DEPOSITED	1,694	20	3711 Buena Vista Dr.				
TOTAL	5,019	61	Orlando, FL 32811-1314	BY	*James Michaels*		
AMT. THIS CHECK	1,478	18	⑆063112094⑆ 000⑆632475⑆				
BAL. CAR'D FOR'D	3,541	43					

Checks and Stubs

Entering Banking Transactions. A depositor should keep a record of the transactions completed with the bank. The checkbook stubs, as shown in the illustration above, serve this purpose because they contain detailed information concerning each check written. The amount column on the check stub is used to record (1) the balance brought forward, (2) the amount of deposits to be added, and (3) the amount of each check to be subtracted. This information keeps a current record of all deposits made and checks issued. It also keeps the balance current in the checking account.

As the amount of each check is entered in the journal, a check mark is placed immediately after the account title written on the stub to indicate that the check has been entered. When the canceled check is subsequently received from the bank, the amount shown on the stub can be checkmarked to indicate that the canceled check has been received.

Records Kept by a Bank. The usual transactions completed by a bank with a depositor are:

1. Accepting deposits made by the depositor.
2. Paying checks issued by the depositor.
3. Lending money to the depositor.

4. Collecting the amounts of various kinds of commercial paper, such as matured notes or bonds and bond interest coupons, for the account of the depositor.
5. Buying and selling securities and insurance for the depositor.

The bank keeps an account for each depositor. These accounts represent liabilities of the bank. Thus, when the bank accepts a deposit, the account of the depositor is credited for the amount of the deposit. The deposit increases the bank's liability to the depositor. When the bank pays a check that has been drawn on the bank, it debits the account of the depositor for the amount of the check because this decreases the bank's liability to the depositor. If the bank makes a collection for the depositor, it credits the account of the depositor for the net amount of the collection. At the same time, the bank notifies the depositor that the collection has been made using a form (**credit advice**) similar to the illustration below.

Credit	⚡ **WIZARD BANK** 3711 Buena Vista Dr. Orlando, FL 32811-1314	
Statement Copy Items received for deposit or collection are accepted under the terms and conditions of this Bank, now in effect or as may be amended from time to time.	**Date** April 18, 19--	
Redemption of Treasury Bill Less collection charge		$20,000.00 20.00
Deposited for Credit of	We Credit your Account Number	**Total** $19,980.00
James Michaels	16-3247-5	Dept. Loan
		By D.K.
	⑆063112094⑆ 0001632475⑈	

Credit Advice

Bank Statement.   A statement of account issued to each depositor once a month by a bank is called a **bank statement**. An illustration of a bank statement is shown on page 176. Some banks provide statements that also present information regarding savings accounts and loan accounts, for those depositors who have such accounts. Very commonly, however, a separate statement is furnished for each type of account.

The statement illustrated is for a checking account. It is a report showing (1) the balance on deposit at the beginning of the period, (2) deposits and other amounts added during the period (credits), (3) withdrawals by check and other amounts subtracted during the period (debits), (4) the balance on deposit at the end of the period, (5) the average daily balance during the period, and (6) the minimum balance during the period. Besides the bank statement, the depositor also receives all checks paid by the bank during the period and any other forms representing items charged to the account.

Statement

⚡ WIZARD BANK

James Michaels
4112 Weber St.
Orlando, FL 32818-1123

Reference Number	16 3247 5
Statement Date	Nov. 21, 19--
Statement Instructions	

Page Number

Beginning Balance $2,721.51	No. of Deposits and Credits 2	We have added these deposits and credits totaling $2,599.31	No. of Withdrawals and Charges 15	We have subtracted these withdrawals and charges totaling $3,572.73	Resulting in a statement balance of $1,748.09
Document Count 17	Average daily balance this statement period $2,258.18		Minimum balance this statement period	Date 11/18/--	Amount $1,748.09

If your account does not balance, please see reverse side and report any discrepancy to our Customer Service Department

Date	Description	Amount	Balance
10/15	Beginning Balance		2,721.51
10/27	Check No. 210	-242.00	2,479.51
10/28	Check No. 211	-68.93	2,410.58
10/28	Check No. 212	-58.00	2,352.58
10/29	Deposit	867.00	3,219.58
11/3	Deposit	1,732.31	4,951.89
11/3	Check No. 214	-19.88	4,932.01
11/3	Check No. 215	-228.11	4,703.90
11/3	Check No. 217	-452.13	4,251.77
11/3	Check No. 219	-94.60	4,157.17
11/10	Check No. 220	-2,000.00	2,157.17
11/10	Check No. 221	-32.42	2,124.75
11/10	Check No. 223	-64.08	2,060.67
11/10	Check No. 225	-210.87	1,849.80
11/18	Check No. 227	-18.00	1,831.80
11/18	Check No. 228	-23.31	1,808.49
11/18	Check No. 229	-58.60	1,749.89
11/19	Service Charge	-1.80	1,748.09

EC - Error Correction		TR - Wire Transfer
OD - Overdrawn	RC - Return Check Charge	D/N-Day/Night

Bank Statement

Reconcile a bank statement.

▬ Reconciling the Bank Statement. The depositor's records of transactions must be brought into agreement with the bank's records of transactions at periodic intervals—usually once a month. After a bank statement is received, the depositor should try to make it agree with the bank balance record kept on the check stubs. This procedure is known as **reconciling the bank statement**. The balance shown on the bank statement may not be the same as the amount shown on the check stubs for one or more of the following reasons:

1. Checks issued during the period may not have been presented to the bank for payment before the statement was prepared. These are known as **outstanding checks**.

2. Deposits may not have been entered by the bank on the bank statement. These are known as **deposits in transit**. Such a deposit may have been mailed, or placed in the automated teller or night deposi-

tory and not entered by the bank until the day following the date of the statement.

3. The bank may have credited the depositor's account for an amount collected, but the depositor may not as yet have noted it on the check stubs since the credit advice has not yet been received.

4. Service charges or other charges may appear on the bank statement that the depositor has not entered on the check stubs.

5. The depositor may have made an error in keeping the bank account record.

6. The bank may have made an error in keeping its account with the depositor.

Each bank usually provides a form for completing the bank reconciliation on the back of the bank statement. If a depositor is unable to reconcile the bank statement, the bank should be notified immediately.

The following is a suggested procedure in reconciling the bank statement:

1. The amount of each deposit entered on the bank statement is compared with the amount entered on the check stubs. Any deposit entered on the check stub but not entered on the bank statement should be added to the bank statement balance as a deposit in transit.

2. The amount of each canceled check is compared both with the amount entered on the bank statement and with the amount entered on the depositor's check stubs. When making this comparison, it is a good plan to place a check mark by the amount entered on each check stub to indicate that the canceled check has been returned by the bank and its amount verified.

3. The outstanding checks are listed, totaled, and deducted from the bank balance. The information needed for this list may be obtained by examining the check stubs and noting the amounts that have not been checkmarked.

4. The amounts of any items listed on the bank statement that represent credits or charges to a depositor's account which have not been entered on the check stubs are added to or deducted from the balance on the check stubs. They are then entered in the journal that is being used for cash receipts and payments.

5. Any error discovered on the check stubs or bank statement will require an adjustment to the check stub balance or bank balance depending on the nature of the error. A journal entry might also be necessary to correct any check stub errors.

After completing the procedures for reconciling the bank statement, the adjusted balance shown on the check stubs should equal the adjusted bank balance. A reconciliation of the bank balance shown in the statement reproduced on page 176 with the most recent check stub balance is as follows:

example

James Michaels
Bank Reconciliation
November 21, 19--

1. Balance per bank statement, November 21		$1,748.09
2. Add deposit in transit, November 21		782.91
		$2,531.00
3. Deduct outstanding checks, November 21:		
No. 525	$163.00	
No. 530	28.47	
No. 532	247.20	438.67
4. Adjusted bank balance, November 21		$2,092.33
5. Balance per check stub, November 21		$2,095.03
6. Deduct: Bank service charge	$1.80	
7. Error on stub for Check No. 503	.90	2.70
8. Adjusted check stub balance		$2,092.33

In making the reconciliation of the James Michaels bank statement as of November 21, 19--, the following steps, which correspond with the numbers in the reconciliation, were completed:

1. The November 21 bank balance, $1,748.09, was copied from the bank statement.

2. A deposit of $782.91 not shown on the bank statement was added to the November 21 bank balance to agree with the check stub that reflected the deposit on that date.

3. The outstanding Checks Nos. 525, 530, and 532 were listed, totaled, and $438.67 was subtracted from the bank balance. These checks had not been presented to the bank for payment and thus were not returned with the bank statement.

4. The adjusted bank balance as of the close of business November 21 was calculated as $2,092.33.

5. The check stub balance as of November 21 was copied from the last check stub bearing that date, in the amount of $2,095.03.

6. A bank service charge of $1.80 shown at the bottom of the bank statement was subtracted from the check stub balance.

7. A checkbook error was discovered. Check No. 503 was written for $19.88 and entered in the check stub as $18.98. This error required the check stub balance to be decreased by $.90.

8. The adjusted check stub balance as of the close of business, November 21, was calculated as $2,092.33 and was equal to the adjusted November 21 bank balance.

In step number 6, a bank service charge was mentioned. A service charge may be made by a bank for the handling of checks and other items. The basis and the amount of such charges vary with different banks in different localities.

When a bank statement indicates that a service charge has been made, the depositor should enter the amount of the service charge in the journal by debiting an expense account, such as Miscellaneous Expense, and by crediting Cash.

Miscellaneous Expense...............................	1.80	
Cash..		1.80
Bank service charge for November.		

The error noted in step number 7 was discovered when the canceled checks that were returned were matched against the check stubs. It was found that, although Check No. 503 had been written for $19.88, the amount was shown as $18.98 on its stub. This is called a **transposition error**, because the "9" and the "8" were transposed; i.e., their order was reversed. On Stub No. 503, and the others that followed, the balance shown was $.90 overstated. The correct amount, $19.88, should be shown on Stub No. 503, and the balance shown on the stub of the last check used should be corrected by reducing the amount by $.90. If Check No. 503 was in payment of a telephone bill and a journal entry had been made for the same amount as shown on the stub ($18.98), an entry should be made debiting Telephone Expense and crediting Cash. Alternatively, since such a small amount was involved, the debit might be made to Miscellaneous Expense.

Telephone Expense (or Miscellaneous Expense)..........	.90	
Cash..		.90
Correction of checkbook error.		

Savings Account

Describe procedures for use of a bank savings account.

When a savings account is opened in a bank, a signature card must be signed by the depositor. By signing the signature card, the depositor agrees to abide by the rules and regulations of the bank. At this time, a **passbook** may be given to the depositor. This is a small book in which the bank teller enters the date and amount of each deposit or withdrawal. The passbook is to be presented at the bank or mailed to the bank along with a deposit or withdrawal slip, each time money is deposited or withdrawn from the account. An alternative practice to the passbook is to give the depositor a small register for recording deposits and withdrawals and a pad of deposit-withdrawal forms. Each time a deposit or withdrawal is made from a savings account, the appropriate part of one of the forms is filled in, signed, entered in the register and presented or mailed to the bank with deposit items or other documents. The bank gives a machine-printed receipt to the depositor or returns it by mail. There should be a separate savings account in the ledger to enter these activities.

At least once each quarter, the bank mails a credit advice to the depositor, indicating the amount of interest credited to the account. This should be entered in the depositor's register upon receipt. If a passbook is used, it should be presented or mailed to the bank, so that the credit advice can be entered by a teller. The depositor also should enter the amount in the journal by a debit to Cash and a credit to Interest Earned, as shown below. The interest is revenue earned and is taxable to the depositor.

```
Cash-Savings Account .............................      xxx
  Interest Earned ...................................           xxx
    Quarterly interest earned.
```

Traditionally, there are two principal differences between a savings account and a checking account. First, interest is paid regularly by the bank on a savings account. Second, withdrawals from a savings account can be made only at the bank or by mail by the depositor or an authorized agent. Depositors use checking accounts primarily as a convenient means of making payments, while savings accounts are used primarily as a means of accumulating funds with interest.

An increasingly common practice is for the bank to combine savings and checking accounts. The bank obtains the depositor's permission to make automatic transfers of funds from the savings portion to the checking portion whenever the latter falls below a specified minimum balance. This practice allows the depositor to earn interest on his or her account.

Interest-Earning Checking Accounts

Many checking accounts now earn interest on their average daily balances. The amount of such interest usually is determined and reported monthly on the depositor's bank statement. Such accounts commonly specify that a minimum balance must be maintained, and higher rates of interest may be offered if depositors agree to maintain larger minimum balances.

Electronic Funds Transfer

Electronic funds transfer (EFT) uses a computer rather than money or checks to complete transactions with the bank. Increasingly, this approach is being used to meet payrolls, process social security payments, and pay for retail purchases.

If employees agree to sign authorization forms, each pay period their employers will send a magnetic tape containing payroll information directly to the bank. The bank's computer will then debit the employer's account for the total payroll and credit each employee's checking account. The U.S. government will, on authorization, process social security payments in a similar manner. Customers of retail stores can insert special pre-coded plastic cards in store terminals and automatically transfer cash from their checking accounts to the store's checking account at the bank in payment for their purchases.

Building Your Accounting Knowledge

1. Name the five requirements with which a check must comply in order to be negotiable.
2. Why do banks usually require a new depositor to fill out a signature card? Why may more than one name appear on a signature card?
3. Describe the use of MICR numbers in the electronic processing of checks.
4. Briefly describe the functioning of a night depository.
5. Briefly describe how a depositor uses an automated teller machine.
6. Name the six major dollar amounts summarized on a bank statement.
7. If a depositor is unable to reconcile a bank statement, what should be done?
8. What journal entry should a depositor make when a bank statement indicates that there has been a service charge?
9. Explain how the traditional differences between a savings account and a checking account are changing.
10. Name three applications of electronic funds transfer in current use.

Assignment Box

To reinforce your understanding of the preceding text materials, you may complete the following:

　　　　Study Guide: Part B
　　　　Textbook: Exercises 5A5 through 5A7 or 5B5 through 5B7
　　　　　　　　　Problems 5A3 through 5A4 or 5B3 through 5B4

Expanding Your Business Vocabulary

What is the meaning of each of the following terms?

ABA numbers (p. 168)
automated teller machines (p. 171)
bank (p. 166)
bank statement (p. 175)
blank endorsement (p. 167)
cash (p. 156)
cash items (p. 156)
cash on hand (p. 156)
cash payments (p. 158)
cash receipts (p. 156)
cash register (p.157)
Cash short and over (p. 160)
check (p. 166)
check stub (p. 172)
checkwriter (p. 173)
compound entry (p. 165)
credit advice (p. 175)
debit advice (p. 170)

deposit ticket (p. 168)
deposits in transit (p. 176)
dishonored check (p. 170)
drawee (p. 167)
drawer (p. 167)
electronic funds transfer (p. 180)
embezzlement (p. 157)
endorsing (p. 167)
imprest method (p. 162)
internal control (pp. 157)
MICR numbers (p. 168)
NSF checks (p. 170)
negotiable (p. 167)
outstanding checks (p. 176)
overdraft (p. 170)
passbook (p. 179)
payee (p. 167)
petty cash fund (p. 161)

Demonstration Problem

Jason Kuhn's check stubs indicated a balance of $4,573.12 on March 31. This included a record of a deposit of $926.10 mailed to the bank on March 30 but not credited to Kuhn's account until April 1. In addition, the following checks were outstanding on March 31:

No. 462, $524.26	No. 473, $543.58
No. 465, $213.41	No. 476, $351.38
	No. 477, $197.45

The bank statement showed a balance of $5,419.00 as of March 31. The bank included a service charge on its March 31 statement with the date of 3/29 in the amount of $4.10. In matching the canceled checks and record of deposits with the stubs, it was discovered that Check No. 456, to Office Suppliers, Inc., for $93 was erroneously recorded on the stub for $39, causing the bank balance on that stub and those following to be $54 too large.

Jason Kuhn maintains a $200.00 petty cash fund. His petty cash payments record showed the following totals at the end of March of the current year.

Automobile Expense	$ 32.40
Postage Expense	27.50
Charitable Contributions Expense	35.00
Telephone Expense	6.20
Travel & Entertainment Expense	38.60
Miscellaneous Expense	17.75
Jason Kuhn, Drawing	40.00
Total	$197.45

This left a balance of $2.55 in the petty cash fund.

Required:

1. Prepare a bank reconciliation statement for Jason Kuhn as of March 31, 19--.
2. Journalize the entries that should be made by Jason Kuhn on his books as of March 31, 19--: (a) as a result of the bank reconciliation and (b) to replenish the petty cash fund.
3. Show proof that, after these entries, the total of the cash and petty cash account balances equals $4,715.02.

Solution

1.

Jason Kuhn
Bank Reconciliation
March 31, 19--

Balance per bank statement, March 31		$5,419.00
Add deposit in transit, March 30		926.10
		$6,345.10
Deduct outstanding checks		
No. 462.....................................	$524.26	
No. 465.....................................	213.41	
No. 473.....................................	543.58	
No. 476.....................................	351.38	
No. 477.....................................	197.45	1,830.08
Adjusted bank balance, March 31.........................		$4,515.02
Balance, per check stub, March 31		$4,573.12
Deduct: Bank service charge	$ 4.10	
Error on stub for Check No. 456	54.00	58.10
Adjusted check stub balance		$4,515.02

2. a. Mar. 31 Miscellaneous Expense 4.10
        Accounts Payable—Office Suppliers, Inc. 54.00
        Cash................................... 58.10
        Bank transactions for March.

     b. Mar. 31 Automobile Expense 32.40
        Postage Expense 27.50
        Charitable Contributions Expense 35.00
        Telephone Expense 6.20
        Travel & Entertainment Expense 38.60
        Miscellaneous Expense 17.75
        Jason Kuhn, Drawing 40.00
        Cash 197.45
        Replenishment of petty cash fund—
        Check No. 477

3. Cash in bank:

Check stub balance, March 31	$4,573.12
Less bank charges	58.10
Adjusted cash in bank	$4,515.02

Cash on hand:

Petty cash fund	$ 2.55
Add replenishment	197.45
Adjusted cash on hand	$ 200.00
Total cash in bank and petty cash on hand	$4,715.02

Note: Now that you have reviewed the Demonstration Problem and Solution you may complete the **Mastery Problem** at the end of the chapter activities.

Applying Accounting Concepts

Series A

Exercise 5A1—Journal Entries for Cash Transactions. José Calderon is a financial consultant. He keeps three cash accounts in his ledger: (1) Cash On Hand; (2) Cash in Regal Bank; and (3) Cash in Township Bank. Prepare the appropriate journal entry for each of the following transactions:

Sept. **4** Received $2,500.00 in professional fees from clients.
   12 Deposited $500.00 in the Regal Bank account.
   14 Deposited $1,000.00 in the Township Bank account.
   18 Paid Consultants Supply Co. (accounts payable) by check on Regal Bank, $125.00.
   21 Paid Office Equipment Co. (accounts payable) by check on Township Bank, $750.00
   29 Recorded bank service charges (miscellaneous expense) as follows: Regal Bank, $1.90; Township Bank, $2.25.

Exercise 5A2—Journal Entries for Cash Short & Over. (a) In attempting to prove cash, a shortage of $16.80 is found. Prepare the appropriate journal entry to recognize this shortage. (b) Assume that cash was found to be over by $4.50. Prepare the appropriate journal entry to recognize the overage.

Exercise 5A3—Journal Entry to Establish and Replenish Petty Cash. (a) On January 1, Betty Jane's Dance Studio established a petty cash fund for $300. Prepare the journal entry for this transaction. (b) The following payments were made from the fund during January:

Telephone Expense	$10.20
Automobile Expense	66.80
Charitable Contributions Expense	54.50
Postage Expense	27.80
Miscellaneous Expense	30.00
Total payments	$189.30

Prepare the journal entry to replenish the fund on January 31.

Exercise 5A4—Petty Cash Payments Record. David Castens, a computer consultant, completed the following petty cash transactions during the month of November.

Nov. 1 Issued check for $250.00 payable to Carolyn Landry, a part-time employee who serves as petty cash fund cashier. The check is cashed by Carolyn and the proceeds placed in a petty cash fund.

3 Reimbursed Castens $13.25 for amount spent entertaining a client at lunch. Petty Cash Voucher No. 1.

6 Paid $24.60 to Breier Auto for servicing company automobile. Petty Cash Voucher No. 2.

10 Gave Castens $25.00 for personal use. Petty Cash Voucher No. 3. (Use special amount column at extreme right side of petty cash payments record.)

13 Gave the American Heart Association a $20.00 donation. Petty Cash Voucher No. 4.

15 Paid $16.30 for typewriter repairs. Petty Cash Voucher No. 5 (Miscellaneous Expense).

16 Paid $9.75 for mailing a package. Petty Cash Voucher No. 6.

21 Reimbursed Castens $5.75 for a long distance telephone call. Petty Cash Voucher No. 7.

24 Paid $22.00 for postage stamps. Petty Cash Voucher No. 8.

27 Donated $15.00 to Grace Hill Settlement House. Petty Cash Voucher No. 9.

30 Paid Paul Powell $6.50 for washing the company automobile. Petty Cash Voucher No. 10.

Open a petty cash payments record for the month of November, 19-- with the following column headings:

Day	Description	Voucher No.	Total Amount	Auto Expense	Postage Expense	Charitable Contributions Expense

Telephone Expense	Travel & Entertainment Expense	Miscellaneous Expense	Account	Amount

Record the preceding petty cash transactions in the petty cash payments record. Then, foot all of the amount columns, determine the total needed to replenish the fund, and complete the record assuming the petty cash fund is replenished on November 30.

Exercise 5A5—Deposit Ticket Preparation. Kimberly J. Dykas is preparing a daily deposit for her checking account in the Wizard Bank at the close of business on August 15, 19--. She has the following items to deposit:

$20 bills - 25	500.	quarters - 45	11.25
$10 bills - 40	40.	dimes - 20	2.00
$ 5 bills - 30	150	nickels - 35	1.75
$ 1 bills - 65	65.	pennies - 60	.60
half dollars - 5	2.50		

cur 755.
18.10 coin

Checks from customers were in the following amounts:

$620.25
$370.75
$440.00

1431.

Complete the following information for Dykas' deposit ticket:

Date _____
Currency _____
Coins _____
Checks _____
_____
_____
_____

Total deposit _____

Exercise 5A6—Reconciliation of Bank Statement. The following information relates to the bank account of Brenda's Bridal Shop on October 31:

Balance per check stub, October 31		$4,482.12
Balance per bank statement, October 31		3,911.08
October 31 deposit not shown on bank statement		1,390.00
Bank service charge shown on bank statement		4.50
Outstanding checks, October 31:		
No. 220	$295.00	
No. 223	76.28	
No. 231	452.18	823.46

Prepare a bank reconciliation as of October 31.

Exercise 5A7—Journal Entries for Bank Reconciliation. (a) A depositor's bank statement shows a service charge of $6.30 (Miscellaneous Expense). Prepare the journal entry for this service charge. (b) Comparison of the canceled checks with the check stubs revealed that Check No. 121 which had been written for $43.94 was shown as $34.94 on the check stub. Check No. 121 was used to pay an electric bill of $43.94 (Utilities Expense). Prepare the journal entry to correct this error.

Series B

Exercise 5B1—Journal Entries for Cash Transactions. Deborah Douglas is an attorney. She keeps three cash accounts in her ledger: (1) Cash on Hand; (2) Cash in Cougar Bank; and (3) Cash in Lemay Bank. Prepare the appropriate journal entry for each of the following transactions:

Aug. 3 Received $3,500.00 in legal fees from clients.
11 Deposited $1,500.00 in the Cougar Bank account.
15 Deposited $750.00 in the Lemay Bank account.
21 Paid Legal Supply Co. (accounts payable) by check on Cougar Bank, $250.00.
24 Paid Edox Equipment Co. (accounts payable) by check on Lemay Bank, $500.00.
31 Recorded bank service charges (miscellaneous expense) as follows: Cougar Bank, $2.65; Lemay Bank, $1.80.

Exercise 5B2—Journal Entries for Cash Short & Over. (a) In attempting to prove cash, a shortage of $12.60 is found. Prepare the appropriate journal entry to recognize this shortage. (b) Assume that cash was found to be over by $3.40. Prepare the appropriate journal entry to recognize the overage.

Exercise 5B3—Journal Entry to Establish and Replenish Petty Cash. (a) On July 1, Billy Bob's Photo Studio established a petty cash fund for $225.00. Prepare the journal entry for this transaction. (b) The following payments were made from the fund in July.

Telephone Expense	$ 7.65
Automobile Expense	50.10
Supplies	41.30
Postage Expense	19.85
Miscellaneous Expense	$ 22.50
Total payments	$141.40

Prepare the journal entry to replenish the fund on July 31.

Exercise 5B4—Petty Cash Payments Record. Susan Zachary, a management consultant, completed the following petty cash transactions during the month of May:

May 1 Issued check for $200.00 payable to Steven Michelstein, a part-time employee who serves as petty cash fund cashier. The check is cashed by Steven and the proceeds placed in a petty cash fund.

4 Paid $22.75 to Auto Tune for servicing company automobile. Petty Cash Voucher No. 1.

8 Reimbursed Zachary $12.50 for amount spent entertaining a client at lunch. Petty Cash Voucher No. 2.

11 Gave the American Cancer Society a $15.00 donation. Petty Cash Voucher No. 3.

12 Gave Zachary $30.00 for personal use. Petty Cash voucher No. 4. (Use special amount column at extreme right side of petty cash payments record.)

15 Paid $9.25 for mailing a package. Petty Cash Voucher No. 5.

17 Paid $17.60 for typewriter repairs. Petty Cash Voucher No. 6 (Miscellaneous Expense).

19 Donated $25.00 to Camp Wyman. Petty Cash Voucher No. 7.

23 Reimbursed Zachary $6.25 for a long distance telephone call. Petty Cash Voucher No. 8.

26 Paid Gene McNary $5.75 for washing the company automobile. Petty Cash Voucher No. 9.

31 Paid $44.00 for postage stamps. Petty Cash Voucher No. 10.

Open a petty cash payments record for the month of May, 19-- with the following column headings:

Day	Description	Voucher No.	Total Amount	Auto Expense	Postage Expense	Charitable Contributions Expense

Telephone Expense	Travel & Entertainment Expense	Miscellaneous Expense	Account	Amount

Record the preceding petty cash transactions in the petty cash payments record. Then, foot all of the amount columns, determine the total needed to replenish the fund, and complete the record assuming the petty cash fund is replenished on May 31.

Exercise 5B5—Deposit Ticket Preparation. Thomas J. Carmody is preparing a daily deposit for his checking account in The Wizard Bank at the close of business on March 16, 19--. He has the following items to deposit:

$20 bills - 30	quarters - 55
$10 bills - 35	dimes - 30
$ 5 bills - 40	nickels - 45
$ 1 bills - 72	pennies - 85
half dollars - 4	

Checks from customers were in the following amounts:

$760.00
$420.00
$447.85

Complete the following information for Carmody's deposit ticket:

Date	_____
Currency	_____
Coins	_____
Checks	_____
	_____
	_____
	_____
Total deposit	_____

Exercise 5B6—Reconciliation of Bank Statement. The following information relates to the bank account of Bruce's Bicycle Shop on April 30:

Balance per check stub, April 30		$1,120.65
Balance per bank statement, April 30		977.77
April 30 deposit not shown on bank statement		347.50
Bank service charge shown on bank statement		1.25
Outstanding checks, April 30:		
No. 430	$73.75	
No. 434	19.07	
No. 442	113.05	205.87

Prepare a bank reconciliation as of April 30.

Exercise 5B7—Journal Entries for Bank Reconciliation. (a) A depositor's bank statement shows a service charge of $5.25 (Miscellaneous Expense). Prepare the journal entry for this service charge. (b) Comparison of the cancelled checks with the check stubs revealed that Check No. 309 which had been written for $25.20 was shown as $22.50 on the check stub. Check No. 309 was used to pay a telephone bill of $25.20 (Telephone Expense). Prepare the journal entry to correct this error.

Series A

Problem 5A1 — Journal Entries for Cash Transactions; Posting to Ledger; Trial Balance

Rich Lambakis operates an appliance repair business called Rich's Renewal Shop. Lambakis's book of original entry is a general journal. A petty cash fund of $300.00 is maintained.

The following transactions occurred during the month of June:

June 2 Paid the June shop rent, $720.00.
3 Received a check for $320.00 from Ken Watt for repairing his refrigerator.
6 Paid Holdman's Hardware $134.00 for supplies.
9 Paid $127.00 for new soldering iron.
10 Received a check for $268.00 from Marietta Romak for repairing her dryer.
13 Withdrew $200.00 for personal use.
16 Gave the Epilepsy Foundation $50.00.
17 Paid the June telephone bill, $58.00.
20 Received a check for $236.00 from J. Little for repairing his washer.
23 Paid garage bill of $58.00 for servicing delivery truck.
27 Paid B & G Company $150.00 on account.
30 Received a check for $228.00 from Jan Laski for repairing her dishwasher.
30 Replenished the petty cash fund. In order to make this journal entry you must use the petty cash data given below.

Petty Cash Data

Telephone Expense	$ 5.20
Supplies	48.40
Truck Expense	57.40
Charitable Contributions Expense	20.00
Postage Expense	29.80
Miscellaneous Expense	9.50

30 In attempting to prove cash, a shortage of $16.72 was found. The cause of the shortage could not be determined.

Chart of Accounts

Account	Account No.	June 1 Balance
Cash..	111	$ 3,480.00 dr.
Petty Cash.................................	112	300.00 dr.
Supplies....................................	151	929.80 dr.
Equipment.................................	181	5,900.00 dr.
Truck......................................	185	11,000.00 dr.
Accounts Payable.........................	218	1,220.00 cr.
Rich Lambakis, Capital....................	311	14,542.60 cr.
Rich Lambakis, Drawing...................	312	1,650.00 dr.
Repairing Fees............................	411	12,480.00 cr.
Rent Expense..............................	541	3,600.00 dr.
Telephone Expense........................	545	360.40 dr.
Truck Expense.............................	546	675.00 dr.
Charitable Contributions Expense..........	557	80.00 dr.
Postage Expense...........................	564	137.60 dr.
Cash Short & Over........................	569	12.20 cr.
Miscellaneous Expense.....................	572	142.00 dr.

Required:

1. Using four-column ledger accounts, enter the preceding beginning balances in each of the accounts as of June 1, 19--.
2. Journalize the June transactions. Number the journal beginning with page 4.
3. Post the journal entries to the ledger accounts.
4. Prepare a trial balance as of June 30, 19--.

Problem 5A2   Petty Cash Payments Record

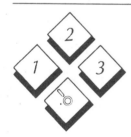

Robin Lonsbury, who operates a pre-owned clothing business, had a balance of $300 in the petty cash fund as of November 1. During November the following petty cash transactions were completed.

Nov. 1 Paid $18.00 for stamps. Petty Cash Voucher No. 61.
      2 Paid $9.15 for typewriter ribbons. Petty Cash Voucher No. 62.
      6 Paid $14.85 for lubricating car. Petty Cash Voucher No. 63.
      7 Made a donation to Easter Seals, $35.00. Petty Cash Voucher No. 64.
      8 Paid $5.25 for October newspapers. Petty Cash Voucher No. 65.
     13 Paid $12.15 for office supplies. Petty Cash Voucher No. 66.
     14 Paid $13.60 for repairing tire. Petty Cash Voucher No. 67.
     20 Donated $15.00 to the Salvation Army. Petty Cash Voucher No. 68.
     21 Paid $16.42 for office supplies. Petty Cash Voucher No. 69.
     22 Reimbursed Lonsbury $12.00 for entertaining a customer. Petty Cash Voucher No. 70.
     27 Paid $18.00 for newspaper ad. Petty Cash Voucher No. 71.
     27 Paid the postman $1.56 for postage due. Petty Cash Voucher No. 72.

28 Paid $60.00 for a filing cabinet found at a garage sale. Petty Cash Voucher No. 73. (Charge to Office Equipment.)

29 Reimbursed Lonsbury $4.80 for a long distance phone call. Petty Cash Voucher No. 74.

29 Paid $22.83 for typewriter servicing. Petty Cash Voucher No. 75.

30 Rendered report of petty cash payments for month and replenished the fund.

Required:

1. Enter the petty cash payments for November on page 11 of a petty cash payments record with the following columns:

Day	Description	Voucher No.	Total Amount	Auto Expense	Postage Expense	Charitable Contributions Expense

Telephone Expense	Supplies Expense	Miscellaneous Expense	Account	Amount

2. Prove the petty cash payments record by footing the amount columns and proving the totals. Enter the totals and rule the amount columns with single and double lines.

3. Bring down the balance in the petty cash fund below the ruling in the Description column, enter the amount received to replenish the fund, and enter the total amount to be forwarded to the top of a new page for December.

Problem 5A3   Signature Card Preparation; Check and Stub Preparation; Reconciliation of Bank Statement

---

Note: Working papers are required to work this problem.

Assume that you are engaged in the professional practice of public accounting. Your office is located at 1010 Market St., St. Louis, MO 63166-5024. You begin your practice with an initial investment of $10,000 in cash. In completing this problem, you are required to open a checking account, make deposits, write checks and reconcile a bank statement. The working papers consist of the following:

> A signature card.
> Blank checks (with stubs) to be issued during October.
> Checks received from clients during October.
> A blank deposit ticket.
> The bank statement for October.
> Statement paper to prepare a bank reconciliation.

During the month of October the following bank transactions were completed. The title of the account to be debited for each check is given in parentheses.

Oct. 2 Issued Check No. 1 to the Romito Realty Co. for October rent, $1,000. (Rent Expense)

   9 Issued Check No. 2 to Dennis Supply Co. in payment of stationery and supplies purchased, $254.65. (Stationery and Supplies)

  12 Issued Check No. 3 to Speed-E-Tax Service Co. in full settlement of its account, $966. (Accounts Payable)

  16 Issued Check No. 4 to Midwest Telephone Co. in payment of telephone bill, $102.50. (Telephone Expense)

  20 Issued Check No. 5 to Nolan Office Interiors in payment of office equipment purchased $1,422.35. (Office Equipment)

  23 Issued Check No. 6 to Steve's Garage in payment for automobile service, $57.12. (Automobile Expense)

  27 Issued Check No. 7 payable to Cash, for personal use, $300. (Student, Drawing)

  30 Deposited coins amounting to $41.34, currency amounting to $324, and the checks from clients reproduced in the working papers. Prepare the deposit ticket.

  31 Issued Check No. 8 to Jubilee Janitorial Service in payment of their account, $93.75. (Accounts Payable)

Required:

1. On October 2, you open a checking account in the Wizard Bank with a deposit of $10,000. Fill out the required signature card. Your account number is 15-4273-6.
2. Enter the amount of the initial deposit on the first stub of your checkbook.
3. Fill in the stubs and write the checks as indicated by the narrative of bank transactions.
4. Prepare a bank reconciliation as of October 31.

Problem 5A4   Reconciliation of Bank Statement

George Sachs' check stubs indicated a balance of $8,142.84 on July 31. This included a record of a $1,400.00 deposit mailed to the bank on July 30 but not credited to Sachs' account until August 1. In addition, the following checks were outstanding on July 31.

No. 283, $422.00	No. 291, $215.52
No. 289, $93.96	No. 294, $34.60

In matching the canceled checks and record of deposits with the stubs, it was discovered that Check No. 278 for $1,100.00 was improperly recorded on the stub as $1,010.00, causing the bank balance on that stub and those following to be $90.00 too large.

Required:

Based on the information above, prepare a reconciliation of Sachs' check stub balance with the bank statement balance shown below. Note the service charge on July 28.

Statement				🎩 WIZARD BANK	

George Sachs
3615 Harmann Estate Dr.
Orlando, FL 32811-5256

Reference Number	25 6319 2	Page Number

Statement Date | July 31, 19--

Statement Instructions

Beginning Balance $8,320.16	No. of Deposits and Credits 3	We have added these deposits and credits totaling $5,163.20	No. of Withdrawals and Charges 14	We have subtracted these withdrawals and charges totaling $6,068.14	Resulting in a statement balance of $7,415.22
Document Count	Average daily balance this statement period		Minimum balance this statement period	Date	Amount

If your account does not balance, please see reverse side and report any discrepancy to our Customer Service Department

Date	Description	Amount	Balance
7/1	Beginning Balance		8,320.16
7/3	Check No. 281	-270.22	8,049.94
7/4	Check No. 282	-1,403.66	6,646.28
7/4	Check No. 284	-403.32	6,242.96
7/7	Deposit	2,220.00	8,462.96
7/10	Check No. 285	-132.30	8,330.66
7/12	Deposit	1,600.00	9,930.66
7/12	Check No. 287	-673.44	9,257.22
7/12	Check No. 288	-232.80	9,024.42
7/14	Check No. 286	-1,100.00	7,924.42
7/17	Check No. 290	-376.00	7,548.42
7/19	Deposit	1,343.20	8,891.62
7/19	Check No. 292	-596.32	8,295.30
7/21	Check No. 295	-30.60	8,264.70
7/24	Check No. 293	-195.78	8,068.92
7/28	Service Charge	-3.70	8,065.22
7/28	Check No. 296	-500.00	7,565.22
7/31	Check No. 297	-150.00	7,415.22

EC - Error Correction		TR - Wire Transfer
OD - Overdrawn	RC - Return Check Charge	D/N-Day/Night

Series B

Problem 5B1   Journal Entries for Cash Transactions; Posting to Ledger; Trial Balance

Fred Cohen operates a furniture refinishing business called Fred's Furniture Finishers. Cohen's book of original entry is a general journal. A petty cash fund of $225.00 is maintained.

A narrative of transactions occurring during the month of July appears below.

July 3 Paid the July shop rent, $450.00.
5 Received a check for $420.00 from Morris Arky for refinishing an antique chest of drawers.
6 Paid Smith Hardware $110.00 for supplies.
7 Paid $130.00 for new finishing tool.
10 Received a check for $335.00 from N. Carmody for refinishing her dining table and chairs.
12 Withdrew $150.00 for personal use.
14 Gave the Kidney Foundation $35.00.
17 Paid the July telephone bill, $42.00.
21 Received a check for $211.00 from A. McManus for refinishing his bedroom suite.
24 Paid garage bill of $47.00 for servicing delivery truck.
27 Paid L & W Company $110.00 on account.
28 Received a check for $214.00 from Martin Koshner for refinishing his fireplace mantel.
31 Replenished the petty cash fund. In order to make this journal entry you must use the petty cash data given below.

Petty Cash Data

Telephone Expense	$ 3.90
Supplies	36.30
Truck Expense	43.05
Charitable Contributions Expense	15.00
Postage Expense	21.35
Miscellaneous Expense	7.25

31 In attempting to prove cash, a shortage of $12.54 was found. The cause of the shortage could not be determined.

Chart of Accounts

Account	Account No.	July 1 Balance
Cash	111	$ 2,610.00 dr.
Petty Cash	112	225.00 dr.
Supplies	151	697.35 dr.
Equipment	181	4,425.00 dr.
Truck	185	8,250.00 dr.
Accounts Payable	218	915.00 cr.
Fred Cohen, Capital	311	10,906.95 cr.
Fred Cohen, Drawing	312	1,237.50 dr.
Repairing Fees	411	9,360.00 cr.
Rent Expense	541	2,700.00 dr.
Telephone Expense	545	270.30 dr.
Truck Expense	546	506.25 dr.
Charitable Contributions Expense	557	60.00 dr.
Postage Expense	564	103.20 dr.
Cash Short & Over	569	9.15 cr.
Miscellaneous Expense	572	106.50 dr.

Required:

1. Using four-column ledger accounts, enter the preceding beginning balances in each of the accounts as of July 1, 19--.
2. Number the journal beginning with page 4. Journalize the July transactions.
3. Post the journal entries to the ledger accounts.
4. Prepare a trial balance as of July 31, 19--.

Problem 5B2   Petty Cash Payments Record

Thelma Caskey, who operates a greeting card business, had a balance of $250.00 in the petty cash fund as of December 1. During December the following petty cash transactions were completed.

Dec.		
	1	Paid $15.00 for stamps. Petty Cash Voucher No. 71.
	3	Paid $7.60 for typewriter ribbons. Petty Cash Voucher No. 72.
	5	Paid $12.45 for lubricating car. Petty Cash Voucher No. 73.
	7	Made a donation to Christmas Seals, $30.00. Petty Cash Voucher No. 74.
	8	Paid $4.40 for November newspapers. Petty Cash Voucher No. 75.
	12	Paid $10.25 for office supplies. Petty Cash Voucher No. 76.
	14	Paid $11.30 for repairing tire. Petty Cash Voucher No. 77.
	19	Donated $10.00 to Red Cross. Petty Cash Voucher No. 78.
	21	Paid $13.75 for office supplies. Petty Cash Voucher No. 79.
	22	Reimbursed Caskey $10.00 for entertaining a customer. Petty Cash Voucher No. 80.
	26	Paid $15.00 for newspaper ad. Petty Cash Voucher No. 81.
	27	Paid the postman $1.28 for postage due. Petty Cash Voucher No. 82.
	28	Paid $50.00 for a filing cabinet. Petty Cash Voucher No. 83. (Charge to Office Equipment.)
	29	Reimbursed Caskey $4.05 for a long distance phone call. Petty Cash Voucher No. 84.
	29	Paid $18.16 for typewriter servicing. Petty Cash Voucher No. 85.
	29	Rendered report of petty cash payments for month and replenished the fund.

Required:

1. Enter the petty cash payments for December on page 12 of a petty cash payments record with the following columns:

Day	Description	Voucher No.	Total Amount	Auto Expense	Postage Expense	Charitable Contributions Expense

Telephone Expense	Supplies	Misc. Expense	Account	Amount

2. Prove the petty cash payments record by footing the amount columns and proving the totals. Enter the totals and rule the amount columns with single and double lines.

3. Bring down the balance in the petty cash fund below the ruling in the Description column, enter the amount received to replenish the fund, and enter the total amount to be forwarded to the top of a new page for January.

Problem 5B3   Signature Card Preparation; Check and Stub Preparation; Reconciliation of Bank Statement

---

Note: Working papers are required to work this problem.

Assume that you are engaged in the professional practice of public accounting. Your office is located at 230 Vine St., Hannibal, MO 63401-5972. You begin your practice with an initial investment of $12,000 in cash. In completing this problem, you are required to open a checking account, make deposits, write checks, and reconcile a bank statement. The working papers consist of the following:

> A signature card.
> Blank checks (with stubs) to be issued during September.
> Checks received from clients during September.
> A blank deposit ticket.
> The bank statement for September.
> Statement paper to prepare a bank reconciliation.

During the month of September the following bank transactions were completed. The title of the account to debited for each check is given in parentheses.

Sept. 1 Issued Check No. 1 to the Mays Realty Co. for September rent, $1,400.00 (Rent Expense)

8 Issued Check No. 2 to Finley Supply Co. in payment of stationery and supplies purchased, $339.54. (Stationery and Supplies)

12 Issued Check No. 3 to Compu-Tax Service Co. in full settlement of its account, $1,288.00. (Accounts Payable)

15 Issued Check No. 4 to MoKan Telephone Co. in payment of telephone bill, $83.36. (Telephone Expense)

20 Issued Check No. 5 to Haworth Office Outfitters in payment of office equipment purchased, $1,867.50. (Office Equipment)

22 Issued Check No. 6 to Sam's Super Service in payment of automobile service, $76.22. (Automobile Expense)

27 Issued Check No. 7 payable to Cash, for personal use, $400.00 (Student, Drawing)

28 Deposited coins amounting to $45.12, currency amounting to $432.00, and the checks from clients reproduced in the working papers. Prepare the deposit ticket.

29 Issued Check No. 8 to Killian Janitorial Service in payment on account, $125.00. (Accounts Payable)

Required:

1. On September 1, you open a checking account in the Wizard Bank with a deposit of $12,000. Fill out the required signature card. Your account number is 20-12107-73.

2. Enter the amount of the initial deposit on the first stub of your checkbook.

3. Fill in the stubs and write the checks as indicated by the narrative of bank transactions.

4. Prepare a bank reconciliation as of September 30.

Problem 5B4   Reconciliation of Bank Statement

John Calhoun's check stubs indicated a balance of $6,069.40 on June 30. This included a record of a $1,050.00 deposit mailed to the bank on June 29 but not credited to Calhoun's account until July 1. In addition, the following checks were outstanding on June 30:

No. 383, $316.50	No. 391, $161.64
No. 389, $ 70.47	No. 394, $ 25.95

In matching the canceled checks and record of deposits with the stubs, it was discovered that check No. 378 for $852.00 was improperly recorded on the stub as $825.00, causing the bank balance on that stub and those following to be $27.00 too large.

Required:

Based on the information above, prepare a reconciliation of Calhoun's check stub balance with the bank statement balance shown on page 198. Note the service charge on June 28.

**Mastery
Problem**

Turner Excavation maintains a checking account and has decided to open a petty cash fund.

Statement   ⚡ **WIZARD BANK**

John Calhoun
3 Westerly Lane
Winter Park, FL 32789-2397

Reference Number	24 6438 7	Page Number
Statement Date	June 30, 19--	
Statement Instructions		

Beginning Balance $6,240.12	No. of Deposits and Credits 3	We have added these deposits and credits totaling $3,872.40	No. of Withdrawals and Charges 14	We have subtracted these withdrawals and charges totaling $4,548.16	Resulting in a statement balance of $5,564.36
Document Count	Average daily balance this statement period		Minimum balance this statement period	Date	Amount

If your account does not balance, please see reverse side and report any discrepancy to our Customer Service Department

Date	Description	Amount	Balance
6/1	Beginning Balance		6,240.12
6/2	Check No. 380	-202.66	6,037.46
6/5	Check No. 382	-1,052.75	4,984.71
6/5	Check No. 381	-302.49	4,682.22
6/7	Deposit	1,665.00	6,347.22
6/8	Check No. 384	-99.23	6,247.99
6/12	Deposit	1,200.00	7,447.99
6/12	Check No. 387	-505.08	6,942.91
6/12	Check No. 385	-174.60	6,768.31
6/15	Check No. 388	-825.00	5,943.31
6/16	Check No. 386	-282.00	5,661.31
6/19	Deposit	1,007.40	6,668.71
6/19	Check No. 392	-447.24	6,221.47
6/22	Check No. 390	-22.95	6,198.52
6/26	Check No. 393	-144.06	6,054.46
6/28	Service Charge	-2.60	6,051.86
6/28	Check No. 396	-375.00	5,676.86
6/30	Check No. 395	-112.50	5,564.36

EC - Error Correction
OD - Overdrawn

RC - Return Check Charge

TR - Wire Transfer
D/N-Day/Night

Required:

1. Record each of the following transactions in either a two-column journal or a petty cash payments record:

July 2 Established a petty cash fund by issuing Check No. 301 for $100.00.

5 Issued Check No. 302 to pay office rent, $650.00.

5 Paid $25.00 out of the petty cash fund for postage. Voucher No. 1.

7 Paid $30.00 out of the petty cash fund for delivery of flowers for the secretaries (Miscellaneous Expense). Voucher No. 2.

8 Paid $20.00 out of the petty cash fund to repair a tire on the company truck. Voucher No. 3.

12 Paid $22.00 out of the petty cash fund for a newspaper advertisement. Voucher No. 4.

13 Issued Check No. 303 to replenish the petty cash fund. Foot, prove, total, and rule the petty cash payments record. Record the balance

and the amount needed to replenish the fund in the Description column of the petty cash payment record.

15 Issued Check No. 304 for office equipment, $525.00.

17 Issued Check No. 305 for the purchase of supplies, $133.00.

18 Issued Check No. 306 to pay attorney fees, $1,000.

20 Paid $26.00 out of the petty cash fund to reimburse an employee for expenses incurred to repair the company truck. Voucher No. 5.

24 Paid $12.50 out of the petty cash fund for telephone calls made from a phone booth. Voucher No. 6.

28 Paid $25.00 out of the petty cash fund as a contribution to the YMCA. Voucher No. 7.

30 Issued Check No. 307 to the Times Newspaper for an advertisement, $200.20.

31 Issued Check No. 308 to replenish the petty cash fund. Foot, prove, total, and rule the petty cash payments record. Record the balance and the amount needed to replenish the fund in the Description column of the petty cash payments record.

2. The following bank statement was received in the mail. Deposits were made on July 6 for $3,500.00 and on July 29 for $2,350.00. The checkbook balance on July 31 is $4,331.55. Prepare a bank reconciliation statement and

Statement — **Merchant's National Bank**

Turner Excavation
220 Main St
Oakhurst, NJ 07755-1461

Reference Number 16 3247 5 · Statement Date July 31, 19--

Beginning Balance	No. of Deposits and Credits	We have added these deposits and credits totaling	No. of Withdrawals and Charges	We have subtracted these withdrawals and charges totaling	Resulting in a statement balance of
$1,250.25	1	$3,500.00	6	$1,512.50	$3,237.75

Date	Description	Amount	Balance
7/1	Beginning Balance		1,250.25
7/5	Check No. 301	-100.00	1,150.25
7/8	Check No. 302	-655.00	495.25
7/9	Deposit	3,500.00	3,995.25
7/15	Check No. 303	-97.00	3,898.25
7/20	Check No. 304	-525.00	3,373.25
7/28	Check No. 305	-133.00	3,240.25
7/31	Service Charge	-2.50	3,237.75

EC - Error Correction · OD - Overdrawn · TR - Wire Transfer · RC - Return Check Charge · D/N-Day/Night

Depositor agrees and Bank accepts business upon the terms and conditions of Bank's rules and regulations now in effect or as may be hereafter adopted.

make any necessary journal entries. Notice the discrepancy in Check No. 302 that cleared the bank for $655.00. This check was written on July 5th for rent expense, but was incorrectly entered on the check stub and in the journal as $650.00.

CHAPTER 6

Accounting for Purchases and Payments

Careful study of this chapter should enable you to:

- Explain why the cash, or modified cash basis of periodic income determination usually is unsuited to a merchandising business, and why the accrual basis gives a more meaningful measure of periodic income.

- Describe and use the following source documents:

  1. Purchase requisition
  2. Purchase order
  3. Purchase invoice
  4. Freight bill
  5. Credit memorandum

- Define and explain the purpose of and compute trade discounts and cash discounts and describe the most common terms of purchase.

- Define and explain the purpose of the following accounts used in the calculation of cost of goods sold: purchases, purchases discounts, purchases discounts lost, purchases returns and allowances, and merchandise inventory.

- Explain and use the gross-price and net-price methods of entering purchase invoices and processing such invoices for payment.

- Describe the accounts payable control account in the general ledger and subsidiary records that support amounts in general ledger accounts, specifically—

  1. A file of unpaid suppliers' invoices—the "invoice" method, or
  2. A subsidiary accounts payable ledger—the "ledger account" method.

- Explain and use a special journal for purchases of merchandise on account.

- Explain and use a special journal for all cash payments.

- Prepare a schedule of accounts payable.

In Chapters 3 and 4 the modified cash basis of accounting for a personal service enterprise was illustrated. Except for depreciation and supplies, the net income for the year was calculated on the cash basis.

Revenue was recorded when cash was received for services performed. Similarly, most expenses were recorded when cash was paid. Since it is unrealistic to consider the entire cost of an asset such as office equipment (expected to be used for many years) to be an expense only of the month or year of purchase, an exception to this practice was made for depreciation. The cost of plant and equipment is allocated as an expense over their expected useful lives. Similarly, a distinction was made between supplies used during the period and those remaining at year end. The supplies used were reported as an expense on the income statement and those remaining at the end of the period were reported as an asset on the balance sheet.

The modified cash basis is not technically perfect, but it is simple to use and easy to understand. This accounting method has proved to be quite satisfactory for most personal service enterprises. In the case of business enterprises whose major activity is the purchase of merchandise for resale, however, the modified cash basis of periodic income determination usually does not give a meaningful or useful measure of net income or net loss. There are two reasons why this is true. First, merchandising businesses commonly purchase and sell merchandise "on account" or "on credit"—meaning that payment is postponed a few days or weeks. The amount of cash paid to suppliers in any accounting period is almost never the same as purchases for the period. Similarly, cash received from customers does not necessarily represent the revenue earned from sales during the period. Second, merchandising businesses normally start and end each period with a stock of goods on hand for resale. This inventory should be reported on the Balance Sheet as an asset. The cost of the inventory sold during the period should be reported on the Income Statement as an expense. By matching the cost of the goods actually sold against the revenue earned from those sales, a more meaningful measure of net income can be obtained.

The purpose of this chapter is to describe and explain the accrual basis of accounting for purchases of merchandise, and the subsequent payment of invoices for such purchases. Commonly used source documents for purchases and payments will be discussed and illustrated, and special journals for purchases and cash payments will be introduced and explained.

Explain why the cash, or modified cash basis of periodic income determination usually is unsuited to a merchandising business, and why the accrual basis gives a more meaningful measure of periodic income.

Purpose of the chapter

Source Documents and Associated Records for Purchases and Payments

Merchandise for resale and other property for use in the operation of a business enterprise may be purchased either for cash or on account. In a small enterprise the buying may be done by the owner or by an employee, and may require only part-time attention. In a large enterprise a purchasing department may be needed with a manager and staff who devote their entire time to buying activities. The successful operation of a purchasing department requires an efficient organization as well as the proper equipment.

A flowchart showing some of the major documents commonly used in the purchases function of a merchandise business is presented below. Each of these documents is explained in the following sections.

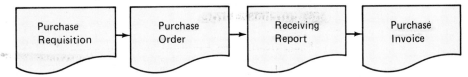

The Purchase Requisition

Describe and use
various source
documents.

A form used to request the responsible person or department to purchase merchandise or other property is known as a purchase requisition. Such requests may come from any authorized person or department of an enterprise. Purchase requisitions should be numbered consecutively to prevent the loss or misuse of the forms. Usually they are prepared in duplicate; the original copy is sent to the person responsible for purchasing and the duplicate copy is retained by the person or department originating the requisition.

The following purchase requisition is for computer software. The merchandising business known as Northern Micro is owned by Gary L. Fishel. It is organized into several store areas. Requisitions for merchandise originate with the salespersons responsible for the particular areas.

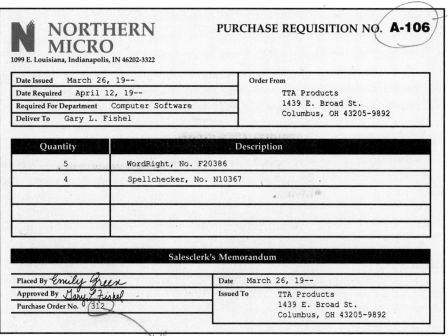

Purchase Requisition

After the purchase requisition was approved by Fishel, an order was placed with TTA Products, a manufacturer of computer software, as indicated by the memorandum at the bottom of the form. The purchase requisition, when approved, is the authority to order the merchandise or other property described in the requisition.

The Purchase Order

A written order by a buyer for merchandise or other property specified in a purchase requisition is known as a purchase order. A purchase order may be prepared on a printed stock form, on a specially designed form, or on an order blank furnished by a supplier of goods or services. Purchase orders should be numbered consecutively and prepared with multiple copies. The original copy is sent to a supplier or vendor—a person or firm from whom the merchandise or other property is ordered. Sometimes the duplicate copy also goes to the supplier as an "acknowledgment copy." The acknowledgment copy has a space for the supplier's signature to indicate the acceptance of the order. Such acceptance creates a formal contract. The signed acknowledgment copy is then returned to the ordering firm. Sometimes a copy of the purchase order is sent to the salesperson or department of the company that requisitioned the purchase. In many organizations a copy of the purchase order is sent to a receiving clerk. Some firms require that the accounting department receive a copy of the purchase order to provide a basis for verifying the charges made by the supplier. A variety of practices are followed with respect to requisitioning purchases, placing orders, verifying goods received and charges made, recording purchases, and paying suppliers. Each business adopts procedures best suited to its particular needs.

The purchase order at the top of page 205 shows the same quantity and description of the merchandise ordered as specified in the purchase requisition reproduced on page 203. The unit prices shown in the purchase order are those quoted by the supplier and it is expected that the merchandise will be billed at such prices.

The Purchase Invoice

A source document prepared by the seller that lists the items shipped, their cost, and the method of shipment is commonly referred to as an invoice. From the viewpoint of the seller, it is considered a sales invoice; from the viewpoint of the buyer, it is considered a purchase invoice.

A purchase invoice may be received by the buyer before or after delivery of the merchandise or other property ordered. As invoices are received, it is customary for the buyer to number them consecutively. These numbers should not be confused with the suppliers' numbers, which represent their sale numbers. After being numbered, each purchase invoice is compared with a copy of the purchase order to determine that the quantity, description, prices, and the terms agree. Also, the method of shipment and the date of delivery are compared with the instructions and specifications on the invoice. A separate approval form

N NORTHERN MICRO		**PURCHASE ORDER NO.** 312

1099 E. Louisiana, Indianapolis, IN 46202-3322

Date March 26, 19- **Deliver By** April 12, 19--		
Terms 2/10, n/30		TTA Products
Ship By Ajax Transfer Co.		1439 E. Broad St.
FOB Columbus		Columbus, OH 43205-9892

Quantity	Description	Unit Price
5	WordRight, No. F20386	180.00
4	Spellchecker, No. N10367	75.00

Mary L. Fishel

Purchase Order

may be used, or approval may be stamped on the invoice by means of a rubber stamp. If a separate approval form is used, it may be stapled to or pasted on the invoice form.

The illustration on page 206 is an example of a purchase invoice. A rubber stamp was used to imprint the approval form on the face of the invoice. When the merchandise is received, the salesperson may compare the contents of the shipment with a copy of the purchase order, or may prepare a receiving report indicating the contents of the shipment. In the latter event, the receiving report and the purchase order must be compared by someone from either the purchasing or the accounting area. After the prices and extensions are verified, the invoice is kept in an unpaid invoice file until it is paid.

Back Orders. If the supplier is unable to ship part or all of the merchandise ordered, the portions not shipped are known as back orders. Nevertheless, the supplier may send an invoice for the complete order, indicating on it what has been back ordered and when such items will be shipped. The purchase invoice reproduced on page 206 indicates that while 5 copies of WordRight were ordered, only 3 were shipped by TTA Products. Notice of this shortage was indicated on the invoice. In this instance, only the items shipped were billed.

Trade Discounts. Many manufacturers and wholesalers quote list prices (printed prices) which are subject to special discounts. Special discounts on list prices granted to customers to encourage their patronage

Explain the purpose of and compute trade discounts.

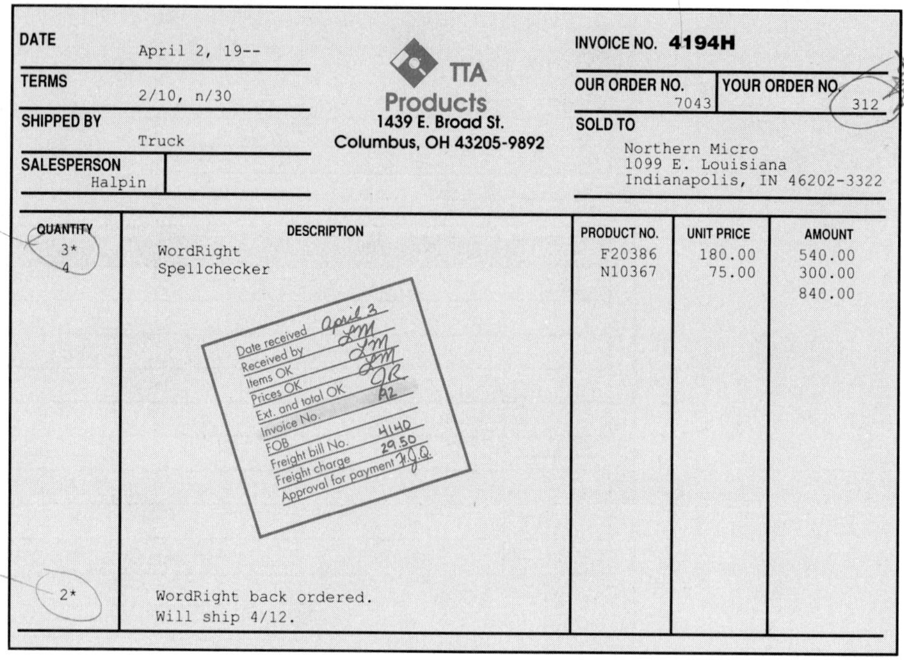

(margin handwriting) TTA Invoice #

(left margin handwriting) only got 3 were ordered

(left margin handwriting) I not yet reviewed

DATE	April 2, 19--				INVOICE NO. **4194H**	

TTA
Products
1439 E. Broad St.
Columbus, OH 43205-9892

TERMS	2/10, n/30
SHIPPED BY	Truck
SALESPERSON	Halpin

OUR ORDER NO. 7043   YOUR ORDER NO. 312

SOLD TO
Northern Micro
1099 E. Louisiana
Indianapolis, IN 46202-3322

QUANTITY	DESCRIPTION	PRODUCT NO.	UNIT PRICE	AMOUNT
3*	WordRight	F20386	180.00	540.00
4	Spellchecker	N10367	75.00	300.00
				840.00

(stamp, handwritten)
Date received April 3
Received by LM
Items OK LM
Prices OK QR
Ext. and total OK A2
Invoice No.
FOB 4140
Freight bill No. 29.50
Freight charge
Approval for payment QQ

2*   WordRight back ordered.
Will ship 4/12.

Purchase Invoice

are known as <u>trade discounts</u>. The use of trade discounts makes it possible for businesses to publish catalogs with prices that will not be subject to frequent changes. Some firms, such as those dealing in hardware and jewelry, publish catalogs listing thousands of items. Such catalogs are costly, and considerable loss might be involved when price changes occur if it were not for the fact that discount rates may be changed without changing the listed prices. Another advantage of using trade discounts is that retail dealers can display catalogs to their customers without revealing what the items of merchandise cost them.

When an invoice is subject to a trade discount, the discount is usually shown as a deduction from the total amount of the invoice. For example, the invoice on page 207 is subject to a trade discount of 10%. This information is stated in the body of the invoice.

The amount to be entered in the accounting records for an invoice subject to a trade discount is the net amount, $756.00, after deducting the trade discount of $84.00. Trade discounts represent a reduction in the price of the merchandise and should not be entered in the accounts of either the seller or the buyer.

Sometimes a series or chain of trade discounts is allowed. For example, if the list prices are subject to discounts of 20%, 10%, and 5%, each discount is computed separately on the successive net amounts. Assume that the gross amount of an invoice is $100 and discounts of 20%, 10%, and 5% are allowed. The net amount is determined as follows:

Gross amount of invoice	$100.00
Less 20%	20.00
Balance	$ 80.00
Less 10%	8.00
Balance	$ 72.00
Less 5%	3.60
Net amount	$ 68.40

In entering this invoice only the net amount, $68.40, is used.

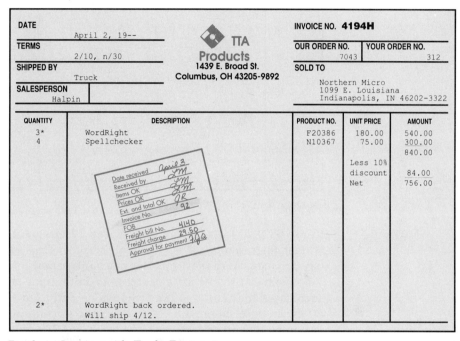

Purchase Invoice with Trade Discount

Do not Book Trade Discounts (handwritten)

Explain the purpose of and compute cash discounts.

Cash Discounts. Many firms follow the practice of allowing cash discounts, which are discounts from quoted prices, as an inducement for prompt payment of invoices. The terms of payment should be clearly indicated on the invoice. The terms specified on the invoice reproduced on page 208 are "2/10, n/30." This means that a discount of 2% will be allowed if payment is made within 10 days from the date of the invoice (April 2), that is, if payment is made by April 12.

If the invoice is paid on or before April 12, 2% of $840 or $16.80, is deducted and a check for $823.20 may be issued in full settlement of the invoice. After April 12, no discount will be allowed and the total amount of $840 must be paid not later than 30 days after the date of invoice, that is, by May 2.

The 2% discount associated with purchase invoice terms of 2/10, n/30 may not seem like a significant savings for paying within the discount period. However, when viewed as a finance charge of $16.80 for the right

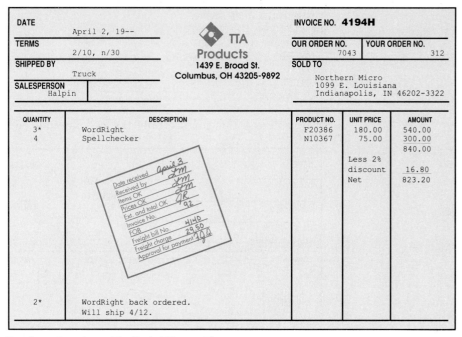

Purchase Invoice with Cash Discount

to use $823.20 for a 20 day period, the 2% discount actually represents an annual interest rate of approximately 37%. Thus, it is very important to pay for merchandise within the discount period.

Sometimes an invoice is subject to both trade and cash discounts. In such cases the trade discount should be deducted from the gross amount of the invoice before the cash discount is computed and deducted. For example, the invoice reproduced on page 209 is subject to a trade discount of 10% and the terms are 2/10, n/30. The net amount payable within 10 days from the date of the invoice should be computed in the following manner:

Amount of invoice	$840.00
Less trade discount, 10%	84.00
Amount subject to cash discount	$756.00
Less cash discount, 2%	15.12
Net amount payable	$740.88

Purchase Invoice Terms. The terms commonly used in connection with purchase invoices are interpreted as follows:

Describe the most common terms of purchase.

30 days	The amount of the invoice must be paid within 30 days from its date.
2/10, n/30	A discount of 2% is allowed if payment is made within 10 days from the date of the invoice; otherwise, the total amount of the invoice must be paid within 30 days from its date.

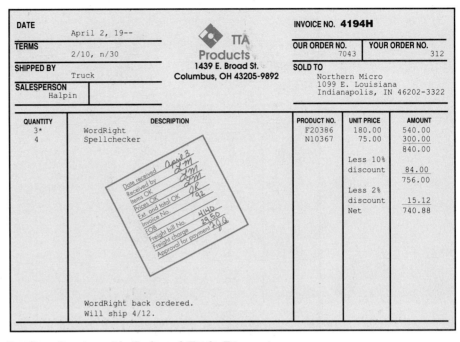

Purchase Invoice with Cash and Trade Discounts

2/EOM, n/60
: A discount of 2% is allowed if payment is made before the end of the month; otherwise, the total amount of the invoice must be paid within 60 days from its date.

4/10 EOM
: A discount of 4% is allowed if payment is made within 10 days after the end of the current month.

COD
: Collect on delivery. The amount of the invoice must be paid at the time the merchandise is delivered.

FOB Shipping Point
: Free on board at point of origin of the shipment. Under such terms the buyer must pay all transportation costs and assume all risks from the time the merchandise is accepted for shipment by the carrier.

FOB Destination
: Free on board at destination of the shipment. The seller will pay the transportation costs and will assume all responsibility for the merchandise until it reaches the carrier's delivery point at destination.

■■■■ **Payment of Invoice.** If Northern Micro pays the April 2 invoice of TTA Products on April 12, the purchase invoice is removed from the unpaid invoice file. A rubber stamp is used to imprint the notation "Paid" and the date of payment "4/12/—" on the face of the invoice. The check number and amount paid are then entered on the proper lines, and the check is issued to the supplier. The illustration on page 210 shows the "paid" invoice and related check. Note that the check is for $740.88 (the invoice amount of $756.00 less the 2% cash discount).

After the check is mailed to the supplier, the purchase invoice is placed in a "paid invoice" file in alphabetical order by supplier's name.

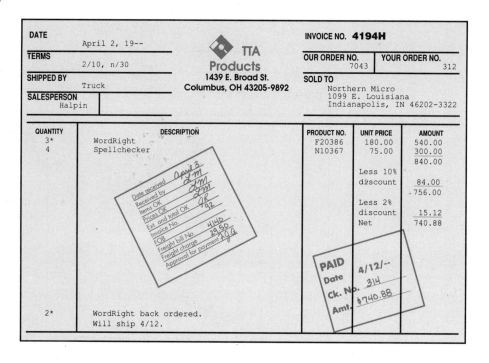

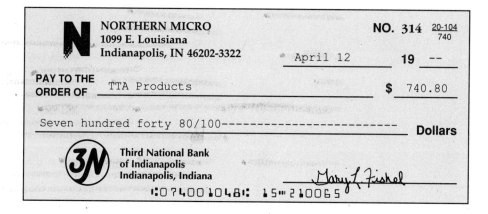

Paid Invoice with Related Check

COD Purchases. Merchandise or other property may be purchased on COD terms, that is, collect on delivery or cash on delivery. COD shipments may be received by parcel post, express mail, or freight. When shipments are received by parcel post or express mail, the recipient must pay for the property at the time of delivery. The bill may include transportation charges and COD fees. In any event, the total amount paid represents the cost of the property purchased.

When COD shipments are made by freight, the amount to be collected by the transportation company is entered immediately below the description of the merchandise on the bill. A copy of the sales invoice may be inserted in an envelope which is pasted to the outside of the package, carton, or case. The transportation company then collects the amount specified, plus a COD collection fee, at the time of delivering the merchandise, and remits the amount to the shipper.

The Freight Bill

Describe and use a freight bill.

When merchandise or other property is delivered to a transportation company for shipment, an agent of the transportation company prepares a document known as a waybill. A waybill describes the shipment, shows the point of origin and destination, and indicates any special handling that may be required. The original copy is forwarded to the transportation officer at the location to which the shipment is directed. When the shipment arrives at the destination, a bill for the transportation charges is prepared, which is known as a freight bill. Sometimes the recipient of the shipment is required to pay the freight bill before the property can be obtained. The following is an example of a freight bill.

TO	Northern Micro 1099 E. Louisiana Indianapolis, IN 46202-3322	Ajax Transfer Co. 1530 E. Mason Columbus, OH 43205-8919				
		ORIGINAL FREIGHT BILL		NUMBER **4140**		
FROM	TTA Products 1439 E. Broad St. Columbus, OH 43205-9892	CODE 3	TERMINAL Columbus		SHIPPER NO. C 02473	
		FOR OFFICE USE ONLY NAME			PRO	DIV
		DATE April 3, 19--				
PIECES	DESCRIPTION	WEIGHT	RATE	PREPAID		COLLECT
2	Packages Software	2 lbs.	14.75			29.50
		C.O.D. AMOUNT		FEE		DRIVER COLLECT
ARTICLES LISTED HAVE BEEN RECEIVED IN GOOD CONDITION BY *L.M.* DATE *April 5*						

Freight Bill

Trucking companies usually make what is known as a "store-to-door delivery." Freight shipments made by railroad or airline may also be delivered to the recipient's place of business at no extra charge. If such service is not rendered by the transportation company, it may be necessary for the recipient to employ a local drayage company to transport the merchandise from the freight warehouse to the place of business. In such a case, the drayage company will submit a bill for its services, which is known as a drayage bill.

The Credit Memorandum

Describe and use a credit memorandum.

Sometimes a buyer may want to return part or all of the merchandise or other property to the supplier for various reasons, such as the following:

Sales return

1. It may not conform to the specifications in the purchase order.
2. A mistake may have been made in placing the order and the supplier may give permission for it to be returned.
3. It may have been delayed in shipment and thus, the buyer cannot dispose of it. This sometimes happens with seasonal goods, such as style merchandise handled by a clothing store.

If the merchandise received is damaged or unsatisfactory or the prices charged are not in accord with an existing agreement, an adjustment, called an allowance, may be made.

When merchandise is to be returned to the supplier for credit, a debit memorandum is usually issued by the buyer for the purchase price of the merchandise returned. A debit memorandum is a formal request for credit to be granted by the supplier. (This document is referred to as a debit memorandum because the buyer is requesting permission to debit Accounts Payable.) Upon receipt of the returned merchandise, the supplier usually issues a document, known as a credit memorandum, confirming the amount of the credit allowed. (The seller refers to this document as a credit memorandum because it indicates that Accounts Receivable has been credited. This account will be discussed in Chapter 7.) A filled-in credit memorandum is reproduced below. This form indicates that TTA Products has given Northern Micro credit for the return of one Spellchecker software package. Note that TTA Products has shown on the face of the credit memorandum both the gross and net amount of the credit.

♦ TTA Products
1439 E. Broad St.
Columbus, OH 43205-9892

CREDIT MEMORANDUM

DATE   April 9, 19--

TO   Northern Micro
1099 E. Louisiana
Indianapolis, IN 46202-3322

WE CREDIT YOUR ACCOUNT AS FOLLOWS

DESCRIPTION	QUANTITY	UNIT PRICE	EXTENSION	TOTAL
Spellchecker	1	75.00	75.00	75.00
Less 2% discount				1.50
Net credit				73.50

Credit Memorandum

Building Your Accounting Knowledge

1. What are the major reasons why the cash basis of accounting does not result in a useful measure of net income or net loss for a merchandising business?
2. Why should purchase requisitions be numbered consecutively?
3. Why should a purchase invoice be compared with a copy of the related purchase order after having been numbered consecutively upon receipt?
4. How is a trade discount usually shown on an invoice?
5. If an invoice is subject to both trade and cash discounts, which type of discount should be deducted from the gross invoice amount first?
6. What is done with the purchase invoice at the time of its payment?
7. What is the purpose of a waybill?
8. When does a buyer usually issue a debit memorandum?
9. When does a supplier usually issue a credit memorandum?

Assignment Box

To reinforce your understanding of the preceding text materials, you may complete the following:
> Study Guide: Part A
> Textbook: Exercise 6A1 or 6B1
> > Problems 6A1 through 6A4 or 6B1 through 6B4

Accrual Accounting Procedures for Purchases and Payments

Define and explain the purpose of the accounts used in the calculation of cost of goods sold.

Under the accrual basis of accounting, revenues are recognized in the period they are earned and expenses are recognized in the period they are incurred, regardless of when cash is received or paid. Proper recognition of revenues from the selling of merchandise will be discussed in Chapter 7. In this chapter, the accounting for cost of goods sold, a major expense incurred as the result of selling merchandise, will be addressed.

Goods held for resale are known as merchandise inventory. Determining the value of this inventory at the beginning and end of the accounting period is an important factor in the periodic determination of net income for a merchandising business.

The word purchase can refer to the act of buying almost anything or, if used as a noun, to the item that is bought. For a merchandising business, however, the term usually refers to merchandise. A reference to "purchases for the year," unless qualified in some way, relates to the merchandise purchased for resale, stock in trade.

Net purchases is the cost of merchandise purchased during the period less:

(1) the amount of any discounts—purchases discounts—granted by suppliers to encourage prompt payment of their invoices;

(2) the cost of goods returned—purchases returns—to suppliers because they have proved to be unsatisfactory or unwanted; and

(3) the amount of any allowances—purchases allowances—(price reductions for damaged or defective goods received) made by suppliers.

Under the accrual basis of accounting, the cost of goods sold must be calculated periodically so that it can be matched against the net sales revenue of the same period. Adding net purchases to the beginning inventory equals the cost of the merchandise that was available for sale during the period—goods available for sale. Subtracting the ending inventory, merchandise inventory still on hand at the end of the period, from goods available for sale equals cost of goods sold. A general format for the calculation of cost of goods sold is provided below.

Cost of goods sold:			
Merchandise inventory, beginning of period			xx
Purchases		xx	
Less: Purchases discounts	xx		
Purchases returns and allowances	xx	xx	
Net purchases			xx
Goods available for sale			xx
Less merchandise inventory, end of period			xx
Cost of goods sold			xx

To enter transactions associated with the purchasing of merchandise, it is desirable to keep at least the following accounts:

1. Purchases
2. Purchases Discounts Lost (or Purchases Discounts)
3. Purchases Returns and Allowances

Purchases

The purchases account is a temporary owner's equity account in which the cost of all merchandise purchased during the accounting period is entered. The account is debited for the cost of the merchandise purchased.

Purchases	
Debit to enter the cost of merchandise purchased.	

If the purchase is for cash, the cash account is credited; if purchased on account, Accounts Payable should be credited. For example, when Northern Micro purchased merchandise on account from TTA Products Inc. for $840, the following entry was made.

Purchases	840	
Accounts Payable		840

The purchases account may also be debited for any transportation charges, such as freight, express mail, and parcel post charges, that increase the cost of the merchandise purchased. The common practice, however, is to charge these items to a separate account.

Purchases Discounts

Cash discounts often are not entered in the books at the same time as purchase invoices are entered, even though it may be the policy of a firm to pay all invoices in time to get the benefit of any cash discounts offered. For example, the invoice reproduced on page 206 shows that an amount of $840 was entered in the books. If there was a cash discount taken at time of payment, it would be accounted for by crediting a contra account, purchases discounts, at the time of recording the check issued in payment of the invoice.

Purchases Discounts	
	Credit for cash discounts taken

Explain and use the gross-price method of entering purchase invoices and processing such invoices for payment.

The purchases discounts account represents a reduction in the cost of goods purchased and is classified as a contra account to purchases. At the end of the period, the credit balance of this account is shown on the income statement as a deduction from purchases when calculating net purchases. This approach to accounting for purchases, which is known as the gross-price method, is illustrated in the following example. If Northern Micro made the purchase on April 3 for $840 with no trade discount and terms of 2/10, n/30, the following entry would be made:

April 3 Purchases..................................	840.00	
Accounts Payable		840.00

If the invoice was paid on April 12, the following entry would be made:

April 12 Accounts Payable	840.00	
Cash		823.20
Purchases Discounts		16.80

On the other hand, if the invoice was not paid until April 20, the following entry would be made:

April 20 Accounts Payable	840.00	
Cash		840.00

Purchases Discounts Lost

Define and explain the purpose of the Purchases Discounts Lost account.

An alternative approach to accounting for purchases that is being used by a growing number of businesses today is the net-price method. The net-price basis of entering purchase invoices assumes that nearly all discounts will be taken. The purchases are therefore entered at invoice price less all available discounts. If the purchase invoice is not paid within the discount period, the amount of the discount is debited to a special purchases discounts lost account at the time that the invoice is paid.

The purchases discounts lost account is an expense account and is reported on the income statement with the other expenses. The balance of the account reflects the amount of finance charges incurred by a business as the result of failing to pay invoices within the discount period. Although purchases discounts lost could be debited directly to Purchases, it is better to debit the account Purchases Discounts Lost. This separate record allows the business to keep account of the expense of careless invoice payment. If discounts lost are large in proportion to gross purchases, a business may want to take necessary action to make sure that bills are paid within the discount period.

Purchases Discounts Lost

Debit to enter the expense of discounts lost because of late payment of invoices	

Explain and use the net-price method of entering purchase invoices and processing such invoices for payment.

In the case of the invoice previously described for $840 with terms 2/10, n/30, the April 3 entry under the net-price method is shown below.

April 3 Purchases....................................	823.20	
Accounts Payable		823.20

If the invoice was paid on April 12, the following entry would be made:

| April 12 Accounts Payable .... | 823.20 | |
| Cash .... | | 823.20 |

However, if the invoice was not paid until April 20, the following entry would be made:

April 20 Accounts Payable	823.20	
Purchases Discounts Lost...................	16.80	
Cash		840.00

When the net-price method is used, care must be taken to see that the amount on the face of the invoice agrees with the amount entered in the accounts. Not all suppliers report the gross and net amounts on the invoice. This potential problem is solved if the buyer simply enters on the face of the invoice the discount in dollars and the net amount due at the time the invoice is received.

By comparing the entries made under the net- and gross-price methods, the main benefit of the net-price method becomes apparent. Under the gross-price method, finance charges incurred, by failing to pay within the discount period, are included in the purchases account with the actual cost of the merchandise acquired. This means that this account includes two kinds of information: costs incurred for merchandise *and* for finance charges. Under the net-price method, the purchases account contains only the cost of the merchandise. Any finance charges incurred for late payment are reported in a separate account, Purchases Discounts Lost. When analyzing the relationship between the cost of the goods sold and the revenues earned from sales during the period, the net-price method can provide a more accurate picture.

Purchases Returns and Allowances Account

Purchases Returns and Allowances is classified as a contra account to purchases. It is reported as a deduction from purchases in the cost of goods sold section of the Income Statement. The account is credited for the cost of any merchandise returned to suppliers and for any allowances received from suppliers that decrease the cost of the merchandise purchased. The offsetting debit is to Accounts Payable if the goods were purchased on account, or to Cash if a refund is received because the purchase was originally for cash. Allowances may be received from suppliers for merchandise delivered in poor condition or for merchandise that does not meet specifications as to quality, weight, size, color, grade, or style.

Purchases Returns and Allowances

Credit to enter the cost of merchandise returned and allowances received.

Although any purchases returns and allowances may be credited directly to Purchases, it is better to credit the account Purchases Returns and Allowances. By using a contra account to Purchases, businesses can keep a record of the amount of gross purchases and the total amount of returns and allowances. If returns and allowances are large in proportion to gross purchases, a weakness in purchasing operations is indicated. Better sources of supply may need to be sought or purchase specifications may need to be stated more clearly.

As an example, consider the credit memorandum for $75.00 illustrated on page 212. In this credit memorandum, TTA Products is giving Northern Micro credit for one Spellchecker software package. As explained on page 212, since Northern Micro uses the net-price method for entering purchases, this credit memorandum should be entered at the net price amount of $73.50 in a two-column journal as follows:

Accounts Payable	73.50	
Purchases Returns and Allowances		73.50

Firms using the gross-price method would enter the transaction using $75.00. If a separate accounts payable subsidiary ledger is kept, this amount should also be posted as a debit to the individual account of TTA Products, in that ledger. This procedure will be discussed further in the next section.

Accounts Payable

Describe the Accounts Payable control account in the general ledger.

It is important that the owner or manager know both the amount owed to the individual suppliers (sometimes referred to as "creditors"), and the total amount owed to all suppliers. Thus, it is necessary to keep an individual record for each supplier and a summary or controlling ledger account indicating the total liability owed to the creditors. The summary account in the general ledger that represents the total liability to all the suppliers at any point in time is known as Accounts Payable.

It is also necessary to keep a record of the transactions completed with each supplier in order to know the amount owed to each supplier and when each invoice should be paid. Two widely used methods of accounting for purchases on account are described in the following paragraphs.

The Invoice Method. Under the invoice method, it is customary to keep a chronological record of the purchase invoices received and to file them systematically by due date in an "unpaid invoices" file. All documents relating to invoices such as returns or allowances are filed with the purchase invoices. The "unpaid invoices" file represents a detailed listing of the liabilities to individual suppliers for individual invoices. The total amount of unpaid invoices should equal the balance in the accounts payable account. After an invoice is paid, it is filed alphabetically by the supplier name in a "paid invoices" file with any related documents. Special filing equipment or computerized files facilitate the use of this method.

The unpaid invoice file is usually arranged with a division for each month with folders numbered 1 to 31 in each division. This makes it possible to file each unpaid invoice according to its due date which facilitates payment of the invoices on or before their due dates. Since certain invoices may be subject to discounts, it is important that they are filed in such a manner that payment is made in sufficient time to get the benefit of the discounts.

If a partial payment is made on an invoice, a notation of the payment should be made on the invoice, and it should be retained in the unpaid invoice file until paid in full. If credit is received because of returns and allowances, a notation of the amount of the credit should be made on the invoice so that the adjusted balance due will be indicated. As mentioned earlier, when an invoice is paid in full, the payment should be noted on the invoice, and the invoice then transferred from the unpaid invoice file to the paid invoice file. It is considered a good policy to pay each invoice in full because it simplifies the accounting process for both the buyer and the seller.

Subsidiary Ledger Account Method. When the volume of business and the number of transactions is great, it may be advisable to subdivide the ledger. A common approach is to separate the accounts with suppliers from the other accounts and keep them in a separate ledger called a subsidiary accounts payable ledger.

A special account form known as the three-column account form is widely used in keeping suppliers' accounts in the subsidiary accounts payable ledger. The three-column account form has three parallel amount columns for entering debits, credits, and balances. After each entry, the new balance should be determined and entered in the Balance column. The nature of the account determines whether its normal balance is a debit or a credit. Accounts with suppliers usually have credit balances. If a supplier's account has a debit balance, the balance may be bracketed or the term "Dr." entered next to the figure in the Balance column. The total of the accounts with debit balances should be deducted from the

Describe subsidiary records that support amounts in the general ledger accounts: The Invoice Method.

Describe subsidiary records that support amounts in the general ledger accounts: The Subsidiary Ledger Account Method.

Describe and use a three-column ledger account.

More commonly used

total of the accounts with credit balances to determine the total accounts payable balance in the subsidiary ledger.

NAME						
ADDRESS						
DATE	ITEM	POST. REF.	DEBIT	CREDIT	BALANCE	

Three-Column Account Form

Purchases Journal

Explain and use a special journal for purchases of merchandise on account.

All of the transactions of a merchandising business can be entered in an ordinary two-column journal or in a combination journal. However, in many enterprises purchases of merchandise occur frequently. Since most purchases are made on account, such transactions may be entered advantageously in a special journal. A journal designed for entering only purchases of merchandise on account is called a purchases journal. A sample purchases journal is provided at the top of page 221. In this type of journal, each transaction can be entered on one horizontal line.

Note that in entering each purchase invoice, the following information is placed in the purchases journal:

1. Date on which the invoice is received
2. Number of the invoice, i.e., the number assigned by the buyer
3. From whom purchased (the supplier)
4. Amount of the invoice

If an individual ledger account is not kept for each supplier, the purchase invoices should be filed immediately after they have been entered in the purchases journal. It is preferable that they are filed according to the due date in an unpaid invoice file. If an individual ledger account is kept for each supplier, the invoices normally are used to post to the supplier accounts (as explained below), after which the invoices are properly filed.

Posting from the Purchases Journal

At the end of the month, the column titled "Purchases Dr. and Accounts Payable Cr." of the purchases journal is totaled and the ruling completed. A process referred to as summary posting is then performed by posting the total as a debit to Purchases and as a credit to Accounts Payable. The summary posting from Northern Micro's purchases journal to the ledger accounts on April 30 is illustrated on page 221. The numbers "(511)(218)" under the total of the purchases journal indicate that the

Purchase Journal

Put into subsidiary ledger

		PURCHASES JOURNAL			Page 8
Date	Invoice No.	From Whom Purchased	Post. Ref.		Purchases Dr. Accts. Pay. Cr.
19-- Apr. 4	631	Compucraft	✔	—	6,300.00
8	632	Maxisoft	✔	—	2,500.15
9	633	EZX Corp.	✔	—	8,765.12
17	634	Printpro Corp.	✔	—	10,800.20
23	635	Televax, Inc.	✔	—	5,250.50
30					33,615.97
					(511) (218)

E.O.M.

ACCOUNTS PAYABLE SUBSIDIARY LEDGER (Partial)

NAME Compucraft, Inc.
ADDRESS 2100 West Main Street

Date	Item	Post. Ref.	Debit	Credit	Balance
19-- Apr. 4		P8		6,300.00	6,300.00

NAME Maxisoft
ADDRESS 210 Kirkwood

Date	Item	Post. Ref.	Debit	Credit	Balance
19-- Apr. 8		P8		2,500.15	2,500.15

NAME EZX Corp.
ADDRESS 312 South College

Date	Item	Post. Ref.	Debit	Credit	Balance
19-- Apr. 9		P8		8,765.12	8,765.12

NAME Printpro Corp.
ADDRESS 1200 Chambers Pike

Date	Item	Post. Ref.	Debit	Credit	Balance
19-- Apr. 17		P8		10,800.20	10,800.20

NAME Televax, Inc.
ADDRESS 1500 North Walnut Street

Date	Item	Post. Ref.	Debit	Credit	Balance
19-- Apr. 23		P8		5,250.50	5,250.50

GENERAL LEDGER (Partial)

ACCOUNT Accounts Payable   **ACCOUNT NO.** 218

Date	Item	Post. Ref.	Debit	Credit	Balance Debit	Balance Credit
19-- Apr. 1	Bal.	✔				8,850.12
30		P8		33,615.97		42,466.09

ACCOUNT Purchases   **ACCOUNT NO.** 511

Date	Item	Post. Ref.	Debit	Credit	Balance Debit	Balance Credit
19-- Apr. 30		P8	33,615.97		33,615.97	

homework — may 17,
Exer. 6A2-6A4, 6A6
Prob. 6A5

total was posted twice—to Purchases, Account No. 511, as a debit, and to Accounts Payable, Account No. 218, as a credit. A proper cross-reference should be completed by entering the page of the purchases journal preceded by the initial "P" in the Posting Reference column of the general and subsidiary ledger accounts.

The Invoice Method. Under the invoice method of accounting for purchases on account, individual posting from the purchases journal is not required. When this plan is followed, it is customary to place a check mark in the Posting Reference column of the purchases journal at the time each invoice is entered.

The Subsidiary Ledger Account Method. If a subsidiary ledger account is kept for each supplier, all transactions entered in the purchases journal should be posted individually to the proper subsidiary account. The posting, usually done with the aid of electronic equipment, will be completed directly from the purchase invoices and other vouchers or documents. As the individual supplier accounts are posted, a check mark ($\sqrt{}$) should be placed in the Posting Reference column of the purchases journal. For cross-reference purposes, the journal page preceded by the initial "P" is entered in the posting reference column of the subsidiary account. This procedure is illustrated for Northern Micro on page 221.

A flowchart of the major documents used in the purchases function was presented near the beginning of the chapter. That flowchart can now be updated to include the following accounting procedures:

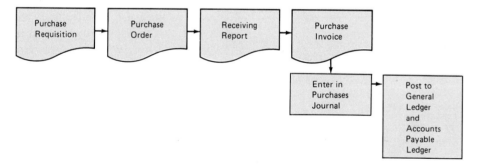

Cash Payments Journal

Explain and use a special journal for all cash payments.

Just as purchase transactions occur frequently in many enterprises, it follows that payment of suppliers' invoices and other obligations of the business will cause cash payment transactions to occur frequently. These cash transactions may be entered in a special journal called a **cash payments journal**. A cash payments journal is shown on page 224.

Note that every entry in the cash payments journal includes the following information:

1. Date of the cash payment
2. Number of the check issued
3. Amount of the cash payment, entered in the Cash Cr. column

In addition, the General Dr. column is used to enter debits to accounts other than Accounts Payable and Purchases. The Account Debited column is used to enter the name of the appropriate account when the General Dr. column is used, and to identify the supplier name when the Accounts Payable Dr. column is used.

Five types of transactions commonly entered in a cash payments journal, and proper procedures for entering each transaction are presented below. The entries are illustrated in the cash payments journal on page 224.

1. **Payment of an expense**—The name of the expense account is entered in the Account Debited column and the debit amount is entered in the General Dr. column.
2. **Cash purchase**—The debit amount is entered in the Purchases Dr. column. Note that the Account Debited column is left blank because neither the General Dr. column nor any supplier account is affected by this transaction.
3. **Payment to a supplier**—The name of the supplier is entered in the Account Debited column and the debit amount is entered in the Accounts Payable Dr. column. If the invoice is past due, "Purchases Discounts Lost/ name of supplier" is entered in the Account Debited column. The amount of the discount lost is entered in the General Dr. column. (In some cases, a special column entitled Purchases Discounts Lost Dr. is added to the cash payments journal.) The net amount of the invoice is entered in the Accounts Payable Dr. column, and Cash is credited for the full invoice amount. The check mark ($\sqrt{}$) entered in the Posting Reference column indicates that the amount in the Accounts Payable Dr. column has been posted to the accounts payable subsidiary ledger.
4. **Payment of a liability**—The name of the liability account is entered in the Account Debited column and the debit amount is entered in the General Dr. column.
5. **Withdrawal by the owner**—The name of the drawing account is entered in the Account Debited column and the debit amount is entered in the General Dr. column.

Posting From the Cash Payments Journal

Three different types of postings must be made from the cash payments journal. Each of these postings is described below and illustrated on page 224.

First, each amount in the General Dr. column of the cash payments journal is posted individually to the ledger account named in the Account Debited column. The notation "CP12" is entered in the Post. Ref. column

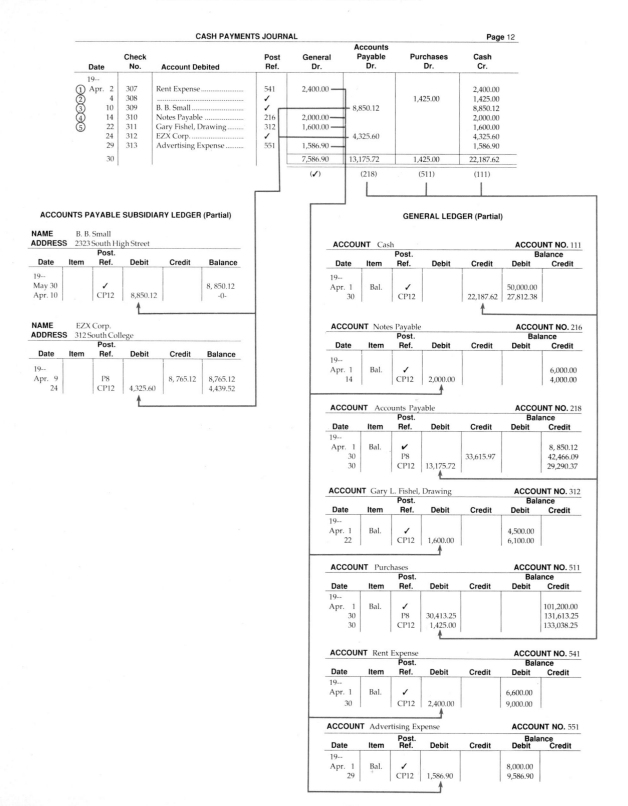

CASH PAYMENTS JOURNAL   Page 12

Date	Check No.	Account Debited	Post Ref.	General Dr.	Accounts Payable Dr.	Purchases Dr.	Cash Cr.
19--							
① Apr. 2	307	Rent Expense	541	2,400.00			2,400.00
② 4	308	....	✓			1,425.00	1,425.00
③ 10	309	B. B. Small	✓		8,850.12		8,850.12
④ 14	310	Notes Payable	216	2,000.00			2,000.00
⑤ 22	311	Gary Fishel, Drawing	312	1,600.00			1,600.00
24	312	EZX Corp.	✓		4,325.60		4,325.60
29	313	Advertising Expense	551	1,586.90			1,586.90
30				7,586.90	13,175.72	1,425.00	22,187.62
				(✓)	(218)	(511)	(111)

ACCOUNTS PAYABLE SUBSIDIARY LEDGER (Partial)

NAME B. B. Small
ADDRESS 2323 South High Street

Date	Item	Post. Ref.	Debit	Credit	Balance
19--					
May 30		✓			8, 850.12
Apr. 10		CP12	8,850.12		-0-

NAME EZX Corp.
ADDRESS 312 South College

Date	Item	Post. Ref.	Debit	Credit	Balance
19--					
Apr. 9		P8		8,765.12	8,765.12
24		CP12	4,325.60		4,439.52

GENERAL LEDGER (Partial)

ACCOUNT Cash   **ACCOUNT NO.** 111

Date	Item	Post. Ref.	Debit	Credit	Balance Debit	Balance Credit
19--						
Apr. 1	Bal.	✓			50,000.00	
30		CP12		22,187.62	27,812.38	

ACCOUNT Notes Payable   **ACCOUNT NO.** 216

Date	Item	Post. Ref.	Debit	Credit	Balance Debit	Balance Credit
19--						
Apr. 1	Bal.	✓				6,000.00
14		CP12	2,000.00			4,000.00

ACCOUNT Accounts Payable   **ACCOUNT NO.** 218

Date	Item	Post. Ref.	Debit	Credit	Balance Debit	Balance Credit
19--						
Apr. 1	Bal.	✓				8, 850.12
30		P8		33,615.97		42,466.09
30		CP12	13,175.72			29,290.37

ACCOUNT Gary L. Fishel, Drawing   **ACCOUNT NO.** 312

Date	Item	Post. Ref.	Debit	Credit	Balance Debit	Balance Credit
19--						
Apr. 1	Bal.	✓			4,500.00	
22		CP12	1,600.00		6,100.00	

ACCOUNT Purchases   **ACCOUNT NO.** 511

Date	Item	Post. Ref.	Debit	Credit	Balance Debit	Balance Credit
19--						
Apr. 1	Bal.	✓				101,200.00
30		P8	30,413.25			131,613.25
30		CP12	1,425.00			133,038.25

ACCOUNT Rent Expense   **ACCOUNT NO.** 541

Date	Item	Post. Ref.	Debit	Credit	Balance Debit	Balance Credit
19--						
Apr. 1	Bal.	✓			6,600.00	
30		CP12	2,400.00		9,000.00	

ACCOUNT Advertising Expense   **ACCOUNT NO.** 551

Date	Item	Post. Ref.	Debit	Credit	Balance Debit	Balance Credit
19--						
Apr. 1	Bal.	✓			8,000.00	
29		CP12	1,586.90		9,586.90	

of the affected ledger account at the time that the item is posted, and the appropriate account number is entered in the Post. Ref. column of the cash payments journal.

Second, each amount in the Accounts Payable Dr. column must be posted to the specific supplier's account in the accounts payable subsidiary ledger. The notation "CP12" is entered in the Post. Ref. column of the affected subsidiary ledger account at the time that the item is posted. A check mark ($\sqrt{}$) is then entered in the Post. Ref. column of the cash payments journal to indicate that the entry was posted to the subsidiary ledger.

Third, at the end of the month, the amount columns of the cash payments journal are totaled and the ruling completed as illustrated. The summary posting is then performed by posting the total of the Accounts Payable Dr. column as a debit to Account No. 218, the total of the Purchases Dr. column as a debit to Account No. 511, and the total of the Cash Cr. column as a credit to Account No. 111. As each total is posted, the notation "CP12" is entered in the Post. Ref. column of the affected ledger account, and the number of that account is entered in parentheses below the appropriate column total in the cash payments journal. A check mark ($\sqrt{}$) is entered in parentheses below the total of the General Dr. column to indicate that its total is not posted to the ledger.

Schedule of Accounts Payable

Prepare a Schedule of Accounts Payable.

A list showing the amount due to each supplier as of a specified date is known as a schedule of accounts payable. It is usually advisable to prepare such a schedule at the end of each month. An example of a schedule of accounts payable for Northern Micro as of April 30, 19--, is provided on page 226. This schedule can be easily prepared from the list of supplier accounts in the subsidiary accounts payable ledger or from the supplier names and amounts due in the unpaid invoice file. If the total of the schedule does not agree with the balance of the accounts payable control account, the error may be in either the subsidiary ledger, the file, or the control account. The subsidiary ledger could be incorrect because of an error in posting. The file may be incorrect in that one or more paid invoices have not been removed or one or more unpaid ones are missing. Another possibility is that a memorandum of a partial payment was overlooked in preparing the schedule. The accounts payable control account could be incorrect because of an error in posting or because of an error in a journal from which the purchases were posted. In any event, the postings, journals, and invoices must be examined until the reason for the discrepancy is found so that the necessary correction can be made.

Cash Purchases

Cash purchases of merchandise are entered in the cash payments journal by debiting the purchases account (using the "Purchases Dr." column) and by crediting the cash account. Usually cash purchases are not

Northern Micro
Schedule of Accounts Payable
April 30, 19--

TTA Products, Inc.	$ 6,300.00
Maxisoft	2,500.15
E.Z.X. Corp	4,439.52
Printpro	10,800.20
Televax	5,250.50
	$29,290.37

posted to the individual accounts of suppliers. However, if it is desired to post cash purchases to the individual accounts of suppliers, such transactions may be entered both in the purchases journal and in the cash payments journal. In other words, invoices received in connection with cash purchases may be processed in the same manner as invoices for purchases on account. Northern Micro follows the practice of entering cash purchases of merchandise in the cash payments journal and purchases on account in the purchases journal.

COD Purchases

When property is purchased on COD terms, payment must be made before possession of the property can be obtained. It is customary to treat such transactions the same as cash purchases. Thus, the check issued in payment of a COD purchase is entered in the cash payments journal by debiting the proper account and crediting the cash account. The proper account to debit depends upon the kind of property purchased. If merchandise is purchased, the purchases account is debited for the cost of the merchandise and the transportation account is debited for the amount of any transportation charges paid. If plant or equipment assets are purchased, the proper asset account is debited for the total cost, including COD fees and transportation charges. If supplies are purchased, the proper supplies account is debited for the total cost of the supplies, including COD fees and transportation charges.

Transportation Charges

Express and freight charges may be prepaid by the seller or may be paid by the buyer at the time of delivery. Parcel post charges must be prepaid by the seller. Store-to-door delivery of freight shipments may be made by the transportation companies. However, when freight shipments are not delivered to the buyer's place of business by the transportation company, the buyer either calls for the goods at a nearby freight warehouse or employs a truck to deliver the goods.

▦ **Transportation Charges Prepaid.**   If the transportation charges are prepaid by the seller, the amount may or may not be added to the invoice, depending upon the terms of the sale. If the seller has quoted prices FOB destination, it is understood that the prices quoted include transportation charges either to the buyer's place of business or to a nearby freight warehouse and that no additional charge will be made for any transportation charges paid by the seller.

If the seller has quoted prices FOB shipping point, it is understood that the prices quoted do not include the transportation charges and that the buyer is expected to pay the transportation costs. If these transportation charges are prepaid by the seller, the charges will be added to the invoice, and the seller will be reimbursed by the buyer when the invoice is paid.

▦ **Transportation Charges Collect.**   If prices are quoted FOB shipping point and shipment is made collect, the buyer pays the transportation charges before obtaining possession of the shipment. Such transportation charges represent an addition to the cost of the merchandise or other property purchased. The method of entering the transportation charges in this case is the same as if the charges had been prepaid by the seller and added to the invoice.

If prices are quoted FOB destination but for some reason shipment is made collect, the buyer pays the transportation charges to obtain possession of the shipment. In such cases the transportation charges paid by the buyer are entered as a debit to Accounts Payable and the subsidiary account of the supplier from whom the merchandise or other property was ordered.

▦ **Transportation Accounts.**   It is common practice to enter transportation charges on incoming merchandise in a separate account, which may be entitled Freight-In or Transportation-In. Under these circumstances, a special Freight-In or Transportation-In column is included in the purchases journal, or this type of transaction can be entered in a two-column journal. This account is reported in the cost of goods sold section of the income statement as an addition to net purchases, as follows:

```
Cost of goods sold:
Merchandise inventory, beginning of period......................      xx
Purchases.........................................          xx
Less: Purchases discounts .......................      xx
        Purchases returns and allowances.........      xx  xx
        Net purchases............................          xx
Add freight-in ..................................          xx
Cost of goods purchased..........................              xx
Goods available for sale.........................              xx
Less merchandise inventory, end of period........              xx
Cost of goods sold ..............................              xx
```

Transportation charges applicable to equipment, such as office equipment, store equipment, or delivery equipment, are treated as an addition to the cost of the equipment. It is immaterial whether the freight charges are prepaid by the seller and added to the invoice or whether shipment is made collect. If the freight is prepaid and added to the invoice, the total cost, including the invoice price and the transportation charges, is entered as a debit to the equipment account in one amount. On the other hand, if shipment is made freight collect, the amount of the invoice and the amount of the freight charges are posted as separate debits to the equipment account.

Parcel Post Insurance. Merchandise or other property mailed parcel post may be insured against loss or damage in transit. If the cost of insurance is charged to the customer and is added to the invoice, it represents an addition to the cost of the merchandise or other property purchased. Thus, if an invoice is received for merchandise purchased and the merchandise is billed at a total cost of $225 plus postage of $3 and insurance of 90 cents, the total cost of the merchandise is $228.90.

The cost of insurance is seldom entered separately in the accounts of the buyer. It is either charged directly to the purchases account or is included with transportation charges and charged to Freight-In.

Building Your Accounting Knowledge

1. Describe how to compute the cost of goods sold.
2. Define each of the following accounts and describe briefly how each is used: (1) Purchases, (2) Purchases Discounts Lost, (3) Purchases Discounts, (4) Purchases Returns and Allowances.
3. Explain the advantages and disadvantages of the gross-price and net-price methods of accounting for purchases.
4. What does the net-price basis of entering purchase invoices assume with regard to the taking of all available discounts? Why is this assumption made?
5. Discuss the two major methods of keeping records of the transactions completed with individual suppliers.
6. List four items of information about each purchase normally entered in the purchases journal.
7. List four items of information about each cash payment normally entered in the cash payments journal.
8. List five kinds of transactions requiring varying entry procedures in the cash payments journal.
9. In what journal does Northern Micro enter cash purchases?
10. Are COD purchases handled the same as cash purchases or the same as purchases on account?
11. If transportation charges are billed collect under normal FOB shipping point terms, what do such charges represent as far as the buyer is concerned?
12. If transportation charges are billed collect under FOB destination terms, how should the buyer treat the payment of these charges?
13. Indicate two alternative means of entering the cost of parcel post insurance.

Assignment Box

To reinforce your understanding of the preceding text materials, you may complete the following:

Study Guide: Part B
Textbook: Exercises 6A2 through 6A7 or 6B2 through 6B7
Problems 6A5 through 6A7 or 6B5 through 6B7

Expanding Your Business Vocabulary

What is the meaning of each of the following items?

Accounts Payable (p. 218)
accrual basis of accounting (p. 213)
allowance (p. 212)
back orders (p. 205)
cash discounts (p. 207)
cash payments journal (p. 222)
COD (p. 209)
cost of goods sold (p. 214)
credit memorandum (p. 212)
debit memorandum (p. 212)
drayage bill (p. 211)
FOB destination (p. 209)
FOB shipping point (p. 209)
freight bill (p. 211)
goods available for sale (p. 214)
gross-price method (pp. 215)
invoice (p. 204)
invoice method (p. 219)
list prices (p. 205)
Merchandise Inventory (p. 213)
net-price method (p. 216)
net purchases (p. 213)
purchase (p. 213)
purchase invoice (p. 204)
purchase order (p. 204)
purchase requisition (p. 203)
purchases account (p. 214)
purchases allowances (p. 214)
purchases discounts (p. 214)
purchases discounts lost (p. 216)
purchases journal (p. 220)
purchases returns (p. 214)
Purchases Returns and Allowances (p. 217)
receiving report (p. 205)
sales invoice (p. 204)
schedule of accounts payable (p. 225)
stock in trade (p. 213)
subsidiary accounts payable ledger (p. 219)
subsidiary ledger account method (p. 219)
summary posting (p. 220)
supplier or vendor (p. 204)
trade discounts (p. 206)
waybill (p. 211)

Demonstration Problem

Jodi Rutman operates a retail pharmacy. The books of original entry include: (1) a purchases journal, in which purchases of merchandise on account are entered using the gross price method; (2) a cash payments journal, in which all cash payments (except petty cash) are entered; and (3) a two-column journal, in which entries such as purchases returns and allowances are made. The subsidiary ledger method of accounting is used for purchases on account. Following are the transactions related to purchases and cash payments for the month of June:

June 1 Purchased merchandise from Sullivan Co. on account, $234.20. Invoice No. 71, dated June 1, terms, 2/10, n/30.

2 Issued Check No. 536 for $1,000.00 in payment of rent (Rent Expense) for June.

5 Purchased merchandise from Amfac Drug Supply on account, $562.40. Invoice No. 72, dated June 2, terms, 1/15, n/30.

7 Purchased merchandise from University Drug Co. on account, $367.35. Invoice No. 73, dated June 5, terms, 3/10 EOM.

9 Issued Check No. 537 to Sullivan Co. in payment of Invoice No. 71, less 2% discount.

12 Received a credit memorandum from Amfac Drug Supply for $46.20 for merchandise returned to them that was purchased on June 5.

14 Purchased merchandise from Mutual Drug Co. on account, $479.40, Invoice No. 74, dated June 14, terms, 2/10, n/30.

15 Received a credit memorandum from University Drug Co. for $53.70 for merchandise returned to them that was purchased on June 7.

16 Issued Check No. 538 to Amfac Drug Supply in payment of Invoice No. 72, less the credit memorandum of June 12, and less 1% discount.

23 Issued Check No. 539 to Mutual Drug Co. in payment of Invoice No. 74, less 2% discount.

27 Purchased merchandise from Flites Pharmaceuticals on account, $638.47. Invoice No. 75, dated June 27, terms, 2/10 EOM.

30 Issued Check No. 540 for $270.20 to Dolgin Candy Co. for a cash purchase of merchandise.

Required:

1. Enter the transactions in a purchases journal, a five-column cash payments journal, and a two-column journal. Enter the totals and rule the purchases and cash payments journals.

2. Post from the journals to the general ledger accounts and the accounts payable subsidiary ledger. (In posting from these three journals, the page number, preceded by the initials "J," "P," or "CP" should be placed in the Post. Ref. column of the general or subsidiary ledger account involved.) Then, update the account balances.

3. Show proof that the difference between the June 1 balance and the June 30 balance of the accounts payable control account (No. 218) is equal to the sum of the balances of the accounts payable subsidiary ledger accounts as of June 30. (Only a portion of the subsidiary ledger is illustrated in this problem.)

Solution

1.

		Purchases Journal		Page 2

Date	Invoice No.	From Whom Purchased	Post Ref.	Purchases Dr. Accts. Pay. Cr.
19--				
June 1	71	Sullivan Co.	√	234.20
5	72	Amfac Drug Supply	√	562.40
7	73	University Drug Co.	√	367.35
14	74	Mutual Drug Co.	√	479.40
27	75	Flites Pharmaceuticals	√	638.47
30				2,281.82
				(511) (218)

	Journal		Page 4	

Date	Description	Post Ref.	Debit	Credit
19--				
June 12	Accounts Payable (Amfac Drug Supply)	218/√	46.20	
	Purchases Returns & Allow.	511.1		46.20
15	Accounts Payable (University Drug Co.)	218/√	53.70	
	Purchases Returns & Allow.	511.1		53.70

		Cash Payments Journal						Page 4

Date	Ck. No.	Account Debited	Post Ref.	General Dr.	Accounts Payable Dr.	Purchases Dr.	Purchases Discount Cr.	Cash Cr.
19--								
June 2	536	Rent Expense		1,000.00				1,000.00
9	537	Sullivan Co.	√		234.20		4.68	229.52
16	538	Amfac Drug Supply	√		516.20		5.16	511.04
23	539	Mutual Drug Co.	√		479.40		9.59	469.81
30	540	Dolgin Candy Co.	√			270.20		270.20
30				1,000.00	1,229.80	270.20	19.43	2,480.57
				(√)	(218)	(511)	(511.2)	(111)

2. *Account* Cash   *Acct. No.* 111

Date	Item	Post. Ref.	Debit	Credit	Balance Debit	Balance Credit
19--						
June 1	Balance	√			9,180.00	
30		CP4		2,480.57	6,699.43	

Account Accounts Payable   Acct. No. 218

Date	Item	Post. Ref.	Debit	Credit	Balance Debit	Balance Credit
19--						
June 1 Balance		√				6,217.69
12		J4	46.20			6,171.49
15		J4	53.70			6,117.79
30		P2		2,281.82		8,399.61
30		CP4	1,229.80			7,169.81

Account Purchases   Acct. No. 511

Date	Item	Post. Ref.	Debit	Credit	Balance Debit	Balance Credit
19--						
June 1 Balance		√			13,826.25	
30		P2	2,281.82		16,108.07	
30		CP4	270.20		16,378.27	

Account Purchases Returns and Allowances   Acct. No. 511.1

Date	Item	Post. Ref.	Debit	Credit	Balance Debit	Balance Credit
19--						
June 1 Balance		√				312.63
12		J4		46.20		358.83
15		J4		53.70		412.53

Account Purchases Discount   Acct. No. 511.2

Date	Item	Post. Ref.	Debit	Credit	Balance Debit	Balance Credit
19--						
June 1 Balance		√				211.45
30		CP4		19.43		230.88

Accounts Payable Ledger

Account Amfac Drug Supply

Date	Item	Post. Ref.	Debit	Credit	Balance
19--					
June 5		P2		562.40	562.40
12		J4	46.20		516.20
16		CP4	516.20		-0-

Account Flites Pharmaceuticals

Date	Item	Post. Ref.	Debit	Credit	Balance
19--					
June 27		P2		638.47	638.47

Account Mutual Drug Co.

Date	Item	Post. Ref.	Debit	Credit	Balance
19--					
June 14		P2		479.40	479.40
23		CP4	479.40		-0-

Account Sullivan Co.

Date	Item	Post. Ref.	Debit	Credit	Balance
19--					
June 1		P2		234.20	234.20
9		CP4	234.20		-0-

Account University Drug Co.

Date	Item	Post. Ref.	Debit	Credit	Balance
19--					
June 7		P2		367.35	367.35
15		J4	53.70		313.65

3. Balance of Accounts Payable, June 30 . . . . $7,169.81
   Less Balance of Accounts Payable, June 1 . . . . 6,217.69
   Difference . . . . $ 952.12

   Flites Pharmaceuticals . . . . $ 638.47
   University Drug Co. 313.65
   Total . . . . $ 952.12

*Note: Now that you have reviewed the Demonstration Problem and Solution you may complete the **Mastery Problem** at the end of the chapter activities.

Applying Accounting Concepts

Series A

Exercise 6A1—Interpretation of Invoice Terms. The following are some commonly used invoice terms. For each one, determine the due date and amount to be paid on a purchase invoice dated (not a leap year) February 2, 19--. The amount of $945.60 is subject to a cash discount. If two options exist as to dates and amounts, show both options.

(a) 30 days   (c) 2/EOM, n/60
(b) 2/10, n/30 (d) 4/10 EOM

' **Exercise 6A2—Journal Entries; Gross-Price Basis.** The following transactions occurred for Datamax Office Systems during the month of September:

Sept. 5   Purchased merchandise on account as follows:

15 Electronic printing calculators	$ 49.25 each
10 Electric self-correcting typewriters	795.00 each
5 Microcomputers.......................................	1,925.00 each

The amount of the purchase is subject to a trade discount of 10% and credit terms of 2/10, n/30.

Sept. 15   Issued a check for the amount due.

1. Journalize the transactions in two-column journal form using the gross-price basis of entering invoices.
2. Make the appropriate two-column journal entry if the payment is not made until October 5.

Exercise 6A3—Journal Entries; Net-Price Basis. Using the information from Exercise 6A2:

1. Journalize the transactions that occurred on September 5 and September 15 in two-column journal form using the net-price basis.
2. Make the appropriate journal entry if the payment is not made until October 5.

Exercise 6A4—Journal Entries; Net-Price Basis. The following transactions occurred for Club Heating and Air Conditioning in May and June:

May 26   Purchased merchandise on account from Albelene Sheet Metal, gross price, $4,048; terms 4/10, n/30. (Club uses net-price basis.)

June 26   Paid the balance due to Albelene Sheet Metal. (Take into account the amount of discount lost.)

Journalize the preceding transactions in two-column journal form.

Exercise 6A5—Calculation of Cost of Goods Sold. Determine the cost of goods sold based on the following data taken from the accounts of Essen Hardware, a small retail business.

Merchandise inventory, beginning of the period	$ 32,000
Purchases during the period	148,000
Purchases discounts lost during the period	460
Purchases returns and allowances during the period	8,400
Merchandise inventory, end of the period	35,000

Exercise 6A6—Entries in Purchases Journal. Maurice Williams, who operates Williams Pharmacy, completed the following transactions related to purchases of merchandise on account.

Aug. 3   Purchased medicine from Goldsmith Medicines, $490, terms, n/30. Invoice No. 260.

    3 Purchased jewelry from Romantique Company, $150, terms, n/30. Invoice No. 261.

  10 Purchased greeting cards from The Card Castle, $228, terms, n/30. Invoice No. 262.

  16 Purchased film from Clayton Camera, $114, terms, n/30. Invoice No. 263.

  18 Purchased medicines from Stewart Pharmacal Supplies, $778, terms, n/30. Invoice No. 264.

1. Prepare a purchases journal using the same format and account titles as illustrated in the chapter. Enter the purchases in the purchases journal.

2. Total and rule the journal.

Exercise 6A7—Entries in Cash Payments Journal.

1. Prepare a cash payments journal using the same format and account titles as illustrated in the chapter. Enter the payments of the transactions from Exercise 6A6 in the cash payments journal. Assume that payments were made 30 days after the date of purchase. Number the checks beginning with 575.

2. Enter the following transactions:

Sept. 20 Issued Check No. 580 for $700 to Center Delivery Service in payment of delivery service for drug store.

      25 Issued Check No. 581 for $266 to Butler Brothers for a cash purchase of medicines.

3. Total and rule the journal.

Series B

Exercise 6B1—Interpretation of Invoice Terms. The following are some commonly used invoice terms. For each one, determine the due date and amount to be paid on a purchase invoice dated January 2, 19--, (not a leap year) with an amount subject to cash discount of $654.90. If two options exist as to dates and amounts, show both options.

(a) 60 days   (c) 1/EOM, n/60
(b) 3/10, n/30 (d) 2/10 EOM

Exercise 6B2—Journal Entries; Gross-Price Basis. The following transactions occurred for Info Support Center during October:

Oct. 3 Purchased merchandise on account as follows:

25	Electronic printing calculators	$ 39.95 each
15	Electric self-correcting typewriters	755.00 each
10	Microcomputers	1,910.00 each

The amount of the purchase is subject to a trade discount of 5% and credit terms of 1/15, n/30.

Oct. 18   Issued a check for the amount due.

1. Journalize the transactions in two-column journal form using the gross-price basis of entering invoices.
2. Make the appropriate two-column journal entry if the payment is not made until November 2.

Exercise 6B3—Journal Entries; Net-Price Basis.   Using the information from Exercise 6B2:

1. Journalize the transactions that occurred on October 3 and October 18 in two-column journal form using the net-price basis.
2. Make the appropriate journal entry if the payment is not made until November 2.

Exercise 6B4—Journal Entries; Net-Price Basis.   The following transactions occurred for Beckmann Heating and Cooling in April and May:

April 25   Purchased merchandise on account from Alco Valve, gross price, $3,036; terms 3/10, n/30. (Beckmann uses net-price basis.)

May 25   Paid the balance due to Alco Valve. (Take into account the amount of discount lost.)

Journalize the preceding transactions in two-column journal form.

Exercise 6B5—Calculation of Cost of Goods Sold.   Determine the cost of goods sold based on the following data taken from the accounts of Paradise Paints, a small retail business.

Merchandise inventory, beginning of the period	$ 24,000
Purchases during the period	111,000
Purchases discounts lost during the period	3,450
Purchases returns and allowances during the period	6,300
Merchandise inventory, end of the period	26,250

Exercise 6B6—Entries in Purchases Journal.   Carl Schmitt, who operates Schmitt's Hardware, completed the following transactions related to purchases of merchandise on account.

July 3   Purchased formica from Azeno Sales, $360, terms, n/30. Invoice No. 350.

5   Purchased locks from Exotic Brass, $125, terms, n/30. Invoice No. 351.

10   Purchased tools from Tab-Buffalo, $180, terms, n/30. Invoice No. 352.

14   Purchased door frames from H & G Sales, $575, terms, n/30. Invoice No. 353.

18   Purchased nails from New Market Hardware, $580, terms, n/30. Invoice No. 354.

1. Prepare a purchases journal using the same format and account titles as illustrated in the chapter. Enter the purchases in the purchases journal.
2. Total and rule the journal.

Exercise 6B7—Entries in Cash Payments Journal.

1. Prepare a cash payments journal using the same format and account titles as illustrated in the chapter. Enter the payments of the transactions from Exercise 6B6 in the cash payments journal. Assume that payments were made 30 days after the date of purchase. Number the checks beginning with 465.
2. Enter the following transactions:

Aug. 21 Issued Check No. 470 for $525 to Kempermann Delivery Service in payment of delivery service for the hardware store.
   25 Issued Check No. 471 for $200 to Henges Brothers for a cash purchase of hardware.

3. Total and rule the journal.

Series A

Problem 6A1   Flow Chart Labeling

A partially completed flowchart showing some of the major documents commonly used in the purchases function of a merchandise business is presented below.

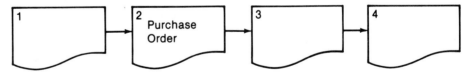

Required:
Identify documents 1, 3, and 4.

Problem 6A2   Purchase Requisition Preparation

If the working papers for this textbook are not used, omit Problems 6A2, 6A3, and 6A4.

You are employed by Heritage Garden & Crafts as manager of the Yard and Garden Department. You requisition the following merchandise on Sept. 1.

18 All steel rubber-tire wheelbarrows
30 Garden hose, 50 ft.
 3 Power mowers, 21" cut
 6 Heavy duty rototillers
18 Spade shovels
 9 Long-handle space shovels
18 Spade forks

Required:

Using the form provided in the working papers, prepare Requisition No. 204 for the preceding merchandise.

Specify that delivery is desired within 10 days and that you are to be notified upon receipt of the merchandise.

NOTE: *The department manager's memorandum at the bottom of the form should not be completed until after the purchase order is placed in Problem 6A3.*

Problem 6A3   Purchase Order Preparation

Sept. 2.   You are acting as purchasing agent for Heritage Garden & Crafts, and you are to order the merchandise specified on Requisition No. 204 in Problem No. 6A2; prices as follows:

All steel rubber-tire wheelbarrows	$ 22.50 ea.
Garden hose, 50 ft.	5.75 ea.
Power mower, 21" cut	187.45 ea.
Heavy duty rototillers	295.00 ea.
Spade shovels	7.95 ea.
Long-handle spade shovels	8.95 ea.
Spade forks	8.25 ea.

Required:

1. Using the purchase order form provided in the working papers (Purchase Order No. 631), order the merchandise on Requisition No. 204 from Problem No. 6A2. The merchandise is being ordered from Gardener's Supply, 1200 N. Milwaukee St., Milwaukee, WI, 53204-9868.
2. Specify shipment by Gateway Transfer FOB St. Louis; terms, 2/10, n/40.
3. After preparing the purchase order, fill in the department manager's memorandum at the bottom of Purchase Requisition No. 204. Assume that the requisition was approved by Isham Jones.

Problem 6A4   Purchase Invoice Verification

The following purchase invoice received from Gardeners' Supply has been referred to you for verification.

Required:

1. Compare it with Purchase Order No. 631 in Problem No. 6A3, and verify (a) the quantities ordered, (b) the quantities shipped, (c) the unit prices, (d) the extensions, and (e) the total amount of the invoice.
2. For each item that has been verified, report any discrepancies detected.

SOLD TO Heritage Garden & Crafts 8035 N. Broadway St. Louis, MO 63147-3274		SHIP TO same		INVOICE NO. **1540**	

GARDENER'S SUPPLY   𝓰𝓼
1200 N. Milwaukee St., Milwaukee, Wisconsin 53204-9868

YOUR ORDER NO. & DATE	INVOICE DATE
631 Sept. 2, 19--	Sept. 7, 19--
REQUISITION NO.	DATE SHIPPED
204	Sept. 7, 19--

TERMS 2/10,n/40	FOB St. Louis	CAR INITIALS & NO.	HOW SHIPPED & ROUTE Gateway Transfer	SHIPPED FROM Milwaukee

QUANTITY SHIPPED	DESCRIPTION	UNIT PRICE	EXTENSION
18	All steel rubber-tire wheelbarrows	22.50	405.00
30	Garden hose, 50 ft.	5.75	172.50
6	Power mower, 21" cut	187.45	1,124.70
6	Heavy duty rototillers	295.00	1,770.00
18	Spade shovels	7.95	153.40
9	Long-handle spade shovels	8.25	74.25
18	Spade forks	8.95	161.10
			3,860.95

Problem 6A5   Entries in Purchases Journal and Two-Column Journal; Posting to Selected Ledger Accounts

Tom Holling operates a business under the name of Tom's Toggery. The books of original entry include a purchases journal in which purchases of merchandise on account are entered using the gross price method and a two-column journal in which entries such as purchases returns and allowances are made. The invoice method of accounting is used for purchases on account; hence, in entering purchase invoices in the purchases journal, a check mark should be placed in the

Posting Reference column to indicate that individual posting is not required. Following are the transactions related to purchases for the month of March:

March 3 Purchased merchandise from Levin Jobbers on account, $797.28. Invoice No. 21, dated March 1; terms, 10 days.

6 Purchased merchandise from Hart, Schaffner, & Marx on account, $1,360.22. Invoice No. 22, dated March 6; terms, 30 days. Goods were shipped FOB shipping point and the invoice included $14.50 in freight charges. (Tom's charges freight costs to Purchases.)

10 Purchased merchandise from Povaratti's Imports on account, $3,237.30. Invoice No. 23, dated March 8; terms, 30 days.

14 Purchased merchandise from Tiger Supply Co., on account, $1,311.48. Invoice No. 24, dated March 9; terms, 30 days.

17 Received a credit memorandum from Bittle Co. for $57.00 for merchandise returned that had been purchased on account.

20 Purchased merchandise from Levin Jobbers for $1,085.86 on account. Invoice No. 25, dated March 17; terms, 10 days.

22 Received a credit memorandum from Levin Jobbers for $30.40 for merchandise returned that had been purchased on account.

27 Purchased merchandise from the Primo Sales Co. for $1,886.22 on account. Invoice No. 26, dated February 27; terms, 30 days. Goods were shipped FOB destination. The freight charges of $24.00 were paid by Primo and not included in the invoice.

Required:

1. Enter the transactions in a purchases journal and in a two-column journal. Total and rule the purchases journal.

2. Complete the summary posting of the purchases journal and the individual posting of the two-column journal to the following four-column ledger accounts:

Accounts Payable, Acct. No. 218,
   March 1 balance, $11,613.48
Purchases, Acct. No. 511,
   March 1 balance, $ 8,479.60
Purchases Returns and Allowances, Acct. No. 511.1
   March 1 balance, $416.84

Then, update the account balances. (In posting from the two journals, the page number preceded by the initials "P" or "J" should be placed in the Posting Reference column of the ledger account involved.)

Problem 6A6   Entries in Cash Payments Journal: Posting to Selected Ledger Accounts (Gross-Price Basis)

Judy Carter operates a retail shoe store. The books of original entry include a purchases journal in which all merchandise purchases on account are entered on

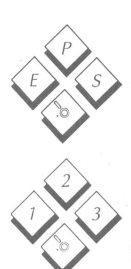

a gross-price basis and a cash payments journal in which all cash payments (except petty cash) are entered. Following are the transactions related to cash payments for the month of May:

May 1 Issued Check No. 47 for $1,200 in payment of rent (Rent Expense) for May.

3 Issued Check No. 48 to Robin's Shoes in payment on account, $960 less 2% discount.

9 Issued Check No. 49 to In-Step in payment on account, $1,050 less 3% discount.

12 Issued Check No. 50 for $146.25 to Supreme Electric for electrical repairs just completed (Repairs Expense).

19 Issued Check No. 51 to Omni Co. in payment for cash purchase, $595.

22 Issued Check No. 52 to Rockport Shoe in payment on account, $840. A discount of 2% was lost because Carter neglected to pay the invoice within the discount period.

26 Issued Check No. 53 to Seliga Co. in payment on account, $765 less 2% discount.

29 Issued Check No. 54 to Voss Co. in payment for cash purchases, $360.

Required:

1. Enter the transactions in a five-column cash payments journal. Number the journal page 4. Enter the totals and rule the journal.

2. Complete the summary posting of the cash payments journal to the following four-column ledger accounts:

    Cash, Account No. 111, May 1 balance, $12,240.00
    Accounts Payable, Account No. 218, May 1 balance, $8,290.26
    Purchases, Account No. 511, May 1 balance, $18,435.00
    Purchases Discount, Account No. 511.2, May 1 balance, $281.94

Then, update the account balances. (In posting from this journal, the page number preceded by the initials "CP" should be placed in the Posting Reference column of the ledger account involved.) (Use the five-column cash payments journal and the ledger accounts found in the working papers.)

19.2

Problem 6A7   Entries in Cash Payments Journal; Posting to Selected Ledger Accounts (Net-Price Basis)

See Problem No. 6A6. Assume that Carter enters all purchases on account on a net-price basis.

Required:

1. Enter the transactions listed in Problem No. 6A6 in a five-column cash payments journal. Enter the totals and rule the journal.

2. Open the following general ledger accounts. Then, complete the summary posting of the cash payments journal.

Cash, Account No. 111, May 1 balance, $12,240.00
Accounts Payable, Account No. 218, May 1 balance, $8,205.10
Purchases, Account No. 511, May 1 balance, $18,252.30
Purchases Discounts Lost, Account No. 555, May 1 balance, $10.28.
(Use the five-column cash payments journal and the ledger accounts found in the working papers.)

Series B

Problem 6B1   Flow Chart Labeling

A partially completed flowchart showing some of the major documents commonly used in the purchases function of a merchandise business is presented below.

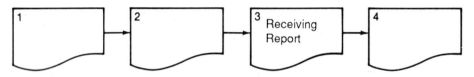

Required:
Identify documents 1, 2 and 4.

Problem 6B2   Purchase Requisition Preparation

If the working papers for this textbook are not used, omit Problems 6B2, 6B3, and 6B4.

You are employed by Winchester Hardware, a retail hardware business, as manager of the Lawn and Garden Department. You requisition the following merchandise on Oct. 2.

24 All steel rubber-tire wheelbarrows
40 Garden hose, 50 ft.
 4 Power mowers, 21" cut
 8 Heavy duty rototillers
24 Spade shovels
12 Long-handle spade shovels
24 Spade forks

Required:

Using the form provided in the working papers, prepare Requisition No. 306 for the preceding merchandise. Specify that delivery is desired within 10 days and that you are to be notified upon receipt of the merchandise.

NOTE: The department manager's memorandum at the bottom of the form should not be completed until after the purchase order is placed in Problem 6B3.

Problem 6B3　　Purchase Order Preparation

Oct. 3. You are acting as purchasing agent for Winchester Hardware, and you are to order the merchandise specified on Requisition No. 306 in Problem No. 6B2; prices as follows:

All steel rubber-tire wheelbarrows	$27.75 ea.
Garden hose, 50 ft.	6.35 ea.
Power mower, 21" cut	246.50 ea.
Heavy duty rototillers	395.00 ea.
Spade shovels	9.95 ea.
Long-handle spade shovels	10.95 ea.
Spade forks	10.25 ea.

Required:

1. Using the purchase order form provided in the working papers (Purchase Order No. 526), order the merchandise on Requisition No. 306 from Problem No. 6B2. The merchandise is being ordered from Howard's Hardware, 4064 Laclede Ave., St. Louis, MO 63108-9868.
2. Specify shipment by Transmart, Inc., FOB St. Louis; terms, 2/10, n/30.
3. After preparing the purchase order, fill in the department manager's memorandum at the bottom of Purchase Requisition No. 306. Assume that the requisition was approved by George Olsen.

Problem 6B4　　Purchase Invoice Verification

The purchase invoice at the top of page 244 received from Howard's Hardware has been referred to you for verification.

Required:

1. Compare it with Purchase Order No. 526 in Problem No. 6B3, and verify (a) the quantities ordered, (b) the quantities shipped, (c) the unit prices, (d) the extensions, and (e) the total amount of the invoice.
2. For each item that has been verified, report any discrepancies detected.

INVOICE NO. 1275	SOLD TO Winchester Hardware 224 W. Argonne St. St. Louis, MO 63122-3274		SHIP TO same	

Howard's Hardware 4064 Laclede Ave. St. Louis, MO 63108-9868	INVOICE DATE Oct. 9, 19--	YOUR ORDER NO & DATE 526 Oct. 3, 19--
	REQUISITION NO. 306	DATE SHIPPED Oct. 8, 19--

TERMS 2/10, n/30	FOB St. Louis	CAR INITIALS & NO.	HOW SHIPPED & ROUTE Transmart, Inc.	SHIPPED FROM St. Louis

QUANTITY SHIPPED	DESCRIPTION	UNIT PRICE	EXTENSION
24	All steel rubber-tire wheelbarrows	27.75	666.00
40	Garden hose, 50 ft.	6.35	254.00
8	Power mower, 21" cut	246.50	1,972.00
8	Heavy duty rototillers	395.00	3,160.00
24	Spade shovels	9.95	288.30
12	Long-handle spade shovels	10.25	123.00
24	Spade forks	10.95	262.80
			6,726.10

Problem 6B5   Entries in Purchases Journal and Two-Column Journal; Posting to Selected Ledger Accounts.

Joanne Tackes operates a business under the name of Joanne's Juvenile Shop. The books of original entry include a purchases journal in which purchases of merchandise on account are entered using the gross price method and a two-column journal in which entries such as purchases returns and allowances are recorded. The invoice method of accounting is used for purchases on account; hence, in entering purchase invoices in the purchases journal, a check mark should be placed in the Posting Reference column to indicate that individual posting is not required. Following are the transactions related to purchases for the month of January:

Jan. 3   Purchased merchandise from Britney on account, $597.96. Invoice No. 41, dated January 2; terms, 10 days.

4   Purchased merchandise from Royer Mfg. Co. on account, $1,020.15. Invoice No. 42, dated January 4; terms, 30 days. Goods were shipped FOB shipping point and the invoice included $10.85 in freight charges. (Joanne's charges freight costs to Purchases.)

11   Purchased merchandise from Contadore's Imports on account, $2,427.95. Invoice No. 43, dated January 9; terms, 30 days.

13 Purchased merchandise from Verona Supply Co., on account $983.61. Invoice No. 44, dated January 11; terms, 30 days.

17 Received a credit memorandum from Millie's Apparel for $42.75 for merchandise returned that had been purchased on account.

18 Purchased merchandise from Britney for $814.40 on account. Invoice No. 45, dated January 17; terms, 10 days.

23 Received a credit memorandum from Britney for $22.80 for merchandise returned that had been purchased on account.

25 Purchased merchandise from the Lamberti Sport Co. for $1,414.66 on account. Invoice No. 46, dated January 25; terms, 30 days. Goods were shipped FOB destination. The freight charges of $18.00 were paid by Lamberti and not included in the invoice.

Required:

1. Enter the transactions in a purchases journal and in a two-column journal. Total and rule the purchases journal.

2. Complete the summary posting of the purchases journal and the individual posting of the two-column journal to the following 4-column ledger accounts:
   Accounts Payable, Acct. No. 218,
     Jan. 1 balance, $8,710.11
   Purchases, Acct. No. 511,
     Jan. 1 balance, $6,359.70
   Purchases Returns and Allowances, Acct. No. 511.1
     Jan. 1 balance, $312.63

   Then, update the account balances. (In posting from the two journals, the page number preceded by the initials "P" or "J" should be placed in the Posting Reference column of the ledger account involved.)

Problem 6B6   **Entries in Cash Payments Journal; Posting to Selected Ledger Accounts (Gross-Price Method)**

Ray Sobocinski operates a retail variety store. The books of original entry include a purchases journal in which all merchandise purchases on account are entered on a gross-price basis and a cash payments journal in which all cash payments (except petty cash) are entered. Following are the transactions related to cash payments for the month of April:

April 3 Issued Check No. 87 for $1,000.00 in payment of rent (Rent Expense) for April.

4 Issued Check No. 88 to Acme Premium Supply in payment on account, $320.00 less 2% discount.

10 Issued Check No. 89 to Fairway Mfg. in payment on account, $350.00 less 3% discount.

14 Issued Check No. 90 for $48.25 to Chapnick Electric for electrical repairs just completed (Repairs Expense).

19   Issued Check No. 91 to Giuliani Co. in payment for cash purchase, $185.00.

24   Issued Check No. 92 to Custom Sports in payment on account, $210.00. A discount of 2% was lost because Sobocinski neglected to pay the invoice within the discount period.

27   Issued Check No. 93 to The Puzzle Box in payment on account, $255.00, less 2% discount.

28   Issued Check No. 94 to Leftie's Corner in payment for cash purchases, $120.00.

Required:

1.   Enter the transactions in a five-column cash payments journal. Enter the totals and rule the journal.

2.   Complete the summary posting of the cash payments journal to the following four-column ledger accounts:

   Cash, Account No. 111, Apr. 1 balance, $3,060.00
   Accounts Payable, Account No. 218, Apr. 1 balance, $2,072.56
   Purchases, Account No. 511, Apr. 1 balance, $4,608.75
   Purchases Discount, Account No. 511.2, Apr. 1 balance, $70.48

Then, update the account balances. (In posting from this journal, the page number preceded by the initials "CP" should be placed in the Posting Reference column of the ledger account involved.) (Use the five-column cash payments journal and the ledger accounts found in the working papers.)

Problem 6B7   Entries in Cash Payments Journal; Posting to Selected Ledger Accounts (Net-Price Basis)

See Problem 6B6. Assume that Sobocinski enters all purchases on account on a net-price basis.

Required:

1.   Enter the transactions listed in Problem No. 6B6 in a five-column cash payments journal. Enter the totals and rule the journal.

2.   Open the following general ledger accounts. Then, complete the summary posting of the cash payments journal.

   Cash, Account No. 111, Apr. 1 balance, $3,060.00
   Accounts Payable, Account No. 218, Apr. 1 balance, $2,051.25
   Purchases, Account No. 511, Apr. 1 balance, $4,563.10
   Purchases Discounts Lost, Account No. 555, Apr. 1 balance, $2.55.

(Use the five-column cash payments journal and the ledger accounts found in the working papers.)

Mastery Problem

If the working papers for the textbook are not used, omit the Mastery Problem.

Michelle French owns and operates "Books and More," a retail book store. The following purchases and cash payments transactions took place during the month of June. French uses the net-price method of accounting for purchases of inventory.

June 1 Purchased books on account from Irving Publishing Company for $2,100.00, terms, 2/10, n/30, FOB destination. Issued Invoice No. 101.

2 Made payment on account to North-Eastern Publishing Company for goods purchased on May 23, terms, 2/10, n/30. Issued Check No. 300 for $2,000.00.

3 Purchased books on account from Broadway Publishing Inc. for $3,200.00, subject to 20% and 10% trade discounts and invoice terms of 3/10, n/30; FOB shipping point. Issued Invoice No. 102.

3 Paid shipping charges to Mayday Shipping for delivery from Broadway Publishing Company, $250.00. Issued Check No. 301.

4 Paid rent for the month of June, $625.00. Issued Check No. 302

8 Purchased books on account from North-Eastern Publishing Company for $5,825.00, terms, 2/EOM, n/60, FOB destination. Issued Invoice No. 103.

9 Made payment to Bonzi Shipping Company for books delivered from North-Eastern Publishing Company, FOB destination on June 8th. Issued Check No. 303 for $400.00.

10 Received a credit memorandum from Irving Publishing Company for $550.00 (gross-price). Books had been returned because the covers were on upside down.

13 Made payment on account to Broadway Publishing Inc. for the purchase made on June 3. Check No. 304 was issued.

28 Made the purchases listed below:

Inv. No.	Company	Amount	Terms
104	Broadway Pub. Inc.	$2,350.00	2/10, n/30; FOB Destination
105	North-Eastern Pub. Co.	4,200.00	2/EOM, n/60; FOB Destination
106	Riley Publishing Co.	3,450.00	3/10, n/30; FOB Destination

30 Paid utilities for month of June, to Taylor County Utility Co. Issued Check No. 305 for $325.00.

30 French withdrew $4,500.00 for personal use. Issued Check No. 306.

30 Made payment on account to Irving Publishing Company for purchase made on June 1, less returns made on June 10. Check No. 307 was issued.

30 Made payment to North-Eastern Publishing Company for purchase made on June 8th. Issued Check No. 308.

30 Purchased books at an auction. Issued Check No. 309 for $1,328.00.

Required:

1. Enter the above transactions in the appropriate journals.

2. Total and rule the purchases journal and cash payments journal.
3. Post from the journals to the general ledger accounts and the accounts payable subsidiary ledger.
4. Prepare a schedule of accounts payable.
5. If merchandise inventory was $35,523.00 on January 1 and $42,100.00 as of June 30, prepare the cost of goods sold section of the income statement for the six months ended June 30, 19--.

CHAPTER 7

Accounting for Sales and Collections

Chapter
Objectives

Careful study of this chapter should enable you to:

- Describe various types of sales and explain how to process them.

- Describe retail sales taxes and the related accounting procedures.

- Describe commonly followed practices in processing incoming orders for merchandise, including the use of the following source documents:

  1. Customer purchase order
  2. Sales ticket or invoice
  3. Customer's check
  4. Credit memorandum

- Define the terms sale, sales discounts, sales returns and allowances.

- Enter sales transactions with discounts, returns and allowances.

- Determine net sales and gross margin (gross profit).

- Describe two methods of maintaining subsidiary records for accounts receivable:

  1. the "sales ticket" method
  2. the accounts receivable ledger method.

- Explain and use a special journal for sales of merchandise on account.

- Explain and use a special journal for all cash receipts.

- Prepare a schedule of accounts receivable.

I n the calculation of periodic income under the accrual basis, revenues earned during a period are matched against expenses incurred as a result of the efforts made to produce the revenues. Revenues are considered to have been realized once the firm receives cash or a collectible claim to cash as the result of selling a product or providing a service.

The purpose of this chapter is to describe and explain the accrual method of accounting for sales of merchandise and the subsequent collection of remittances for such sales. The setting is the same small retail enterprise introduced in Chapter 6. Commonly used source documents for sales and collections will be discussed and illustrated, and special journals for sales and cash receipts will be introduced and explained.

Source Documents and Associated Records for Sales And Collections

Define the term sale.

A sale is the transfer of the ownership of merchandise from one business or individual to another in exchange for something of value, typically cash or the promise to pay cash at a later date. To understand the role of the various source documents and associated records for sales, it is helpful to know the nature of the underlying sales transactions. A variety of types of sales can be identified in the retail business world.

Types of Sales

Describe various types of sales and explain how to process them.

Eight types of sales will be discussed here: (1) cash sales; (2) sales on account; (3) bank credit card sales; (4) COD sales; (5) sales on approval; (6) layaway sales; (7) installment sales; and (8) consignment sales.

■ **Cash Sales.** Some businesses sell merchandise for cash only, while others sell merchandise either for cash or on account. A variety of practices are followed in the handling of **cash sales**. If such transactions are numerous, it is probable that one or more types of electronic cash register will be used. In this instance, the original entry of the sales is made in the register. Often, registers have the capability of accumulating more than one total. This means that by using the proper key, each amount that is entered in the register can be classified by type of merchandise, by department, or by salesperson. Where sales tax is involved, the amount of the tax may be separately entered.

In many retail establishments, salesclerks prepare sales tickets in triplicate for cash sales. (Sales tickets will be discussed and illustrated in a subsequent section.) Sometimes the preparation of the sales tickets involves the use of a cash register that enters the amount of the sale directly on the ticket. Modern electronic cash registers serve as input terminals that are "on line" with computers, that is, in direct communication with the central processor. At the end of each day the cash received is compared with the record that the register provides. The receipts may also be compared with the total of the cash-sales tickets, if the system makes use of the latter. (A daily summary of a cash register tape is illustrated on page 251. The colored numbers in parentheses refer to the different types of sales.)

■ **Sales on Account.** **Sales on account** are often referred to as "charge sales" because the seller exchanges merchandise for the buyer's promise to pay. This promise to pay represents an asset to the seller called accounts receivable. Selling goods on account is common practice at the retail level of the distribution process. Firms that sell goods on account should investigate the financial reliability of those to whom they sell. A business of some size may have a separate credit department whose major function is to establish credit policies and decide upon requests for credit from persons and firms who wish to buy goods on account. Sea-

```
        (1)
    CASH SALES          327.79 +
        (3)
    MCARD/VISA          550.62 +
        (6)
    LAYAWAY              79.50 +
    TOTAL CASH          957.91 *
        (2)
    CHARGE SALES        543.84 +
        (5)
    APPROVAL            126.58 +
    TOTAL CHARGE        670.42 *

    TOTAL SALES       1,628.33 G*
    SALES TAX            81.42 +
                         81.42 *

    REC'D ON ACCT.      324.51 +
                        324.51 *

    PAID OUT             76.51 +
                         76.51 *

    NO SALE               0.00 +
                          0.00 *

    *   SUB-TOTAL
    G*  GRAND TOTAL
```

Cash Register Tape Summary

soned judgment is needed to avoid a credit policy that is so stringent that profitable business may be refused, or a credit policy that is so liberal that uncollectible account losses may become excessive.

Generally, no goods are delivered until the salesclerk has been assured that the buyer has established credit—that there is an account for this customer with the company. In the case of many retail businesses, customers with established credit are provided with credit cards or charge plates, which provide evidence that the buyer has an account. These are used in mechanical or electronic devices to print the customer's name and other identification on the sales tickets. For orders received by mail or by phone, verification of the buyer's status can be handled as a routine matter before the goods are delivered.

Bank Credit Card Sales. Retail sales of certain types of goods and services to customers using bank credit cards are referred to as bank credit card sales. The two most widely used credit cards of this type in the United States are the VISA card and the MasterCard. Several thousand banks participate in each of these programs. The two systems have much in common.

Participating banks encourage their depositors and other customers to obtain the cards by supplying the necessary information to establish their credit reliability. When this is accomplished, a small plastic card containing the cardholder's name, an identifying number, and an expiration date is issued to the applicant. Validation of a credit card sale can be obtained through an on-line computer system at the register that verifies the card number, records the amount of sale, and grants approval. Both VISA and

MasterCard also furnish participating businesses with lists of expired or otherwise invalid credit cards at frequent intervals. Merchants and other businesses are invited to participate in the program.

The sales slips for the bank credit card sales must be filled out according to the conditions set by the bank. The bank will only accept for deposit properly completed and signed copies of sales slips (also called "tickets" or "drafts") for goods sold or services rendered to cardholders. The bank, in effect, either "buys" the tickets at a discount (commonly 4%, though it may be more or less depending upon various factors) immediately, or gives the merchant immediate credit for the full amount of the tickets. If the latter practice is used, then once a month the bank charges the merchant's account with the total amount of the discount, at the agreed rate. This latter practice is more common.

For the merchant, bank credit card sales are nearly the equivalent of cash sales. The service is performed or the goods are sold, and the money is secured. It is then up to the bank to collect from the buyer or bear the loss, if the account proves to be uncollectible.

In most respects, accounting for bank credit card sales is very similar to accounting for regular cash sales. A regular sales ticket may be prepared as well as the credit card form of invoice. Usually the transactions are accounted for as sales for the full price, with the amount of the discount being treated as an expense when the bank makes the monthly charge or immediately discounts the tickets. Entries for both methods of handling the discount are illustrated below.

Entries when the bank gives full credit for the sales and then charges a 4% fee once a month:

Cash...	100,000	
Sales...		100,000

Bank Credit Card Expense	4,000	
Cash..		4,000

Entry when the bank deducts a 4% discount at the time the sales invoices are deposited:

Cash..	96,000	
Bank Credit Card Expense	4,000	
Sales...		100,000

Although VISA and MasterCard are the most widely used credit cards, other forms of retail credit cards exist. These forms include cards used by petroleum companies, the American Express Card, and the Diner's Club card. Sales involving these cards are similar in many respects to bank credit card sales.

COD Sales. Collect on Delivery sales (COD sales), are sales of merchandise or other property for which payment must be made at the time the goods are delivered to the buyer by the seller or the agent. The agent usually is an employee of the seller but may also be a messenger, the postal service, an express company, or any common carrier (railroad, truck line, airline, etc.).

In retail merchandising, COD sales tickets are separated each day and a COD list is prepared for control purposes. The merchandise is then delivered to the customer and the sale price is collected upon delivery. When the money is turned in to the seller, the driver or other agent is given credit for the collection on the COD list and the sale is entered in the same manner as a cash sale. If the customer refuses to accept the merchandise, it is returned to stock and no entries are made. Under this plan of handling COD sales, title to the merchandise does not pass to the customer until the goods are delivered and collection has been made; therefore, the merchandise is considered to be part of the inventory of the seller until a remittance is received.

Sales on Approval. Sales that give the customer the right to return the goods within a specified time are called sales on approval. Typically these sales are handled the same as ordinary cash sales. No journal entries are made until it is definitely known that the goods will be retained by the customer. Until this can be determined, a separate record of customers who have purchased merchandise on approval is maintained. When the money is received, the sale is entered in the books. If the goods are returned, they are placed back in stock and no entries are made.

Layaway Sales. Sales on approval should not be confused with layaway sales. Layaway sales may be made for cash or on account, but in either case the customer agrees to accept the goods at a later date. Sometimes a deposit is made by the buyer with the understanding that the merchandise will be held until some future date. On or before this date, the buyer either picks up the merchandise or requests that the merchandise be delivered. If the customer requests delivery on a COD basis, a COD slip is made for the proper amount. When the remittance is received, it is entered in the same manner as if the customer had picked up the merchandise and paid cash.

Although businesses account for deposits on layaway sales in different ways, a common accounting method is to enter the deposits in the same manner as cash sales. When this method is used, a charge sales ticket is prepared for the balance due and is entered by debiting a special accounts receivable control account and crediting the sales account. Individual accounts with layaway customers may be kept in a special subsidiary ledger, sometimes referred to as a layaway ledger.

At the end of the accounting period, the total amount due from customers who made deposits on layaway sales is treated as ordinary accounts receivable. The cost of the merchandise that is being held is not included in the inventory because it is considered to be the property of the customer.

Installment Sales. A sale in which a buyer places a down payment on goods or services and agrees to pay the remainder of the sales price in installments is called an installment sale. These payments, sometimes referred to as installment payments, are arranged in fractional amounts over an extended period of time. Usually, an interest component is added to these payments.

When the seller carries the account rather than requiring the buyer to borrow the money elsewhere, it is desirable to use a special form of subsidiary ledger account for entering installment transactions. A different subsidiary ledger account is kept for each buyer. Together these subsidiary ledger accounts comprise what is called an "installment ledger." This installment ledger contains the details of the general ledger account entitled **Installment Accounts Receivable**.

Normal accounting practice is to regard installment sales as regular sales on account. This means that all revenue from an installment sale is considered to be realized at the point of sale. For income tax purposes, however, an alternative method is available which basically postpones the recognition of the revenue from the sale until cash is received. This "installment method" of accounting is somewhat complex and typically covered in upper-level accounting courses.

Consignment Sales. An arrangement in which one business, known as the consignor, ships goods to another business, known as the consignee, without any change in the legal ownership of the goods, is called a consignment sale. The consignee acts as an agent for the consignor and attempts to sell the goods, usually at prices specified by the consignor. If the goods are sold, the consignee receives an agreed commission, which is deducted from the proceeds of the sales when remittance of the amount due is made to the consignor. Consigned goods in the hands of the consignee at the end of the accounting period are a part of the consignor's inventory until sold and should be included in that account balance. Sale of such goods is entered by the consignor when they are sold by the consignee.

Sometimes, each party keeps a set of memorandum accounts for consignment transactions. These accounts are used to maintain a record of consignment transactions, but are not part of the "official" accounting records and would not appear on the financial statements. In other cases, no entries are made until the goods have been sold. Consignment selling is not a widespread practice.

Retail Sales Tax

Describe retail sales
taxes.

A tax imposed by many cities and states upon retail sales of tangible personal property at retail is known as a retail sales tax. The tax usually is a percentage of the gross sales price. Retail sales taxes may also be imposed upon services, in which case the tax is a percentage of the cost of such services. The rates of the tax vary considerably. In most states the tax is a general sales tax. However, in some states the tax is imposed only on specific items, such as automobiles, cosmetics, radios, television sets, and playing cards. Food items and medicines are often exempt from tax. To avoid fractions of cents and to simplify the determination of the tax, it is customary to use a sales tax table or schedule. For example, where the rate is 5%, the tax may be calculated as shown in the schedule below.

Amount of Sale	Amount of Tax
1¢ to 10¢	None
11¢ to 29¢	1¢
30¢ to 49¢	2¢
50¢ to 69¢	3¢
70¢ to 89¢	4¢
90¢ to $1.09	5¢

and so on

The amount of the tax imposed under the schedule approximates the legal rate. Retail sales tax reports accompanied by remittances for the amounts due must be filed periodically, either monthly or quarterly, depending upon the law of the state or city in which the business is located.

Customer Purchase Order

Describe commonly
followed practices in
processing orders for
merchandise.

The following flowchart shows some of the major documents and procedures commonly used in the sales function of a merchandising business. Each of these documents and procedures is explained in the following sections.

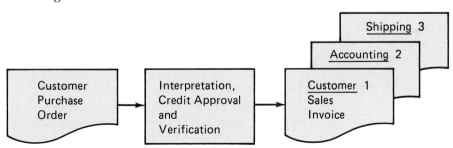

Sales by merchants often occur from purchase orders received by mail or telephone. Orders received by mail may be entered on the purchase order form, letterhead, or other stationery of the buyer or on an order blank furnished by the seller. An illustration of a typical purchase order form was shown on page 205. Usually when an order is received, a rubber stamp impression with spaces to show the date received, credit approval, approval of prices shown, and date of billing is stamped on its face. The person or persons handling the order fill in the appropriate data on the stamped form. Orders received by telephone are entered on forms provided for that purpose.

Procedure for Handling Incoming Purchase Orders. The procedures for handling purchase orders vary widely with different firms. Every business should establish a well-organized set of procedures to promote efficiency. Also by adhering to these procedures, the business will be able to maintain an internal check that will help in preventing mistakes in handling orders. The following five steps constitute the core of such procedures.

Interpretation. Each purchase order received should be interpreted as to (a) identity of the customer and (b) quantity and description of items ordered. Orders may be received from old or new customers. Sometimes it is difficult to identify a new customer, particularly if there has been no previous correspondence or the customer has not been contacted by the seller's representative. In some cases, it is difficult to identify the items ordered because customers frequently are careless in describing the merchandise. Different items of merchandise may be specified by name or stock number. Care should be used to make sure that the stock number agrees with the description of the item.

Credit Approval. All purchase orders received that involve credit in any form, should be referred to the office manager or credit department for approval before any goods are shipped. COD orders should also be approved because some customers have a reputation for not accepting COD shipments. COD shipments are then returned at the seller's expense. Customers who abuse the COD privilege may be required thereafter to send cash with the order, either in full or partial payment. Some firms follow this policy for all merchandise to be shipped COD.

Verification of Purchase Orders. The unit prices specified on purchase orders should be verified, proper extensions should be made, and the total should be entered. Persons performing this function usually use electronic calculating machines.

Shipping. In handling each purchase order, it is necessary to determine how shipment will be made and how the transportation charges will be handled. Shipment may be made by parcel post, express, or freight. Parcel post packages may be insured. Express shipments may be made by rail or air. Freight shipments may be made by rail, air, truck, or water.

The transportation charges must be prepaid on shipments made by parcel post. The transportation charges on express and freight shipments may be prepaid by the seller or may be paid by the customer upon receipt of the shipment. When transportation charges are prepaid by the seller, they may or may not be added to the invoice, depending upon whether prices have been quoted FOB shipping point or FOB destination.

If shipment is made by freight, it is also necessary to determine the routing of the shipment. The buyer may specify how shipment should be made. When the buyer does not indicate any preference, the seller must determine whether to make shipment by rail, truck, air, or water. The seller must also decide on what transportation company to use. Shipment to certain points may be made via a variety of different trucking companies, airlines, or railroads.

A retail merchant like Northern Micro would seldom incur transportation charges in connection with its sales. If any such charges are incurred, they can be charged to an operating expense account entitled Freight Out and entered in the cash payments journal.

Billing. The last step in the handling of an order is preparing the sales ticket or invoice. The sales ticket or invoice usually is prepared on a typewriter, billing machine, or computer-printer. Sales invoices should be numbered consecutively. By using some form of copying equipment, additional copies may be prepared. At least three copies usually are considered necessary. The original should go to the customer as an acknowledgement of the order; a copy should go to accounting personnel for data entry purposes; and a copy should be used as authority for packing and shipping the merchandise.

Additional copies of the sales ticket or invoice may also be used for the following purposes by larger organizations:

1. One copy may go to the salesperson in whose territory the sale is made.
2. One copy may go to a branch office, if the sale is made in a territory served by such an office.
3. One copy may serve as a label to be secured to the carton or package in which shipment is made. Usually this copy is perforated so that only that part containing the name and the address of the customer is used.

Sales Ticket

The source document of a sales transaction is called a sales ticket or sales invoice. Whether merchandise is sold for cash or on account, a sales ticket should be prepared. When the sale is for cash, the ticket may be printed by the cash register at the time that the sale is keyed in. However, some stores prefer to use individually prepared sales tickets whether the sale is for cash or on account. The same flexibility does not exist for entering charge sales; a sales ticket or charge slip must be prepared for every sale on account. In preparing a charge sales ticket the date, the name and address of the customer, the quantity, a description of the items sold, the unit prices, the total amount of the sale, and the amount of the sales tax should be entered. Each salesperson may be provided with a separate pad of consecutively numbered sales tickets. Each pad has a different letter or number on it that identifies the clerk. This code helps in determining the amount of goods sold by each clerk.

The following sales ticket shows the type of information usually obtained.

N NORTHERN MICRO		206B
1099 E. Louisiana, Indianapolis, IN 46202-3322		

Account No.	Sold by	Date
		4/10/--

Sold to Bill Darson
Address 429 S. Holiday Dr.
City South Bend   State IN   Zip 46615-1928

Send to same
Address
City   State   Zip

Rec'd. on Acct. ☐   Charge Sale ☒   Sales Ret./Allow. ☐

Quantity	Articles	Amount	
15	Double-sided, double-density diskette	12	00
	Tax		60
		12	60

Bill Darson
CUSTOMER'S SIGNATURE
All claims & returned goods MUST be accompanied by this bill.

Sales Ticket

Define sales discounts, sales returns and allowances

■ **Discounts.** Trade discounts allowed on sales are usually shown as deductions in determining the total of the sales ticket or invoice. Such discounts should not be entered in the accounts of the seller, since they only represent a reduction in the selling price of the merchandise. The use of trade discounts helps the supplier avoid the frequent publication of catalogs.

Cash discounts offered by the seller to encourage prompt payment are called sales discounts and should be indicated in the terms of the sale.

Retailers seldom offer sales discounts, while wholesalers often use this technique. When sales discounts are offered, they may be accounted for separately in a contra revenue account called Sales Discounts.

■ **Customer's Check.** Assume that on April 14 TTA Products collects the April 2 invoice of $756.00, illustrated below. A copy of the invoice is removed from an "uncollected invoices" file, and a rubber stamp is used to imprint the notation "Received" and the date of collection "4/14/--" on the face of this copy. The check number and amount received are

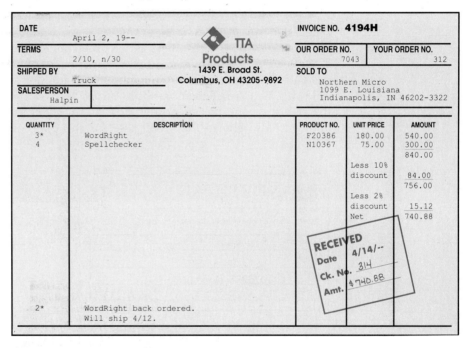

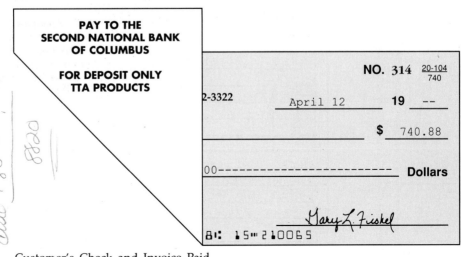

Customer's Check and Invoice Paid

then entered on the proper lines as shown at the top of page 259. Note that the amount received is $740.88, the invoice amount of $756.00 less the 2% cash discount.

The check received from the customer is endorsed for deposit with another rubber stamp, as shown at the bottom of page 259, and deposited in the bank. The copy of the invoice is then placed in a "collected invoices" file in alphabetic order by customer's name.

Credit Memorandum

Articles of merchandise returned by the customer for a refund are called sales returns. Reductions in the price of the merchandise granted by the seller due to defects or other problems are called sales allowances. If credit is given for merchandise returned or an allowance is made, it is customary to issue a credit memorandum for the amount involved. The following is a credit memorandum issued by Northern Micro, authorizing the return of one box of printer ribbons by Harry Sitler. The credit memorandum also shows the credit due for the price of the ribbons and the sales tax.

NORTHERN MICRO			72
1099 E. Louisiana, Indianapolis, IN 46202-3322			

Date April 28, 19--			
Name Harry Sitler			
Address 2730 Bent Brook Dr.			
City Indianapolis State IN Zip 46250-1998			

Sales Number		OK	
Cash Refund	Mdse Order	Charge ✓	Gift	Amount 102.90

Quantity	Articles	Amount
1 Box	Printer ribbons	98.00
	Tax	4.90
		102.90

One hundred two 90/100 ————— Dollars
Reason Not needed
Rec'd. Stock By Laura Murphy
x Harry Sitler
Customer's Signature

(handwritten note in margin: show they owe you your own money Two)

Credit Memorandum

If a customer is given credit for merchandise returned or given an allowance, the amount of credit and the remaining balance should be noted on the charge sales ticket to which the credit relates. If a credit memorandum is issued to a customer, it should be prepared in duplicate and a copy should be attached to the sales ticket on which the amount is noted.

Statement of Account

When merchandise is sold on account, it is customary to send a monthly bill to each charge customer. An itemized bill, showing the amount still owed from the previous month and the detailed charges and credits to the customer's account during the current month, is known as a statement of account. Usually the statements are mailed as soon as they can be completed following the close of each month or at a time during the month determined by the billing cycle. The use of "billing cycles" is limited, generally, to businesses with hundreds or thousands of customers. When a remittance is not received from the customer within the usual credit period, a copy of the statement of account may be sent to the credit department for the credit manager to review.

The following is Vivian Winston's statement of account for the month ended March 31. It shows (1) the balance at the beginning of the month amounting to $800.00; (2) a charge of $1,500.00 made on March 29; (3) a

NORTHERN MICRO

STATEMENT

1099 E. Louisiana, Indianapolis, IN 46202-3322

Account Number
0619 7238 9174 6

Previous Balance	Charges	Credits	Balance
$800.00	$1,500.00	$800.00	$1,500.00

Vivian Winston
50 Monument Circle
Indianapolis, IN 46206-1285

$

Amount paid

Please detach this portion and return with your remittance

Please save this portion for your records

Date	Description	Charges	Credits	Balance
3/1/--				800.00
3/29/--	Merchandise	1,500.00		2,300.00
3/31/--	Payment Rec'd		800.00	1,500.00

Statement of Account

credit of $800.00 for cash received on March 31; and (4) the balance at the close of the month amounting to $1,500.00. Note that the customer is asked to tear off the upper portion of the statement, fill in the amount of the remittance, and return it along with the remittance.

Building Your Accounting Knowledge

1. How is periodic income calculated under the accrual basis of accounting?
2. In what two ways does a bank accept copies of bank credit card sales invoices or tickets for deposit?
3. In what ways do layaway sales differ from sales on approval?
4. Briefly describe the nature of consignment sales.
5. What is the usual basis of measurement for a retail sales tax?
6. What five steps constitute the core of a set of procedures for the proper handling of customer purchase orders?
7. If a sales ticket is prepared in triplicate, what distribution should be made of the copies?
8. What is done with the sales invoice at the time of its collection?
9. Under what circumstances is it customary for a seller of merchandise to issue a credit memorandum?
10. Explain the purpose of a statement of account.

▨ Assignment Box

To reinforce your understanding of the preceding text materials, you may complete the following:
  Study Guide: Part A
  Textbook: Exercises 7A1 through 7A4 or 7B1 through 7B4
        Problems 7A1 through 7A3 or 7B1 through 7B3

Accrual Accounting Procedures for Sales and Collections

A major advantage of accrual basis accounting is the ability to match the cost of goods sold against revenues earned from sales, rather than simply matching cash received from customers with cash paid to suppliers. In Chapter 6 accrual accounting procedures for purchases and payments and the calculation of cost of goods sold were discussed. In this chapter, the focus will be on accrual accounting for sales and collections and the proper measurement of revenue from the sale of merchandise.

In entering transactions concerned with sales of merchandise, it is desirable to keep the following accounts:

1. Sales
2. Sales Tax Payable

3. Sales Returns and Allowances
4. Sales Discounts

The following sections include a discussion of each of these accounts, an explanation and illustration of the computation of gross margin, and a discussion of the sales and cash receipts journals.

Sales Account

The sales account is a temporary owner's equity account in which the revenue earned from the sale of merchandise is entered. The account is credited for the selling price of all merchandise sold during the accounting period.

ASSET

Sales
Credit to enter the selling price of merchan- dise sold.

If sales are for cash, the credit to Sales is offset by a debit to Cash; if the sales are on account, the debit is made to an asset account, Accounts Receivable, as shown below.

Cash or Accounts Receivable	xxx	
Sales		xxx

Sales Tax Payable Account

Describe accounting procedures for sales taxes.

When sales tax is imposed on merchandise sold, it is advisable to keep an account for Sales Tax Payable. This is a liability account which is credited for the amount of tax collected or imposed on sales. The account should be debited for the amount of the tax paid to the proper taxing authority or for the amount of the tax on merchandise returned by customers. A credit balance in the account, Sales Tax Payable, indicates the amount of the liability owed to the tax authority for taxes.

LIABILITY

Sales Tax Payable	
Debit	Credit
to enter payment of tax to the proper taxing authority or adjustment of tax on merchandise returned by customers	to enter tax collect- ed or imposed on sales.

As shown below, when merchandise is sold for cash in a state or a city which has a retail sales tax, the transaction results in an increase in cash, offset by an increase in sales and an increase in sales tax payable.

```
Cash Sale:  Cash ......................................  10,500
               Sales......................................          10,000
               Sales Tax Payable ............................            500
```

When merchandise is sold on account in such a state or city, the following entry is made.

```
Sale on Account:  Accounts Receivable ......................  10,500
                     Sales ....................................          10,000
                     Sales Tax Payable ......................            500
```

The debit to Accounts Receivable indicates that the amount owed by customers to the firm has increased. Since the buyer has accepted the merchandise and promised to pay a specific amount, revenue is recognized by crediting the sales account. Also, the amount of sales tax owed to a government agency has increased and is entered by crediting Sales Tax Payable.

An alternative procedure that is permissible under some sales tax laws is to credit the total of both the sales and the tax to the sales account, as follows:

```
Cash or Accounts Receivable ......................  10,500
   Sales........................................          10,500
```

Periodically (usually at the end of each month) a calculation is made to determine how much of the balance of the sales account is presumed to be tax. An entry is then made to remove this amount from the sales account and transfer it to the sales tax payable account. Suppose, for example, that the tax rate is 5%, and that the sales account includes the tax collected or charged, along with the amount of the sales. In this event, 100/105 of the balance of the account is presumed to be the amount of the sales, and 5/105 of the balance is the amount of the tax. If the sales account had a balance of $10,500, the tax portion would be $500 (5/105 of $10,500). As shown below, a debit to Sales and a credit to Sales Tax Payable of $500 would remove the tax from the sales account and transfer it to the sales tax payable account.

```
Sales...........................................  500
   Sales Tax Payable ............................            500
```

Sales tax accounting may be complicated by such factors as (1) sales returns and allowances and (2) exempt sales. As mentioned above, if the tax is entered at the time the sale is entered, it will be necessary to adjust for the tax when entering sales returns and allowances. If some sales are exempt from the tax, it will be necessary to distinguish between the taxable and the nontaxable sales. A common example of nontaxable sales is sales to out-of-state customers.

Sales Discounts

Enter sales transactions with discounts, returns and allowances.

Some businesses offer cash discounts to encourage prompt payment. As discussed in Chapter 6, the buyer views these discounts as purchases discounts. To the seller, these discounts are considered sales discounts. As discussed earlier, a contra account to Sales called Sales Discounts may be established to account for any cash discounts allowed. This account is reported as a deduction from Sales on the income statement.

To illustrate, assume that merchandise with a retail price of $100 is sold 2/10, n/30 and cash is received within the discount period. These transactions may be entered as follows:

Accounts Receivable	100	
Sales		100

Cash	98	
Sales Discounts	2	
Accounts Receivable		100

Sales Returns and Allowances Account

This account is a contra revenue account in which sales returns and allowances are entered. When sales taxes are accounted for separately, Sales Returns and Allowances is debited for the selling price (less sales tax) of any merchandise returned by customers and Sales Tax Payable is debited for the amount of tax on the item sold. The offsetting credit is to Accounts Receivable if the goods were sold on account, or to Cash if a refund was made because the sale was originally for cash. Sales allowances reduce the selling price of the merchandise sold and are accounted for in a similar fashion. Such allowances may be granted to customers for merchandise delivered in poor condition or for merchandise that does not meet specifications as to quality, weight, size, color, grade, or style.

Sales Returns and Allowances

Debit	
to enter returns and allowances.	

While sales returns and allowances can be debited directly to Sales, it is better to debit Sales Returns and Allowances. As a contra revenue account, Sales Returns and Allowances is deducted from Sales on the income statement. By using both accounts, the amount of gross sales and the amount of returns and allowances can be reported. If returns and allowances are large in proportion to gross sales, a weakness in the merchandising operations is indicated and the trouble should be determined and corrected.

As an example of accounting for sales returns and allowances, consider the credit memorandum illustrated on page 260 for $163.80 which was issued to Harry Sitler for one dozen printer ribbons (sales price of merchandise, $156; tax, $7.80). The entry for this transaction is as follows:

Sales Returns and Allowances	156.00	
Sales Tax Payable.................................	7.80	
Accounts Receivable (Harry Sitler)		163.80

If an accounts receivable ledger is maintained, $163.80 should be credited to the individual account of Harry Sitler in that ledger. This procedure will be discussed further in a subsequent section.

Computation of Net Sales and Gross Margin

Compute Net Sales and Gross Margin

An important step in the determination of net income for a merchandising business is the calculation of what is called the gross margin. Gross margin (also known as gross profit) is the difference between net sales and cost of goods sold. Net sales is the total sales: (1) less the sales price of any goods returned by customers (**sales returns**), (2) less any reduction in price (**sales allowances**) given to customers, and (3) less cash discounts (**sales discounts**) allowed by the seller. As explained in Chapter 6, cost of goods sold is determined by adding the amount of beginning inventory to the net purchases (purchases less purchases discounts, returns and allowances) and then subtracting the amount of ending inventory. To illustrate the calculation of the gross margin consider the following information:

Sales price of all goods sold and delivered to customers during the current period	$122,000
Sales price of goods returned by customers	3,000
Sales (cash) discounts allowed on merchandise sold	5,000

Cost of merchandise (goods) on hand, beginning of period	18,000
Cost of merchandise purchased during the period (gross)	96,000
Cost of goods returned to the supplier or allowances made by the supplier (not ordered, damaged or soiled, etc.)	2,000
Purchases (cash) discounts taken	3,000
Cost of merchandise (goods) on hand, end of period	23,000

Based on this information, the gross margin for the period is calculated as follows:

Sales			$122,000
Less:			
Sales returns and allowances		$ 3,000	
Sales discounts		5,000	8,000
Net sales			$114,000
Cost of goods sold:			
Merchandise inventory, beginning of period		$ 18,000	
Add purchases	$96,000		
Less:			
Purchases returns and allowances	2,000		
Purchases discounts	3,000		
Net purchases		91,000	
Merchandise available for sale		$109,000	
Less merchandise inventory, end of period		23,000	
Cost of goods sold			86,000
Gross margin on sales			$ 28,000

Accounts Receivable

It is important that the owner or manager know both the amount owed by individual customers and the total amount owed by all customers. Thus, it is necessary to keep an individual record for each customer and a summary or controlling ledger account indicating the total receivable. The summary account in the general ledger that represents the total to be received from all customers at any point in time is known as **Accounts Receivable.**

It is necessary to maintain a record of the transactions completed with each customer so that the amount due from each customer may be readily available at all times. The following methods of accounting for charge sales are widely used.

Describe two methods of maintaining subsidiary records for Accounts Receivable.

■■■ **The Sales Ticket Method.** This method is similar to the invoice method of accounting for purchases, discussed in Chapter 6. Under this method, it is customary to file the charge sales tickets systematically by customer. All other related source documents representing transactions with customers should be filed with the appropriate sales tickets. Special filing equipment facilitates the use of this method. In some cases, a chronological record of the charge sales tickets is kept as a means of control.

■■■ **The Accounts Receivable Ledger Method.** When the volume of business and the number of transactions is great, it may be advisable to subdivide the ledger. A common approach is to separate the accounts with customers from the other accounts and keep them in a separate ledger called a subsidiary accounts receivable ledger. This method is similar to the subsidiary ledger account method of accounting for purchases on account, discussed in Chapter 6. Under this method, an accounts receivable ledger is maintained with separate accounts for each customer listed in alphabetical order. Since all transactions affecting the accounts receivable account in the general ledger also affect an account in the subsidiary ledger, the sum of the receivables entered in the subsidiary ledger should equal the balance of the accounts receivable account. Special electronic equipment may be used in maintaining a permanent file of the charge sales tickets and other documents supporting the accounting records.

Sales Journal

Explain and use a special journal for sales of merchandise on account.

As discussed earlier, transactions involving the sale of merchandise on account can be entered in an ordinary two-column journal. However, in merchandising businesses where many sales transactions are made on account, such transactions may be entered advantageously in a special journal. A journal designed for entering only sales on account is called a sales journal. If the business is operated in an area where no sales taxes are imposed, all sales on account can be entered in a sales journal with only one amount column as shown.

SALES JOURNAL   PAGE

	DATE	SALE No.	TO WHOM SOLD	POST. REF.	AMOUNT	
1						1
2						2
3						3

If the business is operated in an area where sales taxes are imposed, a sales journal with three amount columns, as illustrated below, is more appropriate. Often, such a journal has both account titles and account numbers in the column headings, or just account numbers as headings. In computer-based accounting systems, account numbers virtually replace account names, except for statement purposes.

SALES JOURNAL   PAGE

	DATE	SALE No.	TO WHOM SOLD	POST. REF.	ACCOUNTS RECEIVABLE DR.	SALES CR.	SALES TAX PAYABLE CR.	
1								1
2								2
3								3

The transactions entered in the journal were completed by Northern Micro during the month of April. The store is located in a state that imposes a tax of 5% on the retail sale of all merchandise whether sold for cash or on account.

Note that the following information regarding each charge sales ticket is entered in the sales journal:

1. Date
2. Number of the sales ticket and salesclerk code
3. To whom sold (the customer)
4. Amount charged to customer (debit to Accounts Receivable)
5. Amount of sale (credit to Sales)
6. Amount of sales tax (credit to Sales Tax Payable)

With this form of sales journal, each transaction can be entered on one horizontal line. The sales ticket should provide all the information needed in entering each charge sale.

If a subsidiary ledger account is not kept for each customer, the charge sales tickets should be filed by customer's name after they have been entered in the sales journal. There are numerous types of devices on the market for filing charge sales tickets by customer name. Such devices are designed to save time and to offer an accurate means of keeping track of the transactions with each charge customer. If a subsidiary ledger account is kept for each customer, the sales tickets normally are used to post the customer accounts. They should then be properly filed.

Posting from the Sales Journal

At the end of the month, the amount columns of the sales journal are footed. The sum of the totals of the credit columns should be equal to the total of the debit column. The totals are then entered in normal-size figures and the ruling completed as illustrated on page 270. The totals should be posted to the general ledger accounts indicated in the column headings. This summary posting should be completed in the following order:

1. Debit Accounts Receivable for the total of the Accounts Receivable Dr. column.
2. Credit Sales for the total of the Sales Cr. column.
3. Credit Sales Tax Payable for the total of the Sales Tax Payable Cr. column.

A proper cross-reference should be provided by entering the page of the sales journal preceded by the initial "S" in the Posting Reference column of the ledger. Also, the account number should be entered immediately below the column total of the sales journal. The proper method of completing the summary posting from the Northern Micro sales journal on April 30 is shown on page 270.

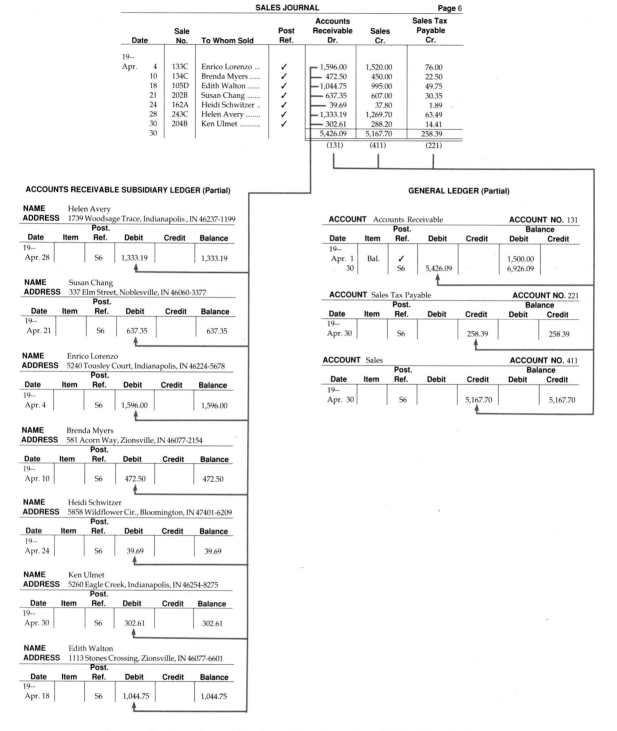

Postings from Sales Journal to General and Subsidiary Ledgers

The Sales Ticket Method. Under the sales ticket method of accounting for sales on account, individual posting from the sales journal is not required. When this method is followed, it is customary to place a check mark in the Posting Reference column of the sales journal at the time of entering each sale.

The Accounts Receivable Ledger Method. If a subsidiary ledger account is kept for each customer, all transactions affecting the amount due from each customer should be posted individually to the proper account. The posting, usually done with electronic equipment, is completed directly from the charge sales tickets and other documents. As the individual customer accounts are posted, a check mark ($\sqrt{}$) is placed in the Posting Reference column of the sales journal. For cross-reference purposes, the journal page preceded by the initial "S" is entered in the posting reference column of the subsidiary account. This procedure is illustrated on page 270.

A flowchart of the major documents and procedures commonly used in the sales function was presented earlier in the chapter. That flowchart can now be updated to include the additional accounting procedures as follows:

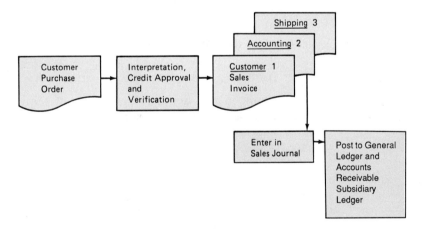

Cash Receipts Journal

Explain and use a special journal for all cash receipts.

Just as sales transactions occur frequently in many enterprises, it follows that cash receipt transactions will also occur frequently. These transactions may be entered in a special journal called a cash receipts journal. The illustration on page 273 shows a cash receipts journal.

Note that every entry in the cash receipts journal includes the following information:

1. Date of the cash receipt
2. Amount of the cash receipt, entered in the Cash Dr. column.

In addition, the General Cr. column is used to enter credits to accounts other than Accounts Receivable, Sales, and Sales Tax Payable. The Account Credited column is used to enter the name of the appropriate account when the General Cr. column is used, and to identify the customer name when the Accounts Receivable Cr. column is used.

The following types of cash receipt transactions are illustrated in the Cash Receipts Journal on Page 273.

1. Collections from customers—the name of the customer is entered in the Account Credited column and the credit amount is entered in the Accounts Receivable Cr. column. The check mark ($\checkmark$) entered in the Post. Ref. column indicates that this transaction has been posted to the accounts receivable ledger.

2. Cash and bank credit card sales—the total amount of such sales is entered in the Sales Cr. column, and the amount of the sales tax is entered in the Sales Tax Payable Cr. column. Note that the Account Credited column is left blank because neither the General Cr. column, nor any customer account is affected by this transaction.

3. Receipt of revenue—the name of the revenue account is entered in the Account Credited column and the credit amount is entered in the General Cr. column. In this case, Northern Micro has rented a computer on a short-term basis to a customer and has received rent for the month of April.

4. Receipt of cash from a bank loan—the name of the liability account is entered in the Account Credited column and the credit amount is entered in the General Cr. column

Posting from the Cash Receipts Journal

Each amount in the General Cr. column of the cash receipts journal is posted individually to the ledger account named in the Account Credited column. The notation "CR7" is entered in the Post. Ref. column of the affected ledger account at the time that the item is posted, and the appropriate account number is entered in the Post. Ref. column of the cash receipts journal.

If a subsidiary ledger is used, each amount in the Accounts Receivable Cr. column must be posted to the specific customer's account in the Accounts Receivable Ledger. The notation "CR7" is entered in the Post. Ref. column of the affected subsidiary ledger account at the time that the item is posted. A check mark ($\checkmark$) is then entered in the Post. Ref. column of the cash receipts journal to indicate that the entry was posted to the subsidiary ledger.

When a subsidiary ledger is not used, sales tickets paid in full should be receipted and may either be given to the customer or be transferred to another file for future reference. When a customer makes a partial payment on an account, the amount of the payment should be noted on the most recent charge sales ticket and the new balance should be indicated.

At the end of the month, the five amount columns of the cash receipts journal are totaled and the ruling completed as illustrated. The summary posting involves posting the total of the Accounts Receivable Cr. column as a credit to Account No. 131, the total of the Sales Cr. column as a

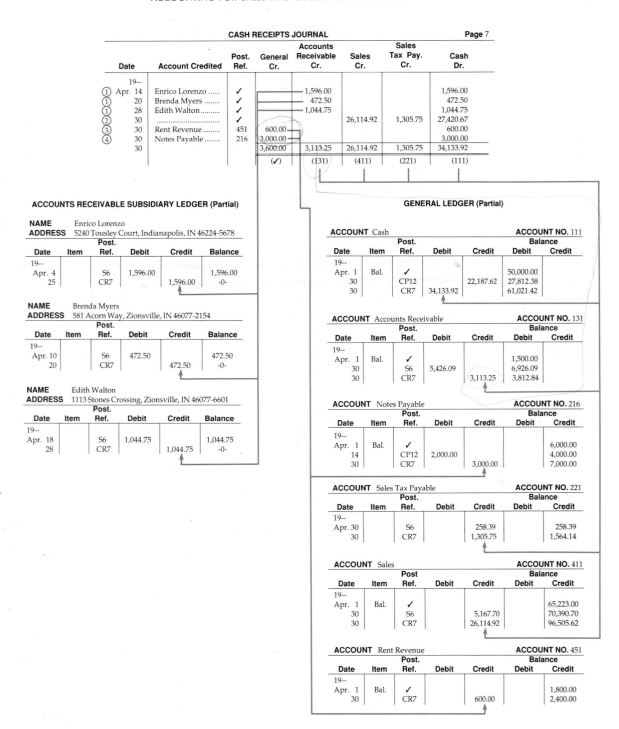

Postings from Cash Receipts Journal to General and Subsidiary Ledgers

credit to Account No. 411, the total of the Sales Tax Payable Cr. column as a credit to Account No. 221, and the total of the Cash Dr. column as a debit to Account No. 111.

As each total is posted, the notation "CR7" is entered in the Post. Ref. column of the affected ledger account, and the number of that account is entered in parentheses below the appropriate column total in the cash receipts journal. A check mark (√) is entered in parentheses below the total of the General Cr. column to indicate that its total is not posted to the ledger.

The individual and summary postings from Northern Micro's cash receipts journal to the general and subsidiary ledger accounts on April 30 are illustrated on page 273.

Schedule of Accounts Receivable

Prepare a schedule of accounts receivable.

A list showing the amount due from each customer as of a specified date is known as a schedule of accounts receivable. It is usually advisable to prepare such a schedule at the end of each month. An example of a schedule of accounts receivable for Northern Micro as of April 30, 19--, is shown below.

**Northern Micro
Schedule of Accounts Receivable
April 30, 19--**

Helen Avery	$1,333.19
Susan Chang	637.35
Heidi Schwitzer	39.69
Ken Ulmet	302.61
Vivian Winston	1,500.00
	$3,812.84

This schedule can be easily prepared from the list of customer accounts in the accounts receivable ledger or from the customer names and amounts due in the sales tickets file. If the total of the schedule does not agree with the balance of the summary accounts receivable account, the error may be in the subsidiary ledger, the file, or the ledger account. The subsidiary ledger could be incorrect because of an error in posting. The file may be incorrect in that one or more collected sales tickets have not been removed or one or more uncollected ones are missing. Another possibility is that a notation of a partial collection was overlooked in preparing the list. The accounts receivable account could be incorrect because of an error in posting or because of an error in a journal from which the totals were posted. In any event, the postings, journals, and sales tickets must be reviewed until the reason for the discrepancy is found so that the necessary correction can be made.

Building Your Accounting Knowledge

1. Describe how each of the following accounts is used: (1) Sales, (2) Sales Tax Payable, (3) Sales Discounts, and (4) Sales Returns and Allowances.
2. The gross margin is the difference between what two dollar amounts?
3. Describe the sales ticket method of keeping records of the transactions completed with individual customers.
4. Describe the ledger account method of keeping records of the transactions completed with individual customers.
5. List six items of information about each sale normally entered in the sales journal.
6. In what order should the summary posting from the sales journal to the general ledger be completed?
7. List two items of information about each cash receipt normally entered in the cash receipts journal.
8. List four kinds of transactions requiring varying entry procedures in the cash receipts journal.
9. In what journal does Northern Micro enter cash and bank credit card sales?
10. If the schedule of accounts receivable does not agree in total with the balance of the summary accounts receivable account, what major error possibilities exist?

Assignment Box

To reinforce your understanding of the preceding text materials, you may complete the following:
   Study Guide: Part B
   Textbook: Exercises 7A5 through 7A7 or 7B5 through 7B7
             Problems 7A4 through 7A6 or 7B4 through 7B6

Expanding Your Business Vocabulary

What is the meaning of each of the following terms?

accounts receivable (p. 250)
accounts receivable ledger (p. 268)
bank credit card sales (p. 251)
cash receipts journal (p. 271)
cash sales (p. 250)
COD sales (p. 253)
consignee (p. 254)
consignment sale (p. 254)
consignor (p. 254)

cost of goods sold (p. 266)
credit cards/charge plates (p. 251)
credit memorandum (p. 260)
gross margin/gross profit (p. 266)
installment accounts receivable (p. 254)
installment sales (p. 254)
layaway ledger (p.254)

Demonstration Problem

Karen Hunt operates an audio-video store. The books of original entry include a sales journal, a cash receipts journal, and a two-column journal. The following transactions related to sales on account and cash receipts occurred during April.

April 3 Sold merchandise on account to Susan Haberman, $159.50, plus tax of $11.17, Sale No. 41.

4 Sold merchandise on account to Glenn Kelly, $299.95, plus tax of $21.00, Sale No. 42.

6 Received $69.50 from Tera Scherrer on account.

7 Issued a credit memorandum for $42.75 which included the tax of $2.80 to Kenneth Watt for merchandise returned that had been sold on account.

10 Received $99.95 from Kellie Cokley on account.

11 Sold merchandise on account to Victor Cardona, $499.95, plus tax of $35.00, Sale No. 43.

14 Received $157.00 from Kenneth Watt in full settlement of account.

17 Sold merchandise on account to Susan Haberman, $379.95, plus tax of $26.60, Sale No. 44.

19 Sold merchandise on account to Tera Scherrer, $59.95, plus tax of $4.20, Sale No. 45.

21 Issued a credit memorandum for $53.45 which included the tax of $3.50 to Glenn Kelly for merchandise returned that had been sold on account.

24 Received $299.95 from Victor Cardona on account.

25 Sold merchandise on account to Kellie Cokley, $179.50, plus tax of $12.57, Sale No. 46.

26 Received $250.65 from Susan Haberman on account.

28 Sold merchandise on account to Kenneth Watt, $49.95, plus tax of $3.50, Sale No. 47.

28 Cash and bank credit card sales for the month, $3,220, plus tax of $225.40.

Hunt had the following general ledger account balances as of April 1:

Cash, Account No. 111, 4/1 Balance, $5,000.00
Accounts Receivable, Account No. 131, 4/1 Balance, $1,208.63
Sales Tax Payable, Account No. 221, 4/1 Balance, $72.52.
Sales, Account No. 411, 4/1 Balance, $8,421.49.
Sales Returns & Allowances, Account No. 411.1, 4/1 Balance, $168.43.

Hunt also had the following accounts receivable ledger account balances as of April 1:

Victor Cardona, 6115 Washington Blvd., St. Louis, MO 63130-9523
4/1 Balance, $299.95
Kellie Cokley, 6666 Kingsbury Blvd., St. Louis, MO 63130-1645
4/1 Balance, $99.95
Susan Haberman, 9421 Garden Ct., Kirkwood, MO 63122-1878
4/1 Balance, $79.98
Glenn Kelly, 6612 Arundel Pl., Clayton, MO 63105-9266
4/1 Balance, $379.50
Tera Scherrer, 315 W. Linden St., Webster Groves, MO 63119-9881
4/1 Balance, $149.50
Kenneth Watt, 11742 Fawnridge Dr., St. Louis, MO 63131-1726
4/1 Balance, $199.75

Required:

1. Open a T account general ledger and a T account subsidiary accounts receivable ledger for Hunt's Audio-Video Store as of April 1 of the current year. Enter the April 1 balance of each of the above accounts in the T accounts on the appropriate side, with a check mark to the left of each balance.
2. Enter each transaction either in a three-column sales journal, a five-column cash receipts journal, or a two-column journal.
3. Post directly from each of the three journals to the proper customers' accounts in the subsidiary accounts receivable ledger. Each subsidiary ledger account should show the initials "S," "CR," or "J" followed by the appropriate journal page number as a posting reference for each transaction.
4. Enter the totals and rule the sales journal and the cash receipts journal. Foot the two-column journal to prove the equality of debits and credits. Complete the summary posting of the cash receipts and sales journals and the individual posting of the two-column journal to the proper general ledger accounts. Each general ledger account should show the initials "S," "CR," or "J" followed by the appropriate journal page number as a posting reference for each transaction.
5. Foot and balance all general and subsidiary ledger accounts.
6. Prove the balance of the summary accounts receivable account by preparing a schedule of accounts receivable as of April 30, based on the subsidiary accounts receivable ledger.

Solution

2, 3 & 4.

			Sales Journal			Page 5	
Date	Sale No.	To Whom Sold	Post Ref.	Accounts Receivable Dr.	Sales Cr.	Sales Tax Payable Cr.
19--						
Apr. 3	41	Susan Haberman	√	170.67	159.50	11.17
4	42	Glenn Kelly	√	320.95	299.95	21.00
11	43	Victor Cardona	√	534.95	499.95	35.00
17	44	Susan Haberman	√	406.55	379.95	26.60
19	45	Tera Scherrer	√	64.15	59.95	4.20
25	46	Kellie Cokley	√	192.07	179.50	12.57
28	47	Kenneth Watt	√	53.45	49.95	3.50
30				1,742.79	1,628.75	114.04
				(131)	(411)	(221)

	Cash Receipts Journal						Page 8	
Date	Account Credited	Post Ref.	General Cr.	Accounts Receiv. Cr.	Sales Cr.	Sales Tax Payable Cr.	Cash Dr.
19--							
Apr. 6	Tera Scherrer	√		69.50			69.50
10	Kellie Cokley	√		99.95			99.95
14	Kenneth Watt	√		157.00			157.00
24	Victor Cardona	√		299.95			299.95
26	Susan Haberman	√		250.65			250.65
30					3,220.00	225.40	3,445.40
				877.05	3,220.00	225.40	4,322.45
				(131)	(411)	(221)	(111)

	Journal			Page 7
19--				
Apr. 7	Sales Returns & Allowances............	411.1	39.95	
	Sales Tax Payable	221	2.80	
	Accounts Receivable (K. Watt).........	131		42.75
21	Sales Returns & Allowances............	411.1	49.95	
	Sales Tax Payable	221	3.50	
	Accounts Receivable (G. Kelly)........	131		53.45
			96.20	96.20

1., 3., 4. & 5.   ACCOUNTS RECEIVABLE LEDGER

	Victor Cardona								Kellie Cokley				
19--					19--				19--				19--
Apr. 1	Bal.	√	299.95		Apr. 24	CR8	299.95		Apr. 1	Bal.	√	99.95	Apr. 10 CR8 99.95
11		S5	534.95						25		S5	192.07	
			834.90									292.02	
	534.95									192.07			

Susan Haberman

19--				19--			
Apr.	1	Bal.	√	79.98	Apr. 26	CR8	250.65
	3		S5	170.67			
	17		S5	406.55			
				657.20			
			406.55				

Tera Scherrer

19--				19--			
Apr.	1	Bal.	√	149.50	Apr. 6	CR8	69.50
	19		S5	64.15			
				213.65			
		144.15					

Glenn Kelly

19--				19--			
Apr.	1	Bal.	√	379.50	Apr. 21	J7	53.45
	4		S5	320.95			
				700.45			
		647.00					

Kenneth Watt

19--				19--			
Apr.	1	Bal.	√	199.75	Apr. 7	J7	42.75
	28		S5	53.45		14	CR8	157.00
				253.20			199.75
		53.45					

GENERAL LEDGER

Cash——Acct. No. 111

19--				
Apr.	1	Bal.	√	5,000.00
	30		CR8	4,322.45
				9,322.45

Accounts Receivable——Acct. No. 131

19--					19--			
Apr.	1	Bal.	√	1,208.63	Apr.	7	J7	42.75
	30		S5	1,742.79		21	J7	53.45
						30	CR8	877.05
				2,951.42				973.25
		1,978.17						

Sales Tax Payable——Acct. No. 221

19--				19--			
Apr.	7	J7	2.80	Apr.	1	Bal.	√	72.52
	21	J7	3.50		30		S5	114.04
					30		CR8	225.40
			6.30					411.96
						405.66	

Sales——Account No. 411

		19--			
		Apr.	1	Bal.	√	8,421.49
			30		S5	1,628.75
			30		CR8	3,220.00
						13,270.24

Sales Returns & Allow.——Account No. 411.1

19--			
Apr.	1	Bal. √	168.43
	7	J7	39.95
	21	J7	49.95
			258.33

6.

Hunt's Audio-Video Store
Schedule of Accounts Receivable
April 30, 19--

Victor Cardona	534.95
Kellie Cokley	192.07
Susan Haberman	406.55
Glenn Kelly	647.00
Tera Scherrer	144.15
Kenneth Watt	53.45
	1,978.17

*Note: Now that you have reviewed the Demonstration Problem and Solution you may complete the **Mastery Problem** at the end of the chapter activities.

Applying Accounting Concepts

Series A

Exercise 7A1—Sales Tax and Price Determination. To simplify the determination of tax, Eaton's Novelty Shop uses a sales tax table for calculating the amount of tax to be charged on sales. The rate is 5%. Using the section of a sales tax table presented below, determine the amount of tax that would be added to the price of each item sold. Then find the total to be collected on each individual sale.

Amount of Sale	Amount of Tax
. . . .	. . .
$1.10 to 1.29	.06
1.30 to 1.49	.07
1.50 to 1.69	.08
1.70 to 1.89	.09
1.90 to 2.09	.10
2.10 to 2.29	.11
2.30 to 2.49	.12
2.50 to 2.69	.13
2.70 to 2.89	.14
2.90 to 3.09	.15
. . . .	. . .

Sale Number	Item	Price	Tax	Total
50	Pen	$1.79	$	$
51	Monogrammed cup	$1.99	$	$
52	Paper napkins	$3.05	$	$
53	Birthday candles	$1.59	$	$
54	Birthday card	$1.25	$	$

Exercise 7A2—Sales Tax and Price Determination. Baker Beauty Supply follows the practice of entering sales tax in the sales account. Periodically, the sales tax is determined and forwarded to the state government. The sales account has a balance of $6,454.50. The sales tax rate is 7%.

Determine (a) the amount of sales tax that was included in the sales account and (b) the price of the merchandise sold.

Exercise 7A3—Sales Return Refund Determination. Claudia Spiller returned merchandise for a cash refund. The cost of the returned merchandise was $164.71, excluding the sales tax of 6%.

Determine the total amount that should be refunded to Spiller.

Exercise 7A4—Flow Chart Labeling. The following flowchart shows some of the major documents and procedures commonly used in the sales function of a merchandising business. Fill in the blank spaces.

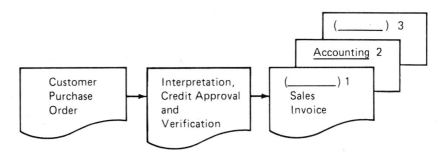

Exercise 7A5—Calculation of Gross Margin on Sales. The following information is from the accounting records of the Pampered Pantry Kitchen Center.

Sales price of all goods sold and delivered to customers during the current period	$366,000
Sales price of goods returned by customers	24,000
Cost of merchandise (goods) on hand, beginning of the period.......	54,000
Cost of merchandise purchased during the period	288,000
Cost of goods returned to the supplier or allowances made by the supplier	1,500
Cost of merchandise (goods) on hand, end of current period	69,000

Based on this data, determine the gross margin on sales. Show the calculation using the format illustrated in the chapter.

Exercise 7A6—Entries in Sales Journal. Anita Rao Renovators complete the following transactions related to sales of merchandise on account. Sales tax of 6% was included in the amount of each sale.

April 3 Sold wallpaper supplies to Harper Homes, $95.65, terms, n/30. Sale No. 335.

12 Sold paint to David Altman, $95, terms, n/30. Sale No. 336.

21 Sold miniblinds to Sharon Meiman, $148.13, terms, n/30. Sale No. 337.

24 Sold decorator items to Melissa Sands, $35.24, terms, n/30. Sale No. 338.

25 Sold paint to Kathryn Biggs, $17.45, terms, n/30. Sale No. 339.

1. Enter the above transactions using a sales journal with the same format and account titles as illustrated in the chapter.
2. Total and rule the journal.

Exercise 7A7—Entries in Cash Receipts Journal. Assume Anita Rao Renovators received the full amount of each sale 30 days after the date of sale, as indicated in Exercise 7A6.

1. Enter the receipt of cash for each transaction, using a cash receipts journal with the same format and account titles as illustrated in the chapter.
2. Enter the following transaction:
   May 29 Deposited cash and bank credit card sales, $1,872.53 (includes sales tax).
3. Total and rule the journal.

Exercise 7B1—Sales Tax and Price Determination. To smplify the determination of tax, Patti's Paper Products uses a sales tax table for calculating the amount of tax to be charged on sales. The rate is 6%. Using the section of a sales tax table presented below, determine the amount of tax that would be added to the price of each item sold. Then find the total to be collected on each individual sale.

Amount of Sale	Amount of Tax
. . . .	. . .
$1.09 to 1.24	.07
1.25 to 1.40	.08
1.41 to 1.56	.09
1.57 to 1.72	.10
1.73 to 1.88	.11
1.89 to 2.04	.12
2.05 to 2.20	.13
2.21 to 2.36	.14
2.37 to 2.52	.15
2.53 to 2.68	.16
. . . .	. . .

Sale Number	Item	Price	Tax	Total
26	Paper cups	$2.29	$	$
27	Paper plates	2.65	$	$
28	Paper napkins	1.99	$	$
29	Plastic forks	2.45	$	$
30	Plastic spoons	1.79	$	$

Exercise 7B2—Sales Tax and Price Determination. Berger Barber Supply follows the practice of entering sales tax in the sales account. Periodically, the sales tax is determined and forwarded to the state government. The sales account has a balance of $3,227.25. The sales tax rate is 5%.

Determine (a) the amount of sales tax that was included in the sales account and (b) the price of the merchandise sold.

Exercise 7B3—Sales Return Refund Determination. Jon Bergman returned merchandise for a cash refund. The cost of the returned merchandise was $82.35, excluding the sales tax of 7%.

Determine the total amount that should be refunded to Bergman.

Exercise 7B4—Flow Chart Labeling. The following flowchart shows some of the major documents and procedures commonly used in the sales function of a merchandising business. Fill in the blank spaces.

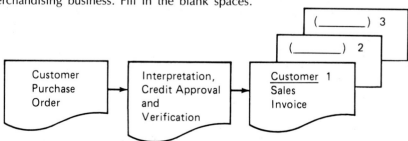

Exercise 7B5—Calculation of Gross Margin on Sales. The following information is from the accounting records of the Old Orchard Garden Center.

Sales price of all goods sold and delivered to customers during the current period	$549,000
Sales price of goods returned by customers	36,000
Cost of merchandise (goods) on hand, beginning of the period	81,000
Cost of merchandise purchased during the period	432,000
Cost of goods returned to the supplier or allowances made by the supplier	2,250
Cost of merchandise (goods) on hand, end of current period	103,500

Based on this data, determine the gross margin on sales. Show the calculation using the format illustrated in the chapter.

Exercise 7B6—Entries in Sales Journal. Heinlein Hardware completes the following transactions related to sales of merchandise on account. Sales tax of 7% was included in the amount of each sale.

March　2　Sold hardware supplies to Paradise Homes, $59.65, terms, n/30. Sale No. 175.

　　　　13　Sold paint to David Aiken, $65.00, terms, n/30. Sale No. 176.

　　　　23　Sold lumber to Jennifer Livoti, $184.31, terms, n/30. Sale No. 177.

　　　　24　Sold glass to Mike Vehaskari, $43.52, terms, n/30. Sale No. 178.

　　　　27　Sold paint to Marcia Solomon, $15.74, terms, n/30. Sale No. 179.

1. Enter the above transactions using a sales journal with the same format and account titles as illustrated in the chapter.

2. Total and rule the journal.

Exercise 7B7—Entries in Cash Receipts Journal. Assume Heinlein Hardware received the full amount of each sale 30 days after the date of sale, as indicated in Exercise 7B6.

1. Enter the receipt of cash for each transaction, using a cash receipts journal with the same format and account titles as illustrated in the chapter.

2. Enter the following transaction:

　　Apr. 28　Deposited cash and bank credit card sales, $1,725.38 (includes sales tax).

3. Total and rule the journal.

Series A

Problem 7A1　　Sales Invoice Preparation

If the working papers for this textbook are not used, omit Problem 7A1.

Following is a reproduction of a purchase order received from Behan Building Co. by Hill Building Supplies, Inc. dated August 15.

Required:

Assuming that you are employed by Hill Building Supplies, Inc., prepare a sales invoice (No. 271) as of August 18, billing Behan Building Co. for the items specified in their order No. A309. The unit prices are as follows: #6 insulated steel doors, $329.00 each and #14 wooden louvered doors, $63.00 each. Indicate terms of 30 days and add prepaid express charges, $74.60. Use the invoice form found in the working papers.

Purchase Order		Order No. **A309**

Behan Building Co.
6515 Page Blvd.
St. Louis, MO 63133-2287

Date: August 15, 19--

Terms: 30 days

Ship Via: Prepaid express

Please enter our order for the following:

To: Hill Building Supplies, Inc.
833 S. Kirkwood Rd.
Kirkwood, MO 63122-3663

Quantity	Description	Price
10	#6 Insulated steel doors	329.00
15	#14 Wooden louvered doors	63.00

Deliver no goods without a written order on this form.   **By** *R. King*

Problem 7A2   Credit Memorandum Preparation

If the working papers for this textbook are not used, omit Problem 7A2.

Behan Building Company returned 1 #6 Insulated Steel Door to Hill Building Supplies, Inc., for credit on August 28.

Required:

Using the blank form found in the working papers, prepare a credit memorandum (No. 27) covering the cost of the door sold on Aug. 18.

Problem 7A3   Sales Invoice Preparation; Telegraphic Order

If the working papers for this textbook are not used, omit Problem 7A3.

The following telegram ordering dictionaries was received by Eden Publishing House from a charge customer on October 12. Following the telegram is a reproduction of a page of the price list of the Eden Publishing House.

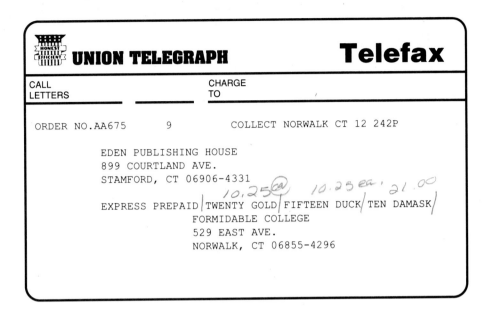

Required:

Interpret the telegraphic order and prepare a sales invoice, using the blank form found in the working papers. In preparing the sales invoice, use the stock numbers and descriptions indicated. Allow a trade discount of 10% and add $25.50 for prepaid express charges. Use Invoice No. 847.

Price List

Stock No.	Description	Code Word	List Price
	Dictionary		
	For Group Use (School Classrooms, Libraries)		
	Regular Style Size, 7 × 10 × 2⅝ inches. Weight, 5 lbs.		
No. 7	Cloth, indexed	Gold	$10.25
No. 8	Buckram, marbled edges, indexed	Golden	13.50
	For Individual Use		
	Thin-Paper Style Size, 6 × 8⅞ × 1½ lines. Weight, 2½ lbs.		
	Printed on Bible paper, from the plates as the Regular Style.		
No. 9	Special Cloth, dark blue, sprinkled edges, indexed	Duck	$10.25
No. 10	Fabrikoid, rich dark brown, gilt edges, indexed . .	Delight	14.50
No. 11	Leather, Levant Grain, black, gilt edges, indexed	Damask	21.00
No. 11A	Limp Pigskin, dark blue, gilt edges, round corners, indexed	Decorate	22.50
No. 11B	Limp Pigskin, natural, gilt edges, round corners, indexed	Design	22.50

Problem 7A4	**Partial Income Statement for Gross Margin Determination**

Gloria Santana is the owner of a small retail store known as Gloria's Confectionery. The following information is taken from Santana's records and books of account.

Cost of merchandise (goods) on hand, beginning of year	$ 13,500
Cost of merchandise purchased during the year	106,000
Cost of goods returned to suppliers	1,600
Cash payments during the year for goods purchased both in prior years and in the current year	82,350
Sales price of all goods sold and delivered to customers during the current year	145,000
Sales price of goods returned by customers	5,500
Cash received from customers during the year for sales both of prior years and the current year	129,000
Cost of merchandise (goods) on hand, end of year	14,650

Required:

Select from the above information the appropriate amounts to complete the partial income statement illustrated below.

Gloria's Confectionery
Partial Income Statement
For The Year Ended December 31, 19--

Sales		*145,000*
Less sales returns and allowances	*(5,500)*	
Net sales		*139,500*
Cost of goods sold:		
Merchandise inventory, January 1, 19--	*13,500*	
Add purchases	*106,000*	
Less purchases returns and allowances	*(1,600)*	
Net purchases	*117,900*	
Cost of goods available for sale	*103,250*	
Less merchandise inventory, December 31, 19--	*14,650*	
Cost of goods sold		*88,600*
Gross margin on sales		*50,900*

36,250.00

Problem 7A5	**Entries in Sales Journal and Two-Column Journal; Posting to Selected Ledger Accounts; Schedule of Accounts Receivable**

Stephen DeBarry operates a book store. The books of original entry include a sales journal in which sales on account are entered and a two-column journal in which entries such as sales returns and allowances are recorded. Following are the transactions related to sales on account for the month of July.

July 3 Sold merchandise on account to T. W. Bassett, $73.75, plus tax of $4.43. Sale No. 21.

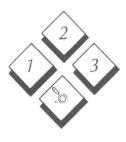

145.000

5 Sold merchandise on account to S.M. Davis, $16.50, plus tax of $.99. Sale No. 22.

6 Sold merchandise on account to J.B. Field, $42.50, plus tax of $2.55. Sale No. 23.

10 Sold merchandise on account to K.L. Hollenberg, $73.95, plus tax of $4.44. Sale No. 24.

12 Sold merchandise on account to D.A. Seay, $50.00, plus tax of $3.00. Sale No. 25.

13 Issued a credit memorandum for $6.36, including tax of $.36, to S.M. Davis for merchandise returned that had been sold on account.

17 Sold merchandise on account to A.J. Silver, $32.19, plus tax of $1.93. Sale No. 26.

19 Sold merchandise on account to T.W. Bassett, $42.05, plus tax of $2.52. Sale No. 27.

21 Sold merchandise on account to K.L. Hollenberg, $30.00, plus tax of $1.80. Sale No. 28.

24 Issued a credit memorandum for $10.60, including tax of $.60, to T.W. Bassett for merchandise returned that had been sold on account.

25 Sold merchandise on account to D.A. Seay, $55.55, plus tax of $3.33. Sale No. 29.

27 Sold merchandise on account to S.M. Davis, $103.95, plus tax of $6.24. Sale No. 30.

28 Sold merchandise on account to J.B. Field, $44.15, plus tax of $2.65. Sale No. 31.

31 Sold merchandise on account to T.W. Bassett, $34.75, plus tax of $2.09. Sale No. 32.

Required:

1. Enter each transaction in a sales journal or in a two-column journal.

2. Post directly from the sales journal and the two-column journal to the proper customer accounts in a subsidiary accounts receivable ledger. The subsidiary ledger should be in three-column format. The following customer accounts are required:

T.W. Bassett, 7104 Forsyth Blvd., St. Louis, MO 63105-5013, 7/1 Balance, $130.00.

S.M. Davis, 317 Ballman, St. Louis, MO 63135-5313, 7/1 Balance, $107.80.

J.B. Field, 613 Yorkshire Dr., Washington, IL 61571-1751, 7/1 Balance, $153.50.

K.L. Hollenberg, 6111 Pershing Ave., St. Louis, MO 63112-2113, 7/1 Balance, $84.00.

D.A. Seay, 6515 Wydown Blvd., Clayton, MO 63105-5102, 7/1 Balance, $47.05.

A.J. Silver, 6615 University Ave., University City, MO 63130-1421, 7/1 Balance, -0-.

(In posting from these journals, the page number preceded by the initials "S" or "J" should be placed in the Posting Reference column of the ledger account involved.)

3. Enter the totals and rule the sales journal. Foot the two-column journal to prove the equality of the debits and credits. Complete the summary posting of the sales journal and the individual posting of the two-column journal to the proper general ledger accounts. The general ledger should be in the four-column format and contain the following accounts:

Accounts Receivable	Account No. 131, 7/1 Balance, $522.35.
Sales Tax Payable	Account No. 221, 7/1 Balance, $222.28.
Sales	Account No. 411, 7/1 Balance, $3,704.65.
Sales Returns & Allowances	Account No. 411.1, 7/1 Balance, $74.50.

(In posting from these journals, the page number preceded by the initials "S" or "J" should be placed in the Posting Reference column of the ledger account involved.)

4. Prove the balance of the summary accounts receivable account by preparing a schedule of accounts receivable as of July 31, based on the subsidiary accounts receivable ledger.

(Sales and two-column journal paper, general and subsidiary ledger account forms, and ruled paper for the schedule of accounts receivable can be found in the working papers.)

Problem 7A6   Entries in Cash Receipts Journal and Two-Column Journal; Posting to Selected Ledger Accounts

Lisa Ross operates a dress shop. The books of original entry include a cash receipts journal and a two-column journal. The following transactions related to sales and cash receipts occurred during September.

Sept. 5 Received $194.80 from R. Weber on account.
     11 Received $208.50 from J. Maier on account.
     12 M. Siegel returned merchandise for credit. Sales price, $116.00, plus tax of $5.80. (Enter in two-column journal.)
     18 Received $150.90 from A. Weinhaus on account.
     21 Received $131.80 from S. Gilfix on account.
     25 C. Sanderson returned merchandise for credit. Sales price, $145.00, plus tax of $7.25.
     27 Received $175.30 from J. Laski on account.
     29 Cash and bank credit card sales for the month, $8,440.00, plus tax of $422.00.

Required:

1. Enter the transactions in a cash receipts journal or a two-column journal. Total and rule the cash receipts journal. Foot the amount columns of the two-column journal to prove the equality of debits and credits.

2. Complete the summary posting of the cash receipts journal and the individual posting of the two-column journal to the following four-column general ledger accounts:

    Cash, Account No. 111, 9/1 Balance, $60,000.00.
    Accounts Receivable, Account No. 131, 9/1 Balance, $4,300.90.
    Sales Tax Payable, Account No. 221, 9/1 Balance, $628.08
    Sales, Account No. 411, 9/1 Balance, $62,146.94.
    Sales Returns & Allowances, Account No. 411.1, 9/1 Balance, $1,569.72.

(In posting from the cash receipts journal, the page number preceded by the initials "CR" should be placed in the Posting Reference column of the ledger account involved.) Then, update the account balances.

(Cash receipts and two-column journal paper and general ledger account forms can be found in the working papers.)

Series B

Problem 7B1   Sales Invoice Preparation

If the working papers for this textbook are not used, omit Problem 7B1.

Following is a reproduction of a purchase order received from Vincento Construction Co. by Custom Builders Corporation dated July 14.

Purchase Order		Order No. **B107**

Vincento Construction Co.
436 Hill Ave.
Hamilton, OH 45014-1407

Date: July 14, 19--

Terms: 30 days

TO: Custom Builders Corporation
119 Long St.
Hamilton, OH 45011-6321

Ship Via: Prepaid express

Please enter our order for the following:

Quantity	Description	Price
10	#15 Aluminum awnings	99.00
15	#22 Aluminum windows	289.00

Deliver no goods without a written order on this form.   *V. Albers*

Required:

Assuming that you are employed by Custom Builders Corporation, prepare a sales invoice (No. 321) as of July 17, billing Vincento Construction Co. for the items specified in their order No. B107. The unit prices are as follows: #15 aluminum awnings, $99.00 each and #22 removable windows, $289.00 each. Indicate terms of 30 days and add prepaid express charges, $87.60.

Problem 7B2   Credit Memorandum Preparation

If the working papers for this textbook are not used, omit Problem 7B2.

Vincento Construction Co. returned 1 #15 aluminum awning to Custom Builders Corporation for credit on July 27.

Required:

Using the blank form found in the working papers, prepare a credit memorandum (No. 32) covering the cost of the items sold on July 17.

Problem 7B3	**Sales Invoice Preparation; Telegraphic Order**

If the working papers for this textbook are not used, omit Problem 7B3.

The telegram on page 291 ordering dictionaries was received by Corner Publishing House from a charge customer on September 13. A reproduction of a page of the price list of the Corner Publishing House appears below.

Required:

Interpret the telegraphic order and prepare a sales invoice, using the blank form found in the working papers. In preparing the sales invoice, use the stock numbers and descriptions indicated. Allow a trade discount of 10% and add $32.25 for prepaid express charges. Use Invoice No. 462.

Price List

Stock No.	Description	Code Word	List Price
	Dictionary		
	For Group Use (School Classrooms, Libraries)		
	Regular Style Size, 7 × 10 × 2⅝ inches. Weight, 5 lbs.		
No. 3	Cloth, indexed	Gold	$10.25
No. 4	Buckram, marbled edges, indexed	Golden	13.50
	For Individual Use		
	Thin-Paper Style Size, 6 × 8⅞ × 1½ inches. Weight, 2½ lbs.		
	Printed on Bible paper, from the plates as the Regular Style.		
No. 5	Special Cloth, dark blue, sprinkled edges, indexed	Duck	$10.25
No. 6	Fabrikoid, rich dark brown, gilt edges, indexed . . .	Delight	14.50
No. 7	Leather, Levant Grain, black, gilt edges, indexed . .	Damask	21.00
No. 7A	Limp Pigskin, dark blue, gilt edges, round corners, indexed	Decorate	22.50
No. 7B	Limp Pigskin, natural, gilt edges, round corners, indexed	Design	22.50

Problem 7B4	**Partial Income Statement for Gross Margin Determination**

Juan Alvarez is the owner of a small retail store known as Juan's Pipe Shoppe. The following information is taken from Alvarez's records and books of account.

Cost of merchandise (goods) on hand, beginning of year	$ 16,200
Cost of merchandise purchased during the year	127,200

BEECHER TELEGRAPH   **Telefax**

CALL LETTERS	CHARGE TO

```
ORDER NO.AC222      9        COLLECT ROCKVILLE MD 13 242P

        CORNER PUBLISHING HOUSE
        8529 CEDAR AVE.
        BALTIMORE, MD 21227-6597

        EXPRESS PREPAID THIRTY GOLDEN TEN DELIGHT TEN DESIGN
                    WILLIAM JEWELL COLLEGE
                    371 BRENT RD.
                    ROCKVILLE, MD 20850-1521
```

Problem 7B4 (Concluded)

Cost of goods returned to suppliers	$ 1,920
Cash payments during the year for goods purchased both in prior years and in the current year	98,820
Sales price of all goods sold and delivered to customers during the current year	174,000
Sales price of goods returned by customers	6,600
Cash received from customers during the year for sales both of prior years and the current year	154,800
Cost of merchandise (goods) on hand, end of year	17,580

Required:

Select from the above information the appropriate amounts to complete the partial income statement illustrated below.

Juan's Pipe Shoppe
Partial Income Statement
For The Year Ended December 31, 19--

Sales ....

Less sales returns and allowances...................................

Net sales ....

Cost of goods sold:

    Merchandise inventory, January 1, 19-- ....

    Add purchases ....

    Less purchases returns and allowances ....

    Net purchases ....

    Cost of goods available for sale..................................

    Less merchandise inventory, December 31, 19--.....................

    Cost of goods sold ....

Gross margin on sales ....

Problem 7B5   Entries in Sales Journal and Two-Column Journal; Posting to Selected Ledger Accounts; Schedule of Accounts Receivable

Shellie Suffriti operates a specialty shop. The books of original entry include a sales journal in which sales on account are entered and a two-column journal in which entries such as sales returns and allowances are recorded. Following are the transactions related to sales on account for the month of June.

June 1 Sold merchandise on account to S.M. Aronson, $295.00, plus tax of $14.75. Sale No. 61.
2 Sold merchandise on account to W.R. Davis, $66.00, plus tax of $3.30. Sale No. 62.
6 Sold merchandise on account to D.H. Gordon, $170.00, plus tax of $8.50. Sale No. 63.
9 Sold merchandise on account to N.J. Haffner, $295.80, plus tax of $14.79. Sale No. 64.
12 Sold merchandise on account to R.J. Klein, $200.00, plus tax of $10.00. Sale No. 65.
13 Issued a credit memorandum for $25.20, including tax of $1.20, to W.R. Davis for merchandise returned that had been sold on account.
16 Sold merchandise on account to A.M. Zala, $128.76, plus tax of $6.44. Sale No. 66.
19 Sold merchandise on account to S.M. Aronson, $168.20, plus tax of $8.41, Sale No. 67.
21 Sold merchandise on account to N.J. Haffner, $120.00, plus tax of $6.00. Sale No. 68.
22 Issued a credit memorandum for $42.00, including tax of $2.00, to S.M. Aronson for merchandise returned that had been sold on account.
26 Sold merchandise on account to R.J. Klein, $222.20, plus tax of $11.11. Sale No. 69.
27 Sold merchandise on account to W.R. Davis, $415.80, plus tax of $20.79. Sale No. 70.
28 Sold merchandise on account to D.H. Gordon, $176.60, plus tax of $8.83. Sale No. 71.
30 Sold merchandise on account to S.M. Aronson, $139.00, plus tax of $6.95. Sale No. 72.

Required:
1. Enter each transaction in a sales journal or in a two-column journal.
2. Post directly from the sales journal and the two-column journal to the proper customer accounts in a subsidiary accounts receivable ledger. The subsidiary ledger should be in three-column format. The following customer accounts are required:
   S.M. Aronson, 8544 Everett Ave., Richmond Heights, MO 63117-2131, 6/1 Balance, $520.00.
   W.R. Davis, 8821 Eager Rd., Brentwood, MO 63144-4413, 6/1 Balance, $431.30.
   D.H. Gordon, 1016 Winwood Dr., Ladue, MO 63124-5621, 6/1 Balance, $614.00.
   N.J. Haffner, 7540 Maryland Ave., Clayton, MO 63105-5013, 6/1 Balance, $336.00.

R.J. Klein, 11988 Mark Twain Ln., Bridgeton, MO 63044-7126, 6/1 Balance, $188.20.

A.M. Zala, 7 Wrenwood Ct., Webster Groves, MO 63119-8721, 6/1 Balance, -0-.

(In posting from these journals, the page number preceded by the initials "S" or "J" should be placed in the Posting Reference column of the ledger account involved.)

3. Enter the totals and rule the sales journal. Foot the two-column journal to prove the equality of the debits and credits. Complete the summary posting of the sales journal and the individual posting of the two-column journal to the proper general ledger accounts. The general ledger should be in the four-column format and contain the following accounts:

    Accounts Receivable, Account No. 131, 6/1 Balance, $2,089.50.

    Sales Tax Payable, Account No. 221, 6/1 Balance, $889.12.

    Sales, Account No. 411, 6/1 Balance, $14,818.66.

    Sales Returns & Allowances, Account No. 411.1, 6/1 Balance, $298.00.

    (In posting from these journals, the page number preceded by the initials "S" or "J" should be placed in the Posting Reference column of the ledger account involved.)

4. Prove the balance of the summary accounts receivable account by preparing a schedule of accounts receivable as of June 30, based on the subsidiary accounts receivable ledger.

    (Sales and two-column journal paper, general and subsidiary ledger account forms, and ruled paper for the schedule of accounts receivable can be found in the working papers.)

Problem 7B6   Entries in Cash Receipts Journal and Two-Column Journal; Posting to Selected Ledger Accounts

---

Jim Mapp operates an auto accessories store. The books of original entry include a cash receipts journal and a two-column journal. The following transactions related to sales and cash receipts occurred during August.

Aug. **4** Received $48.70 from T. Schiff on account.

10 Received $52.10 from M. Moran on account.

14 M. Stiebel returned merchandise for credit. Sales price, $29.00, plus tax of $1.45. (Enter in two-column journal.)

18 Received $37.75 from N. Wilson on account.

21 Received $32.95 from R. Ryan on account.

24 B. Pretzel returned merchandise for credit. Sales price, $36.25, plus tax of $1.81.

28 Received $43.80 from B. Levenson on account.

31 Cash and bank credit card sales for the month, $2,110.00, plus tax of $105.50.

Required:

1. Enter the transactions in a cash receipts journal or a two-column journal. Total and rule the cash receipts journals. Foot the amount columns of the two-column journal to prove the equality of debits and credits.

2. Complete the summary posting of the cash receipts journal and the individual posting of the two-column journal to the following four-column general ledger accounts:

Cash, Account No. 111, 8/1 Balance, $15,000.00.
Accounts Receivable, Account No. 131, 8/1 Balance, $1,075.25.
Sales Tax Payable, Account No. 221, 8/1 Balance, $157.02.
Sales, Account No. 411, 8/1 Balance, $15,536.73.
Sales Returns & Allowances, Account No. 411.1, 8/1 Balance, $392.43.

(In posting from the cash receipts journal, the page number preceded by the initials "CR" should be placed in the Posting Reference column of the ledger account involved.) Then, update the account balances.

(Cash receipts and two-column journal paper and general ledger account forms can be found in the working papers.)

Mastery Problem

If the working papers for this textbook are not used, omit the Mastery Problem.

Geoff and Sandy Harland own and operate Wayward Kennel and Pet Supply where the motto is "if your pet is not becoming to you, he should be coming to us." The following sales and cash collections took place during the month of September. The Harlands prefer to maintain a sales tax payable account throughout the month to account for the 6% sales tax. They use a sales journal, cash receipts journal, and a two-column journal.

Sept. 1 Sold a fish aquarium on account to Ken Shank for $125.00 plus tax of $7.50, terms, n/30. Sale No. 101.

3 Sold dog food on account to Nancy Truelove for $68.25 plus tax of $4.10, terms, n/30. Sale No. 102.

5 Sold a bird cage on account to Jean Warkentin for $43.95 plus tax of $2.64, terms, n/30. Sale No. 103.

8 Cash sales for the week were $2,332.45 plus tax of $139.95.

10 Cash received for boarding and grooming services, $625.00 plus tax of $37.50.

11 Jean Warkentin stopped by the store to point out a minor defect in the bird cage recently purchased. The Harlands offered a sales allowance of $10.00 on the price of the cage which seemed to satisfy Jean Warkentin.

12 Sold a cockatoo on account to Tully Shaw for $1,200.00 plus tax of $72.00, terms, n/30. Sale No. 104.

14 Received cash from Jayne Brown on account, $256.00.

15 Jayne Brown returned merchandise sold for $93.28, including sales tax.

16 Received cash from Nancy Truelove on account, $58.25.

17 Cash sales for the week were $2,656.85 plus tax of $159.41.

18 Cash received for boarding and grooming services, $535.00 plus tax of $32.10.

19 Received cash from Ed Cochran on account, $63.25.

20 Sold pet supplies on account to Susan Hays for $83.33 plus tax of $5.00, terms, n/30. Sale No. 105.

21 Sold three labrador retriever puppies to All American Day Camp for $375.00 plus tax of $22.50, terms, n/30. Sale No. 106.

22 Cash sales for the week were $3,122.45 plus tax of $187.35.

23 Cash received for boarding and grooming services, $515.00 plus tax of $30.90.

25 Received cash from Ken Shank on account, $132.50.

26 Received cash from Nancy Truelove on account, $72.35.

27 Received cash from Joe Gloy on account, $273.25.

28 Borrowed $11,000.00 to be used for the purchase of a pet limousine.

29 Cash sales for the week were $2,835.45 plus tax of $170.13.

30 Cash received for boarding and grooming services, $488.00 plus tax of $29.28.

Required:

1. Enter the transactions for the month of September in the proper journals.
2. Enter the totals and rule the journals where appropriate.
3. Post the entries to the general and subsidiary ledgers.
4. Prepare a schedule of accounts receivable.
5. Compute the net sales for the month of September.

CHAPTER 8

Payroll Accounting

Chapter Objectives

Careful study of this chapter should enable you to:

- Explain and perform the three major steps in payroll accounting: (1) calculation of employee earnings and deductions; (2) calculation of employer payroll taxes; (3) proper entry of the expenses, liabilities, and cash payments in connection with (1) and (2).

- Explain the government laws and regulations that primarily affect payroll accounting.

- Describe and prepare selected forms and records that are required or desirable in payroll accounting.

- Explain selected record-keeping methods and procedures used in the payroll area in a computer-based accounting information system.

Employers need to maintain detailed and accurate payroll accounting records for both financial and legal reasons. The financial reason is that payroll expenditures are a major part of the total expenditures of most companies. Payroll accounting records provide data useful in the analysis, classification, and control of these expenditures. In addition, payroll accounting information is invaluable in contract discussions with labor unions, in the settlement of company-union grievances, and in determining employee pension benefits.

The legal reason for maintaining payroll accounting records is that employers are required by federal, state, and local laws to do so. Companies must accumulate payroll data both for the business as a whole and for each employee. Clearly, accurate payroll accounting is essential to the survival of most businesses.

Employee Earnings and Deductions

The first step in determining the amount to be paid to an employee is to calculate the employee's total or gross earnings for the pay period. The second step is to determine the amounts of deductions that are required either by law or by specific agreement between the em-

Explain and perform the calculation of employee earnings and deductions.

ployer and the employee. Depending upon a variety of circumstances, these steps may be relatively simple or quite complicated. An examination of the factors that must be considered in performing these two steps follows.

Employees and Independent Contractors

Not every individual who performs services for a business is considered to be an employee. A public accountant, lawyer, or management consultant who sells services to a business does not necessarily become its employee. Neither does a plumber nor an electrician who is hired to make specific repairs or installations on business property. These people are told what to do, but not how to do it, and the compensation that they receive for their services is called a fee. Any person who agrees to perform a service for a fee and is not subject to the control of those for whom the service is performed is called an independent contractor.

In contrast, an employee is one who is under the control and direction of an employer with regard to the performance of services. The difference between an independent contractor and an employee is an important legal distinction. The nature and extent of the responsibilities of the contractor and the client to each other and to third parties are quite different from the mutual obligations of the employer and the employee. Of particular importance for payroll accounting purposes is the fact that the various government laws and regulations regarding employee deductions, employer payroll taxes, records, and reports apply only to employees.

Types of Compensation

Compensation for managerial or administrative services usually is called salary. A salary normally is expressed in biweekly, monthly, or annual terms. Compensation either for skilled or for unskilled labor usually is referred to as wages. Wages ordinarily are expressed in terms of hours, weeks, or units produced. The terms salaries and wages often are used interchangeably in practice.

Although compensation for services is usually monetary, it sometimes may take the form of goods, lodging, meals, or other property. This type of compensation is measured by the fair market value of the property or service given in payment for the employee's efforts.

In addition to compensation, employers often provide additional incentives in the form of supplements. Supplements to the basic salaries or wages of employees include bonuses, commissions, cost-of-living adjustments, pension and profit sharing plans, and vacation pay. This chapter demonstrates proper accounting for basic salaries and wages of employees paid in cash.

Determination of Total Earnings

An employee's earnings commonly are based on the time worked during the payroll period. Sometimes earnings are based on units of output or of sales during the period. Compensation based on time requires a record of the time worked by each employee. If there are only a few employees, a record of times worked may be kept in a memorandum book. When there are many employees, time clocks are commonly used to record time spent on the job each day. A time clock uses time cards provided for each employee, to record arrival and departure times. Alternatively, plastic cards or badges encoded with basic employee data are now being used in computer-based timekeeping systems. Whatever method is used, the total time worked during the payroll period must be computed.

Employees often are entitled to compensation at more than their regular rate of pay. If the employer is engaged in interstate commerce, the Fair Labor Standards Act (commonly known as the Federal Wage and Hour Law) provides that all employees covered by the act must be paid $1\frac{1}{2}$ times the regular rate for all hours worked over 40 hours per week. Also, labor-management agreements often require extra pay for certain hours or days. In such cases, hours worked in excess of eight per day or work on Sundays and specified holidays may be paid for at higher rates.

To illustrate, assume that the company pays Hela Chiopi time and a half for all hours worked in excess of 40 hours per week and double time for work on Sunday. Chiopi's regular rate is $12 per hour; and during the week ended April 11, Chiopi worked 9 hours each day Monday through Friday, 6 hours on Saturday and 4 on Sunday. Chiopi's total earnings or gross pay for the week ended April 11, is computed as follows:

40 hours @ $12	$480
11 hours @ $18 (1 1/2 × $12 = $18)	198*
4 hours (on Sunday) @ $24 (2 × $12 = $24)	96
Total earnings for the week	$774

*Chiopi worked 9 hours each day Monday through Friday and 6 hours on Saturday—a total of 51 hours. 40 hours would be paid for at the regular rate and 11 hours at time and a half.

An employee who is paid a regular biweekly, monthly or annual salary may also be entitled to premium pay for any overtime. If this is the case, it is necessary to compute the regular hourly rate of pay before computing the overtime rate. To illustrate, assume that Karl Schmidt receives a regular salary of $2,000 a month and that Schmidt is entitled to overtime pay at the rate of $1\frac{1}{2}$ times the regular hourly rate for any time worked in excess of 40 hours per week. Schmidt's overtime pay is computed as follows:

$2,000 × 12 months	$24,000 annual pay
$24,000 / 52 weeks	$461.54 pay per week
$461.54 / 40 hours	$11.54 pay per regular hour
$11.54 × 1 1/2	$17.31 overtime pay per hour

Deductions from Total Earnings

An employee's take-home or **net pay** is typically less than the total earnings or gross pay. The difference between an employee's gross and net pay generally can be explained by three factors: (1) employee FICA (Federal Insurance Contributions Act) tax withheld by the employer, (2) employee federal income taxes (and state and city income taxes where applicable) withheld by the employer, and (3) other deductions based on special agreements between the employer and the employee.

Explain the government laws and regulations that primarily affect payroll accounting.

▨ **Employees' FICA Tax Withheld.** The Federal Insurance Contributions Act (FICA) requires most employers to withhold certain amounts from employees' earnings. The amount withheld, commonly referred to as social security tax, is the employee's contribution to the federal programs for old-age, survivors, and disability insurance (OASDI) and health insurance for the aged (HIP). These withheld amounts are commonly referred to as FICA taxes.

The earnings base, against which the FICA tax is applied, and the tax rate have been changed several times since the law was first enacted and can be changed by Congress at any time in the future. These base and rate changes, however, do not affect the accounting principles and procedures for payroll. Therefore, for the sake of convenience in this chapter, the rate is assumed to be 6.0% of taxable wages paid during the calendar year for OASDI plus 1.5% for HIP for a total FICA rate of 7.5%. It is also assumed that the first $50,000 of earnings paid to each employee in any calendar year is subject to the FICA tax.

▨ **State and Local Taxes.** In addition to the federal requirements, a few states require employers to withhold a percentage of the employees' wages for unemployment compensation benefits or for disability benefits. In some states and cities, employers are also required to withhold a percentage of the employees' wages for other types of payroll taxes.

▨ **Employees' Income Tax Withheld.** Under federal law, employers are required to withhold certain amounts from the total earnings of each employee. These withholdings are applied toward the payment of the employee's federal income tax. The amount to be withheld each pay period is based on (1) the total earnings of the employee, (2) the marital status of the employee, (3) the number of withholding allowances claimed by the employee, and (4) the length of the employee's pay period.

Each employee is required to furnish the employer with an Employee's Withholding Allowance Certificate, Form W-4, showing marital status and the number of allowances claimed. The marital status of the taxpayer and the number of allowances claimed determine the dollar amount of earnings subject to withholding. A **withholding allowance** is an allowance of a specific dollar amount on which no federal income tax is withheld from the employee's pay. Each federal income tax payer is permitted one personal withholding allowance, one for a spouse, and one for each dependent satisfying certain legal requirements. A taxpayer can also qualify for a **special withholding allowance** depending on the taxpayer's marital status, number of jobs held, whether the taxpayer's spouse works, and the amounts earned on the jobs held. Finally, **additional withholding allowances** are permitted to taxpayers who expect to have tax credits or large itemized deductions.

An allowance certificate completed by Ken Stone is shown below. Stone is married, has a spouse who is not employed, and has one dependent child. He qualifies for the special withholding allowance and two additional withholding allowances. On line 1 of the W-4 form, Stone claims 6 allowances, calculated as follows:

Personal allowances:
Self		1
Wife		1	2
Allowance for dependent		1
Special withholding allowance		1
Additional withholding allowances		2
Total withholding allowances		6

----------------- Cut here and give the certificate to your employer. Keep the top portion for your records. -----------------

Form **W-4** Department of the Treasury Internal Revenue Service	**Employee's Withholding Allowance Certificate** ▶ For Privacy Act and Paperwork Reduction Act Notice, see reverse.	OMB No. 1545-0010 19--

1 Type or print your first name and middle initial Ken M.	Last name Stone	2 Your social security number 393-58-8194

| Home address (number and street or rural route) 1546 Swallow Drive | 3 Marital Status | ☐ Single   ☒ Married |
| City or town, state, and ZIP code St. Louis, MO 63144-4752 | | ☐ Married, but withhold at higher Single rate. Note: *If married, but legally separated, or spouse is a nonresident alien, check the Single box.* |

4 Total number of allowances you are claiming (from line G above or from the Worksheets on back if they apply) . . . **4** | 6

5 Additional amount, if any, you want deducted from each pay . . . . **5** $

6 I claim exemption from withholding and I certify that I meet **ALL** of the following conditions for exemption:
  • Last year I had a right to a refund of **ALL** Federal income tax withheld because I had **NO** tax liability; **AND**
  • This year I expect a refund of **ALL** Federal income tax withheld because I expect to have **NO** tax liability; **AND**
  • This year if my income exceeds $500 and includes nonwage income, another person cannot claim me as a dependent.
If you meet all of the above conditions, enter the year effective and "EXEMPT" here . . . . ▶ **6** | 19

7 Are you a full-time student? *(Note: Full-time students are not automatically exempt.)* . . . . **7** ☐ Yes ☒ No

Under penalties of perjury, I certify that I am entitled to the number of withholding allowances claimed on this certificate or entitled to claim exempt status.

Employee's signature ▶ *Ken M. Stone*   Date ▶ January 3   , 19--

8 Employer's name and address (**Employer:** Complete 8 and 10 only if sending to IRS) | 9 Office code (optional) | 10 Employer identification number

Withholding Allowance Certificate (Form W-4)

Most employers use the **wage-bracket method** to determine the amount of tax to be withheld from an employee's pay. Employers trace the employee's gross pay for a specific time period into the appropriate wage-bracket table provided by the Internal Revenue Service. These tables cover various time periods, and there are separate tables for single and married taxpayers. Copies may be obtained from any local Internal Revenue Service office. A portion of a weekly income tax wage-bracket withholding table for married persons is illustrated on page 301. To use this table, assume that Ken Stone (who claims 6 allowances) had gross earnings of $425 for the week ending December 19, 19--. On the line showing the tax on wages of "at least $420, but less than $430," in the column

WEEKLY Payroll Period—Employee MARRIED

And the wages are-		And the number of withholding allowances claimed is—										
At least	But less than	0	1	2	3	4	5	6	7	8	9	10 or more
		The amount of income tax to be withheld shall be—										
310	320	38	33	27	22	16	10	5	0	0	0	0
320	330	40	34	29	23	17	12	6	1	0	0	0
330	340	41	36	30	25	19	13	8	2	0	0	0
340	350	43	37	32	26	20	15	9	4	0	0	0
350	360	44	39	33	28	22	16	11	5	0	0	0
360	370	46	40	35	29	23	18	12	7	1	0	0
370	380	47	42	36	31	25	19	14	8	2	0	0
380	390	49	43	38	32	26	21	15	10	4	0	0
390	400	50	45	39	34	28	22	17	11	5	0	0
400	410	52	46	41	35	29	24	18	13	7	1	0
410	420	53	48	42	37	31	25	20	14	8	3	0
420	430	55	49	44	38	32	27	21	16	10	4	0
430	440	56	51	45	40	34	28	23	17	11	6	0
440	450	58	52	47	41	35	30	24	19	13	7	2
450	460	59	54	48	43	37	31	26	20	14	9	3
460	470	61	55	50	44	38	33	27	22	16	10	5
470	480	62	57	51	46	40	34	29	23	17	12	6
480	490	64	58	53	47	41	36	30	25	19	13	8
490	500	65	60	54	49	43	37	32	26	20	15	9
500	510	67	61	56	50	44	39	33	28	22	16	11
510	520	68	63	57	52	46	40	35	29	23	18	12
520	530	70	64	59	53	47	42	36	31	25	19	14
530	540	71	66	60	55	49	43	38	32	26	21	15
540	550	73	67	62	56	50	45	39	34	28	22	17
550	560	74	69	63	58	52	46	41	35	29	24	18
560	570	76	70	65	59	53	48	42	37	31	25	20
570	580	77	72	66	61	55	49	44	38	32	27	21
580	590	79	73	68	62	56	51	45	40	34	28	23
590	600	80	75	69	64	58	52	47	41	35	30	24
600	610	82	76	71	65	59	54	48	43	37	31	26
$610	$620	$83	$78	$72	$67	$61	$55	$50	$44	$38	$33	$27
620	630	85	79	74	68	62	57	51	46	40	34	29
630	640	87	81	75	70	64	58	53	47	41	36	30
640	650	90	82	77	71	65	60	54	49	43	37	32
650	660	93	84	78	73	67	61	56	50	44	39	33
660	670	95	85	80	74	68	63	57	52	46	40	35
670	680	98	88	81	76	70	64	59	53	47	42	36
680	690	101	91	83	77	71	66	60	55	49	43	38
690	700	104	93	84	79	73	67	62	56	50	45	39
700	710	107	96	86	80	74	69	63	58	52	46	41

Federal Withholding Tax Tables

headed "6 withholding allowances," $21.00 is given as the amount to be withheld.

Whether the wage-bracket method or some other method is used in computing the amount of tax to be withheld, the sum of the taxes withheld from an employee's wages is only an approximation. An employee may be liable for a tax larger than the amount withheld. This additional tax will be remitted with the employee's federal income tax return. On the other hand, the amount of the taxes withheld by the employer may be greater than the employee's actual tax liability. In such an event, the employee will be entitled to a refund of the excess taxes withheld, or the excess can be applied to the employee's tax liability for the following year.

Several states and cities have adopted state and city income tax procedures. Some of these states and cities supply employers with withholding allowance certificate forms and income tax withholding tables that are similar in concept and appearance to those used by the federal Internal Revenue Service. Other states determine the amount to be withheld merely by applying a fixed percentage to the federal withholding amount.

■■■ **Other Deductions.** In addition to the mandatory deductions from employee earnings for FICA and income taxes, there are many other possible deductions. These deductions generally are voluntary and depend on specific agreements between the employee and employer. Some examples of these deductions are for:

1. United States savings bond purchases.
2. Life, accident, dental, or health insurance premiums.
3. Credit union deposits.
4. Pension plan payments.
5. Charitable contributions.

Payroll Records

Describe and prepare selected forms and records that are required or desirable in payroll accounting.

The needs of management and the requirements of various federal and state laws make it necessary for employers to keep records that will provide the following information for each employee:

1. Name, address, and social security number.
2. The gross amount of earnings, the date of payment, and the period of employment covered by each payroll.
3. The gross amount of earnings accumulated since the first of the year.
4. The amount of any taxes or other items withheld.

Regardless of the number of employees or type of business, three types of payroll records usually need to be prepared by the employer. They are: (1) the payroll register or payroll journal; (2) the payroll check with earnings statement attached; and (3) the earnings record of the individual employee (on a weekly, monthly, quarterly, or annual basis). While these records can be prepared either by manual or by automated methods, payroll is a major application of computer-based accounting systems. For the sake of convenience and in order to avoid duplication, the illustrations in this chapter are based on a computer system only. The forms and procedures illustrated are equally applicable to a manual or a mechanical system.

PAYROLL

| | | | | EARNINGS | | | | TAXABLE EARNINGS | |
NAME	EMP. NO.	NO. OF ALLOW.	M/S	REGULAR	OVERTIME	TOTAL	CUMULATIVE TOTAL	UNEMPLOY. COMP.	FICA
COLLINS, PAMELA D.	1	4	M	520.00		520.00	26,320.00		520.00
GUNTHER, JAMES B.	2	1	S	360.00	40.00	400.00	20,400.00		400.00
STONE, KEN M.	3	6	M	425.00		425.00	22,025.00		425.00
PROW, MARY F.	4	2	M	650.00	75.00	725.00	35,850.00		725.00
RAINES, RUSSELL J.	5	3	M	440.00		440.00	22,340.00		440.00
SWANEY, LINDA L.	6	2	S	450.00	50.00	500.00	25,000.00		500.00
TAMIN, PAUL	7	5	M	490.00		490.00	25,650.00		490.00
WILES, HARRY	8	1	S	300.00		300.00	6,300.00	300.00	300.00
				3,635.00	165.00	3,800.00	183,885.00	300.00	3,800.00

Payroll Register—Computer Prepared (left page)

▓▓ **Payroll Register.** A **payroll register** is a multi-column form used to assemble, compute, and summarize the data required at the end of each payroll period. The computerized payroll register used by Westly, Inc., for the payroll period ended December 19, 19--, is illustrated below. The columnar headings are self-explanatory. Detailed information on earnings, taxable earnings, deductions, and net pay is summarized for each employee.

Westly, Inc., has eight employees. The first $50,000 of earnings received by an employee in any calendar year is subject to FICA tax. The Cumulative Total column, under the earnings category, shows that none of the eight employees has exceeded this limit. The columns for taxable earnings are needed for determining the employer's payroll taxes in addition to determining FICA tax. The payroll taxes are discussed on pages 299-301.

Regular deductions are made from the earnings of employees for FICA tax, federal income tax, and city earnings tax. In addition, voluntary deductions are made for the company pension plan (which is a voluntary plan), health insurance, the company credit union, and for the United Way contribution, according to agreement with individual employees. Gunther and Prow have each authorized Westly, Inc., to withhold $20 each week for their United Way contributions.

After the data for each employee have been entered, the amount columns in the payroll register should be footed and the footings verified as shown below. In a computer-based accounting system, the software package for the payroll application will perform this proof without need for separate verification. An error in the payroll register could cause the payment of an incorrect amount to an employee. It also could result in the sending of an incorrect amount to the companies or government agencies for whom funds are deducted from the employees' gross pay.

REGISTER

			DEDUCTIONS							
FICA TAX	FEDERAL INCOME TAX	CITY TAX	PENSION PLAN	HEALTH INS.	CREDIT UNION	UNITED WAY	TOTAL	DATE	NET PAY	CK. NO.
39.00	47.00	9.40	10.00		7.50		112.90	12/19/--	407.10	409
30.00	51.00	10.20			7.50	20.00	118.70	12/19/--	281.30	410
31.88	21.00	4.20		10.00			67.08	12/19/--	357.92	411
54.38	91.00	18.20	12.00	13.00	7.50	20.00	216.08	12/19/--	508.92	412
33.00	41.00	8.20	12.00	13.00	7.50		114.70	12/19/--	325.30	413
37.50	70.00	14.00	8.50				130.00	12/19/--	370.00	414
36.75	32.00	6.40		10.00	7.50		92.65	12/19/--	397.35	415
22.50	37.00	9.40					66.90	12/19/--	233.10	416
285.00	390.00	80.00	42.50	46.00	37.50	40.00	919.00		2,881.00	

Payroll Register—Computer Prepared (right page)

Regular earnings		$3,635.00
Overtime earnings		165.00
Gross earnings		$3,800.00
Deductions:		
FICA tax	$285.00	
Federal income tax	390.00	
City earnings tax	78.00	
Pension plan	42.50	
Health insurance premiums	46.00	
Credit union	37.50	
United Way	40.00	919.00
Net amount of payroll		$2,881.00

▨ **Payroll Check.** Employees may be paid in cash or by check. In some cases today, the employee does not even handle the paycheck. Rather, salary is paid via **direct deposit** or electronic funds transfer (EFT), by the employer to the employee's bank. The employee receives the deduction stub from the check and a printed deposit receipt. Payment by check or direct deposit is strongly preferred because it provides better internal accounting control. Many businesses prepare a single check for the net amount of the total payroll and deposit it in a special payroll bank account. Individual paychecks are then drawn on that account for the amount due to each employee. Data needed to prepare an individual paycheck for each employee are contained in the payroll register. (In a computer-based system, the paychecks normally are prepared at the same time as the payroll register.) The employer furnishes a statement of payroll deductions to each employee along with each wage payment. Paychecks with detachable stubs, like the one for Ken Stone illustrated on page 305, are widely used for this purpose. Before such a check is deposited or cashed, the stub should be detached and retained by the employee as a permanent record of earnings and payroll deductions.

▨ **Employee's Earnings Record.** A separate record of each employee's earnings is called an **employee's earnings record.** This record provides the information needed in preparing the various federal, state, and local reports required of employers. A computer-prepared employee's earnings record used by Westly, Inc., for Ken M. Stone during the last two quarters of the current calendar year is illustrated on pages 306 and 307.

This record usually is kept on separate sheets or cards, which may be filed alphabetically or by employee number for easy reference. The information printed on this form is obtained from the payroll register. In a computer-based system, the employee's earnings record can be updated simultaneously with the preparation of the payroll register. This is done with multiple-copy forms and special paper, which can be machine-separated after printing.

Stone's earnings for the last half of the year up to December 19 are shown on this form. The entry for the pay period ended December 19 is the same as that in the payroll register illustrated on pages 302 and 303.

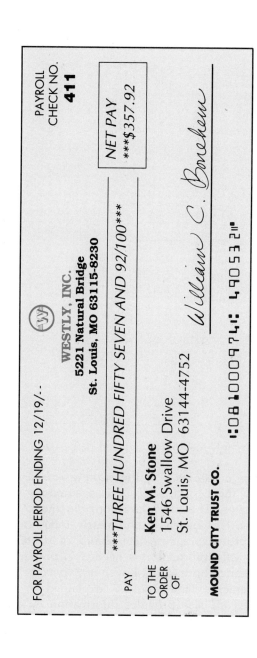

FOR PAYROLL PERIOD ENDING 12/19/--

PAYROLL
CHECK NO.
411

WESTLY, INC.
5221 Natural Bridge
St. Louis, MO 63115-8230

NET PAY
***$357.92

PAY

THREE HUNDRED FIFTY SEVEN AND 92/100

TO THE
ORDER
OF

Ken M. Stone
1546 Swallow Drive
St. Louis, MO 63144-4752

William C. Borchers

MOUND CITY TRUST CO.

⑈0810009741: 49053 2⑈

WESTLY, INC.
ST. LOUIS, MO.
STATEMENT OF EARNINGS

	Earnings			Deductions									
Date	Regular	Overtime	Total	Fica Tax	Federal Inc. Tax	City Tax	Pension Plan	Health Ins.	Credit Union	United Way	Total	Net Pay	Ck. No.
12/19/--	425.00		425.00	31.88	21.00	4.20		10.00			67.08	357.92	411
Year-to-Date	20,375.00	1,650.00	22,025.00	1,651.88	1,138.00	227.60		484.00			3,501.48	18,523.52	

Paycheck and Deduction Stub—Computer Prepared

```
                                                            EMPLOYEE'S

    NAME        Ken M. Stone                 SEX               Male
    ADDRESS     1546 Swallow Dr.             MARITAL STATUS     Married
    CITY        St. Louis, MO  63144-4752    NUMBER OF ALLOWANCES  6
```

REGULAR	OVERTIME	TOTAL	CUMULATIVE TOTAL	UNEMPLOY. COMP.	FICA
425.00		425.00	11,365.00		425.00
425.00		425.00	11,790.00		425.00
425.00		425.00	12,215.00		425.00
425.00		425.00	12,640.00		425.00
425.00		425.00	13,065.00		425.00
425.00		425.00	13,490.00		425.00
425.00		425.00	13,915.00		425.00
425.00		425.00	14,340.00		425.00
425.00		425.00	14,765.00		425.00
425.00		425.00	15,190.00		425.00
425.00		425.00	15,615.00		425.00
425.00		425.00	16,040.00		425.00
425.00		425.00	16,465.00		425.00
THIRD QUARTER					
5,525.00		5,525.00			5,525.00
425.00		425.00	16,890.00		425.00
425.00		425.00	17,315.00		425.00
425.00		425.00	17,740.00		425.00
425.00		425.00	18,165.00		425.00
425.00	50.00	475.00	18,640.00		475.00
425.00	60.00	485.00	19,125.00		485.00
425.00	50.00	475.00	19,600.00		475.00
425.00	75.00	500.00	20,100.00		500.00
425.00	75.00	500.00	20,600.00		500.00
425.00	75.00	500.00	21,100.00		500.00
425.00	75.00	500.00	21,600.00		500.00
425.00		425.00	22,025.00		425.00
FOURTH QUARTER					
YEARLY TOTAL					

Earnings / Taxable Earnings

Employee's Earnings Record—Computer Prepared (left page)

The payroll register is a summary of the earnings of all employees for each pay period, while the earnings record is a summary of the annual earnings of each employee. The earnings record illustrated above and on page 307 is designed so that quarterly and yearly totals can be accumulated. Thus the form provides a complete record of the earnings of an employee for the year. This information is needed in preparing an annual report to the employee and the Internal Revenue Service on a form called a Wage and Tax Statement. This report is explained in the following section. The earnings record also provides information on an employee's quarterly earnings, which is needed for filing quarterly reports to government agencies. These reports will be discussed later in this chapter.

Wage and Tax Statement

Not later than January 31 of each year, the law requires employers to furnish each employee with an annual report called a Wage and Tax

EARNINGS RECORD

DEPARTMENT	Maintenance	SOCIAL SECURITY NUMBER	393-58-8194
OCCUPATION	Service	DATE OF BIRTH	August 17, 1964
PAY RATE	$425 weekly	DATE EMPLOYED	January 3, 1987
EMPLOYEE NO.	3	DATE EMPLOYMENT TERMINATED	

DEDUCTIONS

FICA TAX	FEDERAL INCOME TAX	CITY TAX	PENSION PLAN	HEALTH INS.	CREDIT UNION	UNITED WAY	TOTAL	DATE	NET PAY	CK. NO.
31.88	21.00	4.20		10.00			67.08	7/4/--	357.92	219
31.88	21.00	4.20		10.00			67.08	7/11/--	357.92	227
31.88	21.00	4.20		10.00			67.08	7/18/--	357.92	235
31.88	21.00	4.20		10.00			67.08	7/25/--	357.92	243
31.88	21.00	4.20		10.00			67.08	8/1/--	357.92	251
31.88	21.00	4.20		10.00			67.08	8/8/--	357.92	259
31.88	21.00	4.20		10.00			67.08	8/15/--	357.92	267
31.88	21.00	4.20		10.00			67.08	8/22/--	357.92	275
31.88	21.00	4.20		10.00			67.08	8/29/--	357.92	283
31.88	21.00	4.20		10.00			67.08	9/5/--	357.92	291
31.88	21.00	4.20		10.00			67.08	9/12/--	357.92	299
31.88	21.00	4.20		10.00			67.08	9/19/--	357.92	307
31.88	21.00	4.20		10.00			67.08	9/26/--	357.92	315
414.44	273.00	54.60		130.00			872.04		4,652.96	
31.88	21.00	4.20		10.00			67.08	10/3/--	357.92	323
31.88	21.00	4.20		10.00			67.08	10/10/--	357.92	331
31.88	21.00	4.20		10.00			67.08	10/17/--	357.92	339
31.88	21.00	4.20		10.00			67.08	10/24/--	357.92	347
35.63	29.00	5.80		10.00			80.43	10/31/--	394.57	355
36.38	30.00	6.00		10.00			82.38	11/7/--	402.62	363
35.63	29.00	5.80		10.00			80.43	11/14/--	394.57	371
37.50	33.00	6.60		10.00			87.10	11/21/--	412.90	379
37.50	33.00	6.60		10.00			87.10	11/28/--	412.90	387
37.50	33.00	6.60		10.00			87.10	12/5/--	412.90	395
37.50	33.00	6.60		10.00			87.10	12/12/--	412.90	403
31.88	21.00	4.20		10.00			67.08	12/19/--	357.92	411

Employee's Earnings Record—Computer Prepared (right page)

Statement, Form W-2. This form shows the total amount of wages paid to the employee and the amount of tax withheld during the preceding calendar year. Presented on page 308 is a completed Form W-2.

If the employee's wages are subject to FICA tax as well as federal, state, or local income tax, the employer must report total wages paid and the amounts deducted both for income tax and for FICA tax. Information for this purpose is contained in the employee's earnings record.

The Wage and Tax Statement is a six-part combined federal/state form. It is printed in sets of six copies so that copies are available for filing with different federal, state, and city agencies, and for the employer's and employee's records.

The **employer's identification number** appearing on the Wage and Tax Statement is an identification number assigned to the employer by the Internal Revenue Service. An employer who employs one or more persons must file for an identification number. This number must be shown

1 Control number	22222	For Paperwork Reduction Act Notice, see back of Copy D. OMB No. 1545-0008	For Official Use Only ▶		
2 Employer's name, address, and ZIP code Westly, Inc. 5221 Natural Bridge St. Louis, MO 63115-8230			3 Employer's identification number 43 0211630	4 Employer's state I.D. number 21 686001	
			5 Statutory employee ☐ Deceased ☐ Pension plan ☐ Legal rep. ☐	942 emp. ☐ Subtotal ☐ Deferred compensation ☐ Void ☐	
			6 Allocated tips	7 Advance EIC payment	
8 Employee's social security number 393-58-8194	9 Federal income tax withheld $1,159.00		10 Wages, tips, other compensation $22,450.00	11 Social security tax withheld $1,683.75	
12 Employee's name (first, middle, last) Ken M. Stone			13 Social security wages $22,450.00	14 Social security tips	
			16 (See Instr. for Forms W-2/W-2P)	16a Fringe benefits incl. in Box 10	
1546 Swallow Drive St. Louis, MO 63144-4752			17 State income tax	18 State wages, tips, etc.	19 Name of state
15 Employee's address and ZIP code			20 Local income tax $231.80	21 Local wages, tips, etc. $22,450.00	22 Name of locality St. Louis Co.

Form **W-2** **Wage and Tax Statement**   Copy A For Social Security Administration   Dept. of the Treasury—IRS

Wage and Tax Statement (Form W-2)

on all reports required of Westly, Inc., under the Federal Insurance Contributions Act.

Explain selected record-keeping methods and procedures used in the payroll area in a computer-based accounting information system.

■ **Record-Keeping Methods.** A purely manual system is one in which all records, journals and ledgers are prepared by hand. Such systems are rare today. Even very small businesses use cash registers and other machines in performing accounting tasks. In this sense, virtually all accounting information systems today are at least partially automated, i.e., they use some kind of machines in the accounting process.

In a manual system, all employee data on the payroll records, such as name, address, social security number, pay rate, hours worked, current earnings, and taxes withheld, are determined, calculated, and entered by hand. In such a system, it is often necessary to enter the same data a number of times. For example, identical employee earnings amounts would be entered on the payroll register, paycheck, and earnings record.

Automated systems can be broken down into two types: mechanical and electronic. A mechanical system is one in which various types of accounting machines are used for posting accounts, billing customers, entering payroll, and printing paychecks. An electronic system is one in which data are processed using electronic computers. On previous pages, a payroll register, payroll check, and individual employee's earnings record that were prepared using a microcomputer were illustrated.

In a mechanical system, much of the payroll information is entered simultaneously on the payroll register, paycheck, and earnings record. This is an example of the write-it-once principle. It is often desirable to enter data on a number of documents and records at the same time, because each time the same information is recopied there is a chance for error. Many accounting machines are available that perform these functions. Most of these machines also are capable of performing the arithmetic operations necessary in preparing the payroll. Each pay period, accounting personnel still need to provide input to the machines indicating such information as employee name, social security number, gross earnings, taxes withheld, and other deductions.

In a system using electronic computers, not only are the payroll register, paycheck, and earnings record generated simultaneously, but a number of inputs need not be repeated each pay period. Computers have the ability to store internally large amounts of information, such as employee names, social security numbers, withholding allowances, pay rates, FICA and income tax withholding rates, and earnings to date. They can also perform the arithmetic and logic functions required in payroll accounting. Based on inputs of employee social security numbers and hours worked, the computer can supply each employee's gross earnings, all appropriate deductions, and net pay. The computer can then print the paychecks and the payroll register, and update the employee's earnings records.

Both mechanical and electronic processing systems are also available through companies external to an employer's business. These companies, known as **service bureaus** (or automation companies), perform payroll accounting, in addition to other accounting functions, for businesses on a contract basis. The employer provides a service bureau with whatever inputs the employer would need if the payroll were being prepared on the employer's own mechanical or electronic payroll system. The service bureau then processes these inputs and provides the employer with the completed payroll register, paychecks, and updated employee earnings records. The use of service bureaus is decreasing as a result of rapid growth in the use of personal computer systems.

Computers are also used with payroll accounting systems on a **time sharing** basis. This refers to the use of a single computer by a number of small- to medium-sized businesses who share time on the computer. Thus it is possible for businesses that cannot afford their own computer to have the use of one by sharing it with other companies. Companies using time sharing have record keeping and processing situations similar to those for companies having their own computers. The main difference is that communication between time sharing users and the computer is normally by means of special telephone lines, remote computer terminals, and other electronic devices at each business location. Time sharing is also diminishing in use due to the increased use of personal computer systems.

An important point to note in connection with this discussion of payroll record-keeping methods is that the same inputs and outputs are required in all of the different systems. Even with an electronic computer with substantial data stored in its memory, the data required for payroll processing have to be inputted into the system at some point in time. The outputs in the form of a payroll register, paychecks, and employee earnings records are basically the same under all of the different systems.

Accounting for Employee Earnings and Earnings Deductions

Explain and perform proper entry of the expenses, liabilities, and cash payments for employee earnings and deductions.

In accounting for employee earnings and deductions from earnings, it is desirable to keep separate accounts for (1) earnings and (2) earnings deductions. Various account titles are used in entering wages, such as Payroll Expense, Salaries Expense, and Salaries and Commissions Expense. The accounts needed in entering earnings deductions depend upon the deductions involved. It helps in understanding the accounting for these deductions if we recognize that in withholding amounts from employees' earnings, the employer is serving as an agent for various groups such as the federal government, insurance companies, and credit unions. Amounts that are withheld and deducted from an employee's gross earnings must be paid by the employer to these groups. Therefore, a separate account should be kept for the liability incurred under each type of deduction. Examples of several of the major accounts involved in payroll accounting and of a typical journal entry for payroll are presented in the following sections.

Payroll Expense. This is an expense account which is debited for the total amount of the gross earnings of all employees for each pay period. Sometimes separate payroll accounts are kept for the employees of different departments. Thus separate accounts may be kept for Office Salaries Expense, Sales Salaries Expense, and Factory Payroll Expense.

Payroll Expense	
Debit	Credit
to enter gross earnings of employees for each pay period.	

FICA Tax Payable. This is a liability account which is credited for (1) the FICA tax withheld from employees' earnings and (2) the FICA tax imposed on the employer. FICA taxes imposed on the employer are discussed later in the chapter. The account should be debited for amounts paid to the Internal Revenue Service. When all of the FICA taxes have been paid, the account will have a zero balance.

FICA Tax Payable	
Debit	Credit
to enter payment of FICA tax previously withheld or imposed.	to enter FICA taxes (1) withheld from employees' earnings and (2) imposed on the employer.

▬▬ **Employees Income Tax Payable.** This is a liability account which should be credited for the total income tax withheld from employees' earnings. The account is debited for amounts paid to a bank depository for the Internal Revenue Service. When all of the income taxes withheld have been paid, the account will have a zero balance. A city or state earnings tax payable account is used in a similar manner.

Employees Income Tax Payable	
Debit	Credit
to enter payment of income tax previously withheld.	to enter income tax withheld from employees' earnings.

▬▬ **Other Deductions.** Pension Plan Deductions Payable is a liability account which is credited with amounts withheld from employees' earnings for any pension plan contributions. The account should be debited for the subsequent payment of these amounts to the pension plan trustee. Accounts for health insurance premiums payable, credit union contributions payable, and United Way contributions payable are similarly used.

▬▬ **Journalizing Payroll Transactions.** The information needed to properly enter the payment of employee wages and salaries is contained in the payroll register. The totals at the bottom of the columns of the payroll register on pages 302 and 303 provide the basis for the following two-column journal entry for wages paid on December 19, 19--:

Dec. 19 Payroll Expense	3,800.00	
FICA Tax Payable........................		285.00
Employees Income Tax Payable		390.00
City Earnings Tax Payable		78.00
Pension Plan Deductions Payable............		42.50
Health Insurance Premiums Payable		46.00
Credit Union Contributions Payable		37.50
United Way Contributions Payable		40.00
Cash....................................		2,881.00
Payroll for week ended December 19.		

These amounts are posted to payroll expense and liability accounts such as those illustrated in the preceding paragraphs.

Building Your Accounting Knowledge

1. Why is it important for payroll accounting purposes to distinguish between an employee and an independent contractor?

2. Name three factors that generally explain the difference between an employee's gross pay and net pay.

3. Identify the four factors that determine the amount of federal income tax that is withheld from an employee's pay each pay period.

4. Describe how to determine the number of regular withholding allowances to which a taxpayer is entitled.

5. Identify the three types of payroll records usually needed by an employer.

6. Describe the information contained in the payroll register.

7. Why is it important to foot and verify the footings of the payroll register after the data for each employee have been entered?

8. Distinguish between the payroll register and the employee earnings record.

9. Explain what an employer does with the amounts withheld from an employee's pay.

Assignment Box

To reinforce your understanding of the preceding text materials, you may complete the following:

      Study Guide: Part A

      Textbook: Exercises 8A1 through 8A2 or 8B1 through 8B2

              Problems 8A1 through 8A2 or 8B1 through 8B2

Payroll Taxes Imposed on the Employer

Explain and perform the calculation of employer payroll taxes.

The various taxes discussed thus far have had one thing in common—they all were levied on the employee. The employer withholds them from the employees' earnings only for the purpose of subsequently paying them to some agency or organization. They do not represent any additional expense of the employer.

In addition to these employee taxes, however, certain taxes are also imposed directly on the employer. Most employers are subject to FICA taxes and FUTA (Federal Unemployment Tax Act) taxes. An employer may also be subject to state unemployment taxes. All of these employer taxes represent additional payroll expenses of the employer, as will be demonstrated in subsequent sections.

Employer's FICA Tax

Explain the government laws and regulations that primarily affect payroll accounting.

FICA taxes are levied on employers at the same rate and on the same earnings base as employees. As explained on page 299, the rate and the taxable earnings base of the tax may be changed by Congress at any time. It was assumed in this chapter that the combined rate (OASDI and HIP) is 7.5% and the base is $50,000. Thus, the employer would be required to pay the employer's share of the FICA tax at a rate of 7.5% on the first $50,000 of each employee's earnings. (Note that a total of 15% of each employee's taxable earnings—the employer's share and the employee's share—must be paid periodically to an authorized bank or the Internal Revenue Service.)

Self-Employment Tax

Individuals who own and run their own business are considered self-employed. These individuals can be viewed as both the employer and employee. They do not receive salary or wages from the business, but they do have earnings in the form of the business net income. Self-employment income is the net income of a trade or business conducted by an individual. The law requires persons earning self-employment income of $400 or more to pay a self-employment tax. Self-employment tax is a contribution to the federal social security (FICA) program. The tax rate is about 5% more than the prevailing FICA rate, and is applied to the same income base as is used for the FICA tax. In this textbook, a rate of 13% on a net income base of $50,000 will be assumed.

Since the self-employment tax is a personal expense of the owner of the business, it does not usually affect the accounting records of the business. If the tax is paid with business funds, the amount should be charged to the owner's drawing account.

Employer's FUTA Tax

Under the Federal Unemployment Tax Act, a payroll tax, called the FUTA tax, is levied on employers for the purpose of financing the administration cost of the federal/state unemployment compensation program. This tax is levied only on employers and is not deducted from employees' earnings. Employers who employ one or more persons for at least one day in each of 20 or more calendar weeks in a calendar year, or who pay wages of $1,500 or more in any calendar quarter are subject to this tax. The federal law imposes a specific rate of tax on a specific earnings base but allows a substantial credit against this levy for amounts paid into state unemployment compensation programs. Since all states have such programs, the amounts actually paid to the federal government by most employers are substantially less than the legal maximum.

As in the case of the FICA tax, Congress can change both the rate and the taxable base of the FUTA tax. A rate of 6.2% with a credit of 5.4% for payments to state unemployment programs is assumed. The difference, 0.8% (6.2% − 5.4%) is the effective federal rate. Further, the taxable base is the first $7,000 of compensation paid to each employee during the calendar year. Note that both the rate and base are substantially lower than the 7.5% and $50,000 for the FICA tax. It is also important to note that all of the payroll taxes relate to gross wages *paid*—not to wages *earned*. Sometimes wages are earned in one quarter or year, but not paid until the following period.

Employer's State Unemployment Tax

All of the states as well as the District of Columbia have enacted unemployment compensation laws providing for the payment of benefits to qualified unemployed workers. The funds for these benefits are provided by payroll taxes imposed under the state unemployment compensation laws. These taxes are known as **State Unemployment Taxes**. As explained in the previous section, the administrative costs of the unemployment compensation program are borne by the federal government. Thus, the entire amount paid into the state funds can be used for the payment of benefits to qualified workers. Although there is considerable uniformity in the provisions of the state laws, there are still many variations in coverage, rates of tax imposed, and benefits payable to qualified workers. The date unemployment taxes are paid also varies from state to state, and a penalty is generally imposed on the employer for late payment. Not all employers are covered by both the Federal Unemployment Tax Act and state unemployment compensation laws, though most employers are covered by the federal law.

Under the laws of most states there is a merit-rating system which provides a tax-saving incentive to employers to stabilize employment. This system allows an employer's rate to be considerably less than the maximum rate if steady work is provided for the employees, i.e., if none or very few of the employer's workers have applied for unemployment compensation. If an employer is qualified for a lower state rate, the full credit of 5.4% would still be allowed in computing the federal unemployment tax due.

To illustrate the merit-rating system and the functioning of the federal/state unemployment tax program as a whole, assume that an employer has a favorable merit rating and is required to pay only 2.0% rather than 5.4% to the state government. If an employee earns $5,000, this employer would be required to pay a total of $140 in unemployment taxes; $100 to the state government and $40 to the federal government, calculated as follows:

Taxable earnings	$5,000
State unemployment tax rate................................	× 2.0%
State unemployment tax.....................................	$ 100
Taxable earnings	$5,000
Total FUTA rate 6.2%	
Credit for state program 5.4%	
	× 0.8%
Federal unemployment tax..................................	$ 40

For purposes of the payroll discussions that follow in this textbook, assume that a favorable merit rating exists and employers are required to pay only 2.7% rather than 5.4% to the state unemployment programs.

Accounting for Employer Payroll Taxes

Explain and perform proper data entry of the expenses, liabilities, and cash payments for employer payroll taxes.

In accounting for employer payroll taxes, it is acceptable either to use separate accounts for FICA Tax Expense, FUTA Tax Expense, and State Unemployment Tax Expense, or to enter all of these taxes in a single account such as Payroll Taxes Expense. Liabilities for FICA, FUTA, and state unemployment taxes normally should be entered in separate accounts. Examples of the payroll taxes expense and liability accounts and a typical journal entry for payroll taxes are presented in the following sections.

▨▨ **Payroll Taxes Expense.** All of the payroll taxes imposed on an employer under the federal and state social security laws are an expense of the employer. For the purpose of this discussion, it is assumed that a single account entitled Payroll Taxes Expense is used in summarizing such taxes. This is an expense account which is debited for all payroll taxes imposed on the employer.

Payroll Taxes Expense	
Debit to enter FICA, FUTA, and state unemployment taxes imposed on the employer.	

▨▨ **FICA Tax Payable.** This is the same liability account that was illustrated on page 310 and was used to recognize the FICA tax withheld from employees' earnings. The account is credited to enter the FICA tax imposed on the employer and is debited when the tax is paid to the Internal Revenue Service. When all of the FICA taxes have been paid, the account will have a zero balance.

FICA Tax Payable	
Debit to enter payment of FICA tax.	Credit to enter FICA taxes (1) withheld from employees' earnings and (2) imposed on the employer.

▨▨ **FUTA Tax Payable.** When entering the federal unemployment tax, it is customary to keep a separate liability account entitled FUTA Tax Payable. This is a liability account which is credited for the tax imposed on employers under the Federal Unemployment Tax Act. The account is debited for amounts paid for such taxes. When all of the FUTA taxes have been paid, the account will have a zero balance.

FUTA Tax Payable

Debit	Credit
to enter payment of FUTA tax.	to enter FUTA tax imposed on the employer.

▪▪▪ **State Unemployment Tax Payable.** When entering the tax imposed under state unemployment compensation laws, it is customary to keep a separate liability account entitled State Unemployment Tax Payable. This is a liability account which is credited for the tax imposed on employers under the state unemployment compensation laws. The account is debited for the amount paid for such taxes. When all of the state taxes have been paid, the account will have a zero balance. Some employers who are subject to taxes imposed under the laws of several states keep a separate liability account for the tax imposed by each state.

State Unemployment Tax Payable

Debit	Credit
to enter state unemployment tax paid.	to enter state unemployment tax imposed on the employer.

▪▪▪ **Journalizing Employer's Payroll Taxes.** The payroll taxes imposed on employers may be entered periodically, such as monthly or quarterly. It is common to enter payroll taxes at the time that wages are paid so that the employer's liability for such taxes and related expenses may be entered in the same period as the wages on which the taxes are based.

The information needed to properly enter employer payroll taxes is contained in the payroll register such as the one illustrated on pages 306 and 307. The totals at the bottom of the two columns headed Unemployment Compensation and FICA, under the Taxable Earnings category, indicate the total employee earnings on which employer taxes would be levied. The FICA taxable earnings for that pay period amounted to $3,800.00. Assuming that the combined rate of the tax imposed on the employer was 7.5%, which is the same as the rate of the tax imposed on each employee, the tax would amount to $285.00. The only earnings in the payroll register that were subject to unemployment compensation taxes were Wiles' earnings for the year because they had not exceeded the $7,000 taxable base. Wiles just started working for Westly, Inc., on July 28 of the current year. Federal and State unemployment taxes in this situation can be computed as follows:

State unemployment tax, 2.7% of $300 .... $ 8.10
FUTA tax, 0.8% of $300 .... 2.40
Total unemployment taxes $10.50

The following two-column journal entry would therefore be made for the employer payroll taxes expense on wages paid on December 19. These amounts would be posted to Payroll Taxes Expense and to liability accounts such as those illustrated in the preceding paragraphs.

Dec. 19 Payroll Taxes Expense	295.50	
FICA Tax Payable		285.00
FUTA Tax Payable		2.40
State Unemployment Tax Payable		8.10
Employer payroll taxes for the week ended December 19.		

It is important to note the total cost incurred by an employer in order to employ a person. The employer must pay the gross wages of an employee, either in whole or in part to the employee, or in part to various government agencies and other organizations. In addition to these gross wages, however, the employer must pay payroll taxes on wages paid to an employee up to certain dollar limits. To illustrate, assume that an employee earns $25,000 for a year. The total cost of this employee to the employer can be calculated as follows:

Gross wages $25,000
Employer FICA tax, 7.5% of $25,000 1,875
State unemployment tax, 2.7% of $7,000 189
FUTA tax, 0.8% of $7,000 56
$27,120

Thus, the total cost to an employer of employing a person whose stated compensation is $25,000 is $27,120. Employer payroll taxes clearly are a significant cost of doing business.

Filing Returns and Making Payroll Tax Payments

Describe and prepare selected forms and records that are required or desirable in payroll accounting, and perform proper entry of cash payments.

Employer responsibilities for filing reports and making payroll tax payments can be broken down into two areas: (1) responsibility with respect to FICA and federal income taxes, and (2) responsibility with respect to state and federal unemployment taxes. These two areas are discussed in the following sections.

Responsibilities for FICA and Federal Income Taxes. Federal reporting and payment regulations deal jointly with requirements for employee FICA taxes withheld, federal income taxes withheld, and employer FICA taxes. When the cumulative amount withheld from employees for FICA and income tax purposes plus the cumulative amount of employer FICA tax exceeds certain specified dollar amounts as of particular dates, an employer is required to deposit the amount in a Federal Reserve bank or branch or in some other authorized commercial bank depository. The dollar amounts and dates have been changed several times in recent years and are subject to change at any time in the future. In general, large employers are required to make deposits about every four days. Medium-size employers generally are required to make deposits by the 15th of the following month. In contrast, very small employers need not make a deposit but must pay the accumulated liability at the end of the following month. For the sake of convenience in this chapter, it is assumed that the cumulative amount of FICA and income taxes at the end of each month must be deposited by the 15th of the following month.

When a tax deposit is made, the employer should submit to the depository bank a completed copy of the Federal Tax Deposit Form 8109. An example of this form is shown below.

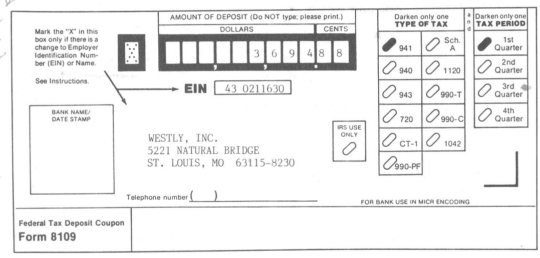

Federal Tax Deposit Coupon (Form 8109)

The accounting procedure for entering the payment of employees' FICA and income taxes withheld and employer's FICA tax is illustrated below. Assume that on January 26, Westly, Inc., issued a check to pay the following taxes imposed on wages paid during the first four payroll weeks of January:

Employees' income tax withheld from wages		$1,654.80
FICA tax:		
Withheld from employees' wages	$1,020.04	
Imposed on employer	1,020.04	2,040.08
Amount of check		$3,694.88

The journal entry for this transaction would be as follows:

> Jan. 26 FICA Tax Payable 2,040.08
>   Employees Income Tax Payable 1,654.80
>   Cash 3,694.88
>   Remitted $3,694.88 in payment of taxes.

Another major form that the employer must file in connection with employee FICA and income taxes withheld and cumulative employer FICA taxes is Form 941. This is the Employer's Quarterly Federal Tax Return which must be filed with the Internal Revenue Service by the end of the month following the end of each quarter involved. A completed copy of Form 941 used by Westly, Inc., on April 30, 19--, to file for the quarter ended March 27, 19--, is shown on page 320. This form summarizes employee FICA and federal income taxes withheld and employer FICA taxes due for the quarter. Portions of the information needed to complete Form 941 are obtained from the payroll register.

■■■ **Responsibilities for State and Federal Unemployment Taxes.** The amount of the tax imposed on employers under the state unemployment compensation laws must be remitted to the proper state office by the end of the month following the close of each calendar quarter involved. Each state provides an official form to be used in making a return of the taxes due. The accounting procedure for entering the payment of state unemployment taxes is illustrated below. Assume that a check for $842.40 was issued on April 30 in payment of state unemployment compensation taxes on wages paid during the preceding quarter ended March 27. This transaction would be entered in a two-column journal as follows:

> Apr. 30 State Unemployment Tax Payable 842.40
>   Cash 842.40
>   Paid state unemployment tax.

Federal unemployment tax must be computed on a quarterly basis. If the amount of the employer's liability under the Federal Unemployment Tax Act during any quarter is more than $100, the total must be paid to a Federal Reserve Bank or some other authorized depository. The total is due the last day of the first month following the close of the quarter. If the amount is $100 or less, no deposit is necessary, but this amount must be added to the amount subject to deposit for the next quarter. When a federal unemployment tax deposit is made, the employer should submit to the bank a completed copy of the Federal Tax Deposit of Unemployment Taxes, Form 508. This form is similar to Form 8109, which was illustrated on page 318.

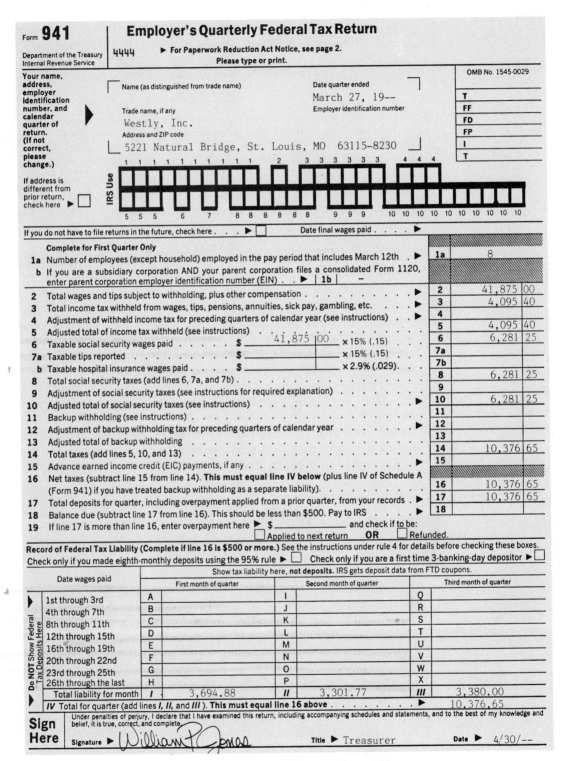

Form **941**		**Employer's Quarterly Federal Tax Return**	

Department of the Treasury Internal Revenue Service 4444 ► For Paperwork Reduction Act Notice, see page 2. Please type or print.

OMB No. 1545-0029

Your name, address, employer identification number, and calendar quarter of return. (If not correct, please change.)

Name (as distinguished from trade name)

Date quarter ended
March 27, 19--

Employer identification number

T
FF
FD
FP
I
T

Trade name, if any
Westly, Inc.
Address and ZIP code
5221 Natural Bridge, St. Louis, MO 63115-8230

If address is different from prior return, check here ►

IRS Use

1 1 1 1 1 1 1 1 1 1   2   3 3 3 3 3   4 4 4 4

5 5 5   6   7   8 8 8 8 8 8   9 9 9   10 10 10 10 10 10 10 10 10

If you do not have to file returns in the future, check here . . . ►   Date final wages paid . . . . ►

Complete for First Quarter Only

1a	Number of employees (except household) employed in the pay period that includes March 12th . ►	**1a**	8
b	If you are a subsidiary corporation AND your parent corporation files a consolidated Form 1120, enter parent corporation employer identification number (EIN) . . ► **1b** —		
2	Total wages and tips subject to withholding, plus other compensation . . . . ►	**2**	41,875 00
3	Total income tax withheld from wages, tips, pensions, annuities, sick pay, gambling, etc. . . ►	**3**	4,095 40
4	Adjustment of withheld income tax for preceding quarters of calendar year (see instructions) . .	**4**	
5	Adjusted total of income tax withheld (see instructions)	**5**	4,095 40
6	Taxable social security wages paid . . . . $ 41,875 00 × 15% (.15) . . .	**6**	6,281 25
7a	Taxable tips reported . . . . $ _____ × 15% (.15) . . .	**7a**	
b	Taxable hospital insurance wages paid . . . . $ _____ × 2.9% (.029). . .	**7b**	
8	Total social security taxes (add lines 6, 7a, and 7b)	**8**	6,281 25
9	Adjustment of social security taxes (see instructions for required explanation)	**9**	
10	Adjusted total of social security taxes (see instructions) . . . . ►	**10**	6,281 25
11	Backup withholding (see instructions)	**11**	
12	Adjustment of backup withholding tax for preceding quarters of calendar year	**12**	
13	Adjusted total of backup withholding	**13**	
14	Total taxes (add lines 5, 10, and 13)	**14**	10,376 65
15	Advance earned income credit (EIC) payments, if any . . . . ►	**15**	
16	Net taxes (subtract line 15 from line 14). **This must equal line IV below** (plus line IV of Schedule A (Form 941) if you have treated backup withholding as a separate liability).	**16**	10,376 65
17	Total deposits for quarter, including overpayment applied from a prior quarter, from your records ►	**17**	10,376 65
18	Balance due (subtract line 17 from line 16). This should be less than $500. Pay to IRS . . .	**18**	
19	If line 17 is more than line 16, enter overpayment here ► $ _____ and check if to be:		

Applied to next return   **OR**   Refunded.

Record of Federal Tax Liability (Complete if line 16 is $500 or more.) See the instructions under rule 4 for details before checking these boxes.
Check only if you made eighth-monthly deposits using the 95% rule ►   Check only if you are a first time 3-banking-day depositor ►

Show tax liability here, **not deposits.** IRS gets deposit data from FTD coupons.

Date wages paid		First month of quarter		Second month of quarter		Third month of quarter
1st through 3rd	A		I		Q	
4th through 7th	B		J		R	
8th through 11th	C		K		S	
12th through 15th	D		L		T	
16th through 19th	E		M		U	
20th through 22nd	F		N		V	
23rd through 25th	G		O		W	
26th through the last	H		P		X	
Total liability for month	I	3,694.88	II	3,301.77	III	3,380.00

IV Total for quarter (add lines **I, II,** and **III**). **This must equal line 16 above** . . . . ►   10,376.65

Do NOT Show Federal Tax Deposits Here

Sign Here

Under penalties of perjury, I declare that I have examined this return, including accompanying schedules and statements, and to the best of my knowledge and belief, it is true, correct, and complete.

Signature ► *William P. Jonas*   Title ► Treasurer   Date ► 4/30/--

Employer's Quarterly Federal Tax Return (Form 941)

In addition to these quarterly reports and deposits, employers are required to submit an annual report of federal unemployment tax on Form 940. This form must be sent to the District IRS Center by the end of the month following the close of the calendar year. Form 940 is not illustrated here. Any federal unemployment tax due for the last quarter or for other periods during the year would be submitted with Form 940.

The accounting procedure for payment of federal unemployment tax is illustrated below. Assume that a check for $87.20 was issued on January 30 in payment of federal unemployment tax on wages paid during the preceding three quarters ended December 26. This transaction would be entered in a two-column journal as follows:

Jan. 30 FUTA Tax Payable	87.20
Cash	87.20
Paid federal unemployment tax.	

Building Your Accounting Knowledge

1. Why do employer payroll taxes represent an additional expense to the employer, whereas the various employee payroll taxes do not?
2. What is the purpose of the FUTA tax and who must pay it?
3. Why is most of the total amount of the tax levied under the FUTA program typically paid to the state governments?
4. Describe how a state merit-rating system works to reduce an employer's unemployment tax rate.
5. Identify all items that are debited or credited to the FICA Tax Payable account.
6. What accounts are affected when employer payroll tax expenses are properly recorded?
7. Explain why an employee whose gross salary is $20,000 costs an employer more than $20,000 to employ.
8. What is the purpose of the Employer's Quarterly Federal Tax Return Form 941?

Assignment Box

To reinforce your understanding of the preceding text materials, you may complete the following:

  Study Guide: Part B
  Textbook: Exercises 8A3 through 8A7 or 8B3 through 8B7
       Problems 8A3 through 8A4 or 8B3 through 8B4

Expanding Your Business Vocabulary

What is the meaning of each of the following terms?

additional withholding allowances (p. 300)
automated systems (p. 308)
direct deposit (p. 304)
electronic system (p. 308)
employee (p. 297)
employee's earnings record (p. 304)
employer's identification number (p. 307)
fee (p. 297)
FICA taxes (p. 299)
FUTA tax (p. 313)
gross pay (p. 299)
independent contractor (p. 297)
manual system (p. 308)

mechanical system (p. 308)
merit-rating system (p. 314)
net pay (p. 299)
payroll register (p. 303)
salary (p. 297)
self-employment income (p. 313)
self-employment tax (p. 313)
service bureaus (p. 309)
special withholding allowance (p. 300)
State Unemployment Taxes (p. 314)
time sharing (p. 309)
wage-bracket method (p. 300)
wages (p. 297)
withholding allowance (p. 299)
write-it-once principle (p. 308)

Demonstration Problem

Carole Vohsen operates a beauty salon known as Carole's Coiffures, and has five employees. All are paid on a weekly basis. Carole's Coiffures uses a payroll register, individual employee's earnings records, a two-column journal, and standard general ledger accounts.

Carole's Coiffures uses a weekly federal income tax withholding table. The payroll data for each employee for the week ended January 21, 19-- are given below. Employees are paid time and a half for work over 40 hours a week, and double time for work on Sunday.

Name	Employee No.	No. of Allowances	Marital Status	Total Hours Worked Jan. 15-21	Rate	Total Earnings Jan. 1-14
DeNourie, Katie	1	2	M	44	$11.50	$1,058.00
Garriott, Pete	2	1	M	40	12.00	1,032.00
Martinez, Sheila	3	3	M	39	12.50	987.50
Parker, Nancy	4	4	M	42	11.00	957.00
Shapiro, John	5	2	M	40	11.50	931.50

Sheila Martinez is the assistant manager of Carole's Coiffures. Her social security number is 500-88-4189, and she was born April 12, 1959. Sheila was employed September 1 of last year.

FICA Tax is withheld at the rate of 7.5%, and city earnings tax at the rate of 1%, both applied to gross pay. Garriott and Parker each have $10 withheld this payday for group life insurance. All employees, except Shapiro, have $4.00 withheld this payday for health insurance. DeNourie, Martinez and Shapiro each have $15 withheld this payday to be invested in the beautician's credit union. Garriott and Shapiro each have $18.75 withheld this payday under a savings bond purchase plan.

Carole's Coiffures' payroll is met by drawing checks on its regular bank account. This week, the checks were issued in sequence, beginning with No. 811.

Payroll raxes are imposed on the employer as follows:
FICA tax, 7.5%
FUTA tax, 0.8%
State unemployment tax, 2.5%.

Required:

1. Prepare a payroll register for Carole's Coiffures for the week ended January 21, 19--. Foot the amount columns, prove the footings, enter the totals, and rule with single and double lines.
2. Prepare an employee's earnings record for Sheila Martinez for the week ended January 21, 19--.
3. Assuming that the wages for the week ended January 21 were paid on January 23, prepare a two-column journal entry for the payment of this payroll.
4. Prepare a two-column journal entry for the employer's payroll taxes for the week ended January 21, as of January 23.
5. Post the entries in (3.) and (4.) to the affected T accounts in the ledger of Carole's Coiffures.

Solution

1.

Name	Employee No.	No. of Allow	Marital Status	Earnings				Taxable Earnings	
				Regular	Overtime	Total	Cumula-tive Total	Unemploy Comp.	FICA
DeNourie, Katie	1	2	M	460.00	69.00	529.00	1,587.00	529.00	529.00
Garriott, Pete	2	1	M	480.00		480.00	1,512.00	480.00	480.00
Martinez, Sheila	3	3	M	487.50		487.50	1,475.00	487.50	487.50
Parker, Nancy	4	4	M	440.00	33.00	473.00	1,430.00	473.00	473.00
Shapiro, John	5	2	M	460.00		460.00	1,391.50	460.00	460.00
				2,327.50	102.00	2,429.50	7,395.50	2,429.50	2,429.50

FICA Tax	Fed. Inc. Tax	City Tax	Life Ins.	Deductions Health Ins.	Credit Union	Other		Total	Net Pay	Ck. No.
39.68	59.00	5.29		4.00	15.00			122.97	406.03	811
36.00	58.00	4.80	10.00	4.00		U.S. Savings Bond	18.75	131.55	348.45	812
36.56	47.00	4.88		4.00	15.00			107.44	380.06	813
35.48	40.00	4.73	10.00	4.00				94.21	378.79	814
34.50	50.00	4.60			15.00	U.S. Savings Bond	18.75	122.85	337.15	815
182.22	254.00	24.30	20.00	16.00	45.00		37.50	579.02	1,850.48	

2.

EMPLOYEE'S EARNINGS RECORD

19 - - Period Ending	Earnings				Taxable Earnings		Deductions	
	Regular	Over-Time	Total	Cumulative Total	Unemploy. Comp.	FICA	FICA Tax	Federal Inc. Tax
1/7								
1/14								
1/21	487 50		487 50	1,475 00	487 50	487 50	36 56	47 00
1/28								

	Sex		Department	Occupation	Social Security No.	Marital Status	Exemp-tions
	M	F ✔	Beauty Salon	Asst. Manager	500-88-4189	M	3

FOR PERIOD ENDED   January 21, 19 - -

City Tax	Life Ins.	Deductions Health Ins.	Credit Union	Other		Total	Net Pay Ck. No.	Amount
4 88		4 00	15 00			107 44	813	380 06

Pay Rate	Date of Birth	Date Employed	Name- Last	First	Middle	Emp. No.
$12.50	4/12/59	9/1/- -	Martinez	Sheila		3

	Journal			Page 49
Date	*Description*	*Post Ref.*	*Debit*	*Credit*
3. 19--				
Jan 23	Payroll Expense	542	2,429.50	
	FICA Tax Payable	211		182.22
	Employees' Inc. Tax Payable	214		254.00
	City Earnings Tax Payable	225		24.30
	Life Insurance Premiums Payable	226		20.00
	Health Insurance Premiums Payable	227		16.00
	Credit Union Contributions Payable	228		45.00
	Savings Bond Deductions Payable	229		37.50
	Cash	111		1,850.48
	Payroll for week ended January 21.			
4.				
23	Payroll Taxes Expense	552	262.40	
	FICA Tax Payable	211		182.22
	FUTA Tax Payable	212		19.44
	State Unemployment Tax Payable	213		60.74
	Payroll taxes for week ended Jan. 21.			

5.

Cash—Acct. No. 111

19--		
Jan. 23	49	1,850.48

FICA Tax Payable—Acct. No. 211

19--		
Jan. 23	49	182.22
23	49	182.22

FUTA Tax Payable—Acct. No. 212

19--		
Jan. 23	49	19.44

State Unemployment Tax Payable—Acct. No. 213

19--		
Jan. 23	49	60.74

Employees' Income Tax Payable—Acct. No. 214

19--		
Jan. 23	49	254.00

Life Insurance Premiums Payable—Acct. No. 226

19--		
Jan. 23	49	20.00

Health Insurance Premiums Payable—Acct. No. 227

19--		
Jan. 23	49	16.00

Credit Union Contributions Payable—Acct. No. 228

19--		
Jan. 23	49	45.00

Savings Bond Deductions Payable—Acct. No. 229

19--		
Jan. 23	49	37.50

Payroll Expense—Acct. No. 542

19--		
Jan. 23	49	2,429.50

City Earnings Tax Payable—Acct. No. 225	Payroll Taxes Expense—Acct. No. 552
19-- Jan. 23 49 24.30	19-- Jan. 23 49 262.40

*Note: Now that you have reviewed the Demonstration Problem and Solution you may complete the **Mastery Problem** at the end of the chapter activities.

Applying Accounting Concepts

Series A

Exercise 8A1—Computation of Weekly Gross Pay. Elaine Mandel's regular hourly rate is $10.00. She receives time and a half for any time worked over 40 hours a week, and double time for work on Sunday. During the past week, Mandel worked 8 hours each day Monday through Thursday, 10 hours on Friday, and 6 hours on Sunday.

Compute Mandel's gross pay for the past week.

Exercise 8A2—Journal Entry for Payroll. The payroll register of ABF Company for the payroll period ended December 8 showed the following column totals:

Regular earnings	$7,960.00
Overtime earnings	412.00
Deductions:	
FICA tax	$ 628.08
Federal income tax	1,255.80
City earnings tax	250.22
Pension plan	106.90
Health insurance	115.00
Credit union	94.00
United Way	100.00

Based on these amounts, prepare the two-column journal entry for the payment of wages on December 8.

Exercise 8A3—Computation of State and Federal Unemployment Tax. Terry Duggan operates a business in a state with a maximum state unemployment tax rate of 5.4%, but he qualifies for a 1.2% rate because of his merit rating. The gross payroll for the period ending April 14 is $8,000, all of which is subject to state and federal unemployment taxes.

Compute (a) the state unemployment tax and (b) the federal unemployment tax for Duggan's payroll for the period ending April 14. (Assume a total FUTA tax rate of 6.2%.)

Exercise 8A4—Journal Entry for Employer Payroll Tax Expense. LC Company's gross payroll for the period ending May 12 is $9,000. All of the earnings are subject to FICA tax at a rate of 7.5%. Only $4,800 of the earnings are subject to state unemployment tax at a rate of 2.5% and FUTA tax at a rate of 0.8%.

Prepare the two-column journal entry for LC Company's employer payroll taxes expense for wages paid on May 12.

Exercise 8A5—Total Cost of Employee for Year. Helen Duncan employs John Ernest at a salary of $40,000 a year. Duncan is subject to employer FICA taxes at a rate of 7.5% on the salary. In addition, Duncan must pay state unemployment tax at a rate of 2.2% and federal unemployment tax at a rate of 0.8% on the first $7,000 of Ernest's salary.

Compute the total cost to Duncan of employing Ernest for the year.

Exercise 8A6—Journal Entry for Payment of Withheld and Imposed Taxes. On June 15, Taussig Company paid the following taxes imposed on the wages paid in the four preceding weekly payrolls:

Employees' income tax withheld from wages		$2,434.80
FICA tax:		
Withheld from employees' wages	$1,402.60	
Imposed on employer	1,402.60	2,805.20
Amount of check		$5,240.00

Prepare the two-column journal entry for the payment of these taxes.

Exercise 8A7—Journal Entry for Payment of Unemployment Taxes. On January 30, Taussig Company paid the following state unemployment taxes for the previous quarter and federal unemployment tax for the previous three quarters:

State unemployment taxes	$1,123.20
Federal unemployment taxes	89.40

Prepare two two-column journal entries for the payment of these taxes. The tax expense was recognized when the wages were earned.

Series B

Exercise 8B1—Computation of Weekly Gross Pay. Dave Abernathy's regular hourly rate is $12.00. He receives time and a half for any time worked over 40 hours a week, and double time for work on Sunday. During the past week Abernathy worked 8 hours each day Monday through Thursday, 10 hours on Friday, and 6 hours on Sunday.

Compute Abernathy's gross pay for the past week.

Exercise 8B2—Journal Entry for Payroll. The payroll register of PDT Company for the payroll period ended November 3 showed the following column totals:

Regular earnings	$5,970.00
Overtime earnings	309.00
Deductions:	
FICA tax	$ 471.06
Federal income tax	857.88
City earnings tax	187.63
Pension plan	80.18
Health insurance	86.25
Credit union	70.50
United Way	75.00

Based on the foregoing payroll register amounts, prepare the two-column journal entry for the payment of wages on November 3.

Exercise 8B3—Computation of State and Federal Unemployment Tax. Kim Greenwood operates a business in a state with a state unemployment tax rate of 5.4%, but she qualifies for a 1.5% rate because of her merit rating. The gross payroll for the period ending March 17 is $6,000, all of which is subject to state and federal unemployment taxes.

Compute (a) the state unemployment tax and (b) the federal unemployment tax for Greenwood's payroll for the period ending March 17. (Assume a total FUTA tax rate of 6.2%.)

Exercise 8B4—Journal Entry for Employer Payroll Tax Expense. JS Company's gross payroll for the period ending April 14 is $6,800. All of the earnings are subject to FICA tax at a rate of 7.5%. Only $3,600 of the earnings are subject to state unemployment tax at a rate of 2.2%, and FUTA tax at a rate of 0.8%.

Prepare the two-column journal entry for JS Company's employer payroll taxes expense for wages paid on April 14.

Exercise 8B5—Total Cost of Employee for Year. C. Limmer employs Barry Dix at a salary of $30,000 a year. Limmer is subject to employer FICA taxes at a rate of 7.5% on the salary. In addition, Limmer must pay state unemployment tax at a rate of 2.5% and federal unemployment tax at a rate of 0.8% on the first $7,000 of Dix's salary.

Compute the total cost to Limmer of employing Dix for the year.

Exercise 8B6—Journal Entry for Payment of Withheld and Imposed Taxes. On September 15, Manley Company paid the following taxes imposed on the wages paid in the four preceding weekly payrolls:

Employees' income tax withheld from wages		$1,826.10
FICA tax:		
Withheld from employees' wages	$1,051.95	
Imposed on employer	1,051.95	2,103.90
Amount of check		$3,930.00

Prepare the two-column journal entry for the payment of these taxes.

Exercise 8B7—Journal Entry for Payment of Unemployment Taxes. On January 27, Manley Company paid the following state unemployment taxes for the previous quarter and federal unemployment taxes for the previous three quarters:

State unemployment taxes.. $842.40
Federal unemployment taxes .... $ 67.05

Prepare two two-column journal entries for the payment of these taxes. The tax expense was recognized when the wages were earned.

Series A

Problem 8A1   Payroll Register and Entry for Payment of Payroll

Craig Kuhl operates a business known as C.K. Enterprises. Kuhl's business uses a payroll register. All hours worked in excess of 40 a week are paid for at the rate of time and a half.

The employer uses a weekly federal income tax withholding table. A portion of this weekly table is reproduced in the chapter. FICA tax at the rate of 7.5% is also withheld. City earnings tax is withheld at the rate of 1% of gross pay. DeFrancesco, Gilbert, Levy, and Parker each have $14.00 withheld this payday for group life insurance. Each employee, except Greene, has $5.50 withheld this payday for health insurance. Gilbert, Levy, and Wolff each have $10.00 withheld this payday to be invested in the company credit union. Blasberg and Turner each have $18.75 withheld this payday under a savings bond purchase plan. The payroll data for each employee for the week ended January 14 are given below.

Name	Employee No.	No. of Allowances	Marital Status	Total Hours Worked Jan. 8-14	Rate	Cumulative Total Earnings Jan. 1-7
Blasberg, Will	1	1	M	42	12.50	550.00
Davis, Michael	2	3	M	40	11.00	440.00
DeFrancesco, Joan	3	2	M	40	13.00	520.00
Gilbert, Jeff	4	4	M	39	14.00	532.00
Greene, Carolyn	5	2	M	42	11.00	473.00
Levy, Ira	6	1	M	45	14.00	665.00
Parker, George	7	2	M	32	13.00	416.00
Steber, Barbara	8	1	M	40	12.50	500.00
Turner, Amelia	9	3	M	45	12.50	575.00
Wolff, Sanford	10	2	M	36	11.00	396.00

C.K. Enterprises follows the practice of drawing a single check for the net amount of the payroll and depositing the check in a special payroll account at the bank. Individual paychecks are then drawn for the amount due each employee. The checks issued this payday were numbered consecutively beginning with No. 721.

Required:

1. Using the form illustrated in the chapter, prepare a payroll register, foot the amount columns, prove the footings, enter the totals, and rule with single and double lines.
2. Assuming that the wages for the week ended January 14 were paid on January 16, prepare a two-column journal entry for the payment of this payroll.

Problem 8A2   Earnings Record Preparation

Refer to Problem 8A1. C.K. Enterprises keeps employee earnings records.

Required:

For the week ended January 14, complete such a record for Joan DeFrancesco whose social security number is 392-16-4651. DeFrancesco is employed as manager in the order department. She was born August 14, 1958 and employed November 1 of last year.

Problem 8A3   Journal Entries for Payroll Transactions;
Post to General Ledger

Kelly Richeson, proprietor of the Richeson Agency, has five employees. All are paid on a monthly basis. The fiscal year of the business is October 1 to September 30. Payroll taxes are imposed as follows:

FICA tax to be withheld from employees' wages, 7.5%.
FICA tax imposed on the employer, 7.5%.
State unemployment contributions, 2.7%.
FUTA tax imposed on the employer, 0.8%.

The accounts kept by the Richeson Agency include the following:

Cash, Acct. No. 111, Oct. 1 balance, $86,700.00.
FICA Tax Payable, Acct. No. 211, Oct. 1 balance, $2,340.00.
FUTA Tax Payable, Acct. No. 212, Oct. 1 balance, $298.40.
State Unemployment Tax Payable, Acct. No. 213, Oct. 1 balance, $370.00.
Employees' Income Tax Payable, Acct. No. 214, Oct. 1 balance, $2,155.20.
Savings Bond Deductions Payable, Acct. No. 261, Oct. 1 balance, $700.00.

Payroll Expense, Acct. No. 542, Oct. 1 balance, $-0-.
Payroll Taxes Expense, Acct. No. 552, Oct. 1 balance, $-0-.

Following is a narrative of certain selected transactions relating to payrolls and payroll taxes that occurred during the months of October, November, December, and January.

Oct. 27 Paid $4,495.20 covering the following September taxes:

FICA tax *payable*	$ 2,340.00
Employees' income tax withheld *payable*	2,155.20
Total	$ 4,495.20

27 Paid state unemployment tax for the third quarter, $370.00.

31 October payroll: *EXPENSE*

Total payroll expense		$16,000.00
Less amounts withheld:		
FICA tax	$1,200.00	
Employees' income tax	$2,196.80	
Savings bond deductions	800.00	4,196.80
Net amount paid		$11,803.20

31 Purchased savings bonds for employees, $900.00.

31 Data for computing employer's social security taxes for October: *2.7%*
   FICA taxable wages, $16,000.00.
   FUTA and state unemployment taxable wages, $3,600.00.

Nov. 15 Paid $4,596.80 covering the following October taxes:

FICA tax	$ 2,400.00
Employees' income tax withheld	2,196.80
Total	$ 4,596.80

30 November payroll:

Total payroll expense		$17,200.00
Less amounts withheld:		
FICA tax	$1,290.00	
Employees' income tax	2,275.00	
Savings bond deductions	800.00	4,365.00
Net amount paid		$12,835.00

30 Purchased savings bonds for employees, $850.00.

30 Data for computing employer's social security taxes for November:
   FICA taxable wages, $17,200.00.
   FUTA and state unemployment taxable wages, $1,600.00.

Dec. 15 Paid $4,855.00 covering the following November taxes:

FICA tax	$ 2,580.00
Employees' income tax withheld	2,275.00
Total	$ 4,855.00

29 December payroll:

Total payroll expense		$18,000.00
Less amounts withheld:		
FICA tax	$1,350.00	
Employees' income tax	2,390.60	
Savings bond deductions	800.00	4,540.60
Net amount paid		$13,459.40

Dec. 29 Purchased savings bonds for employees, $800.00.

Data for computing employer's social security taxes for December:
FICA taxable wages, $18,000.00.
FUTA and state unemployment taxable wages, -0-.

Jan. 26 Paid $5,090.60 covering the following December taxes:

FICA tax	$ 2,700.00
Employees' income tax withheld	2,390.60
Total	$ 5,090.60

26 Paid state unemployment tax for quarter ended December 31, $140.40.

26 Paid FUTA tax for year ended December 31, $340.00.

Required:

1. Journalize the preceding transactions, using two-column journal paper.
2. From the list of accounts given above, open the necessary general ledger accounts and post the journal entries to them.

Problem 8A4   Computation and Journal Entry for Employer's Payroll Taxes

V.A. Paladin, proprietor of Paladin Interiors, has three employees. Headings and summary totals from Paladin's payroll register for the month of April are reproduced below. Employer payroll taxes are imposed on Paladin as follows:

FICA Tax...	7.5%
State unemployment contributions...................................	2.7%

(The maximum rate in Paladin's state is 5.4%, but Paladin qualifies for a 2.7% rate because of its special merit rating.)

FUTA tax (Supply proper rate) .... _____

Payroll Register

				Earnings				Taxable Earnings	
Name	Em. No.	No. of All.	Ma. St.	Regular	Over-Time	Total	Cumulative Total	Unemploy Comp.	FICA
Total				5,900.00	387.00	6,287.00	30,881.20	5,580.00	5,900.00

For Period Ended April 30 19--

Deductions									
FICA Tax	Federal Inc. Tax	City Tax	Life Ins.	Health Ins.	Credit Union	Other	Total	Net Pay	Ck. No.
442.50	680.00	122.10	96.00		60.00		1,400.60	4,886.40	

Required:

1. Compute Paladin's employer payroll taxes for FICA, state unemployment contributions, and FUTA for the month of April on a separate sheet of paper and record the results.
2. Prepare the two-column journal entry to record Paladin's employer payroll taxes.

Series B

Problem 8B1   Payroll Register and Entry for Payment of Payroll

Carol Kring operates a business known as K.R. Enterprises. Kring's business uses a payroll register. All hours worked in excess of 40 a week are paid for at the rate of time and a half.

The employer uses a weekly federal income tax withholding table. A portion of this weekly table is reproduced in the chapter. FICA tax at the rate of 7.5% is also withheld. City earnings tax is withheld at the rate of 1% of gross pay. Ligon, Linhardt, Miller and Price each have $11.00 withheld this payday for group life insurance. Each employee, except Lodato, has $3.75 withheld this payday for health insurance. Linhardt, Miller, and Werling each have $15.00 withheld this payday to be invested in the company credit union. Boettcher and Tucker each have $18.25 withheld this payday under a savings bond purchase plan. The payroll data for each employee for the week ended January 14 are given below.

Name	Employee No.	No. of Allowances	Marital Status	Total Hours Worked Jan. 8-14	Rate	Total Earnings Jan. 1-7
Boettcher, Lee	1	2	M	45	13.00	598.00
Gregorich, Ken	2	3	M	40	12.50	500.00
Ligon, Mary	3	1	M	38	11.00	418.00
Linhardt, Hanford	4	4	M	42	13.00	598.00
Lodato, Sally	5	2	M	40	14.00	560.00
Miller, Guy	6	1	M	45	11.00	473.00
Price, Edward	7	2	M	40	14.00	560.00
Robinson, Martha	8	1	M	36	11.00	396.00
Tucker, Alex	9	3	M	42	12.50	550.00
Werling, Lynda	10	2	M	39	12.50	475.00

K.R. Enterprises follows the practice of drawing a single check for the net amount of the payroll and depositing the check in a special payroll account at the bank. Individual paychecks are then drawn for the amount due each employee. The checks issued this payday were numbered consecutively beginning with No. 541.

Required:

1. Using the form illustrated in the chapter, prepare a payroll register, foot the amount columns, prove the footings, enter the totals, and rule with single and double lines.
2. Assuming that the wages for the week ended January 14 were paid on January 16, prepare a two-column journal entry for the payment of this payroll.

Problem 8B2   Earnings Record Preparation

Refer to Problem 8B1. K.R. Enterprises keeps employee earnings records.

Required:

For the week ended January 14, complete such a record for Mary Ligon whose social security number is 395-16-8795. She is employed as manager in the billing department. Ligon was born September 9, 1967 and employed September 1 of last year.

Problem 8B3   Journal Entries for Payroll Transactions;
Post to General Ledger

Eric Lindhorst, proprietor of the Lindhorst Construction Co., has five employees. All are paid on a monthly basis. The fiscal year of the business is October 1 to September 30. Payroll taxes are imposed as follows:

FICA tax to be withheld from employees' wages, 7.5%.
FICA tax imposed on the employer, 7.5%.
State unemployment contributions, 2.7%.
FUTA tax imposed on the employer, 0.8%.

The accounts kept by the Lindhorst Construction Co. include the following:

Cash, Acct. No. 111, Oct. 1 balance, $65,025.00.
FICA Tax Payable, Acct. No. 211, Oct. 1 balance, $1,755.00.
FUTA Tax Payable, Acct. No. 212, Oct. 1 balance, $223.80.
State Unemployment Tax Payable, Acct. No. 213, Oct. 1 balance, $277.50.
Employees' Income Tax Payable, Acct. No. 214, Oct. 1 balance, $1,616.40.
Savings Bond Deductions Payable, Acct. No. 261, Oct. 1 balance, $525.00.
Payroll Expense, Acct. No. 542, Oct. 1 balance, -0-.
Payroll Taxes Expense, Acct. No. 552, Oct. 1 balance, -0-.

Following is a narrative of selected transactions relating to payrolls and payroll taxes that occurred during the months of October, November, December, and January.

Oct. 27 Paid $3,371.40 covering the following September taxes:

FICA tax	$ 1,755.00
Employees' income tax withheld	1,616.40
Total	$ 3,371.40

    27 Paid state unemployment tax for the third quarter, $277.50

    31 October payroll:

Total payroll expense		$12,000.00
Less amounts withheld:		
FICA tax	$ 900.00	
Employees' income tax..................	1,647.60	
Savings bond deductions	600.00	3,147.60
Net amount paid		$ 8,852.40

Oct. 31 Purchased savings bonds for employees, $675.00.

    31 Data for computing employer's social security taxes for October:
FICA taxable wages, $12,000.00.
FUTA and state unemployment taxable wages, $2,700.00.

Nov. 15 Paid $3,447.60 covering the following October taxes:

FICA tax	$ 1,800.00
Employees' income tax withheld	1,647.60
Total	$ 3,447.60

    30 November payroll:

Total payroll expense		$12,900.00
Less amounts withheld:		
FICA tax	$ 967.50	
Employees' income tax..................	1,706.25	
Savings bond deductions	600.00	3,273.75
Net amount paid		$ 9,626.25

    30 Purchased savings bonds for employees, $637.50.

    30 Data for computing employer's social security taxes for November:
FICA taxable wages, $12,900.00.
FUTA and state unemployment taxable wages, $1,200.00.

Dec. 15 Paid $3,641.25 covering the following November taxes:

FICA tax	$ 1,935.00
Employees' income tax withheld	1,706.25
Total	$ 3,641.25

    29 December payroll:

Total payroll expense		$13,500.00
Less amounts withheld:		
FICA tax	$1,012.50	
Employees' income tax..................	1,792.95	
Savings bond deductions	600.00	3,405.45
Net amount paid		$10,094.55

    29 Purchased savings bonds for employees, $600.00.

    29 Data for computing employer's social security taxes for December:
FICA taxable wages, $13,500.00.
FUTA and state unemployment taxable wages, -0-.

Jan. 26 Paid $3,817.95 covering the following December taxes:

FICA tax .... $ 2,025.00
Employees' income tax withheld 1,792.95
Total .... $ 3,817.95

26 Paid state unemployment tax for quarter ended December 31, $105.30.

26 Paid FUTA tax for year ended December 31, $255.00.

Required:

1. Journalize the preceding transactions, using two-column journal paper.
2. From the list of accounts given above, open the necessary general ledger accounts and post the journal entries to them.

Problem 8B4 — Computation and Journal Entry for Employer's Payroll Taxes

Karen Cade, proprietor of Cade Catering, has three employees. Headings and summary totals from Cade's payroll register for the month of May are reproduced below. Employer payroll taxes are imposed on Cade as follows:

FICA Tax 7.5%
State unemployment contributions 3.0%
(The maximum rate in Cade's state is 5.4%, but Cade qualifies for a 3.0% rate because of its special merit rating.)
FUTA tax (Supply proper rate) .... ____

Payroll Register

Name	Em. No.	No. of All.	Ma. St.	Regular	Over-Time	Total	Cumulative Total	Unemploy Comp.	FICA
						Earnings		Taxable Earnings	
Total				4,425.00	290.25	4,715.25	23,160.90	4,185.00	4,425.00

For Period Ended 19--

FICA Tax	Federal Inc. Tax	City Tax	Life Ins.	Health Ins.	Credit Union	Other	Total	Net Pay	Ck. No.
				Deductions					
331.88	510.00	91.57	72.00		45.00		1,050.45	3,664.80	

Required:

1. Compute Cade's employer payroll taxes for FICA, state unemployment contributions, and FUTA for the month of May on a separate sheet of paper and record the results.
2. Prepare the two-column journal entry to record Cade's employer payroll taxes.

Mastery Problem

Abigail Trenkamp owns and operates a collection agency. Listed below are the name, number of allowances claimed, information from time cards on hours worked each day, and the hourly rate of each employee. All employees are married. All hours worked in excess of 8 hours on week days are paid at the rate of time and a half. All weekend hours are paid at double time.

The employer uses a weekly federal income tax withholding table. A portion of this weekly table is provided in the chapter. Earnings are subject to tax for unemployment compensation insurance on the first $7,000 earned. FICA tax at the rate of 7.5% is also withheld from the first $50,000 earned. State income tax is withheld at the rate of 2.5% of gross earnings and a city earnings tax is withheld at the rate of 1% of gross pay. Berling, Salzman, and Thompson each have $20.00 withheld this payday for group life insurance. Each employee, except Merz and Menick, has $5.00 withheld this payday for health insurance. All of the employees use direct deposit to the Credit Union for varying amounts as listed below. Heimbrock, Townsley, and Morris each have $18.25 withheld this payday under a savings bond purchase plan.

Trenkamp Collection Agency
Payroll Information for the Week Ended November 18, 19--

Name	Empl. No.	Allow.	Marital Status	S	S	M	T	W	T	F	Regular Hourly Rate	Deposit Credit Union	Toal Earnings 1/1-11/11
Berling, James	1	3	M	2	2	9	8	8	9	10	12.00	129.60	30,525.00
Merz, Linda	2	4	M	4	3	8	8	8	8	11	10.00	117.00	28,480.00
Goetz, Ken	3	5	M	0	0	6	7	8	9	10	11.00	91.30	25,500.00
Menick, Judd	4	2	M	8	8	0	0	8	8	9	11.00	126.50	22,625.00
Morris, Ruth	5	3	M	0	0	8	8	8	6	8	13.00	98.80	28,730.00
Heimbrock, Jacob	6	2	M	0	0	8	8	8	8	8	17.00	136.00	49,800.00
Townsley, Sarah	7	2	M	4	0	6	6	6	6	4	9.00	64.80	21,425.00
Salzman, Ben	8	4	M	6	2	8	8	6	6	6	11.00	110.00	6,635.00
Layton, Esther	9	4	M	0	0	8	8	8	8	8	11.00	88.00	5,635.00
Thompson, David	10	5	M	0	2	10	9	7	7	10	11.00	108.90	29,635.00
Wissman, Celia	11	2	M	8	0	4	8	8	8	9	13.00	139.10	24,115.00

The Trenkamp Collection Agency follows the practice of drawing a single check for the net amount of the payroll and depositing the check in a special payroll account at the bank. Individual paychecks are then drawn for the amount due each employee. The checks issued this payday were numbered consecutively beginning with No. 331.

Required:

1. Complete the payroll register, foot the amount columns, prove the footings, enter the totals, and rule with single and double lines.
2. Assuming that the wages for the week ended November 18 were paid on November 21, enter the payment in the two-column journal using ruled paper.
3. The company operates in a state with a state unemployment tax rate of 5.4%, but Trenkamp qualifies for a 2.2% rate because of the company's merit rating. Compute the employer's payroll taxes that must be paid for state and federal unemployment taxes and FICA tax.
4. Prepare the entry for payroll taxes in a general journal.

5. The current employee's earnings record for Ben Salzman is provided in the working papers. Update Salzman's earnings record to reflect the November 18 payroll. Although this information should have been entered earlier, complete the required information at the bottom of the earnings record. The necessary information is provided below.

Name	Ben F. Salzman
Sex	Male
Department	Administration
Occupation	Office Manager
S.S. No.	446-46-6321
Marital Status	Married
Exemptions	4
Pay Rate	$11.00 per hour
Birth Date	3/4/59
Date Employed	7/22/--

CHAPTER 9

Accounting for a Small Retail Business

Chapter Objectives

Careful study of this chapter should enable you to:

- Describe accrual accounting.
- Explain the application of accrual accounting principles in accounting for:
  1. Uncollectible accounts
  2. Prepaid expenses
  3. Accrued expenses
  4. Depreciation
- Apply accrual accounting and the data processing phases of the accounting cycle to a small retail business.
- Prepare a ten-column end-of-year work sheet for a retail business, including the following adjustments:
  1. The two adjustments needed for the beginning and ending merchandise inventory components of cost of goods sold.

2. The adjustment needed for accrued interest expense.
3. The adjustment needed for accrued bank credit card expense.
4. The adjustments needed for supplies expense and insurance expense applicable to the year just ended.
5. The adjustment needed for uncollectible accounts expense expected to result from the past year's charge sales.
6. The adjustment needed for depreciation of property, plant, and equipment during the past year.

A business enterprise that purchases and sells goods on account, maintains a stock of merchandise, and has property, plant or equipment must account for periodic income or loss on the accrual basis. This is necessary to measure the success of the business and to comply with federal and state income tax laws. Several features of accrual accounting were introduced in the preceding chapters. A more detailed consideration

339

of these procedures and an introduction of other major practices that constitute accrual accounting will be presented here and in Chapter 10.

As an aid in applying the principles and procedures involved in keeping the accounts of a merchandising business on the accrual basis, a system of accounts for the retail computer business called Northern Micro, owned and operated by Gary L. Fishel, will be described. In addition, the use of a ten-column work sheet at the end of an accounting period will be explained and illustrated. Most of the principles and procedures discussed and illustrated for Northern Micro are equally applicable to many other types of business.

Accrual Accounting Principles and Procedures

A blend of accounting principles and practices will be discussed in this chapter. It is important to keep in mind that principles relate to goals and objectives, while practices are designed to attain these goals and objectives. Double-entry accounting procedures with the use of source documents, journals, and ledger accounts help make the processing of accounting data complete, orderly, and as error-free as possible. While most accounting principles are broad enough to allow flexibility, it is in the area of practices that wide latitude is found. Within limits, the records for each business can be styled to meet the particular requirements and practices of the management.

Accrual Accounting

Describe accrual accounting.

As explained in Chapters 6 and 7, under the accrual basis of accounting, revenue is recognized in the accounting period in which it is earned whether or not cash has been received. Likewise expense is recognized in the accounting period in which it is incurred as a result of efforts to produce revenue whether or not cash has been paid. The cash basis of accounting, on the other hand, recognizes revenue only when cash is received and recognizes expense only when cash is paid.

Under accrual accounting, revenues are recognized when services have been performed or goods provided in exchange for something of value. Generally, services or goods are exchanged for money or the legal claim to money in the future, but they might also be exchanged for other assets. A merchant normally recognizes revenue when the customer buys goods and either pays or agrees to pay for them.

Under accrual accounting, expenses are recognized when incurred as the result of efforts made to produce revenues. Expenses generally cause a reduction or outflow of assets, or an increase in liabilities. For example, expenses are incurred as the useful lives of long-term assets are consumed, merchandise is sold, and wages and salaries are earned by employees.

The accrual basis of accounting is widely used by enterprises because it involves the period-by-period matching of revenue with the expenses that helped to produce that revenue. For example, the revenue from sales must be matched against the cost of the goods sold and the various other expenses that were incurred in earning the revenue. A simple matching of cash received from customers during a period with the cash paid for goods purchased in that period would be almost meaningless in most cases. The collections might relate to sales of a prior period and the payments to purchases of the current period, or vice versa. The expense related to plant and equipment does not occur immediately when such assets are acquired. Rather, the expense is spread over the time the assets are used. In computing net income for a specified period, the accrual basis recognizes changes in many types of assets and liabilities—not just changes in the cash account.

In processing business data, accountants must think in terms of time intervals so that revenue and expense are accounted for in the proper accounting period. This can be difficult with certain types of revenue and expense. For example, the wages of an employee accrue minute by minute during each working day, but no entry is made of the expense until the employee is paid. If the end of the period occurs before the employee is paid, the accountant should enter the payroll expense and the liability that has accrued up to that time. If delays occur in entering revenue and expense within the accounting period, steps must be taken at the end of the period to enter all revenue earned and expenses incurred. These steps consist of making **end-of-period adjustments** in the accounts. Three types of expenses that require such adjustments are described in the following sections.

Accounting for Uncollectible Accounts Receivable

Explain the application of accrual accounting principles in accounting for uncollectible accounts.

Businesses that sell goods or services on account often cannot collect all that a customer may owe. The amounts that cannot be collected from charge customers are called uncollectible accounts expense or bad debts expense. The amount of such expense often depends upon the credit policy of the business. If a seller has a credit policy that is too liberal, uncollectible accounts may become excessive. Also, if a seller has a credit policy that is too tight, uncollectible accounts may be minimized at the sacrifice of a larger volume of sales and greater net income. These extremes should be avoided in defining a credit policy.

A common method of accounting for uncollectible accounts receivable is to estimate the amount of uncollectible accounts that will eventually result from the sales of a period and to treat that amount as an expense of that same period. This treatment, known as the allowance method, provides a proper periodic matching of revenue and expense. Under this method, the estimated expense is debited in the current period and a credit is made to a contra account entitled Allowance for Doubtful Accounts or Allowance for Bad Debts. The allowance for doubtful accounts is contra to the accounts receivable account, which means its balance is deducted from the total of the accounts receivable on the balance sheet.

A simple approach to estimating the allowance for doubtful accounts is to base the estimate on a percentage of the sales on account for the period. The adjusting entry is made by debiting Uncollectible Accounts Expense and crediting Allowance for Doubtful Accounts. Any balance already existing in the allowance account is ignored in determining the amount of this entry. To illustrate, assume that in view of past experience it is expected that one half of one percent of the sales on account during the year 19-A will be uncollectible. If the sales on account amounted to $200,000, the estimated uncollectible accounts expense would be $1,000 ($200,000 x .005). This amount should be entered at the end of 19-A as follows:

Dec. 31 Uncollectible Accounts Expense   1,000
       Allowance for Doubtful Accounts   1,000
        Uncollectible accounts expense provision for
        the year.

The credit part of the adjusting entry cannot be made directly to a specific receivable account because, at the time the entry is made, there is no way of knowing exactly which debtors will not pay.

The amount of the debit balance in the uncollectible accounts expense account is reported in the income statement as an operating expense. The amount of the credit balance in the allowance for doubtful accounts is reported in the balance sheet as a deduction from the receivables, as follows:

Accounts receivable. $60,000
Less allowance for doubtful accounts. 1,000 $59,000

When it is determined that a certain account will not be collected, an entry should be made to write off the account and to charge the amount against the allowance. For example, assume that on June 24, 19-B, it is determined that $95 owed by J. C. Karlin cannot be collected. The following journal entry should be made:

June 24 Allowance for Doubtful Accounts   95
       Accounts Receivable.   95
        To write off account of J. C. Karlin found to
        be uncollectible.

Accounting for Prepaid Expenses

Explain the application of accrual accounting principles in accounting for prepaid expenses.

The term prepaid expense is used to describe an item that is considered to be an asset when acquired, and which will become an expense when it is consumed or used up in the near future. Supplies of various sorts and unexpired insurance are good examples. At the end of the period, the portions of such assets that have expired or have been consumed must be determined, and entries debiting the expense accounts and crediting the prepaid expense accounts must be made. For example, assume a company purchased office supplies for $850 and made the following entry:

Office Supplies	850	
Cash		850
To enter the purchase of office supplies.		

If at the end of the accounting period a physical count indicated that there were $150 of office supplies on hand, it can be determined that $700 ($850-$150) of supplies would have been used. The following adjusting entry should be made:

Office Supplies Expense	700	
Office Supplies		700
To enter office supplies used.		

Similarly, assume that a company purchased a three-year fire insurance policy for $390 and made the following entry:

Prepaid Insurance	390	
Cash		390
To enter the purchase of insurance.		

If the insurance policy had been in effect since the beginning of the fiscal year, $130 ($390/3 years) of the prepaid insurance would have been consumed during the year. The following adjusting journal entry should be made:

Insurance Expense	130	
Prepaid Insurance		130
To enter insurance expired for the year.		

Accounting for Accrued Expenses

Explain the application
of accrual accounting
principles in
accounting for accrued
expenses.

An accrued expense is an expense that has been incurred but not paid at the end of the accounting period. The related liability is commonly referred to as an accrued liability. To properly match expenses with the revenues they helped produce, accrued expenses must be recognized. Interest expense and wages expense are good examples. Assume a company borrowed $2,000 at the beginning of December, with the loan plus interest of $120 due the end of the following May. As of December 31, 19--, interest expense of $20 ($120/6) would have been incurred for the use of the $2,000 for one month. The following adjusting journal entry should be made to recognize the accrued interest expense:

Interest Expense	20	
Accrued Interest Payable		20

Accrued salary and wage expense is handled in a similar manner. Assume a company pays its hourly employees at the end of each week, and that the last pay period of the year ends Saturday, December 27. As of the end of the year, the company would have accrued wages expense for the work done by employees from December 29 through 31. If this amount is $360, the following adjusting journal entry should be made to recognize the accrued wages payable:

Wages Expense	360	
Accrued Wages Payable		360

Accounting for Depreciation

Explain the application
of accrual accounting
principles in
accounting for
depreciation.

Depreciation accounting is the process of allocating the cost of plant and equipment to the periods expected to benefit from the use of these assets. This is done by matching the expense associated with the expiration of the asset's useful life with the revenues the asset helps to produce each period. The expiration of the asset's useful life generally is the result of physical wear and tear, obsolescence, or becoming inadequate for the firm's needs. Once an asset is no longer capable of producing future benefits, it should be removed from the books.

In computing depreciation, no consideration is given to what the assets might bring if they were to be sold. Assets of this type are acquired to be used and not to be sold. During their useful lives any current resale value is of no consequence unless the business is about to end. For a continuing business, the idea is to allocate the depreciable cost of an asset over the years that it is expected to serve. Depreciable cost is the original cost less estimated scrap or salvage value. Since an asset's useful life and salvage value cannot be predicted exactly, depreciation expense is only an estimate. However, with past experience as a guide, the estimates can be reasonably reliable.

There are several ways of calculating the periodic depreciation writeoff. In the traditional **straight-line method**, the amount of depreciation expense for each year is found by dividing the depreciable cost of an asset by the number of years that the asset is expected to serve. It is common practice to express depreciation as a percentage of the depreciable cost of the asset. For example, in the case of an asset with a 10-year life, 10% of the depreciable cost should be written off each year.

$$100\% \ / \ 10 \ \text{years} \ = \ 10\% \ \text{per year.}$$

If it has a 20-year life, 5% should be written off.

$$100\% \ / \ 20 \ \text{years} \ = \ 5\% \ \text{per year.}$$

In part because of its simplicity, the straight-line method has been popular for many years.

As alternatives to the straight-line method, there are numerous depreciation methods that involve larger depreciation charges in the earlier years of an asset's life and smaller charges in succeeding years. These are known as **accelerated** or **reducing-charge methods**. Special types of accelerated methods called **Accelerated Cost Recovery System** (ACRS) and **Modified ACRS** are permitted by the Internal Revenue Code for federal income tax purposes. Many businesses use this method for tax purposes because it leads to lower calculated net income. However, the method is not allowed for financial reporting purposes.

Depreciation expense is handled by an end-of-period adjusting entry that involves debiting one or more depreciation expense accounts and crediting one or more accumulated depreciation accounts. For example, assume that a company purchased a lawn tractor for $3,500 at the beginning of the year, and estimates that it has a useful life of 5 years with no salvage value. The annual depreciation of the lawn tractor under the straight-line method of depreciation would be $700 ($3,500 / 5 years). The entry upon purchase of the equipment would be:

Equipment-Tractor	3,500	
Cash		3,500
To enter purchase of equipment.		

The adjusting entry for the depreciation at the end of the year would be:

Depreciation Expense..............................	700	
Accumulated Depreciation-Equipment		700
To enter annual depreciation of equipment.		

The accumulated depreciation account is a contra account; its balance is deducted from the related asset that is being depreciated. In theory, credits could be made directly to the asset accounts being depreciated in the same way that they are made to the asset accounts for prepaid expenses. However, the depreciation is credited to contra accounts so that both the original cost and the amount of depreciation recognized thus far in the assets' useful lives can be reported. By reporting both amounts, the reader is able to estimate the approximate ages of the assets. The amounts of the credit balances of the contra accounts are reported in the balance sheet as deductions from the costs of the assets to which they relate, as follows:

Equipment		$3,500
Less accumulated depreciation	700	$2,800

The credit balances in the accumulated depreciation accounts increase year by year. When these amounts are equal to the depreciable cost of the related assets, no more depreciation may be taken.

Illustration of Accounting Procedure

Apply accrual accounting and the data processing phases of the accounting cycle to a small retail business.

To apply accrual accounting and the data processing phases of the accounting cycle, the operations of Northern Micro, a small retail business, will be used in this and the following chapter. All of the journals and ledgers used by Northern Micro were described and illustrated in previous chapters, so the illustrations in this chapter will be in abbreviated form. The primary objective is to show how the journals, ledgers, and auxiliary records discussed in previous chapters can be brought together in a complete accounting system for a small retail business. The transactions and illustrations will be sufficient to achieve that objective, but neither the journals nor the ledgers will be illustrated completely.

The Chart of Accounts. The importance of classifying accounts was discussed in preceding chapters. A **chart of accounts** is an orderly and systematic list of accounts that identifies each account by means of an assigned number. The chart is used in locating the account in the ledger. The chart of accounts for Northern Micro is shown on page 347.

The chart of accounts usually is arranged in financial statement order—balance sheet accounts followed by income statement accounts. The bold-type headings in the chart of accounts represent major divisions of the financial statements. Interest Expense is classified as "Other Expense" instead of being listed under "Operating Expenses" because it represents the expense of obtaining money with which to do business, rather than an expense directly associated with operating the business.

The nature of many of the accounts included in the chart of accounts for Northern Micro should be apparent because they have been described and their use has been illustrated in preceding chapters. In addition, the chart includes certain accounts that are needed in entering several types of transactions and events that were described in the preceding sections of this chapter.

Northern Micro
Chart of Accounts

Assets*
Current Assets
111 Cash
112 Petty Cash Fund
131 Accounts Receivable
131.1 Allowance for Doubtful
      Accounts
141 Merchandise Inventory
151 Supplies
155 Prepaid Insurance
Property, Plant and Equipment
181 Store Equipment
181.1 Accumulated Depreciation-
      Store Equipment
Liabilities
211 FICA Tax Payable
213 State Unemployment Tax
    Payable
214 Employees Income Tax Payable
215 Accrued Bank Credit Card
    Payable
216 Notes Payable
217 Accrued Interest Payable
218 Accounts Payable
221 Sales Tax Payable
Owner's Equity
311 Gary L. Fishel, Capital
312 Gary L. Fishel, Drawing
331 Expense and Revenue
    Summary

Revenue
411 Sales
411.1 Sales Returns and
      Allowances
Cost of Goods Sold
511 Purchases
511.1 Purchases Returns and
      Allowances
Operating Expenses
541 Rent Expense
542 Salaries and Commissions
    Expense
543 Supplies Expense
545 Telephone Expense
547 Depreciation Expense
548 Insurance Expense
549 Heating and Lighting
    Expense
551 Advertising Expense
552 Payroll Taxes Expense
553 Bank Credit Card Expense
554 Uncollectible Accounts Expense
555 Purchases Discounts Lost
557 Charitable Contributions
    Expense
572 Miscellaneous Expense
Other Expenses
581 Interest Expense

*Words in bold type represent headings and not account titles.

Books of Account. The accounting system used by Northern Micro includes the following books of account:

Books of Original Entry	*Books of Final Entry*	*Auxiliary Records*
Purchases journal	General ledger	Petty cash payments record
Sales journal	Accounts receivable subsidiary ledger	Checkbook
Cash receipts journal	Accounts payable subsidiary ledger	Employees' earnings records
Cash payments journal		
General journal		

With the exception of the checkbook and the employees' earnings records, a portion of each of these books and records is illustrated on pages 354-359 of this chapter.

Purchases Journal. The purchases journal used by Northern Micro is the same as the one illustrated on page 221 and described in detail in Chapter 6. All transactions involving the purchase of merchandise on account are entered in this journal. The individual credits are posted daily to supplier accounts in the accounts payable ledger. The total purchases for each month are posted to the general ledger accounts at the end of each month. This involves a debit to Purchases, Account No. 511, and a credit to Accounts Payable, Account No. 218.

Sales Journal. The sales journal used by Northern Micro is the same as the one illustrated on page 270 and described in detail in Chapter 7. All transactions involving the sale of merchandise on account are entered in this journal. The individual charges are posted daily to customer accounts in the accounts receivable ledger. The total sales for each month are posted to the general ledger accounts at the end of each month. This involves a debit to Accounts Receivable, Account No. 131, and credits to Sales, Account No. 411, and to Sales Tax Payable, Account No. 221.

Cash Receipts Journal. The cash receipts journal used by Northern Micro is the same as the one illustrated on page 273 and described in detail in Chapter 7. Only transactions involving the receipt of cash are entered in this journal. The individual credits are posted daily to customer accounts in the accounts receivable ledger. All amounts entered in the General Cr. column are posted individually at the end of each week as credits to the accounts named in the Account Credited column; the total is not posted. The totals of the four right-hand amount columns are posted at the end of each month as credits to Accounts Receivable, Account No. 131, Sales, Account No. 411, and Sales Tax Payable, Account No. 221, and as a debit to Cash, Account No. 111.

Cash Payments Journal. The cash payments journal used by Northern Micro is the same as the one illustrated on page 224 and described in detail in Chapter 6. All transactions involving the disbursement of cash but only such transactions are entered in this journal. Debits to individual supplier accounts are posted to the supplier accounts in the accounts payable ledger daily. All amounts entered in the General Dr. column are posted individually at the end of each week as debits to the accounts named in the Account Debited column, and the total is not posted. The totals of the three right-hand amount columns are posted at the end of each month as debits to Accounts Payable, Account No. 218, and Purchases, Account No. 511, and as a credit to Cash, Account No. 111.

General Journal. A **general journal** is used by Northern Micro to enter all transactions that cannot be entered in the special journals. A two-column journal is used for this purpose. Entries affecting general ledger accounts are posted separately to the accounts named in the Description column at the end of each week. Entries affecting subsidiary ledger accounts are posted daily. The totals of this journal are for the purpose of proof only, and are not posted.

General Ledger. A general ledger with the accounts arranged in numerical order is used by Northern Micro. A chart of accounts appears on page 347. The four-column account form is used in the general ledger.

Accounts Receivable Subsidiary Ledger. An accounts receivable ledger with the accounts for customers arranged in alphabetic order is used by Northern Micro. The three-column account form is used in this ledger. Posting to the individual accounts with customers is done daily. As each item is posted, the balance is extended immediately so that the account balance of any customer can be referenced at any time. This is important since it is often necessary to determine the status of a particular customer's account before extending additional credit.

Accounts Payable Subsidiary Ledger. An accounts payable ledger with the accounts for suppliers arranged in alphabetic order is used by Northern Micro. The three-column account form is used in this ledger also. Posting to the individual accounts with suppliers is done daily. As each item is posted, the balance is extended immediately so that the account balance of any supplier can be referenced at any time.

Auxiliary Records. As previously stated, auxiliary records include a petty cash payments record, a checkbook, and employees' earnings records. The form of petty cash payments record is similar to that illustrated on pages 164 and 165. At the end of each month, when the summary postings from the cash receipts and cash payments journals are completed, the balance of the cash account in the ledger should be the same as the balance entered on the check stubs. The earnings record maintained for each of Northern Micro's five employees is similar to the one illustrated on pages 306 and 307.

Accounting Procedure. The partial books of account, containing selected transactions completed during the month of December, are reproduced on pages 354-359. These books include the purchases journal, sales journal; cash receipts journal, cash payments journal, general journal, petty cash payments record, general ledger, accounts receivable ledger, and accounts payable ledger. Before entering the transactions for December, the balance in the petty cash fund was entered in the petty cash payments record. The balance at the beginning of the month of December is shown in each of the selected accounts in the general, accounts receivable, and accounts payable ledgers. These balances, along with those at the end of the month, are summarized in the trial balance and schedules reproduced on pages 360-361.

Presented below is a narrative of selected transactions completed during December. As each new type of transaction is introduced, it is analyzed to explain its effect on the accounts. Entry of these transactions in the books of account is illustrated on pages 354-359.

All of the journals and ledgers illustrated include appropriate posting references. These posting references were made at the time the entries were posted to the general and subsidiary ledgers.

NORTHERN MICRO—Narrative of Selected Transactions

Monday, December 1
Issued checks as follows:
- **(a)** No. 257, Burger Realty Co., $2,000, in payment of December rent.
- **(b)** No. 258, The Burlington Express, $287.75, in payment of freight on merchandise purchased.
- **(c)** No. 259, A&J Office Supply Co., $560.25, in payment of invoice of November 2, no discount.

Analysis: Each of these checks was entered in the cash payments journal. Check No. 257 was entered by a debit to Rent Expense and a credit in the Cash Cr. column. The rent expense account title was entered in the Account Debited column. The account number for Rent Expense (No. 541) was inserted in the Posting Reference column when the individual posting was completed at the end of the week.

Check No. 258 was entered by a debit in the Purchases Dr. column and a credit in the Cash Cr. column. The purchases account was debited because the freight charge increases the cost of the merchandise. A check mark was placed in the Posting Reference column to indicate that individual posting of this amount is not necessary. This amount is posted as part of the summary posting of the Purchases Dr. column total at the end of the month.

Check No. 259 was entered by a debit in the Accounts Payable Dr. column and a credit in the Cash Cr. column. The name of the supplier was written in the Account Debited column. A check mark was placed in the Posting Reference column immediately after the payment was posted to A&J Office Supply Co.'s account in the accounts payable ledger.

Tuesday, December 2
1. Received the following invoices for purchases on account:
   - **(a)** Diskco, 1700 29th Street, Bakersfield, CA 93301-4747, $1,315, per Invoice No. 94 of November 30. Terms, 2/10,n/30.
   - **(b)** Compumate, Inc., 6500 9th Street, New Orleans, LA 70115-1122, $6,494, per Invoice No. 95 of November 30. Terms, 2/10 EOM.
   - **(c)** TTA Products, 1439 E. Broad St., Columbus, OH 43205-9892, $1,416, per Invoice No. 96 of November 30. Terms, 2/10, n/30.

Analysis: These transactions were entered net of any discounts in the purchases journal. The names of the suppliers were entered in the From Whom Purchased column. The invoices were then posted to the subsidiary ledger and filed in an unpaid invoice file according to their due dates. The check marks were placed in the Posting Reference column when these transactions were posted at the end of the day to the suppliers' accounts in the accounts payable ledger.

2. Received a notice from the Colonel Bank that $3,800.00 had been deducted from Northern Micro's account. This amount was deducted because a check from Stephanie Johnson, deposited a few days before, had not been paid at Johnson's bank due to insufficient funds. Johnson's check was enclosed with the notice.

Analysis: This transaction was entered in the cash payments journal by a debit to Accounts Receivable—Stephanie Johnson and a credit in the Cash Cr. column. (Although the reduction in the Cash balance was not accompanied by issuing a check, the effect was the same. The amount was subtracted on the next check stub.) Note that when the amount was posted to Stephanie Johnson's account in the accounts receivable ledger, the notation "NSF" (not sufficient funds) was inserted in the ledger.

Wednesday, December 3

1. Received check from James Revol, $3,891.50.

Analysis: This remittance was entered in the cash receipts journal by a debit in the Cash Dr. column and a credit in the Accounts Receivable Cr. column. The name of the customer was entered in the Account Credited column.

2. Received a notice from the Colonel Bank that $2,156.54 had been deducted from Northern Micro's account. This amount represented the discount (at 4%) of the net amount of Northern Micro's Visa and MasterCard vouchers for the previous month's sales.

Analysis: This transaction was entered in the cash payments journal as a debit to Bank Credit Card Expense and a credit in the Cash Cr. column. The amount was subtracted on the next check stub.

Thursday, December 4

1. Sold merchandise on account as follows:
   (a) No. 71A, James Revol, 429 S. Holiday Dr., South Bend, IN 46615-1928, $2,995, tax, $149.75.
   (b) No. 57B, Helen Armstrong, 1739 Woodsage Trace, Indianapolis, IN 46237-1199, $1,355, tax, $67.75.
   (c) No. 35C, Mark Ewing, 2730 Bent Brook Drive, Indianapolis, IN 46250-1998, $980, tax, $49.

Analysis: These transactions were entered in the sales journal by a debit in the Accounts Receivable Dr. column and credits in the Sales Cr. and Sales Tax Payable Cr. columns. The customer names were entered in the To Whom Sold column.

2. Issued checks as follows:
   (a) No. 260, AB Electronics, $2,730.78, in payment of invoice of November 25, $2,815.23 less discount of $84.45.
   (b) No. 261, Diskco, $588.83, in payment of invoice of November 5. Discount of $11.78 was lost because the invoice was not paid within the ten day discount period.

Analysis: These checks were entered in the cash payments journal. Check No. 260 was entered as a debit in the Accounts Payable Dr. column and a credit in the Cash Cr. column. The original purchase on November 25 was entered net of the available discount, so the payment was simply entered at the net amount of $2,730.78.

Check No. 261 was entered on two lines as a debit to Purchases Discounts Lost, a debit in the Accounts Payable Dr. column, and a credit in the Cash Cr. column. The original purchase on November 5 was entered net of the available discount, but the account was not paid within the discount period. The gross amount of the invoice, $588.83, therefore had to be paid. The difference between the gross payment of $588.83 and the net amount of $577.05 that had been recognized as a liability at the time the goods were purchased is the purchase discount lost of $11.78 ($588.83-$577.05).

Friday, December 5
1. Received Credit Memorandum No. 91 for $93.25 from A&J Office Supply Co., for merchandise returned; to be applied on Invoice No. 89 received on November 28.

    Analysis: This transaction was entered in the general journal by debiting Accounts Payable—A&J Office Supply Co. and crediting Purchases Returns and Allowances.

2. Made petty cash payments as follows: Postage stamps, $20.00—Petty Cash Voucher No. 83. Messenger fee, $6.00—Petty Cash Vou. No. 84.

    Analysis: All payments from the petty cash fund are entered in the petty cash payments record. This record is designed to classify each expenditure. Note that the cost of the postage stamps was entered as a charge to Supplies and the messenger fees were charged to Miscellaneous Expense.

Saturday, December 6
1. Issued Credit Memorandum No. 32 for $315.00 to Helen Armstrong for merchandise returned. (Sales price, $300.00, tax, $15.00)

    Analysis: This transaction was entered in the general journal by debiting Sales Returns and Allowances and Sales Tax Payable, and crediting Accounts Receivable—Helen Armstrong.

2. Cash (including bank credit card) sales for the week:

Salesperson	Merchandise	Tax	Total
A	$ 3,093.38	$154.67	$ 3,248.05
B	2,651.46	132.57	2,784.03
C	3,977.10	198.86	4,175.96
D	2,651.58	132.58	2,784.16
	$12,373.52	$618.68	$12,992.20

Analysis: As each cash sale was completed, a sales ticket and a Visa or MasterCard ticket, if necessary, were prepared. The ticket provides the information needed in entering the amount of the sale on the cash register. Each amount was added to the previous total of cash sales made by each salesperson on an electronic accumulator in the register. Usually the total cash sales are entered daily, but to save time and avoid unnecessary duplication of entries in this illustration, the total cash sales are entered at the end of each week and on the last day of the month. This transaction was entered in the cash receipts journal by a debit in the Cash Dr. column for $12,992.20 and credits in the Sales Cr. column for $12,373.52 and the Sales Tax Payable Cr. column for $618.68.

End-of-the-Week Work

(1) Proved the footings of the sales journal.
(2) Proved the footings of the cash receipts journal.
(3) Proved the footings of the cash payments journal.
(4) Deposited $16,883.70 in the Colonel Bank and proved the cash balance, $42,093.83 (Beginning balance, $37,334.28 + cash debits from cash receipts journal, $16,883.70 − cash credits from cash payments journal, $12,124.15 = $42,093.83).
(5) Posted each entry individually from the General Dr. (Cr.) column of the cash payments journal and from the general journal to the proper general ledger accounts.

(Transactions from December 8 through December 14 were similar to those illustrated for December 1-6 and are not illustrated here.)

Monday, December 15

1. Issued Check No. 271 for $3,327.86 to the Colonel Bank, a U.S. depository, in payment of the following taxes:

Employees' income tax withheld during November		$1,045.90
FICA tax imposed:		
On employees (withheld during November)	$1,140.98	
On the employer...................................	1,140.98	2,281.96
Total		$3,327.86

Analysis: This transaction was entered in the cash payments journal as debits to FICA Tax Payable for $2,281.96 and Employees Income Tax Payable for $1,045.90, and a credit in the Cash Cr. column for $3,327.86.
Issued Check No. 272 payable to Payroll for $2,981.29.

2. Northern Micro follows the policy of paying employees on the 15th and last day of each month. The following statement was prepared from the payroll register:

Payroll Statement for Period Ended December 15

Total salaries and commissions earned during period		$4,001.72
Employees' taxes to be withheld:		
Employees' income tax	$720.30	
FICA tax, 7.5% of $4,001.72...........................	300.13	1,020.43
Net amount payable to employees		$2,981.29
Employer's payroll taxes:		
FICA tax, 7.5% of $4,001.72...........................		$ 300.13
Unemployment compensation taxes:		
State unemployment tax, 2.7% of $546.30		14.75
FUTA tax, 0.8% of $546.30...........................		4.37
Total		$ 319.25

Analysis: None of the earnings of the five employees had reached the $50,000 point. Accordingly, all of the salaries and commissions earned during the period were subject to the FICA tax. All but one employee (a part-time employee) reached the $7,000 maximum state unemployment and FUTA tax limits in an earlier month. As a result, only $546.30 of salaries and commissions earned during the period were subject to these unemployment taxes.

Two entries were required for the payroll. (1) An entry was made in the cash payments journal for the total earnings of the employees, the amounts withheld for FICA tax and income tax, and the net amount paid. (The credits to FICA Tax Payable and Employees' Income Tax Payable are entered in the General Dr. (Cr.) column in brackets, to indicate that they are to be posted as **credits** to these two accounts.) (2) An entry was made in the general journal for the payroll taxes imposed on the employer.

(Transactions from December 16 through December 31 were similar to those illustrated for December 1-6 and 15, and are not illustrated here.)

Routine End-of-the-Month Work

(1) Proved the footings and entered the totals in the sales journal, cash receipts journal, cash payments journal, and general journal; entered the total in the purchases journal.

(2) Deposited $7,525.06 in the Colonel Bank and proved the bank balance, $58,260.55.

(3) Completed the individual posting from the General Dr. (Cr.) column of the cash payments journal and from the general journal.

(4) Completed the summary posting of the column totals of the purchases journal, sales journal, cash receipts journal, and cash payments journal to the proper accounts in the general ledger. When the summary postings were made from the sales journal, cash receipts journal, purchases journal and cash payments journal, the account numbers were placed in parentheses beneath the column totals. A check mark was placed in parentheses beneath the General Cr. and General Dr. column totals in the cash receipts journal and the cash payments journal to indicate that summary posting of these columns is not necessary.

(5) Entered appropriate rulings in the purchases journal, sales journal, cash receipts journal, cash payments journal, and general journal.

(6) Prepared a trial balance and schedules of accounts receivable and accounts payable.

The following journals show partial transactions for the month of December. However the totals reflect all transactions.

PURCHASES JOURNAL   PAGE 22

	DATE		INVOICE No.	FROM WHOM PURCHASED	POST. REF.	PURHASES DR. ACCTS. PAY CR.	
1	19-- Dec.	2	94	Diskco	✓	1 2 8 8 70	1
2		2	95	Compumate, Inc.	✓	6 3 6 4 12	2
3		2	96	TTA Products	✓	1 3 8 7 68	3
						36 5 6 3 32	
						(511) (218)	

Northern Micro—Purchases Journal (Partial)

SALES JOURNAL   PAGE 34

DATE	SALE NO.	TO WHOM SOLD	POST. REF.	ACCOUNTS RECEIVABLE DR.	SALES CR.	SALES TAX PAYABLE CR.
19-- Dec. 4	71A	James Revol	✓	3144 75	2995 00	149 75
4	57B	Helen Armstrong	✓	1422 75	1355 00	67 75
4	35C	Mark Ewing	✓	1029 00	980 00	49 00
				5596 50	5330 00	266 50
				31958 64	30436 80	1521 84
				(131)	(411)	(221)

Northern Micro—Sales Journal (Partial)

CASH RECEIPTS JOURNAL   PAGE 42

DATE	ACCOUNT CREDITED	POST. REF.	GENERAL CR.	ACCOUNTS RECEIV. CR.	SALES CR.	SALES TAX PAY CR.	CASH DR.
19-- Dec. 3	James Revol	✓		3891 50			3891 50
6					12373 52	618 68	12992 20
				14573 38	66660 79	3342 94	84577 11
				(131)	(411)	(221)	(111)

Northern Micro—Cash Receipts Journal (Partial)

CASH PAYMENTS JOURNAL   PAGE 48

DATE	CK. NO.	ACCOUNT DEBITED	POST. REF.	GENERAL DR.	ACCOUNTS PAYABLE DR.	PURCHASES DR.	CASH CR.
19-- Dec. 1	257	Rent Expense	541	2000 00			2000 00
1	258		✓			287 75	287 75
1	259	A&J Office Supply	✓		560 25		560 25
2		Accts. Rec. S. Johnson	131/✓	3800 00			3800 00
3		Bank Cr. Card Expense	553	2156 54			2156 54
4	260	AB Electronics	✓		2730 78		2730 78
4	261	Purch. Discount Lost	555	11 78			
		Diskco	✓		577 05		588 83
				7968 32	3868 08	287 75	12124 15
15	271	FICA Tax Payable	211	2281 96			
		Emp.Inc.Tax Payable	214	1045 90			3327 86
15	272	Salaries & Comm. Ex.	542	4001 72			
		FICA Tax Payable	211	(300 13)			
		Emp.Inc.Tax Payable	214	(720 30)			2981 29
				31207 60	32155 49	287 75	63650 84
				(✓)	(218)	(511)	(111)

Northern Micro—Cash Payments Journal (Partial)

PAGE		PETTY CASH PAYMENTS							
	DAY	DESCRIPTION	VOU. NO.	TOTAL AMOUNT		DRAWING		SUPPLIES EXPENSE	
1		Amounts Forwarded		250.00					
2	5	Postage stamps	83	20	00			20	00
3	5	Messenger fee	84	6	00				
						169	85	50	00	55	25
	31	Balance		80.15					
	31	Received in fund		169.85					
		Total		250.00					

Northern Micro—Partial Petty Cash Payments Record (left page)

JOURNAL

PAGE 27

	DATE		DESCRIPTION	POST. REF.	DEBIT				CREDIT				
1	19-- Dec.	5	Accounts Pay.—A&J Office Supply	218/√		9	3	25					1
2			Purchases Returns and Allow.	511.1						9	3	25	2
3		6	Sales Returns and Allowances	411.1	3	0	0	00					3
4			Sales Tax Payable	221		1	5	00					4
5			Accounts Rec.—Helen Armstrong	131/√					3	1	5	00	5
6		15	Payroll Taxes Expense	552	3	1	9	25					6
7			FICA Tax Payable	211					3	0	0	13	7
8			FUTA Tax Payable	212						4	37		8
9			State Unemployment Tax Payable	213					1	4	75		9

Northern Micro—General Journal (Partial)

GENERAL LEDGER

ACCOUNT Cash   ACCOUNT NO. 111

DATE		ITEM	POST. REF.	DEBIT					CREDIT					BALANCE							
														DEBIT					CREDIT	
19-- Dec.	1	Balance	√											37	3	3	4	28		
	31		CR42	84	5	7	7	11						121	9	1	1	39		
	31		CP48						63	6	5	0	84	58	2	6	0	55		

ACCOUNT Accounts Receivable   ACCOUNT NO. 131

DATE		ITEM	POST. REF.	DEBIT					CREDIT					BALANCE							
														DEBIT					CREDIT	
19-- Dec.	1	Balance	√											14	7	4	3	48		
	2		CP48	3	8	0	0	00						18	5	4	3	48		
	6		J27						3	1	5	00		18	2	2	8	48		
	31		S34	31	9	5	8	64						50	1	8	7	12		
	31		CR42						14	5	7	3	38	35	6	1	3	74		

FOR MONTH OF *December*   **19--**   PAGE *18*

		DISTRIBUTION OF DEBITS					
ADVERTISING EXPENSE	CHARITABLE CONT. EXP.	MISC. EXPENSE			ACCOUNT	AMOUNT	
							1
							2
		6 00					3
28 00	20 00	16 60					

Northern Micro—Partial Petty Cash Payments Record (right page)

ACCOUNT *Accounts Payable*   ACCOUNT NO. *218*

DATE		ITEM	POST. REF.	DEBIT	CREDIT	BALANCE DEBIT	BALANCE CREDIT
19-- Dec.	1	Balance	✓				11 5 5 1 63
	5		J27	9 3 25			11 4 5 8 38
	31		P22		36 5 6 3 32		48 0 2 1 70
	31		CP48	32 1 5 5 49			15 8 6 6 21

ACCOUNT *Sales Tax Payable*   ACCOUNT NO. *221*

DATE		ITEM	POST. REF.	DEBIT	CREDIT	BALANCE DEBIT	BALANCE CREDIT
19-- Dec.	1	Balance	✓				3 9 0 5 36
	6		J27	1 5 00			3 8 9 0 36
	8		CP48	3 8 9 0 36		- 0 -	- 0 -
	10		CP48	1 9 95		1 9 95	
	31		S34		1 5 2 1 84		1 4 8 6 89
	31		CR42		3 3 4 2 94		4 8 2 9 83

ACCOUNT *Sales*   ACCOUNT NO. *411*

DATE		ITEM	POST. REF.	DEBIT	CREDIT	BALANCE DEBIT	BALANCE CREDIT
19-- Dec.	1	Balance	✓				793 6 4 6 60
	31		S34		30 4 3 6 80		824 0 8 3 40
	31		CR42		66 6 6 0 79		890 7 4 4 19

ACCOUNT *Purchases*   ACCOUNT NO. *511*

DATE		ITEM	POST. REF.	DEBIT	CREDIT	BALANCE DEBIT	BALANCE CREDIT
19-- Dec.	1	Balance	✓			566 3 1 5 20	
	31		P22	36 5 6 3 32		602 8 7 8 52	
	31		CP48	2 8 7 75		603 1 6 6 27	

ACCOUNT **Salaries and Commissions Expense** ACCOUNT NO. *542*

DATE		ITEM	POST. REF.	DEBIT	CREDIT	BALANCE DEBIT	BALANCE CREDIT
19-- Dec.	1	Balance	√			79 68 7 62	
	15		CP48	4 00 1 72		83 68 9 34	
	31		CP48	3 96 1 70		87 65 1 04	

Northern Micro—Partial General Ledger (Concluded)

ACCOUNTS RECEIVABLE LEDGER

NAME *Helen Armstrong*

ADDRESS *1739 Woodsage Trace, Indianapolis, IN 46237-1199*

DATE		ITEM	POST. REF.	DEBIT	CREDIT	BALANCE
19-- Dec.	4		S34	1 4 2 2 75		1 4 2 2 75
	6		J27		3 1 5 00	1 1 0 7 75

NAME *Mark Ewing*

ADDRESS *2730 Bent Brook Dr., Indianapolis, IN 46250-2876*

DATE		ITEM	POST. REF.	DEBIT	CREDIT	BALANCE
19-- Dec.	4		S34	1 0 2 9 00		1 0 2 9 00

NAME *Stephanie Johnson*

ADDRESS *6010 South Eaton Ave., Indianapolis, IN 46259-6789*

DATE		ITEM	POST. REF.	DEBIT	CREDIT	BALANCE
19-- Dec.	2	NSF	CP48	3 8 0 0 00		3 8 0 0 00

NAME *James Revol*

ADDRESS *429 South Holiday Dr., South Bend, IN 46615-1928*

DATE		ITEM	POST. REF.	DEBIT	CREDIT	BALANCE
19-- Dec.	1	Dr. Balance	√			3 8 9 1 50
	3		CR1		3 8 9 1 50	- 0 -
	4		S34	3 1 4 4 75		3 1 4 4 75
	26		S34	6 3 7 8 75		9 5 2 3 50

Northern Micro—Accounts Receivable Ledger (Partial)

ACCOUNTS PAYABLE LEDGER

NAME *A&J Office Supply Co.*

ADDRESS *2805 South Meridian, Indianapolis, IN 46225-3460*

DATE		ITEM	POST. REF.	DEBIT	CREDIT	BALANCE
19-- Dec.	1	Cr. Balance	√			8 0 0 25
	1		CP48	5 6 0 25		2 4 0 00
	5		J27	9 3 25		1 4 6 75
	17	12/13—n/30	P22		5 6 3 25	7 1 0 00

NAME *AB Electronics*

ADDRESS *399 Goodman, Cincinnati, OH 45219-2901*

DATE		ITEM	POST. REF.	DEBIT	CREDIT	BALANCE
19-- Dec.	1	Cr. Balance	√			2 7 3 0 78
	4		CP48	2 7 3 0 78		- 0 -
	30	12/27-3/10, n/45	P22		4 4 1 9 32	4 4 1 9 32

NAME *Compumate, Inc.*

ADDRESS *6500 9th Street, New Orleans, LA 70115-1122*

DATE		ITEM	POST. REF.	DEBIT	CREDIT	BALANCE
19-- Dec.	2	11/30-2/10EOM	P22		6 3 6 4 12	6 3 6 4 12
	10		CP48	6 3 6 4 12		- 0 -
	30	12/27-2/10EOM	P22		4 3 0 8 08	4 3 0 8 08

NAME *Diskco*

ADDRESS *1700 29th Street, Bakersfield, CA 93301-4747*

DATE		ITEM	POST. REF.	DEBIT	CREDIT	BALANCE
19-- Dec.	1	Cr. Balance	√			5 7 7 05
	2	11/30-2/10, n/30	P22		1 2 8 8 70	1 8 6 5 75
	4		CP48	5 7 7 05		1 2 8 8 70

NAME *TTA Products*

ADDRESS *1439 East Broad St., Columbus, OH 43205-9892*

DATE		ITEM	POST. REF.	DEBIT	CREDIT	BALANCE
19-- Dec.	2	11/30-2/10EOM	P22		1 3 8 7 68	1 3 8 7 68
	10		CP48	1 3 8 7 68		- 0 -

Northern Micro—Accounts Payable Ledger (Partial)

Northern Micro

Trial Balance

	ACCOUNT TITLE	ACCT. NO.	November 30, 19-- DEBIT	November 30, 19-- CREDIT	December 31, 19-- DEBIT	December 31, 19-- CREDIT	
1	Cash	111	37334 28		58260 55		1
2	Petty Cash Fund	112	250 00		250 00		2
3	Accounts Receivable	131	14743 48		35613 74		3
4	Allow. for Doubtful Accts.	131.1		590 00		590 00	4
5	Merchandise Inventory	141	97083 80		97083 80		5
6	Supplies	151	1965 55		2020 80		6
7	Prepaid Insurance	155	3060 29		3060 29		7
8	Store Equipment	181	23548 10		23548 10		8
9	Accum. Depr.-Store Equip.	181.1		5493 64		5493 64	9
10	FICA Tax Payable	211		2281 96		1194 52	10
11	FUTA Tax Payable	212		26 98		35 68	11
12	State Unemploy. Tax Pay.	213		123 50		152 86	12
13	Employees Inc. Tax Pay.	214		1045 90		1433 40	13
14	Notes Payable	216		34000 00		34000 00	14
15	Accounts Payable	218		11551 63		15866 21	15
16	Sales Tax Payable	221		3905 36		4829 83	16
17	Gary L. Fishel, Capital	311		156030 53		156030 53	17
18	Gary L. Fishel, Drawing	312	82500 00		88050 00		18
19	Sales	411		793646 60		890744 19	19
20	Sales Returns and Allow.	411.1	12702 85		13401 85		20
21	Purchases	511	566315 20		603166 27		21
22	Purchases Ret. and Allow.	511.1		8460 45		8553 70	22
23	Rent Expense	541	22000 00		24000 00		23
24	Salaries and Comm. Exp.	542	79687 62		87651 04		24
25	Telephone Expense	545	1428 32		1546 72		25
26	Heating and Light Expense	549	5096 08		5515 36		26
27	Advertising Expense	551	35775 24		39233 69		27
28	Payroll Taxes Expense	552	7443 72		8079 04		28
29	Bank Credit Card Expense	553	22348 57		24505 11		29
30	Purchases Discounts Lost	555	70 58		82 36		30
31	Charitable Contrib. Exp.	557	1250 00		1270 00		31
32	Miscellaneous Expense	572	1933 17		1966 14		32
33	Interest Expense	581	619 70		619 70		33
34			1017156 55	1017156 55	1118924 56	1118924 56	34
35							35
36							36
37							37
38							38
39							39

Northern Micro—Trial Balance

Northern Micro

Schedule of Accounts Receivable

	Nov. 30 19--	Dec. 31 19--
Helen Armstrong		1 1 0 7 75
Mark Ewing		1 0 2 9 00
Stephanie Johnson	3 8 0 0 00	3 8 0 0 00
	14 7 4 3 48	35 6 1 3 74

Northern Micro—Schedule of Accounts Receivable (Partial)

Northern Micro

Schedule of Accounts Payable

	Nov. 30 19--	Dec. 31 19--
A&J Office Supply Co.	8 0 0 25	7 1 0 00
AB Electronics	2 7 3 0 78	4 4 1 9 32
Compumate, Inc		4 3 0 8 08
	11 5 5 1 63	15 8 6 6 21

Northern Micro—Schedule of Accounts Payable (Partial)

Building Your Accounting Knowledge

1. When should revenue be recognized in accrual accounting? In cash accounting?
2. When should expense be recognized in accrual accounting? In cash accounting?
3. How does the allowance method of accounting for uncollectible accounts receivable provide a proper periodic matching of revenue and expense?
4. Why is the amount of depreciation only an estimate?
5. In recognizing depreciation, why are the credits made to accumulated depreciation accounts rather than to the asset accounts themselves?
6. In Northern Micro's chart of accounts, why is interest expense classified as "Other Expense" instead of being listed as part of "Operating Expenses"?
7. What kinds of transactions are entered in Northern Micro's purchases journal? In Northern Micro's sales journal? In Northern Micro's cash receipt's journal? In Northern Micro's cash payments journal?
8. What kinds of transactions are entered in Northern Micro's general journal?
9. What are the names and account forms of the three ledgers used by Northern Micro?

10. Why are check marks placed in the Posting Reference columns of Northern Micro's purchases and sales journals?

11. Why are check marks placed below the totals of the General Debit and General Credit columns of Northern Micro's cash payments and cash receipts journals?

Assignment Box

To reinforce your understanding of the preceding text materials, you may complete the following:

        Study Guide: Part A
        Textbook: Exercises 9A1 through 9A5 or 9B1 through 9B5
                  Problems 9A1 through 9A2 or 9B1 through 9B2

End-of-Period Work Sheet

One of the major reasons for having an accounting system is to accumulate information for the preparation of periodic summaries such as the income statement, statement of owner's equity, and balance sheet. A trial balance of the general ledger accounts provides most of the information required for these financial statements. However, the trial balance does not supply the data in a form that is easily interpreted. Further, many of the accounts must be adjusted to reflect changes that are not the result of ordinary transactions with other businesses. Therefore, at the end of the fiscal period, a work sheet is generally prepared.

As was explained in Chapter 3, an **end-of-period work sheet** is a device that assists the accountant in three ways. It facilitates (1) the making of needed adjustments in the accounts, (2) the preparation of the financial statements, and (3) the closing of the temporary owner's equity accounts. Work sheets are not financial statements. Ordinarily, it is only the accountant who uses a work sheet. For this reason, a work sheet is usually prepared in pencil or with the aid of a microcomputer.

The Ten-Column Work Sheet

Prepare a ten-column end-of-year work sheet for a retail business.

While an end-of-period work sheet can be in any one of several forms, a common and widely used arrangement involves ten amount columns consisting of five pairs. The first pair of amount columns is for the trial balance. The data to be entered consist of the name, number, and debit or credit balance of each account. Debit balances should be entered in the left-hand column and credit balances in the right-hand column. The second pair of amount columns is used to enter end-of-period adjustments. The third pair of amount columns is used to show the adjusted account balances. This pair of amount columns is entitled "Adjusted Trial Balance" because its purpose is to show that the adjusted debit and credit account balances are equal in amount. The fourth pair of columns is for the adjusted balances of the expense and revenue accounts and is entitled "Income Statement." The fifth and last pair is entitled "Balance Sheet." These columns show the adjusted balances for accounts that will be reported in the balance sheet and for the drawing account. A ten-column end-of-year work sheet for Northern Micro is illustrated on pages 364-365.

The only difference between this work sheet and the eight-column work sheet presented in Chapter 3 is that this work sheet includes the "Adjusted Trial Balance" columns. The purpose of these columns is to verify the mathematical correctness of the adjusted account balances before extending them to the Income Statement and Balance Sheet columns. If an error were made in combining the trial balance and adjustments columns, the debits and credits of the adjusted trial balance columns would not be equal. There are many more adjustments in this work sheet than there were in the work sheet in Chapter 3, so the risk of error is greater. It is therefore worth using the additional pair of columns.

To illustrate the preparation and use of the end-of-period work sheet, the Northern Micro example will be continued. The use of a work sheet as a device for summarizing the data used in the financial statements will be demonstrated. The partial journals and ledgers of Northern Micro for the month of December, needed for the work sheet, were illustrated previously in the chapter.

The Work Sheet for Northern Micro

Following is a description and discussion of the steps taken in the preparation of the work sheet on pages 364-365. Each step should be studied carefully with frequent reference to the work sheet.

Trial Balance Columns. The balances of the general ledger accounts as of December 31 are entered in the first pair of amount columns. This trial balance is the same as the one shown on page 360 except that all of the account titles shown in the chart of accounts on page 347 are included in the work sheet list even though some of the accounts have zero balances at this point.

The Trial Balance Debit and Credit columns are then totaled. The totals should be equal. If not, the discrepancy must be found and corrected before the work sheet can be prepared.

Adjustments Columns. The second pair of amount columns on the work sheet is used to make entries that reflect changes that occurred during the year. In this case, adjustments are needed: (a) to remove the amount of the beginning-of-year merchandise inventory and (b) to enter the amount of the end-of-year inventory; (c) to enter the amount of interest expense incurred but not paid; (d) to enter the amount of bank credit card expense for December that will not be deducted from the bank account until early in the following month; (e) and (f) to enter the portions

Northern
Work
For the Year

#	ACCOUNT TITLE	ACCT. NO.	TRIAL BALANCE DEBIT	TRIAL BALANCE CREDIT	ADJUSTMENTS DEBIT	ADJUSTMENTS CREDIT
1	Cash	111	5 8 2 6 0 55			
2	Petty Cash Fund	112	2 5 0 00			
3	Accounts Receivable	131	3 5 6 1 3 74			
4	Allow. for Doubtful Accs.	131.1		5 9 0 00		(g) 3 0 1 2 63
5	Merchandise Inventory	141	9 7 0 8 3 80		(b) 10 2 6 9 5 20	(a) 9 7 0 8 3 80
6	Supplies	151	2 0 2 0 80			(e) 1 2 2 0 80
7	Prepaid Insurance	155	3 0 6 0 29			(f) 1 5 3 0 15
8	Store Equipment	181	2 3 5 4 8 10			
9	Accum. Depr.—Store Equip.	181.1		5 4 9 3 64		(h) 2 3 5 4 81
10	FICA Tax Payable	211		1 1 9 4 52		
11	FUTA Tax Payable	212		3 5 68		
12	State Unemp. Tax Pay.	213		1 5 2 86		
13	Employees Inc. Tax Pay.	214		1 4 3 3 40		
14	Accrued Bank Cr. Card Pay.	215				(d) 9 2 99
15	Notes Payable	216		3 4 0 0 0 00		
16	Accrued Interest Payable	217				(c) 2 8 3 33
17	Accounts Payable	218		1 5 8 6 6 21		
18	Sales Tax Payable	221		4 8 2 9 83		
19	Gary L. Fishel, Capital	311		15 6 0 3 0 53		
20	Gary L. Fishel, Drawing	312	8 8 0 5 0 00			
21	Exp. & Rev. Summary	331			(a) 9 7 0 8 3 80	(b) 10 2 6 9 5 20
22	Sales	411		89 0 7 4 4 19		
23	Sales Ret. and Allow.	411.1	1 3 4 0 1 85			
24	Purchases	511	60 3 1 6 6 27			
25	Purchases Ret. and Allow.	511.1		8 5 5 3 70		
26	Rent Expense	541	2 4 0 0 0 00			
27	Salaries and Comm. Exp.	542	8 7 6 5 1 04			
28	Supplies Expense	543			(e) 1 2 2 0 80	
29	Telephone Expense	545	1 5 4 6 72			
30	Depreciation Expense	547			(h) 2 3 5 4 81	
31	Insurance Expense	548			(f) 1 5 3 0 15	
32	Heating and Lighting Exp.	549	5 5 1 5 36			
33	Advertising Expense	551	3 9 2 3 3 69			
34	Payroll Taxes Expense	552	8 0 7 9 04			
35	Bank Credit Card Exp.	553	2 4 5 0 5 11		(d) 9 2 99	
36	Uncollectible Accts. Exp.	554			(g) 3 0 1 2 63	
37	Purchases Discounts Lost	555	8 2 36			
38	Charitable Contr. Exp.	557	1 2 7 0 00			
39	Miscellaneous Expense	572	1 9 6 6 14			
40	Interest Expense	581	6 1 9 70		(c) 2 8 3 33	
41			111 8 9 2 4 56	111 8 9 2 4 56	20 8 2 7 3 71	20 8 2 7 3 71
42	Net Income					
43						

Micro

Sheet

Ended December 31, 19--

ADJUSTED TRIAL BALANCE		INCOME STATEMENT		BALANCE SHEET		
DEBIT	CREDIT	DEBIT	CREDIT	DEBIT	CREDIT	
5 8 2 6 0 55				5 8 2 6 0 55		1
2 5 0 00				2 5 0 00		2
3 5 6 1 3 74				3 5 6 1 3 74		3
	3 6 0 2 63				3 6 0 2 63	4
10 2 6 9 5 20				10 2 6 9 5 20		5
8 0 0 00				8 0 0 00		6
1 5 3 0 14				1 5 3 0 14		7
2 3 5 4 8 10				2 3 5 4 8 10		8
	7 8 4 8 45				7 8 4 8 45	9
	1 1 9 4 52				1 1 9 4 52	10
	3 5 68				3 5 68	11
	1 5 2 86				1 5 2 86	12
	1 4 3 3 40				1 4 3 3 40	13
	9 2 99				9 2 99	14
	3 4 0 0 0 00				3 4 0 0 0 00	15
	2 8 3 33				2 8 3 33	16
	1 5 8 6 6 21				1 5 8 6 6 21	17
	4 8 2 9 83				4 8 2 9 83	18
	15 6 0 3 0 53				15 6 0 3 0 53	19
8 8 0 5 0 00				8 8 0 5 0 00		20
9 7 0 8 3 80	10 2 6 9 5 20	9 7 0 8 3 80	10 2 6 9 5 20			21
	89 0 7 4 4 19		89 0 7 4 4 19			22
1 3 4 0 1 85		1 3 4 0 1 85				23
60 3 1 6 6 27		60 3 1 6 6 27				24
	8 5 5 3 70		8 5 5 3 70			25
2 4 0 0 0 00		2 4 0 0 0 00				26
8 7 6 5 1 04	·	8 7 6 5 1 04				27
1 2 2 0 80		1 2 2 0 80				28
1 5 4 6 72		1 5 4 6 72				29
2 3 5 4 81		2 3 5 4 81				30
1 5 3 0 15		1 5 3 0 15				31
5 5 1 5 36		5 5 1 5 36				32
3 9 2 3 3 69		3 9 2 3 3 69				33
8 0 7 9 04		8 0 7 9 04				34
2 4 5 9 8 10		2 4 5 9 8 10				35
3 0 1 2 63		3 0 1 2 63				36
8 2 36		8 2 36				37
1 2 7 0 00		1 2 7 0 00				38
1 9 6 6 14		1 9 6 6 14				39
9 0 3 03		9 0 3 03				40
122 7 3 6 3 52	122 7 3 6 3 52	91 6 6 1 5 79	100 1 9 9 3 09	31 0 7 4 7 73	22 5 3 7 0 43	41
		8 5 3 7 7 30			8 5 3 7 7 30	42
		100 1 9 9 3 09	100 1 9 9 3 09	31 0 7 4 7 73	31 0 7 4 7 73	43

of supplies used and prepaid insurance expired during the year; (g) to enter the estimated amount of expected uncollectible accounts expense; and (h) to enter the estimated depreciation expense for the year.

Eight complete entries are made in the Adjustments columns to reflect these changes. When an account is debited or credited, the amount is entered on the same horizontal line as the name of the account and in the appropriate Adjustments Debit or Credit column. Each adjusting entry made on the work sheet is identified by a small letter in parentheses to facilitate cross-reference. An explanation of each entry found in the work sheet is provided below.

Entry (a) REMOVE INVENTORY BEG OF YEAR.

Prepare the two adjustments needed for the beginning and ending merchandise inventory components of cost of goods sold.

Expense and Revenue Summary	97,083.80	
Merchandise Inventory		97,083.80

This entry is the first of two entries that adjust for the cost of goods sold. To help understand these entries, recall that when merchandise is purchased, Purchases is debited, and when merchandise is sold, Sales is credited. Thus the balance in the merchandise inventory account prior to the adjusting entries is the same amount that was in the account at the beginning of the year. The amount of the beginning merchandise inventory must be removed from the asset account and at the same time included in the determination of net income for the current year. This is done by debiting Expense and Revenue Summary and crediting Merchandise Inventory for $97,083.80. The amount of the beginning merchandise inventory is debited to Expense and Revenue Summary because it is a part of the cost of goods sold.

Entry (b)

Merchandise Inventory	102,695.20	
Expense and Revenue Summary		102,695.20

The second entry to adjust for the cost of goods sold recognizes the calculated cost of the merchandise on hand December 31 (often referred to as the year-end inventory). The calculation was based on a physical count of the merchandise in stock at the close of the year. The cost of the merchandise in stock at year end is entered by debiting Merchandise Inventory and crediting Expense and Revenue Summary for $102,695.20. The amount of ending inventory is credited to Expense and Revenue Summary because this amount is a deduction in the calculation of the cost of goods sold, as follows:

Merchandise inventory, January 1		$ 97,083.80
Purchases	$603,166.27	
Less purchases returns and allowances	8,553.70	
Net purchases		594,612.57
Merchandise available for sale.....................		$691,696.37
Less merchandise inventory, December 31		102,695.20
Cost of goods sold		$589,001.17

The relationship between the amounts in the cost of goods sold calculation presented above and the amounts on the work sheet can be seen by focusing on the income statement columns of the work sheet, as follows:

	Income Statement	
	Debit	*Credit*
Expense and Revenue Summary	97,083.80	102,695.20
Purchases	603,166.27	
Purchases Returns and Allowances..................		8,553.70

Note that the debit and credit amounts for Expense and Revenue Summary are extended to the Income Statement columns. By following this procedure, the total of the debits (Expense and Revenue Summary, $97,083.80 + Purchases, $603,166.27) less the total of the credits (Expense and Revenue Summary, $102,695.20 + Purchases Returns and Allowances, $8,553.70) equals $589,001.17, the cost of goods sold. In other words, the beginning inventory of $97,083.80 *plus* the purchases of $603,166.27 *less* the purchases returns and allowances of $8,553.70 and *less* the ending inventory of $102,695.20 equals the cost of goods sold of $589,001.17.

Entry (c)

Prepare the adjustment needed for accrued interest expense.

Interest Expense	283.33	
Accrued Interest Payable		283.33

This accrual adjustment enters the accrued interest expense that was incurred but not paid by debiting Interest Expense and crediting Accrued Interest Payable for $283.33. The $34,000 note payable in the December 31 trial balance represents money borrowed on December 1. The loan plus interest of $1,700 are due at the end of the following May. Thus, interest expense of $283.33 ($1,700/6) has been incurred for the use of the $34,000 for one month.

Entry (d)

Prepare the adjustment needed for accrued bank credit card expense.

Bank Credit Card Expense	92.99	
Accrued Bank Credit Card Payable		92.99

This accrual adjustment enters the expense for the deduction that will be made by the bank during January for Visa and MasterCard vouchers deposited during December. These deposits amounted to $2,324.76. The bank will deduct 4% of this amount, or $92.99 ($2,324.76 x .04), from the checking account. Since this $92.99 is really an expense for the year just ended, the adjustment is needed to include the expense in the calculation of net income for the past year. The adjustment is recorded by a debit to Bank Credit Card Expense and a credit to Accrued Bank Credit Card Payable.

Entry (e)

Prepare the adjustments needed for supplies expense and insurance expense.

Supplies Expense	1,220.80	
Supplies		1,220.80

This adjustment enters the calculated cost of the supplies used during the year by debiting Supplies Expense and crediting Supplies for $1,220.80. This amount was determined as follows: The December 31 trial balance shows that Supplies has a debit balance of $2,020.80, which is the cost of supplies on hand at the start of the year, plus the cost of supplies purchased during the year. A physical count made of the supplies on December 31 determined the cost of the supplies on hand to be $800. Thus, the cost of the supplies used during the year amounted to $1,220.80 ($2,020.80 − $800.00).

Entry (f)

Insurance Expense	1,530.15	
Prepaid Insurance		1,530.15

This adjustment enters the insurance expense for the year by debiting Insurance Expense and crediting Prepaid Insurance for $1,530.15. The December 31 trial balance shows that Prepaid Insurance has a debit balance of $3,060.29. This amount is the cost of a 2-year policy dated January 2 of the year under consideration. By December 31, one year had elapsed; therefore one half of the premium paid had become an expense.

Entry (g)

Prepare the adjustment for the amount of uncollectible accounts expense.

Uncollectible Accounts Expense	3,012.63	
Allowance for Doubtful Accounts		3,012.63

This adjustment enters the estimated uncollectible accounts expense for the year by debiting Uncollectible Accounts Expense and crediting Allowance for Doubtful Accounts for $3,012.63. Based on past experience, Northern Micro estimated that uncollectible account losses would be approximately one percent of the total sales on account for the year. Investigation of the records revealed that such sales amounted to $301,262.73. One percent of this amount is $3,012.63.

Entry (h)

Prepare the adjustment needed for depreciation of property, plant, and equipment.

Ex. 9A6-9A7

Pro. 9A2-A4

Depreciation Expense	2,354.81	
Accumulated Depreciation—Store Equipment		2,354.81

This adjustment enters the depreciation expense for the year by debiting Depreciation Expense and crediting Accumulated Depreciation—Store Equipment for $2,354.81. The December trial balance shows that Store Equipment has a debit balance of $23,548.10. This balance represents the cost of various items that have been owned the entire year. This equipment is being depreciated at the rate of 10% a year, or $2,354.81 ($23,548.10 x .10).

After making the required entries in the Adjustments columns of the work sheet, the columns are totaled to prove the equality of the debit and credit entries.

Prepare a ten-column end-of-year work sheet for a retail business.

Adjusted Trial Balance Columns. The third pair of amount columns of the work sheet is for the adjusted trial balance, which is a trial balance after the adjustments have been applied. To determine the balance of each account after making the required adjustments, it is necessary to take into consideration the amounts entered in the first two pairs of amount columns (Trial Balance and Adjustments columns).

When an account balance is not affected by entries in the Adjustments columns, the amount in the Trial Balance columns is extended directly to the Adjusted Trial Balance columns. When an account balance is affected by an entry in the Adjustments columns, the balance to be entered in the Adjusted Trial Balance columns is increased or decreased by the amount of the adjusting entry. For example, Accumulated Depreciation—Store Equipment is listed in the Trial Balance Credit column as $5,493.64. Since there is an entry of $2,354.81 in the Adjustments Credit column, the amount extended to the Adjusted Trial Balance Credit column is $7,848.45

($5,493.64 + $2,354.81). Prepaid Insurance is listed in the Trial Balance Debit column as $3,060.29. Since there is an entry of $1,530.15 in the Adjustments Credit column, the amount extended to the Adjusted Trial Balance Credit column is $1,530.14 ($3,060.29 − $1,530.15).

There is one exception to the procedure just described that relates to the debit and the credit in the Adjustments columns for Expense and Revenue Summary. The excess of the $102,695.20 credit over the $97,083.80 debit is $5,611.40. This excess amount could be extended to the Adjusted Trial Balance Credit column. It is better, however, to extend both the debit amount, which represents the beginning inventory, and the credit amount, which represents the ending inventory, into the Adjusted Trial Balance columns. The reason is that both the beginning and ending inventory amounts are used in the preparation of the cost of goods sold section on the income statement, as explained in the discussion of entries (a) and (b) above. Therefore, both amounts should appear in the Income Statement columns.

The Adjusted Trial Balance columns are then totaled to prove the equality of the debits and the credits.

▨▨▨ **Income Statement Columns.** The fourth pair of columns of the work sheet shows the amounts that will be reported in the income statement. The manner of extending both the debit and credit amounts on the line for Expense and Revenue Summary was described previously. The amounts for sales and purchases returns and allowances are extended to the Income Statement Credit column. The amounts for sales returns and allowances, purchases, and all expenses are extended to the Income Statement Debit column.

The Income Statement columns are then totaled. The difference between the totals of these columns is the net income or net loss during the accounting period. If the total of the credits exceeds the total of the debits, the difference represents the increase in owner's equity due to net income. If the total of the debits exceeds the total of the credits, the difference represents the decrease in owner's equity due to net loss.

The Income Statement columns of Northern Micro's work sheet on page 365 show that the total of the credits amounts to $1,001,993.09 and the total of the debits amounts to $916,615.79. The difference, $85,377.30, is the net income for the year.

▨▨▨ **Balance Sheet Columns.** The fifth pair of columns of the work sheet shows the amounts that will be reported in the balance sheet. The amounts for assets and drawing are extended to the Balance Sheet Debit column. The amounts for liabilities and owner's equity are extended to the Balance Sheet Credit column.

The Balance Sheet columns are then totaled. The difference between the totals of these columns also is the amount of net income or net loss for the accounting period. If the total of the debits exceeds the total of the credits, the difference represents net income; if the total of the credits exceeds the total of the debits, the difference represents net loss. This difference should be the same as the difference between the totals of the Income Statement columns.

The Balance Sheet columns of the work sheet of Northern Micro show that the total of the debits amounts to $310,747.73 and the total of the credits amounts to $225,370.43. The difference of $85,377.30 represents the amount of net income for the year.

Completing the Work Sheet. The difference ($85,377.30) between the totals of the Income Statement columns and the totals of the Balance Sheet columns is entered on the next horizontal line below the totals. Since the difference represents net income, it is entered in the Income Statement Debit and in the Balance Sheet Credit columns. If a net loss resulted, the amount would be so designated and entered in the Income Statement Credit and in the Balance Sheet Debit columns. After the net income (or net loss) has been entered, double rulings are placed immediately below the totals.

Proving the Work Sheet. The work sheet provides proof of the arithmetical accuracy of the data that it summarizes. First, it verifies the equality of the debits and credits in the Trial Balance columns, the Adjustments Columns, and the Adjusted Trial Balance columns. Second, it shows that the difference between the debits and credits in the Income Statement columns is the same as the difference between the debits and credits in the Balance Sheet columns.

The reason why the same amount will balance both the Income Statement columns and the Balance Sheet columns is provided by an understanding of (1) the real nature of net income (or net loss) and (2) the basic difference between the income statement accounts and the balance sheet accounts. The reality of net income is that the assets have increased, or that the liabilities have decreased, or that some combination of both events has taken place during a period of time. Most of these changes are entered day after day in the asset and liability accounts in order that they may be kept up to date. However, the effect of the changes on the owner's equity element is not entered in the permanent owner's equity account. Instead, the changes are entered in the temporary owner's equity accounts—the revenue and expense accounts.

At the end of the period after the asset and liability accounts have been adjusted, each of these accounts reflects all of the changes of the period. In contrast, all of the changes in owner's equity for the period are reflected in the revenue and expense accounts and in the drawing account.

As applied to the work sheet, this means that the Balance Sheet column totals are out of balance by the amount of the change in owner's equity due to net income or net loss for the period involved. In other words, the asset and liability accounts reflect the net income of the period, but the owner's capital account at this point does not. It is only after the temporary accounts are closed at the end of the period and the amount of the net income for the period has been transferred to the owner's capital account that this account reflects the net income of the period.

The owner's capital account lacks two things to bring its balance up to date: (1) the decrease due to any withdrawals during the period, which is reflected in the debit balance of the drawing account and (2) the increase due to any net income (or the decrease due to any net loss) for the period. On the work sheet, the debit balance of the drawing account is extended to the Balance Sheet Debit column. Thus, all that is needed to cause the Balance Sheet columns to be equal is the amount of the net income (or loss) for the year. This amount is the difference between the totals of the Income Statement columns.

Building Your Accounting Knowledge

1. In what three ways does an end-of-period work sheet assist the accountant?
2. Explain the purpose of each of the eight adjustments on the Northern Micro work sheet.
3. What two amounts from the Income Statement Debit column are added and what two amounts from the Income Statement Credit column are then subtracted to determine the cost of goods sold?
4. Why are both the debit and credit amounts in the Adjustments columns on the Expense and Revenue Summary line of the work sheet extended to the Adjusted Trial Balance columns?
5. What does the difference between the totals of the Income Statement columns represent? What does the difference between the Balance Sheet column totals represent?
6. What two things does the owner's capital account lack to bring its balance up to date?

Assignment Box

To reinforce your understanding of the preceding text materials, you may complete the following:
　　　　Study Guide: Part B
　　　　Textbook: Exercises 9A6 through 9A7 or 9B6 through 9B7
　　　　　　　　　Problems 9A3 through 9A4 or 9B3 through 9B4

Expanding Your Business Vocabulary

Accelerated Cost Recovery System (p. 345)
accelerated methods (p. 345)
accrual basis of accounting (p. 340)
accrued expense (p. 344)
accrued liability (pp. 344)
adjusted trial balance (p. 369)
allowance method (p. 341)

bad debts expense (p. 341)
cash basis of accounting (pp. 340)
chart of accounts (p. 346)
depreciable cost (p. 344)
depreciation accounting (p. 344)
end-of-period adjustments (p. 341)
end-of-period work sheet (p. 362)

general journal (p. 349)
prepaid expense (p. 343)
reducing-charge methods (p. 345)
straight-line method (p. 345)
uncollectible accounts expense (p. 341)

Demonstration Problem

Keith Kirchoff is in the retail hardware business operating Kirchoff Hardware. The accounts are kept on the basis of a fiscal year ending on January 31. Merchandise is sold for cash and on account. A retail sales tax of 5% is imposed on sales. All sales on account are payable on or before the 10th of the following month. Kirchoff Hardware is subject to FICA tax, FUTA tax, and state unemployment compensation tax.

Listed below are representative transactions for the month of January of the current year.

Jan. 3 Kirchoff invested an additional $10,600 in the business.
3 Borrowed $24,000 from the bank, to be repaid on April 1 of next year plus $540 interest.
5 Paid store rent, $1,050, Check No. 701.
9 Purchased merchandise on account from Ace Homart for $46,000, terms, 2/10, n/30, Invoice No. 231. (Kirchoff uses the net-price method of entering purchases of merchandise on account.)
10 Purchased merchandise on account from Clyde's Lumber Co. for $36,000, terms, 3/10, n/30, Invoice No. 232.
11 Sold a riding lawn mower on account to Gary Stoff for $3,600 plus $180 sales tax, Sale No. 25b.
12 Received $4,400 from a customer, Wendy Clark, on account.
16 Made cash purchases from Empire Hardware Supply Co., $44,600. Issued Check No. 702.
16 Kirchoff serviced several furnaces, receiving cash of $1,806.
17 The $370 owed by Stan Vroman, a customer, has been classified as uncollectible. Kirchoff uses the allowance method of accounting for bad debts.
18 Kirchoff received a credit memo for defective merchandise that was returned to Empire Hardware Supply Co., $2,550.
19 Paid for the merchandise purchased on account from Ace Homart on January 9. Issued Check No. 703.
20 Made cash and bank credit card sales amounting to $106,400, sales tax $5,320.
23 Paid $7,200 for a three-year fire insurance policy covering merchandise and store equipment beginning February 1 of the current year. Issued Check No. 704.

Jan. 24 Kirchoff issued a credit memo to Leroy Sommer for merchandise returned, $3,020 including 5% sales tax. Kirchoff maintains a separate Sales Tax Payable Account.

26 Paid for merchandise purchased on account from Clyde's Lumber Co. Issued Check No. 705.

30 Sold merchandise on account to Patty Busic, $4,600, plus sales tax of $230. Sale No. 18d.

31 Paid the payroll as follows:

Total employee earnings for January		$18,500
Taxes to be withheld:		
Employees' Federal Income Tax	$2,776	
Employees' State Income Tax	370	
FICA tax	1,388	4,534
Net amount payable to employees		$13,966
Employer's payroll taxes:		
FICA tax		$ 1,388
Federal unemployment tax		74
State unemployment tax		268
		$ 1,730

The trial balance as of January 31 of the current year is reproduced on the next page.

Required:

1. Enter the January transactions in the appropriate special or general journal.
2. Prove the footings and enter the totals of the purchases, cash payments, sales, cash receipts, and general journals.
3. Complete a ten-column work sheet, proceeding as follows:
   (A) Enter the trial balance in the Trial Balance columns.
   (B) Make the necessary entries in the Adjustments columns for the following items:
      (a) Transfer beginning inventory to Expense and Revenue Summary.
      (b) Year-end merchandise inventory, $37,688.00.
      (c) Interest accrued on notes payable, $53.15.
      (d) Accrued bank credit card payable, $230.40.
      (e) Prepaid insurance unexpired, $517.50.
      (f) Supplies on hand, $63.00.
      (g) Depreciation of store equipment, 10% a year.
      (h) Uncollectible accounts expense. (Increase allowance by $261.00 to provide for estimated loss.)
   (C) Extend the adjusted account balances to the Adjusted Trial Balance columns and total these columns.
   (D) Extend the account balances from the Adjusted Trial Balance columns to the proper financial statement columns and total these

Kirchoff Hardware
Trial Balance
January 31, 19--

Account	Acct. No.	Debit	Credit
Cash	111	$ 12,162.15	
Petty Cash Fund	112	75.00	
Accounts Receivable	131	3,507.83	
Allowance for Doubtful Accounts	131.1		$ 122.25
Merchandise Inventory	141	34,202.55	
Supplies	151	326.02	
Prepaid Insurance	155	723.94	
Store Equipment	181	5,955.00	
Accum. Depr.—Store Equipment	181.1		1,488.75
FICA Tax Payable	211		275.39
FUTA Tax Payable	212		74.58
State Unemployment Tax Payable	213		105.90
Employees Income Tax Payable	214		319.12
Accrued Bank Credit Card Payable	215		-0-
Notes Payable	216		4,125.00
Accrued Interest Payable	217		-0-
Accounts Payable	218		4,585.35
Sales Tax Payable	221		1,050.31
Keith Kirchoff, Capital	311		30,305.82
Keith Kirchoff, Drawing	312	22,301.25	
Expense and Revenue Summary	331	-0-	-0-
Sales	411		250,100.00
Sales Returns and Allowances	411.1	3,838.65	
Purchases	511	161,895.11	
Purchases Returns and Allowances	511.1		1,876.09
Purchases Discount	511.2		3,237.90
Rent Expense	541	6,750.00	
Salaries and Commissions Expense	542	25,682.96	
Supplies Expense	543	-0-	
Telephone Expense	545	339.90	
Depreciation Expense	547	-0-	
Insurance Expense	548	-0-	
Heating and Lighting Expense	549	923.40	
Advertising Expense	551	12,495.23	
Payroll Taxes Expense	552	2,293.50	
Bank Credit Card Expense	553	3,016,80	
Uncollectible Accounts Expense	554	-0-	
Miscellaneous Expense	572	910.95	
Interest Expense	581	266.22	
		$297,666.46	$297,666.46

columns. Determine the net income or net loss for the fiscal year, enter it in two places, total and rule the four financial statement columns.

4. Compute the Cost of Goods Sold for Kirchoff Hardware.

Solution

1. & 2.

Purchases Journal   Page

Date	Invoice No.	From Whom Purchased	Post. Ref.	Purchases Dr. Accts. Pay. Cr.
19--				
Jan. 9	231	Ace Homart		45,080.00
10	232	Clyde's Lumber Co.		34,920.00
				80,000.00

Cash Payments Journal   Page

Date	Ck. No.	Account Debited	Post. Ref.	General Dr.	Accounts Payable Dr.	Purchases Dr.	Purchases Disc. Lost Dr.	Cash Cr.
19--								
Jan. 5	701	Rent Expense...............		1,050.00				1,050.00
16	702	....				44,600.00		44,600.00
19	703	Ace Homart			45,080.00			45,080.00
23	704	Prepaid Insurance		7,200.00				7,200.00
26	705	Clyde's Lumber Co.			34,920.00		1,080.00	36,000.00
31	706	Salaries & Comm. Expense		18,500.00				
		Employees Income Tax Payable		(3,146.00)				
		FICA Tax Payable		(1,388.00)				13,966.00
				22,216.00	80,000.00	44,600.00	1,080.00	147,896.00

Sales Journal   Page

Date	Sale No.	To Whom Sold	Post. Ref.	Accounts Receivable Dr.	Sales Cr.	Sales Tax Payable Cr.
19--						
Jan. 11	25b	Gary Stoff		3,780.00	3,600.00	180.00
30	18d	Patty Busic		4,830.00	4,600.00	230.00
				8,610.00	8,200.00	410.00

Cash Receipts Journal   Page

Date	Account Credited	Post. Ref.	General Cr.	Accounts Receivable Cr.	Sales Cr.	Sales Tax Payable Cr.	Cash Dr.
19--							
Jan. 3	K. Kirchoff, Capital..............		10,600.00				10,600.00
3	Notes Payable		24,000.00				24,000.00
12	Wendy Clark			4,400.00			4,400.00
16	....				1,806.00		1,806.00
20	....				106,400.00	5,320.00	111,720.00
			34,600.00	4,400.00	108,206.00	5,320.00	152,526.00

Date	Journal Description	Post. Ref.	Debit	Page Credit
	Journal			**Page**

Date	Description	Post. Ref.	Debit	Credit
19--				
Jan. 17	Allowance for Doubtful Accounts		370.00	
	Accounts Receivable—S. Vroman			370.00
18	Accounts Payable—Empire		2,550.00	
	Purchases Returns & Allowances			2,550.00
24	Sales Returns & Allowances		2,876.19	
	Sales Tax Payable		143.81	
	Accounts Receivable—L. Sommer			3,020.00
	(3,020/1.05 = 2,876.19)			
31	Payroll Taxes Expense		1,730.00	
	FICA Tax Payable			1,388.00
	FUTA Tax Payable			74.00
	State Unemployment Tax Payable			268.00
			7,670.00	7,670.00

3. The worksheet can be found on pages 378-379.

4.

Merchandise Inventory, 1/1/--			$ 34,202.55
Purchases		$161,895.11	
Less:			
Returns & Allowances	$1,876.09		
Discount	3,237.90	5,113.99	
Net Purchases			156,781.12
Goods Available for Sale			$190,983.67
Merchandise Inventory, 12/31/--			37,688.00
Cost of Goods Sold			$153,295.67

*Note: Now that you have reviewed the Demonstration Problem and Solution you may complete the **Mastery Problem** at the end of the chapter activities.

Applying Accounting Concepts

Series A

Exercise 9A1—Journal Entry for Uncollectible Accounts Expense. Based on past experience, Fae's Fabulous Fashions expects to have an uncollectible accounts expense in an amount equal to one half of one percent of the sales on account during the year. Sales on account amounted to $360,000. Give the end-of-period adjusting entry in general journal form to enter the estimate for uncollectible accounts expense.

Exercise 9A2—Journal Entry for Write-Off of Uncollectible Account. Grand National Suppliers follows the practice of adjusting at the end of the year for an amount estimated to be uncollectible accounts expense. On April 14 of the next year, Maxine Pratt's account in the amount of $453 has been determined to be uncollectible due to bankruptcy. Give the entry in general journal form to write off Pratt's account.

3.

Kirchoff

Work

For the Year

	ACCOUNT TITLE	ACCT. NO.	TRIAL BALANCE DEBIT	TRIAL BALANCE CREDIT	ADJUSTMENTS DEBIT	ADJUSTMENTS CREDIT
1	Cash	111	12162 15			
2	Petty Cash Fund	112	75 00			
3	Accounts Receivable	131	3507 83			
4	Allow. for Doubtful Accs.	131.1		122 25		(h) 261 00
5	Merchandise Inventory	141	34202 55		(b)37688 00	(a)34202 55
6	Supplies	151	326 02			(f) 263 02
7	Prepaid Insurance	155	723 94			(e) 206 44
8	Store Equipment	181	5955 00			
9	Accum. Depr. Store Equip.	181.1		1488 75		(g) 595 50
10	FICA Tax Payable	211		275 39		
11	FUTA Tax Payable	212		74 58		
12	State Unemp. Tax Pay.	213		105 90		
13	Employees Inc. Tax Pay.	214		319 12		
14	Accrued Bank Cr. Card Pay.	215				(d) 230 40
15	Notes Payable	216		4125 00		
16	Accrued Interest Payable	217				(c) 53 15
17	Accounts Payable	218		4585 35		
18	Sales Tax Payable	221		1050 31		
19	Keith Kirchoff, Capital	311		30305 82		
20	Keith Kirchoff, Drawing	312	22301 25			
21	Exp. and Rev. Summary	331			(a)34202 55	(b)37688 00
22	Sales	411		250100 00		
23	Sales Ret. and Allow.	411.1	3838 65			
24	Purchases	511	161895 11			
25	Purchases Ret. and Allow.	511.1		1876 09		
26	Purchases Discount	511.2		3237 90		
27	Rent Expense	541	6750 00			
28	Salaries and Comm. Exp.	542	25682 96			
29	Supplies Expense	543			(f) 263 02	
30	Telephone Expense	545	339 90			
31	Depreciation Expense	547			(g) 595 50	
32	Insurance Expense	548			(e) 206 44	
33	Heating and Lighting Exp.	549	923 40			
34	Advertising Expense	551	12495 23			
35	Payroll Taxes Expense	552	2293 50			
36	Bank Credit Card Exp.	553	3016 80		(d) 230 40	
37	Uncollectible Accts. Exp.	554			(h) 261 00	
38	Miscellaneous Expense	572	910 95			
39	Interest Expense	581	266 22		(c) 53 15	
40			297666 46	297666 46	73500 06	73500 06
41	Net Income					
42						

Hardware

Sheet

Ended Janaury 31, 19--

ADJUSTED TRIAL BALANCE		INCOME STATEMENT		BALANCE SHEET		
DEBIT	CREDIT	DEBIT	CREDIT	DEBIT	CREDIT	
1 2 1 6 2 15				1 2 1 6 2 15		1
7 5 00				7 5 00		2
3 5 0 7 83				3 5 0 7 83		3
	3 8 3 25				3 8 3 25	4
3 7 6 8 8 00				3 7 6 8 8 00		5
6 3 00				6 3 00		6
5 1 7 50				5 1 7 50		7
5 9 5 5 00				5 9 5 5 00		8
	2 0 8 4 25				2 0 8 4 25	9
	2 7 5 39				2 7 5 39	10
	7 4 58				7 4 58	11
	1 0 5 90				1 0 5 90	12
	3 1 9 12				3 1 9 12	13
	2 3 0 40				2 3 0 40	14
	4 1 2 5 00				4 1 2 5 00	15
	5 3 15				5 3 15	16
	4 5 8 5 35				4 5 8 5 35	17
	1 0 5 0 31				1 0 5 0 31	18
	3 0 3 0 5 82				3 0 3 0 5 82	19
2 2 3 0 1 25				2 2 3 0 1 25		20
3 4 2 0 2 55	3 7 6 8 8 00	3 4 2 0 2 55	3 7 6 8 8 00			21
	25 0 1 0 0 00		25 0 1 0 0 00			22
3 8 3 8 65		3 8 3 8 65				23
16 1 8 9 5 11		16 1 8 9 5 11				24
	1 8 7 6 09		1 8 7 6 09			25
	3 2 3 7 90		3 2 3 7 90			26
6 7 5 0 00		6 7 5 0 00				27
2 5 6 8 2 96		2 5 6 8 2 96				28
2 6 3 02		2 6 3 02				29
3 3 9 90		3 3 9 90				30
5 9 5 50		5 9 5 50				31
2 0 6 44		2 0 6 44				32
9 2 3 40		9 2 3 40				33
1 2 4 9 5 23		1 2 4 9 5 23				34
2 2 9 3 50		2 2 9 3 50				35
3 2 4 7 20		3 2 4 7 20				36
2 6 1 00		2 6 1 00				37
9 1 0 95		9 1 0 95				38
3 1 9 37		3 1 9 37				39
33 6 4 9 4 51	33 6 4 9 4 51	25 4 2 2 4 78	29 2 9 0 1 99	8 2 2 6 9 73	4 3 5 9 2 52	40
		3 8 6 7 7 21			3 8 6 7 7 21	41
		29 2 9 0 1 99	29 2 9 0 1 99	8 2 2 6 9 73	8 2 2 6 9 73	42

Exercise 9A3—Journal Entries with Adjustments for Office Supplies and Insurance. During the year Gaines Air Conditioning and Heating purchased office supplies for $590 and a two-year fire insurance policy for $746. Give the following entries related to these expenditures in general journal form.

1. Give the entry for the purchase of the office supplies and insurance for cash.
2. Give the end-of-period adjusting entry that would be made if there were $260 of office supplies on hand.
3. Give the end-of-period adjusting entry that would be made if the insurance policy had been in effect since the beginning of the fiscal year.

Exercise 9A4—Journal Entries for Acquisition and Depreciation of Long-Term Asset. On January 4, the beginning of the year, Gravois Glass and Mirror purchased a truck on account for $12,500 and estimates that it has a useful life of 4 years with no salvage value.

1. Give the appropriate entry in general journal form for the purchase of the truck.
2. Assuming that Gravois Glass and Mirror uses the straight-line method of depreciation, give the adjusting entry in general journal form to enter the depreciation at the end of the year.

Exercise 9A5—Identification of Proper Journals for Recording Transactions. Green Thumb Nursery uses the following journals: sales, purchases (only for merchandise purchased on account), cash receipts, cash payments, and general. Identify the appropriate journal or journals in which each of the following transactions would be recorded.

(a) Cash sales for the week
(b) Issued check in payment of invoice for merchandise purchased on account
(c) Received check from a customer for merchandise sold on account
(d) Sold merchandise on account
(e) Received a notice from the bank for an amount deducted from the company's bank account for Bank Credit Card Expense related to Visa and MasterCard sales
(f) Received an invoice for merchandise purchased on account
(g) Replenished the petty cash fund
(h) Received credit memorandum for merchandise returned that was purchased on account by the company earlier in the month
(i) Issued check payable to Payroll for weekly payroll and entered liability for payroll taxes

Exercise 9A6—Adjusting Journal Entries. Provide the adjusting entries in general journal form that are needed for the following situations. The end of the accounting period is December 31, 19--.

1. The supplies account has a balance of $550.00. An inventory of the supplies on hand indicates that $175.00 is available at the end of the year.
2. Interest of $41.67 is owed on a $2,500.00, 10%, 80-day note payable.
3. Visa and MasterCard vouchers in the amount of $7,285.00 were deposited on December 29. The vouchers are subject to a bank credit card expense of 4%.

(handwritten margin notes: 868.00 ÷ 8; USED 3 month from 2 yrs; ⅛ USED 108.50)

4. The prepaid insurance account has a balance of $868.00. This represents the premium for a two-year fire policy. The policy was effective as of October 1 of the current year.

5. The office equipment is depreciated at the rate of 10%. The balance in the office equipment account is $6,358.00.   *635.8*

6. Sales on account for the year totaled $89,620.00. Based on past experience, uncollectible accounts expense is estimated to be three-fourths of 1% of sales on account.   *× .0075 = 672.15   ¾ × 1%*

Exercise 9A7—Account Classification by Financial Statement and Nature of Account Balance. Identify the financial statement (or statements) on which each of the following items would be shown. Copy the item numbers and on the same line write an "I" if the item goes on the income statement, an "OE" if the item goes on the statement of owner's equity, and/or a "B" if the item goes on the balance sheet. (More than one statement may be indicated.) Indicate next to the financial statement designation(s) a dr. or a cr. to show the normal balance of the item.

(handwritten legend: INCOME — I; OWNERS EQUITY — OE; BALANCE — B; DR or CR; NORMAL BAL.)

1. Accounts Payable *B, CR*
2. Accounts Receivable *B dr*
3. Accumulated Depreciation—Store Equipment *B, CR*
4. Accrued Bank Credit Card Payable *B cr* *Liability*
5. Accrued Interest Payable *B, cr*
6. Allowance for Doubtful Accounts *B, cr*
7. Advertising Expense *I, dr*
8. Bank Credit Card Expense *I, dr*
9. Cash *B, dr*
10. D.H. Sinclair, Capital *B, cr • OE cr*
11. Depreciation Expense *I dr*
12. D.H. Sinclair, Drawing *B, OE, dr*
13. Employees' Income Tax Payable *B cr*
14. FICA Tax Payable *B cr*
15. FUTA Tax Payable *B cr*
16. Insurance Expense *I dr*
17. Merchandise Inventory (beginning of the period) *B dr* *B dr*
18. Payroll Taxes Payable *B CR*
19. Petty Cash Fund *B de*
20. Prepaid Insurance *B dr*
21. Purchases *I dr*
22. Purchases Returns and Allowances *I cr*
23. Purchases Discounts *I CR*
24. Revenue from Fees *CR, I*
25. Sales *I, CR*
26. Sales Returns and Allowances *I, dr*
27. Sales Discounts *I, dr*
28. Sales Tax Payable *B cr*
29. Store Equipment *B, dr*
30. Uncollectible Accounts Expense *I, dr*

Series B

Exercise 9B1—Journal Entry for Uncollectible Accounts Expense. Based on past experience, Kyle's Kite Store expects to have an uncollectible accounts expense in an amount equal to 3/4 of 1 percent of the sales on account during the year. Sales on account amounted to $270,000. Give the end-of-period adjusting entry in general journal form to enter the estimate for uncollectible accounts expense.

Exercise 9B2—Journal Entry for Write-Off of Uncollectible Account. Mound City Suppliers follows the practice of adjusting at the end of the year for an amount estimated to be uncollectible accounts expense. On May 16 of the next year, Peter Barbuto's account in the amount of $569 has been determined to be uncollectible due to bankruptcy. Give the entry in general journal form to write off Barbuto's account.

Exercise 9B3—Journal Entries with Adjustments for Office Supplies and Insurance. During the year Protzel Heating and Cooling purchased office supplies for

$840 and a two-year fire insurance policy for $874. Give the following entries related to these expenditures in general journal form.

1. Give the entry for the purchase of the office supplies and insurance for cash.
2. Give the end-of-period adjusting entry that would be made if there were $320 of office supplies on hand.
3. Give the end-of-period adjusting entry that would be made if the insurance policy had been in effect since the beginning of the fiscal year.

Exercise 9B4—Journal Entries for Acquisition and Depreciation of Long-Term Asset.   On January 3, the beginning of the year, Dellwood Art Glass purchased a truck on account for $16,400 and estimates that it has a useful life of 4 years with no salvage value.

1. Give the appropriate entry in general journal form for the purchase of the truck.
2. Assuming that Dellwood Art Glass uses the straight-line method of depreciation, give the adjusting entry in general journal form to enter the depreciation at the end of the year.

Exercise 9B5—Identification of Proper Journals for Recording Transactions.   Hartke's Exteriors uses the following journals: sales, purchases (only for merchandise purchased on account), cash receipts, cash payments, and general. Identify the appropriate journal or journals in which each of the following transactions would be recorded:

(a) Received credit memorandum for merchandise returned that was purchased on account by the company earlier in the month
(b) Issued check payable to Payroll for weekly payroll and entered liability for payroll taxes
(c) Replenished the petty cash fund
(d) Received a notice from the bank for an amount deducted from the company's bank account for Bank Credit Card Expense related to Visa and MasterCard sales
(e) Received an invoice for merchandise purchased on account
(f) Received check from a customer for merchandise sold on account
(g) Sold merchandise on account
(h) Recorded cash sales for the week
(i) Issued check in payment of invoice for merchandise purchased on account

Exercise 9B6—Adjusting Journal Entries.   Provide the adjusting entries in general journal form that are needed for the following situations. The end of the accounting period is December 31, 19--.

1. The supplies account has a balance of $785.00. An inventory of the supplies on hand indicates that $235.00 is available at the end of the year.
2. Interest of $83.33 is owed on a $5,000.00, 10%, 90-day note payable.
3. Visa and MasterCard vouchers in the amount of $8,527.00 were deposited on December 28. The vouchers are subject to a bank credit card expense of 4%.
4. The prepaid insurance account has a balance of $464.00. This represents the premium for a two-year fire policy. The policy was effective as of August 1 of the current year.

5. The office equipment is depreciated at the rate of 10%. The balance in the office equipment account is $5,863.00.
6. Sales on account for the year totaled $62,980.00. Based on past experience, uncollectible accounts expense is estimated to be three-fourths of 1% of sales on account.

Exercise 9B7—Account Classification by Financial Statement and Nature of Account Balance. Identify the financial statement (or statements) on which each of the following items would be shown. Copy the item numbers and on the same line write an "I" if the item goes on the income statement, an "OE" if the item goes on the statement of owner's equity, and/or a "B" if the item goes on the balance sheet. (More than one statement may be indicated.) Indicate next to the financial statement designation(s) a dr. or a cr. to show the normal balance of the item.

1.	Uncollectible Accounts Expense	17.	FICA Tax Payable
2.	Store Equipment	18.	Employees' Income Tax Payable
3.	Sales Tax Payable	19.	B.J. White, Drawing
4.	Sales Discounts	20.	Depreciation Expense
5.	Sales Returns and Allowances	21.	B.J. White, Capital
6.	Sales	22.	Cash
7.	Revenue from Fees	23.	Bank Credit Card Expense
8.	Purchases Discounts	24.	Advertising Expense
9.	Purchases Returns and Allowances	25.	Allowance for Doubtful Accounts
10.	Purchases	26.	Accrued Interest Payable
11.	Prepaid Insurance	27.	Accrued Bank Credit Card Payable
12.	Petty Cash Fund	28.	Accumulated Depreciation— Store Equipment
13.	Payroll Taxes Payable	29.	Accounts Receivable
14.	Merchandise Inventory (beginning of the period)	30.	Accounts Payable
15.	Insurance Expense		
16.	FUTA Tax Payable		

Series A

Problem 9A1 Journal Entries with Adjustments for Office Supplies, Insurance, and Long-Term Assets

The following situations occurred at the Slay Store:

(a) At the beginning of the current year, the Slay Store purchased office supplies for $2,850 and a two-year liability insurance policy for $1,500.
(b) At the end of the year, a physical count showed that Slay had $240 of office supplies on hand. Determine the office supplies used, assuming there was no beginning balance in the supplies account.
(c) At the end of the year, determine the insurance expense for the year.
(d) At the beginning of the current year, Slay purchased store fixtures for $6,000.

(e) Assuming that the store fixtures have an estimated useful life of 5 years and a salvage value of $400, determine the depreciation at the end of the year using the straight-line method.

Required:
Prepare journal entries for each of the preceding situations.

Problem 9A2   Journal Entries in Five Journals and Calculations for Making Adjusting Entries.

Listed below are various transactions that occurred during the month of April at The Nash Shop.

April 2 Emily Nash invested $50,000.00 cash in a retail merchandising enterprise known as The Nash Shop.

2 Paid rent, $1,000.00, Check No. 1.

3 Purchased store equipment on account from the Flowers Company, $13,600.00, terms, 2/30, n/60. (Use the net-price basis and the general journal for this transaction.)

7 Purchased merchandise from Flawless Company for $3,620.00, terms, 3/10, n/30. (Use the net-price basis.)

9 Made cash and bank credit card sales totaling $1,400.00, plus tax of $70.00.

9 Received a notice from the Trust-in-Us Bank that $380.90 had been deducted from The Nash Shop account, representing a 4 percent discount on the net amount of Visa and MasterCard tickets that had been deposited by Nash relating to such sales to date.

11 Paid for advertising, $650.00, Check No. 2.

13 Sold J.U. Elmer merchandise on 30 days' credit, $1,410.00, plus tax of $70.50.

13 Purchased merchandise for cash, $1,480.00, Check No. 3.

16 Purchased store equipment for cash, $8,200.00, Check No. 4.

17 Paid Flawless Company for merchandise purchased 10 days ago by issuing Check No. 5 for $3,511.40. (See the transaction of April 7.)

18 Received $690.00 from a customer, Mark Risk, on account.

20 Paid a premium of $1,560.00 for a 2-year insurance policy, dated April 1, on merchandise and equipment, Check No. 6.

24 Sold Rita Fialka merchandise on 30 days' credit, $1,220.00, plus tax of $61.00.

25 Borrowed $16,000.00 at the Trust-in-Us Bank on a 90-day, 12% note.

27 Sheila Jones, a customer, owes $406.00. The account has been found to be uncollectible and is, therefore, considered worthless. Assume that an allowance for doubtful accounts is maintained.

30 Following is the payroll statement for the monthly pay period:

Total earnings of employees for period		$3,020.00
Taxes to be withheld:		
Employees' income tax	$393.40	
FICA tax	226.50	619.90
Net amount payable to employees		$2,400.10

Employer's payroll taxes:		
FICA tax		$ 226.50
Unemployment taxes:		
State (2.7%)	$ 81.54	
Federal (0.8%)	24.16	105.70
Total		$ 332.20

Issued Check No. 7 for the net amount of the payroll and entered the employer's payroll taxes.

Required:

1. Journalize the preceding transactions using purchases, sales, cash receipts, cash payments, and general journals.
2. Total and rule the journals as appropriate.
3. Based on the information provided, make the necessary calculations to determine the answers to the following questions:
   (a) Refer to the transaction of April 20. By the end of April, how much of the cost of the insurance policy will have become an expense?
   (b) If the store equipment purchased on April 3 is expected to serve for 10 years and to have no salvage value, what will be the amount of depreciation expense for this equipment for each *full* year?
   (c) If the store equipment purchased on April 16 is expected to serve for 8 years and, at the end of 8 years, have a salvage value of $600.00, what will be the depreciation expense on this equipment for each *full* year of the 8-year period?
   (d) Refer to the transaction of April 3. If Nash did not pay for this equipment within the discount period, what amount of discount would be lost because of this?
   (e) Refer to the second transaction of April 9. What must have been the gross amount of bank credit card tickets deposited by The Nash Shop during the first week in April? (Hint: $380.90 is 4% of what amount?)

1560.00 APRIL 1 (30DAY)

Problem 9A3   Ten-Column Work Sheet

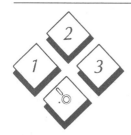

Dennis Rasmussen is in a retail merchandising business operating as The Rasmussen Sales Company. The accounts are kept on the basis of a fiscal year ending on July 31. Merchandise is sold for cash and on account. A retail sales tax of 5% is imposed on sales. All sales on account are payable on or before the 10th of the following month. The firm is subject to FICA tax, FUTA tax, and state unemployment compensation tax.

The trial balance taken on July 31 of the current year is reproduced below.

The Rasmussen Sales Company
Trial Balance
July 31, 19--

Account	Acct. No.	Debit	Credit
Cash	111	32,432.40	
Petty Cash Fund	112	200.00	
Accounts Receivable	131	9,354.22	
Allowance for Doubtful Accounts	131.1		326.00
Merchandise Inventory	141	91,206.80	
Supplies	151	869.40	
Prepaid Insurance	155	1,930.50	
Store Equipment	181	(15,880.00) 12.5%	
Accum. Depr.—Store Equipment	181.1	1985.00	3,970.00
FICA Tax Payable	211		734.38
FUTA Tax Payable	212		198.88
State Unemployment Tax Payable	213		282.40
Employees' Income Tax Payable	214		851.00
Accrued Bank Credit Card Payable	215		-0-
Notes Payable	216		11,000.00
Accrued Interest Payable	217		-0-
Accounts Payable	218		12,227.60
Sales Tax Payable	221		2,800.82
Dennis Rasmussen, Capital	311		80,815.52
Dennis Rasmussen, Drawing	312	59,470.00	
Expense and Revenue Summary	331	-0-	-0-
Sales	411		666,933.34
Sales Returns & Allowances	411.1	10,236.40	
Purchases	511	431,720.30	
Purchases Returns & Allowances	511.1		5,002.90
Purchases Discount	511.2		8,634.40
Rent Expense	541	18,000.00	
Salaries and Commissions Expense	542	68,487.90	
Supplies Expense	543	-0-	
Telephone Expense	545	906.40	
Depreciation Expense	547	-0-	
Insurance Expense	548	-0-	
Heating and Lighting Expense	549	2,462.40	
Advertising Expense	551	33,320.60	
Payroll Taxes Expense	552	6,116.00	
Bank Credit Card Expense	553	8,044.80	
Uncollectible Accounts Expense	554	-0-	
Miscellaneous Expense	572	2,429.20	
Interest Expense	581	709.92	
		793,777.24	793,777.24

Required:

As accountant for Rasmussen, complete a ten-column work sheet, proceeding as follows:

1. Enter the trial balance in the Trial Balance columns.
2. Make the necessary entries in the Adjustments columns for the following items:

(a) Transfer of beginning inventory to Expense and Revenue Summary.
(b) Merchandise inventory at the end of the year, $100,502.00.
(c) Interest accrued on notes payable, $141.60.
(d) Accrued bank credit card payable, $614.40.
(e) Prepaid insurance unexpired, $1,380.00.
(f) Supplies on hand, $168.00.
(g) Depreciation: Store equipment, 12.5% a year.
(h) Uncollectible accounts expense.
    (Increase allowance for doubtful accounts an additional $696.00 to provide for estimated loss.)

3. Extend the account balances to the Adjusted Trial Balance columns and extend the adjusted balance of each account to the proper column.
4. Total all of the amount columns. Determine the net income or the net loss for the year and enter it in the proper columns. Enter the totals and complete the ruling.

Problem 9A4　　Ten-Column Work Sheet

On October 1, Cathy Charalambous started a fabric shop in a neighborhood shopping center. She calls her store "Cathy's." On that same day various pieces of store equipment were delivered and installed, and an insurance policy was purchased. Cathy's has sales for cash and on account. All sales are subject to a 5% retail sales tax.

A trial balance of the general ledger of Cathy's is given below.

Required:

Prepare a ten-column work sheet (for the 3 months ended December 31) taking the following factors into account:

(a) A physical inventory was taken at the close of business, December 31. The cost of goods found to be on hand was $25,663.80.
    (Note: Since this is the end of the first period's operation, there is no beginning inventory.)
(b) An inventory of store and office supplies was taken on December 31. The cost of such items remaining on hand was $67.85.
(c) The store equipment is expected to serve for 12 years with no remaining salvage value. (Charalambous follows the policy of writing off a full year's depreciation on store equipment assets acquired and held for 3 months or more and charging no depreciation on such assets acquired and held for less than 3 months or on such assets disposed of during the year.)
(d) Charalambous estimates that uncollectible accounts expense on sales on account made during the period will be approximately $175.00.
(e) The insurance premium paid on October 1 was for a 2-year policy. (One eighth has therefore expired.)
(f) The note payable of $5,700.00 has accrued interest expense of $95.00.
(g) Accrued bank credit card payable, $155.60.

Cathy's
Trial Balance
December 31, 19--

Account	Acct. No.	Debit	Credit
Cash	111	5,960.74	
Accounts Receivable	131	2,260.58	
Allowance for Doubtful Accounts	131.1		-0-
Merchandise Inventory	141	-0-	
Store and Office Supplies	151	198.06	
Prepaid Insurance	155	414.00	
Store Equipment	181	6,300.00	
Accum. Depr.—Store Equipment	181.1		-0-
FICA Tax Payable	211		133.22
FUTA Tax Payable	212		54.06
State Unemployment Tax Payable	213		72.08
Employees' Income Tax Payable	214		145.08
Accrued Bank Credit Card Payable	215		-0-
Notes Payable	216		5,700.00
Accrued Interest Payable	217		-0-
Accounts Payable	218		6,297.11
Sales Tax Payable	221		552.14
Cathy Charalambous, Capital	311		13,105.50
Cathy Charalambous, Drawing	312	2,475.00	
Expense and Revenue Summary	331	-0-	-0-
Sales	411		28,258.25
Sales Returns & Allowances	411.1	460.59	
Purchases	511	31,079.65	
Purchases Returns and Allowances	511.1		929.79
Rent Expense	541	1,800.00	
Salaries and Commissions Expense	542	2,954.62	
Store and Office Supplies Expense	543	-0-	
Utilities and Telephone Expense	545	161.40	
Depreciation Expense	547	-0-	
Insurance Expense	548	-0-	
Advertising Expense	551	323.77	
Payroll Taxes Expense	552	253.09	
Bank Credit Card Expense	553	531.13	
Uncollectible Accounts Expense	554	-0-	
Miscellaneous Expense	572	74.60	
Interest Expense	581	-0-	
		55,247.23	55,247.23

Series B

Problem 9B1   Journal Entries with Adjustments for Office Supplies, Insurance, and Long-Term Assets

The following situations occurred at the Grey Store:

(a)   At the beginning of the current year, the Grey Store purchased office supplies for $2,135 and a two-year liability insurance policy for $1,125.

(b)   At the end of the year, a physical count showed that Grey had $180 of
office supplies on hand. Determine the office supplies used.

(c)   At the end of the year, determine the insurance expense for the year. (See
item No. 1.)

(d)   At the beginning of the current year, Grey purchased store fixtures for
$4,500.

(e)   Assuming that the store fixtures have an estimated useful life of 4 years and
a salvage value of $300, determine the depreciation at the end of the year
using the straight-line method.

Required:
Prepare journal entries for each of the preceding situations.

Problem 9B2   Journal Entries in Five Journals and Calculations for
Making Adjusting Entries

In solving this problem, you are required to journalize the following transactions.

May 1   Edith Gould invested $35,000.00 cash in a retail merchandising enter-
prise known as The Gould Shop.

1   Paid rent, $800.00, Check No. 1.

2   Purchased store equipment on account from the Bayless Company,
$10,200.00, terms, 2/30, n/60. (Use the net-price basis and the general
journal for this transaction.)

7   Purchased merchandise from Spence Company for $2,715.00, terms, 3/
10, n/30. (Use the net-price basis.)

9   Made cash and bank credit card sales totaling $1,000.00, plus tax of
$50.00.

9   Received a notice from the Crusader Bank that $285.65 had been de-
ducted from the Gould Shop account. This amount represented a 4%
discount on the net amount of Visa and MasterCard tickets that had
been deposited by Gould relating to such sales to date.

11   Paid for advertising, $490.00, Check No. 2.

14   Sold merchandise to R.G. Foland on 30 days' credit, $1,050.00, plus
tax of $52.50.

14   Purchased merchandise for cash, $1,120.00, Check No. 3.

16   Purchased store equipment for cash, $6,200.00, Check No. 4.

17   Paid Spence Company for merchandise purchased 10 days ago by issuing Check No. 5 for $2,633.55. (See the transaction of May 7.)

18   Received $520 from a customer, Elinor Coyle, on account.

21   Paid a premium of $1,170.00 for a 2-year insurance policy, dated May
1, on merchandise and equipment, Check No. 6.

21   Sold Patty Towle merchandise on 30 days' credit, $915.00, plus tax of
$45.75.

22   Borrowed $12,000.00 at the Crusader Bank on a 60-day, 11% note.

28 Gerry Virgil, a customer, owes $305.00. The account has been found to be uncollectible and is, therefore, considered worthless. Assume that an allowance for doubtful accounts is maintained.

31 Following is the payroll statement for the monthly pay period:

Total earnings of employees for period..........		$2,265.00
Taxes to be withheld:		
Employees' income tax	$295.05	
FICA tax	169.88	464.93
Net amount payable to employees		$1,800.07
Employer's payroll taxes:		
FICA tax		$ 169.88
Unemployment taxes:		
State (2.7%).............................	$ 61.16	
Federal (0.8%)..........................	18.12	79.28
Total		$ 249.16

Issued Check No. 7 for the net amount of the payroll and entered the employer's payroll taxes.

Required:

1. Journalize the preceding transactions using purchases, sales, cash receipts, cash payments, and general journals.

2. Total and rule the journals as appropriate.

3. Based on the information provided, make the necessary calculations to determine the answers to the following questions:

(a) Refer to the first transaction of May 21. By the end of May, how much of the cost of the insurance policy will have become an expense?

(b) If the store equipment purchased on May 2 is expected to serve for 10 years and to have no salvage value, what will be the amount of depreciation expense for this equipment for each *full* year?

(c) If the store equipment purchased on May 16 is expected to serve for 8 years and, at the end of 8 years, have a salvage value of $450.00, what will be the depreciation expense on this equipment for each *full* year of the 8-year period?

(d) Refer to the transaction of May 2. If Gould did not pay for this equipment within the discount period, what amount of discount would be lost because of this?

(e) Refer to the second transaction of May 9. What must have been the gross amount of bank credit card tickets deposited by The Gould Shop during the first week in May? (Hint: $285.65 is 4% of what amount?)

Problem 9B3   Ten-Column Work Sheet

Rod Herper is in a retail merchandising business operating as The Herper Sales Company. The accounts are kept on the basis of a fiscal year ending on June 30. Merchandise is sold for cash and on account. A retail sales tax of 5% is imposed on sales. All sales on account are payable on or before the 10th of the following month. The firm is subject to FICA tax, FUTA tax, and state unemployment compensation tax.

The trial balance taken on July 31 of the current year is reproduced below.

The Herper Sales Company
Trial Balance
June 30, 19--

Account	Acct. No.	Debit	Credit
Cash	111	24,324.30	
Petty Cash Fund	112	150.00	
Accounts Receivable	131	7,015.66	
Allowance for Doubtful Accounts	131.1		244.50
Merchandise Inventory	141	68,405.10	
Supplies	151	652.05	
Prepaid Insurance	155	1,447.88	
Store Equipment	181	11,910.00	
Accum. Depr.—Store Equipment	181.1		2,977.50
FICA Tax Payable	211		550.78
FUTA Tax Payable	212		149.16
State Unemployment Tax Payable	213		211.80
Employees' Income Tax Payable	214		638.25
Accrued Bank Credit Card Payable	215		-0-
Notes Payable	216		8,250.00
Accrued Interest Payable	217		-0-
Accounts Payable	218		9,170.70
Sales Tax Payable	221		2,100.62
Rod Herper, Capital	311		60,611.64
Rod Herper, Drawing	312	44,602.50	
Expense and Revenue Summary	331	-0-	-0-
Sales	411		500,200.00
Sales Returns and Allowances	411.1	7,677.30	
Purchases	511	323,790.22	
Purchases Returns & Allowances	511.1		3,752.17
Purchases Discount	511.2		6,475.80
Rent Expense	541	13,500.00	
Salaries and Commissions Expense	542	51,365.92	
Supplies Expense	543	-0-	
Telephone Expense	545	679.80	
Depreciation Expense	547	-0-	
Insurance Expense	548	-0-	
Heating & Lighting Expense	549	1,846.80	
Advertising Expense	551	24,990.45	
Payroll Taxes Expense	552	4,587.00	
Bank Credit Card Expense	553	6,033.60	
Uncollectible Accounts Expense	554	-0-	
Miscellaneous Expense	572	1,821.90	
Interest Expense	581	532.44	
		595,332.92	595,332.92

Required:

As accountant for Herper, complete a ten-column work sheet, proceeding as follows:

1. Enter the trial balance in the Trial Balance columns.
2. Make the necessary entries in the Adjustments columns for the following items:

    (a)   Transfer of beginning inventory to Expense and Revenue Summary.

    (b)   Merchandise inventory at the end of the year, $75,376.00.

    (c)   Interest accrued on notes payable, $106.20.

    (d)   Accrued bank credit card payable, $460.80.

    (e)   Prepaid insurance unexpired, $1,035.00.

    (f)   Supplies on hand, $126.00.

    (g)   Depreciation: Store equipment, 10% a year.

    (h)   Uncollectible accounts expense.

           (Increase allowance for doubtful accounts an additional $522.00 to provide for estimated loss.)

3. Extend the account balances to the Adjusted Trial Balance columns and extend the adjusted balance of each account to the proper column.

4. Total all of the amount columns. Determine the net income or the net loss for the year and enter it in the proper columns. Enter the totals and complete the ruling.

Problem 9B4   Ten-Column Work Sheet

On October 1, Burt Kloth started a clothes shop in a neighborhood shopping center. He calls his store "Burt's." On that same day various pieces of store equipment were delivered and installed, and an insurance policy was purchased. Burt has sales for cash and on account. All sales are subject to a 5% retail sales tax.

A trial balance of the general ledger of "Burt's" is given below.

Required:

Prepare a ten-column work sheet for the 3 months ended December 31, taking the following factors into account:

    (a)   A physical inventory was taken at the close of business, December 31. The cost of goods found to be on hand was $38,495.70.

           (Note: Since this is the end of the first period's operation, there is no beginning inventory.)

    (b)   An inventory of store and office supplies was taken on December 31. The cost of such items remaining on hand was $101.78.

    (c)   The store equipment is expected to serve for 10 years. (Kloth follows the policy of writing off a full year's depreciation on store equipment assets acquired and held for 3 months or more and charging no depreciation on such assets acquired and held for less than 3 months or on such assets disposed of during the year.)

    (d)   Kloth estimates that uncollectible accounts expense on sales on account made during the period will be approximately $262.50.

    (e)   The insurance premium paid on October 1 was for a 1-year policy. (One-fourth has therefore expired.)

    (f)   The note payable of $8,550.00 has accrued interest expense of $71.25.

    (g)   Accrued bank credit card payable, $233.40.

Burt's
Trial Balance
December 31, 19--

Account	Acct. No.	Debit	Credit
Cash	111	8,941.11	
Accounts Receivable	131	3,390.87	
Allowance for Doubtful Accounts	131.1		-0-
Merchandise Inventory	141	-0-	
Store and Office Supplies	151	297.09	
Prepaid Insurance	155	621.00	
Store Equipment	181	9,450.00	
Accum. Depr.—Store Equipment	181.1		-0-
FICA Tax Payable	211		199.83
FUTA Tax Payable	212		81.09
State Unemployment Tax Payable	213		108.12
Employees' Income Tax Payable	214		217.62
Accrued Bank Credit Card Payable	215		-0-
Notes Payable	216		8,550.00
Accrued Interest Payable	217		-0-
Accounts Payable	218		9,445.66
Sales Tax Payable	221		828.21
Burt Kloth, Capital	311		19,658.25
Burt Kloth, Drawing	312	3,712.50	
Expense and Revenue Summary	331	-0-	-0-
Sales	411		42,387.38
Sales Returns & Allowances	411.1	690.88	
Purchases	511	46,619.48	
Purchases Returns and Allowances	511.1		1,394.68
Rent Expense	541	2,700.00	
Salaries and Commissions Expense	542	4,430.93	
Store and Office Supplies Expense	543	-0-	
Utilities and Telephone Expense	545	242.10	
Depreciation Expense	547	-0-	
Insurance Expense	548	-0-	
Advertising Expense	551	486.65	
Payroll Taxes Expense	552	379.64	
Bank Credit Card Expense	553	796.69	
Uncollectible Accounts Expense	554	-0-	
Miscellaneous Expense	572	111.90	
Interest Expense	581	-0-	
		82,870.84	82,870.84

Mastery Problem

If the working papers for this textbook are not used, omit the Mastery Problem.

Ted Wright owns and operates "The Wright Stuff Stove Store." In addition to selling wood burning stoves and fireplace inserts, Wright dons his top hat and coat and performs as a chimney sweep. Listed below are selected transactions for the month of December 19-D.

Dec. **1**   Wright invested an additional $5,300 in the business.

1   Borrowed $12,000 from the bank, promising to repay the loan on March 1, 19-E plus $270 interest.

3   Paid rent on store, $525, Check No. 501.

5   Purchased merchandise on account from Abraham's Wood Stoves for $23,000, terms, 2/10, n/30. Invoice No. 121. (Wright uses the net-price method of entering purchases of merchandise on account.)

7   Purchased merchandise on account from Cramer Stoves for $18,000, terms, 3/10, n/30. Invoice No. 122.

9   Sold a wood burning stove on account to Lee Root for $1,800 plus $90 sales tax, Sale No. 15a.

10   Received $2,200 from a customer, Julie Rimmer, on account.

11   Made cash purchases from Black Hills Stoves, $22,300. Issued Check No. 502.

12   Wright cleaned several chimneys and received cash of $903.

13   The $185 owed by a customer, Freda Mooey, has been classified as uncollectible. Wright uses the allowance method of accounting for bad debts.

14   Wright received a credit memo for defective merchandise that was returned to Black Hills Stoves, $1,275.

15   Paid for the merchandise purchased on account from Abraham's Wood Stoves on December 5. Issued Check No. 503.

16   Made cash and credit card sales amounting to $53,200, plus sales tax $2,660.

17   Paid the payroll based on the following information. Issued Check No. 504.

Total earnings of employees for period		$9,250
Taxes to be withheld:		
Employees' Federal Income Tax	1,388	
Employees' State Income Tax	185	
FICA Tax	694	2,267
Net amount payable to employees		6,983
Employer's payroll taxes:		
FICA tax		$694
Unemployment taxes: (All employees have earned		
more than $7,000.)		0
		$694

20   Paid $3,600 for a three-year fire insurance policy that covers merchandise and store equipment beginning January 1, 19-D. Issued Check No. 505.

23   Wright issued a credit memo to Phil Delay for merchandise returned, $1,510 including 5% sales tax. Wright maintains a separate sales tax payable account.

28   Paid for merchandise purchased on account from Cramer Stoves. Issued Check No. 506.

29   Sold merchandise on account to Jill Hill, $2,300, plus sales tax of $115, Sale No. 12c.

Additional Information:

(a-b) Merchandise inventory on December 31, 19-D is $53,255.

(c) Sales on account for the year were $468,500. Bad debts are expected to amount to 2% of all credit sales.

(d) An end-of-year inventory of the office supplies on hand indicates that supplies costing $420 remain.

(e) On January 1, 19-B, a $3,300 premium was paid for a three-year fire insurance policy. Prepaid Insurance was debited at that time.

(f) Store equipment costing $45,800 with a salvage value of $5,800 was acquired at the beginning of 19-A. The estimated useful life of the equipment is 20 years. Wright uses straight-line depreciation.

(g) Bank credit card sales made during the last few days in December and deposited on December 29 amounted to $4,800. The bank will deduct 4% of this amount as a collection fee.

(h) Interest of $90 has accrued on the note signed December 1.

Required:

1. Enter the December transactions in the appropriate special or general journals.
2. Total and rule the journals, as appropriate.
3. The Trial Balance columns of a ten-column work sheet for The Wright Stuff Stove Store have been provided in the working papers. Complete the work sheet.
4. Compute the cost of goods sold for The Wright Stuff Stove Store.

CHAPTER 10

Accounting for a Small Retail Business II

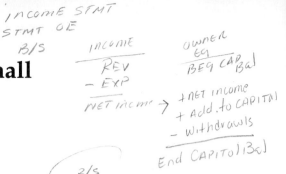

Chapter Objectives

Careful study of this chapter should enable you to:

- Prepare financial statements for a retail merchandising business with the aid of a ten-column work sheet.

- Analyze a company's financial performance and condition for a single period and between periods using the following measures:

  1. Income statement components in comparative form.
  2. Balance sheet components in comparative form.
  3. Current ratio.
  4. Quick ratio.
  5. Working capital.
  6. Return on owner's equity.
  7. Accounts receivable turnover.
  8. Inventory turnover.

- Journalize and post adjusting entries.

- Journalize and post closing entries.

- Prepare a post-closing trial balance.

- Describe, explain the purpose of, journalize, and post reversing entries.

The purpose of this chapter is to complete the illustration of accounting for the operations of a small retail business that was begun in Chapter 9. The ten-column work sheet is used to facilitate preparing the income statement, statement of owner's equity, and balance sheet. Various techniques that can be used in analyzing the financial statements are then described and illustrated. Finally, end-of-period activities in the accounting cycle that involve adjusting and closing entries, preparation of the post-closing trial balance, and reversing entries are illustrated.

The adjusting and closing entries prepare the ledger for the new accounting period. These entries transfer the results of current operations from the revenue, expense, and drawing accounts to the permanent owner's equity account. The post-closing trial balance serves as an end-of-period accuracy check, and the reversing entries simplify the accounting process in the following accounting period.

The Financial Statements

The financial statements of a small retail business usually include (1) an income statement, (2) a statement of owner's equity, and (3) a balance sheet. In larger enterprises, a fourth statement, called a statement of cash flows, is normally prepared. Only the first three statements are discussed in this chapter.

The purpose of an income statement is to summarize the results of operations during an accounting period. The income statement provides information as to the sources of revenue, types of expenses, and the amount of the net income or net loss for the period. The statement of owner's equity summarizes all changes in the owner's equity during the period, including the net income or loss, and additional investments or withdrawals of assets by the owner. The purpose of a balance sheet is to provide information as to the status of a business at a specified date. The balance sheet shows the types and amounts of assets and liabilities, and the owner's equity in the business at a specified point in time—usually at the close of business on the last day of the accounting period.

The Income Statement

Prepare an income statement for a retail merchandising business.

Purpose of Income Statement →

A formal statement of the results of the operation of a business during an accounting period is called an income statement. Other titles commonly used for this statement include statement of earnings, operating statement, and profit and loss statement. The purpose of this statement is to show the types and amounts of revenue and expenses that occurred during the accounting period, and the resulting net income or net loss for this period.

Importance of the Income Statement. The income statement is generally considered to be the most important financial statement of a business. It is essentially a "report card" of the enterprise which provides a basis for judging the overall effectiveness of the management. Decisions as to whether to continue a business, to expand it, or to reduce it are often based upon the results reported in the income statement. Actual and potential creditors are interested in income statements to determine if a business is profitable. Based on this information, creditors can decide to extend credit or grant loans.

Various government agencies are also interested in income statements of businesses for a variety of reasons. Regulatory bodies are concerned with the earnings of the enterprises they regulate, such as airlines, banks, insurance companies, public utilities, and railroads, because a part of the regulation usually relates to the prices, rates, or fares that may be charged. If the enterprise is either exceptionally profitable or unprofitable, a change in the allowed prices or rates may be needed. Income tax authorities have an interest in business income statements. The determination of taxable income differs somewhat from the calculation of net income for financial reporting purposes, but for a variety of reasons, the tax authorities are interested in both sets of calculations.

Form of the Income Statement. The proper heading of the income statement consists of three lines. The name of the business (or of the individual if it is a professional practice or is named for the owner) should be shown first. The name of the statement is then shown followed by the period of time that the statement covers, for example, "For the Year Ended December 31, 19--."

The body of the income statement depends, in part, upon the type of business. Two types of income statement forms commonly used are the single step and the multiple step. The **single-step form** of income statement lists all revenue items and their total first, followed by all expense items and their total. The difference, which is either net income or net loss, is then calculated.

The **multiple-step form** of income statement is commonly used for merchandising businesses. The term "multiple-step" is used because the final net income is calculated on a step-by-step basis. Gross sales is shown first less sales returns and allowances. This difference is called **net sales**. (Many published income statements begin with the amount of net sales.) Cost of goods sold is next subtracted to arrive at **gross margin** (sometimes called **gross profit**). Operating expenses are listed next, and the total of their amounts is subtracted from the gross margin to arrive at the amount of **operating income**. Finally, the amounts of any other revenue are added and any other expenses are subtracted to arrive at the final amount of net income (or net loss).

The multiple-step income statement for Northern Micro for the year ended December 31, 19-B, is shown on the next page. The information needed in preparing the statement was obtained from the work sheet shown on pages 364-365 of Chapter 9. Note that the operating expenses are arranged in descending size order (except for Miscellaneous Expense). This order is a fairly common alternative to the work sheet order used in Chapter 4.

The Statement of Owner's Equity

Prepare a statement of owner's equity for a retail merchandising business.

A formal statement of the changes in owner's equity during an accounting period is called a **statement of owner's equity**. The purpose of the statement is to show in summary form the factors that caused the owner's equity to change during the period. These changes result in the end-of-period balance shown on this statement and the balance sheet.

Importance of the statement of owner's equity. The statement of owner's equity is probably the least important financial statement for a small business because much of the information it contains can be found in other financial statements. The components of the statement of owner's equity are: (1) the owner's equity at the beginning of the period, (2) the net income or loss for the period, (3) the additional investments for the period, (4) the withdrawals for the period, and (5) the owner's equity at the end of the period. The beginning and ending owner's equity balances can be obtained from the prior and current period balance

Northern Micro
Income Statement
For the Year Ended December 31, 19-B

Operating revenue:			
Sales			$890,744.19
Less sales returns and allowances			13,401.85
Net sales			$877,342.34
Cost of goods sold:			
Merchandise inventory, January 1		$ 97,083.80	
Purchases	$603,166.27		
Less purchases returns and allowances	8,553.70		
Net purchases		594,612.57	
Merchandise available for sale		$691,696.37	
Less merchandise inventory, December 31		102,695.20	
Cost of goods sold			589,001.17
Gross margin on sales			$288,341.17
Operating expenses:			
Salaries and commissions expense		$ 87,651.04	
Advertising expense		39,233.69	
Bank credit card expense		24,598.10	
Rent expense		24,000.00	
Payroll taxes expense		8,079.04	
Heating and lighting expense		5,515.36	
Uncollectible accounts expense		3,012.63	
Depreciation expense		2,354.81	
Telephone expense		1,546.72	
Insurance expense		1,530.15	
Charitable contributions expense		1,270.00	
Supplies expense		1,220.80	
Purchases discounts lost		82.36	
Miscellaneous expense		1,966.14	
Total operating expenses			202,060.84
Operating income			$ 86,280.33
Other expenses:			
Interest expense			903.03
Net income			$ 85,377.30

Northern Micro—Income Statement

sheets. The net income or loss appears in the current period income statement. Only the additional investments and withdrawals during the period cannot be found in the other financial statements. Thus, the main contributions of the statement of owner's equity are: (1) to disclose additional investments and withdrawals during the period, and (2) to present all factors causing the change in owner's equity in an organized, single statement.

▦ **Sources of information for the statement of owner's equity.** To prepare the statement of owner's equity for Northern Micro, two sources of information are needed: (1) the work sheet illustrated in Chapter 9, and (2) Gary Fishel's capital account (No. 311) in the general ledger. The work sheet shows net income of $85,377.30 and withdrawals of $88,050.00 during the year. The balance in Gary Fishel's capital account in the general ledger (not illustrated here) at the beginning of the year was $146,030.53. An additional $10,000 was invested in the business in February of the current year.

▦ **Form of the statement of owner's equity.** The proper heading of the statement of owner's equity consists of three lines: (1) the name of the business, (2) the name of the statement, and (3) the period of time that the statement covers.

The statement of owner's equity for Northern Micro for the year ended December 31, 19-B is shown below. Note that the body of the statement consists of the five components identified on page 398.

Northern Micro
Statement of Owner's Equity
For the Year Ended December 31, 19-B

Gary L. Fishel, capital, January 1, 19-B		$146,030.53
Net income for the year	$ 85,377.30	
Add: Additional investments	10,000.00	
Deduct: Withdrawals	(88,050.00)	
Increase in owner's equity		7,327.30
Gary L. Fishel, capital, December 31, 19-B		$153,357.83

Northern Micro—Statement of Owner's Equity

The Balance Sheet

Prepare a balance sheet for a retail merchandising business.

A formal statement of the assets, liabilities, and owner's equity of a business at a specified date is known as a **balance sheet**. The term "balance sheet" is derived from the equality of the elements, that is, the sum of the assets equals the sum of the liabilities plus owner's equity. Sometimes the balance sheet is called a **statement of financial position**, a **statement of condition**, or a **statement of assets and liabilities**. Many accountants believe that the title "statement of financial position" describes more appropriately the items on the balance sheet. Occasionally, other titles are used.

▦ **Importance of the Balance Sheet.** Various people are interested in the information provided in a balance sheet. The owner or owners of a business use the balance sheet to determine the types and amounts of assets and liabilities. These owners are also interested in determining the amount of the owner's equity. Creditors and potential creditors of the business use the balance sheet to determine the financial position of an enterprise. With this information they can determine if assets are available for prompt payment of debts. They can also decide whether to extend credit or to grant loans to a business. Persons considering buying an ownership interest in a business use the balance sheet to determine the character and amount of the assets and liabilities of the business. These people are also concerned with the future earnings possibilities of the business. Finally, various regulatory bodies use balance sheets to determine the financial position of businesses that are under their jurisdiction. With this information regulators can evaluate existing regulations.

Form of the Balance Sheet. The proper heading of the balance sheet consists of three lines: (1) the name of the business, (2) the name of the statement, and (3) the month, day, and year. Remember that the balance sheet relates to a particular moment of time, whereas the income statement and statement of owner's equity relate to a particular period of time.

Traditionally, balance sheets have been presented either in account form or in report form. Each of these forms was discussed briefly in Chapter 4. In the account form, the assets are listed on the left side of the page and the liabilities and owner's equity are listed on the right. This form is similar to the debit-side and credit-side arrangement of the standard ledger account. The balance sheet of John Wendt, Attorney, as of June 30, 19-- is illustrated in account form on page 55 of Chapter 2. The data for the preparation of the statement were taken from the work sheet.

more common → The report form of the balance sheet lists the assets, liabilities, and owner's equity elements in consecutive order on a page. The balance sheet of Northern Micro as of December 31, 19-B in report form is illustrated on page 402. The data for the preparation of this statement were taken from the work sheet.

Classification of Data in the Balance Sheet. The purpose of the balance sheet and all other financial statements is to convey as much information as possible. Proper classification of data helps to accomplish this purpose. On the balance sheet, assets and liabilities are classified into current and non-current (long-term) categories.

Current Assets. **Current assets** include cash and all other assets that may reasonably be expected to be converted into cash or consumed within one year or the normal operating cycle of the business, whichever is longer. In a merchandising business, the current assets usually include cash, receivables (such as accounts receivable), merchandise inventory, and temporary investments. Since prepaid expenses, such as unused supplies and unexpired insurance, are likely to be consumed within a year, they also are reported as current assets.

Northern Micro
Balance Sheet
December 31, 19-B
Assets

Current assets:

Cash		$ 58,510.55
Accounts receivable	$35,613.74	
Less allowance for doubtful accounts	3,602.63	32,011.11
Merchandise inventory		102,695.20
Supplies		800.00
Prepaid insurance		1,530.14
Total current assets		$195,547.00

Property, plant, and equipment:

Store equipment	$23,548.10	
Less accumulated depreciation	7,848.45	
Total property, plant, and equipment		15,699.65
Total assets		$211,246.65

Liabilities

Current liabilities:

FICA tax payable	$ 1,194.52	
FUTA tax payable	35.68	
State unemployment tax payable	152.86	
Employees income tax payable	1,433.40	
Accrued bank credit card payable	92.99	
Notes payable	34,000.00	
Accrued interest payable	283.33	
Accounts payable	15,866.21	
Sales tax payable	4,829.83	
Total current liabilities		$ 57,888.82

Owner's Equity

Gary L. Fishel, capital:		153,357.83
Total liabilities and owner's equity		$211,246.65

Northern Micro—Balance Sheet

The asset, cash, may be represented by one or more accounts. These accounts can include bank checking accounts, bank savings accounts, or a petty cash fund. In the Northern Micro balance sheet above, cash is listed at $58,510.55. This amount is made up of two items as shown in the work sheet on pages 364-365: the balance in the checking account at the Third National Bank, $58,260.55, and the amount of the petty cash fund, $250.

Temporary investments are those assets that have been acquired with money that would otherwise have been temporarily idle and unproductive. Such investments usually include corporate stocks, bonds, notes, or any of several types of government bonds, notes, or bills. Quite often, businesses invest in securities that can be liquidated in a short time with little chance of loss. The account entitled **Marketable Securities** is frequently used to describe temporary investments.

Investments may be owned by a business for many years. Under such circumstances, they would be classified as long-term investments and included in a separate asset classification entitled **Investments**. The intention of the business determines whether the investments are to be classified as current or long-term. Presently, Northern Micro has no investments, but Fishel might be well advised to invest a portion of the large cash balance in high-yield short-term securities.

Property, Plant, and Equipment.   Assets that are used in the operation of a business, such as land, buildings, office equipment, store equipment, and delivery equipment are called **property, plant, and equipment.** Of these assets, only land is permanent; however, all of these assets have a useful life that is comparatively long.

The balance sheet of Northern Micro shows that store equipment is the only property, plant, and equipment asset. The amount of the accumulated depreciation is shown as a deduction from the cost of the equipment. The difference represents the **undepreciated cost** of the equipment. This amount less any salvage value will be written off as depreciation expense in future periods.

Current Liabilities. Current liabilities include those obligations that are due within one year or the normal operating cycle of the business, whichever is longer, and will be paid with money provided by the current assets. As of December 31, the current liabilities of Northern Micro consist of FICA tax payable, FUTA tax payable, state unemployment tax payable, employees income tax payable, accrued bank credit card payable, notes payable, accrued interest payable, accounts payable, and sales tax payable.

Long-Term Liabilities. Long-term liabilities include those obligations that will extend beyond one year or the normal operating cycle, whichever is longer. The most common long-term liability is a mortgage payable.

Mortgage Payable is an account that is used to reflect a debt or an obligation that is secured by a mortgage on certain property. A **mortgage** is a written agreement specifying that if the borrower does not repay a debt, the lender has the right to take over the property to satisfy the debt. When the debt is paid, the mortgage becomes void. A mortgage payable is similar to an account payable or a note payable except that the creditor holds the mortgage as security for the payment of the debt. Usually, debts secured by mortgages run for a longer period of time than ordinary notes payable or accounts payable. A mortgage payable is classified as a long-term liability if the maturity date extends beyond one year or the normal operating cycle of the business. Northern Micro has no long-term liabilities.

Owner's Equity. Accounts relating to owner's equity may be either permanent or temporary. The permanent owner's equity accounts are determined by the type of organization, that is, whether the enterprise is organized as a sole proprietorship, as a partnership, or as a corporation.

In a sole proprietorship, one or more accounts representing the owner's equity may be kept. Northern Micro uses three owner's equity accounts, as follows:

> Gary L. Fishel, Capital—Account No. 311
> Gary L. Fishel, Drawing—Account No. 312
> Expense and Revenue Summary—Account No. 331

Only the capital account is a permanent owner's equity account. The drawing account is debited for any withdrawals during the year, and is closed to the capital account at the end of the year. The expense and revenue summary account is used only at the close of the year to adjust the merchandise inventory account and to close the revenue and expense accounts. The expense and revenue summary account is then closed to the capital account. Thus, the only owner's equity account that appears in Northern Micro's balance sheet is Gary L. Fishel, Capital.

Analysis of Financial Statements

Analyze a company's financial performance and condition.

Many procedures can be used to interpret financial statements. These procedures help evaluate the financial performance and condition of a business. In this section, selected procedures are presented that focus on the different financial statement items.

Analyze financial performance using income statement components in comparative form.

Income Statement Analysis. One approach to analyzing the income statement is to prepare in comparative form the statement for two or more periods of comparable length. In the comparative income statement the figures for the two periods are shown in adjacent columns. A third column is used to show the amount of increase or decrease in each element. Significant changes in the financial performance of the business can be easily seen in the third column.

The condensed comparative income statement for Northern Micro is on the next page. This statement includes the current year results from page 399 and the prior year results which were not previously illustrated.

This comparative statement reveals that Northern Micro's operating income and net income decreased in 19-B. This decrease occurred because the cost of goods sold increased almost as much as the net sales and there was very little additional gross margin to cover the increased operating expenses.

Another approach to analyzing the income statement involves expressing all or at least the major items on the statement as a percent of net sales. These percentages are then compared for two or more periods. The condensed comparative income statement for Northern Micro in which each item is presented both in dollars and as a percent of net sales is shown at the bottom of page 405.

Northern Micro
Comparative Income Statement
For the Years Ended December 31, 19-B and 19-A

	19-B	19-A	Increase (Decrease)
Net sales	$877,342.34	$832,380.70	$ 44,961.64
Less cost of goods sold	589,001.17	545,107.38	43,893.79
Gross margin on sales	$288,341.17	$287,273.32	$ 1,067.85
Operating expenses	202,060.84	190,726.41	11,334.43
Operating income	$ 86,280.33	$ 96,546.91	$(10,266.58)
Interest expense	903.03	920.15	(17.12)
Net income	$ 85,377.30	$ 95,626.76	$(10,249.46)

Northern Micro—Comparative Income Statement

Comparison of the percentages for 19-B and 19-A reveals that cost of goods sold as a percent of net sales has increased from 65.49% to 67.13%, causing a decrease in the gross margin percentage from 34.51% to 32.87%. Although this decrease appears small, bear in mind that just 1% of Northern Micro's net sales is $8,773.42 (1% × $877,342.34 = $8,773.42). In fact, it is the decrease in the gross margin percentage that is primarily responsible for the decrease in Northern Micro's net income from 19-A to 19-B, even though sales increased by $44,961.64, as shown above. More information on Northern Micro's financial performance could be gained by comparing these percentages with income statement data for retail computer businesses of about the same size with respect to assets and net sales. Such data are available from the U.S. Department of Commerce.

Northern Micro
Comparative Income Statement
For the Years Ended December 31, 19-B and 19-A

	19-B		19-A	
Net sales	$877,342.34	100.00%	$832,380.70	100.00%
Less cost of goods sold	589,001.17	67.13	545,107.38	65.49
Gross margin on sales	$288,341.17	32.87	$287,273.32	34.51
Operating expenses	202,060.84	23.03	190,726.41	22.91
Operating income	$ 86,280.33	9.84	$ 96,546.91	11.60
Interest expense	903.03	0.10	920.15	0.11
Net income	$ 85,377.30	9.74	$ 95,626.76	11.49%

Northern Micro—Comparative Income Statement

Analyze financial
condition using
balance sheet
components in
comparative form.

Balance Sheet Analysis. Balance sheets can be prepared in comparative form for two or more dates. The amounts at the different dates are listed in parallel columns, similar to the way the comparative income statement was presented on page 405. If balance sheets as of the close of two consecutive calendar years are compared, it is possible to determine the amount of the increase or decrease during the intervening period in any of the accounts or groups of accounts involved. If the comparison reveals a large increase or decrease in key accounts, further investigation might be warranted.

Too much emphasis should not be placed upon an increase or decrease in cash. Some individuals are inclined to judge the results of operations largely by the cash balance. This practice may be misleading. The net results of operations can be properly determined only by the comparison of all assets and liabilities.

Another approach to analyzing the balance sheet is to express each asset item as a percent of total assets and each liability and owner's equity item as a percent of total liabilities and owner's equity. These percentages can be compared for two or more periods, similar to the way the comparative income statement was presented on page 405. In this way, important changes can be readily identified.

Analyze financial
condition using the
current ratio.

The ability of a business to meet its current obligations may be evaluated by an analysis of its current assets and current liabilities. In a merchandising enterprise in which the capital invested is a major revenue-producing factor, the current ratio, which is the ratio of the current assets to the current liabilities, may be important.

$$\text{Current ratio} = \frac{\text{Current assets}}{\text{Current liabilities}}$$

The balance sheet on page 402 shows total current assets of $195,547.00 and total current liabilities of $57,888.82, a ratio of 3.38 to 1 ($195,547.00 / $57,888.82). This ratio is quite high, which indicates a very favorable financial position. The rough "rule of thumb" traditionally has been that a current ratio should be about 2 to 1, but many businesses operate successfully on a minimum current ratio of 1.5 to 1.

Banks often consider the ratio of current assets to current liabilities when evaluating a loan application, since it is not expected that the property, plant and equipment assets will be sold to obtain sufficient funds with which to pay a short-term loan. If the balance sheet seems to indicate that a sufficient amount of cash will not be realized from the collection of accounts receivable or from the sales of merchandise or services to repay a loan at maturity, the bank may not approve the loan.

Analyze financial
condition using the
quick ratio.

Other measures sometimes used in analyzing a firm's ability to meet its current obligations are the quick ratio and the amount of working capital. **Quick assets** include cash and all other current assets that are readily realizable in cash, such as accounts receivable, and temporary investments in the form of marketable securities and short-term certificates of

Working = current assets − current Liab
greater 195,000 − 57,800
= working capital

deposit. The ratio of quick assets to current liabilities is called the quick ratio.

more likely cash
turn" CASH / A/R & n/R then ↑ current ratio

$$\text{Quick ratio} = \frac{\text{Quick assets}}{\text{Current liabilities}}$$

> 1 greater

Balance

The balance sheet on page 402 shows total quick assets of $90,521.66, which means that the quick ratio is 1.56 to 1 ($90,521.66 / $57,888.02). This indicates that quick assets are more than adequate to meet current obligations. The rough "rule of thumb" traditionally has been that a quick ratio should be about 1 to 1, but many businesses operate successfully on a minimum quick ratio of 0.6 to 1.

Analyze financial condition using working capital.

Balance

The amount of current assets minus the amount of current liabilities is called working capital.

$$\text{Working capital} = \text{Current assets} - \text{Current liabilities}$$

greater > 0

Working capital indicates the funds available for current business operations. Northern Micro's working capital at year end amounts to $137,658.18 ($195,547.00 − $57,888.82), which is nearly 90% ($137,658.18 / $153,357.83) of owner's equity. This represents a very favorable working capital position.

It is difficult to estimate what the proper current ratio, quick ratio, or amount of working capital should be, because of the variations in enterprises and industries. A 2 to 1 ratio of current assets to current liabilities, while more than sufficient in some enterprises, may be inadequate in others. In the milk distribution business, for example, a 1 to 1 ratio of current assets to current liabilities is considered satisfactory. This ratio is satisfactory because very little capital is tied up in inventory and the amount of accounts receivable is comparatively small. Also, the terms on which the milk is purchased from farmers are such that settlements are slow and comparatively large amounts are due to farmers at all times. Another reason is that a large amount of capital is invested in property, plant and equipment needed for treating the milk and delivering it to customers.

Analyze financial performance using return on owner's equity.

Interstatement Analysis. A comparison of the relationships between certain amounts in the income statement and the balance sheet may be informative. A good example of interstatement analysis is the ratio of net income to owner's equity in the business. This ratio is known as return on owner's equity.

Income

$$\text{Return on owner's equity} = \frac{\text{Net Income}}{\text{Owner's equity}} = \%$$

Beg 156 + END / AVG.

The owner's equity of Northern Micro was $146,030.53 on January 1. The net income for the year of $85,377.30 is 58% ($85,377.30 / $146,030.53) of the owner's equity. A comparison of this ratio with the

·return on owner's equity in prior years should be of interest to the owner. It may also be of interest to compare the return on owner's equity of Northern Micro with the same ratio for other stores of comparable nature and size. It is important to note, however, that the net income of Northern Micro was computed without regard to any salary or other compensation for the services of Fishel. In comparing the results of operations of Northern Micro with those of other retail computer businesses, some appropriate adjustment of the salary and other compensation data might be needed in order to impute the value of Fishel's services and make the comparison valid.

Analyze financial performance using accounts receivable turnover.

A second ratio involving both income statement and balance sheet accounts is the rate of accounts receivable turnover—the number of times the accounts receivable turned over or were collected during the accounting period. The rate of accounts receivable turnover is calculated as follows:

$$\frac{\text{Net credit sales for the period}}{\text{Average accounts receivable (net) of allowance for uncollectible accounts)}}$$

The accounts receivable turnover for Northern Micro for the year ended December 31, 19-B is computed as follows:

Net accounts receivable balance, Jan. 1, 19-B $29,864.53
Net accounts receivable balance, Dec. 31, 19-B 32,011.11
Net credit sales for the year (determined from the
   accounting records) 341,213.79

Average net accounts receivable =

$$\frac{\text{Beginning balance}(\$29,864.53) \ + \ \text{Ending balance}(\$32,011.11)}{2}$$

$$= \$30,937.82$$

$$\text{Rate of turnover} = \frac{\text{Net credit sales for year } (\$341,213.79)}{\text{Average net accounts receivable } (\$30,937.82)}$$

$$= \underline{11.03}$$

The number of days in the year divided by this rate of turnover shows that Northern Micro's credit customers are taking about 33 days to pay for their purchases.

$$365 \text{ days} / 11.03 = \underline{33.1} \text{ days}$$

If Northern Micro allows credit terms of n/30, this means that customers generally are paying on a timely basis.

Analyze financial performance using inventory turnover.

A third ratio involving both income statement and balance sheet accounts is the rate of inventory turnover for each accounting period—the number of times the merchandise inventory turned over or was sold during the accounting period. The rate of inventory turnover is calculated as follows:

$$\frac{\text{Cost of goods sold for the period}}{\text{Average inventory}}$$

If inventory is taken only at the end of each accounting period, the average inventory for the period can be calculated by adding the beginning and ending inventories and dividing their sum by two. The turnover of Northern Micro for the year ended December 31, is computed as follows:

Beginning inventory . . . . $ 97,083.80
Ending inventory 102,695.20
Cost of goods sold for the period 589,001.17

Average inventory =

$$\frac{\text{Beginning inventory (\$97,083.80) + Ending inventory (\$102,695.20)}}{2}$$

$$= \$99,889.50$$

$$\text{Rate of turnover} = \frac{\text{Cost of goods sold for the period (\$589,001.17)}}{\text{Average inventory (\$99,889.50)}}$$

$$= \underline{5.9}$$

The number of days in the year divided by this rate of turnover shows that Northern Micro's inventory turned over about once every two months.

$$365 \text{ days} / 5.9 = \underline{61.9} \text{ days}$$

The higher the rate of turnover, the smaller the margin needs to be on each dollar of sales to produce a satisfactory total dollar amount of gross margin. This is because the increase in numbers of units sold offsets the smaller amount of gross margin earned per unit. Evaluation of Northern Micro's rate of inventory turnover would require comparison with prior years, other companies, or its industry.

Building Your Accounting Knowledge

1. Explain why the income statement is essentially a "report card" of the enterprise.
2. Describe the nature of the two forms of income statement.
3. What are the main contributions of the statement of owner's equity?
4. How did the title "balance sheet" originate? What title do many accountants believe is more appropriate?
5. What is the major difference between the two forms of a balance sheet?

6. Describe two major approaches to analyzing the income statement.
7. Explain why it is difficult to say what is a proper ratio of current assets to current liabilities.
8. Describe the use of the return on owner's equity ratio; the use of the rate of accounts receivable turnover ratio; the use of rate of inventory turnover ratio.

Assignment Box

To reinforce your understanding of the preceding text materials, you may complete the following:

Study Guide: Part A
Textbook: Exercises 10A1 through 10A5 or 10B1 through 10B5
Problems 10A1 through 10A4 or 10B1 through 10B4

The Adjusting, Closing, and Reversing Process

Four steps remain in the illustration of accounting for the operations of Northern Micro: (1) journalizing and posting the adjusting entries, (2) journalizing and posting the closing entries, (3) preparing a post-closing trial balance, and (4) journalizing and posting the reversing entries. The first three steps were illustrated in Chapter 4. They are repeated in this chapter to show how to perform them in a retail merchandising business and to reinforce the earlier presentation in a more complex setting. The fourth step is a new and final step in the accounting cycle that is useful in accrual accounting.

Adjusting Entries

Journalize and post adjusting entries.

Entries required at the end of an accounting period to bring certain account balances up to date are known as adjusting entries. In preparing the work sheet for Northern Micro (reproduced on pages 364-365), adjustments were made to accomplish the following purposes:

1. To transfer the amount of the beginning-of-year merchandise inventory to the expense and revenue summary account
2. To enter the amount of the end-of-year merchandise inventory
3. To enter the amount of interest accrued on notes payable
4. To enter the amount of accrued bank credit card payable
5. To enter the cost of supplies used during the year
6. To enter the amount of insurance premium expired during the year
7. To enter the estimated amount of uncollectible accounts expense resulting from the credit sales made during the year
8. To enter the estimated amount of depreciation expense for the year

The effect of these adjustments was reflected in the financial statements reproduced on pages 399-402. However, the adjustments made on the work sheet have not been reflected in the general ledger accounts. To bring the ledger into agreement with the financial statements, the adjustments must be journalized and posted to the proper accounts.

Journalizing the Adjusting Entries. Adjusting entries are made in a general journal. The following is a portion of a general journal showing the adjusting entries of Northern Micro. Since the heading "Adjusting Entries" explains the nature of the entries, a separate explanation of each adjusting entry is unnecessary. The information needed in journalizing the adjustments was obtained from the Adjustments columns of the work sheet reproduced on pages 364-365.

JOURNAL   PAGE 28

	DATE		DESCRIPTION	POST. REF.	DEBIT	CREDIT	
1			*Adjusting Entries*				1
2	19-- Dec.	31	Expense and Revenue Summary	331	97 0 8 3 80		2
3	(A)		Merchandise Inventory	141		97 0 8 3 80	3
4		31	Merchandise Inventory	141	102 6 9 5 20		4
5	(B)		Expense and Revenue Summary	331		102 6 9 5 20	5
6		31	Interest Expense	581	2 8 3 33		6
7			Accrued Interest Payable	217		2 8 3 33	7
8		31	Bank Credit Card Expense	553	9 2 99		8
9			Accrued Bank Credit Card Payable	215		9 2 99	9
10		31	Supplies Expense	543	1 2 2 0 80		10
11			Supplies	151		1 2 2 0 80	11
12		31	Insurance Expense	548	1 5 3 0 15		12
13			Prepaid Insurance	155		1 5 3 0 15	13
14		31	Uncollectible Accounts Expense	554	3 0 1 2 63		14
15			Allowance for Doubtful Accounts	131.1		3 0 1 2 63	15
16		31	Depreciation Expense	547	2 3 5 4 81		16
17			Accumulated Depr.-Store Equip.	181.1		2 3 5 4 81	17

Northern Micro—Adjusting Entries

Posting the Adjusting Entries. The adjusting entries are posted individually to the proper ledger accounts. The accounts of Northern Micro that were affected by the first three adjusting entries are reproduced on page 412. The posting of the other adjusting entries was handled in the same manner, so the additional accounts are not reproduced here. The number of the general journal page on which the adjusting entries appear was entered in the Posting Reference column of the general ledger accounts, and the account numbers were entered in the Posting Reference column of the general journal as the posting was completed. This provided a cross-reference between the books.

ACCOUNT **Merchandise Inventory**   ACCOUNT NO. **141**

DATE		ITEM	POST. REF.	DEBIT	CREDIT	BALANCE DEBIT	BALANCE CREDIT
19-- Dec.	1	Balance	√			97 0 8 3 80	
	31		J28		97 0 8 3 80	- 0 -	- 0 -
	31		J28	102 6 9 5 20		102 6 9 5 20	

ACCOUNT **Accrued Interest Payable**   ACCOUNT NO. **217**

DATE		ITEM	POST. REF.	DEBIT	CREDIT	BALANCE DEBIT	BALANCE CREDIT
19-- Dec.	31		J28		2 8 3 33		2 8 3 33

ACCOUNT **Expense and Revenue Summary**   ACCOUNT NO. **331**

DATE		ITEM	POST. REF.	DEBIT	CREDIT	BALANCE DEBIT	BALANCE CREDIT
19-- Dec.	31		J28	97 0 8 3 80		97 0 8 3 80	
	31		J28		102 6 9 5 20		5 6 1 1 40

ACCOUNT **Interest Expense**   ACCOUNT NO. **581**

DATE		ITEM	POST. REF.	DEBIT	CREDIT	BALANCE DEBIT	BALANCE CREDIT
19-- Dec.	1	Balance	√			6 1 9 70	
	31		J28	2 8 3 33		9 0 3 03	

Northern Micro—Selected General Ledger Accounts After Posting Adjusting Entries

Closing Entries

Journalize and post closing entries.

Temporary accounts are used to accumulate the amounts of revenues, expenses, and withdrawals for each period. After the adjusting entries have been posted, all of the temporary owner's equity accounts should be closed. Closing entries are entries used at the end of each period to accomplish two purposes. First, the balances of the temporary owner's equity accounts are transferred to the permanent owner's equity account. Second, the balances in the temporary accounts are reduced to zero so that a new accumulation process can begin for the next period.

The closing process consists of the same four procedures that were described in Chapter 4.

1. All income statement accounts with credit balances are debited, with an offsetting credit to Expense and Revenue Summary.
2. All income statement accounts with debit balances are credited, with an offsetting debit to Expense and Revenue Summary.

3. The resulting balance in the Expense and Revenue Summary, which is the net income or loss for the period, is transferred to the permanent owner's equity account.
4. The balance in the owner's drawing account is transferred to the permanent owner's equity account.

The following flow chart illustrates these four procedures and the accounts involved for Northern Micro.

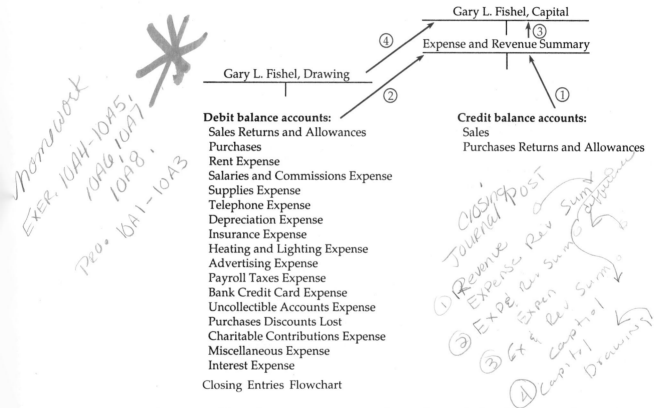

Closing Entries Flowchart

After the temporary owner's equity and drawing accounts are transferred to the permanent owner's equity account, only the asset, liability, and permanent owner's equity accounts will have balances. The sum of the balances of the asset accounts (less balances of any contra accounts) will be equal to the sum of the balances of the liability accounts plus the balance of the permanent owner's equity account. The accounts will agree exactly with what is shown in the balance sheet as of the close of the period.

Journalizing the Closing Entries. Closing entries, like adjusting entries, are entered in a general journal. A portion of a general journal showing the closing entries for Northern Micro is shown on page 414. Since the heading "Closing Entries" explains the nature of the entries, a

JOURNAL

PAGE 29

	DATE		DESCRIPTION	POST. REF.	DEBIT	CREDIT	
1			*Closing Entries*				1
2	19-- Dec.	31	Sales	411	890 7 4 4 19		2
3			Purchases Returns and Allowances	511.1	8 5 5 3 70		3
4			Expense and Revenue Summary	331		899 2 9 7 89	4
5		31	Expense and Revenue Summary	331	819 5 3 1 99		5
6			Sales Returns and Allowances	411.1		13 4 0 1 85	6
7			Purchases	511		603 1 6 6 27	7
8			Rent Expense	541		24 0 0 0 00	8
9			Salaries and Commissions Expense	542		87 6 5 1 04	9
10			Supplies Expense	543		1 2 2 0 80	10
11			Telephone Expense	545		1 5 4 6 72	11
12			Depreciation Expense	547		2 3 5 4 81	12
13			Insurance Expense	548		1 5 3 0 15	13
14			Heating and Lighting Expense	549		5 5 1 5 36	14
15			Advertising Expense	551		39 2 3 3 69	15
16			Payroll Taxes Expense	552		8 0 7 9 04	16
17			Bank Credit Card Expense	553		24 5 9 8 10	17
18			Uncollectible Accounts Expense	554		3 0 1 2 63	18
19			Purchases Discounts Lost	555		8 2 36	19
20			Charitable Contributions Expense	557		1 2 7 0 00	20
21			Miscellaneous Expense	572		1 9 6 6 14	21
22			Interest Expense	581		9 0 3 03	22
23		31	Expense and Revenue Summary	331	85 3 7 7 30		23
24			Gary L. Fishel, Capital	311		85 3 7 7 30	24
25		31	Gary L. Fishel, Capital	311	88 0 5 0 00		25
26			Gary L. Fishel, Drawing	312		88 0 5 0 00	26

Northern Micro—Closing Entries

separate explanation of each closing entry is not necessary. The information required in preparing the closing entries was obtained from the Income Statement columns of the work sheet illustrated on pages 364-365.

The first closing entry was made to close the sales and purchases returns and allowances accounts. Since these accounts have credit balances, each account must be debited for the amount of its balance in order to close it. The debits to these two accounts are offset by a credit of $899,297.89 to Expense and Revenue Summary.

The second closing entry was made to close the sales returns and allowances, purchases, and all of the expense accounts. Since these accounts have debit balances, each account must be credited for the amount of its balance in order to close it. The credits to these accounts are offset by a debit of $819,531.99 to Expense and Revenue Summary.

The posting of the first two adjusting entries and the first two closing entries causes the expense and revenue summary account to have a credit balance of $85,377.30. This amount is the net income for the year. At this point, the account has served its purpose and must be closed. The third closing entry accomplishes this by debiting the expense and revenue summary account and crediting Gary L. Fishel, Capital, for $85,377,30. The fourth closing entry was made to close Gary L. Fishel, Drawing. Since this account has a debit balance, a credit is required to close it. The offsetting debit of $88,050.00 is to Gary L. Fishel, Capital.

Posting the Closing Entries. Closing entries are posted in the usual manner and proper cross-references are provided by using the Posting Reference columns of the general journal and the ledger accounts. Selected accounts of Northern Micro that were affected by the closing entries are reproduced below and on page 416. Posting of the closing entries to the other accounts was handled in the same manner. Note that as each account was closed, the symbol "-0-" for a zero balance was placed in each column.

The first two adjusting entries described and illustrated on pages 410-412 serve to adjust the merchandise inventory account by removing the amount of the beginning inventory and by entering the amount of the ending inventory. These two entries also facilitate the closing process in that they cause the two amounts that are used for the calculation of net income or net loss to be entered in the Expense and Revenue Summary. Once the expense and revenue summary account has been closed to the owner's equity account, the income and expense accounts are ready to be used in the following period.

ACCOUNT *Gary L. Fishel, Drawing*   ACCOUNT NO. *312*

DATE		ITEM	POST. REF.	DEBIT	CREDIT	BALANCE DEBIT	BALANCE CREDIT
19-- Dec.	1	Balance	✓			82 5 0 0 00	
	23		CP48	5 5 0 0 00		88 0 0 0 00	
	31		CP48	5 0 00		88 0 5 0 00	
	31		J29		88 0 5 0 00	- 0 -	- 0 -

ACCOUNT *Expense and Revenue Summary*   ACCOUNT NO. *331*

DATE		ITEM	POST. REF.	DEBIT	CREDIT	BALANCE DEBIT	BALANCE CREDIT
19-- Dec.	31		J28	97 0 8 3 80		97 0 8 3 80	
	31		J28		102 6 9 5 20		5 6 1 1 40
	31		J29		899 2 9 7 89		904 9 0 9 29
	31		J29	819 5 3 1 99			85 3 7 7 30
	31		J29	85 3 7 7 30		- 0 -	- 0 -

ACCOUNT **Sales**　　　　　　ACCOUNT NO. **411**

DATE		ITEM	POST. REF.	DEBIT	CREDIT	BALANCE DEBIT	BALANCE CREDIT
19-- Dec.	1	Balance	✓				793 6 4 6 60
	31		S34		30 4 3 6 80		824 0 8 3 40
	31		CR42		66 6 6 0 79		890 7 4 4 19
	31		J29	890 7 4 4 19		- 0 -	- 0 -

ACCOUNT **Sales Returns and Allowances**　　　　　　ACCOUNT NO. **411.1**

DATE		ITEM	POST. REF.	DEBIT	CREDIT	BALANCE DEBIT	BALANCE CREDIT
19-- Dec.	1	Balance	✓			12 7 0 2 85	
	6		J27	3 0 0 00		13 0 0 2 85	
	10		CP48	3 9 9 00		13 4 0 1 85	
	31		J29		13 4 0 1 85	- 0 -	- 0 -

ACCOUNT **Purchases**　　　　　　ACCOUNT NO. **511**

DATE		ITEM	POST. REF.	DEBIT	CREDIT	BALANCE DEBIT	BALANCE CREDIT
19-- Dec.	1	Balance	✓			566 3 1 5 20	
	31		P22	36 5 6 3 32		602 8 7 8 52	
	31		CP48	2 8 7 75		603 1 6 6 27	
	31		J29		603 1 6 6 27	- 0 -	- 0 -

ACCOUNT **Purchases Returns and Allowances**　　　　　　ACCOUNT NO. **511.1**

DATE		ITEM	POST. REF.	DEBIT	CREDIT	BALANCE DEBIT	BALANCE CREDIT
19-- Dec.	1	Balance	✓				8 4 6 0 45
	5		J27		9 3 25		8 5 5 3 70
	31		J29	8 5 5 3 70		- 0 -	- 0 -

Northern Micro—Selected General Ledger Accounts After Posting Closing Entries

Post-Closing Trial Balance

Prepare a post-closing trial balance.

A trial balance of the general ledger accounts taken after the temporary owner's equity accounts have been closed is usually referred to as a **post-closing trial balance**. The purpose of the post-closing trial balance is to prove that the general ledger is in balance at the beginning of a new accounting period before any transactions for the new accounting period are entered.

A post-closing trial balance of the general ledger of Northern Micro is shown on page 417. The post-closing trial balance may be dated either as of the close of the old accounting period or as of the beginning of the new accounting period. In this illustration, the trial balance is dated December 31, 19-B, the end of the period.

Northern Micro

Post-Closing Trial Balance

December 31, 19-B

Account	Acct. No.	Dr. Balance	Cr. Balance
Cash	111	58 2 6 0 55	
Petty Cash Fund	112	2 5 0 00	
Accounts Receivable	131	35 6 1 3 74	
Allowance for Doubtful Accounts	131.1		3 6 0 2 63
Merchandise Inventory	141	102 6 9 5 20	
Supplies	151	8 0 0 00	
Prepaid Insurance	155	1 5 3 0 14	
Store Equipment	181	23 5 4 8 10	
Accumulated Depreciation-Store Equipment	181.1		7 8 4 8 45
FICA Tax Payable	211		1 1 9 4 52
FUTA Tax Payable	212		3 5 68
State Unemployment Tax Payable	213		1 5 2 86
Employees Income Tax Payable	214		1 4 3 3 40
Accrued Bank Credit Card Payable	215		9 2 99
Notes Payable	216		34 0 0 0 00
Accrued Interest Payable	217		2 8 3 33
Accounts Payable	218		15 8 6 6 21
Sales Tax Payable	221		4 8 2 9 83
Gary L. Fishel, Capital	311		153 3 5 7 83
		222 6 9 7 73	222 6 9 7 73

Northern Micro—Post-Closing Trial Balance

Completing the Accounting Cycle

Describe, journalize, and post reversing entries.

In Chapter 4, page 130, the nine steps involved in handling all of the transactions and events completed during an accounting period, beginning with entries in the books of original entry and ending with a post-closing trial balance, were referred to collectively as the **accounting cycle**. A tenth step—journalizing and posting reversing entries—needs to be added if the accrual basis of accounting is being used.

■ **Use of Reversing Entries.** The primary purpose of reversing entries is to simplify the entering of transactions in the succeeding accounting period. These entries also help to assure that the proper amounts of revenue and expense are recognized in each period. Reversing entries are not required; even a very complicated accounting system can function without them. They simply are intended to make the accounting process easier and to reduce the chance of making errors in entering everyday transactions.

As demonstrated in this chapter and Chapter 9, under accrual accounting numerous adjusting entries are needed at the end of the period to bring the account balances up to date. Some of these entries need to be reversed. As its name implies, a **reversing entry** is the reverse or opposite of the adjusting entry to which it relates.

Not all adjusting entries need to be reversed, and it is not always obvious whether reversal of a particular entry is appropriate. Fortunately, for the types of adjustments made by Northern Micro, a clear rule can be followed: All accrual adjustments should be reversed.

Two accrual adjustments were made by Northern Micro: (1) for accrued interest expense, and (2) for accrued bank credit card expense. These adjustments can be used to demonstrate reversing entries and to show why such entries help simplify the accounting process in the succeeding period.

Accrued Interest Expense. To adjust for accrued interest expense on December 31, 19-B, the following entry was made by Northern Micro.

Interest Expense	283.33	
Accrued Interest Payable		283.33

As explained in Chapter 9, the $283.33 represents the interest accrued on a $34,000 note issued on December 1, 19-B, and due May 31, 19-C. The interest expense account was then closed as part of the closing process at the end of 19-B.

To simplify the entry for the payment of the note and interest in 19-C, the adjusting entry for 19-B needs to be reversed at the beginning of 19-C, as follows:

Accrued Interest Payable	283.33	
Interest Expense		283.33

After the adjusting and closing entries at the end of 19-B and the reversing entry at the beginning of 19-C have been posted, the accounts affected appear as follows:

ACCOUNT *Accrued Interest Payable*   ACCOUNT NO. *217*

DATE	ITEM	POST. REF.	DEBIT	CREDIT	BALANCE DEBIT	BALANCE CREDIT
19-B Dec. 31		J28		2 8 3 33		2 8 3 33
19-C Jan. 1		J30	2 8 3 33		- 0 -	- 0 -

ACCOUNT **Interest Expense**   ACCOUNT NO. **581**

DATE		ITEM	POST. REF.	DEBIT	CREDIT	BALANCE DEBIT	BALANCE CREDIT
19-B Dec.	1	Balance	✓			6 1 9 70	
	31		J28	2 8 3 33		9 0 3 03	
	31		J29		9 0 3 03	- 0 -	- 0 -
19-C Jan.	1		J30		2 8 3 33		2 8 3 33

Northern Micro—Accrued Interest Payable and Interest Expense After Posting of Reversing Entry

Note that after posting the reversing entry, the account, Accrued Interest Payable, has a zero balance and the account, Interest Expense, has a *credit* balance of $283.33. If the note for $34,000 plus $1,700 interest is paid on May 31, the payment will be entered as follows:

```
Notes Payable...................................  34,000.00
Interest Expense................................   1,700.00
  Cash..........................................             35,700.00
```

After posting this entry, the interest expense account will have a debit balance of $1,416.67 ($1,700 minus $283.33). This balance of $1,416.67 represents the amount of interest expense incurred in the year in which the note matures. If the adjusting entry were not reversed, an analysis would have to be made before entering the payment on May 31 to determine the amount of interest expense incurred in the preceding year and the amount of interest expense incurred in the current year. This information then would have been used in preparing the following journal entry on May 31, 19-C:

```
Notes Payable...................................  34,000.00
Accrued Interest Payable........................     283.33
Interest Expense................................   1,416.67
  Cash..........................................             35,700.00
```

The entry on May 31 is simpler and easier to prepare if the reversing entry is made at the beginning of 19-C.

The reversal procedure is particularly useful if the year-end adjustment for accrued interest payable relates to interest accrued on several interest-bearing obligations. When the adjustment is reversed, all future payments of interest can be debited to the interest expense account without any concern as to when the expense for each amount paid was incurred. The portion of any payments that is an expense of the new period will automatically emerge as the balance of the interest expense account.

Accrued Bank Credit Card Expense. To adjust for accrued bank credit card expense on December 31, 19-B, the following entry was made by Northern Micro.

Bank Credit Card Expense	92.99	
Accrued Bank Credit Card Payable		92.99

The bank credit card expense account was then closed as part of the closing process at the end of 19-B.

The adjusting entry for 19-B needs to be reversed at the beginning of 19-C, as follows:

Accrued Bank Credit Card Payable	92.99	
Bank Credit Card Expense		92.99

After the adjusting and closing entries at the end of 19-B and the reversing entry at the beginning of 19-C have been posted, the accounts affected appear as follows:

ACCOUNT **Accrued Bank Credit Card Payable**   ACCOUNT NO. 215

DATE		ITEM	POST. REF.	DEBIT	CREDIT	BALANCE DEBIT	BALANCE CREDIT
19-B Dec.	31		J28		9 2 99		9 2 99
19-C Jan.	1		J30	9 2 99		- 0 -	- 0 -

ACCOUNT **Bank Credit Card Expense**   ACCOUNT NO. 553

DATE		ITEM	POST. REF.	DEBIT	CREDIT	BALANCE DEBIT	BALANCE CREDIT
19-B Dec.	1	Balance	√			22 3 4 8 57	
	3		CP48	2 1 5 6 54		24 5 0 5 11	
	31		J28	9 2 99		24 5 9 8 10	
	31		J29		24 5 9 8 10	- 0 -	- 0 -
19-C Jan.	1		J30		9 2 99		9 2 99

Northern Micro—Accrued Bank Credit Card Payable and Bank Credit Card Expense After Posting of Reversing Entry

Note that after posting the reversing entry the account, Accrued Bank Credit Card Payable, has a zero balance and the account, Bank Credit Card Expense, has a *credit* balance of $92.99. When the bank credit card statement arrives in January, the bank's deduction of $92.99 in credit card fees is entered as follows:

Bank Credit Card Expense	92.99
Cash	92.99

After this entry is posted, Bank Credit Card Expense will have a zero balance. This reflects the fact that this amount is an expense of the year just ended, 19-B, and not of the new year, 19-C. If the reversing entry had not been made, the accountant would have had to remember that the January debit had to be different from the other eleven months. This is not a serious problem, but whenever possible it is better not to disturb the regular routine of entering transactions. Reversing entries for accrual adjustments help to accomplish this objective.

Journalizing the Reversing Entries. Reversing entries, like adjusting and closing entries, are made in a general journal. A portion of the general journal showing the reversing entries of Northern Micro is reproduced below. Usually the reversing entries are made immediately after closing the books at the end of an accounting period. However, the entries should be dated as of the first day of the succeeding accounting period. Thus, the reversing entries for Northern Micro are dated January 1. Since the heading "Reversing Entries" explains the nature of the entries, a separate explanation of each reversing entry is unnecessary.

JOURNAL   PAGE *30*

	DATE		DESCRIPTION	POST. REF.	DEBIT	CREDIT	
1			*Reversing Entries*				1
2	19-C Jan.	1	Accrued Interest Payable	217	2 8 3 33		2
3			Interest Expense	581		2 8 3 33	3
4		1	Accrued Bank Credit Card Payable	215	9 2 99		4
5			Bank Credit Card Expense	553		9 2 99	5

Northern Micro—Reversing Entries

Posting the Reversing Entries Reversing entries are posted in the usual manner and proper cross-references are provided by using the Posting Reference columns of the general journal and the ledger accounts. After the reversing entries have been posted, the accounts affected appear as shown on pages 418-420.

Building Your Accounting Knowledge

1. Why do the adjustments that were made in the work sheet need to be journalized and posted?
2. In what type of journal are adjusting entries made?

3. Where is the information obtained that is needed in journalizing the adjustments?
4. When is the account number of each adjusted ledger account entered in the Posting Reference column of the general journal?
5. In the posting process, how is a cross-reference provided between the general journal and the general ledger?
6. Where is the information obtained that is needed in journalizing the closing entries?
7. Explain the function of each of the four closing entries made by Northern Micro.
8. What is the purpose of a post-closing trial balance?
9. What is the primary purpose of reversing entries?
10. What is the customary date for reversing entries?

Assignment Box

To reinforce your understanding of the preceding text materials, you may complete the following:

> Study Guide: Part B
> Textbook: Exercises 10A6 through 10A10 or 10B6 through 10B10
>   Problems 10A5 through 10A9 or 10B5 through 10B9

Expanding Your Business Vocabulary

What is the meaning of each of the following terms?

account form (p. 401)
accounting cycle (p. 417)
accounts receivable turnover (p. 408)
adjusting entries (p. 410)
balance sheet (p. 400)
closing entries (p. 412)
current assets (p. 401)
current liabilities (p. 403)
current ratio (p. 406)
gross margin/gross profit (p. 398)
income statement (p. 397)
inventory turnover (p. 408)
Investments (p. 403)
long-term liabilities (p. 403)
Marketable Securities (p. 403)
mortgage (p. 403)
Mortgage Payable (p. 403)
multiple-step form (p. 398)
net sales (p. 398)
operating income (p. 398)

operating statement (p. 397)
post-closing trial balance (p. 416)
profit and loss statement (p. 397)
property, plant, and equipment
    (p. 403)
quick assets (p. 406)
quick ratio (p. 407)
report form (p. 401)
return on owner's equity (p. 407)
reversing entry (p. 418)
single-step form (p. 398)
statement of assets and liabilities
    (p. 400)
statement of condition (p. 400)
statement of earnings (p. 397)
statement of financial position (p. 400)
statement of owner's equity (p. 398)
temporary investments (p. 402)
undepreciated cost (p. 403)
working capital (p. 407)

Demonstration Problem

Joe Emerson operates a retail merchandising business called Emerson's. Shown below is a portion of the work sheet for the three months ended December 31, the first year of operations:

Emerson's
Work Sheet
For the Three Months Ended December 31, 19--

Account	Adjustments Debit	Adjustments Credit	Income Statement Debit	Income Statement Credit	Balance Sheet Debit	Balance Sheet Credit
Cash					23,842.96	
Accounts Receivable					9,042.32	
Allow. for Doubtful Accts.		(d) 700.00				700.00
Merchandise Inventory	(a)49,655.20				49,655.20	
Store and Office Supplies		(b) 520.88			271.38	
Prepaid Insurance		(e) 138.00			1,518.00	
Store Equipment					25,200.00	
Accum. Depr.—Store Equipment		(c) 2,520.00				2,520.00
FICA Tax Payable						532.90
FUTA Tax Payable						216.26
State Unemp. Tax Pay.						288.32
Employees Inc. Tax Pay.						580.30
Accrued Bank Credit Card Payable		(g) 622.40				622.40
Notes Payable						22,800.00
Accrued Interest Payable		(f) 380.00				380.00
Accounts Payable						27,610.44
Sales Tax Payable						2,208.58
Joe Emerson, Capital						50,000.00
Joe Emerson, Drawing					9,900.00	
Exp. and Rev. Summary		(a)49,655.20	49,655.20			
Sales				113,033.00		
Sales Ret. and Allow.			1,842.36			
Purchases			124,318.60			
Pur. Ret. and Allow.				3,719.16		
Rent Expense			3,450.00			
Sal. and Comm. Exp.			11,818.48			
Store and Office Supplies Expense	(b) 520.88		520.88			
Utilities and Telephone Expense			645.60			
Depreciation Expense	(c) 2,520.00		2,520.00			
Insurance Expense	(e) 138.00		138.00			
Advertising Expense			5,045.10			
Payroll Taxes Expense			1,012.36			
Bank Credit Card Expense	(g) 622.40		2,746.92			
Uncoll. Accts. Exp.	(d) 700.00		700.00			
Miscellaneous Expense			298.40			
Interest Expense	(f) 380.00		380.00			
	54,536.48	54,536.48	155,436.70	166,407.36	119,429.86	108,459.20
Net Income			10,970.66			10,970.66
			166,407.36	166,407.36	119,429.86	119,429.86

Required:

1. Prepare an income statement for the three months ended December 31. (Arrange operating expenses in descending dollar size order, except for Miscellaneous Expense.)
2. Prepare a statement of owner's equity for the three months ended December 31, and a balance sheet as of December 31 in report form. The $50,000 balance in Joe Emerson, Capital on the work sheet is Emerson's initial investment in the business on October 1, 19--.
3. Compute the following ratios:
   a. current ratio
   b. quick ratio
   c. working capital
   d. return on owner's equity
   e. accounts receivable turnover (credit sales for three-month period were $16,800.00)
   f. inventory turnover
4. Prepare journal entries for the seven adjustments.
5. Prepare journal entries to close the temporary owner's equity accounts.
6. Prepare a post-closing trial balance as of December 31.
7. Prepare any necessary reversing entries as of January 1.

Solution

1. & 2. Solutions can be found on pages 425-426.

3. (a) Current Ratio $= \dfrac{\text{Current Assets}}{\text{Current Liabilities}}$

   $= \$83,629.86 \ / \ \$55,239.20 = 1.51 \text{ to } 1$

   (b) Quick Ratio $= \dfrac{\text{Quick Assets}}{\text{Current Liabilities}}$

   Quick Assets $=$ Cash and Net Receivables
   $= \$23,842.96 + \$8,342.32 = \$32,185.28$

   Quick Ratio: $\$32,185.28 \ / \ \$55,239.20 = .58 \text{ to } 1$

   (c) Working Capital $=$ Current Assets $-$ Current Liabilities
   $= \$83,629.86 - \$55,239.20 = \$28,390.66$

   (d) Return on Owner's Equity $=$ Net Income / Owner's Equity
   $= \$10,970.66 \ / \ \$50,000.00 = 21.94\%$

   (e) Accounts Receivable Turnover $= \dfrac{\text{Net Credit Sales for Quarter}}{\text{Average Net Accounts Receivable}}$

   $= \dfrac{\$16,800}{(0 + \$8,342.32) \ / \ 2}$

   $= \$16,800 \ / \ \$4,171.16 = 4.03$

   92 days in quarter / 4.03 = 22.83 days.
   This is the average number of days to collect an account receivable.

1.   **Emerson's**
Income Statement
For the Three Months Ended December 31, 19--

Operating revenue:			
Sales			$113,033.00
Less sales returns & allowances ..			1,842.36
Net sales			$111,190.64
Cost of goods sold:			
Merchandise inventory October 1		-0-	
Purchases	$124,318.60		
Less purchases returns & allowances	3,719.16		
Net purchases		$120,599.44	
Merchandise available for sale		$120,599.44	
Less merchandise inventory,			
December 31		49,655.20	
Cost of goods sold			70,944.24
Gross margin on sales			$ 40,246.40
Operating expenses:			
Salaries and commissions expense		$11,818.48	
Advertising expense		5,045.10	
Rent expense		3,450.00	
Bank credit card expense		2,746.92	
Depreciation expense		2,520.00	
Payroll taxes expense		1,012.36	
Uncollectible accounts expense....		700.00	
Utilities and telephone expense ...		645.60	
Store and office supplies expense		520.88	
Insurance expense		138.00	
Miscellaneous expense		298.40	
Total operating expenses			28,895.74
Operating income			$ 11,350.66
Other expenses:			
Interest expense			380.00
Net income			$ 10,970.66

3.   (Concluded)

$$\text{(f) Inventory Turnover} = \frac{\text{Cost of Goods Sold}}{\text{Average Inventory}}$$

$$= \frac{\$70,944.24}{(0 + 49,655.20) / 2}$$

$$= \$70,944.24 / \$24,827.60$$

$$= 2.86$$

92 days in quarter / 2.86 = 32.17.
On average, it takes about 32 days to sell inventory.

2.

Emerson's
Statement of Owner's Equity
For the Three Months Ended December 31, 19--

Joe Emerson, capital, October 1, 19--		$ 50,000.00
Net income for quarter	$10,970.66	
Less withdrawals	9,900.00	
Increase in owner's equity		$ 1,070.66
Joe Emerson, capital, December 31, 19--		$51,070.66

Emerson's
Balance Sheet
December 31, 19--

Assets

Current assets:		
Cash		$ 23,842.96
Accounts receivable	$ 9,042.32	
Less allowance for doubtful accounts	700.00	8,342.32
Merchandise inventory		49,655.20
Store and office supplies		271.38
Prepaid insurance		1,518.00
Total current assets		$83,629.86
Property, plant, and equipment:		
Store equipment	$25,200.00	
Less accumulated depreciation	2,520.00	
Total property, plant, and equipment		22,680.00
Total assets		$106,309.86

Liabilities

Current liabilities:		
FICA tax payable	$ 532.90	
FUTA tax payable	216.26	
State unemployment tax payable	288.32	
Employees income tax payable	580.30	
Accrued bank credit card payable	622.40	
Notes payable	22,800.00	
Accrued interest payable	380.00	
Accounts payable	27,610.44	
Sales tax payable	2,208.58	
Total current liabilities		$ 55,239.20

Owner's Equity

Joe Emerson, capital, December 31		51,070.66
Total liabilities and owner's equity		$106,309.86

4.   **Journal**   **Page 3**

Date	Description	Post Ref.	Debit	Credit
	Adjusting Entries			
19--				
Dec. 31	Merchandise Inventory		49,655.20	
	Expense and Revenue Summary			49,655.20
31	Store and Office Supplies Expense		520.88	
	Store and Office Supplies			520.88
31	Depreciation Expense		2,520.00	
	Accum. Depr.—Store Equipment			2,520.00
31	Uncollectible Accounts Expense		700.00	
	Allowance for Doubtful Accounts			700.00
31	Insurance Expense		138.00	
	Prepaid Insurance			138.00
31	Interest Expense		380.00	
	Accrued Interest Payable			380.00
31	Bank Credit Card Expense		622.40	
	Accrued Bank Credit Card payable			622.40

5.   **Journal**   **Page 4**

Date	Description	Post Ref.	Debit	Credit
	Closing Entries			
19--				
Dec. 31	Sales		113,033.00	
	Purchases Returns & Allowances		3,719.16	
	Expense & Revenue Summary			116,752.16
31	Expense & Revenue Summary		155,436.70	
	Sales Returns & Allowances			1,842.36
	Purchases			124,318.60
	Rent Expense			3,450.00
	Salaries and Commissions Expense			11,818.48
	Store and Office Supplies			520.88
	Utilities and Telephone Expense			645.60
	Depreciation Expense			2,520.00
	Insurance Expense			138.00
	Advertising Expense			5,045.10
	Payroll Taxes Expense			1,012.36
	Bank Credit Card Expense			2,746.92
	Uncollectible Accounts Expense			700.00
	Miscellaneous Expense			298.40
	Interest Expense			380.00
31	Expense & Revenue Summary		10,970.66	
	Joe Emerson, Capital			10,970.66
31	Joe Emerson, Capital		9,900.00	
	Joe Emerson, Drawing			9,900.00

6.

Emerson's
Post-Closing Trial Balance
December 31, 19--

Account	Acct. No.	Dr. Balance	Cr. Balance
Cash		$ 23,842.96	
Accounts Receivable		9,042.32	
Allowance for Doubtful Accounts			$ 700.00
Merchandise Inventory		49,655.20	
Store and Office Supplies		271.38	
Prepaid Insurance		1,518.00	
Store Equipment		25,200.00	
Accumulated Depr.—Store Equipment			2,520.00
FICA Tax Payable			532.90
FUTA Tax Payable			216.26
Store Unemployment Tax Payable			288.32
Employee's Income Tax Payable			580.30
Accrued Bank Credit Card Payable			622.40
Notes Payable			22,800.00
Accrued Interest Payable			380.00
Accounts Payable			27,610.44
Sales Tax Payable			2,208.58
Joe Emerson, Capital			51,070.66
		$109,529.86	$109,529.86

7.   **Journal**   **Page 5**

Date	Description	Post Ref.	Debit	Credit
	Reversing Entries			
19--				
Jan. 1	Accrued Interest Payable		380.00	
	Interest Expense			380.00
1	Accrued Bank Credit Card Payable		622.40	
	Bank Credit Card Expense			622.40

*Note: Now that you have reviewed the Demonstration Problem and Solution you may complete the **Mastery Problem** at the end of the chapter activities.

Applying Accounting Concepts

Series A

Exercise 10A1—Income Statement Preparation. The adjusted trial balance for Fabric Bazaar is shown below:

Fabric Bazaar
Adjusted Trial Balance
For the Year Ended December 31, 19--

	Debit	Credit
Cash	$ 11,014	
Accounts Receivable	24,620	
Allowance for Doubtful Accounts		$ 738
Merchandise Inventory	87,580	
Supplies	2,570	
Prepaid Insurance	1,968	
Office Equipment	17,500	
Accumulated Depreciation—Office Equipment		7,000
Accrued Bank Credit Card Payable		128
Notes Payable		9,250
Accrued Interest Payable		150
S.J. Ellston, Capital		110,464
S.J. Ellston, Drawing	14,400	
Expense and Revenue Summary	103,752	87,580
Sales		309,474
Sales Returns and Allowances	7,430	
Purchases	192,476	
Purchases Returns and Allowances		10,824
Salaries and Commissions Expense	61,500	
Depreciation Expense	3,500	
Insurance Expense	656	
Bank Credit Card Expense	4,378	
Uncollectible Accounts Expense	690	
Interest Expense	1,274	
Miscellaneous Expense	300	
Totals	$535,608	$535,608

Prepare a multiple-step form of income statement for Fabric Bazaar.

Exercise 10A2—Statement of Owner's Equity. Refer to Exercise 10A1. Prepare a statement of owner's equity as of December 31 for Fabric Bazaar.

Exercise 10A3—Balance Sheet Preparation. Refer to Exercise 10A1. Prepare a balance sheet in report form with classified assets and liabilities as of December 31 for Fabric Bazaar.

Exercise 10A4—Calculation of Operating Ratios. The following amounts were taken from the income statement for Fine Arts Frame Gallery for the month ended September 30, 19--:

Net sales	$586,146
Cost of goods sold	407,280
Operating expenses	73,526
Other expenses	980

Using net sales as the base, calculate the percent of net sales for each of the following items: (a) Net sales; (b) Cost of goods sold; (c) Gross margin on sales; (d) Operating expenses; (e) Operating income; (f) Other expenses; (g) Net income.

Exercise 10A5—Calculation of Financial and Operating Ratios. The following are amounts that were summarized from the April 30, 19--, balance sheet for Oberg Office Products:

Cash	$ 17,012
Accounts receivable (net amount)	6,826
Merchandise inventory, April 1	28,154
Merchandise inventory, April 30	28,584
Total current assets	53,098
Total assets	57,642
Total current liabilities	18,156
A. Oberg, capital, April 1	38,260
Net income	24,760
A. Oberg, drawing	23,534
Cost of goods sold for April	170,810

Determine the following ratios that might be significant in evaluating the status of Oberg Office Products: (a) Current ratio; (b) Quick ratio; (c) Working capital; (d) Return on owner's equity; (e) Rate of inventory turnover.

Exercise 10A6—Adjusting Journal Entries. Patricia Cain is in the process of preparing end-of-period financial statements. The accountant for the company has summarized the following data related to entries that need to be made in order to bring the accounts up to date prior to preparing the statements.

Merchandise inventory, January 1	$46,600
Merchandise inventory, December 31	49,294
Insurance premiums expired	734
Supplies used	586
Interest accrued on notes payable	135
Accrued bank credit card payable	47
Estimated uncollectible accounts (based on sales on account)	1,446
Depreciation on store equipment	1,132

Give the eight adjusting entries in general journal form to bring the accounts up to date.

Exercise 10A7—Analysis and Preparation of Adjusting Journal Entries. A partial work sheet for Gates Office Supplies appears below:

Gates Office Supplies
Partial Work Sheet
For the Year Ended December 31, 19--

Account	Trial Balance Debit	Trial Balance Credit	Adjusted Trial Balance Debit	Adjusted Trial Balance Credit
Cash.........................	$ 58,262		$ 58,262	
Accounts Receivable.............	35,604		35,604	
Allowance for Doubtful Accounts		586		$3,598
Merchandise Inventory...........	97,088		102,694	
Supplies......................	2,038		818	
Prepaid Insurance	3,072		1,542	
Store Equipment	23,542		23,542	
Accumulated Depreciation—Store Equipment....................		5,490		7,844
Accrued Bank Credit Card Payable				92
Notes Payable		3,400		3,400
Accrued Interest Payable.........				282
F.M. Martin, Capital		35,708		35,708
F.M. Martin, Drawing	88,050		88,050	
Expense and Revenue Summary ..			97,088	102,694
Sales.........................		890,756		890,756
Purchases	603,166		603,166	
Supplies Expense...............			1,220	
Depreciation Expense...........			2,354	
Insurance Expense..............			1,530	
Bank Credit Card Expense	24,500		24,592	
Uncollectible Accounts Expense ..			3,012	
Interest Expense................	618		900	
Totals	$935,940	$935,940	$1,044,374	$1,044,374

Analyze the trial balance and the adjusted trial balance to enter the eight end-of-period adjustments that were made. (a) Determine the change in each balance (increase, decrease, or no change). (b) Determine if the change is a debit or credit. (c) Locate the related debit and credit. For example, insurance expense and prepaid insurance would be related accounts. (d) Enter in general journal form the eight entries that were made to adjust the trial balance totals to obtain the amounts shown in the adjusted trial balance.   900

Exercise 10A8—Closing Journal Entries. Refer to the adjusted trial balance of Gates Office Supplies in Exercise 10A7. (a) Prepare ledger accounts for Expense and Revenue Summary and for F.M. Martin, Capital. Post the beginning and ending inventory amounts to Expense and Revenue Summary and the beginning balance to the capital account. (b) Prepare in general journal form the closing entries that would be made. (c) As you journalize, post all closing entries that affect the expense and revenue summary and capital accounts.

Exercise 10A9—Post-Closing Trial Balance. Refer to Exercises 10A7 and 10A8. Prepare a post-closing trial balance as of December 31 for Gates Office Supplies.

Exercise 10A10—Reversing Journal Entries. Refer to Exercise 10A7. Enter in general journal form the reversing entries that Gates Office Supplies would make as of January 1 of the next year so that the transactions involving the adjusting entries for accruals might be entered in a routine manner.

Series B

Exercise 10B1—Financial Statement Preparation. The adjusted trial balance for Calico Corners is shown below:

Calico Corners
Adjusted Trial Balance
For the Year Ended December 31, 19--

	Debit	Credit
Cash	$ 8,260	
Accounts Receivable	18,465	
Allowance for Doubtful Accounts		$ 553
Merchandise Inventory	65,685	
Supplies	1,928	
Prepaid Insurance	1,476	
Office Equipment	13,125	
Accumulated Depreciation—Office Equipment		5,250
Accrued Bank Credit Card Payable		96
Notes Payable		6,938
Accrued Interest Payable		115
P.K. Pickard, Capital		82,846
P.K. Pickard, Drawing	10,800	
Expense and Revenue Summary	77,814	65,685
Sales		232,105
Sales Returns and Allowances	5,572	
Purchases	144,357	
Purchases Returns and Allowances		8,118
Salaries and Commissions Expense	46,125	
Depreciation Expense	2,625	
Insurance Expense	492	
Bank Credit Card Expense	3,283	
Uncollectible Accounts Expense	518	
Interest Expense	956	
Miscellaneous Expense	225	
Totals	$401,706	$401,706

Prepare a multiple-step form of income statement for Calico Corners.

Exercise 10B2—Statement of Owner's Equity. Refer to Exercise 10B1. Prepare a statement of owner's equity as of December 31 for Calico Corners.

Exercise 10B3—Balance Sheet Preparation. Refer to Exercise 10B1. Prepare a balance sheet in report form with classified assets and liabilities as of December 31 for Calico Corners.

Exercise 10B4—Calculation of Operating Ratios. The following amounts were taken from the income statement for Executive Framing for the month ended June 30, 19--:

Net sales	$439,609
Cost of goods sold	305,460
Operating expenses	55,145
Other expenses	735

Using net sales as the base, calculate the percent of net sales for each of the following items: (a) Net sales; (b) Cost of goods sold; (c) Gross margin on sales; (d) Operating expenses; (e) Operating income; (f) Other expenses; (g) Net income.

Exercise 10B5—Calculation of Financial and Operating Ratios. The following are amounts that were summarized from the June 30, 19--, balance sheet for Parton Paper Products:

Cash	$ 12,759
Accounts receivable (net amount)	5,120
Merchandise inventory, June 1	21,115
Merchandise inventory, June 30	21,438
Total current assets	39,824
Total assets	43,232
Total current liabilities	13,617
D.L. Parton, capital, June 1	28,695
Net income	18,570
D.L. Parton, drawing	17,650
Cost of goods sold for June	128,108

Determine the following ratios that might be significant in evaluating the status of Parton Paper Products: (a) Current ratio; (b) Quick ratio; (c) Working capital; (d) Return on owner's equity; (e) Rate of inventory turnover.

Exercise 10B6—Adjusting Journal Entries. WTU Collection Service is in the process of preparing end-of-period financial statements. The accountant for the company has summarized the following data related to entries that need to be made in order to bring the accounts up to date prior to preparing the statements.

Merchandise inventory, January 1	$31,066
Merchandise inventory, December 31	32,862
Insurance premiums expired	490
Supplies used	395
Interest accrued on notes payable................................	90
Accrued bank credit card payable	32
Estimated uncollectible accounts (based on sales on account)	965
Depreciation on store equipment	754

Give the eight adjusting entries in general journal form to bring the accounts up to date.

Exercise 10B7—Analysis and Preparation of Adjusting Journal Entries A partial work sheet for Color-Craft Shop appears below:

Color-Craft Shop
Work Sheet
For the Year Ended December 31, 19--

Account	Trial Balance Debit	Trial Balance Credit	Adjusted Trial Balance Debit	Adjusted Trial Balance Credit
Cash..................................	43,696		43,696	
Accounts Receivable....................	26,703		26,703	
Allowance for Doubtful Accounts		440		2,698
Merchandise Inventory	72,816		77,021	
Supplies..............................	1,528		613	
Prepaid Insurance	2,304		1,156	
Store Equipment	17,657		17,657	
Accumulated Depreciation—Store Equipment...........................		4,118		5,883
Accrued Bank Credit Card Payable.......				70
Notes Payable		2,550		2,550
Accrued Interest Payable				212
L.H. Craft, Capital.....................		26,780		26,780
L.H. Craft, Drawing	66,038		66,038	
Expense and Revenue Summary			72,816	77,021
Sales.................................		668,067		668,067
Purchases	452,375		452,375	
Supplies Expense......................			915	
Depreciation Expense..................			1,765	
Insurance Expense.....................			1,148	
Bank Credit Card Expense	18,375		18,445	
Uncollectible Accounts Expense			2,258	
Interest Expense......................	463		675	
Totals...............................	701,955	701,955	783,281	783,281

Analyze the trial balance and the adjusted trial balance to enter the eight end-of-period adjustments that were made. (a) Determine the change in each balance (increase, decrease, or no change). (b) Determine if the change is a debit or credit. (c) Locate the related debit and credit. For example, insurance expense and prepaid insurance would be related accounts. (d) Enter in general journal form the eight entries that were made to adjust the trial balance totals to obtain the amounts shown in the adjusted trial balance.

Exercise 10B8—Closing Journal Entries. Refer to the Adjusted Trial Balance of Color-Craft Shop in Exercise 10B7. (a) Prepare ledger accounts for Expense and Revenue Summary and for L.H. Craft, Capital. Post the beginning and ending inventory amounts to Expense and Revenue Summary and the beginning balance to the capital account. (b) Prepare in general journal form the closing entries that would be made. (c) As you journalize, post all closing entries that affect the expense and revenue summary and capital accounts.

Exercise 10B9—Post-Closing Trial Balance. Refer to Exercises 10B7 and 10B8. Prepare a post-closing trial balance as of December 31 for Color-Craft Shop.

Exercise 10B10—Reversing Journal Entries. Refer to Exercise 10B7. Enter in general journal form the reversing entries that Color-Craft Shop would make as of January 1 of the next year so that the transactions involving the adjusting entries for accruals might be entered in a routine manner.

Series A

Problem 10A1   Financial Statement Preparation and Ratio Analysis

Ellen Massey operates a retail merchandising enterprise. The results of operations for the calendar quarter ended March 31 of the current year are reflected in the partial work sheet reproduced below. Massey organized the business on January 1 and has been operating for only 1 quarter.

Ellen Massey
Work Sheet (Partial)
For the Quarter Ended March 31, 19--

Account Title	Acct. No.	Income Statement Debit	Credit	Balance Sheet Debit	Credit
Cash	111			48,443.50	
Accounts Receivable	131			97,628.86	
Allowance for Doubtful Accounts	131.1				3,482.28
Merchandise Inventory	141			97,676.16	
Prepaid Insurance	155			2,812.60	
Store Equipment	181			22,480.00	
Accum. Depr.—Store Equipment	181.1				449.60
Office Equipment	191			14,496.00	
Accum. Depr.—Office Equipment	191.1				362.40
FICA Tax Payable	211				1,323.58
FUTA Tax Payable	212				283.80
State Unemployment Tax Payable	213				706.20
Employees' Income Tax Payable	214				1,089.00
Accrued Bank Credit Card Payable	215				842.32
Accounts Payable	218				83,327.82
Sales Tax Payable	221				2,086.16
Ellen Massey, Capital	311				189,206.72
Ellen Massey, Drawing	312			9,600.00	
Expense and Revenue Summary	331	113,098.70	97,676.16		
Sales	411		282,969.00		
Purchases	511	193,205.52			
Rent Expense	541	13,800.00			
Salaries and Commissions Expense	542	31,990.00			
Depreciation Expense	547	812.00			
Insurance Expense	548	378.20			
Advertising Expense	551	5,511.20			
Payroll Taxes Expense	552	1,034.32			
Bank Credit Card Expense	553	3,422.64			
Uncollectible Accounts Expense	554	3,482.28			
Miscellaneous Expense	572	3,933.06			
		370,667.92	380,645.16	293,137.12	283,159.88
Net Income		9,977.24			9,977.24
		380,645.16	380,645.16	293,137.12	293,137.12

Massey has 2 employees and is subject to FICA tax, FUTA tax, and state unemployment tax.

Required:

1. Prepare an income statement for the calendar quarter ended March 31.
2. Treating sales as 100%, compute the percentages of cost of goods sold, total operating expenses, and net income for the period covered by the income statement. Make the computations on a separate sheet of paper and enter the results immediately following Massey's income statement.
3. Prepare a statement of owner's equity for the calendar quarter ended March 31 and a balance sheet as of March 31 in report form.
4. As an aid in interpreting Massey's balance sheet, compute the following ratios and enter the results immediately following Massey's balance sheet. Make the computations on a separate sheet of paper.
   (a) Ratio of current assets to current liabilities.
   (b) Ratio of total assets to total liabilities.

Problem 10A2   Financial Statement Preparation and Ratio Analysis

---

Steve Yamamoto operates a retail merchandising business. Following is a reproduction of a portion of the work sheet for the current year ended December 31. Merchandise Inventory at the beginning of the year was $73,798.00.

Required:

1. Prepare an income statement for the year ended December 31.
2. Treating net sales as 100%, compute the percentages of cost of goods sold, total operating expenses, and net income for the period covered by the income statement. Make the computations on a separate sheet of paper and enter the results immediately following Yamamoto's income statement.
3. Prepare a statement of owner's equity for the year ended December 31, and a balance sheet in report form as of December 31.
4. As an aid in interpreting Yamamoto's balance sheet, compute the following ratios, and enter the results immediately following Yamamoto's balance sheet.
   (a) Ratio of current assets to current liabilities.
   (b) Ratio of total assets to total liabilities.

Steve Yamamoto
Work Sheet
For the Year Ended December 31, 19--

Account Title	Acct. No.	Income Statement		Balance Sheet	
		Debit	Credit	Debit	Credit
Cash	111			68,458.00	
Accounts Receivable	131			122,698.00	
Allowance for Doubtful Accounts	131.1				4,866.00
Merchandise Inventory	141			54,286.00	
Office Supplies	152			944.00	
Prepaid Insurance	155			1,684.00	
Office Equipment	191			15,980.00	
Accum. Depr.—Office Equipment	191.1				1,598.00
FICA Tax Payable	211				738.00
FUTA Tax Payable	212				76.00
State Unemployment Tax Payable	213				218.00
Employees' Income Tax Payable	214				566.00
Accrued Bank Credit Card Payable	215				818.00
Notes Payable	216				18,000.00
Accrued Interest Payable	217				216.00
Accounts Payable	218				55,684.00
Sales Tax Payable	221				2,336.00
Steve Yamamoto, Capital	311				176,000.00
Steve Yamamoto, Drawing	312			46,820.00	
Expense and Revenue Summary	331	73,798.00	54,286.00		
Sales	411		364,286.00		
Sales Returns and Allowances	411.1	1,426.00			
Purchases	511	227,680.00			
Purchases Returns and Allowances	511.1		4,360.00		
Rent Expense	541	16,800.00			
Salaries and Commissions Expense	542	34,332.00			
Office Supplies Expense	543	2,224.00			
Depreciation Expense	547	1,598.00			
Insurance Expense	548	1,718.00			
Advertising Expense	551	4,590.00			
Payroll Taxes Expense	552	1,112.00			
Bank Credit Card Expense	553	3,134.00			
Uncollectible Accounts Expense	554	1,794.00			
Charitable Contributions Expense	557	1,050.00			
Miscellaneous Expense	572	1,226.00			
Interest Expense	581	696.00			
		373,178.00	422,932.00	310,870.00	261,116.00
Net Income		49,754.00			49,754.00
		422,932.00	422,932.00	310,870.00	310,870.00

Problem 10A3   Analysis of Comparative Income Statements

Condensed comparative income statements for Manchester Fitness Equipment are provided below.

Manchester Fitness Equipment
Comparative Income Statement
For the Years Ended December 31, 19-B and 19-A

	19-B	19-A
Net sales	$651,376	$627,574
Less cost of goods sold	377,801	334,133
Gross margin on sales	$273,575	$293,441
Operating expenses..................................	171,934	177,640
Operating income	$101,641	$115,801
Interest expense	3,514	3,760
Net income	$ 98,127	$112,041

Required:

Prepare a statement showing:

(a) The dollar increase or decrease for each item on the income statement.

(b) All income statement items for each period as a percent of net sales.

Problem 10A4   Analysis of Comparative Balance Sheets.

Comparative balance sheets in report form for Ellisville Lighting Fixtures are provided below:

Ellisville Lighting Fixtures
Comparative Balance Sheets
December 31, 19-B and 19-A

Assets	19-B		19-A	
Current assets:				
Cash		$ 51,200		$ 53,810
Accounts receivable	$ 77,960		$ 81,908	
Less allowance for doubtful accts.	8,400	69,560	8,870	73,038
Merchandise inventory		132,840		139,532
Supplies		17,340		18,258
Prepaid insurance		11,200		11,810
Total current assets		$282,140		$296,448
Property, plant, and equipment:				
Store equipment	$170,800		$170,800	
Less accumulated depreciation.....	64,000	$106,800	48,000	$122,800
Delivery equipment	$ 44,000		$ 44,000	
Less accumulated depreciation.....	30,000	14,000	20,000	24,000
Total property, plant and equipment..................		$120,800		$146,800
Total assets		$402,940		$443,248

Liabilities

Current liabilities:

FICA tax payable	$ 2,460	$ 2,348
FUTA tax payable...............	90	96
State unemployment tax payable ...	300	296
Notes payable	10,000	30,000
Accrued interest payable	1,600	1,530
Accounts payable	24,000	55,600
Total current liabilities	$ 38,450	$ 89,870

Owner's Equity

M. Ellis, Capital..................	364,490	353,378
Total liabilities and owner's equity ..	$402,940	$443,248

Required:

Compute the dollar increase or decrease for each item. (Use net amounts for receivables and plant assets)

Problem 10A5   Journalizing and Posting Adjusting Entries

The adjustments columns of the work sheet for the quarter ended March 31 for the business of Ellen Massey are reproduced on page 441.

Required:

1. Using a general journal, prepare journal entries for the six adjustments.
2. Post the adjusting entries to the general ledger accounts listed below. (Enter the March 31 balances first where given.)

Ellen Massey
Partial List of General Ledger Accounts
March 31, 19--

Account Title	Acct. No.	Debit Balance
Allowance for Doubtful Accounts	131.1	-0-
Merchandise Inventory.................................	141	113,098.70
Prepaid Insurance	155	3,190.80
Accum. Depr.—Store Equipment	181.1	-0-
Accum. Depr.—Office Equipment	191.1	-0-
Accrued Bank Credit Card Payable.......................	215	-0-
Expense and Revenue Summary	331	-0-
Depreciation Expense..................................	547	-0-
Insurance Expense.....................................	548	-0-
Bank Credit Card Expense	553	2,580.32
Uncollectible Accounts Expense	554	-0-

Account Title	Acct. No.	Adjustments Debit	Adjustments Credit
Cash.....................................	111		
Accounts Receivable.....................	131		
Allowance for Doubtful Accounts	131.1		(c) 3,482.28
Merchandise Inventory	141	(b) 97,676.16	(a) 113,098.70
Prepaid Insurance	155		(d) 378.20
Store Equipment	181		
Accum. Depr.—Store Equipment	181.1		(e) 449.60
Office Equipment	191		
Accum. Depr.—Office Equipment	191.1		(e) 362.40
FICA Tax Payable	211		
FUTA Tax Payable	212		
State Unemployment Tax Payable	213		
Employees Income Tax Payable............	214		
Accrued Bank Credit Card Payable..........	215		(f) 842.32
Accounts Payable	218		
Sales Tax Payable	221		
Ellen Massey, Capital	311		
Ellen Massey, Drawing	312		
Expense and Revenue Summary	331	(a) 113,098.70	(b) 97,676.16
Sales...................................	411		
Purchases	511		
Rent Expense	541		
Salaries and Commissions Expense	542		
Depreciation Expense....................	547	(e) 812.00	
Insurance Expense.......................	548	(d) 378.20	
Advertising Expense	551		
Payroll Taxes Expense	552		
Bank Credit Card Expense	553	(f) 842.32	
Uncollectible Accounts Expense	554	(c) 3,482.28	
Miscellaneous Expense...................	572		
		216,289.66	216,289.66

Problem 10A6   Adjusting Journal Entries; Statement of Cost of Goods Sold

The following account balances appeared in the general ledger of The Smith Store, owned by P. Smith, at the close of the fiscal year ended July 31:

Merchandise Inventory, beginning of year (August 1), debit, $85,914.
Purchases, debit, $292,800.
Purchases Returns and Allowances, credit, $1,512.

The merchandise inventory taken at the end of the year amounted to $118,864. In preparing a work sheet at the end of the year, the accountant made the adjusting entries required to transfer the beginning inventory to the expense and revenue summary account and to enter the ending inventory.

Required:

1. Prepare entries in general journal form for the above adjustments in general ledger accounts.
2. Prepare a statement of cost of goods sold as it would appear in the income statement for the year.

Problem 10A7   Adjusting Journal Entries

In preparing the work sheet for The Smith Store at the close of the fiscal year ended July 31, it was also necessary to adjust the accounts for the following:

Interest accrued on notes payable, July 31, $190.
Insurance expired during the year, $386.
Estimated depreciation of property, plant, and equipment during the year:
  Store equipment, $778.
  Office equipment, $1,226.
Uncollectible accounts expense, $1,628.
Bank credit card expense, $714.

Required:
Prepare entries in general journal form for the above adjustments in the general ledger accounts.

Problem 10A8   Closing and Reversing Journal Entries

The partial work sheet of Ellen Massey for the calendar quarter ended March 31, 19-- is reproduced on page 436. The general ledger accounts affected by the closing process are listed on the following page, along with their March 31 balances prior to closing.

Required:

1. Using a general journal, prepare the entries necessary to close the temporary owner's equity accounts. Post the closing entries to the affected general ledger accounts. (Enter the March 31 balances first.)
2. Prepare the necessary reversing entry related to accrued bank credit card payable. Post the entry.

Ellen Massey
Work Sheet (Partial)
For The Quarter Ended March 31, 19--

Account Title	Acct. No.	Income Statement Debit	Income Statement Credit	Balance Sheet Debit	Balance Sheet Credit
Cash	111			48,443.50	
Accounts Receivable	131			97,628.86	
Allowance for Doubtful Accounts	131.1				3,482.28
Merchandise Inventory	141			97,676.16	
Prepaid Insurance	155			2,812.60	
Store Equipment	181			22,480.00	
Accum. Depr.—Store Equipment	181.1				449.60
Office Equipment	191			14,496.00	
Accum. Depr.—Office Equipment	191.1				362.40
FICA Tax Payable	211				1,323.58
FUTA Tax Payable	212				283.80
State Unemployment Tax Payable	213				706.20
Employees Income Tax Payable	214				1,089.00
Accrued Bank Credit Card Payable	215				842.32
Accounts Payable	218				83,327.82
Sales Tax Payable	221				2,086.16
Ellen Massey, Capital	311				189,206.72
Ellen Massey, Drawing	312			9,600.00	
Expense and Revenue Summary	331	113,098.70	97,676.16		
Sales	411		282,969.00		
Purchases	511	193,205.52			
Rent Expense	541	13,800.00			
Salaries and Commissions Expense	542	31,990.00			
Depreciation Expense	547	812.00			
Insurance Expense	548	378.20			
Advertising Expense	551	5,511.20			
Payroll Taxes Expense	552	1,034.32			
Bank Credit Card Expense	553	3,422.64			
Uncollectible Accounts Expense	554	3,482.28			
Miscellaneous Expense	572	3,933.06			
		370,667.92	380,645.16	293,137.12	283,159.88
Net Income		9,977.24			9,977.24
		380,645.16	380,645.16	293,137.12	293,137.12

Ellen Massey
Partial List of General Ledger Accounts
March 31, 19--

Account Title	Acct. No.	Balance Dr. (Cr.)
1 Accrued Bank Credit Card Payable......................	215	$ (842.32)
2 Ellen Massey, Capital.................................	311	(189,206.72)
3 Ellen Massey, Drawing	312	9,600.00
4 Expense and Revenue Summary*......................	331	15,422.54
5 Sales...	411	(282,969.00)
6 Purchases	511	193,205.52
7 Rent Expense	541	13,800.00
8 Salaries and Commissions Expense	542	31,990.00
9 Depreciation Expense.................................	547	812.00
10 Insurance Expense....................................	548	378.20
11 Advertising Expense	551	5,511.20
12 Payroll Taxes Expense	552	1,034.32
13 Bank Credit Card Expense**...........................	553	3,422.64
14 Uncollectible Accounts Expense	554	3,482.28
15 Miscellaneous Expense................................	572	3,933.06

*You will need to enter in the ledger account the beginning inventory of $113,098.70 as a debit and the ending inventory of $97,676.16 as a credit to produce this balance. (DO NOT enter this balance directly.)

**You will need, to enter in a ledger account a beginning balance of $2,580.32, followed by a debit adjustment of $842.32 (which is reversed as of April 1) to produce this balance. (DO NOT enter this balance directly.)

Problem 10A9   Journalizing and Posting Closing Entries; Post-Closing Trial Balance; Reversing Entries

Frank Trotter is the proprietor of The Trotter Store. Following is a reproduction of the Income Statement columns of the work sheet for the fiscal year ended June 30 of the current calendar year.

Required:

1. Using general journal paper, prepare the entries required to close the temporary owner's equity accounts, except for the drawing account.
2. Prepare the general ledger using the accounts listed on the following page with their June 30 balances prior to closing. Then, post the closing entries to the proper general ledger accounts.
3. Prepare a post-closing trial balance to prove that the general ledger is in balance after closing.
4. Prepare the general journal entries as of July 1 to reverse the adjustments that were made on June 30 for accrued interest payable and accrued bank credit card payable. Post the reversing entries to the general ledger accounts.

The Trotter Store
Work Sheet
For the Year Ended June 30, 19--

Account Title	Acct. No.	Income Statement Debit	Credit
Expense and Revenue Summary	331	64,823.00	62,391.60
Sales	411		282,447.60
Sales Returns and Allowances	411.1	2,596.00	
Purchases	511	147,974.30	
Rent Expense	541	15,600.00	
Salaries and Commissions Expense	542	40,990.00	
Depreciation Expense	547	3,816.00	
Advertising Expense	551	3,692.00	
Payroll Taxes Expense	552	1,418.00	
Bank Credit Card Expense	553	7,300.00	
Uncollectible Accounts Expense	554	1,460.78	
Miscellaneous Expense	572	842.94	
Interest Expense	581	391.68	
		290,904.70	344,839.20
Net Income		53,934.50	
		344,839.20	344,839.20

The Trotter Store
General Ledger Accounts
June 30, 19--

Account Title	Acct. No.	Balance Dr. (Cr.)
Cash	111	$ 38,982.36
Accounts Receivable	131	50,445.50
Allowance for Doubtful Accounts	131.1	(1,125.60)
Merchandise Inventory	141	62,391.60
Store Equipment	181	14,824.36
Accum. Depr.—Store Equipment	181.1	(3,702.32)
Office Equipment	191	8,596.00
Accum. Depr.—Office Equipment	191.1	(3,396.00)
FICA Tax Payable	211	(346.44)
FUTA Tax Payable	212	(145.90)
State Unemployment Tax Payable	213	(299.60)
Employees' Income Tax Payable	214	(2,182.40)
Accrued Bank Credit Card Payable	215	(594.24)
Notes Payable	216	(14,000.00)
Accrued Interest Payable	217	(152.36)
Accounts Payable	218	(10,195.60)
Sales Tax Payable	221	(499.60)
Frank Trotter, Capital	311	(84,665.26)
Expense and Revenue Summary*	331	(2,431.40)
Sales	411	(282,447.60)
Sales Returns and Allowances	411.1	2,596.00
Purchases	511	147,974.30

Rent Expense 541   15,600.00
Salaries and Commissions Expense 542   40,990.00
Depreciation Expense 547   3,816.00
Advertising Expense 551   3,692.00
Payroll Taxes Expense 552   1,418.00
Bank Credit Card Expense 553   7,300.00
Uncollectible Accounts Expense 554   1,460.78
Miscellaneous Expense 572   842.94
Interest Expense 581   391.68

*You will need to enter in the ledger account the beginning inventory of $64,823.00 as a debit and the ending inventory of $62,391.60 as a credit to produce this balance. (DO NOT enter this balance directly.)

Series B

Problem 10B1   Financial Statement Preparation and Ratio Analysis

Jean Emory operates a retail merchandising enterprise. The results of operations for the calendar quarter ended March 31 of the current year are reflected in the partial work sheet reproduced on the following page. Emory organized the business on January 1 and has been operating for only 1 quarter.

Emory has 2 employees and is subject to FICA tax, FUTA tax, and state unemployment tax.

Required:

1. Prepare an income statement for the calendar quarter ended March 31.
2. Treating sales as 100%, compute the percentages of cost of goods sold, total operating expenses, and net income for the period covered by the income statement. Make the computations on a separate sheet of paper and enter the results immediately following Emory's income statement.
3. Prepare a statement of owner's equity for the calendar quarter ended March 31 and a balance sheet as of March 31 in report form.
4. As an aid in interpreting Emory's balance sheet, compute the following ratios and enter the results immediately following Emory's balance sheet. Make the computations on a separate sheet of paper.
   (a) Ratio of current assets to current liabilities.
   (b) Ratio of total assets to total liabilities.

Jean Emory
Work Sheet (Partial)
For the Quarter Ended March 31, 19--

Account Title	Acct. No.	Income Statement		Balance Sheet	
		Debit	Credit	Debit	Credit
Cash	111			36,332.62	
Accounts Receivable	131			73,221.65	
Allowance for Doubtful Accounts	131.1				2,611.71
Merchandise Inventory	141			73,257.12	
Prepaid Insurance	155			2,109.45	
Store Equipment	181			16,860.00	
Accum. Depr.—Store Equipment	181.1				337.20
Office Equipment	191			10,872.00	
Accum. Depr.—Office Equipment	191.1				271.80
FICA Tax Payable	211				992.68
FUTA Tax Payable	212				212.85
State Unemployment Tax Payable	213				529.65
Employees' Income Tax Payable	214				816.75
Accrued Bank Credit Card Payable	215				631.74
Accounts Payable	218				62,495.87
Sales Tax Payable	221				1,564.62
Jean Emory, Capital	311				141,905.04
Jean Emory, Drawing	312			7,200.00	
Expense and Revenue Summary	331	84,824.02	73,257.12		
Sales	411		212,226.75		
Purchases	511	144,904.14			
Rent Expense	541	10,350.00			
Salaries and Commissions Expense	542	23,992.50			
Depreciation Expense	547	609.00			
Insurance Expense	548	283.65			
Advertising Expense	551	4,133.40			
Payroll Taxes Expense	552	775.74			
Bank Credit Card Expense	553	2,566.98			
Uncollectible Accounts Expense	554	2,611.71			
Miscellaneous Expense	572	2,949.80			
		278,000.94	285,483.87	219,852.84	212,369.91
Net Income		7,482.93			7,482.93
		285,483.87	285,483.87	219,852.84	219,852.84

Problem 10B2   Financial Statement Preparation and Ratio Analysis

Wayne Stumph operates a retail merchandising business. Following is a reproduction of a portion of the work sheet for the current year ended December 31.
Merchandise Inventory at the beginning of the year was $55,348.00.

Wayne Stumph
Work Sheet
For the Year Ended December 31, 19--

Account Title	Acct. No.	Income Statement Debit	Income Statement Credit	Balance Sheet Debit	Balance Sheet Credit
Cash	111			51,343.00	
Accounts Receivable	131			92,024.00	
Allowance for Doubtful Accounts	131.1				3,649.00
Merchandise Inventory	141			40,714.00	
Office Supplies	152			708.00	
Prepaid Insurance	155			1,263.00	
Office Equipment	191			11,985.00	
Accum. Depr.—Office Equipment	191.1				1,199.00
FICA Tax Payable	211				553.00
FUTA Tax Payable	212				57.00
State Unemployment Tax Payable	213				163.00
Employees' Income Tax Payable	214				425.00
Accrued Bank Credit Card Payable	215				613.00
Notes Payable	216				13,500.00
Accrued Interest Payable	217				162.00
Accounts Payable	218				41,763.00
Sales Tax Payable	221				1,752.00
Wayne Stumph, Capital	311				132,000.00
Wayne Stumph, Drawing	312			35,115.00	
Expense and Revenue Summary	331	55,348.00	40,714.00		
Sales	411		273,215.00		
Sales and Returns and Allowances	411.1	1,070.00			
Purchases	511	170,760.00			
Purchases Returns and Allowances	511.1		3,270.00		
Rent Expense	541	12,600.00			
Salaries and Commissions Expense	542	25,749.00			
Office Supplies Expense	543	1,668.00			
Depreciation Expense	547	1,198.00			
Insurance Expense	548	1,288.00			
Advertising Expense	551	3,442,00			
Payroll Taxes Expense	552	834.00			
Bank Credit Card Expense	553	2,350.00			
Uncollectible Accounts Expense	554	1,346.00			
Charitable Contributions Expense	557	788.00			
Miscellaneous Expense	572	920.00			
Interest Expense	581	522.00			
		279,883.00	317,199.00	233,152.00	195,836.00
Net Income		37,316.00			37,316.00
		317,199.00	317,199.00	233,152.00	233,152.00

Required:

1. Prepare an income statement for the year ended December 31.
2. Treating net sales as 100%, compute the percentages of cost of goods sold, total operating expenses, and net income for the period covered by the income statement. Make the computations on a separate sheet of paper and enter the results immediately following Stumph's income statement.
3. Prepare a statement of owner's equity for the year ended December 31, and a balance sheet in report form as of December 31.
4. As an aid in interpreting Stumph's balance sheet, compute the following ratios and enter the results immediately following Stumph's balance sheet.
   (a) Ratio of current assets to current liabilities.
   (b) Ratio of total assets to total liabilities.

Problem 10B3   Analysis of Comparative Income Statements

Condensed comparative income statements for Scheben's Sporting Goods are provided below:

Scheben's Sporting Goods
Comparative Income Statement
For the Years Ended December 31, 19-B and 19-A

	19-B	19-A
Net sales	$395,826	$382,544
Less cost of goods sold	232,681	205,480
Gross margin on sales	$163,145	$177,064
Operating expenses	103,760	112,584
Operating income	$ 59,385	$ 64,480
Interest expense	2,508	2,656
Net income	$ 56,877	$ 61,824

Required:

Prepare a statement showing:

(a) The dollar increase or decrease for each line of the income statement.
(b) All income statement items for each period as a percent of net sales.

Problem 10B4   Analysis of Comparative Balance Sheets

Comparative balance sheets in report form for Mullins' Fish Market are provided below:

Mullins' Fish Market
Comparative Balance Sheets
December 31, 19-B and 19-A

Assets	19-B		19-A	
Current assets:				
Cash............................		$ 30,720		$ 32,286
Accounts receivable	$ 46,776		$ 49,145	
Less allowance for doubtful				
accounts	5,040	41,736	5,322	43,823
Merchandise inventory		79,704		83,719
Supplies........................		10,404		10,955
Prepaid insurance		6,720		7,086
Total current assets		$169,284		$177,869
Property, plant, and equipment:				
Store equipment	$102,480		$102,480	
Less accumulated depreciation.....	38,400	$ 64,080	28,800	$ 73,680
Delivery equipment	$ 26,400		$ 26,400	
Less accumulated depreciation.....	18,000	8,400	12,000	14,400
Total property, plant &				
equipment..................		$ 72,480		$ 88,080
Total assets.....................		$241,764		$265,949
Liabilities				
Current liabilities:				
FICA tax payable	$ 1,476		$ 1,409	
FUTA tax payable...............	54		58	
State unemployment tax payable ...	180		177	
Notes payable	6,000		18,000	
Accrued interest payable	960		918	
Accounts payable	14,400		33,360	
Total current liabilities		$ 23,070		$ 53,922
Owner's Equity				
D. Mullins, Capital................		218,694		212,027
Total liabilities and owner's equity ...		$241,764		$265,949

Required:

Compute the dollar increase or decrease for each item. (Use net amounts for receivables and plant assets.)

Problem 10B5   Journalizing and Posting Adjusting Entries

The adjustments columns of the work sheet for the quarter ended March 31 for the business of Jean Emory are reproduced below.

Required:

1. Using a general journal, prepare journal entries for the six adjustments.
2. Post the adjusting entries to the general ledger accounts listed below and on the following page. (Enter the March 31 balances first where given.)

Account Title	Acct. No.	Adjustments Debit	Adjustments Credit
Cash.....................................	111		
Accounts Receivable.......................	131		
Allowance for Doubtful Accounts	131.1		(c) 2,611.71
Merchandise Inventory	141	(b) 73,257.12	(a) 84,824.02
Prepaid Insurance	155		(d) 283.65
Store Equipment	181		
Accum. Depr.—Store Equipment	181.1		(e) 337.20
Office Equipment	191		
Accum. Depr.—Office Equipment	191.1		(e) 271.80
FICA Tax Payable	211		
FUTA Tax Payable	212		
State Unemployment Tax Payable	213		
Employees Income Tax Payable.............	214		
Accrued Bank Credit Card Payable..........	215		(f) 631.74
Accounts Payable	218		
Sales Tax Payable	221		
Jean Emory, Capital	311		
Jean Emory, Drawing	312		
Expense and Revenue Summary	331	(a) 84,824.02	(b) 73,257.12
Sales....................................	411		
Purchases	511		
Rent Expense	541		
Salaries and Commissions Expense	542		
Depreciation Expense......................	547	(e) 609.00	
Insurance Expense........................	548	(d) 283.65	
Advertising Expense	551		
Payroll Taxes Expense	552		
Bank Credit Card Expense	553	(f) 631.74	
Uncollectible Accounts Expense	554	(c) 2,611.71	
Miscellaneous Expense.....................	572		
		162,217.24	162,217.24

Jean Emory
Partial List of General Ledger Accounts
March 31, 19--

Account Title	Acct. No.	Debit Balance
Allowance for Doubtful Accounts	131.1	-0-
Merchandise Inventory	141	$84,824.02
Prepaid Insurance	155	2,393.10
Accum. Depr.—Store Equipment	181.1	-0-
Accum. Depr.—Office Equipment	191.1	-0-

Account Title	Acct. No.	Debit Balance
Accrued Bank Credit Card Payable........................	215	-0-
Expense and Revenue Summary	331	-0-
Depreciation Expense...................................	547	-0-
Insurance Expense......................................	548	-0-
Bank Credit Card Expense	553	1,935.24
Uncollectible Accounts Expense	554	-0-

Problem 10B6   Adjusting Journal Entries; Statement of Cost of Goods Sold

The following account balances appeared in the general ledger of The Scaggs Store, owned by Leslie Scaggs, at the close of the fiscal year ended July 31:

Merchandise Inventory, beginning of year (August 1), debit, $64,435.
Purchases, debit, $219,600.
Purchases Returns and Allowances, credit, $1,134.

The merchandise inventory taken at the end of the year amounted to $89,148. In preparing a work sheet at the end of the year, the accountant made the adjusting entries required to transfer the beginning inventory to the expense and revenue summary account and to enter the ending inventory.

Required:

1. Prepare entries in general journal form for the above adjustments in general ledger accounts.
2. Prepare a statement of cost of goods sold as it would appear in the income statement for the year.

Problem 10B7   Adjusting Journal Entries

In preparing the work sheet for The Scaggs Store at the close of the fiscal year ended July 31, it was also necessary to adjust the accounts for the following:

Interest accrued on notes payable, July 31, $142.
Insurance expired during the year, $290.
Estimated depreciation of property, plant, and equipment during the year:
  Office equipment, $919
  Store equipment, $584.
Uncollectible accounts expense, $1,221.
Bank credit card expense, $535.

Required:

Prepare entries in general journal form for the above adjustments in the general ledger accounts.

Problem 10B8   Closing and Reversing Journal Entries

The partial work sheet of Jean Emory for the calender quarter ended March 31, 19-- is reproduced on page 454. The general ledger accounts affected by the closing process are listed below, along with their March 31 balances prior to closing.

Required:

1. Using a general journal, prepare the entries necessary to close the temporary owner's equity accounts. Foot the journal columns. Post the closing entries to the affected general ledger accounts. (Enter the March 31 balances first.)
2. Using a general journal, prepare the necessary reversing entry related to accrued bank credit card payable. Post the entry.

Jean Emory
Partial List of General Ledger Accounts
March 31, 19--

Account Title	Acct. No.	Balance Dr. (Cr.)
Accrued Bank Credit Card Payable	215	$ (631.74)
Jean Emory, Capital	311	(141,905.04)
Jean Emory, Drawing	312	7,200.00
Expense and Revenue Summary*	331	11,566.90
Sales	411	(212,226.75)
Purchases	511	144,904.14
Rent Expense	541	10,350.00
Salaries and Commissions Expense	542	23,992.50
Depreciation Expense	547	609.00
Insurance Expense	548	283.65
Advertising Expense	551	4,133.40
Payroll Taxes Expense	552	775.74
Bank Credit Card Expense**	553	2,566.98
Uncollectible Accounts Expense	554	2,611.71
Miscellaneous Expense	572	2,949.80

*You will need to enter in the ledger account the beginning inventory of $84,824.02 as a debit and the ending inventory of $73,257.12 as a credit to produce this balance. (DO NOT enter this balance directly.)

**You will need to enter in the ledger account a beginning balance of $1,935.24, followed by a debit adjustment of $631.74 (which is reversed as of April 1) to produce this balance. (DO NOT enter this balance directly.)

Jean Emory
Work Sheet (Partial)
For the Quarter Ended March 31, 19--

Account Title	Acct. No.	Income Statement		Balance Sheet	
		Debit	Credit	Debit	Credit
Cash	111			36,332.62	
Accounts Receivable	131			73,221.65	
Allowance for Doubtful Accounts	131.1				2,611.71
Merchandise Inventory	141			73,257.12	
Prepaid Insurance	155			2,109.45	
Store Equipment	181			16,860.00	
Accum. Depr.—Store Equipment	181.1				337.20
Office Equipment	191			10,872.00	
Accum. Depr.—Office Equipment	191.1				271.80
FICA Tax Payable	211				992.68
FUTA Tax Payable	212				212.85
State Unemployment Tax Payable	213				529.65
Employees Income Tax Payable	214				816.75
Accrued Bank Credit Card Payable	215				631.74
Accounts Payable	218				62,495.87
Sales Tax Payable	221				1,564.62
Jean Emory, Capital	311				141,905.05
Jean Emory, Drawing	312			7,200.00	
Expense and Revenue Summary	331	84,824.02	73,257.12		
Sales	411		212,226.75		
Purchases	511	144,904.14			
Rent Expense	541	10,350.00			
Salaries and Commissions Expense	542	23,992.50			
Depreciation Expense	547	609.00			
Insurance Expense	548	283.65			
Advertising Expense	551	4,133.40			
Payroll Taxes Expense	552	775.74			
Bank Credit Card Expense	553	2,566.98			
Uncollectible Accounts Expense	554	2,611.71			
Miscellaneous Expense	572	2,949.80			
		278,000.94	285,483.87	219,852.84	212,369.91
		7,482.93			7,482.93
Net Income		285,483.87	285,483.87	219,852.84	219,852.84

Problem 10B9   Journalizing and Posting Closing Entries; Post-Closing Trial Balance; Reversing Entries.

James O'Donnell is the proprietor of The O'Donnell Store. Following is a reproduction of the Income Statement columns of the work sheet for the fiscal year ended September 30 of the current calendar year.

The O'Donnell Store
Work Sheet (Partial)
For the Year Ended September 30, 19--

Account Title	Acct. No.	Income Statement Debit	Credit
Expense and Revenue Summary	331	48,617.25	46,793.70
Sales	411		211,835.70
Sales Returns and Allowances	411.1	1,947.00	
Purchases	511	110,980.72	
Rent Expense	541	11,700.00	
Salaries and Commissions Expense	542	30,742.50	
Depreciation Expense	547	2,862.00	
Advertising Expense	551	2,769.00	
Payroll Taxes Expense	552	1,063.50	
Bank Credit Card Expense	553	5,475.00	
Uncollectible Accounts Expense	554	1,095.59	
Miscellaneous Expense	572	632.20	
Interest Expense	581	293.76	
		218,178.52	258,629.40
Net Income		40,450.88	
		258,629.40	258,629.40

Required:

1. Using general journal paper, prepare the entries required to close the temporary owner's equity accounts, except for the drawing account.
2. Prepare a general ledger using the accounts listed on the following page with their September 30 balances prior to closing. Then, post the closing entries to the proper general ledger accounts.
3. Prepare a post-closing trial balance to prove that the general ledger is in balance after closing.
4. Prepare the general journal entries as of October 1 to reverse the adjustments that were made on September 30 for accrued interest payable and accrued bank credit card payable. Post the reversing entries to the general ledger accounts.

The O'Donnell Store
General Ledger Accounts
September 30, 19--

Account Title	Acct. No.	Balance Dr. (Cr.)
Cash	111	$ 29,236.77
Accounts Receivable	131	37,834.12

Account Title	Acct. No.	Balance Dr. (Cr.)
Allowance for Doubtful Accounts	131.1	(844.20)
Merchandise Inventory	141	46,793.70
Store Equipment	181	11,118.27
Accumulated Depr.—Store Equipment	181.1	(2,776.74)
Office Equipment	191	6,447.00
Accumulated Depr.—Office Equipment	191.1	(2,547.00)
FICA Tax Payable	211	(259.83)
FUTA Tax Payable	212	(109.42)
State Unemployment Tax Payable	213	(224.70)
Employees' Income Tax Payable	214	(1,636.80)
Accrued Bank Credit Card Payable.....................	215	(445.68)
Notes Payable	216	(10,500.00)
Accrued Interest Payable	217	(114.27)
Accounts Payable	218	(7,646.70)
Sales Tax Payable	221	(374.70)
James O'Donnell, Capital	311	(63,498.94)
Expense and Revenue Summary*	331	(1,823.55)
Sales...	411	(211,835.70)
Sales Returns and Allowances	411.1	1,947.00
Purchases	511	110,980.72
Rent Expense	541	11,700.00
Salaries and Commissions Expense	542	30,742.50
Depreciation Expense................................	547	2,862.00
Advertising Expense	551	2,769.00
Payroll Taxes Expense	552	1,063.50
Bank Credit Card Expense	553	5,475.00
Uncollectible Accounts Expense	554	1,095.59
Miscellaneous Expense...............................	572	632.20
Interest Expense.....................................	581	293.76

*You will need to enter in the ledger account the beginning inventory of $48,617.25 as a debit and the ending inventory of $46,793.70 as a credit to produce this balance. (DO NOT enter this balance directly.)

Mastery Problem

If the working papers for this textbook are not used, omit the Mastery Problem.

Dominique Fouque owns and operates Dominique's Doll House. She has a small shop in which she sells new and antique dolls and is particularly well known for her collection of antique Ken and Barbie dolls. On occasion, she will refurbish dolls for a fee or for a commission on the sale. A complete work sheet for 19-C has been prepared on pages 458-459.

Required:

1. Prepare a multiple-step income statement.
2. Prepare a statement of owner's equity.
3. Prepare a balance sheet.
4. Prepare a condensed comparative income statement reporting dollar increases (decreases) in net sales, cost of goods sold, gross margin, operating expenses, operating income, interest expense, and net income. Information for 19-B is provided in the partially completed statement found in the working papers.
5. Prepare a condensed comparative income statement reporting cost of goods sold, gross margin, operating expenses, operating income, interest expense, and net income as a percentage of net sales. Information for 19-B is provided in the partially completed statement found in the working papers.
6. Prepare a condensed comparative balance sheet reporting the dollar increase or decrease in current assets; property, plant, and equipment; total assets; current liabilities; owner's equity; and total liabilities and owner's equity. Information for 19-B is provided in the partially completed statement found in the working papers.
7. Compute the following ratios for 19-C.
   a. current ratio
   b. quick ratio
   c. working capital
   d. return on owner's equity
   e. accounts receivable turnover (Net credit sales for 19-C were $35,300 and net receivables on January 1, were $2,500.) and the average number of days to collect an account receivable.
   f. inventory turnover and average number of days to sell inventory
8. Prepare adjusting entries in the general journal.
9. Prepare closing entries in the general journal.
10. Prepare reversing entries for the adjustments made for bank credit card expense and interest expense.
11. Post the adjusting, closing, and reversing entries to the general ledger.
12. Prepare a post-closing trial balance.

Dominique's

Work

For the Year Ended

	ACCOUNT TITLE	ACCT. NO.	TRIAL BALANCE DEBIT	TRIAL BALANCE CREDIT	ADJUSTMENTS DEBIT	ADJUSTMENTS CREDIT
1	Cash	111	5,200.00			
2	Accounts Receivable	131	3,200.00			
3	Allowance for Doubtful Accounts	131.1		50.00		(c) 250.00
4	Merchandise Inventory	141	22,300.00		(b)24,600.00	(a)22,300.00
5	Office Supplies	152	800.00			(d) 600.00
6	Prepaid Insurance	155	1,200.00			(e) 400.00
7	Store Equipment	181	25,400.00			
8	Accum. Dep.—Store Equipment	181.1		15,000.00		(f) 5,000.00
9	Accrued Bank Credit Card Payable	215				(g) 90.00
10	Notes Payable	216		6,000.00		
11	Accrued Interest Payable	217				(h) 150.00
12	Accounts Payable	218		5,500.00		
13	Sales Tax Payable	221		855.00		
14	Dominique Fouque, Capital	311		33,577.00		
15	Dominique Fouque, Drawing	312	21,000.00			
16	Expense & Revenue Summary	331			(a)22,300.00	(b)24,600.00
17	Sales	411		125,776.00		
18	Sales Returns and Allowances	411.1	975.00			
19	Purchases	511	72,000.00			
20	Purchases Discounts	511.2		1,155.00		
21	Rent Expense	541	6,000.00			
22	Salaries Expense	542	22,000.00			
23	Office Supplies Expense	543			(d) 600.00	
24	Telephone Expense	545	678.00			
25	Depreciation Expense	547			(f) 5,000.00	
26	Insurance Expense	548			(e) 400.00	
27	Utility Expense	549	4,680.00			
28	Bank Credit Card Expense	553	2,480.00		(g) 90.00	
29	Uncollectible Accounts Expense	554			(c) 250.00	
30	Interest Expense	581			(h) 150.00	
31			187,913.00	187,913.00	5,339.00	5,339.00
32	Net Income					
33						
34						
35						
36						
37						
38						
39						
40						

Doll House

Sheet

December 31, 19-C

ADJUSTED TRIAL BALANCE		INCOME STATEMENT		BALANCE SHEET		
DEBIT	CREDIT	DEBIT	CREDIT	DEBIT	CREDIT	
5 2 0 0 00				5 2 0 0 00		1
3 2 0 0 00				3 2 0 0 00		2
	3 0 0 00				3 0 0 00	3
24 6 0 0 00				24 6 0 0 00		4
2 0 0 00				2 0 0 00		5
8 0 0 00				8 0 0 00		6
25 4 0 0 00				25 4 0 0 00		7
	20 0 0 0 00				20 0 0 0 00	8
	9 0 00				9 0 00	9
	6 0 0 0 00				6 0 0 0 00	10
	1 5 0 00				1 5 0 00	11
	5 5 0 0 00				5 5 0 0 00	12
	8 5 5 00				8 5 5 00	13
	33 5 7 7 00				33 5 7 7 00	14
21 0 0 0 00				21 0 0 0 00		15
22 3 0 0 00	24 6 0 0 00	22 3 0 0 00	24 6 0 0 00			16
	125 7 7 6 00		125 7 7 6 00			17
9 7 5 00		9 7 5 00				18
72 0 0 0 00		72 0 0 0 00				19
	1 1 5 5 00		1 1 5 5 00			20
6 0 0 0 00		6 0 0 0 00				21
22 0 0 0 00		22 0 0 0 00				22
6 0 0 00		6 0 0 00				23
6 7 8 00		6 7 8 00				24
5 0 0 0 00		5 0 0 0 00				25
4 0 0 00		4 0 0 00				26
4 6 8 0 00		4 6 8 0 00				27
2 5 7 0 00		2 5 7 0 00				28
2 5 0 00		2 5 0 00				29
1 5 0 00		1 5 0 00				30
218 0 0 3 00	218 0 0 3 00	137 6 0 3 00	151 5 3 1 00	80 4 0 0 00	66 4 7 2 00	31
		13 9 2 8 00			13 9 2 8 00	32
		151 5 3 1 00	151 5 3 1 00	80 4 0 0 00	80 4 0 0 00	33
						34
						35
						36
						37
						38
						39
						40

INDEX